T0311635

The Economics
of
International
Migration

World Scientific Studies in International Economics
(ISSN: 1793-3641)

The complete list of the published volumes in the series can be found at
http://www.worldscientific.com/series/wssie

49

World Scientific
Studies in
International
Economics

The Economics
of
International
Migration

Giovanni Peri

UC Davis

World Scientific

NEW JERSEY · LONDON · SINGAPORE · BEIJING · SHANGHAI · HONG KONG · TAIPEI · CHENNAI · TOKYO

Published by

World Scientific Publishing Co. Pte. Ltd.
5 Toh Tuck Link, Singapore 596224
USA office: 27 Warren Street, Suite 401-402, Hackensack, NJ 07601
UK office: 57 Shelton Street, Covent Garden, London WC2H 9HE

Library of Congress Cataloging-in-Publication Data
Names: Peri, Giovanni, author.
Title: The economics of international migration / Giovanni Peri.
Description: New Jersey : World Scientific, 2015. | Series: World scientific studies in
    international economics ; v. 49 | Includes bibliographical references.
Identifiers: LCCN 2015047853 | ISBN 9789814719896 (hardcover)
Subjects: LCSH: Emigration and immigration--Economic aspects. | Immigrants--
    Economic conditions. | Emigration and immigration--Cross-cultural studies.
Classification: LCC JV6217 .P47 2015 | DDC 304.8--dc23
LC record available at http://lccn.loc.gov/2015047853

British Library Cataloguing-in-Publication Data
A catalogue record for this book is available from the British Library.

First published 2016 (Hardcover)
Reprinted 2017 (in paperback edition)
ISBN 978-981-3224-88-9

In-house Editor: Philly Lim

Typeset by Stallion Press
Email: enquiries@stallionpress.com

Printed in Singapore

Dedication

To Claudia, Fabio and Dante;

who will make the world a better place.

Preface

As I am writing this preface to the book *The Economics of Immigration* the first pages of European newspapers have been covered for the last months with news on the "Syrian refugee crisis" and the US presidential campaign has been ignited with promises of "building a wall" and deporting millions of undocumented immigrants to Mexico. As it happens periodically the potential economic costs and benefits of immigration are hot news. The temptation to motivate the importance of the economic analysis of immigration with the currency of newsworthiness is high. The view emerging from the analysis of this book is, however, different. Immigration has been and is a very powerful and fundamental force that modifies the demographic and economic structure of countries whose effects are only apparent over decades. Most of all, immigration is an extraordinary economic opportunity for developed countries and for the migrants themselves. Understanding the economic motivation of migrants and the economic impact they have on the receiving economy is a very important input in building the best policies to manage migration flows. The ability of rich countries to manage immigration flows for growth and productivity will be one extremely important factor determining their economic success in the next decades.

During the last decades when international migration, and especially migration from poor to rich countries, increased substantially, the research on the economic determinants and effects of migrations blossomed too. Together with several coauthors I have been part of this revival in the economic analysis of migration. Our research agenda helped renew research in the area and pushed economists to look at different aspects and different economic implications of immigration. First, we understood that the "canonical model" with a homogeneous labor factor supplied by natives and immigrants was too simplistic to understand some crucial interactions in the labor markets between natives and immigrants. Second we explored the possibility that immigration stimulates responses in native workers and firms that may affect productivity and growth. Third we emphasized the importance of long-run analysis and possibly growth effects of high skilled immigrants. Finally we started to focus on the importance of understanding immigration policies and estimating their impact on immigration.

This volume collects our seminal and most relevant papers on these topics written and published during the last seven years plus a brand new introductory chapter, written for this volume, that emphasizes the fundamental correlations in the data between immigrants and labor market outcomes in the US. Together these papers provide a multifaceted analysis of the effect of immigrants on wages, employment, productivity considering the US, Europe and OECD countries as receiving economies and analyzing state, city and country level economies over years and decades. The picture emerging is that important adjustments take place in the receiving economies and while potential cost for some groups may exist, immigration generates significant gains for the natives especially in the long run. As immigration is relatively slow and adjustments take place at a comparable pace as immigrants are integrated in the receiving economy the resulting effects on natives are mainly positive. While certainly some disagreement still exist among economists on the specific effects of immigration, the research presented in this volume has indicated approaches and methodologies that seem to have become mainstream in this literature. I hope that reading these papers collected in one volume will inspire young economists to continue and advance research in migration economics.

I am grateful to my several brilliant coauthors in these papers, some of which I had the fortune of having as classmates and friends for a while such as Gianmarco Ottaviano and Frederic Docquier. Others are graduate advisees turned into coauthors and collaborators such as Chad Sparber, Greg Wright and Kevin Shih. All of them, including Francesc Ortega, Francesco D'Amuri, Caglar Ozden and Ilse Ruyssen have been excellent collaborators and coauthors. Without them I would certainly not have been able to write the papers and learn much from doing that. Certainly this book is only and intermediate step, as I am still actively working with these coauthors in the field of migration economics and I hope to continue contributing to its development in the next decades.

Giovanni Peri

October 20, 2015

Acknowledgements

Besides all the co-authors for the papers contained in this volume, the editor would also like to acknowledge and thank the following publishers, for granting the permissions to make this book possible. Grouped by Publishers in alphabetically order:

The American Economic Association

Task Specialization, Immigration and Wages
American Economic Journal: Applied Economics, Volume 1, Issue 3

Immigration, Offshoring and American Jobs
American Economic Review, Volume 103, Issue 5

Elsevier

Openness and Income: The roles of trade and migration
Journal of International Economics, Volume 92, Issue 2

The European Economic Association

Rethinking the Effect of Immigration on Wages
Journal of the European Economic Association, Volume 10, Issue 1

Immigration, Jobs and Labor Market Institutions: Evidence from Europe
European Economic Association, Volume 12, Issue 2

MIT Press

The Effect of Immigration on Productivity: Evidence from U.S. states
The Review of Economics and Statistics, Volume 94, Issue 1

Oxford University Press

The Economic Value of Cultural Diversity: Evidence from U.S. cities
Journal of Economic Geography, Volume 6, Issue 1

The Effect of Income and Immigration Policies on International Migrations
Migration Studies, Volume 1 Issue 1

Royal Economic Society

The Labor Market Effects of Immigration and Emigration in OECD
Countries
The Economic Journal, Volume 124, Issue 579

University of Chicago Press

STEM Workers, H1B Visas and Productivity in U.S. Cities
Journal of Labor Economics, Volume 33, Number S1

Wiley

The Cross-country Determinants of Potential and Actual Migration
International Migration Review, Volume 48, Number S1

About the Editor

 Giovanni PERI is Professor of Economics and Director of the Migration Cluster at UC Davis. He is also a Research Associate of the National Bureau of Economic Research in Cambridge, Massachusetts, IZA affiliate, and Editor of *Regional Science and Urban Economics*. He is in the Editorial Board of the *Journal of the European Economic Association* and the *Journal of Population Economics*. He has published in several academic journals including the *American Economic Review, The Review of Economic Studies*, the *Review of Economics and Statistics, The Economic Journal* and the *Journal of the European Economic Association*. He has done research on human capital, growth and technological innovation. Recently, he has focused on the impact of international migrations on labor markets, housing markets, productivity and innovation of the receiving countries, and on the determinants of international migrations. His research has been featured on *The New York Times, The Economist, The Washington Post*, and several popular blogs and newspapers.

Table of Content

INTRODUCTION

The Association between Immigration and Labor Market Outcomes in the U.S.

With G. Basso

Abstract

In this introductory chapter we present important correlations between immigration and labor market outcomes of native workers in the US. We use data on local labor markets, states and regions from the Census and American Community Survey over the period 1970–2010. We first look at simple correlations and then we use regression analysis with an increasing number of controls for observed and unobserved factors. We review the potential methods to separate the part of this correlation that captures the causal link from immigrants to native labor outcomes and we show estimates obtained with 2SLS method using the popular shift-share instrument. One fact emerging from all the specifications is that the net growth of immigrant labor has a zero to positive correlation with changes in native wages and native employment, in aggregate and by skill group. We briefly review the channels and the mechanisms that allow local economies to absorb immigrants with no negative (and possibly positive) impact on the labor demand for natives.

1. Introduction

The labor market and, more generally, the economic impact of immigrants in the United States are highly researched topics. Several influential articles have been written since the 1980's on immigration and native wages and employment (Grossman 1982, Card 1990, Borjas *et al.* 1997, Friedberg and Hunt 1995, Friedberg 2001). There has been some disagreement on whether the association between immigrant and wages is negative, positive or null (e.g. Borjas 2003, Card 2009, and Ottaviano and Peri 2012). The economics of how immigrants affect native wages and employment can be framed in a very simple labor demand and labor supply model for homogeneous workers.

1

Such a basic canonical model with a negatively sloped labor demand curve implies that in the short run an increase in supply due to immigration, keeping everything else constant, produces a decline in wage and/or in employment for native workers. In the long run as capital adjusts this model predicts no effect on native wages and employment.

There are many reasons, however, to believe that the simple canonical model described above is a gross oversimplification as it omits aspects that are crucial for the issue at hand. Immigrants are not homogeneous to natives, technology and capital adjusts in response to labor, firms create jobs in response to incentives, there are complementarity across different workers, more workers allow for specialization and division of labor that could enhance efficiency, and so on. All these factors imply that the marginal product of *native* labor may change when the supply of *immigrant* changes, and it may change in a direction that offsets or overturns the negative effects implied by the canonical model. In other words, the change in supply of immigrant workers may correspond to an ambiguous change in the *demand* for native workers. It could be positive or negative depending on the relative strength of competition and complementarity/productivity effects.

A second issue limiting the relevance of the "supply shift with-everything-else-constant" paradigm is that we rarely observe "sudden and short lived" changes in immigration rates. The usual scenario is one in which a slow but persistent increase in immigration rates shapes, over decades, the labor markets of the receiving countries. In this context several adjustments take place concurrently with the immigrant inflow. Even the more remarkable examples of immigration "booms" entailed net inflows only around 0.5 to 1% of the population each year. One of these immigration episodes took place in Israel during the period 1990–2000, due to Jewish immigrants from the ex-Soviet Union: in that episode, the share of foreign-born increased by 10 percentage points (pp) of the population in a decade. In another episode, from 1995 to 2008, the share of foreign-born in Spain increased by 11pp due to immigration. By comparison, the period of largest US immigration, namely the years 1990–2010, experienced an increase in the share of foreign-born by 5pp, hence an average of 0.25% of the population each year. Most of the other countries have had much smaller yearly rates for a period of few decades.[1] It is more useful, therefore, to think of a

---

[1]There have been some episodes of large refugee migrations in a short amount of time such as the Bosnians in the mid 1990's, but their flows were not too large.

framework in which the inflow of immigrants changes the long run equilibrium in the labor markets over decades. As both labor demand and labor supply change in the long-run and immigration may affect both dynamics, there is no clear prediction of the sign of the effects.

For these reasons it is useful to go to the data to learn about the long-run correlations between changes in immigrant population and native wages and employment without a pre-conceived expectation about their sign. We analyze these correlations for the US over the period 1970–2010, considering several different dimensions pertaining geographical areas and skill groups in section 2 of this chapter.

There are reasons to think that in the long run the correlation immigrant-native demand can be negative if forces of competition, crowding and decreasing returns prevail. But there are as many reasons to think that a positive correlation will prevail if agglomeration economies, labor and capital complementarity, specialization and skill externalities prevail. By analyzing the long-run correlations between these variables we obtain a picture of their joint movements in equilibrium. While correlations *per se* cannot reveal what is their driving force, and hence they cannot identify the causal effects of immigration, they may suggest some scenarios and rule out others, especially if they are consistent across decades and across geographical units. Moreover, other important long-run forces driving changes in the labor market, such as technology, change in demographic groups and changes in schooling attainments are, at least in part, observable. Thus, we can absorb their variation and only distill the correlation that survives such controls to better approximate the causal link between immigrants and native wages.

With these caveats in mind, we will estimate a series of basic regressions that progressively absorb the variation of confounding (observable and unobservable) factors so as to isolate a partial correlation between immigrant supply and native wages and employment. Overall we find correlations that are positive or not significantly different from 0 and rather stable across different periods, geographical units and specifications. These correlations reveal that, unless specific unobserved factors systematically offset the crowding and competition effects by immigrants, the identified correlations do not support the existence of negative and significant effects of immigration on native labor demand. We present this analysis in section 3.

Even the more sophisticated regression analysis, however, cannot really ensure that we are fully identifying causation from immigration to native labor demand. While the positive correlations are suggestive, and the robustness to controls is encouraging, we need to have a more systematic way to separate the causal link between exogenous changes in immigrant labor supply and native wages and employment. In section 4 we discuss the frequently used method of instrumental variables estimation, and the popular instruments in this context, defined as "shift-share" (or "enclave-based"). That method aims at isolating supply-driven changes in immigrants. We apply this instrumental variable technique to our regression analysis and observe only a small change in the point estimates of the correlation between immigrants and average native wages. The precision of the estimates, however, deteriorates significantly. We also discuss in that section more recent and promising methods that leverage policy changes and their variation across regions or the discontinuity over time of migratory flows as source of exogenous variation of immigrant labor supply. While those methods are interesting and promising, it is hard to find policy changes and push-episodes for all countries and years. Hence the shift-share instrument may still have an important role and it needs to be constructed accurately, paying attention to important details.

Finally, acknowledging that most of the simple and sophisticated correlations and 2SLS correlations between immigrant labor supply and native wages are positive or null, in section 5 we review the literature that identifies channels and mechanisms allowing absorption of immigrant labor with positive effects on native labor demand. This is a good way to lead into the rest of the volume. The first part of the book includes four papers devoted to analyzing the specific channels and mechanisms that can explain the zero or positive effects of immigrants on native labor demand. Then the second part of this volume focuses on the specific effect of immigrants on productivity and efficiency, emphasizing externalities and spillovers. Section 6 concludes this introduction and briefly connects it to the rest of this volume.

2. Basic Aggregate Correlations

We first consider simple correlations between the growth of the foreign-born population and the growth of wages and employment of natives. We aggregate US Census data for 1970 (2% sample), 1980, 1990 and 2000 (5% samples) and the 2008–2012 American Community Survey, which create a 5% sample around 2010 that we use for that year. As main geographical unit of analysis we use 722 Commuting Zones (CZs) that encompass the 48 adjoining US states and are defined as to comprise the same residents and workers within themselves. They approximate local labor markets. We use the definition of Commuting Zone, and the concordance over time, as developed by Autor and Dorn (2013). Alternatively, we use 50 US states or 9 US Census regions as units of analysis. The samples that measure population in working age include all individuals between 18 and 64 years old not residing in group quarters, while those measuring employment only include individuals who worked a positive amount of weeks in the previous year. Finally, the samples constructed to measure wages include working individuals who received strictly positive wage income. We use the logarithm of weekly wages that we define as total income from wages divided by weeks worked in the previous year.[2]

Let us define as FB_{it} the number of foreign-born in working age in location i and Census year t. We then define as USB_{it} the number of US born people in working age in the same location and Census year. Our measure of the increase in immigrants (foreign-born) over an inter-Census decade (for $t = 1970, 1980, 1990, 2000$) is the change in the number of foreign-born standardized by the initial population: $\Delta(immi_{i,t}) = (FB_{i,t+10} - FB_{it})/(FB_{it} + USB_{it})$. This variable captures the increased number of immigrants relative to the local population in working age. Correspondingly, we define as $\Delta \ln(wage_{i,t})^{USB}$ the inter-Census change in the logarithm of average weekly wages of native workers and as $\Delta (empl_{i,t})^{USB}$ the inter-Census change in native employment as share of the population in working age in Census year t. These variables capture the change in native workers' labor market outcomes over the considered decades measured as percentage points of the initial value. Figure 1 shows the variation of $\Delta(immi_{i,t})$ across US CZs considering the whole 1970–2010 change and indicating with darker shades of grey the CZs with larger increase of immigrants. Several CZs in California, Texas and Florida, but also on the East Coast and in the Central States, show the largest values. Parts of the Midwest and some Mountain States show the smallest increases. Figure 2 shows the geography of the variable $\Delta \ln(wage_{i,t})^{USB}$ across CZs also considering

---

[2]The detailed description of the samples, variables and their constructions using the IPUMS Census and ACS data (Ruggles *et al.* 2015) is in the Data Appendix. In general, we have used the same definitions of samples and variables as used in the book *Immigraiton Economics* by George Borjas (2014). All the dollar amounts are expressed in $ as of 1999 adjusted using the BLS CPI-U All Items.

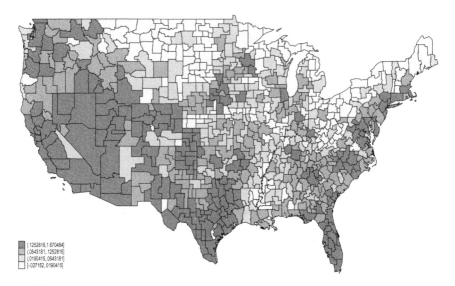

Fig. 1   Change in foreign-born as share of initial population: Commuting Zones, changes 1970–2010.
Note: Our calculations based on Census and ACS data from Census 1970, 80, 90, 2000 and 2010. The definition of the variable represented is given in the text. Units are 722 Commuting Zones.

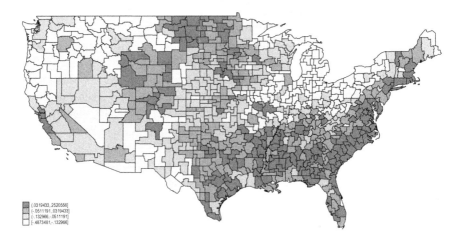

Fig. 2   Change in the logarithm of weekly wages of natives: Commuting Zones, changes 1970–2010.
Note: Our calculations based on Census and ACS data from Census 1970, 80, 90, 2000 and 2010. The definition of the variable represented is given in the text. Units are 722 Commuting Zones.

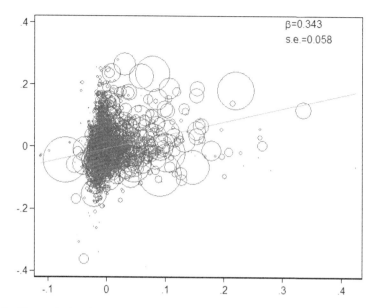

Fig. 3 Change in immigrants and change in weekly wages of natives: Commuting Zones per decade, pooled 1970–2010.
Note: The vertical axis shows the change in logarithmic weekly wages for natives, the horizontal axis shows the change in foreign-born as share of initial population. Unit of observation is a CZ in a decade. The changes are cleaned from the decade average. The size of the circle is proportional to the beginning of decade population in the CZ.

the change for the whole 1970–2010 period. We observe some fast growing wages in CZs of Texas, Florida and on the East Coast, but also in the Mountain States.

As it is hard to discern positive or negative correlations from these maps we show in Figure 3 the scatterplot of the decade changes $\Delta \ln(wage_{i,t})^{USB}$ on the vertical axis versus the change of immigrants, $\Delta(immi_{i,t})$ on the horizontal axis, pooling decades (1970–2010) after we have subtracted common decade averages. The units of observation are CZs in a decade. We also report the regression line, its coefficient (β) and the standard error $(s.e.)$. The size of a circle in the graph is proportional to the population of the CZ. The plot clearly shows a strong and significant positive correlation between immigration and native wage increase. In fact, the coefficient is quite large and it implies that an increase of immigrants by 10pp of the initial population in a CZ is associated to a native wage growth of 3.4%. Figure 4 breaks down the correlation between immigrant inflow and native wages across four decades to see whether such association has changed systematically

Introduction

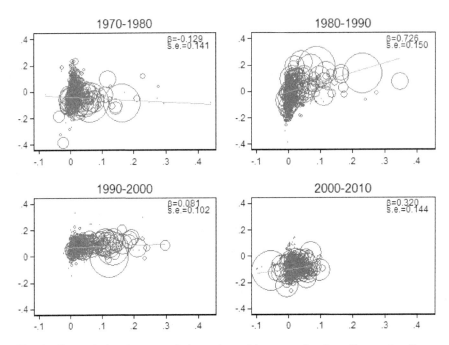

Fig. 4   Change in immigrants and change in weekly wages of natives: Commuting Zones separately by decade.

Note: Each panel shows the decade-change in logarithmic weekly wages for natives (vertical axis), and the decade-change in foreign-born as share of initial population (horizontal axis). Unit of observation is a CZ in a decade. The size of the circle is proportional to the beginning of decade population in the CZ.

over time. The graph shows a non-significant coefficient for the 1970's and 1990's and a positive and significant coefficient for the 1980's and 2000's. While certainly the nature of labor market shocks across CZs has changed over these decades, introducing significant noise, we do not observe a systematic decrease (or increase) in the correlation between immigrants and native wages over time that could imply a systematic change in their role as competitors/complements of native workers. Overall, we observe positive or null correlations, with a fair amount of noise.

Looking at relatively small geographical units such as the CZs can provide an incomplete representation of the phenomenon. First, natives may offset the inflow of immigrants by leaving the area. Second, focussing on larger areas one can internalize some of the potential effects on wages that spilled over to other CZs. To begin exploring these possibilities, therefore, in Figure 5 and 6 we show the correlation between native employment changes

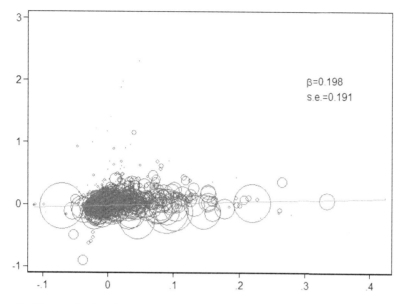

Fig. 5 Change in immigrants and change native employment: Commuting Zones per decade, pooled 1970–2010.

Note: The vertical axis shows the change in native employment relative to total employment at the beginning of the decade. The horizontal axis shows the change in foreign-born as share of initial population. Unit of observation is a CZ in a decade. The changes are cleaned from the decade average. The size of the circle is proportional to the beginning of decade population in the CZ.

and immigration in scatterplots that mirror Figure 3 and 4. A strong role of immigrants in displacing natives would likely produce a negative correlation. A coefficient of −1 would be compatible with a strong displacement effect in which one immigrant replaces one native as worker. When pooling the observations across decades in Figure 5, as well as in the panels of Figure 6 where we show one chart per decade, we see either null or positive correlations between immigration and native employment. The pooled estimates show a positive correlation of 0.20, not significantly different from 0. Across decades one finds a positive and significant coefficient in the 2000's and non significant coefficients in the other decades. Combining these correlation with those with native wages (zero to positive) it is clear that immigration is associated with a positive demand change for native workers across CZs. While the cause of such positive demand change for native workers cannot be inferred from these correlations directly, we can establish two minimal findings. First, locations where immigrants go are those where

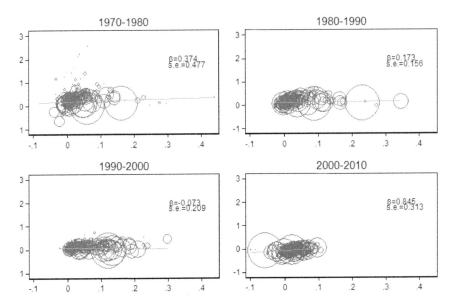

Fig. 6   Change in immigrants and change in native employment: Commuting Zones separately by decade.
Note: Each panel shows the decade-changes in native employment relative to total employment at the beginning of the decade (vertical axis), and the decade-change in foreign-born as share of initial population. Unit of observation is a CZ in a decade. The size of the circle is proportional to the beginning of decade population in the CZ.

native labor markets are growing. This may certainly be driven by other factors, but at least the inflow of immigrants does not reverse the positive demand shock. Second, we have not found evidence of systematically changing correlation between native labor markets outcomes and immigrants over decades.

Before trying to control more systematically for some observed and unobserved determinants of native labor demand we consider an important differentiation in the labor market for native workers. Workers of different skills are subject to different degrees of immigrant competition and their schooling level is an important factor in determining such competition. Workers with different schooling levels can be considered as different and imperfectly substitutable labor inputs (see Borjas 2003, Ottaviano and Peri 2012, and Card 2009). In areas where immigrants are more skilled, highly educated natives could suffer more competition than less educated natives. To the contrary, a larger inflow of low educated immigrants produces competition for less educated natives and possibly complements the skills of

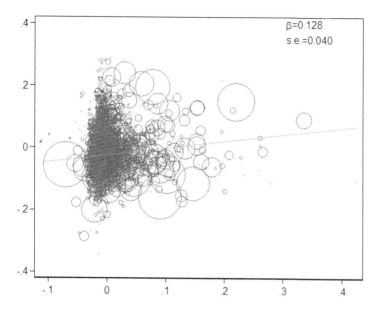

Fig. 7 Change in immigrants and change in weekly wages of non-college educated natives: Commuting Zones per decade, pooled 1970–2010.

Note: The vertical axis shows the change in logarithmic weekly wages for non-college educated natives, the horizontal axis shows the change in foreign-born as share of initial population. Unit of observation is a CZ in a decade. The changes are cleaned from the decade average. The size of the circle is proportional to the beginning of decade population in the CZ.

highly educated. On average, the inflow of immigrants in the US during the considered period (1970–2010) has been largest among workers with no high school degree (low-skilled). Hence separating workers with low education (at most a high school degree) and those with high education (college educated or more), and still considering aggregate immigration in CZs as explanatory variables, we want to see if the correlation with native wages is consistent with a stronger competition effect on less educated natives. Figure 7 and 8 show the scatterplot of the increase of the log of weekly wages for natives with at most a high school diploma (Figure 7), or for natives with a college education (Figure 8) versus the increase in total foreign born as share of the total population. Two facts emerge. First, in both cases the correlation is positive and significant which confirms the idea that immigration is associated to a positive demand change for both types of native workers. Second, the correlation is stronger for college educated. While an increase in immigrants by one percentage point is associated to a

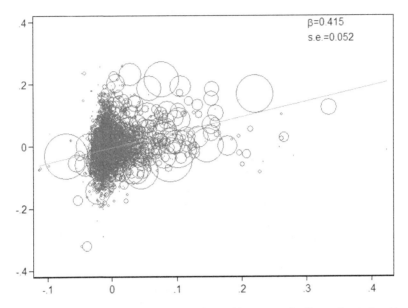

Fig. 8   Change in immigrants and change in weekly wages of college educated natives:
Commuting Zones per decade, pooled 1970–2010.
Note: The vertical axis shows the change in logarithmic weekly wages for natives with
some college education or more, the horizontal axis shows the change in foreign-born
as share of initial population. Unit of observation is a CZ in a decade. The changes are
cleaned from the decade average. The size of the circle is proportional to the beginning
of decade population in the CZ.

0.13 increase in non-college educated wages, college educated show a 0.42%
grow. This is consistent with an overall positive demand (productivity)
change associated with immigrants. If part of this association is causal it
would be consistent with a stronger complementarity effect of immigrants
on highly educated natives.

3.   Correlations and Regression Analysis

In order to analyze more systematically the correlations between immigrants and wage/employment of natives we perform several regressions.
Those regressions allow us to control for an array of omitted variables, some
of them not observable (but common to location over time, or to decades
across locations) and some observable, or at least proxied by variables that
can be constructed, such as measures of technological change. We run two
types of regressions in this section. The first set of regressions analyzes the

impact of aggregate immigration in a location (as proxied by the immigrant share in the working age population of that area) either on native average performance (wage and employment) or on the performance of college educated or non-college educated separately. The estimated regressions are of the following type:

$$\Delta (y_{i,t})^{USB} = \phi_i + \psi_t + \beta\Delta(immi_{i,t}) + \varepsilon_{it}, \tag{1}$$

where $(y_{i,t})^{USB}$ is an outcome (such as wage or employment) for all US born workers, or for an education group within them (college or non-college educated). The terms ϕ_i and ψ_t are fixed location and time effects. The term ε_{it} captures a zero-mean random error. The coefficient of interest is β and it describes the percent increase in the outcome variables associated to an increase of immigrants by one percentage point of the total population. These aggregate regressions aim at capturing the overall association between immigrants as a whole and native outcomes. The limit of these regressions is that, if other factors are not controlled for, the correlation is not informative of the causal effect of immigrants on native outcomes.

A second group of regressions analyzes instead the correlation between immigrants and native outcomes within skill-location cells. The skill cells are defined as four education groups (no degree, high school degree, some college and college degree) by two experience groups (at most twenty years of experience and more than twenty years of experience). By selecting natives and immigrants in the same cell one is considering similar type of workers, more likely to compete for similar jobs. By including fixed terms that control for location-decade effects one is likely to absorb some of the omitted variables that may bias the previous regression (1) hence reducing the risk of spurious correlations. However, such a strategy also absorbs with the fixed effects all the possible cross-skill complementarity and aggregate externalities that immigrants workers generate. Namely, in these regressions we estimate the effect of immigrants in the same skill group and location, considering those in other skill-group in the same location as constant. While these regressions are informative and allow us to include a much larger number of fixed effects as controls, one has to emphasize the *partial* nature of the estimates that they produce. The estimated regressions are of the form:

$$\Delta (y_{i,k,t})^{USB} = \phi_i + \phi_t + \phi_k + \phi_{i,k} + \phi_{i,t} + \phi_{k,t} + \beta\Delta(immi_{i,k,t}) + \varepsilon_{i,k,t}, \tag{2}$$

where the index k denotes the skill groups (eight of them divided into four education by two experience groups) and the fixed effects include area, decade and skill effects plus fixed effects for all the interactions between two of those attributes.[3] The value of β in these type of regressions has been considered as an estimate of the effect of immigrants on natives in some studies (e.g. in Borjas 2014). However, even abstracting from omitted variable bias this is at best, as pointed out in Ottaviano and Peri (2012), a partial, own-skill effect of immigrants, reflecting only the impact on most similar natives' wages and absorbing the cross-skill complementarity and externalities in the area in the time-area effects. If we were to omit the set of $\phi_{i,t}$ effects in the estimates then the regressions might provide an average estimate of the own plus cross effects of immigrants, as long as other omitted variables do not bias those effects.

3.1. *Area regressions: Average effects*

Table 1 shows the estimated coefficient β from the aggregate regressions as in (1) when the dependent variable is the change in logarithm of average weekly wage for natives. The difference between columns is given by the geographical units of observation considered. In column (1) the regression is run using observations for 722 Commuting Zones over four decades. In column (2) we use 50 States over four decades and in column (3) we use 9 Census regions over four decades. Across rows we estimate somewhat different specifications. Row (1) includes only decade fixed effects while row (2) has decade and geographic unit fixed effects. Row (2) is our preferred specification. In the row (3) we omit the earlier decade (1970–80), while in row (4) we include the most recent decade of data (2000–2010) only. Large changes in estimates across samples could reveal a systematically changing nature of the link between immigration and wages consistent, for instance, of significant spillovers out of the smaller geographical units. In the two bottom rows we omit the smallest 10% of CZs and the largest 10% to see if extreme values drive the correlation. Most of the estimated coefficients using CZs are not far from 0.4, and when using larger geographical units the coefficient is also, usually around 0.4, but has some variance as it can be as low as 0.27 and as large as 0.60.[4] In most cases we cannot reject the hypothesis that, for specifications in one row, the coefficients are the

---

[3]As usual, when including the cross-group effects one needs to omit the individual group effects, as they are fully absorbed in the interactions.

[4]The highest value for the region regression is 1.35 in the last row of column (3). As there are only 9 regions the regression is rather imprecise and standard error is quite large.

Table 1 Correlation between change in immigrants and native log weekly wage change: Aggregate area regressions, period 1970–2010.

Dependent variable: Decade change of average native log weekly wage			
Specification	(1) Commuting Zones	(2) States	(3) Census regions
(1) FE: Decade	0.34**	0.29**	0.27
	(0.06)	(0.08)	(0.24)
(2) FE: Decade, Area	0.36**	0.54**	0.38
	(0.04)	(0.13)	(0.21)
(3): As (2) Dropping 1970–80	0.39**	0.60**	0.49
	(0.06)	(0.17)	(0.23)
(4): Only 2000–2010	0.32**	0.34	0.94
	(0.14)	(0.31)	(0.55)
(5): As (2) Trimming bottom 10% in size	0.36**	0.53**	0.38
	(0.04)	(0.13)	(0.22)
(6): As (2) Trimming top 10% in size	0.30	0.64**	1.35*
	(0.16)	(0.46)	(0.44)

Note: Each cell shows the coefficient on the variable "change of immigrants as share of initial population" from a different regression of the type of Equation (1). The units of observations are geographical areas, as specified at the top of the column by decades. Variables are in decadal changes with change in native average log weekly wage as dependent variable and the change in immigrant population as share of initial population as explanatory variable. Regressions are weighted by the total number of individuals in the area at the beginning of the decade. Standard errors clustered at the area unit level. *,** = significant at 5%, 1% confidence level.

same across all geographical units [columns (1) to (3)]. This suggests that spillovers of a potential causal impact of immigrants are not so relevant as to invalidate correlations taken at the level of a labor market. The relationship between immigrants and wages is stable across specifications, geographical units and decades. While imprecision of the estimates limits our confidence in any individual specification, taken together these estimates seems to show a significantly positive correlation coefficient around 0.4.

Table 2 then shows the aggregate correlation between immigrants and native employment. In this case most of the estimates are not significantly different from 0. When focussing on the last decade [row (4)] and on smaller CZs [row (6)] one gets imprecisely estimated positive correlations. Considering our preferred estimates in row (2) we observe stable and consistently small and non-significant estimates of the correlation between immigration and native employment across all geographical units. No systematic difference in the correlation between immigrants and native employment emerged across CZs, States or Census regions when considering specifications in

Table 2 Correlation between change in immigrants and native employment change: Aggregate area regressions, period 1970–2010.

Dependent variable: Change in native employment relative to initial population

Specification	(1) Commuting Zones	(2) States	(3) Census regions
(1) FE: Decade	0.20	0.32	0.46
	(0.19)	(0.29)	(0.36)
(2) FE: Decade, Area	0.02	0.05	0.09
	(0.14)	(0.10)	(0.23)
(3): As (2) Dropping 1970–80	−0.05	−0.02	0.03
	(0.11)	(0.13)	(0.30)
(4): Only 2000–2010	0.84**	1.04**	1.75**
	(0.31)	(0.23)	(0.40)
(5): As (2)	0.02	0.04	0.14
Trimming bottom 10% in size	(0.14)	(0.10)	(0.27)
(6): As (2)	1.11**	0.54*	0.99*
Trimming top 10% in size	(0.40)	(0.27)	(0.39)

Note: Each cell shows the coefficient on the variable "change of immigrants as share of initial population" from a different regression of the type of Equation (1). The units of observations are geographical areas, as specified at the top of the column. Variables are in decadal changes with change in native employment as share of initial population as dependent variable and the change in immigrant population as share of initial population as explanatory variable. Regressions are weighted by the total number of individuals in the area at the beginning of the decade. Standard errors clustered at the regional unit level.
*,** = significant at 5%, 1% confidence level.

row (2). In particular, none of the correlations is suggestive of displacement of natives that would imply a negative and significant coefficient. Combining all wage and employment correlations, the area regressions confirm the impression produced by the simple scatterplots. Immigration is associated, on average, with an increase in demand for native workers and such association exists at the very local (CZs) as well as the broader (Census region) geographical level. If immigrants are purely attracted by aggregate local demand shocks then these effects are consistent with immigrants responding to those as natives do.[5] But can we control for some of those shocks?

---

[5] Recent analysis by Cadena and Kovak (2015) finds that low skilled immigrants respond to local demand shocks more than natives. Their analysis is based on short-run variations but the high mobility of immigrants can certainly be part of the reason for the positive correlation between native share of the population and native wages and employment growth.

And can we analyze if the association between immigration and native labor demand in specific skill groups is very different from this average effect? In the next section we will analyze the skill structure of labor markets and the competition effect of immigrants on similar workers.

3.2. *Area-skill-cell regressions: Partial effects*

Table 3 reports the estimates of coefficient β for different specifications of regression (2). In particular, those differ across columns for the geographical units used as observations (in column (1) the units are Commuting Zones-by-skill in column (2) they are States-by-skill in column (3) they are Census regions-by-skill). They differ across rows for the progressive inclusion of more fixed effects (only area, skill and decade effects in row (1), area-skill interactions and decade effects in row (2), area-skill and skill-decade

Table 3 Correlation between change in immigrants and native log weekly wage change: Partial area-skill regressions, period 1970–2010.

	(1)	(2)	(3)
Dependent variable: Decade change of average native log weekly wage			
Specification	Commuting Zones × skills	States × skills	Census regions × skills
(1) FE: Area, Skill,	0.17**	0.04	−0.03
Decade.	(0.02)	(0.02)	(0.07)
(2) FE: Area-Skill,	0.18**	0.05	−0.03
Decade	(0.02)	(0.04)	(0.09)
(3) FE: Area-Skill,	0.24**	0.18**	0.14
Skill-Decade	(0.03)	(0.05)	(0.12)
(4) FE: Area-Skill,	0.05*	0.04	0.01
Skill-Decade,	(0.02)	(0.03)	(0.08)
Area-Decade			
(5): As (3) dropping	0.28**	0.24**	0.25
1970–80	(0.04)	(0.07)	(0.17)

Note: Each cell shows the coefficient on the variable "change of immigrants as share of initial population" from a different regression. The units of observations are cells at the geographical areas by skill, as specified at the top of the column. Skills are four education by two experience group as defined. Variables are in decade changes with change in native average log weekly wage as dependent variable and the change in immigrant population as share of initial population as explanatory variable. Regressions are weighted by the total number of individuals in the cell (defined as area × skill group) at the beginning of the decade. Standard errors clustered at the area level.
*,** = significant at 5%, 1% confidence level.

interactions in row (3) and all the two-way interactions in row (4)). The last row excludes the 1970–80 decade from the analysis.

The coefficients in row (4) estimate the own-skill partial effect of immigrants in the skill-group and area once we control for total immigration in the area (that is captured by the area-time fixed effects). Those values are close to 0. This is consistent with a framework in which native and immigrants in a skill group are different enough that the competition effect of similar immigrants is balanced by their complementarity effect resulting in no wage impact. The other specifications, not including area-decade effects, identify the average effect of combining own and cross-skill. Those are positive or close to zero. In particular, the effects are attenuated and more imprecisely estimated at the Census region level. This may be due to smaller variation as we are averaging across areas with very different inflows of immigrants.

Table 4 shows the same specifications with the change in native employment as dependent variable. Even in this case we observe positive and significant coefficients in the first two rows, and non-significant coefficients in the other rows. These estimates are consistent with a world in which either complementarity between immigrants and natives prevails, or positive demand shocks for natives accompany inflow of immigrants in the same area and skill group. They are not compatible, however, with a situation in which supply driven changes in immigrants displace natives or depress their wages.

3.3.   *Area regressions for more or less educated natives*

The combination of results from Tables 1 and 2 is consistent with a scenario in which the inflow of immigrants is associated with a positive increase in demand for native workers due to complementarity or externalities, together with a small competition effect on native workers of similar skills. The cell-level analysis is useful to capture the fact that, controlling for overall immigration in an area, skill groups with larger increase of immigrants do not experience especially negative or positive outcomes. Hence a part of the positive aggregate effect in Table 1 must come from cross-group complementarity or externalities. To learn how the complementarity-externality and competition effects (plus potential omitted variables) influence wages and employment of natives in different skill groups, we focus on more and less educated in separate regressions. In Table 5 we show the effect on average log weekly wages of high school educated natives (upper part of the table)

Table 4 Correlation between change in immigrants and native employment change: Partial area-skill regressions, period 1970–2010

Dependent variable: Change in native employment relative to initial population

Specification	(1) Commuting Zones × skills	(2) States × skills	(3) Census regions × skills
(1) FE: Area, Skill,	0.62**	1.75**	2.47**
Decade.	(0.18)	(0.30)	(0.62)
(2) FE: Area-Skill,	0.70*	2.13**	2.94*
Decade	(0.28)	(0.52)	(0.97)
(3) FE: Area-Skill,	−0.02	−0.01	−0.05
Skill-Decade	(0.15)	(0.13)	(0.10)
(4) FE: Area-Skill,	0.16	0.17	0.20*
Skill-Decade,	(0.11)	(0.09)	(0.07)
Area-Decade			
(5): As (3) dropping	−0.09	−0.04	−0.03
1970–80	(0.12)	(0.12)	(0.14)

Note: Each cell shows the coefficient on the variable "change of immigrants as share of initial population" from a different regression. The units of observations are cells at the geographical areas by skill, as specified at the top of the column. Skills are four education by two experience group as defined. Variables are in decade changes with change in native employment as share of the initial total population as dependent variable and the change in immigrant population as share of initial population as explanatory variable. Regressions are weighted by the total number of individuals in the cell (defined as area × skill group) at the beginning of the decade. Standard errors clustered at the area level.
*,** = significant at 5%, 1% confidence level.

and of college educated natives (lower part) separately. We estimate specification (1) with the outcome $\Delta \ln(wage_{i,t})^{USB}$ measured separately for each of the two education groups. If immigration, as it appears so far, is accompanied by constant or increased labor demand for native workers, with a larger boost for college educated natives, we should observe zero or positive estimates in all entries and larger point estimates in the bottom part of the table. This is exactly what we find. In specification (2), across columns, we find correlation consistent with the fact that a 0.2–0.3% increase in less educated wages is associated to one percentage point increase of immigrants in the population, and a 0.4–0.6% increase for college educated native wages is associated to the same increase of immigrants. Limiting ourselves to the last decade, precision is lacking, but we find more balanced effects on the two groups, consistently with the more college-intensive immigration of the recent decade. While only suggestive, these correlations overall

Table 5 Correlation between change in immigrants and native log weekly wages, schooling groups: Aggregate area regressions, period 1970–2010.

Dependent variable: Decade change of average native log weekly wage			
Specification	(1) Commuting Zones	(2) States	(3) Census regions
HIGH SCHOOL OR LESS			
(1) FE: Decade	0.13**	0.12	0.11
	(0.04)	(0.11)	(0.30)
(2) FE: Decade, Area	0.23**	0.33**	0.14
	(0.04)	(0.14)	(0.30)
(3) Only 2000–2010	0.16	0.50	1.28
	(0.12)	(0.31)	(0.72)
COLLEGE OR MORE			
(4) FE: Decade	0.41**	0.41**	0.46**
	(0.05)	(0.05)	(0.14)
(5) FE: Decade, Area	0.42**	0.65**	0.60**
	(0.05)	(0.12)	(0.15)
(6) Only 2000–2010	0.29	0.32	0.84
	(0.15)	(0.31)	(0.56)

Note: Each cell shows the coefficient on the variable "change of immigrants as share of initial population" from a different regression of the type of Equation (1). The units of observations are geographical areas, as specified at the top of the column by decades. Variables are in decadal changes. In the upper part of the table labelled "HIGH SCHOOL OR LESS" the dependent variable is the change in native average log weekly wage for natives with a high school degree or less. In the lower part of the table labelled "COLLEGE OR MORE" the dependent variable is the change in native average log weekly wage for natives with some college education or more. Regressions are weighted by the total number of individuals in the area at the beginning of the decade. Standard errors clustered at the area unit level.
** = significant at 5% confidence level.

are consistent with immigration being beneficial to native labor demand, especially for college educated.

4.   Omitted Variables and Identification of Causality

One important reason for the different performance of labor markets across locations during the last decades has been the very different economic success of different industries. High tech sectors in manufacturing and services have increased much their productivity, propelled by the information and communication technology revolution and their demand for workers especially of highly educated ones has surged. To the contrary part of the manufacturing and service sector, characterized by simple, routine and non-cognitive type of occupations have experienced stagnant wages and employment (e.g. Acemoglu and Autor 2011, Autor and Dorn 2013). As different geographical areas have different specialization, some have suffered more from the decline of low performing industries and other have benefitted more from the expansion of fast growing ones. Here we use the different industry specialization of Commuting Zones in year 1970, and the differential growth of wages across those industries, to construct an index of local sector-driven labor demand. We then include this control that captures sector-driven labor demand growth and we test whether the positive correlation between immigrants and native wage growth survives.

Specifically, we construct an index of sector-specific growth, often called "Bartik" instrument (Bartik 1991), as follows. Let us define as $sh_{ij,1970}^{EMPL}$ the share of employment in industry j in the total employment of CZ i, and let $\Delta \ln wage_{jt}$ be the change of the log weekly average wages for workers in industry j nationally between year $t - 10$ and year t. Then the proxy for industry-driven growth in labor productivity (labor demand) for workers in CZ i will be defined as:

$$\Delta Bartik_{it} = \sum_j \left(sh_{ij,1970}^{EMPL} \Delta \ln wage_{jt} \right), \quad \text{for } t = 1980, 1990, 2000, 2010.$$

$$(3)$$

This index will be included as control in the regressions of Table 5. Table 6 shows the results of specifications (1) and (2) of Table 5, estimated for CZs only and controlling for $\Delta Bartik_{it}$, the proxy for labor demand growth. Considering the more demanding specification (2) we see that, while the demand growth proxied by $\Delta Bartik_{it}$ is itself a very important determinant of native wage growth for college and non-college educated, its inclusion does not eliminate the positive and significant correlation between native wages and growth in immigrant population. We still estimate a 0.2% increase in the wage of non-college educated natives per percentage point of foreigners and a 0.4% increase for wages of college educated natives.

An alternative way of making progress towards identification of the causal effect of immigrants on native labor market outcomes is, rather than controlling for demand changes, to construct a proxy for the supply-driven shifts of the immigrant population. We then use that as an instrumental variable for the changes in immigrants as share of the population. A popular way of doing this is to construct a so-called "shift-share" instrument (as suggested by Altonji and Card 1991, Card 2001, and used in several

Table 6 Immigration and native wages, including "Bartik" controls for change in labor demand: Aggregate area regressions, Commuting Zones period 1970–2010.

Dependent variable: Decade change of average native log weekly wage, CZ level

Specification	(1) All native workers	(2) Native high school or less	(3) Natives college or more
(1) FE: Decade			
Coefficient on Δ(Immi)	0.28**	0.07**	0.36**
	(0.04)	(0.03)	(0.04)
Coefficient on Δ(Bartik)	2.74**	2.65**	2.30**
	(0.29)	(0.40)	(0.26)
(2) FE: Decade, Area			
Coefficient on Δ(Immi)	0.34**	0.20**	0.40**
	(0.06)	(0.06)	(0.05)
Coefficient on Δ(Bartik)	2.52**	2.49**	2.16**
	(0.41)	(0.56)	(0.36)

Note: The units of observations are Commuting Zones. Variables are in decadal changes. In the first column the dependent variable is the change in native average log weekly wage for all natives. In the second column the dependent variable is the change in native average log weekly wage for native workers with a high school degree or less. In the third column the dependent variable is the change in native average log weekly wage for natives with some college education or more. The explanatory variables and specification are described in the first column. Regressions are weighted by the total number of individuals in the area at the beginning of the decade. Standard errors clustered at the area unit level.
** = significant at 5% confidence level.

papers since then) using FB_{i,c,t_0}, the population of immigrants by nationality (c), across US CZs (i) in year t_0, that should be prior to the considered period, and augment these populations by the aggregate growth factor of immigrants from that nationality c in the US between year t_0 and t, $\frac{FB_{c,t}}{FB_{c,t_0}}$. This instrument is based on the idea that the distribution of foreign born of nationality c in CZ i in t_0 is uncorrelated with subsequent demand shifts and productivity changes in that CZ. In our case we would instrument the variable $\Delta(immi_{i,t})$ with the following imputed value:

$$\Delta(\widehat{immi}_{i,t}) = \frac{\widehat{FB_{it+10}} - \widehat{FB_{it}}}{\widehat{FB_{it}} + USB_{it}} \text{ where } \widehat{FB_{it}} = \sum_c FB_{i,c,t_0} * \frac{FB_{c,t}}{FB_{c,t_0}}. \tag{4}$$

We will use in the analysis only the decade changes from 1980 to 2010, and as "initial year" t_0 we choose alternatively 1980 or 1970. The choice

Table 7 Immigration and native wages, using immigrant network instruments: Aggregate area regressions, period 1980–2010 [row (1)], 1990–2010 [row (2)].

Dependent variable: Decade change of average native log weekly wage, CZ level
Instrument: Network based immigration changes

Specification	(1) All native workers	(2) Native high school or less	(3) Natives college or more
(1) FE: Decade	0.25	−0.19	0.38*
1970 based instruments	(0.20)	(0.16)	(0.17)
F-statistics, first stage	92.5	92.5	92.5
(2) FE: Decade	0.23	−0.19	0.36*
1980 based instruments	(0.19)	(0.16)	(0.15)
F-Statistics, First stage	51.5	51.5	51.5

Note: The units of observations are Commuting Zones. Variables are in decadal changes. In the first column the dependent variable is the change in native average log weekly wage for all natives. In the second column the dependent variable is the change in native average log weekly wage for native workers with a high school degree or less. In the third column the dependent variable is the change in native average log weekly wage for natives with some college education or more. The specification and IV are described in the first column. The method of estimation in each specification is 2SLS using the shift-share instruments as described in the text, either using 1970 or 1980 as base year. Regressions are weighted by the total number of individuals in the area. Standard errors clustered at the area unit level.
** = significant at 5% confidence level.

of an earlier year reduces the chance that persistent labor demand shocks drive both the distribution of foreigners by nationality in t_0 and the native worker productivity growth in the subsequent decades. Hence one may think that $t_0 = 1970$ is the better choice. The instruments so constructed are reasonably strong (F-statistics of 92.5 for the one with base-year 1970 and 51.5 for the one based on 1980, as shown in Table 7). One cannot still be sure that the distribution of immigrants in 1980 or even 1970 is fully exogenous to post-1980 demand shocks and hence we still need to be careful in interpreting the results. Past immigrants may have located following past demand shocks and a long-run persistence of these shocks could threaten the exclusion restriction and introduce omitted variable bias. Table 7 shows the 2SLS estimates of the same specification as row (1) of Table 5, for CZs only, including decade fixed effects and using the shift-share instrument. The first row shows estimates using IV based in 1970, while the second row shows the same estimates with IV based in 1980. We only include the three decade changes from 1980 and 2010 in the analysis. Two things emerge. While the

point estimates of the average effect and of the effect on college educated
is very similar to the OLS estimates, the standard error for each coefficient
increases significantly so that two out of four estimates are not any longer
significant, although still positive and large. Second, the point estimates on
the wage of less educated native workers is reduced (now the point estimate
is negative) and the standard error is larger so that we do not estimate any
significant effect on the wage of that group. By better isolating supply
shocks linked to the country of origin of immigrants we may have gotten
closer to a genuine causal estimate (with the caveat mentioned above).
What we observe is a non-significant effect on less educated, a positive effect
on college educated, and an overall positive but non-significant average
effect.

The small and non-significant association of immigrants with wages of
less educated native workers and the positive association with wages of
college educated that emerges from the last 2SLS estimates, are consistent
with the results obtained using a variety of methods and approaches. In
other chapters of the book we will show model based-approaches (Peri and
Sparber 2009, Ottaviano and Peri 2012, Ottaviano *et al.* 2013, D'Amuri and
Peri 2014, Peri 2012) and reduced form approaches (Ottaviano and Peri
2006, Ortega and Peri 2015) and most of them will show a positive average
association of immigration with native wages, and a smaller correlation with
wages of less educated and a larger one with wages of more educated natives.
This book will review several estimates and explore several channels that
may explain such positive correlation. Overall, we think that the series of
simple correlation presented in this chapter, while certainly not exhaustive,
are urging us to understand better how local economies in the US, and the
national economy as a whole, absorb immigrants and generate adjustment
and new options for natives along several margins, which could produce
positive employment and wage effects.

Recent research trying to identify the effect of immigration on native
wages has focussed on the possibility of using new identification strategies, namely changes in the supply of immigrants not simply linked to the
shift-share proxy. Often these papers rely on changes in national policies
that had differential regional effects, or combination of policies and specific push-episodes from countries of origin that produce a sudden supply
shock. The problem is, often, that interesting policy changes and large
push-driven migrations are not available for all countries and hence this
identification strategy is only applicable to some specific cases. In the later
part of this volume we present some studies in which we have tried to

classify systematically immigration policies across countries and we identify episodes of policy changes to see if and how much they affected immigration (Ortega and Peri 2013, Docquier, Peri and Ruyssen 2014) with the intention of creating an international database of policies. Using such data would allow us to use response to policy changes as supply shocks. In recent papers we have used specific policies to that purpose. For instance, Foged and Peri (forthcoming) uses the surge in Bosnian refugees to Denmark during the Bosnian war (1993–1995) and the Danish refugee dispersal policy as exogenous supply shocks across Danish municipalities. The paper can then track the effects of differential refugees inflow on native labor market outcomes and it finds a positive wage impact around 1% for an increase of refugees by one percent of the population. This is due to refugees taking manual jobs and pushing natives to take more complex jobs, with career upgrade and pay increases. Beerli and Peri (2015) uses instead the opening of the Swiss border to mobility of workers from the European Union between 1999 and 2004. Such process had different timing in two types of Swiss regions and the authors use such different timing to perform a difference in difference analysis of immigrant inflows and labor market outcomes. They find very small and not significant average effects on native wages and employment.

Considering all evidence together it appears that to understand the connection between immigration and native wages and employment one needs to envision mechanisms in which local economies respond to immigration with a possible increase in the demand for native workers. We will describe very briefly some of them in the next section, in connection with papers contained in this volume.

5. Mechanisms of Adjustment: A Review

The key factors to understand the potentially positive effects of immigrants on demand for native workers are three. First, immigrant and natives are different types of workers, and they complement each other up to a certain degree. Second, immigrants may induce changes in efficiency, specialization and technology adopted by native firms with positive impact on all workers. Third, immigrants, especially the highly educated, may have positive external effects due to their impact on innovation and new ideas. Let us briefly review these arguments.

First, as pointed out in Ottaviano and Peri (2006), and Ottaviano and Peri (2012), immigrants, even with similar schooling and education as natives, tend to do different jobs from them. They bring different culture, different language skills, different abilities and these factors differentiate them from natives. A natural dimension to think of this differentiation is that immigrants have a comparative advantage in manual tasks relative to language ones (Peri and Sparber 2009). Hence they will not so much compete directly with natives, but they will create conditions for increased specialization where natives do more communication-intensive jobs and immigrants do manual-type of tasks. This can imply gains in productivity (Peri 2012, Ottaviano *et al.* 2013). However, the differentiation may also be along other dimensions. The services that immigrants provide, the products that they manufacture are different from natives'. The complementarity/diversity of tasks may drive efficient specialization and this implies gains in efficiency. But also the increased diversity in productive services itself may be beneficial to production. The added benefits from efficiency and diversity are the second reason that will result in higher wages and more demand for the skills of native workers.

But it is not all. Some immigrants may have an especially positive effects on native productivity and growth of the economy. Highly skilled immigrants are largely scientists and engineers in the US (Peri *et al.* 2015) and their contribution to ideas, innovation and new technologies drives higher productivity and higher income for everybody in the US economy. A positive externality from high human capital (as in Moretti 2004, or Docquier *et al.* 2014), or specifically from their role as scientists and engineers (as in Peri *et al.* 2015), or simply from their diversity in abilities and ideas (as in Ortega and Peri 2014), are likely to be an added boost to US growth. In fact, in a dynamic perspective the growth from more varied and better ideas can be the most important positive contribution of immigrants to the US economy.

6.   Conclusions

In this introductory chapter we have presented a battery of simple, yet increasingly demanding correlations between immigrant population and native wages and employment across areas of the United States. The prevailing fact emerging is an association of immigrants with zero to positive changes in the demand for native workers. This is true at any geographical level, for individual skill-level and in the aggregate and both when using employment and wages. We have tried to rule out spurious determinants of this correlation by including measures of local technology or common geographical factors, and the correlation has remained, possibly attenuated for less educated native workers. Certainly we have not been able to exhaust all omitted variables. Nevertheless, the prevalence of positive correlations implies that we should explore seriously models and frameworks in which the local absorption of immigrants may generates an increase (or no change) in the demand for native workers. This is what we do in the rest of the volume, first in a sequence of four chapters that collect model-based empirical analysis that provides a structural interpretation to the estimated parameters, and uses them to assess the substitutability of immigrants and natives and the impact of immigrants (and emigrants) on the productivity of natives. Then, the following four chapters focus more on the connection immigration-efficiency or immigration-innovation-productivity. They also adopt a "production function based" framework, and search specifically for productivity enhancing effects through spillovers, specialization, innovation. All the chapters try to tackle seriously the identification issue and propose a variety of methods, and instruments. The last two chapters recognize that immigration policies are the leverage that country have to affect immigration and its changes and we try to measure these policies and analyze systematically their impact on migrants. We analyze in those two chapters how immigration policies have affected migration flows in the last decades and which of them appears more effective.

Appendix: Data

The data used to construct our dependent and independent variables are drawn from the US Census public use microdata as available from IPUMS (Ruggles *et al.* 2015). We use data from 1970 (aggregating two 1% metropolitan area samples), 1980, 1990 and 2000 (5% samples), as well as the 2008–2012 American Community Survey, which creates a 5% sample around 2010 that we use for that year. The samples that measure population include all individuals age 18–64 not residing in group quarters, while the employment sample only include individuals who worked a positive amount of weeks in the previous year. The population and employment samples are weighted by the Census personal weight. The samples used to measure wages include individuals age 18–64, who are not attending school at the time of the survey, who worked a positive amount of hours and weeks in the previous year, and who received strictly positive wage income. We also exclude from the wage sample self-employed and unpaid family workers. The measure of wage used throughout the chapter is the logarithm of weekly wages that we define as the total income from wages divided by weeks worked in the previous year. Top-coded income from wages observations are multiplied by 1.5. All the dollar amounts are expressed in $ as of 1999 adjusted using the BLS CPI-U index. The wage samples are weighted by the product of the Census personal weight and the number of weeks worked in the previous year.

All the dependent variables used in the chapter are for the native population only. We define as foreign born, or immigrants, all the individuals who are born abroad, including those who become naturalized citizens. We define low-skilled workers (or "high school or less") as those with either 12 completed years of schooling and/or a high school or equivalent diploma, and as high-skilled workers (or "college or more") those with at least one year of college or more. We also breakdown these definitions further into four groups: high school dropouts (with less than 12 years of schooling), high school graduates (12 years of schooling and/or a high school or equivalent diploma), some college (at least one year of college and/or an Associate's degree), college graduates or more (Bachelor's degree or higher). Finally, we define two experience groups: workers with at most twenty years of experience, and more than twenty years of experience.

We use as main geographical unit of analysis 722 Commuting Zones that encompass the 48 adjoining US states, thus dropping Alaska and Hawaii. Commuting Zones are clusters of counties that are characterized by strong within-cluster and weak between-cluster commuting ties, thus capturing the boundaries of local labor markets. In order to match the geographic information contained in the IPUMS data (County Group in the 1970 and 1980 Census, PUMA in the 1990 and 2000 Census, and in the 2008–2012 ACS) to Commuting Zones we use the crosswalk developed by Autor and Dorn (2013) (as available on David Dorn's website, http://www.ddorn.net/data.htm). Hence we multiply the person weights and labor supply weights described above with an adjustment factor that accounts for the fraction of a County Group/PUMA that maps to a given Commuting Zone. Alternatively, we use 50 US states or 9 US Census regions as geographic units as available in IPUMS.

The description of the "Bartik" instrument, from Bartik (1991), is given in the text. The sector definition is based on 45 industrial sectors that are consistently identifiable in the 1970–2010 IPUMS samples. The wage growth measure is based on the sectoral log weekly average wages, which we defined above. The "enclave" instrument, described in the text, is based on the immigrants' country of birth that we aggregate into 15 country groups consistent across samples.

References

Acemoglu, Daron and David Autor. (2011). "Skills, Tasks and Technologies: Implications for Employment and Earnings." Handbook of Labor Economics, vol. 4B, pages 1043–1171.

Altonji, Joseph G. and David Card (1991). "The Effects of Immigration on the Labor Market Outcomes of Less-skilled Natives," NBER Chapters, in: *Immigration, Trade, and the Labor Market*, pages 201–234 National Bureau of Economic Research, Inc.

Autor, David and David Dorn (2013). The Growth of Low-Skill Service Jobs and the Polarization of the US Labor Market American Economic Review 2013, vol. 103(5), pages 1553–1597.

Bartik, Timothy J. (1991). "The Effects of Metropolitan Job Growth on the Size Distribution of Family Income," Upjohn Working Papers and Journal Articles 91-06, W.E. Upjohn Institute for Employment Research.

Beerli, Andreas and Giovanni Peri (2015). "The Labor Market Effects of Opening the Border: New Evidence from Switzerland," NBER Working Papers 21319, National Bureau of Economic Research, Inc.

Borjas, George J. (2003). "The Labor Demand Curve Is Downward Sloping: Reexamining The Impact Of Immigration On The Labor Market," The Quarterly Journal of Economics, MIT Press, vol. 118(4), pages 1335–1374, November.

Borjas George (2014). "Immigration Economics" Harvard University Press.

Borjas, George J., Richard B. Friedman and Lawrence F. Katz (1997). "How Much Do Immigration and Trade Affect Labor Market Outcomes?," Brookings Papers on Economic Activity, Economic Studies Program, The Brookings Institution, vol. 28(1), pages 1–90.

Cadena, Brian C. and Brian K. Kovak (forthcoming). "Immigrants Equilibrate Local Labor Markets: Evidence from the UK," American Economic Journal: Applied Economics.

Card, David (1990). "The impact of the Mariel boatlift on the Miami labor market," Industrial and Labor Relations Review, ILR Review, Cornell University, ILR School, vol. 43(2), pages 245–257, January.

Card, David (2001). "Immigrant Inflows, Native Outflows, and the Local Labor Market Impacts of Higher Immigration," Journal of Labor Economics, University of Chicago Press, vol. 19(1), pages 22–64, January.

Card, David (2009). "Immigration and Inequality," American Economic Review, American Economic Association, vol. 99(2), pages 1–21, May.

D'Amuri, Francesco and Giovanni Peri (2014). "Immigration, Jobs, And Employ-
    ment Protection: Evidence From Europe Before And During The Great
    Recession," Journal of the European Economic Association, European Eco-
    nomic Association, vol. 12(2), pages 432–464, April.
Docquier, Frédéric, Çağlar Ozden and Giovanni Peri (2014). "The Labour Mar-
    ket Effects of Immigration and Emigration in OECD Countries," Eco-
    nomic Journal, Royal Economic Society, vol. 124(579), pages 1106–1145,
    September.
Docquier, Frédéric, Giovanni Peri and Ilse Ruyssen (2014). "The Cross-country
    Determinants of Potential and Actual Migration," International Migration
    Review, Wiley Blackwell, vol. 48, pages S37–S99, September.
Friedberg, Rachel M. (2001). "The Impact Of Mass Migration On The
    Israeli Labor Market," The Quarterly Journal of Economics, MIT Press,
    vol. 116(4), pages 1373–1408, November.
Friedberg, Rachel M. and Jennifer Hunt (1995). "The Impact of Immigrants on
    Host Country Wages, Employment and Growth," Journal of Economic Per-
    spectives, American Economic Association, vol. 9(2), pages 23–44, Spring.
Foged, Mette and Giovanni Peri (forthcoming). "Immigrants' Effect on Native
    Workers: New Analysis on Longitudinal Data," American Economic Jour-
    nal: Applied Economics.
Grossman, Jean Baldwin (1982). "The Substitutability of Natives and Immi-
    grants in Production," The Review of Economics and Statistics, MIT Press,
    vol. 64(4), pages 596–603, November.
Moreth, Enrico (2004). "Workers' Education, Spillovers, and Productivity: Evi-
    dence from plant-level production function," American Economic Review,
    vol. 94(3), pages 656–690.
Ottaviano, Gianmarco I. P. and Giovanni Peri (2012). "Rethinking The Effect Of
    Immigration On Wages," Journal of the European Economic Association,
    European Economic Association, vol. 10(1), pages 152–197, February.
Ottaviano, Gianmarco I. P., Giovanni Peri and Greg C. Wright (2013). "Immi-
    gration, Offshoring, and American Jobs," American Economic Review,
    American Economic Association, vol. 103(5), pages 1925–59, August.
Ortega, Francesc and Giovanni Peri (2014). "Openness and income: The roles
    of trade and migration," Journal of International Economics, Elsevier,
    vol. 92(2), pages 231–251.
Peri, Giovanni (2012). "The Effect Of Immigration On Productivity: Evidence
    From U.S. States," The Review of Economics and Statistics, MIT Press,
    vol. 94(1), pages 348–358, February.
Peri, Giovanni and Chad Sparber (2009). "Task Specialization, Immigration, and
    Wages," American Economic Journal: Applied Economics, American Eco-
    nomic Association, vol. 1(3), pages 135–69, July.

Peri, Giovanni, Kevin Shih and Chad Sparber (2015). "STEM Workers, H-1B Visas, and Productivity in US Cities," Journal of Labor Economics, University of Chicago Press, vol. 33(S1), pages S225–S255.

Ruggles, Steven, Katie Genadek, Ronald Goeken, Josiah Grover, and Matthew Sobek (2015). "Integrated Public Use Microdata Series: Version 6.0 [Machine-readable database]." Minneapolis: University of Minnesota.

I
IMMIGRANTS
AND LABOR MARKETS

RETHINKING THE EFFECT OF IMMIGRATION ON WAGES

Gianmarco I. P. Ottaviano
London School of Economics and
Bocconi University

Giovanni Peri
University of California, Davis

Abstract
This paper calculates the effects of immigration on the wages of native US workers of various skill levels in two steps. In the first step we use labor demand functions to estimate the elasticity of substitution across different groups of workers. Second, we use the underlying production structure and the estimated elasticities to calculate the total wage effects of immigration in the long run. We emphasize that a production function framework is needed to combine own-group effects with cross-group effects in order to obtain the total wage effects for each native group. In order to obtain a parsimonious representation of elasticities that can be estimated with available data, we adopt alternative nested-CES models and let the data select the preferred specification. New to this paper is the estimate of the substitutability between natives and immigrants of similar education and experience levels. In the data-preferred model, there is a small but significant degree of imperfect substitutability between natives and immigrants which, when combined with the other estimated elasticities, implies that in the period from 1990 to 2006 immigration had a small effect on the wages of native workers with no high school degree (between 0.6% and +1.7%). It also had a small positive effect on average native wages (+0.6%) and a substantial negative effect (−6.7%) on wages of previous immigrants in the long run. (JEL: F22, J61, J31)

1. Introduction

The empirical analysis of cross-city and cross-state evidence in the United States has consistently found small and often insignificant effects of immigration on the wages of native workers.[1] However, two recent influential contributions by Borjas (2003) and Borjas and Katz (2007) have emphasized the importance of estimating the effects of immigration using national level data and have found a significant negative effect of immigration on the wages of natives with no high school

The editor in charge of this paper was Orazio Attanasio.

Acknowledgments: We thank the editor in charge and three anonymous referees for very useful and constructive comments. We thank David Card, Steve Raphael, Chad Sparber and participants to several seminars and presentations for very helpful discussions and comments on previous drafts of this paper. Ottaviano gratefully acknowledges funding from the European Commission and MIUR. Peri gratefully acknowledges funding from the John D. and Catherine T. MacArthur Foundation.

E-mail addresses: g.i.ottaviano@lse.ac.uk (Ottaviano); gperi@ucdavis.edu (Peri)

1. See the influential review by Friedberg and Hunt (1995) and, since then, National Research Council (1997), Card (2001), Friedberg (2001), Lewis (2005), Card and Lewis (2007) and Card (2007).

diploma.[2] These studies have argued that wages across local labor markets are subject to the equalizing pressure that arises from the spatial arbitrage of mobile workers. As a result, the wage effects of immigration are better detected at the national level since one can exploit variation in wages and immigrants across groups of workers with different skills (as captured by education and experience) over time.

The underlying logic is that while it may be relatively easy for a US worker to react to local immigration by changing their residence within the United States it is much harder for her to do so by relocating across the US border or by changing her own skill mix. Accordingly, the estimation of the substitutability among workers with different skills should play a key role in the analysis of the wage effects of immigration. Our aim is to contribute to this approach at the national level in two ways: through an improved estimation of the substitutability among workers with different characteristics and through the clarification of a crucial distinction between the partial and the total wage effects of immigration, a distinction not fully appreciated in the existing literature.

First, in terms of substitutability and in contrast to Borjas (2003) and Borjas and Katz (2007), we estimate the elasticity of substitution between immigrant and native workers within the same education and experience group without assuming ex ante that they are perfectly substitutable. Given that natives and immigrants of similar education and age have different skills, often work in different jobs and perform different productive tasks, their substitutability is an empirical question, the answer to which has important implications since the degree of imperfect substitutability affects the impact that immigrants have on the wage of natives with similar skills.

Some recent papers have also estimated the native–immigrant elasticity of substitution. Card (2007), using US city data for year 2000, Raphael and Smolensky (2008), using US data over 1970–2005, and D'Amuri et al. (2010), using German data, all find small but significant values for the inverse of the native–immigrant elasticity implying less than perfect substitutability between these groups of workers (with an elasticity between 20 and 30).[3] While our estimates are in the same ballpark, a closely related work by Manacorda, Manning, and Wadsworth (this issue) using UK data finds an even smaller substitutability between natives and immigrants (with elasticity between 5 and 10). This may be due to their use of yearly net inflows (rather than the ten-year flows we use) implying that the elasticity of substitution is identified on very recent immigrants, who are likely to be the most different from natives. On the other hand, Borjas, Grogger, and Hanson (2008) show that one can get small and

---

2. See, also, Borjas, Freeman, and Katz 1997.

3. In the older literature, indirect evidence of imperfect substitution between natives and immigrants was found in the form of small wage effects of immigrants on natives and larger negative effects on the wages of previous immigrants (see Longhi, Nijkamp, and Poot, 2005, pp. 468–469, for a discussion of this issue). Until very recently, however, only a very few studies have directly estimated the elasticity of substitution between natives and immigrants. Jaeger (1996) covers metropolitan areas only over 1980–1990, obtaining estimates that may be susceptible to attenuation bias and endogeneity problems related to the use of local data. Cortes (2008) considers low-skilled workers and uses metropolitan area data, finding a rather low elasticity of substitution between US- and foreign-born workers.

insignificant estimates for the inverse of the native–immigrant elasticity, and therefore little evidence of imperfect substitutability, in specifications that are highly saturated with fixed effects.[4]

We also reconsider the substitutability between workers of different schooling and experience levels. We produce new estimates and compare them with those found in the existing literature. In particular, since the inflow of immigrants to the United States in recent decades has been much larger among workers with no high school degree than among high school graduates, we emphasize the importance of distinguishing the substitutability between workers with no high school degree and workers with a high school diploma from the substitutability between those two groups taken together and workers with at least some college education. This distinction has a long tradition since Katz and Murphy (1992) argued that in order to understand the impact of changes in labor supply and demand on the wages of workers with different education levels it is important to consider highly educated and less-educated workers as imperfectly substitutable.[5] This has been motivated by the observation that the wage time series of workers with and without high school degrees move together much more than do the wages of high school dropouts and college educated workers.[6] The substitutability across alternative experience groups has been similarly investigated.[7]

Our second contribution concerns the distinction between partial and total wage effects. While the former refers to the direct impact of immigration on native wages within a skill group given fixed supplies in other skill groups, the latter accounts for the indirect impacts of immigration in all other skill groups. Accordingly, the total wage effects on natives across skill groups depend on the relative sizes of the different skill groups, the relative strength of own- and cross-skill impacts and the pattern of immigration across skill groups.

To clarify the distinction between partial and total wage effects, we introduce an aggregate production function that produces marginal productivity equations that can be used to compute both sorts of effects of immigration on the wage of natives in each skill group. Because we consider a rich set of skills, a large number of cross-skill effects need to be estimated. Doing this with minimal structure is impossible given available data. For example, the 32 education-by-experience groups proposed in Borjas (2003) and Borjas and Katz (2007) imply 992 cross-skill effects. But US Census data only consists of 192 skill-by-year observations on employment and wages. Adding structure, like the nested-CES labor composite we introduce in what follows, allows the

---

4. A more detailed discussion of the results by Borjas, Grogger, and Hanson (2008) is presented in Section 4.1.

5. See also Murphy and Welch 1992; Angrist 1995; Autor, Katz, and Krueger 1998; Johnson 1997; Krusell et al. 2000; Acemoglu 2002.

6. See, for instance, Katz and Murphy (1992), p. 68, and Goldin and Katz (2008) and also Figures 7 and 8 in this paper.

7. Katz and Murphy (1992) consider a simple structure with two groups (young and old) and find an elasticity of substitution between them of around 3.3. Welch (1979) as well as Card and Lemieux (2001) use a symmetric CES structure with several age groups and estimate elasticities between 5 and 10.

plethora of cross-skill effects to be expressed in terms of a limited number of structural parameters that can, in turn, be estimated with available data. In other words, the aggregate production function provides a structural foundation to the wage regressions used to assess workers' substitutability and provides parametric interpretations of the estimated coefficients. That said, economic interpretation of estimates from any reduced-form equation requires assumptions on the form of the cross-skill interactions. So, by explicitly introducing the aggregate production function we are able to get the required estimates and we can discuss the pros and cons of the underlying assumptions.

While the nested-CES approach imposes restrictions on the form of the cross-elasticities, it is still flexible enough to allow for the exploration of alternative nesting structures in terms of number of cells, order of nesting and skill grouping. In particular, we explore four different nesting models, which together span most of the structures used to estimate the substitutability among skill groups in the existing literature. Model A augments the structure proposed by Borjas (2003, Section VII) by allowing for imperfect substitutability between US- and foreign-born workers of equal education and experience. This model assumes the same substitutability between any pair of education groups and between any pair of experience groups with identical education. While the latter assumption is standard in the labor literature, the former is rather unusual as it is more common to divide workers into two broad education groups of workers, those with high education (some college education and more) and those with low education (high school education or less).[8] This alternative partition is considered in model B. Models C and D cover plausible alternatives that are not much used by the existing literature. Model C considers the possibility that some experience groups may be closer substitutes than others by allowing for the elasticity across broad experience groups to differ from the elasticity across narrow experience groups. Finally, in model D the nesting order of education and experience in Borjas (2003, Section VII) is inverted with respect to model A.

We estimate the relevant elasticities of substitution for the four models using data from the Census in 1960, 1970, 1980, 1990, and 2000, and from the American Community Survey (ACS) 2006 downloaded from IPUMS (Ruggles et al. 2009). As this set of data generates only six time-series observations, in order to better estimate the elasticities of substitution between large aggregate groups we also use Current Population Survey (CPS) yearly data for the period 1962–2006 (downloaded from IPUMS-CPS, King et al. 2009). We then use the different nested-CES models to compute the effects of immigration on the wages of natives and previous immigrants in the period 1990–2006 based on the corresponding estimated elasticities.[9]

While overall the elasticity estimates and, therefore, the computed wage effects are somewhat sensitive to model specification, some results are robust across

---

8. See, for example, Welch (1979) as well as Card and Lemieux (2001) on experience groups; Katz and Murphy (1992), Angrist (1995), Krusell et al. (2000), Goldin and Katz (2008) on education groups.

9. In so doing, we focus on the wage effects that materialize in the long run, that is, after capital has fully adjusted to the labor supply shock caused by the inflow of foreign-born workers. See Ottaviano and Peri (2008) for the evaluation of the short-run effects.

specifications. First, we find a small but significant degree of imperfect substitutability between natives and immigrants within the same education and experience group. When we constrain the native–immigrant elasticity to be the same for all education groups, our preferred estimate is 20. It becomes much lower (around 12.5) for less educated workers once we remove that constraint. Using model A, such large but finite elasticities imply that the negative wage impact of immigration on less-educated natives is −1.1% to −2.0% over the period 1990–2006. This model would imply a wage loss of less educated natives of −3.1% when the elasticity of substitution between natives and immigrants is infinite, as in Borjas (2003) and Borjas and Katz (2007). Hence, allowing for imperfect substitutability reduces the impact of immigration on native wages by no less than a third. This imperfect substitutability also implies that, on average, immigrants already in the United States suffer much larger wage losses than natives as a consequence of inflows of new immigrants. Based on model A, their average wage losses due to immigration are calculated to be around 6.7% for the period 1990–2006.

Second, while model A is a useful tool to assess the effects of introducing imperfect native–immigrant substitutability in the framework proposed by Borjas (2003), the data suggest that model B should be preferred instead. The key evidence for this is gathered when the different models are estimated on CPS data. That sample is large enough to allow for the separate estimation of the elasticity of substitution between broad education groups and between narrow education groups. These elasticities are indeed estimated to be quite different from each other, with the first evaluated around 2 and the second evaluated above 10. Using these estimates in model B generates wage effects that are rather different from those obtained from model A. In particular, the effect of immigration on the wages of natives with low education is now a small positive effect (between 0.6% and 1.7%). This result is due to the balanced inflow of immigrants between the broad high-education and low-education groups together with the imperfect substitutability between natives and immigrants, especially those with low education levels.

Finally, there is not much support for model C as the elasticity across broad experience groups is not very different from the elasticity across narrow experience groups (both being estimated around 5). There is no reason to favor model D either, as this leads to similar parameter estimates as model A. Indeed, for given parameter estimates, both models C and D generate wage effects that are very similar to those of model A.

The rest of the paper is organized as follows. In Section 2 we introduce the aggregate production function and the alternative nested-CES models. We also derive the equations used to estimate workers' substitutability as well as those needed to calculate the partial and total effects of immigration on wages. Section 3 presents the data and describes how we compute the relevant variables. Section 4 details the empirical estimation of the relevant elasticities of substitution among different groups of workers. Section 5 uses the estimated elasticities in the alternative models to compute the wage effects of immigration. Section 6 concludes.

2. Theoretical Framework

We treat immigration as a labor supply shock, omitting any productivity impact that it may produce (due, for example, to improved efficiency, choice of better technologies, or scale externalities). We may therefore miss part of its positive impact on wages, often identified as a positive average wage effect on natives in cross-city or cross-state analyses such as Card (2007) and Ottaviano and Peri (2005, 2006b).[10] Moreover, we focus on the effects of immigration on wages in the long run, that is, after capital has fully adjusted to the labor supply shock caused by the inflow of foreign-born workers.[11]

In order to evaluate the effects of immigrants on wages, we need a model of how the marginal productivity of a given type of worker reacts to changes in the supply of other types. The model we adopt is based on the nested-CES approach that has become the workhorse for the evaluation of the wage response to labor supply and demand shocks at the national level (see, for example, Katz and Murphy 1992; Card and Lemieux 2001; Borjas 2003; Borjas and Katz 2007). This is based on an aggregate production function that parameterizes the elasticity of substitution between different types of workers together with a simple theory of capital adjustment.

2.1. Aggregate Production and Capital Accumulation

Aggregate production takes place according to the following constant-returns-to-scale Cobb–Douglas function:

$$Y = AL^{\alpha}K^{1-\alpha}, \tag{1}$$

where Y is aggregate output, A is exogenous total factor productivity (TFP), K is physical capital, L is a CES aggregate of different types of labor (more on this in Section 2.2), and $\alpha \in (0, 1)$ is the income share of labor. All variables are relative to time t but their time dependence is left implicit to alleviate the notational burden. The functional form (1) has been widely used in the macro-growth literature (recently, for instance, by Jones 2005; Caselli and Coleman 2006) and is supported by the empirical observation that the share of income going to labor is rather constant in the long run and across countries (Kaldor 1961; Gollin 2002).[12] Profit maximization under perfect competition implies that the effect of physical capital on wages operates through its effect on the marginal productivity of L whose remuneration absorbs $\alpha A(K/L)^{1-\alpha}$ units of aggregate output.

---

10.   Our method may also miss any potential aggregate negative productivity effect of immigration.

11.   See Ottaviano and Peri (2008) for a discussion of short-run effects.

12.   The Cobb–Douglas functional form implies that physical capital has the same degree of substitutability with each type of worker. Some influential studies (for example, Krusell et al. 2000) have argued that physical capital complements highly educated workers and substitutes for less educated workers. This assumption, however, implies that the income share of capital should have risen over time following the large increase in the supply and the income share of highly educated workers. This has not happened in the United States over the period considered.

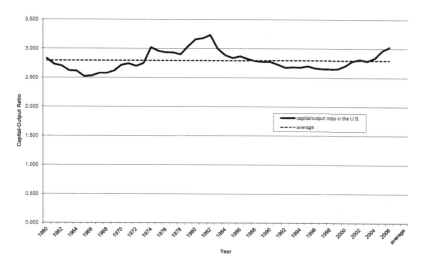

FIGURE 1. US capital–output ratio 1960–2006. Source: Authors' calculations using BEA data on the stock of physical capital and GDP.

When nested into standard Ramsey (1928) or Solow (1956) models, the production function (1) also implies that in the long run the economy follows a balanced growth path, along which the real interest rate and the aggregate capital–output ratio are both constant while the capital–labor ratio K/L grows at a constant rate equal to $1/\alpha$ times the growth rate of TFP. The intuition behind this result is that a rise in labor supply makes capital relatively scarce. This boosts its marginal productivity and depresses the marginal productivity of labor. As a reaction, capital accumulation increases until the capital–labor ratio is brought back to its balanced growth path. This implication is also supported by the data, as the real return to capital and the capital–output ratio in the United States do not exhibit any trend over the long run, while the capital–labor ratio grows at a constant rate. This is shown in Figures 1 and 2 for the period 1960–2004: both the capital–output ratio and the detrended log capital–labor ratio exhibit cyclical movements but also a remarkable mean reversion in the long run. Hence, at the aggregate level the average wage does not depend on labor supply and, therefore, on immigration in the long run. This implication of the model will be maintained throughout the paper.

2.2. *Worker Heterogeneity in a Flexible Nested-CES Model*

As workers are heterogeneous, the zero effect of immigration on the average wage may hide asymmetric effects at more disaggregated levels. In qualitative terms, immigrants should put downward pressure on the wages of workers with similar characteristics and upward pressure on the wages of workers with different characteristics. In quantitative

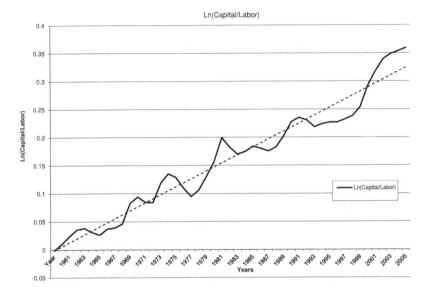

FIGURE 2. Log capital–labor ratio and trend 1960–2006. Source: Authors' calculations using BEA data on the stock of physical capital and BLS data on total nonfarm employment.

terms, these effects on wages should depend on how substitutable workers of different types are and how large the inflow of workers of each type is.

We propose a flexible nested-CES structure that embeds various alternative models studied in the literature as special cases. Though slightly demanding, the chosen notation has the advantage of allowing for recursive expressions of general results. Consider $N + 1$ characteristics numbered $n = 0, \ldots, N$. Characteristic 0 is common to all workers and defines them as such. We first partition workers into groups $i_1 = 1, \ldots, M_1$ that differ according to characteristic 1. Then, each of these groups is itself partitioned into groups $i_2 = 1, \ldots, M_2$ that differ according to characteristic 2, and so on up to characteristic N. This sequential partitioning and its relative notation is illustrated in Figure 3. The index $n = 0, \ldots, N$ identifies the characteristic used to partition workers into the corresponding groups. The figure shows how groups i_{n+1} are *nested* in groups i_n so that we can use n to also index the nesting level along the depicted partitioning structure.

Let us call $i(n)$ a group (*type*) of workers defined by common characteristics up to n, and define as $L_{i(n)}$ the corresponding labor supply. The CES aggregator at the generic level n is then defined:

$$L_{i(n)} = \left[\sum_{i(n+1) \in i(n)} \theta_{i(n+1)} \left(L_{i(n+1)} \right)^{\frac{\sigma_{n+1}-1}{\sigma_{n+1}}} \right]^{\frac{\sigma_{n+1}}{\sigma_{n+1}-1}}, \quad n = 0, \ldots, N, \quad (2)$$

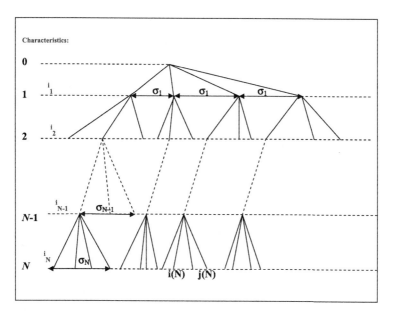

FIGURE 3. Scheme of the CES nests and relative notation.

where $\theta_{i(n)}$ is the relative productivity level of type $i(n)$ standardized so that $\sum_{i(n)\in i(n-1)}\theta_{i(n)} = 1$ and any common multiplying factor is absorbed in the TFP parameter A of (1). Both A and $\theta_{i(n)}$ depend on exogenous technological factors only. The parameter $\sigma_n > 0$ is the elasticity of substitution between types $i(n)$. The fact that the sequential partitioning of workers leads to fewer and fewer heterogeneous groups $i(n)$ as n increases is captured by assuming that $\sigma_{n+1} > \sigma_n$. Since type $i(0)$ includes all workers, we can embed the nested structure defined by (2) in (1) by imposing $L = L_{i(0)}$.

Using this structure and notation, we can calculate the profit-maximizing wage of a worker of type $i(N)$ as the value of her marginal productivity:

$$\ln(w_{i(N)}) = \ln(\alpha A\kappa^{1-\alpha}) + \frac{1}{\sigma_1}\ln(L) + \sum_{n=1}^{N}\ln\theta_{i(n)}$$

$$- \sum_{n=1}^{N-1}\left(\frac{1}{\sigma_n} - \frac{1}{\sigma_{n+1}}\right)\ln(L_{i(n)}) - \frac{1}{\sigma_N}\ln(L_{i(N)}). \qquad (3)$$

This expression holds for $N > 2$ and can be used as the empirical basis for estimating the substitutability parameters σ_n with $n = 1, \ldots, N$. First, focusing on the last level of nesting N and considering two different groups $i(N)$ and $j(N)$ with all characteristics up to $N - 1$ in common, expression (3) implies

$$\ln\left(\frac{w_{i(N)}}{w_{j(N)}}\right) = \ln\frac{\theta_{i(n)}}{\theta_{j(n)}} - \frac{1}{\sigma_N}\ln\left(\frac{L_{i(N)}}{L_{j(N)}}\right). \tag{4}$$

Therefore, $-1/\sigma_N$ can be estimated from observations on wages and employment levels over time, using fixed-type effects to control for $\ln(\theta_{i(n)}/\theta_{j(n)})$. Second, for any other nesting level $m = 1, \ldots, N - 1$, we can define $w_{i(m)}$ as the average wage of a specific group of workers $i(m)$ sharing characteristics up to m. Then, substituting m for N in (3) gives the profit maximizing relation between $w_{i(m)}$ and $L_{i(m)}$. In this case, using observations over time, the estimation of $-1/\sigma_m$ can be achieved by regressing the logarithmic wage of group $i(m)$ on the logarithmic CES aggregate $L_{i(m)}$ with the inclusion of fixed-time effects to capture the variation of the aggregate terms $\ln(\alpha A\kappa^{1-\alpha})$ and $\ln(L)$, and group-specific effects varying only over characteristics up to $m - 1$ and by year in order to absorb the terms $\sum_{n=1}^{m-1}(1/\sigma_n - 1/\sigma_{n+1})\ln(L_{i(n)})$ that do not change with characteristic m.

Once we have estimated the elasticities of substitution between different types of workers, the wage equation (3) can also be used to compute the percentage change in the wage of workers of a certain type $j(N)$ caused by a percentage change in the labor supply of workers of another type $i(N)$. To show this in a compact way let us denote by $s_{i(N)}^n$ type $i(N)$'s share of the labor income among workers exhibiting the same characteristics up to n as that type. Hence, $s_{i(N)}^{n-1} \leq s_{i(N)}^n$ and $s_{i(N)}^N = 1$. Then, we can write the percentage impact of a change in labor supplied by workers of type $i(N)$ on the wage of a worker of type $j(N)$ with the same characteristics up to m as

$$\frac{\Delta w_{j(N)}^0/w_{j(N)}^0}{\Delta L_{i(N)}/L_{i(N)}} = \frac{s_{i(N)}^0}{\sigma_1} > 0, \quad m = 0 \tag{5}$$

and

$$\frac{\Delta w_{j(N)}^m/w_{j(N)}^m}{\Delta L_{i(N)}/L_{i(N)}} = -\sum_{n=0}^{m-1}\frac{s_{i(N)}^{n+1} - s_{i(N)}^n}{\sigma_{n+1}} < 0, \quad m = 1, \ldots, N. \tag{6}$$

Two remarks on equations (5) and (6) are in order. First, an increase in the labor supply of a certain type $i(N)$ causes an increase in the wage of another type $j(N)$ only if the two types differ in terms of characteristic 1. Second, if the two types share at least characteristic 1, then a rise in the labor supply of $i(N)$ always depresses the wage of $j(N)$. This effect is stronger the larger the number of differentiating characteristics $j(N)$ has in common with $i(N)$. Both results rely on the characteristics having been nested, so that $\sigma_{n+1} > \sigma_n$.

2.3. Alternative CES Nesting Structures

The traditional characteristics used in the literature to partition heterogeneous workers are education and experience (see, for example, Borjas 2003; Borjas and Katz 2007).

We consider birthplace ("US-born", "foreign-born") as an additional characteristic differentiating workers in the same education and experience categories.

There are several reasons for adding this new source of heterogeneity since, even when considering workers with equivalent education and experience, natives and immigrants differ in several respects that are relevant to the labor market. First, people who migrate are different from those that do not. Immigrants have skills, motivations and tastes that may set them apart from natives. Second, in manual and intellectual work they have culture-specific skills (for example, cooking, crafting, opera singing, soccer playing) and limits (for example, limited knowledge of the language or culture of the host country), which create comparative advantages in some tasks and comparative disadvantages in others.[13] Third, due to comparative advantages, migration networks, or historical accidents, immigrants tend to choose different occupations with respect to natives, even for given education and experience levels. In particular, new immigrants tend to work disproportionately in those occupations where foreign-born workers are already over-represented.[14] Finally, there is no need to impose perfect substitutability between natives and immigrants ex ante as this elasticity can be estimated. Hence, while exploring alternative nesting structures for education and experience, we always consider the birthplace of the worker as her Nth differentiating characteristic. This allows us to partition each education by experience cell into US-born workers (labeled D, for domestic) and foreign-born workers (labeled F).

In combining education and experience, we borrow different nesting models from the literature and, where possible, we test one against the other to allow the data to identify a preferred one. These alternative models are depicted in Figure 4 as specific cases of the flexible nested-CES model presented in Section 2.2. Model A builds on Borjas (2003) and Borjas and Katz (2007). In this model we have $N = 3$; education is characteristic 1 partitioned into four categories:

$i_1 =$ (No Degree, High School Degree, Some College Education, College Degree);

experience is characteristic 2 partitioned into eight experience categories over a working life of 40 years:

$i_2 =$ (0–5, 6–10, 11–15, 16–20, 21–25, 26–30, 31–35, 36–40);

birthplace is characteristic 3 partitioned, as already mentioned, into two categories $i_3 =$ (D, F).

An alternative partitioning of education is more frequently used in the labor literature.[15] Accordingly, in model B workers are first partitioned in terms of two

---

13. See Peri and Sparber (2009) for evidence supporting the existence of different comparative advantages in production tasks between US- and foreign-born workers.

14. Ottaviano and Peri (2006a) find a positive and very significant correlation between the initial share of immigrants in an occupation and the inflow of new immigrants in that occupation over the subsequent decade.

15. See among others Goldin and Katz 2008; Katz and Murphy 1992; Autor, Katz, and Krueger 1997; Krusell et al. 2000; Card and Lemieux 2001; Acemoglu 2002; Caselli and Coleman 2006.

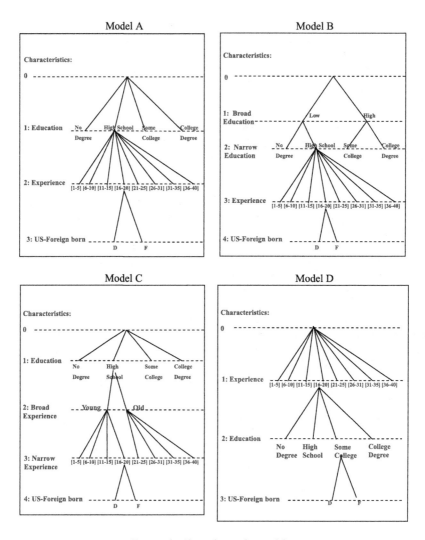

FIGURE 4. Alternative nesting models.

broad educational characteristics, each of which comprises two narrower educational categories. In this case, we have $N = 4$ with broadly defined education being characteristic 1 so that $i_1 = $ (High education, Low education). Narrowly defined education is characteristic 2, with $i_2 = $ (No degree, High school degree) partitioning Low education and $i_2 = $ (Some college education, College degree) partitioning High education. Experience is characteristic 3, still partitioned into the same eight categories as before, and place of birth is characteristic 4.

Model C is based instead on the mirror idea that substitutability may differ across pairs of experience rather than education categories, and will be smaller for groups that are closer in terms of experience. We again have $N = 4$ but there is only one level of educational characteristics, again with four categories as in model A. Broad experience is characteristic 2 with $i_2 = $ (Young, Old) and narrow experience is characteristic 3 with $i_3 = $ (0–5, 6–10, 11–15, 16–20) within the group Young and $i_3 = $ (21–25, 26–30, 31–35, 36–40) within the group Old.

These three models all proceed from the idea that characteristics are chosen to sequentially nest groups that are increasingly substitutable ($\sigma_{n+1} > \sigma_n$). As we will see, this is consistent with our estimates implying that the elasticity of substitution across education groups is generally smaller than across experience groups. If, however, workers of different education levels were more substitutable with each other than workers of different experience levels, an inverted order of nesting would be more appropriate. Hence, we also consider model D, which reverses the nesting order between education and experience. This is a natural check, though we are not aware of previous studies that adopt it. Specifically, model D maintains the same categories as model A for both education and experience but defines experience as characteristic 1 and education as characteristic 2. The structure is completed by the place of birth as a last category so that $N = 3$.

2.4. Partial and Total Wage effects of Immigration

The flexible nested-CES model from Section 2.2 allows us to clarify a crucial distinction between partial and total wage effects. While the former refer to the direct impact of immigration within a given group of workers, the latter also account for the indirect impact of immigration on all other groups of workers. This implies that the total wage effect on natives across groups depends on the relative sizes of the different groups, the relative strength of own- and cross-group impacts, and the actual pattern of immigration across all groups.

Specifically, recall that birthplace is the Nth characteristic in all our nesting structures so that σ_N always represents the elasticity of substitution between native and immigrant workers with similar education and experience. We call the *direct partial wage effect* of immigration the wage impact on native workers due to a change in the supply of immigrants with the same $N - 1$ characteristics, while keeping constant the labor supplies of all other workers. This effect has been the main or only coefficient of interest in most *reduced-form* approaches that regress native wages on the employment of immigrants in the same skill-groups.[16] The direct partial wage effect has been

---

16. For instance, in Borjas (2003, sections II to VI) or in Borjas (2006) and in the studies inspired by these seminal papers, the *direct partial wage effect* of immigration is the main estimated wage effect. Even the recent meta-study by Longhi, Nijkamp, and Poot (2005) considers this partial effect as the relevant estimate across studies.

estimated by panel regressions of $\ln w_{j(N)}^{N-1}$ on $\ln L_{i(N)}$, where the former is the wage of group $j(N)$ of native workers sharing $N - 1$ characteristics (i.e., all but the birthplace) with the group $i(N)$ of immigrants and the latter is the employment of group $i(N)$ of immigrants. Careful econometric specifications (such as Borjas 2003) control for year-specific effects (to absorb the variation of $L = L_{i(0)}$) and characteristic-by-year specific effects (to absorb the variation of $L_{i(n)}$ for $n = 1, \ldots, N - 1$). In terms of our flexible model, the resulting partial elasticity can be written as

$$\varepsilon_{i(N)}^{N-1} = - \left(\frac{1}{\sigma_{N-1}} - \frac{1}{\sigma_N} \right) s_{i(N)}^{N-1}. \tag{7}$$

Note, however, that the direct partial wage effect (7) coincides only with the last among the several terms composing the summation in (6) as this includes both direct and indirect wage effects. This happens because, by construction, the elasticity $\varepsilon_{i(N)}^{N-1}$ captures only the wage effect of a change in labor supply operating through the term $-(1/\sigma_{N-1} - 1/\sigma_N)\ln(L_{i(N-1)})$ in (3).

Hence, two important observations on (7) are in order. First, $\varepsilon_{i(N)}^{N-1}$ is negative whenever the chosen nesting structure is such that the substitutability between immigrants and natives sharing $N - 1$ characteristics is larger than the substitutability between workers sharing only $N - 2$ characteristics (that is, $\sigma_N > \sigma_{N-1}$). Second, the value and the sign of $\varepsilon_{i(N)}^{N-1}$ give incomplete information about the overall effect of immigrant supply changes on the wages of domestic workers. Indeed, (7) includes only the last term of (6), which itself is only one of the terms entering the *total wage effect* for domestic workers of type $j(N)$. In order to evaluate the total wage effect, one has to combine the impacts generated by (6) across all the $i(N)$ that include foreign-born workers for which $L_{i(N)}$ changes due to immigration.

This definition of the total wage effect implies that it cannot be directly estimated from a regression.[17] In particular, one can directly estimate the elasticities σ_1 to σ_N as well as $\varepsilon_{i(N)}^{N-1}$. However, in order to compute the total wage effect of immigration, one needs to combine the estimated elasticities σ_n with the income shares $s_{i(N)}^n$ in equation (6) and aggregate across all groups for which $L_{i(N)}$ changes due to immigrants. Intuitively, this depends on the fact that the total wage effect can only be computed by combining *own*-group effects with the set of *cross*-group effects.

To see how misleading it can be to use the direct partial wage effects to infer the total wage effects of immigration consider, for instance, model A with an elasticity of substitution between experience categories equal to 0.20 and an elasticity of

---

17. Dustmann, Frattini, and Preston (2008) propose an estimate of the *total wage effect* of immigrants on natives in a specific portion (cell) of the native wage distribution by regressing the wage of natives in that cell on the total inflow of immigrants (plus several controls). Such an approach, however, assumes the same wage effect of immigrants in any other group on natives. This is consistent with a one-level CES (which they assume) but not with a nested CES. A nested CES implies different effects depending not only on total immigration but also on the distribution of immigrants across skill groups. Moreover, to obtain enough observations for their estimates, they consider UK provinces as separate labor markets. Considering one national labor market, as we do here, would not provide enough observations (only one per year) to estimate the *total wage effect*.

substitution between natives and immigrants equal to 0.05, which we will use as reasonable estimates for the United States over our observation period 1990–2006. Assume further that the share of immigrant employment in an education group is similar to its share in the wage bill of the group. Then, (7) implies that an inflow of immigrants increasing labor supply in an education–experience group by 1% would produce a -0.15% change in the real wage of native workers in that group. If one failed to realize the partial nature of the above elasticity, one could be tempted to generalize these findings by arguing that, over the period 1990–2006, the increase of 11.4% in total hours worked in the United States due to immigration caused a decrease of $-1.7\% = (-0.15 * 11.4\%)$ in the average wages of natives; or that groups, such as high school dropouts, for which the inflow of immigrants was as high as 23% of initial hours worked, lost -3.4% of their wages. Such generalization would, however, be incorrect since expression (7) only accounts for the effect on wages of immigrants in the same skill group and omits all the cross-group effects. In fact, as we will detail in Section 5, while sharing the same negative partial elasticity, the wage effects on natives were very different across skill groups, depending on the relative size of the groups, the relative strength of cross-group effects, and the actual pattern of immigration across groups. As a result, the values of -1.7% or -3.4% calculated earlier do not bear any resemblance to the total wage effects.

3. Data, Variables and Sample Description

The definitions of variables, their construction and the sample selection coincide exactly with those in Borjas, Grogger, and Hanson (2008).[18] The data we use are downloaded from the integrated public use microdata samples (IPUMS) where the original sources are the US Decennial Census 1960–2000 and the 2006 American Community Survey (Ruggles et al. 2009). Following the Katz and Murphy (1992) tradition we construct two somewhat different samples to produce measures of hours worked (or employment) by cell and average wages by cell. The employment sample is more inclusive as it aims at measuring the hours worked in each education–experience–birthplace cell. The wage sample is more restrictive as it aims at producing a representative average wage (price of labor) in the cell.

To construct the measure of hours worked in each cell and year we consider people aged 18 and older in the Census year not living in group quarters, who worked at least one week in the previous year. We then group them into four schooling groups, eight potential experience groups and two birthplace (US- and foreign-born) groups. Four schooling groups are identified: individuals with no high school degree, high school graduates, individuals with some college education, and college graduates. Years of potential experience are calculated under the assumption that people without

---

18. For further details see Appendix B and the companion technical appendices available online (called Online Appendix). Together with exhaustive information on data, variable definitions and sample selection, the online appendices also provide the files and code needed to reproduce all the results in this paper.

a high school degree enter the labor force at age 17, people with a high school degree enter at 19, people with some college enter at 21, and people with a college degree enter at 23. We group workers into eight five-year experience intervals beginning with those with one to five years of experience and ending with those with 36 to 40 years of experience.[19] The status of *foreign-born* is given to those workers who are noncitizens or are naturalized citizens. We calculate the hours of labor supplied by each worker and then multiply them by the individual weight (PERWT) and aggregate within each education–experience group. This measure of hours worked by cell is the basic measure of labor supply. As an alternative measure of supply, we calculate the employment level (that is, count of employed people) by cell summing up the person weights for all people in the cell.

To construct the average wage in each cell we use a more selective sample. The basic wage sample is a subset of the employment sample where workers who do not report wages (or report 0 wages) and those who are self-employed are eliminated. In a more restrictive wage sample we only include full-time workers, defined as those working at least 40 weeks in the year and at least 35 hours in the usual workweek.[20] The average weekly wage in a cell is constructed by calculating the real weekly wages of individuals (equal to annual salary and income, INCWAGE, deflated using the CPI and adjusted for top-coding, divided by weeks worked in a year) and then taking their weighted average where the weights are the hours worked by the individual times her person weight.

The procedure just described allows us to construct the variables *hours worked* or *employment* and *average weekly wages* for all groups defined by their education, experience, and nativity characteristics in each year *t* (1960, 1970, 1980, 1990, 2000, 2006). The data also allow us to construct the wage bill share of each group and subgroup. When estimating the elasticity parameters, we always use the entire panel of data, 1960–2006. When we compute the effects of immigration on real wages based on those estimates, we focus on the most recent period, 1990–2006.

Table 1 reports the percentage increase in hours worked due to immigrants (column 3) and the percentage change in weekly wages of natives (column 4) for each education–experience group over the period 1990–2006, pooling men and women together. This period is the one on which we focus for our assessment of the total wage effects of immigration. Even a cursory look at the values in column 3 of Table 1 reveals that the inflow of immigrants has been uneven across groups. Focusing on the rows marked All Experience Groups, in each of the four narrow educational groups we notice that the group of workers with no high school degree experienced the largest percentage increase in hours worked due to immigrants over the 1990–2006 period (equal to +23.6%) followed by the group of college graduates (+14.6%), while high

---

19. Workers with 0 years of potential experience or less and with more than 40 years of potential experience are dropped from the sample.

20. This sample excludes workers with low *labor market attachment* who could be different from full-time workers and whose average weekly wage can introduce nonclassical measurement error, as argued by Borjas, Grogger, and Hanson 2008.

TABLE 1. Immigration and changes in native wages: education-experience groups, 1990–2006.

Column 1: Education	Column 2: Experience	Column 3: Percentage change in hours worked in the group due to new immigrants 1990–2006	Column 4: Percentage change in weekly wages, Natives, 1990–2006
No High School Degree (ND)	1 to 5 years	8.5%	0.7%
	6 to 10 years	21.0%	−1.5%
	11 to 15 years	25.9%	0.6%
	16 to 20 years	31.0%	1.6%
	21 to 25 years	35.7%	1.3%
	26 to 30 years	28.9%	−1.6%
	31 to 35 years	21.9%	−8.8%
	36 to 40 years	14.3%	−10.1%
	All Experience groups	**23.6%**	**−3.1%**
High School Degree (HSD)	1 to 5 years	6.7%	−5.3%
	6 to 10 years	7.7%	−1.6%
	11 to 15 years	8.7%	−1.4%
	16 to 20 years	12.1%	1.8%
	21 to 25 years	13.0%	0.6%
	26 to 30 years	11.8%	−0.9%
	31 to 35 years	11.0%	−2.0%
	36 to 40 years	9.3%	−4.0%
	All Experience groups	**10.0%**	**−1.2%**
Low Education (ND+HSD)	All Experience groups	13.2%	−1.5%
Some College Education (SCO)	1 to 5 years	2.6%	−5.4%
	6 to 10 years	2.6%	−2.0%
	11 to 15 years	3.9%	0.1%
	16 to 20 years	6.2%	0.6%
	21 to 25 years	8.4%	−2.5%
	26 to 30 years	12.0%	−3.1%
	31 to 35 years	12.3%	−3.8%
	36 to 40 years	12.7%	−3.0%
	All Experience groups	**6.0%**	**−1.9%**
College Degree (COD)	1 to 5 years	6.8%	0.4%
	6 to 10 years	12.2%	6.5%
	11 to 15 years	13.7%	14.2%
	16 to 20 years	12.2%	17.3%
	21 to 25 years	17.5%	9.1%
	26 to 30 years	24.4%	4.3%
	31 to 35 years	26.1%	1.7%
	36 to 40 years		
	All Experience groups	**14.6%**	**9.3%**
High Education (SCO+COD)	All Experience groups	10.0%	4.5%

school graduates and the group of workers with some college education experienced only a 10% and a 6% increases, respectively. Interestingly, however, such imbalances are drastically reduced if we consider the broad educational categories corresponding to High Education and Low Education as defined in Section 2.3. When we merge workers with a high school degree and those with no degree (see the row in the middle of Table 1) immigrant labor represents a 13.2% increase in hours worked (1990–2006). This is because the group of high school graduates received few immigrants and the group of workers with no degree constitutes only a very small share of the total labor supply.[21] In comparison, merging workers with some college education and those with a college degree implies that immigration represented a 10% increase in hours worked by the High Education group (last row of Table 1). Therefore, it is already clear from these numbers that the substitutability between the group of workers with no degree and those with a high school degree will be very important in determining how much of the downward pressure of immigrants on wages remains localized in the group of workers with no degree and how much is instead diffused to the group of workers with at most a high school degree. This suggests that the extra degree of flexibility allowed by model B in Figure 1 may be very important to correctly evaluate the total wage effects of immigration.

Column 4 of Table 1 shows the percentage change of real weekly wages in each education–experience group between 1990 and 2006. A cursory comparison of columns 3 and 4 of Table 1 suggests that it would be hard to find a strong negative correlation between increases in the share of immigrants and the real wage changes of natives across the narrow education groups. We are now ready to use our model to check whether this obviously superficial and possibly wrong prima facie impression survives deeper scrutiny.

4. Elasticity Estimates

4.1. Place of Birth

We begin with the estimation of the elasticity of substitution between natives and immigrants sharing all education and experience characteristics. As discussed in Section 2.3, in all our nesting models the place of birth is the Nth characteristic and σ_N is the corresponding elasticity of substitution (hence, intuitively N can be seen also as a mnemonic for *nativity*). Moreover, in all our nesting models we have the same 32 skill groups at level $N - 1$ (4 narrow education categories times 8 narrow experience categories). This allows us to implement equation (4) for all models through the following common empirical specification:

$$\ln\left(\frac{w_{Fkt}}{w_{Dkt}}\right) = \varphi_k + \varphi_t - \frac{1}{\sigma_N}\ln\left(\frac{L_{Fkt}}{L_{Dkt}}\right) + u_{it}, \tag{8}$$

---

21. Only 8% of total hours worked in 2006 are supplied by workers with no degree versus 30% by workers with a high school degree.

where w_{Dkt} and w_{Fkt} are the average wages of natives and immigrants in group k with k spanning all the 32 skill (education by experience) groups in Census year t. L_{Dkt} and L_{Fkt} are the corresponding hours worked (or employment). Expression (8) assumes that relative productivity $\ln(\theta_{Fkt}/\theta_{Dkt})$ in skill group k can be represented as $\varphi_k + \varphi_t + u_{it}$ where φ_k is a set of 32 education–experience effects, φ_t is a set of six year effects, and u_{it} are zero-mean random variables uncorrelated with relative labor supply $\ln(L_{Fkt}/L_{Dkt})$ (more on this in what follows). Accordingly, φ_k captures the relative productivity of foreign-born versus natives workers of similar education and experience. We allow relative productivity to have a common component of variation over time φ_t across groups, due for instance to changes in immigration policies. We also assume that the remaining time variation u_{it} is independent of relative labor supply. While imposing specific restrictions on the behavior of relative productivity, these assumptions seem reasonable. First, since we use *ratios* of wages and labor supply within education–experience groups, any variation of group specific efficiency in a Census decade would cancel out. In particular, any biased technological change affecting the productivity of more educated (experienced) workers relative to less educated (experienced) workers would be washed out in the ratios. Second, our assumptions are still less restrictive than those made in the existing literature to similarly estimate the elasticity of substitution between skill groups.[22]

Before commenting on the regression results reported in Table 2, it is useful to have a preliminary look at the data. Figure 5 shows the scatterplot of $\ln(w_{Fkt}/w_{Dkt})$ versus $\ln(L_{Fkt}/L_{Dkt})$ and the corresponding regression line from a simple OLS estimation including all 32 education–experience groups in all the years considered. The negative and significant correlation between relative wages and relative labor supplies provides prima facie evidence of imperfect substitutability. The elasticity σ_N implied by the OLS coefficient is around 20 and precisely estimated. Figure 6 shows the scatterplot restricted to the groups of workers with no degree, which have experienced the largest percentage immigrant inflows over the period. In this case the negative correlation is even stronger and more significant with the OLS coefficient, implying an elasticity of substitution σ_N of about 14.

This first impression of imperfect substitutability between natives and immigrants is confirmed in Table 2 which reports the values of $-1/\sigma_N$ estimated using specification (8). Each entry in the table corresponds to a point estimate from a different regression and the standard errors, reported in parentheses below the estimates, are heteroskedasticity robust and clustered by education–experience group to allow error correlation within group. The method of estimation is Least Squares. In specifications 1, 2, 4, and 5 we weight each cell by its employment in order to down-weight those cells with large sampling errors (due to their small size). Specifically, columns (1) and

---

22. For instance, in estimating the elasticity of substitution between experience groups, Borjas (2003, Section VII.A) and Borjas and Katz (2007, Section 1.4) assume that, within each education category, the experience-specific productivity terms are constant over time. This would correspond to including only φ_k in our regression. In Katz and Murphy (1992) the elasticity of substitution between education groups is estimated by assuming that the evolution of their relative productivity follows a time trend. This would correspond to restricting our φ_t to follow a time trend.

TABLE 2. Estimates of the coefficient $(-1/\sigma_N)$.

Specification	(1) No Fixed Effects	(2) With FE	(3) Not weighted with FE	(4) No Fixed Effects	(5) With FE	(6) Not weighted with FE
Wage Sample:	All workers, weighted by hours			Full time workers only		
	PANEL A Estimates of $(-1/\sigma_N)$.					
Men	−0.053***	−0.033**	−0.045***	−0.063**	−0.048***	−0.059***
	(0.008)	(0.013)	(0.013)	(0.005)	(0.010)	(0.012)
Women	−0.037***	−0.058***	−0.067***	−0.050***	−0.066***	−0.071***
	(0.009)	(0.017)	(0.016)	(0.007)	(0.014)	(0.012)
Pooled Men and Women	−0.032***	−0.024*	−0.026*|	−0.044***	−0.037***	−0.038*
	(0.008)	(0.015)	(0.015)	(0.006)	(0.012)	(0.013)
Men, Labor supply measured as employment	−0.057**	−0.027*|	−0.030*|	−0.066***	−0.040*|	−0.041**
	(0.007)	(0.014)	(0.015)	(0.006)	(0.012)	(0.014)
	PANEL B Separate estimates of $(-1/\sigma_N)$ by education group.					
Men, No degree	−0.073***	−0.070***	−0.070***	−0.085***	−0.084**	−0.081**
	(0.007)	(0.010)	(0.009)	(0.004)	(0.006)	(0.007)
Men, High School Graduates	−0.089***	−0.090***	−0.093***	−0.097***	−0.099***	−0.100***
	(0.016)	(0.020)	(0.018)	(0.013)	(0.015)	(0.015)
Men, Some College education	−0.071**	−0.060	−0.070*	−0.077**	−0.068*	−0.075**
	(0.024)	(0.035)	(0.034)	(0.023)	(0.033)	(0.034)
Men; College Graduates	−0.017	0.006	0.019	−0.024	−0.009	−0.0150
	(0.026)	(0.042)	(0.030)	(0.027)	(0.041)	(0.029)

TABLE 2. Continued.

Specification	(1) No Fixed Effects	(2) With FE	(3) Not weighted with FE	(4) No Fixed Effects	(5) With FE	(6) Not weighted with FE
Wage Sample:	All workers, weighted by hours			Full time workers only		
PANEL C						
Separate estimates of $(-1/\sigma_N)$ by experience group						
Men, 0–10 years of experience	−0.012	−0.14***	−0.15**	−0.037**	−0.151***	−0.157***
	(0.018)	(0.028)	(0.030)	(0.014)	(0.020)	(0.031)
Men, 11–20 years of experience	−0.044**	−0.061***	−0.066**	−0.050***	−0.068***	−0.073***
	(0.011)	(0.014)	(0.013)	(0.011)	(0.014)	(0.014)
Men, 21–30 years of experience	−0.073**	−0.052**	−0.058**	−0.077***	−0.059**	−0.066***
	(0.008)	(0.022)	(0.017)	(0.007)	(0.022)	(0.018)
Men, 31–40 years of experience	−0.094**	−0.065**	−0.063**	−0.096***	−0.064***	0.060**
	(0.013)	(0.014)	(0.016)	(0.013)	(0.015)	(0.018)

Note: National Census and ACS, U.S. data 1960–2006. Each cell reports the estimate of the parameter $-1/\sigma_N$ from specification (8) in the text. Method of estimation is Least Squares. In parentheses we report the heteroskedasticity-robust standard errors, clustered over the 32 education-experience groups. In specifications 1, 2, 4 and 5 we weight each cell by its employment. FE (fixed Effects) include Education by Experience plus time effects in rows one to four. Experience fixed effects are included in rows 5 to 8 and Education fixed effects are in rows 9–12. *** = significant at 1% level; ** = significant at 5% level; * = significant at 10% level.

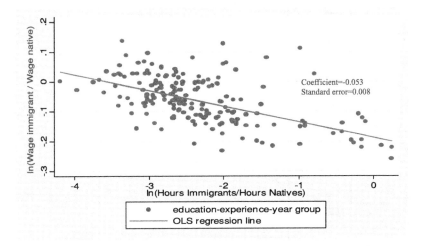

FIGURE 5. Correlation between relative wages and hours worked, immigrant-natives. Cells are education–experience–year groups. Men, 1960–2006.
Note: Each observation corresponds to one of the 32 education–experience group in one of the considered years (1960, 1970, 1980, 1990, 2000, 2006). The horizontal axis measures the logarithm of the relative hours worked in the group by male immigrants relative to natives and the vertical axis measure the logarithm of the weekly wage paid to male immigrants relative to natives.

(4) report the estimates obtained without including the fixed effects φ_k and φ_t in the regression, while other columns always include them. In columns (3) and (6), instead, we use OLS without weighting the cells. Moreover, in columns (1) to (3) all (non-self-employed) workers are used to construct the wage sample while in columns (4) to (6) only full time workers are used. Turning to rows, the top four rows show the coefficient estimates obtained for the whole sample (192 observations), assuming that σ_N is the same for each group. The subsequent rows explore the possibility that σ_N varies across education groups (Rows 5 to 8) or across different experience groups (Rows 9 to 12). In addition, the top four rows show the coefficients obtained by focusing alternatively on male relative wages (Row 1), female relative wages (Row 2) or pooled relative wages (Row 3). Finally, the fourth row uses employment, rather than hours worked, as the measure of the relative labor supply.

Two clear results emerge from the estimates reported in Panel A of Table 2. First, in each case the estimated coefficient $-1/\sigma_N$ is significantly negative at the 5% level, and in most cases at the 1% level. Second, the estimated values range between -0.024 and -0.071. Most of them are around -0.05 implying estimates of σ_N in the neighborhood of 20. Somewhat larger estimates of $-1/\sigma_N$ in absolute value are obtained when using the sample of full-time workers and of women, but these differences are not significant. To test robustness along other dimensions, we have also performed additional estimates (not reported but available upon request): excluding the early period of data (1960s) or the most recent period (2000–2006), clustering the standard errors over education

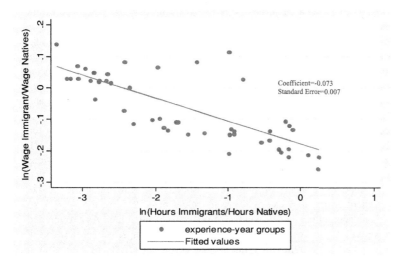

FIGURE 6. Correlation between relative wages and hours worked, Immigrant–natives with no degree; cells are experience–year groups, male with no degree only, 1960–2006
Note: Each observation corresponds to one of the 32 education–experience group in one of the considered years (1960, 1970, 1980, 1990, 2000, 2006). The horizontal axis measures the logarithm of the hours worked in the group by male immigrants relative to natives and the vertical axis measure the logarithm of the weekly wage paid to male immigrants relative to natives.

groups (or experience groups) only, or weighting the cells by hours rather than total employment. None of the resulting estimates is much different in size and statistical significance from those reported in Table 2.

For the estimates of $-1/\sigma_N$ to be consistent, relative productivity have to be uncorrelated with relative labor supplies after controlling for the fixed effects. Our structural model only calls for education–experience fixed effects.[23] Immigrant-biased productivity shocks concentrated in some cells, however, may attract more immigrants to those cells, thus inducing a positive correlation between relative productivity and labor supply. This would cause OLS to be upward biased and the bias would be more severe the larger the correlation. In this case, our estimates would represent an upper bound for the true value of $-1/\sigma_N$ so that the actual elasticity σ_N would be even smaller than what is implied by our estimates.

To control for some systematic types of correlation of the error with the explanatory variables over time and across groups, one can include additional specific effects. Borjas, Grogger, and Hanson (2008) in a specification otherwise similar to (8) include education-by-time and experience-by-time effects. Accordingly, they estimate 102 fixed effects with 192 observations and a very large part of the panel variation is absorbed by the fixed effects. This increases the standard errors, which become mostly

---

23. As in the estimation of the other elasticities, we only include the effects required by the model.

larger than 0.03 and often as large as 0.04, posing problems in identifying a coefficient $-1/\sigma_N$ that is mostly estimated in the neighborhood of -0.05.

Specifically, let us consider their preferred specifications (for pooled men and women) which include all workers, weighted by hours worked, or full time workers only. These are reported in columns (2) and (3) of their Table 4, which show estimates of $-1/\sigma_N$ equal to 0.005 and -0.034 respectively, with associated standard errors of 0.024 and 0.036. Our corresponding estimates can be found in columns (2) and (5) of Panel A of Table 2 and are equal to -0.024 and -0.037 respectively, with associated standard errors of 0.015 and 0.012. An important difference lies in the standard errors, which are significantly larger in Borjas, Grogger, and Hanson (2008), implying that both of our point estimates are well within two standard deviations of theirs. Based on these results, Borjas, Grogger, and Hanson (2008) conclude that there is no compelling evidence of imperfect substitutability. However, given the size of their standard errors, they can rarely reject values of $-1/\sigma_N$ equal to -0.05, so that there is no compelling evidence either of perfect substitutability. As a result, and since, as we will see in Section 5, even a small degree of imperfect substitutability makes a significant difference in terms of the computed effects of immigration on native wages, we prefer our point estimates and standard errors as reported in Table 2.[24]

Imperfect substitutability between immigrants and natives of similar observable characteristics may derive from somewhat different skills among these groups leading to different choices of occupations. Peri and Sparber (2009) suggests that this is particularly true for low levels of education since these immigrants tend to have less English language skill. Since they do have similar physical and manual skills as natives they tend to specialize in manual-intensive tasks. This does not happen at high levels of education because the skills of college-educated workers are more similar between native and immigrants. Moreover, since the difference in skills tends to decrease the longer immigrants stay in the United States, imperfect substitutability could be particularly acute among young workers. For both reasons the estimated elasticity of substitution should be smaller for young and less-educated workers. In Table 2, Panel B shows the estimates of $-1/\sigma_N$ when we restrict the sample to cells including, alternatively, workers with no degree (first row of Panel B), a high school degree (second row), some college education (third row), or a college degree (fourth row). Each of the estimates is based on 48 observations (8 experience groups times 6 years) and controls for experience fixed effects (except specifications in columns (1) and (4)). Interestingly, the estimates of $-1/\sigma_N$ for the groups up to "Some college

---

24. Two recent studies have estimated $-1/\sigma_N$ for countries different from the United States using specifications similar to (8) but relying on even fewer dummies as controls. D'Amuri, Ottaviano, and Peri (2010) for Germany and Manacorda, Manning, and Wadsworth (this issue) for the UK both include only education, experience and time effects. As for their estimated values, while the results in D'Amuri, Ottaviano, and Peri are similar to ours, Manacorda, Manning, and Wadsworth find lower native–immigrant substitutability. This is possibly due to the fact that they identify the native–immigrant elasticity of substitution on yearly data, thus including among immigrants only the newest arrivals, who are likely to be the most different in skills and abilities from natives.

education" are very significant and between -0.06 and -0.10, with an average value around -0.08. They imply an average elasticity of substitution of 12.5. For college educated workers, on the other hand, there is no evidence of imperfect substitutability. Although not very precise, the estimate of $-1/\sigma_N$ for this group is very close to 0. Panel C of Table 2 shows the estimates when pooling education groups and separating cells for workers with potential experience up to 10 years (Row 9), 11 to 20 years (Row 10), 21 to 30 years (Row 11), or 31 to 40 years (Row 12). Each coefficient is estimated using 48 observations (4 education times 2 experience groups times 6 years). The estimates are in this case mostly significant. When we control for education fixed effects we also observe the predicted pattern according to which $-1/\sigma_N$ is larger in absolute value for the youngest group (-0.15 with corresponding elasticity of substitution 6.6) than for the others (-0.06 with corresponding elasticity of substitution 16.6).

To sum up, when the substitutability between natives and immigrants is constrained to be the same across education and experience groups, the estimated elasticity of substitution σ_N is about 20. When we allow for differences across education and experience groups, we find that natives and immigrants have a particularly low substitutability among low educated workers ($\sigma_N = 12.5$) and among young workers ($\sigma_N = 6.6$).

4.2. Education and Experience

We have used equation (8) to estimate $-1/\sigma_N$. From the same regression we also obtain estimates of the fixed effects φ_k. These can be translated into estimates of the systematic (time-invariant) component of immigrant and native productivities, $\hat{\theta}_{F,k} = \exp(\hat{\varphi}_k)/(1 + \exp(\hat{\varphi}_k))$ and $\hat{\theta}_{D,k} = 1/(1 + \exp(\hat{\varphi}_k))$ respectively, which can be used to construct the labor composite $L_{i(N-1)}$ for group $i(N-1)$ using formula (2) for $n = N - 1$.[25] We can then calculate the corresponding average wage $w_{i(N-1)}$ and estimate $-1/\sigma_{N-1}$ by implementing equation (3). In so doing, we include two types of fixed effects. The first controls for the variation of the common aggregate term $\ln(\alpha A \kappa^{1-\alpha}) + (1/\sigma_1)\ln(L)$ and group-specific aggregates $\sum_{n=1}^{N-2} (1/\sigma_n - 1/\sigma_{n+1}) \ln(L_{i(n)})$. The second controls for the systematic variation of group-specific productivities $\ln \theta_{i(N-1)}$.

The first type of fixed effect is dictated by the nested-CES structure and, therefore, depends on the chosen nesting model.[26] The second type is, instead, required by the fact that the variation of $\ln \theta_{i(N-1)}$ may be correlated with $L_{i(N-1)}$, which would affect the consistency of the estimates. As the theoretical framework has no implication as to which specific effects to include in order to control for such a correlation, we simply assume that while $\ln \theta_{i(N-1)}$ may have a systematic component across groups

---

25.   In the derivation of the expressions for $\hat{\theta}_{F,k}$ and $\hat{\theta}_{D,k}$ we have used the standardization $\hat{\theta}_{F,k} + \hat{\theta}_{D,k} = 1$.

26.   For instance, in model A the common aggregate term can be controlled for by time effects whereas $\ln L_{i(N-2)}$ can be captured by education-by-time effects.

potentially correlated with the distribution of $L_{i(N-1)}$, the remaining variation over time is a zero-average random variable uncorrelated with changes in $L_{i(N-1)}$, and we add some structure over time (such as time trends). This method can be iterated upward so that, once we have the estimates of σ_n and $\ln \theta_{i(n)}$, we can construct $L_{i(n-1)}$ and $w_{i(n-1)}$ and proceed to estimate σ_{n-1} by applying (3) to level $n-1$.

Let us emphasize that while we estimate the elasticity σ_{N-1} (and higher level elasticities σ_n with $n = 1, \ldots, N - 2$) by implementing (3), the interpretation of the elasticity σ_{N-1} and the type of fixed effects included depend on the nesting structure chosen. While so far our recursive notation has proved useful in order to embed the alternative nesting models in a single flexible nested-CES framework, the comparative discussion of estimated elasticities across models will benefit from a more intuitive notation. Say, for example, that we want to compare the estimated substitutability between narrow experience groups. Depending on the model, the corresponding elasticity would be σ_{N-1} (models A, B and C) or σ_{N-2} (model D). Hence, from now on we prefer to label the various elasticities by the name of the relevant characteristics rather than by their order in the nesting structure. Of course each elasticity coming from the different nesting models is estimated using the appropriate specification of (3) and includes the appropriate set of fixed effects prescribed by the corresponding structure. Henceforth, σ_{EXP} will denote the elasticity of substitution between five-year experience groups and will be estimated for all models; σ_{Y-O} will denote the elasticity of substitution between twenty-year experience groups and, therefore, will be estimated only for model C; σ_{EDU} will denote the elasticity of substitution between narrow education groups and, therefore, will be estimated for all models; and σ_{H-L} will denote the elasticity of substitution between high- and low-education workers and, therefore, will be estimated only for specification B.

Before presenting our estimates, two comments are in order. First, in the existing literature there are estimates of all these elasticities. In particular, σ_{Y-O} and σ_{EXP} have been estimated by Welch (1979), Katz and Murphy (1992) and Card and Lemieux (2001) while σ_{H-L} and σ_{EDU} have been estimated by Katz and Murphy (1992) and Goldin and Katz (2008). This means that our estimates and those in the literature can be used to inform the choice of parameters for the computation of total wage effects in Section 5. Second, as we estimate elasticities at higher levels of the nesting structure (especially σ_{H-L}), we end up using only a few large labor aggregates for which the Census data provide very few observations over time (six year points only). For this reason, we complement the estimates that use Census data with estimates obtained on data from the Current Population Survey (CPS) 1963–2006, which provides 44 yearly observations.

4.2.1. Census Data.   First, let us discuss our estimates of the elasticities of substitution for experience groups using Census data. Table 3 reports the estimates of the parameters $-1/\sigma_{\mathrm{EXP}}$ and $-1/\sigma_{Y-O}$ obtained for the different nesting structures by implementing the appropriate version of equation (3). All regressions are estimated using 2SLS and immigrant labor supply to instrument total labor supply (measured as

TABLE 3. Estimates of $(-1/\sigma_{\text{EXP}})$.

Structure of the nest	Model A and B	Model C		Model D
Estimated coefficient:	(1) $(-1/\sigma_{\text{EXP}})$	(2) $(-1/\sigma_{\text{EXP}})$	(3) $(-1/\sigma_{\text{Y}-\text{O}})$	(4) $(-1/\sigma_{\text{EXP}})$
Men				
Labor Supply is Hours worked	−0.16***	−0.19**	−0.31*	−0.30***
	(0.05)	(0.08)	(0.15)	(0.06)
Women	−0.05	−0.08*	−0.14	−0.01
Labor Supply is Hours worked	(0.05)	(0.045)	(0.12)	(0.06)
Pooled Men and Women	−0.14***	−0.17**	−0.28**	−0.23***
Labor Supply is Hours worked	(0.04)	(0.06)	(0.12)	(0.05)
Men	−0.13***	−0.18**	−0.26*	−0.22***
Labor Supply is Employment	(0.05)	(0.08)	(0.12)	(0.06)
Cells:	Education-experience-year	Education-experience-year	Education-Young/Old-year	Experience-year
Effects Included	Education by Year and Education by Experience	Education-Young-Year, Education-Old-Year and Education by Experience	Education-Year and Education-Young/Old	Experience effects and year effects
Observations	192	192	96	48

Note: National Census and ACS U.S. data 1960–2006. Each cell reports the estimates from a different regression that implements equation (3) in the text for the appropriate characteristics and using the appropriate aggregate and fixed effects. The method of estimation is 2SLS using immigrant workers' hours as an instrument for total workers' hours. Cells are weighted by their employment. Standard errors are heteroskedasticity robust and clustered at the education-experience level for columns (1) and (2), at the education-young/old level for column (3) and at the experience level for column (4).
*, **, *** = significant at the 10, 5 and 1% level.

Immigrants and Labor Markets

hours worked or employment) in the relevant labor composite[27]. As in Section 4.1, we are assuming that, after controlling for the fixed effects, the variation of immigrants by cell is random and orthogonal to relative productivity changes. As before, rows 1 to 3 report the estimates obtained using men, women, or both in the wage sample whereas row 4 uses employment rather than hours worked as measure of labor supply. The other rows report the cells, the fixed effects, and the number of observations included in the various specifications. In estimating $-1/\sigma_{\mathrm{EXP}}$, models A and B generate exactly the same regression equation, for which estimates are reported in column (1). Model C produces estimates of $-1/\sigma_{\mathrm{EXP}}$ at level $N-1$ and of $-1/\sigma_{Y-O}$ at level $N-2$. These are in columns (2) and (3), respectively. Model D generates estimates of $-1/\sigma_{\mathrm{EXP}}$ at level $N-2$, which are reported in column (4).

There is some variation in the estimates depending on the sample and the model. In particular, estimates using the wage sample of women are never significant. The estimates for men and for the pooled sample are, however, remarkably consistent, always significantly different from 0 and averaging around -0.20. The wage sample of women may have a significant amount of error. Women often have a more discontinuous working career than men, so potential experience may be a noisy proxy of actual experience. For this reason most studies (see, for example, Card and Lemieux 2001) focus on men only and, when considering women, one should expect an attenuation bias. The other estimates vary between -0.13 and -0.31, which is exactly the range previously estimated in the literature for this parameter. In a setup similar to ours with five-year experience categories within education categories, Welch (1979, Tables 7 and 8) finds a value of $-1/\sigma_{\mathrm{EXP}}$ between -0.080 and -0.218. Katz and Murphy (1992, footnote 23) estimate a value of -0.342 using only two experience groups (*young*, equivalent to 1–5 years of experience and *old*, equivalent to 26–35 years of experience). Finally, in the most influential contribution, Card and Lemieux (2001, Table V) use the supply variation due to the baby boomers' cohorts to estimate a value between -0.107 and -0.237. Hence, an estimate of -0.20, which is around the middle of our range, would be also in the middle of the combined ranges of previous estimates. We take this as a reasonable reference value, implying $\sigma_{\mathrm{EXP}} = 5$.

Another overall implication of the estimates in Table 3 is that there is no strong evidence that the elasticity of substitution between broad experience groups (*young* and *old*) is lower than the elasticity between narrow five-year experience groups. The coefficient $-1/\sigma_{\mathrm{EXP}}$ is estimated in the pooled sample at -0.17 with a standard deviation of 0.06 while $-1/\sigma_{Y-O}$ for the same sample is -0.28 with a standard error of 0.12. A formal test does not reject the hypothesis of them being equal at the 10% level.[28] Thus, given that for $1/\sigma_{Y-O} = 1/\sigma_{\mathrm{EXP}}$ model C reduces to model A and no

---

27.   This reflects the idea that changes in immigrants' employment in each skill group, once we control for fixed effects, is mainly driven by supply shocks such as demographic factors and migration costs. Such an assumption is the common one in the literature on the national wage effect of immigrants.

28.   We have also estimated $-1/\sigma_{Y-O}$ and $-1/\sigma_{\mathrm{EXP}}$ on yearly CPS data, using a method similar to Katz and Murphy (1992). This is reported in our online appendices. Doing so, we do not find evidence that those elasticities are statistically different either. Also in this case the point estimates of $-1/\sigma_{Y-O}$ and $-1/\sigma_{\mathrm{EXP}}$ are mostly between -0.1 and -0.2.

previous study has found $1/\sigma_{Y-O}$ different from $1/\sigma_{\text{EXP}}$. We interpret these results as suggesting that *model C can be reasonably absorbed into model A*.

Second, let us discuss our estimates of elasticity of substitution for education groups using Census data. Table 4 shows the estimates of $-1/\sigma_{\text{EDU}}$, reporting the estimates obtained from the appropriate versions of (3) for model A in columns (1) and (2) and those for model D in columns (3) and (4). The estimates for model C (not reported) are essentially identical to those obtained for model A, further confirming the coincidence between these two models. The estimates in Table 4 are very sensitive to the nesting structure adopted and to the fixed effects included. Model A prescribes the inclusion of time effects, so we either include education effects and education-specific time trends (to capture relative changes in education demand) or only education-specific time trends. Model D dictates the inclusion of experience by year effects (column (3)) but we also include education–experience and education–year effects to control for heterogeneous productivity (column (4)). We have also tried several other combinations of fixed effects and trends obtaining mostly negative, non-significant estimates. The specifications that produce significant estimates (column (2) and (3)) show values ranging between -0.22 and -0.43. The literature provides scant guidance for this parameter. The only clear comparisons we can make are with Borjas (2003), whose estimate is -0.759 (with standard error equal to 0.582), and with Borjas and Katz (2007), whose estimate is -0.412 (with standard error equal to 0.312) due to the fact that both papers use the same nesting structure as model A. The estimate in Borjas and Katz (2007) is indeed very close to those reported in column (2) of our Table 4, which uses exactly the same set of dummies and trends that they use.

Most of the literature, however, has assumed a split between two imperfectly substitutable education groups (High and Low) and has produced several estimates of the corresponding elasticity $-1/\sigma_{H-L}$. This is also assumed by our model B. Unfortunately, however, $-1/\sigma_{H-L}$ cannot be estimated with available Census data since by considering high school graduates or less as low-education workers and college-educated or more as high-education workers we are left with only twelve observations to work with. Hence, in order to obtain estimates of $-1/\sigma_{H-L}$, we revert to CPS data.

4.2.2. CPS Data. Writing (3) for model B at the highest level of nesting ($n = 1$) for $i(1) = \text{High}$ and $i(1) = \text{Low}$ and taking the ratio between the resulting expressions, we obtain

$$\ln\left(\frac{w_{Ht}}{w_{Lt}}\right) = \ln\frac{\theta_{Ht}}{\theta_{Lt}} - \frac{1}{\sigma_{H-L}}\ln\left(\frac{L_{Ht}}{L_{Lt}}\right), \tag{9}$$

where w_{Ht} is the average weekly wage of workers with a college degree or more (calculated as an hours-weighted average) and w_{Lt} is the hours-weighted average weekly wage of high school graduates or less. The parameters θ_{Ht} and θ_{Lt} capture the productivities of the two groups and L_{Ht} and L_{Lt} measure their labor supplies. Note that equation (9) is identical to the one estimated by Katz and Murphy (1992) (henceforth, simply KM).

TABLE 4. Estimates of $(-1/\sigma_{\text{EDU}})$.

Specification:	Model A		Model D	
	(1) With education-specific FE and trends	(2) With education-specific trends only	(3) With experience-year FE	(4) With experience-year, education-experience and education-year FE
Men Labor Supply is Hours worked	−0.16 (0.12)	−0.28** (0.10)	−0.22* (0.12)	−0.04 (0.03)
Women Labor Supply is Hours worked	−0.16 (0.15)	−0.34** (0.14)	−0.25** (0.11)	−0.02 (0.04)
Pooled Men and Women Labor Supply is Hours worked	−0.15 (0.10)	−0.30** (0.11)	−0.23** (0.11)	−0.02 (0.03)
Men Labor Supply is employment	−0.17 (0.10)	−0.43** (0.16)	−0.28** (0.09)	−0.03 (0.03)
Cells	Education-Year	Education-Year	Education-Experience-years	Education-Experience-years
Fixed Effects Included:	Education-specific effects, Education-specific trends and Year effects	Education-specific trends and Year effects	Experience by year only	Experience by year, Education by year and education by Experience
Number of observations	24	24	192	192

Note: National Census and ACS, U.S. data 1960–2006. Each cell reports the estimates from a different regression that implements (3) in the text using the appropriate wage as dependent variable and labor aggregate as explanatory variable and the appropriate fixed effects. The method of estimation is 2SLS using immigrant workers as instrument for total workers in the relative skill group. Cells are weighted by their employment. Standard errors are heteroskedasticity robust and clustered at the education level for columns (1) and (2), and at the education-experience level for columns (3) and (4).
*, **, *** = significant at the 10, 5 and 1% level.

We implement (9) on the yearly IPUMS–CPS data from King et al. (2008) with the sample and variable definitions generally identical to those used for the Census data in the previous section.[29] The data cover the period 1963–2006, so we have 44 yearly observations to estimate each elasticity. Assuming that the relative productivity $\ln(\theta_{Ht}/\theta_{Lt})$ can be decomposed into a systematic time trend and a random variable u_t uncorrelated with relative labor supply, we can estimate $-1/\sigma_{H-L}$ using OLS. There are only two small differences between our procedure and the KM one. First, our measures of labor supply L_{Ht} and L_{Lt} are CES labor composites rather than simple sums of hours. The two measures of labor supply, however, turn out to be very highly correlated so that the distinction does not matter much. Second, in KM workers with some college education contribute their hours of work partly to L_{Ht} and partly to L_{Lt} according to some regression weights. In our case all workers with some college education are included in L_{Ht}.

The estimates of $-1/\sigma_{H-L}$ based on (9) are reported in column (1) of Table 5. As in KM, we use the pooled sample of men and women and show both the heteroskedasticity-robust and the Newey–West autocorrelation-robust standard errors (as the time-series data may contain some autocorrelation). Rows 1 and 2 differ in terms of the allocation of hours worked by workers with some college education. Row 1 splits them between the high-education and the low-education groups as in KM whereas row 2 includes all workers in the former group, as implied by our model. In addition, row 3 uses employment rather than hours worked as the measure of labor supply while row 4 omits the 1960s. Finally, parentheses highlight the OLS standard errors while square brackets highlight the Newey–West autocorrelation-robust standard errors.

According to column (1), all estimates of $-1/\sigma_{H-L}$ are between -0.32 and -0.66, with standard errors between 0.06 and 0.09, hence very significantly different from 0. These estimates are close to the value estimated by KM at -0.709 with a standard error of 0.15 and confirm the imperfect substitutability between high- and low-education workers with an elasticity of substitution ranging between 1.5 and 1.8. When workers with some college education are included only in the High Education group (row 2), the estimated $-1/\sigma_{H-L}$ is -0.32, thus somewhat smaller in absolute value and compatible with an elasticity of substitution of 3. All in all, these results suggest that an elasticity around 2 (as frequently used in the literature) represents indeed a reasonable estimate of σ_{H-L}.

The KM method embedded in specification (9) is also useful to estimate the elasticities of substitution $\sigma_{EDU,H}$ and $\sigma_{EDU,L}$ between narrow education categories within the high- and low-education groups. In particular, in model B the ratios of equations (3) at the nesting stage $n = 2$ within the two broad groups produce the two equations that allow estimation of the inverse of those elasticities by regressing the within-group wage ratios on the corresponding within-group employment ratios,

---

29. The IPUMS (Integrated Public Use Microdata Samples) produces comparable variable definitions and names between the CENSUS data (that we used in the previous sections) and CPS data. Additional information on the construction of sample and variables using CPS data can be found in Appendix B and, in greater detail, in the online appendix to this paper.

TABLE 5. Elasticity of substitution between broad and narrow education groups.

| | Model B | | | |
	(1) $-1/\sigma_{\text{H-L}}$	(2) $-1/\sigma_{\text{EDU,L}}$	(3) $-1/\sigma_{\text{EDU,H}}$	Observations
"Some College" split between	−0.54***	−0.029	−0.16*	44
L$_H$ and L$_L$	(0.06)	(0.018)	(0.08)	
	[0.07]	[0.021]	[0.10]	
"Some College" in L$_H$	−0.32***	−0.029	−0.16*	44
	(0.06)	(0.018)	(0.08)	
	[0.08]	[0.021]	[0.10]	
Employment as a Measure of	−0.66***	−0.039	−0.08	44
Labor Supply	(0.07)	(0.020)	(0.09)	
	[0.09]	[0.024]	[0.11]	
1970–2006	−0.52***	0.021	−0.13	36
	(0.06)	(0.028)	(0.08)	
	[0.08]	[0.025]	[0.09]	

Note: CPS data 1962–2006, Pooled Men and Women. Each cell is the estimate from a separate regression using yearly CPS data. In the first column we estimate the relative wage elasticity of the group of workers with a high school degree or less relative to those with some college or more. Method and construction of the relative supply (hours worked) and relative average weekly wages are described in the text in Section 4.2.2. In the first row we split workers with some college education between H and L. In the second row we include them in group H, following the CES nesting in our model. In the second column we consider only the groups of workers with no degree and those with a high school degree (the dependent variable is relative wages and the explanatory is relative hours worked). In the third column we consider only workers with some college education and workers with a college degree or more (the dependent variable is relative wages and the explanatory is relative hours worked). In brackets are the standard errors and in square brackets the Newey-West autocorrelation-robust standard errors. *** = significant at 1% level; ** = significant at 5% level; * = significant at 10% level.

assuming that relative productivities follow a time trend plus a random term uncorrelated with relative supplies. Columns (2) and (3) of Table 5 report the estimates of $-1/\sigma_{\text{EDU},L}$ and $-1/\sigma_{\text{EDU},H}$.[30] Both estimates, and particularly the former, are much smaller in absolute value than $-1/\sigma_{H-L}$. In the majority of cases they are not significantly different from 0. The estimates of $-1/\sigma_{\text{EDU},L}$ are at most equal to −0.039 and a one-sided test can exclude at any confidence level that the estimate is larger than 0.10 in absolute value. The F-test statistic for $-1/\sigma_{\text{EDU},L} = -0.32$ (a value that corresponds to the lowest estimate of $-1/\sigma_{H-L}$) is 258, thus rejecting the null hypothesis of $-1/\sigma_{\text{EDU},L} = -1/\sigma_{H-L}$ at an overwhelming level of confidence. The estimate of $-1/\sigma_{\text{EDU},H}$ is around −0.10. Again, the hypotheses $-1/\sigma_{\text{EDU},H} = -0.32$ and $-1/\sigma_{\text{EDU},H} = -1/\sigma_{H-L}$ are rejected.

Hence, three important results emerge from Table 5. First, the restriction $-1/\sigma_{\text{EDU},H} = -1/\sigma_{\text{EDU},L} = -1/\sigma_{H-L}$ is overwhelmingly rejected by the data. This provides evidence that model *B* better fits the time-series CPS data than model A.

---

30. The corresponding estimates using wages calculated on the male sample only are available in the Table G.5 of the online appendix.

FIGURE 7. Relative supply and relative wages: (college and more)/(high school or less) 1963–2006.

Second, the estimates of $-1/\sigma_{H-L}$ are between -0.32 and -0.66 with an average of -0.50. This implies $\sigma_{H-L} = 2$, which is perfectly in line with the estimates of Katz and Murphy (1992), Angrist (1995), Johnson (1997), and Krusell et al. (2000) which range between 1.5 and 2.5. Third, the estimated value of $-1/\sigma_{\mathrm{EDU},L}$ is between -0.039 and 0, implying an elasticity of substitution between workers with a high school degree and those with no high school degree of 25 or above.

The reason for the extremely different estimates of $-1/\sigma_{\mathrm{EDU},L}$ and $-1/\sigma_{H-L}$ is clear from the detrended time series of relative supplies (thick line) versus relative wages (thin line) of college graduates and more versus high school graduates and less (Figure 7) and of high school graduates versus high school dropouts (Figure 8). In particular, Figure 7 shows clear and strong mirror movements of the relative (detrended) wages and supplies, a clear sign of negative correlation resulting in negative and significant $-1/\sigma_{\mathrm{EDU},H}$. In contrast, Figure 8 shows no movement at all of relative wages vis à vis the very large fluctuations of the relative detrended relative supplies, which are similar in direction and larger in magnitude than those in Figure 7. This results in a value of $-1/\sigma_{\mathrm{EDU},L}$ close to 0.

To sum up, CPS data suggest that reasonable estimates are in the neighborhood of -0.5 for $-1/\sigma_{\mathrm{EDU},H}$ and between -0.10 and 0 for $-1/\sigma_{\mathrm{EDU},L}$ and $-1/\sigma_{\mathrm{EDU},H}$ with the first coefficient closer to 0 and the second closer to -0.10. Accordingly, while one should be cautious in interpreting these values given the sensitivity of the estimates to specifications and nesting structures, the pattern that emerges seems to suggest that model B is preferred by the data to model A, with σ_{H-L} around 2 and $\sigma_{\mathrm{EDU},H}$ and $\sigma_{\mathrm{EDU},L}$ both larger than or equal to 10.

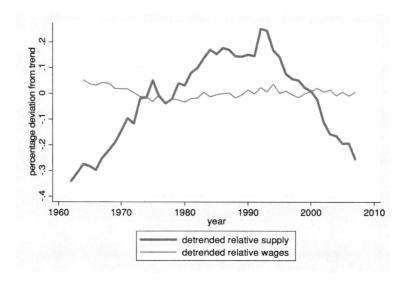

FIGURE 8. Relative supply and relative wages: (college and more)/(high school or less)
1963–2006.

5. Wage Effects of US Immigration

In Section 4 we have presented a new set of estimated elasticities of substitution
between workers with different education, experience, and place of birth. In particular,
we have argued in favor of a common elasticity of substitution σ_{EXP} (in the range
of 5.5 to 6.25) between any pair of experience groups, and for an elasticity of
substitution σ_N around 20 between natives and immigrants with the same education
and experience, with some evidence that if one allows σ_N to vary between more and
less educated, the corresponding elasticities become 33 and 11.1 respectively. The
support for a common σ_{EXP} has led us to subsume model C in model A. Moreover,
the findings against a common elasticity of substitution σ_{EDU} between different pairs
of education groups have led us to prefer model B to both model A and model D
with an elasticity of substitution σ_{H-L} around 2 between broad education groups, and
elasticities of substitution $\sigma_{\text{EDU},H}$ and $\sigma_{\text{EDU},L}$ around 6.25 and 33.3 respectively. On
the other hand, if one still wanted to use models A and D as a robustness check,
it would be reasonable to adopt an estimate of σ_{EDU} from column (2) of Table 4 of
around 3.3.

   Whereas, as discussed in Section 2.4, the previous literature has often focused
on generally uninformative *partial* wage effects, we provide here an assessment of
the *total* wage effects of immigration to the United States in the period 1990–2006
by comparing the implications of models A, B, and D based on the corresponding
estimated elasticities. Specifically, we use the estimated elasticities from Tables 2 to

5 and the data on actual immigrant flows by skill group reported in column 3 of Table 1 (together with the appropriate wage shares) to calculate the percentage impact of immigration in any skill group on the wages of each skill group as implied by expressions (5) and (6). We then aggregate all these impacts to obtain averages for specific sets of workers.[31]

Table 6 reports the simulations of the total long-run wage effects of immigration over the 1990–2006 period, separating US-born workers in panel A and foreign-born workers in panel B. The term *long-run* implies that the simulated effects assume full adjustment of the capital stock of the economy in order to restore the capital–labor ratio as it was before the inflow. We focus on 1990–2006 as this was the period of fastest immigration growth in recent US history.[32] As highlighted in the top row of the table, we consider models A, B, and D due to the fact that, according to the data, model C can be absorbed into model A (see Section 4.2.1). The values of the elasticities used in each simulation are reported in the first six rows of the table. The elasticities are the estimated parameters. They are asymptotically normal and their point estimates and standard deviations are reported in the first rows of Table 6. We consider 1,000 draws from the joint normal parameter distribution with the specified average and standard deviation. Then, using the formulas for the appropriate model, we calculate the total wage effect for each education–experience group for each draw of the parameters. This produces 1,000 simulated effects for each skill group and each parameter configuration. From those simulated realizations we obtain the simulated average total wage effect for the group and its simulated standard error. The reported wage change (and standard error) in each education group for foreign- and US-born workers are obtained by weighting the percentage total wage change (and standard errors) of each experience-education group by its wage share in the education group.[33] This provides the entries in the rows labeled "less than HS", "HS graduates", "Some CO", and "CO graduates", which show the simulated total effects, averaging by education group and their simulated standard error. We also average the changes across education groups for US- and foreign-born workers separately, again weighting the effect in each group (and its standard error) by their wage shares. The resulting values are reported in the rows labeled "Average US-born" and "Average Foreign-Born". Finally, we average the changes for the two groups of US- and foreign-born workers, still using wage share weights, to obtain the overall wage change (and its standard deviation) reported in the last row labeled "Overall Average".

Recall that Table 6 reports the "long-run" effects, after capital has fully adjusted to the labor supply shock caused by immigration. Consistent with our theoretical framework the overall average wage effect is always zero in the long run (as the average wage depends only on the capital–labor ratio and this does not change in

---

31. The detailed formulas relative to model B are described in Appendix A.2. The formulas for the other models are analogous. The STATA code to implement the formulas for all models are available in the online appendix.

32. Net immigration decreased in 2007 and 2008 and it was negative in 2009.

33. Weighting by wage shares is dictated by the nested-CES structure.

Immigrants and Labor Markets

TABLE 6. Calculated long-run wage effects of immigration, 1990–2006. (with simulated standard errors)

Nesting Structures:	Model A/C			Model D		Model B			
Parameter values (std. errors in parentheses):	(1) $1/\sigma_N = 0$	(2) Estimated $1/\sigma_N$	(3) Education specific $1/\sigma_N$	(4) Estimated $1/\sigma_N$	(5) Education specific $1/\sigma_N$	(6) Estimated $1/\sigma_N$	(7) Education specific $1/\sigma_N$	(8) Katz-Murphy $1/\sigma_{HIGH-LOW}$	(9) $1/\sigma_{EXP} = 0.13$
$1/\sigma_{H-L}$	0.30 (0.11)	0.30 (0.11)	0.30 (0.11)	0.28 (0.09)	0.28 (0.09)	0.54 (0.06)	0.54 (0.06)	0.71 (0.15)	0.54 (0.06)
$1/\sigma_{EDU,H}$	0.30 (0.11)	0.30 (0.11)	0.30 (0.11)	0.28 (0.09)	0.28 (0.09)	0.16 (0.08)	0.16 (0.08)	0	0.16 (0.08)
$1/\sigma_{EDU,L}$	0.30 (0.11)	0.30 (0.11)	0.30 (0.11)	0.28 (0.09)	0.28 (0.09)	0.03 (0.02)	0.03 (0.02)	0	0.03 (0.02)
$1/\sigma_{EXP}$	0.16 (0.05)	0.16 (0.05)	0.16 (0.05)	0.30 (0.05)	0.30 (0.05)	0.16 (0.05)	0.16 (0.05)	0.16 (0.05)	0.13 (0.05)
$1/(\sigma_N)_H$	0	0.05 (0.01)	0.03 (0.03)	0.05 (0.01)	0.03 (0.03)	0.05 (0.01)	0.03 (0.03)	0.03 (0.03)	0.03 (0.03)
$1/(\sigma_N)_L$	0	0.05 (0.01)	0.09 (0.01)	0.05 (0.01)	0.09 (0.01)	0.05 (0.01)	0.09 (0.01)	0.09 (0.01)	0.09 (0.01)
PANEL A									
Real percentage change of the wage of us-born workers due to immigration, 1990–2006. (simulated standard errors in parentheses)									
Less than HS	-3.1 (1.0)	-2.0 (1.0)	-1.1 (1.0)	-1.8 (1.0)	-1.0 (1.0)	0.6 (0.4)	1.5 (0.4)	1.7 (0.4)	1.5 (0.5)
HS graduates	0.7 (0.3)	1.1 (0.3)	1.5 (0.3)	1.1 (0.4)	1.5 (0.4)	0.3 (0.1)	0.7 (0.1)	0.6 (0.2)	0.7 (0.1)
Some CO	1.6 (0.5)	1.9 (0.6)	1.8 (0.6)	1.8 (0.5)	1.7 (0.6)	1.3 (0.3)	1.2 (0.4)	0.3 (0.3)	1.1 (0.5)
CO graduates	-1.1 (0.5)	-0.3 (0.5)	-0.6 (0.6)	-0.2 (0.4)	0.5 (0.6)	0.3 (0.4)	0.0 (0.6)	0.6 (0.5)	0.0 (0.6)
Average US-born	0.0 (0.5)	0.6 (0.6)	0.6 (0.6)	0.6 (0.5)	0.6 (0.6)	0.6 (0.3)	0.6 (0.4)	0.6 (0.4)	0.6 (0.5)

TABLE 6. Continued

Nesting Structures:		Model A/C			Model D		Model B		
Parameter values (std. errors in parentheses):	(1) $1/\sigma_N = 0$	(2) Estimated $1/\sigma_N$	(3) Education specific $1/\sigma_N$	(4) Estimated $1/\sigma_N$	(5) Education specific $1/\sigma_N$	(6) Estimated $1/\sigma_N$	(7) Education specific $1/\sigma_N$	(8) Katz-Murphy $1/\sigma_{HIGH-LOW}$	(9) $1/\sigma_{EXP} = 0.13$
PANEL B									
Real percentage change of the wage of foreign-born workers due to immigration, 1990–2006. (simulated standard errors in parenthesis)									
Less than HS	-3.1 (1.0)	-7.4 (1.4)	-10.6 (1.3)	-7.3 (1.3)	-10.5 (1.4)	-4.8 (0.9)	-8.1 (0.9)	-7.8 (0.9)	-8.1 (0.9)
HS graduates	0.7 (0.3)	-6.3 (1.4)	-11.7 (1.4)	-6.3 (1.5)	-11.8 (1.4)	-7.1 (1.4)	-12.6 (1.4)	-12.8 (1.4)	-12.6 (1.4)
Some CO	1.6 (0.5)	-2.9 (1.1)	-1.1 (2.8)	-3.1 (1.1)	-1.1 (2.7)	-3.6 (1.0)	-2.2 (2.7)	-2.6 (2.8)	-1.8 (2.9)
CO graduates	-1.1 (0.5)	-8.8 (1.6)	-5.7 (4.6)	-8.8 (1.6)	-5.6 (4.5)	-8.2 (1.6)	-5.5 (4.4)	-4.6 (4.8)	-5.3 (4.8)
Average Foreign-born	0.0 (0.5)	-6.8 (1.4)	-6.7 (3.0)	-6.8 (1.4)	-6.7 (3.0)	-6.4 (1.3)	-6.7 (2.8)	-6.3 (3.0)	-6.4 (3.0)
Overall average	0.0 (0.4)	0.0 (0.6)	0.0 (0.8)	0.0 (0.6)	0.0 (0.8)	0.0 (0.4)	0.0 (0.6)	0.0 (0.6)	0.0 (0.7)

Note: The percentage wage changes for each education group are obtained averaging the wage change of each education-experience group weighting by the wage share in the education group. The wage change for each group is calculated using the formulas for the appropriate nesting structure. Since the parameters used (listed in the first 6 rows) are normally distributed random variables we proceed as follows. We first generate 1000 extractions per each configuration of the parameters (described in the top of the column) from a joint normal distribution. We then calculate the wage effect for each education-experience group and then we take the average and the std. deviation of the 1000 values. The US-born and foreign-born average changes and their standard errors are obtained by weighting changes (and standard errors) of each education group by its share in the 1990 wage bill of the group. The overall average wage change adds the change of US- and foreign-born weighted for the relative wage shares in 1990 and it is always equal to 0 due to the long-run assumption that the capital-labor ratio adjusts to maintain constant returns to capital.

the long run). However the imperfect substitutability between natives and immigrants implies that there may be a permanent effect of immigration on the average wage of each group (as shown in the last row of panels A and B) which is, in this case, positive for natives (whose relative supply decreases) and negative for immigrants (whose relative supply increases).

Turning to the columns, column (1) shows the simulated wage effects using model A and the parameter combination estimated on Census data using model A (namely the estimates in the third row of column (2) in Table 4 and in the first row of column (1) in Table 3) except for $1/\sigma_N$, which is taken to be 0. Such a combination of parameters is close to that adopted by Borjas (2003) and Borjas and Katz (2007). Columns (2) and (3) present simulations using the same nesting model and parameter combination as column (1), except for $1/\sigma_N$ whose value is estimated. We either impose that $1/\sigma_N$ is equal for all groups, and specifically equal to 0.05 (which is roughly the average estimate in Table 2, panel A), or we allow it to differ across education groups using $1/\sigma_N = 0.09$ for those with a high school degree or less and $1/\sigma_N = 0.03$ for those with some college education or more (column (3)). These are the average estimates from Table 2, panel B. In columns (4) and (5) we use the parameter configuration estimated using model D (first row of specification 4 in Table 3 and fourth row of specification 3 in Table 4) and the formulas from model D to produce the simulated values. Columns (6), (7), and (9) show the results obtained using the parameter configuration estimated with model B when, as estimated in Section 4.2.2, substitutability is significantly lower between broad education groups than between narrow education groups within the same broad group. Specifications 6 and 7 use the estimates from the first row of Table 5 and differ only in their treatment of $1/\sigma_N$ as equal across all groups or as education-specific. Specification 9 uses an alternative, smaller estimate of $1/\sigma_{EXP}$. Finally, column (8) uses the elasticity between education groups from Katz and Murphy (1992) and the other parameters from our model B estimates. Those authors estimate a value of $1/\sigma_{H-L}$ equal to 0.71 and perfect substitution within broad education groups.

Let us first compare the results reported in column (1), in which natives and immigrants are perfect substitutes, with those in columns (2) or (3), in which they are instead imperfect substitutes. Three main differences emerge. First, the wage loss of the least-educated native workers is reduced by 1.1 or 2 percentage points. Given that in column (1) the negative wage impact is estimated at -3.1 percentage points, that loss is reduced between one- and two-thirds of its absolute value. Accounting for the uncertainty of the effects, captured by the simulated standard errors, the wage loss of less-educated natives is not significant in column (3) and marginally significant in column (2). Second, on average, all the other native groups gain a bit more (or lose a bit less) in columns (2) and (3) relative to column (1). In fact, natives as a whole gain 0.6% of their average wage in columns (2) and (3) (although the gain is not significantly different from 0 if we account for the standard error). Third, the gains of natives in columns (2) and (3) relative to column (1) happen at the expense of previous immigrants as these bear most of the competitive pressure from new immigrants due to their perfect substitutability. This is the relevant distributional shift due to immigration and imperfect substitutability: on average, natives gain 0.6 to 0.7% of their wages whereas previous immigrants lose 6.6 to 7% of their wages. The losses of immigrants are statistically significant at a 1% confidence level if we use the simulated standard error and a normal two-sided test.

The results for model D in columns (4) and (5) are quite similar to those of model A. This is because the estimated elasticities across education and nativity groups are similar. Moreover, for given elasticities, the order of nesting between education and experience has little bearing on the wage effects. In particular, the losses of natives with low or intermediate education seem a bit attenuated but the gaps are small. Otherwise, the three main differences with respect to column (1) apply to these cases too.

Finally, columns (6)–(9) report the wage effects in model B, which Section 4.2.2 has shown to be preferred by the data. In light of the estimates in that section, columns (6), (7), and (9) set $1/\sigma_{H-L} = 0.54$, $1/\sigma_{EDU,H} = 0.16$ and $1/\sigma_{EDU,LOW} = 0.03$, assuming imperfect substitutability between natives and immigrants to be either equal across groups (column (6)) or education-specific (columns (7) to (9)). Column (8) uses $1/\sigma_{H-L} = 0.71$, which is the exact estimate from Katz and Murphy (1992), and in column (9) we test how sensitive the results are to changing $1/\sigma_{EXP}$ to 0.13. The wage effects are not too different across all columns. Interestingly, the wage effects on less-educated natives are usually small but are positive and sometimes significant, especially when one allows the lower substitutability between natives and immigrants among less educated workers (columns (7) to (9)). Natives still gain as a group (0.6% of their average wages) and immigrants still lose (-6.1%). The main difference with columns (2) or (3) is that the relative wage changes of more and less educated natives are now much smaller, with the two groups experiencing more homogeneous (usually positive but not very significant) effects. This is because, while from 1990 to 2006 immigration led to rather unbalanced increases in labor supplies between workers with no high school degree (23.6%) and high school graduates (10%), increases were rather balanced between workers with high school or less (13%) and those with some college or more (10%). Hence, the value of $1/\sigma_{EDU,L}$ plays a fundamental role in determining the relative wage effects, and a value as large as 0.3 (column (1)) produces much larger effects relative to the preferred value of 0.03 used in columns (6)–(9). Indeed, in these specifications the negative effect on the least educated natives, due to the fact that the distribution of immigrants is tilted towards lower educational levels, is balanced, or more than balanced, by the positive effects, due to their imperfect substitutability. That is why even the least-educated natives face a small long-run positive effect of immigration. The wage loss of less-educated previous immigrants is between 4.8 and 8.1%. Increasing the value of $\sigma_{EDU,L}$ to infinity (which is never rejected in the estimates of Section 4.2.2) would only marginally change the estimated effect of immigrants on less educated natives.[34]

---

34. The corresponding results are not reported but are available on request.

6. Conclusions

The present paper has extended the *national approach* to the analysis of the effect of immigration on wages in the tradition of Borjas (2003) and Borjas and Katz (2007). In particular, it has argued that a structural model of production, combining workers of different skills with capital, is necessary to assess the effect of immigration on the wages of native workers of different skills in the long run. Estimating a reduced-form or a partial elasticity does not give complete information about the total wage effect of immigration as these estimate only the effect of direct competition, whereas the total wage effect is also determined by indirect complementarities among different types of immigrants and natives. Using a nested-CES framework seems to be a promising way to make progress in understanding the total wage effect of immigration. And while such a framework imposes restrictions on cross-elasticities, it is flexible enough to allow for different nesting structures and, therefore, for testing alternative restrictions.

In this framework we found a small but significant degree of imperfect substitutability between natives and immigrants within education and experience groups. A substitution elasticity of around 20 is supported by our estimates. Allowing this elasticity to vary across education groups results in significantly lower estimates among less educated workers (around 11.1). In the long run, these estimates imply an overall average positive effect of immigration on native wages of about 0.6% and an overall average negative effect on the wages of previous immigrants of about −6%.

We have also argued that the elasticity of substitution between workers with no degree and workers with a high school degree is an important parameter in determining the wage effects of immigration. The established tradition in labor economics of assuming that this elasticity is large (around 33) is strongly supported by the data. Also consistent with the labor literature, we found that the elasticity of substitution between workers with some college education or more and those with a high school education or less is much smaller (around 2). The relatively balanced inflow of immigrants belonging to these two groups from 1990 to 2006 implies very small relative wage effects due to immigration. Varying the nesting or other elasticity assumptions (for example, by inverting education and experience in the nest, or allowing different elasticities of substitution between young and old workers) matter much less in determining the total wage effect of immigration on natives of different educational levels.

All in all, one finding seems robust: once imperfect substitutability between natives and immigrants is allowed for, over the period 1990–2006 immigration to the United States had at most a modest negative long-run effect on the real wages of the least educated natives. This effect is between −2.1% and +1.7% depending on the chosen nesting structure, with the positive results coming from the nesting structure preferred by the data. Our finding at the national level of a small wage effect of immigration on less-educated natives is in line with the findings identified at the city level.

Appendix A: Theory Appendix

A.1. Income Shares in the Nested CES

For parsimony it is useful to consider a situation in which workers' diversity is defined in terms of only one characteristic. This characteristic identifies groups that are numbered $d = 1, \ldots, D$. In this case, the CES labor aggregate in (1) can be defined as follows:

$$L = \left[\sum_{d=1}^{D} \theta_d \, (L_d)^{\frac{\sigma_D - 1}{\sigma_D}} \right]^{\frac{\sigma_D}{\sigma_D - 1}}, \tag{A.1}$$

where L_d is the number of workers in group d, θ_d is the relative productivity level of that group, and $\sigma_D > 0$ is the elasticity of substitution between any two groups. Productivity levels are standardized so that $\sum_d \theta_d = 1$.

Given (A.1), the labor demand for workers in category d is

$$L_d = \frac{(w_d/\theta_d)^{-\sigma_D}}{\sum_d (w_d/\theta_d)^{1-\sigma_D}} \sum_d w_d L_d, \tag{A.2}$$

so that the labor income share of workers with education d can be written as

$$s_d \equiv \frac{w_d L_d}{\sum_d w_d L_d} = \theta_d \frac{(w_d/\theta_d)^{1-\sigma_D}}{\sum_d (w_d/\theta_d)^{1-\sigma_D}}. \tag{A.3}$$

On the other hand, differentiation of (A.1) yields

$$\frac{dL}{dL_d} = \theta_d \left(\frac{L}{L_d} \right)^{\frac{1}{\sigma_D}}. \tag{A.4}$$

Then, (A.2), (A.3) and (A.4) together imply

$$\frac{d \ln L}{d \ln L_d} = \frac{dL}{dL_d} \frac{L_d}{L} = s_d.$$

A.2. Total Wage Effects of Immigration in Model B

We denote the change in the supply of foreign-born due to immigration between two Censuses in group $j(N)$ as $\Delta L_{F,j(N)} = L_{F,j(N),t+10} - L_{F,j(N),t}$. Then, we can use the demand functions (3) and take the total differential with respect to variation in all groups $j(N-1)$ to derive the total effect of immigration on native and immigrant wages. The resulting expressions are

$$\left(\frac{\Delta w_{i(N-1)}^{D}}{w_{i(N-1)}^{D}}\right)^{\text{Total}} = \frac{1}{\sigma_{H-L}} \sum_{H-L} \sum_{\text{EDU}} \sum_{\text{EXP}} \left(s_{j(N-1),F}^{0} \frac{\Delta L_{F,j(N-1)}}{L_{F,j(N-1)}}\right)$$

$$+ \left(\frac{1}{\sigma_{\text{EDU},i}} - \frac{1}{\sigma_{H-L}}\right) \sum_{\text{EDU}} \sum_{\text{EXP}} \left(s_{j(N-1),F}^{1} \frac{\Delta L_{F,j(N-1)}}{L_{F,j(N-1)}}\right)$$

$$+ \left(\frac{1}{\sigma_{\text{EXP}}} - \frac{1}{\sigma_{\text{EDU},i}}\right) \sum_{\text{EXP}} \left(s_{j(N-1),F}^{2} \frac{\Delta L_{F,j(N-1)}}{L_{F,j(N-1)}}\right)$$

$$+ \left(\frac{1}{\sigma_{N}} - \frac{1}{\sigma_{\text{EXP}}}\right) \left(s_{j(N-1),F}^{3} \frac{\Delta L_{F,j(N-1)}}{L_{F,j(N-1)}}\right) \qquad (A.5)$$

and

$$\left(\frac{\Delta w_{i(N-1)}^{F}}{w_{i(N-1)}^{F}}\right)^{\text{Total}} = \frac{1}{\sigma_{H-L}} \sum_{H-L} \sum_{\text{EDU}} \sum_{\text{EXP}} \left(s_{j(N-1),F}^{0} \frac{\Delta L_{F,j(N-1)}}{L_{F,j(N-1)}}\right)$$

$$+ \left(\frac{1}{\sigma_{\text{EDU},i}} - \frac{1}{\sigma_{H-L}}\right) \sum_{\text{EDU}} \sum_{\text{EXP}} \left(s_{j(N-1),F}^{1} \frac{\Delta L_{F,j(N-1)}}{L_{F,j(N-1)}}\right)$$

$$+ \left(\frac{1}{\sigma_{\text{EXP}}} - \frac{1}{\sigma_{\text{EDU},i}}\right) \sum_{\text{EXP}} \left(s_{j(N-1),F}^{2} \frac{\Delta L_{F,j(N-1)}}{L_{F,j(N-1)}}\right)$$

$$+ \left(\frac{1}{\sigma_{N}} - \frac{1}{\sigma_{\text{EXP}}}\right) \left(s_{j(N-1),F}^{3} \frac{\Delta L_{F,j(N-1)}}{L_{F,j(N-1)}}\right) - \frac{1}{\sigma_{N}} \frac{\Delta L_{F,i(N-1)}}{L_{F,i(N-1)}},$$

$$(A.6)$$

where $w_{i(N-1)}^{D}$ is the wage of domestic workers in group $i(N-1)$, $s_{j(N-1),F}^{m}$ is the share of labor income of foreign workers with characteristics $j(N-1)$ among all workers exhibiting the same characteristics up to m.

Using the percentage change in wages for each skill group, we can then aggregate and find the effect of immigration on several representative wages. The average wage for the whole economy in year t, inclusive of natives and immigrants, is given by

$$\bar{w}_t = \sum_{H-L} \sum_{\text{EDU}} \sum_{\text{EXP}} \left(w_{i(N-1)}^{F} \varkappa_{i(N-1),F} + w_{i(N-1)}^{D} \varkappa_{i(N-1),D}\right),$$

where $\varkappa_{i(N-1),F}$ ($\varkappa_{i(N-1),D}$) are the hours worked by immigrants (natives) in group $i(N-1)$ as a share of total hours worked in the economy. Similarly, the average wages of immigrants and natives can be expressed as weighted averages of individual group wages:

$$\bar{w}_{Ft} = \frac{\sum_{H-L} \sum_{\text{EDU}} \sum_{\text{EXP}} \left(w_{i(N-1)}^{F} \varkappa_{i(N-1),F}\right)}{\sum_{H-L} \sum_{\text{EDU}} \sum_{\text{EXP}} \varkappa_{i(N-1),F}}$$

and

$$\bar{w}_{Dt} = \frac{\sum\limits_{H-L}\sum\limits_{\text{EDU}}\sum\limits_{\text{EXP}}\left(w^D_{i(N-1)}\varkappa_{i(N-1),D}\right)}{\sum\limits_{H-L}\sum\limits_{\text{EDU}}\sum\limits_{\text{EXP}}\varkappa_{i(N-1),D}}.$$

The percentage change in the average wage of natives as a consequence of changes in each group's wage due to immigration is given by

$$\frac{\Delta\bar{w}_{Dt}}{\bar{w}_{Dt}} = \frac{\sum\limits_{H-L}\sum\limits_{\text{EDU}}\sum\limits_{\text{EXP}}\left(\frac{\Delta w^D_{i(N-1)}}{w^D_{i(N-1)}}\frac{w^D_{i(N-1)}}{\bar{w}_{Dt}}\varkappa_{i(N-1),D}\right)}{\sum\limits_{H-L}\sum\limits_{\text{EDU}}\sum\limits_{\text{EXP}}\varkappa_{i(N-1),D}}$$

$$= \frac{\sum\limits_{H-L}\sum\limits_{\text{EDU}}\sum\limits_{\text{EXP}}\left(\frac{\Delta w^D_{i(N-1)}}{w^D_{i(N-1)}}\right)s^0_{j(N-1),D}}{\sum\limits_{H-L}\sum\limits_{\text{EDU}}\sum\limits_{\text{EXP}}s^0_{j(N-1),D}}, \qquad (A.7)$$

where $\Delta w^D_{i(N-1)}/w^D_{i(N-1)}$ represents the percentage change in the wage of US-born in group $i(N-1)$ due to immigration, and its expression is given in (A5). Similarly, the percentage change in the average wage of foreign-born workers is

$$\frac{\Delta\bar{w}_{Ft}}{\bar{w}_{Ft}} = \frac{\sum\limits_{H-L}\sum\limits_{\text{EDU}}\sum\limits_{\text{EXP}}\left(\frac{\Delta w^F_{i(N-1)}}{w^F_{i(N-1)}}\frac{w^F_{i(N-1)}}{\bar{w}_{Ft}}\varkappa_{i(N-1),F}\right)}{\sum\limits_{H-L}\sum\limits_{\text{EDU}}\sum\limits_{\text{EXP}}\varkappa_{i(N-1),F}}$$

$$= \frac{\sum\limits_{H-L}\sum\limits_{\text{EDU}}\sum\limits_{\text{EXP}}\left(\frac{\Delta w^F_{i(N-1)}}{w^F_{i(N-1)}}\right)s^0_{j(N-1),F}}{\sum\limits_{H-L}\sum\limits_{\text{EDU}}\sum\limits_{\text{EXP}}s^0_{j(N-1),F}}, \qquad (A.8)$$

where $\Delta w^F_{i(N-1)}/w^F_{i(N-1)}$ represents the percentage change in the wage of foreign-born workers in group $i(N-1)$ due to immigration, and its expression is given in (A.6). Finally, by aggregating the total effect of immigration on the wages of all groups, native and foreign, we can obtain the effect of immigration on average wages:

$$\frac{\Delta\bar{w}_t}{\bar{w}_t} = \sum\limits_{H-L}\sum\limits_{\text{EDU}}\sum\limits_{\text{EXP}}\left(\frac{\Delta w^F_{i(N-1)}}{w^F_{i(N-1)}}s^0_{j(N-1),F} + \frac{\Delta w^D_{i(N-1)}}{w^D_{i(N-1)}}s^0_{j(N-1),D}\right). \qquad (A.9)$$

Recall that the variables $s^0_{j(N-1),F}$ and $s^0_{j(N-1),D}$ represent the group's share in total wages and, as shown in Section A.1, in the nested-CES framework the correct weights in order to obtain the percentage change in average wages are the shares in the wage bill and not the shares in employment. We adopt the same averaging procedure (weighting percentage changes by wage shares) in calculating the effects of immigration on specific groups of US- and foreign-born workers.

Appendix B: Data Appendix

B.1. IPUMS Census Data

We downloaded the IPUMS data on 1 June 2008. The data originate from these samples: 1960, 1% sample of the Census; 1970, 1% sample of the Census; 1980, 5% sample of the Census; 1990, 5% sample of the Census; 2000, 5% sample of the Census; 2006, 1% sample of the ACS. We constructed two datasets that cover slightly different samples. The first aggregates the employment and hours worked by US- and foreign-born males and females in 32 education–experience groups in each Census year. This is called the *employment sample*. The second is called the *wage sample* and is used to calculate the average weekly and hourly wages for US- and foreign-born males and females in the same 32 education–experience groups in each Census year. The first sample is slightly more inclusive than the second.

B.2. IPUMS–CPS Data

We downloaded the IPUMS–CPS data on 28 April 2008, including the years 1963 to 2006 in the extraction. As for the Census data, we constructed an *employment sample* and a *wage sample*. We used the first sample to calculate measures of hours worked and employment, and the second sample to calculate the average weekly wages for US- and foreign-born males and females in each skill group and in each Census year. The first sample is more inclusive than the second. We constructed hours worked, employment and the average wage for each of 4 education groups (workers with no high school, high school graduates, workers with some college, college graduates), following as closely as possible the procedure described in Katz and Murphy (1992), pp. 67–68.

Further details on the definitions of samples and variables that allow the exact reproduction of the sample and results of this paper can be found in the online appendix to the present paper.

Appendices C–G are available online.

References

Acemoglu, Daron (2002). "Directed Technical Change." *Review of Economic Studies*, 69, 781–810.

Angrist, Joshua (1995). "The Economic Returns to Schooling in the West Bank and Gaza Strip." *American Economic Review*, 85, 1065–1087.

Autor, David, Lawrence Katz, and Alan Krueger (1998). "Computing Inequality: Have Computers Changed The Labor Market?" *The Quarterly Journal of Economics*, 113, 1169–1213.

Borjas, George, Richard Freeman, and Larry Katz (1997). "How Much Do Immigration and Trade Affect Labor Market Outcomes?" *Brookings Papers on Economic Activity*, 1997(1), 1–90.

Borjas, George (2003). "The Labor Demand Curve is Downward Sloping: Reexamining the Impact of Immigration on the Labor Market" *Quarterly Journal of Economics*, 118, 1335–1374.

Borjas, George (2006). "Native Internal Migration and the Labor Market Impact of Immigration." *Journal of Human Resources*, 41, 221–258.

Borjas, George, and Lawrence Katz (2007). "The Evolution of the Mexican-Born Workforce in the United States." In *Mexican Immigration to the United States*, edited by George Borjas .National Bureau of Economic Research Conference Report, Cambridge, MA.

Borjas, George, Jeffrey Grogger, and Gordon Hanson (2008). "Imperfect Substitution between Immigrants and Natives: A Reappraisal." National Bureau of Economic Research, Working Paper # 13887, Cambridge, MA.

Card, David, and Thomas Lemieux (2001). "Can Falling Supply Explain the Rising Returns to College for Younger Men? A Cohort Based Analysis." *Quarterly Journal of Economics*, 116, 705–746.

Card, David (2001). "Immigrant Inflows, Native Outflows, and the Local Labor Market Impacts of Higher Immigration." *Journal of Labor Economics*, 19, 22–64.

Card, David (2007). "How Immigration Affects U.S. Cities." CReAM Discussion Paper, no. 11/07, University College London.

Card, David, and Ethan Lewis (2007). "The Diffusion of Mexican Immigrants During the 1990s: Explanations and Impacts." In *Mexican Immigration to the United States*, edited by George Borjas. National Bureau of Economic Research Conference Report, Cambridge, MA.

Caselli, Francesco and Wilbur Coleman (2006). "The World Technology Frontier." *American Economic Review*, 96, 499–522.

Cortes, Patricia (2008). "The Effect of Low-skilled Immigration on US Prices: Evidence from CPI Data." *Journal of Political Economy*, 116, 381–422.

D'Amuri, Francesco, Gianmarco Ottaviano, and Giovanni Peri (2010) "The Labor Market Impact of Immigration in Western Germany in the 1990s." *European Economic Review*, 54, 550–570.

Dustamnn Christian, Tommaso Frattini and Ian Preston (2008) "The Effect of Immigration along the Distribution of Wages." CReAM Discussion Paper 0803, University College London.

Friedberg, Rachel, and Jennifer Hunt (1995). "The Impact of Immigrants on Host Country Wages, Employment and Growth." *Journal of Economic Perspectives*, 9, 23–44.

Friedberg, Rachel (2001). "The Impact of Mass Migration on the Israeli Labor Market." *Quarterly Journal of Economics*, 116, 1373–1408.

Goldin, Claudia and Larry Katz (2008). "The Race Between Education and Technology." Harvard University Press, Cambridge, MA.

Gollin, Douglas (2002). "Getting Income Shares Right." *Journal of Political Economy*, 100, 458–474.

Jaeger, David (1996). "Skill Differences and the Effect of Immigrants on the Wages of Natives." U.S. Bureau of Labor Statistics, Economic Working Paper #273. Washington, DC.

Johnson, George E., (1997). "Changes in Earnings Inequality: The Role of Demand Shifts." *The Journal of Economic Perspectives*, 11, 41–54.

Jones, Charles (2005). "The Shape of Production Functions and the Direction of Technical Change." *Quarterly Journal of Economics*, 120, 517–549.

Kaldor, Nicholas (1961). "Capital Accumulation and Economic Growth." In *The Theory of Capital*, edited by F. A. Lutz and D. C. Hague. St. Martins, New York.

Katz, Larry and Kevin Murphy (1992). "Changes in Relative Wages 1963–1987: Supply and Demand Factors." *Quarterly Journal of Economics*, 107, 35–78.

King, Miriam, Steven Ruggles, Trent Alexander, Donna Leicach, and Matthew Sobek (2009). Integrated Public Use Microdata Series, Current Population Survey: Version 2.0. [Machine-readable database]. Minneapolis, MN: Minnesota Population Center [producer and distributor], http://www.ipums.org.

Krusell, Per, Lee Ohanian, Victor Rios-Rull, and Giovanni Violante (2000). Capital–Skill Complementarity and Inequality: A Macroeconomic Analysis. *Econometrica*, 68, 1029–1053.

Lewis, Ethan (2005). "Immigration, Skill Mix, and the Choice of Technique." Federal Reserve Bank of Philadelphia Working Paper no. 05-08.

Longhi, Simonetta, Peter Nijkamp, and Jacques Poot (2005). "A Meta-Analytic Assessment of the Effect of Immigration on Wages." *Journal of Economic Surveys*, 86, 451–477.

Manacorda Marco, Alan Manning, and John Wadsworth (Forthcoming). "The Impact of Immigration on the Structure of Wages: Theory and Evidence from Britain." *Journal of European Economic Association*, this issue.

Murphy, Kevin and Finis Welch (1992). "The Structure of Wages." *The Quarterly Journal of Economics*, 107, 285–326.

National Research Council (1997). "The New Americans: Economic, Demographic, and Fiscal Effects of Immigration." National Academy Press, Washington, DC.

Ottaviano, Gianmarco, and Giovanni Peri (2005). "Cities and Cultures." *Journal of Urban Economics*, 58, 304–307.

Ottaviano, Gianmarco, and Giovanni Peri (2006a) "Rethinking the Effect of Immigration on Wages" National Bureau of Economic Research, Working Paper # 12496, Cambridge, MA.

Ottaviano, Gianmarco, and Giovanni Peri (2006b). "The Economic Value of Cultural Diversity: Evidence from U.S. Cities." *Journal of Economic Geography*, 6, 9–44.

Ottaviano, Gianmarco, and Giovanni Peri (2008). "Immigration and National Wages: Clarifying the Theory and the Empirics." National Bureau of Economic Research Working Papers # 14188, Cambridge, MA.

Peri, Giovanni and Chad Sparber (2009). "Task Specialization, Immigration, and Wages." *American Economic Journal: Applied Economics, American Economic Association*, 1, 135–169.

Ramsey, Frank (1928). "A Mathematical Theory of Saving." *Economic Journal*, 38, 543–559.

Raphael Steven and Ed Smolensky (2008). "Immigration and Poverty in the Unites States." Working paper, UC Berkeley, April 2008.

Ruggles, Steven, Matthew Sobek, Trent Alexander, Catherine A. Fitch, Ronald Goeken, Patricia Kelly Hall, Miriam King, and Chad Ronnander (2009) Integrated Public Use Microdata Series: Version 4.0 [Machine-readable database]. Minneapolis, MN: Minnesota Population Center [producer and distributor], http://www.ipums.org.

Solow, Robert (1956). "A Contribution to the Theory of Economic Growth." *Quarterly Journal of Economics*, 70, 65–94.

Welch, Finis (1979). "Effects of Cohort Size on Earnings: The Baby Boom Babies Financial Boost." *Journal of Political Economy*, 87, 65–97.

Task Specialization, Immigration, and Wages[†]

By Giovanni Peri and Chad Sparber*

Large inflows of less educated immigrants may reduce wages paid to comparably-educated, native-born workers. However, if less educated foreign- and native-born workers specialize in different production tasks, because of different abilities, immigration will cause natives to reallocate their task supply, thereby reducing downward wage pressure. Using occupational task-intensity data from the O*NET dataset and individual US census data, we demonstrate that foreign-born workers specialize in occupations intensive in manual-physical labor skills while natives pursue jobs more intensive in communication-language tasks. This mechanism can explain why economic analyses find only modest wage consequences of immigration for less educated native-born workers. (JEL J24, J31, J61)

Immigration has significantly affected the US labor market during the last few decades, particularly increasing the supply of workers with low levels of formal schooling. Economists continue to debate the wage effects of these large inflows on native-born workers. If workers' skills are differentiated solely by their level of educational attainment, and if the production technology and productivity of each type of labor are given, then a large inflow of immigrants with limited schooling should alter the relative scarcity of education groups, increase wages paid to highly educated natives, and reduce wages paid to less educated ones. George J. Borjas (2003) and Borjas and Lawrence F. Katz (2007) adopt this intuitive approach and use US national-level data to argue that immigration reduced real wages paid to native-born workers without a high school degree by 4 to 5 percent between 1980 and 2000. Area studies by David Card (2001, 2007), Card and Ethan G. Lewis (2007), and Lewis (2005), in contrast, employ city- and state-level data, and find almost no effect of immigration on the wages of less educated native workers.

Gianmarco I. P. Ottaviano and Peri (2006, 2008) emphasize that the effects of immigration depend upon whether native- and foreign-born workers with similar

*Peri: Department of Economics, University of California-Davis, One Shields Avenue, Davis, CA 95616 (e-mail: gperi@ucdavis.edu); Sparber: Department of Economics, Colgate University, 13 Oak Drive, Hamilton, NY, 13346 (e-mail: csparber@mail.colgate.edu). We thank two anonymous referees for their helpful and constructive comments. We also thank John Bound, David Card, Gordon Hanson, Anamaria Felicia Ionescu, Larry Katz, Peter Lindert, Albert Saiz, Nicole Simpson, and participants at several seminars and conferences for helpful comments and suggestions. Peri gratefully acknowledges the John D. and Catherine T. MacArthur Foundation Program on Global Migration and Human Mobility for generously funding his research on immigration.

† To comment on this article in the online discussion forum, or to view additional materials, visit the articles page at: http://www.aeaweb.org/articles.php?doi=10.1257/app.1.3.135.

136   *AMERICAN ECONOMIC JOURNAL: APPLIED ECONOMICS*   *JULY 2009*

observable characteristics are imperfect substitutes in production. They argue that immigrants and natives of comparable educational attainment and experience possess unique skills that lead them to specialize in different occupations, which mitigates natives' wage losses from immigration.[1] Also, Patricia Cortes (2008), analyzing US cities, finds a significant effect of low-skilled immigration on prices of local nontraded goods, and on wages of previous immigrants, and much smaller effects on wages of low-skilled natives. This implies that low-skilled immigrants and natives are imperfect substitutes.

We advance this literature by developing a theory and performing empirical analysis to demonstrate *how* native- and foreign-born workers are imperfect substitutes in production. We focus on workers with little educational attainment and argue that less educated native and immigrant workers specialize in different production tasks. Immigrants are likely to have imperfect language (or, equivalently, "communication") skills, but they possess physical (or "manual") skills similar to those of native-born workers. Thus, they have a comparative advantage in occupations requiring manual labor tasks, while less educated native-born workers will have an advantage in jobs demanding communication skills. Immigration encourages workers to specialize. Less educated natives respond to immigration by leaving physically demanding occupations for language-intensive ones. Importantly, language-intensive tasks tend to earn a comparatively higher return, and those returns are further enhanced by the increased aggregate supply of complementary manually intensive tasks. Therefore, productivity gains from specialization, coupled with the high compensation paid to communication skills, imply that foreign-born workers do not have a large, adverse effect on the wages paid to less educated natives.

We begin, in Section I, by describing a simple model of comparative advantage and incomplete specialization by workers. Workers' skill endowments imply that immigration reduces the compensation paid for manual tasks and increases the compensation paid for communication tasks. The complementary nature of the two skills, and the reallocation of native workers toward communication tasks, favors wages paid to native workers. The effects compensate (in part or entirely) for the depressing effect of immigration on the wage paid to manual tasks.

Section II describes the decennial data for the 50 US states (plus the District of Columbia) from 1960 to 2000 and the construction of the variables that we use to test our model. Census occupation codes allow us to merge occupational characteristics with individual-level data from the Integrated Public Use Microdata Series (IPUMS) census microdata (Steven Ruggles et al. 2005). To measure the manual and communication skill intensity of occupations, we use the US Department of Labor's *O*NET* dataset on job task requirements. This dataset measures the importance of several physical (dexterity, coordination, and strength) and language (oral and written comprehension and expression) abilities within each census occupation code.

---

[1] Marco Manacorda, Alan Manning, and Jonathan Wadsworth (2007), and Francesco D'Amuri, Ottaviano, and Peri (2008) argue for similar imperfect substitutability between native and immigrant workers in the UK and Germany, respectively. Other important contributions to the literature on immigration and wages include Joseph G. Altonji and Card (1991); Borjas (1994, 1995, 1999, 2003); Borjas, Richard B. Freeman, and Katz (1997); Kristin F. Butcher and Card (1991); Card (1990); Rachel M. Friedberg and Jennifer Hunt (1995); Friedberg (2001); and James P. Smith and Barry Edmonston (1997).

Data values are based on experts' recent assessments and reflect the current use of skills across occupations.[2]

The empirical analysis in Section III strongly supports key implications of our theory. States with large inflows of less educated immigrants, relative to those with small flows, also experienced a greater shift in skill supply among less educated native-born workers toward communication tasks and away from manual ones; a greater decrease in the total supply of communication relative to manual skills; and a greater increase in the compensation paid to communication relative to manual skills. These results are upheld by two-stage least squares (2SLS) regressions that instrument for the variation of less educated immigrants across states using two different sets of exogenous variables, both of which exploit the increased level of Mexican immigration as an exogenous supply shift at the state level. The first follows a strategy similar to Card (2001), Card and John E. DiNardo (2000), and Cortes (2008) by using the imputed share of Mexican workers (based upon 1960 state demographics and subsequent national growth rates) as a proxy for the share of less educated immigrants in a state. The second set of instruments interacts decade indicator variables with the distance of a state's center of gravity to the Mexico-US border and to a border dummy.

Section III also performs a host of robustness checks to ensure that the results are not spuriously driven. We control for possible shifts in the demand for skills, analyze how labor flows affect previous immigrant groups and assess how the effects of immigration vary across demographic groups. The results of these checks again support the implications of our model.

Given the positive wage effect of specializing in language-intensive occupations, native-born workers can protect their wages and mitigate losses due to immigration by reallocating their tasks. In Section IV, we use our model and the empirical estimates to simulate the effects of immigration on average wages paid to native-born employees with a high school degree or less. Combining the task complementarity and the increasing specialization among native-born workers in response to immigrants (estimated in Section III), the simulations imply that the wage impact of immigration on less-educated natives is very small for the United States overall. While less-educated natives in states receiving a disproportionately large number of less-educated immigrants (relative to highly-educated ones) still experience wage losses, the effects are usually small and, in some states, they are even positive. The wage effects for natives and immigrants also allow us to calculate the elasticity of substitution between immigrants and natives implied by our simulated model. We obtain values between 20 and 47, with an average of 33. These figures are very

---

[2] Our analysis ignores changes in the task content of occupations over time. Thus, we might underestimate the effect of immigration on task performance of natives by capturing only the part due to reallocation across occupations. In Peri and Chad Sparber (2008c), we use *Dictionary of Occupational Titles* (*DOT*) and *O*NET* measures of skill intensity. The *DOT* identifies the intensity of skill use in occupations measured in 1977 and 1991, and, therefore, accounts for changes over time. Unfortunately, that dataset contains only two measures of manual skills (eye, hand, and foot coordination, and finger dexterity) and an imperfect measure of communication abilities (the performance of direction, control, and planning activities) that encompass many tasks in addition to language skills. Despite the differences between datasets and skill intensity measures, we found remarkably similar and robust results. We refer the reader to Peri and Sparber (2008c) for a more detailed description of analysis and results using *DOT* variables.

138   *AMERICAN ECONOMIC JOURNAL: APPLIED ECONOMICS*   *JULY 2009*

similar to the elasticity estimated directly by Ottaviano and Peri (2008), regress-ing relative immigrant-native wages on relative hours worked at the national level. Altogether, our findings agree in spirit with those of Card (2001), Card and Lewis (2007), Card (2007), and Cortes (2008), while adding a new dimension and more microfoundations to the structural framework introduced by Borjas (2003) and refined by Ottaviano and Peri (2008).

I. Theoretical Model

We propose a simple general equilibrium model of comparative advantages in task performance to illustrate the effects of immigration on specialization and wages.[3] We briefly describe the model here, and provide more detailed derivations and results in the Appendix. We will test the key qualitative implications of the model in Section III, and use the production structure and empirically-estimated elasticities to simulate the effects of immigration on wages paid to less-educated native-born workers in Section IV.

A. *Production*

Consider an open economy (e.g., a US state) that combines two nontradeable intermediate services, Y_H and Y_L, in a *CES* production function to produce a final tradeable consumption good, Y, according to equation (1).

$$(1) \qquad Y = \left[\beta Y_L^{\frac{\sigma-1}{\sigma}} + (1-\beta)Y_H^{\frac{\sigma-1}{\sigma}} \right]^{\frac{\sigma}{\sigma-1}}.$$

The parameter $\sigma \in (0, \infty)$ measures the elasticity of substitution between Y_H and Y_L. The coefficients β and $(1-\beta)$ capture the relative productivity of these inter-mediate services in the production of good Y. This final consumption good is also the numeraire, so that all prices and wages are expressed in real terms. We assume that it is assembled by perfectly competitive firms that minimize costs and earn no profits. This ensures that the prices of Y_L and Y_H (denoted P_L and P_H) are equal to their marginal products.

The two intermediate services are produced by different workers. Low education workers (with total labor supply equal to L) produce Y_L, and high education workers (H) produce Y_H. The symmetric *CES* production function (1) combining the services of more and less educated workers (i.e., those with and without college experience) is widely used in economics.[4] Some immigration papers, in contrast, separate workers into four education groups: high school dropouts, high school degree holders, those

---

[3] Gene M. Grossman and Esteban Rossi-Hansberg (2008) develop an interesting theory of offshoring that builds upon a process of international task division. David H. Autor and David Dorn (2007) use a model of differ-entiated task performance to analyze the evolution of wages in the 1980s and 1990s related to computer adoption. Those models have features similar to ours.

[4] For instance, the literature on cross-country income differences (Daron Acemoglu and Fabrizio Zilibotti 2001; Francesco Caselli and Wilbur John Coleman, II 2006), technological change (Acemoglu 1998, 2002), and labor economics (Katz and Kevin M. Murphy 1992; Card and Thomas Lemieux 2001) all use a production func-tion similar to (1).

with some college experience, and college graduates. However, Ottaviano and Peri (2008) argue that workers with no degree and workers with a high school diploma were close substitutes between 1960 and 2000, as were workers with some college education and those with a college degree. A recent paper by Claudia Goldin and Katz (2007) also argues that "high school graduates and dropouts are close substitutes today." Most of the literature (including Katz and Murphy 1992; Joshua D. Angrist 1995; George E. Johnson 1997; Goldin and Katz 2007; Ottaviano and Peri 2008) does find a significant degree of imperfect substitutability between workers with a high school diploma or less and those with some college education or more. Thus, we advocate a two-group *CES* model distinguishing between workers with a high school degree or less and workers with some college education or more.

We add to the framework above by assuming that less-educated workers must perform both manual and communication tasks in order to produce Y_L. Manual tasks require the use of physical skills such as dexterity, body coordination, or strength. Communication tasks, such as directing, training, and organizing people, require mostly language skills. Let less-educated workers supply M units of manual-task inputs and C units of communication-task inputs in the aggregate.[5] These tasks combine to produce Y_L according to the *CES* function in equation (2), where $\beta_L \in (0,1)$ captures the relative productivity of manual skills, and $\theta_L \in (0,\infty)$ measures the elasticity of substitution between M and C.

$$(2) \qquad Y_L = \left[\beta_L M^{\frac{\theta_L-1}{\theta_L}} + (1-\beta_L) C^{\frac{\theta_L-1}{\theta_L}} \right]^{\frac{\theta_L}{\theta_L-1}}.$$

Since this paper focuses on the market for less-educated workers, we make the simplifying assumption that highly-educated workers only perform one "analytical" (or equivalently, "cognitive") task in the production of Y_H.[6] Alternatively, one can assume that highly-educated workers provide both analytical and communication tasks (and very few physical tasks), that those two tasks are highly substitutable, and/or that their relative supply and returns are not affected much by the presence of less educated immigrants.[7] By standardizing the units of these tasks, we can assume that Y_H is produced according to a linear technology equal to the total supply of highly-educated working hours. That is, $Y_H = H$.

Competitive labor markets and perfect competition among producers of Y_L and Y_H yield the relative task demand function in equation (3), where w_M and w_C denote the compensation (price) paid for one unit of manual and communication task, respectively.

$$(3) \qquad \frac{C}{M} = \left(\frac{1-\beta_L}{\beta_L} \right)^{\theta_L} \left(\frac{w_C}{w_M} \right)^{-\theta_L}.$$

---

[5] We will use capital letters to denote aggregate values, and lower case letters to denote per capita figures, throughout the text.

[6] For a more careful analysis of task specialization between natives and immigrants among highly educated workers, see Peri and Sparber (2008b).

[7] We provide empirical evidence in Section II and in Table W7, in the Web Appendix, that shows the independence between the task supply among highly-educated workers and the inflow of less-educated immigrants.

140   *AMERICAN ECONOMIC JOURNAL: APPLIED ECONOMICS*   *JULY 2009*

B. *Relative Supply of Tasks: Natives and Immigrants*

Since each highly-educated worker is identical from a productive point of view, the wage paid to these workers equals the marginal productivity of Y_H in (1). That is, $w_H = P_H$. In contrast, less educated workers are heterogeneous and may differ from each other in their relative task productivity. We consider two types of workers: less-educated "domestic" native-born workers (D), and less-educated "foreign-born" immigrant workers (F). We let L_j (for $j = D$ or F) represent the total labor supply of these groups.

Each less-educated worker chooses an occupation and fully allocates one unit of time in order to provide μ_j units of manual tasks, ζ_j units of communication tasks, or some division between the two. Native and immigrant workers differ in that the first has a comparative advantage in communication tasks. Mathematically, this implies $(\zeta_D/\mu_D) > (\zeta_F/\mu_F)$.

Let l_j be the share of a worker's labor endowment (time) spent performing manual tasks in her occupation, implying that $1 - l_j$ is the time spent performing communication tasks. A worker's supply of manual task units is $m_j = (l_j)^\delta \mu_j$, while her supply of communication task units is $c_j = (1 - l_j)^\delta \zeta_j$. The parameter $\delta \in (0, 1)$ captures the decreasing returns from performing a single task, which implies that no one will fully specialize.

Each worker takes the unit compensation paid to tasks (w_M and w_C) as given, and chooses an occupation allocating her time between manual and communication tasks to maximize labor income. Labor income is given in equations (4) and (5) for less-educated native and immigrant workers, respectively.

$$(4) \qquad\qquad w_D = (l_D)^\delta \, \mu_D w_M + (1 - l_D)^\delta \, \zeta_D w_C.$$

$$(5) \qquad\qquad w_F = (1 - d)[(l_F)^\delta \, \mu_F w_M + (1 - l_F)^\delta \, \zeta_F w_C].$$

These equations sum the income from performing manual and interactive tasks. The productivity in each task is specific to the type of worker (F or D). Notice that in (5) we allow wages of immigrants to be a fraction $(1 - d) \in [0, 1]$ of their marginal productivity, allowing for some form of discrimination or reduced bargaining power relative to natives. This feature does not affect the relative (or absolute) supply of tasks by immigrants. It only implies that immigrants may earn lower wages than natives do within a given occupation, which is a feature that we allow in the estimation and is supported by the data.

By maximizing wages with respect to l_j, we can identify the equilibrium relative supply of communication versus manual tasks for natives and immigrants. Equation (6), which depends positively on relative task compensation and on the worker's relative efficiency in performing tasks (ζ_j/μ_j), describes the relative task supply for natives ($j = D$) and immigrants ($j = F$). Equivalently, equation (7) expresses this relationship in terms of the relative time spent performing these tasks.

$$(6) \qquad\qquad \frac{c_j}{m_j} = \left(\frac{w_C}{w_M}\right)^{\frac{\delta}{1-\delta}} \left(\frac{\zeta_j}{\mu_j}\right)^{\frac{1}{1-\delta}}.$$

(7)
$$\frac{l_j}{1 - l_j} = \left(\frac{\zeta_j w_C}{\mu_j w_M}\right)^{\frac{1}{\delta - 1}}.$$

Since each occupation is identified by a unique allocation of time between manual and communication tasks, when a worker chooses an occupation to maximize her wage income, she also reveals her relative efficiency (ζ_j/μ_j) in task performance. Equations (6) and (7) can therefore be interpreted as describing the occupation choice for a worker of type j, establishing a unique and invertible relationship between an individual's relative abilities and her occupation.[8] The existence of a continuum of occupations (for values of l_j between zero and one) allows workers to respond continuously to a marginal increase in the relative compensation of communication tasks (w_C/w_M) by marginally increasing c_j/m_j. That is, by moving to an occupation requiring less time devoted to manual tasks, l_j.

In this simplified model, there is no differentiation of abilities within citizenship groups. All native workers are endowed with task efficiency (ζ_D, μ_D), whereas all foreign-born workers have efficiency (ζ_F, μ_F). This implies that each native supplies (c_D, m_D) task units and each immigrant supplies (c_F, m_F), so that members from each group will choose a common occupation. Each group will choose a new occupation, however, if the relative compensation of tasks changes. Hence, in our notation, j represents the worker type as well as her occupation, since the latter fully reveals the former.[9] The aggregate task supply for native and foreign workers will equal the product of individual task supply and total labor supply $(M_j = L_j m_j$ and $C_j = L_j c_j)$. This implies that if we substitute c_j/m_j with C_j/M_j (by multiplying numerator and denominator by L_j), expression (6) also describes the relative supply of tasks for natives and immigrants.

Equation (8) represents the aggregate relative supply of tasks in the economy obtained by summing the skills provided by each group.

(8)
$$\frac{C}{M} = \frac{C_F + C_D}{M_F + M_D} = \varphi(f) \frac{C_F}{M_F} + (1 - \varphi(f)) \frac{C_D}{M_D}.$$

The term $\varphi(f) = (M_F/(M_F + M_D)) \in (0, 1)$ is the share of manual tasks supplied by foreign-born workers, and is a simple monotonically increasing transformation of the foreign-born share of less-educated workers,[10] $f = L_F/(L_F + L_D)$. Hence, the aggregate relative supply of tasks in the economy is a weighted average of each group's relative supply, and the weights are closely related to the share of each group in employment. Substituting (6) for natives and immigrants in (8), and equating

---

[8] In our empirical implementation, for example, a relative task supply $c_j/m_j = 0.16$ corresponds to the occupation "assembler of electrical equipment." A relative task supply of 3.12 corresponds to the occupation "financial service salesperson."

[9] In a model with heterogeneous abilities (as in Peri and Sparber 2008c), as well as in the empirical implementation, workers with different ζ_j/μ_j choose different occupations within each group. In that case, the index j can be thought of as indexing the worker's relative effectiveness as well as her occupation.

[10] Specifically: $\varphi'(f) > 0$; $\varphi(0) = 0$ and $\varphi(1) = 1$.

relative supply with relative demand (expressed by (3)), one can solve for the equilibrium relative compensation of tasks:

$$(9) \qquad \frac{w_C^*}{w_M^*} = \left(\frac{1-\beta_L}{\beta_L}\right)^{\frac{(1-\delta)\theta_L}{(1-\delta)\theta_L+\delta}} \left[\underset{+}{\frac{\varsigma}{\mu}}\left(\underset{-}{f}, \frac{\varsigma_F}{\mu_F}\right)\right]^{\frac{-1}{(1-\delta)\theta_L+\delta}}.$$

The function $\frac{\varsigma}{\mu}\left(f, \frac{\varsigma_F}{\mu_F}\right)$ is a weighted average of the relative skill endowments among natives and immigrants, and it represents an aggregate measure of communication relative to manual ability in the economy. More specifically, $\frac{\varsigma}{\mu}\left(f, \frac{\varsigma_F}{\mu_F}\right)$ $= [\varphi(f)\,(\varsigma_F/\mu_F)^{1/(1-\delta)} + (1 - \varphi(f))\,(\varsigma_D/\mu_D)^{1/(1-\delta)}]^{(1-\delta)}$. For a given value of the relative skills of natives (ς_D/μ_D), the term $\frac{\varsigma}{\mu}\left(f, \frac{\varsigma_F}{\mu_F}\right)$ depends negatively on f and positively on ς_F/μ_F, as indicated by the signs in equation (9). This is intuitive. Due to the assumption that $\varsigma_F/\mu_F < \varsigma_D/\mu_D$, a larger fraction of immigrants decreases the average relative communication skills of the workforce. Similarly, a decrease in the relative communication ability of immigrants (ς_F/μ_F) for a given share of employment would decrease the average relative communication ability of the workforce.

By substituting the equilibrium wage into the aggregate relative supply for domestic workers, we find their equilibrium relative provision of tasks (equation (10)). The weighted average of C_D^*/M_D^* and C_F^*/M_F^*, according to equation (8), identifies the equilibrium aggregate relative provision of tasks in equation (11).

$$(10) \qquad \frac{C_D^*}{M_D^*} = \left(\frac{1-\beta_L}{\beta_L}\right)^{\frac{\delta\theta_L}{(1-\delta)\theta_L+\delta}} \left(\frac{\varsigma_D}{\mu_D}\right)^{\frac{1}{(1-\delta)}} \left[\underset{+}{\frac{\varsigma}{\mu}}\left(\underset{-}{f}, \frac{\varsigma_F}{\mu_F}\right)\right]^{\frac{-1}{(1-\delta)\theta_L+\delta}\frac{\delta}{1-\delta}}.$$

$$(11) \qquad \frac{C^*}{M^*} = \left(\frac{1-\beta_L}{\beta_L}\right)^{\frac{\delta\theta_L}{(1-\delta)\theta_L+\delta}} \left[\underset{+}{\frac{\varsigma}{\mu}}\left(\underset{-}{f}, \frac{\varsigma_F}{\mu_F}\right)\right]^{\frac{\theta_L}{(1-\delta)\,\theta_L+\delta}}.$$

If we assume that workers also spend their entire wage income to consume Y in each period (there is no capital in the model, so we assume no saving and investment), the equilibrium compensation values w_H, w_M, and w_C fully determine the income, task supply, and consumption of each agent. Hence, the model is a simple general equilibrium static representation of an economy.

C. Model Predictions and Empirical Specifications

It is simple and intuitive to perform some comparative static analyses using the equilibrium expressions (9), (10), and (11). In particular, since the average relative ability $\frac{\varsigma}{\mu}\left(f, \frac{\varsigma_F}{\mu_F}\right)$ depends negatively on the share of immigrants in the population (f), an increase in that share has three effects. First, the return to communication relative to manual tasks increases (equation (9)), which, in turn, implies an increase in the relative supply of communication tasks by natives (equation (10)), while the aggregate relative supply of communication tasks decreases (equation (11)). Similarly,

VOL. 1 NO. 3   PERI AND SPARBER: TASK SPECIALIZATION, IMMIGRATION, AND WAGES   143

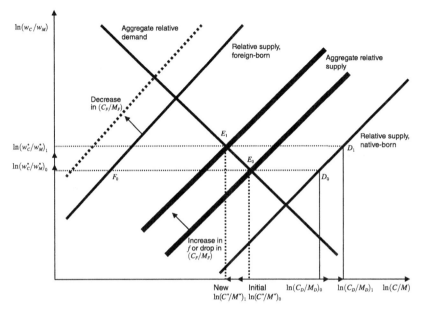

FIGURE 1. RELATIVE COMMUNICATION/MANUAL TASK SUPPLY AND DEMAND

since $\frac{\zeta}{\mu}\left(f, \frac{\zeta_F}{\mu_F}\right)$ depends positively on ζ_F/μ_F, a decrease in that variable produces an increase in the relative return to communication versus manual tasks, an increase in the native relative supply of communication versus manual tasks, and a decrease in the overall relative supply of communication versus manual tasks. Empirically, between 1960 and 2000, the United States experienced an increase in f and an inflow of immigrants with lower ζ_F/μ_F relative to natives.

Figure 1 displays the equilibrium in an economy with native- and foreign-born workers, illustrating the effects of an increase in the share of immigrants and/or a decrease in their relative ζ_F/μ_F abilities using relative supply and demand curves. The downward sloping demand curve represents relative marginal task productivity as expressed by equation (3). Comparative advantage dictates that the relative task supply curve for immigrants is to the left of that for domestic workers. Aggregate relative supply (represented by the thickest line in the panel) is a weighted average of the two. The distance of the average supply curve from those of immigrants and domestic workers is proportional to $\varphi(f)$ and $1 - \varphi(f)$, respectively.

The initial equilibrium relative task compensation $\left(\ln\left(w_C^*/w_M^*\right)\right)$ and provision $\left(\ln\left(C^*/M^*\right)\right)$ is denoted by E_0. The points D_0 and F_0 along the native and immigrant skill-supply curves identify each group's respective initial relative supply of tasks. Either an increase in the foreign-born share of employment or a decrease in ζ_F/μ_F

will shift aggregate supply to the left (the latter also shifts the supply curve for immigrants). This implies a new equilibrium, E_1. The aggregate level of communication versus manual tasks decreases, thus increasing their relative compensation. Natives respond rationally by providing *more* communication versus manual tasks (a move along their relative skill-supply curve to D_1). Hence, a larger share of immigrants among less-educated workers (possibly reinforced by a decrease in their relative communication abilities) pushes less-educated native workers to further exploit their comparative advantage. The economy experiences an increase in the relative compensation of communication versus manual tasks, an increase in natives' relative supply of these tasks, and a decrease in the relative supply of communication versus manual tasks in the aggregate.

In Section III, we empirically test these three predictions by using decennial (year t) US state (s) data for the period 1960–2000. In particular, by log-linearizing the two key equilibrium conditions, (10) and (11), we obtain the two linear empirical specifications expressed below.

$$(12) \qquad \ln\left(\frac{C_D}{M_D}\right)_{st} = \gamma f_{st} + \alpha_s^D + \tau_t^D + \varepsilon_{st}^D .$$

$$(13) \qquad \ln\left(\frac{C}{M}\right)_{st} = \gamma_{TOT} f_{st} + \alpha_s^{TOT} + \tau_t^{TOT} + \varepsilon_{st}^{TOT} .$$

We also invert and log-linearize the relative demand function (3) to obtain a third linear relation given by:

$$(14) \qquad \ln\left(\frac{w_C}{w_M}\right)_{st} = -\frac{1}{\theta_L} \ln\left(\frac{C}{M}\right)_{st} + \alpha_s^w + \tau_t^w + \varepsilon_{st}^w .$$

Each regression includes a noncorrelated zero-mean disturbance term (ε_{st}^D, ε_{st}^{TOT}, and ε_{st}^w). Time fixed effects (τ_t^D, τ_t^{TOT}, and τ_t^w) account for common time-varying technological parameters. The first two capture the term $\left(\delta\theta_L/((1-\delta)\theta_L+\delta)\right) \times \ln\left((1-\beta_L)/\beta_L\right)$ from equations (10) and (11), while τ_t^w controls for $\ln\left((1-\beta_L)/\beta_L\right)$ from the relative labor demand equation. The state fixed effects in each expression (denoted α_s^D, α_s^{TOT}, and α_s^w) account for variation due to unobserved characteristics of the population, including the term $(1/(1-\delta)) \times \ln(\zeta_D/\mu_D)$ from (10).

The remaining terms in these log-linearized expressions represent our theoretical model's central implications. In equation (12), $\gamma \equiv -\left(1/((1-\delta)\theta_L + \delta)\right)\left(\delta/(1-\delta)\right) \times (\partial \ln(\zeta/\mu)/\partial f)$. The model's equation (10) predicts $\gamma > 0$ because a state's foreign-born share of less-educated employment (f_{st}) causes native workers to increase their relative supply of communication tasks. In equation (13), $\gamma_{TOT} \equiv \left(\theta_L/((1-\delta)\theta_L+\delta)\right) \times (\partial \ln(\zeta/\mu)/\partial f)$ is derived from (11), which predicts $\gamma_{TOT} < 0$ since immigration causes the overall relative supply of these tasks to fall. Finally, we use equation (14) to estimate the elasticity of substitution, θ_L, which is predicted to be positive. This specification rearranges the relative demand function for skills (3) so that

$\ln (C/M)_{st}$ represents the explanatory variable. Since $\ln (C/M)_{st}$ is endogenous, we use the results from our regression of (13) and adopt the exogenous shifter of the share of immigrants, f_{st}, as an instrument in estimation of (14).

Sections IIIA, IIIB, and IIIC estimate (12), (13), and (14), respectively. Before showing the results, however, we describe the data and discuss the measures of task supply and task compensation in Section II.

II. Data: Task Variables and Instruments

This section briefly describes how we construct measures of task supply in order to test the main implications of the model.[11] The IPUMS dataset by Ruggles et al. (2005) provides individual-level data on personal characteristics, employment, wages, immigration status, and occupation. We consider data from the decennial census for the period 1960–2000. We include US-born and foreign-born (immigrant) workers who were between 18 and 65 years of age. We calculate the potential experience of workers assuming that those without a degree started working at age 17, and those with a diploma started working at age 19. Whenever we construct aggregate or average variables, we weight each individual by his/her personal census weight, multiplied by the number of hours he/she worked in a year.

Since the immigrant share of employment varies greatly across US states, we interpret states as labor markets and adopt them as the econometric unit of analysis. One critique of this approach is that states are open economies, so the effects of immigration in one state could spill into others through the migration of natives. Most of the literature,[12] however, finds little to no evidence that, in the long run, natives respond to immigration through interstate migration or by exiting employment.[13] Instead, we provide a new explanation for the observed small wage and employment response to immigration. Native-born workers partly protect themselves from competition with immigrants by specializing in language-intensive occupations.

A. Task Variables

Construction and National Trends.—In light of our theoretical model, because of the correspondence expressed in (6), we can interpret j not only as representing different individual types, but also as identifying different occupations. Our quantitative analysis requires measures of the effective supply of manual (m_j) and communicative (c_j) tasks in each occupation. We assume that our task-intensity variables, described below, exactly capture this effective task-supply.[14]

---

[11] A more detailed account of the data, and of the task variable construction, can be found in Sections I–III of the Web Appendix.

[12] E.g., Card (2001, 2007), Card and Lewis (2007), Cortes (2008), Lewis (2005), and Ottaviano and Peri (2007).

[13] We confirm those results with our own analysis of the effect of immigrants on natives' employment reported in Section V of the Web Appendix.

[14] Table W1 in the Web Appendix provides c_j and m_j values for all occupations j.

By merging occupation-specific task values with individuals across census years, we are able to obtain these task supply measures for natives and immigrants by education level, in each state, over time. The US Department of Labor's *O*NET* abilities survey provides information on the characteristics of occupations. This dataset assigns numerical values to describe the importance of 52 distinct employee abilities (which we refer to as "tasks" or "skills") required by each occupation.[15] We merge these occupation-specific values to individuals in the 2000 census. We then rescale each skill variable so that it equals the percentile score in 2000 (between zero and one), representing the relative importance of that skill among all workers in 2000. For instance, an occupation with a score of 0.02 for a specific skill indicates that only 2 percent of workers in the United States in 2000 were supplying that skill less intensely. We then assign these *O*NET* percentile scores to individuals from 1960 to 2000 using the IPUMS variable *occ1990*, which provides an occupational crosswalk over time.[16]

Table A1 in the Appendix lists each of the 52 *O*NET* variables and organizes them into categories that we use to construct our manual and communication skill supply indices. In our "basic" definition of manual skills, we average only the variables capturing an occupation's "movement and strength" requirements.[17] Similarly, our basic definition of communication skills includes only measures of oral and written expression and comprehension.

The basic skill definitions described above manifest most closely the notion of communication and manual skills, and we prefer them. However, as a robustness check, some of our specifications employ an "extended" definition of manual skills, adding "sensory and perception" abilities (i.e., those using the five senses) to the physical skill group (see Table A1 for details). In the Web Appendix, we also show results that use an "extended" definition of communication skills in which we introduce "cognitive and analytical" and "vocal" abilities to that skill group (see Table A1). The simplicity of our two-skill dichotomy forces us to make a few judgment calls when trying to fit all the *O*NET* variables into one of the two categories, especially when using extended definitions. The robustness of our empirical results to the use of our extended definitions, however, lends support to our framework, which summarizes occupations with just two skill measures.

To produce the United States- or state-level variables, we calculate the aggregate supply of manual skills for less-educated immigrants (M_F), natives (M_D), or both groups of workers (M) by summing the values of m_j across individuals (weighted by hours worked). We follow an analogous procedure for aggregate communication skills (creating C_F, C_D, and C).

We now briefly describe how different occupations rank in their use of physical versus language skills according to the *O*NET* task variables, and we present some national trends. Table 1 shows the skill intensity for occupations maintaining the highest, lowest, and average c/m values among occupations with more than 25,000

---

[15] Classified using the standard occupation classification (SOC).

[16] See Barry R. Chiswick and Paul W. Miller (2007) or Sparber (2009) for alternative uses of *O*NET* data.

[17] Those skills can be further divided, as shown in Table A1, into "limb, hand, and finger dexterity;" "body coordination and flexibility;" and "strength."

TABLE 1—OCCUPATIONS, RELATIVE TASK INTENSITY, AND CHANGES IN THE FOREIGN-BORN SHARE
OF LESS-EDUCATED EMPLOYMENT

Occupation	Communication intensity index	Manual intensity index	C/M percentile	Change in foreign-born share of less-educated employment 1970–2000 (percentage points)
Four occupations with highest communication/manual values				
Financial managers	0.83	0.23	0.999	+5.7
Managers of properties and real estate	0.74	0.21	0.997	+1.8
Editors and reporters	0.87	0.27	0.991	+12.2
Operations and systems researchers and analysts	0.64	0.20	0.990	+4.1
Five occupations with average communication/manual values				
Cashiers	0.38	0.73	0.562	+12.0
Cooks, variously defined	0.32	0.67	0.530	+19.9
Hairdressers and cosmetologists	0.30	0.62	0.498	+17.0
Repairers of industrial electrical equipment	0.36	0.77	0.490	+9.5
Kitchen workers	0.28	0.62	0.489	+2.8
Four occupations with lowest communication/manual values				
Vehicle washers and equipment cleaners	0.04	0.72	0.021	+20.6
Furniture and wood finishers	0.01	0.72	0.021	+13.4
Roofers and slaters	0.01	0.64	0.020	+26.4
Drywall installers	0.00	0.72	0.006	+24.2

Notes: Authors' calculations based on *O*NET* task definitions and censuses (1970–2000). The occupations included are those with more than 25,000 employees in each year. Only less-educated wage-earning employees between 18 and 65 years old and not living in group quarters are considered. The basic manual index is constructed averaging 19 measures that capture the intensity of several physical abilities. The basic communication task index is constructed averaging four measures that capture oral and written expression and comprehension. Both are standardized to be between zero and one. The details of their construction are reported in the main text and in the Web Appendix.

less-educated workers in each year. As we might expect, values of c/m are highest among managers, analysts, and clerks while construction workers and cleaners score among the lowest. Cooks, hair-dressers, and cashiers score near the average. Table 1 also reports the change in the foreign-born share of workers with a high school degree or less between 1970 and 2000. In accordance with our theory, the foreign-born share increased, on average, by only 6 percentage points in occupations with high communication versus manual task content, by about 12 percentage points in occupations with average communication-manual content, and by an average of 21 percentage points in those with low c/m values. As we only include less-educated workers in the immigration figures shown in Table 1, the educational distribution of immigrants cannot explain this large difference.

A similar message is conveyed in Figure 2, which reports the national trend (1970–2006) in the relative provision of communication versus manual tasks (C/M) for less-educated natives, recent immigrants (those who have been in the United States ten years or less), and long-term immigrants (those residing in the United

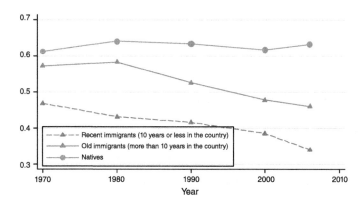

FIGURE 2. COMMUNICATION/MANUAL INTENSITY OF NATIVES, RECENT IMMIGRANTS,
AND LONG-TERM IMMIGRANTS US (1970–2000)
(Workers with a high school degree or less education)

Notes: The relative C/M supply for the US economy is constructed by aggregating individuals' supply of communication and manual skills, weighted by their hours worked. Natives are individuals with US citizenship at birth. Recent immigrants are noncitizens or naturalized citizens who resided in the United States for ten years or less. Long-term immigrants are noncitizens or naturalized citizens who resided in the United States for more than ten years.
Source: Ruggles et al. (2005).

States more than ten years).[18] The graph highlights three stylized facts. First, the level of C/M provided by native workers with a high school degree or less has been higher than that of both recent and long-term immigrants with similar educational attainment. Second, relative skill values are always lowest among new immigrants. Third, cross-group disparities have been growing over time. Less-educated native workers have increased (if only slightly) their C/M supply between 1970 and 2006, while values have decreased among foreign-born workers. Altogether, the trends in Figure 2 do not suggest a common response of natives and immigrants to modified relative demand for skills but rather show increasing specialization of the two groups consistent with the idea that immigration represented an exogenous change in relative skill supply. The increase in the relative specialization in manual tasks of immigrants, combined with substantial growth of the immigrant share of less-educated workers,[19] implies that immigration represented a significant negative contribution to the overall value of C/M for the United States. If our theory is correct, this should have important ramifications for native-born task supply and wage earnings, which we analyze at the state level.

---

[18] Since the variable "year of immigration" is not available in 1960, we cannot extend this figure back to that year. We provide 2006 American Community Survey (ACS) data for comparison, though it is not part of the empirical analysis.
[19] See Figure W1 in the Web Appendix.

State-Level Quantities and Prices.—The empirical analysis of Section III assumes that states represent labor markets and can be used to test the implications of our theory in Section I. To perform the analysis, we must construct state-level skill data for less educated native workers (C_D/M_D) and immigrant workers (C_F/M_F) in each census year between 1960 and 2000. Importantly, we first clean this data of demographic effects since personal characteristics (such as age, education, gender, or race) affect individual (and state-level) task supply and may correlate with immigration. Failing to account for this could generate a spurious correlation between the presence of immigrants and the task supply of natives. Using a first-stage regression (separately for each census year, *O*NET* variable, and native-immigrant group), we obtain an individual's skill cleaned of demographic effects.[20] Averaging the cleaned *O*NET* variables belonging to each skill type, we compute an individual's total manual and communication task supply. We then create state-level averages for native workers $((c_D)_{st}$ and $(m_D)_{st})$, and their ratio $(c_D/m_D = C_D/M_D)$, for each state s and year t by weighting each individual by his or her personal weight (and hours worked). Using these data, panel A of Figure 3 plots the constructed relative task supply (C_D/M_D) for native workers (in differences from the overall 1960–2000 state average) against the immigrant share of less-educated workers for a state and year (also differenced from the overall state average). Panel B graphs the relative task supply and the immigrant share, in levels, for 2000. Both figures show a strong and significantly positive relationship between the two variables. States where the foreign-born presence grew rapidly between 1960 and 2000 were also those in which natives (after controlling for demographic characteristics) shifted their supply more toward communication tasks and away from manual ones. In 2000, there was a strong, positive correlation between the level of relative task supply among natives and the share of immigrants. These correlations constitute preliminary evidence supporting the prediction of our model that an inflow of less-educated immigrants pushes less-educated natives to supply more communication skills relative to manual ones.

The second set of variables needed for our empirical analysis is the unit compensation of communication and manual skills, w_M and w_C, for each state and year. As we did for the skill data, we need to clean for the effect of individual characteristics. Moreover, in the case of wage compensation, we do not observe the unit wage paid to manual or communication tasks, but we only observe the wage paid to workers in each occupation. Hence, we use a two steps procedure for each state and year.[21] We first regress separately by year, the logarithm of individual real weekly wages on individual characteristics for workers with a high school degree or less. These regressions also include occupation by state dummies whose coefficients represent our estimates for the average "cleaned" log-wage, $\ln(\bar{w}_{jst})$, for occupation j, state s, and census year t. In the second step, we transform $\ln(\bar{w}_{jst})$ into levels and regress $\bar{w}_{jst}$ on the occupation-specific measures of manual (m_j) and communication (c_j) skills (obtained from *O*NET*). We allow the coefficients on the skill variables to vary across states. By separately estimating the second-stage regression in equation (15)

---

[20] The first-stage cleaning procedure is described in detail in Section II of the Web Appendix.
[21] Again, Section II of the Web Appendix describes the details of the procedure.

150   *AMERICAN ECONOMIC JOURNAL: APPLIED ECONOMICS*   *JULY 2009*

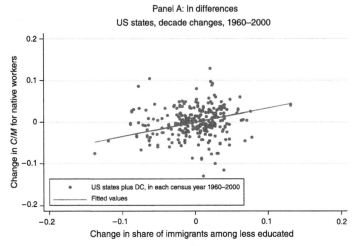

Notes: The construction of C/M is described in detail in Section IIA. Fitted lines are from a weighted least squares regression (weights equal to less educated employment in the state). Slope = 0.34, Standard error = 0.04.

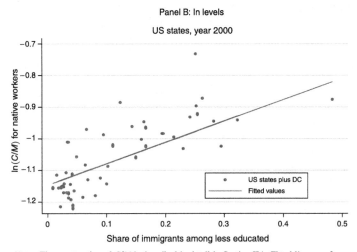

Notes: The construction of C/M is described in detail in Section IIA. Fitted lines are from a weighted least squares regression (weights equal to less educated employment in the state). Slope = 0.67, Standard error = 0.10.

FIGURE 3. SHARE OF IMMIGRANTS AND THE RELATIVE C/M SUPPLY OF LESS-EDUCATED NATIVES

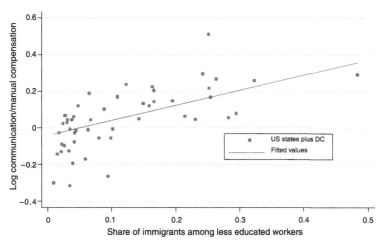

FIGURE 4. LESS EDUCATED IMMIGRANT SHARE AND THE COMPENSATION OF COMMUNICATION RELATIVE TO
MANUAL SKILLS ACROSS US STATES, 2000

Notes: The relative compensation of communication and manual skills is constructed by first running an individual wage regression to clean for individual characteristics and then estimating the compensation of skills to vary across states using the average cleaned occupation wages. A detailed description of the procedure is in Section IIA of the text. The fitted line is from a weighted least square regression (weights equal to employment of less educated in the state). Slope = 0.82, Standard error = 0.13.

for each census year, we can identify the state and year-specific compensation, $(w_M)_{st}$ and $(w_C)_{st}$, received for supplying one unit of manual and communication tasks.

$$(15) \qquad \bar{w}_{jst} = (w_M)_{st} \, m_j + (w_C)_{st} \, c_j + \varepsilon_{jst}.$$

Interpreting m_j and c_j as the effective supply of manual tasks in occupation j (as expressed in the theoretical model), equation (15) implements the relationships in (4) and (5) to infer the values of w_M and w_C in a market (state) from the occupational wages. The fact that we controlled for nativity in the first-stage regression implies that we allow wages to differ between natives and immigrants by proportional factors (such as the discrimination effect in equation (5)). In order to obtain estimated coefficients $\widehat{w_M}_{st}$ and $\widehat{w_C}_{st}$ that could be interpreted as the weekly compensation of a unit of skill (and therefore always assuming positive values), we do not include a constant in (15).[22]

---

[22] Table A2 in the Table Appendix shows some estimates and statistics from implementing regression (15). We report, for each year, the average estimates (at the national level) of $\widehat{w_M}_{st}$ and $\widehat{w_C}_{st}$, the R^2 values, and the number of occupation-state observations used. The table shows that the average compensation to communication tasks was larger than the compensation to manual tasks in each year except for 1980, and since 1980 the premium for communication tasks has increased. It also shows that the model in (15) explains a significant share (30 to 40 percent in each of the years considered) of the cross-occupation variance in wages.

Using the constructed relative task compensation, Figure 4 shows preliminary evidence for another key prediction of our model. The horizontal axis again displays the immigrant share of less-educated foreign-born workers in 2000, and the vertical axis records the constructed relative compensation of communication versus manual tasks $(\hat{w}_C/\hat{w}_M)$ by US state. Consistent with our model, states with a larger immigrant share also have higher $(\hat{w}_C/\hat{w}_M)$ values (this is what drives natives to alter their skill supply). While Section IIIC will more formally establish the relationship between immigration and relative task compensation, this preliminary evidence emphasizes that a correlation (in levels) existed in 2000.

B. *Instrumental Variables*

Our basic empirical specifications in equations (12), (13), and (14) provide a simplified examination of the theoretical model's predictions. To establish whether correlation between the foreign-born employment share and native-born (or aggregate) skill use (and compensation) is causal, we need to ensure that the cross-state variation of less-educated immigrants is driven mostly by supply shifts. One concern is that unobserved technology and demand factors, which may differ across states, might have simultaneously affected the productivity of (demand for) communicative tasks and attracted immigrants. To establish causality, we use two sets of instruments that build on the fact that documented and undocumented Mexican immigration has represented a large share of the increase in the less-educated foreign-born population, beginning in the 1970s. This aggregate inflow was largely independent of state-specific demand shocks and can be exploited as an exogenous supply shift since it differed across states.

Our first instrument for the share of immigrants among less-educated workers is the share of "imputed" Mexicans among all workers. We impute the number of Mexican immigrants in a state based upon their distribution in 1960 and subsequent national growth rates of Mexican immigrants. This methodology[23] produces powerful instruments as new immigrants, especially those with little education, tend to move to the same areas in which previous immigrants from their source country live.[24] Also, unlike previous waves of immigration, a large proportion of immigrants between 1960 and 2000 came from Mexico. Together, these facts allow us to use the location preferences of Mexicans as factors affecting the supply of foreign-born workers across states and time that are uncorrelated with state-specific changes in demand (productivity).

Our second set of instruments similarly relies upon the exogenous increase in Mexican immigration, but is based on geography. We use the distance of each state's population center of gravity to its closest section of the Mexican border interacted with four census year dummies (1970–2000). This captures the fact that distance

---

[23] Card (2001) first used this methodology. Cortes (2008), Lewis (2005), Ottaviano and Peri (2007), and Albert Saiz (2008) followed a similar approach.

[24] This is due to information networks between immigrants and their country of origin, as well as to the immigration policy of the United States. The analysis in Krishna Patel and Francis Vella (2007) also shows evidence of strong "network" effects affecting the supply of immigrants. New immigrants are more likely to settle and work in occupations and areas with a large presence of co-nationals.

from the border had a larger effect in predicting the inflow of less educated workers in decades with larger Mexican immigration. Second, we use a Mexican border dummy interacted with decade indicators to capture the fact that border states had larger inflows of Mexican workers due to undocumented border crossings. Essentially, the use of the geographic instruments is equivalent to a difference-in-difference approach in which the identifying variation stems from differences in the inflow of Mexicans between states close to, and far from, the border in the post-1980 period (when Mexican migration rose dramatically) relative to previous decades.

III. Empirical Results

This section uses the empirical specifications in (12), (13), and (14) to formally test the relationships identified by the theoretical model. Section A assesses the correlation between the foreign-born share of less-educated workers and the relative supply of tasks by native workers across states. Section B tests the effect of immigration on the aggregate supply of relative tasks across states. Section C quantifies the effects of immigration on the relative compensation of manual and communication tasks.

A. *Immigration and the Relative Task Supply of Natives*

We begin by estimating equation (12) using least squares, weighting each observation by employment in the cell (thus, accounting for the large variation in labor market size across states), and clustering standard errors by state. This provides a direct test of our theoretical model by determining if γ is positive. We also ascertain whether immigration has a stronger relationship with the average native-born supply of manual (m_D) or communication (c_D) tasks by separately estimating equations (16) and (17).[25]

$$(16) \qquad \ln(c_D)_{st} = \alpha_s^C + \tau_t^C + \gamma^C f_{st} + \varepsilon_{st}^C.$$

$$(17) \qquad \ln(m_D)_{st} = \alpha_s^M + \tau_t^M + \gamma^M f_{st} + \varepsilon_{st}^M.$$

Columns 1 and 2 of Table 2 present the WLS estimates of γ, γ^C, and γ^M for different definitions of the task variables. Column 1 uses the basic definitions of language and manual ability involving the average of 4 and 19 *O*NET* variables, respectively. Column 2 uses the basic definition for language ability and the extended definition for manual ability (average of 37 *O*NET* variables).[26] Each specification uses the full sample of 255 observations (a decennial panel of 50 states plus the District of Columbia from 1960–2000). Three important results emerge. First, the estimates of γ strongly uphold our theory as the coefficients are between 0.31 and 0.34 and are always significantly positive at the 1 percent confidence level. The estimates in

---

[25] Recall that $m_D = M_D/L_D$ and $c_D = C_D/L_D$.
[26] Table W2 in the Web Appendix shows the WLS estimates using more restrictive and more inclusive definitions of manual and communication abilities. The results are very similar to those reported here.

TABLE 2—FOREIGN-BORN WORKERS AND THE NATIVE SUPPLY OF TASKS
(*Workers with a high school degree or less*)

	Explanatory variable: foreign-born share of workers with a high school degree or less					
	(1)	(2)	(3)	(4)	(5)	(6)
Communication definition	Basic	Basic	Basic	Basic	Basic	Basic
Manual definition	Basic	Extended	Basic	Extended	Basic	Extended
Method of estimation	WLS		2SLS using imputed Mexican share, geographic variables as instruments		2SLS using imputed Mexican share, geographic variables as instruments	
Additional controls	State and year fixed effects		State and year fixed effects		State and year fixed effects, computer use, sector-driven C/M	
Dependent variables						
$\ln(C_D/M_D)$ $\quad\gamma$	0.34***	0.31***	0.37***	0.33***	0.51**	0.44***
	(0.05)	(0.04)	(0.05)	(0.04)	(0.04)	(0.04)
$\ln(c_D)$ $\quad\gamma^C$	0.31***	0.31***	0.33***	0.33***	0.43***	0.43***
	(0.03)	(0.04)	(0.05)	(0.04)	(0.04)	(0.04)
$\ln(m_D)$ $\quad\gamma^M$	−0.03	0.00	−0.04***	0.00	−0.08***	−0.01
	(0.02)	(0.02)	(0.02)	(0.02)	(0.03)	(0.04)
First stage						
Joint F-test of the instruments (p-value)	NA	NA	18.9 (0.00)	18.9 (0.00)	6.9 (0.00)	6.9 (0.00)
Test of over-identifying restrictions	NA	NA	12.5	13.2	10.2	10.4
Probability (χ^2 > test) under the null of instrument exogeneity	NA	NA	0.14	0.11	0.25	0.24
Observations	255	255	255	255	255	255

Notes: Each cell contains estimates from a separate regression. The dependent variable in each is indicated in the first column. To construct the average manual m_D and communication c_D skill supply by native workers in a state-year, we first run individual regressions to control for individual age, experience, gender, and race. The state average (hours-weighted) of this "cleaned" supply represents the values c_D and m_D after controlling for individual demographic characteristics, and C_D/M_D is their ratio. The explanatory variable is the immigrant share of less-educated labor hours worked in the state and year. The units of observation in each regression are US states in a census year (decennial panel of 50 states plus Washington, DC from 1960–2000). All regressions include state and year fixed effects. The method of estimation in specifications (1)–(2) is weighted least squares. Regressions use employment as an analytic weight for each observation, and the standard errors are heteroskedasticity-robust and clustered by state. Specifications (3)–(6) use 2SLS using the imputed share of Mexicans (constructed as described in the main text), the distance between the center of gravity of the state and the Mexican border (inter-acted with decade dummies), and an indicator for states on the Mexican border (also interacted with decade dum-mies) as instruments. Specifications (5) and (6) include the percentage of workers using a computer at work and the sector-driven communication versus manual task-demand as controls.
  ***Significant at the 1 percent level.
  **Significant at the 5 percent level.

column 1 suggest that a 1 percentage-point increase in the foreign-born share of less-educated workers is associated with a 0.34 percent increase in the relative supply of communication versus manual tasks among natives. Second, this relative increase is primarily achieved through a rise in the supply of language skills, rather than a fall in natives' supply of physical labor. The estimate of γ^C in column 1 implies that a

1 percentage-point increase in the foreign-born share is associated with a significant 0.31 percent rise in natives' supply of communication tasks, whereas the estimates of γ^M imply that the native supply of manual tasks would only decline by 0.03 percent, a value not significantly different from 0. Third, the estimates are precise and robust to the different skill definitions used. The basic definition is the one producing the strongest and most significant results, while the definition that includes abilities not strictly related to physical skills produces a smaller value of γ.

In order to argue that our estimates of γ represent the native-born task supply *response* to immigration, the regressions in columns 3 and 4 of Table 2 perform the two-stage least squares counterparts of columns 1 and 2 by employing the instrumental variables introduced in Section IIB. The coefficients γ, γ^C, and γ^M of columns 3 and 4 are estimated by 2SLS using the imputed share of Mexicans and the geographic variables together as instruments, and, alternatively, the basic-basic and the basic-extended definitions for communication and manual skills, respectively[27]. The estimates of γ are still positive and very significant, and not very far from their WLS counterparts. They now range between 0.33 and 0.37. The F-tests reveal that the instruments strongly explain the endogenous variable (f_{st}), and they pass the test for over-identifying restrictions.[28] According to our preferred estimates (of column 3), natives respond to increases in immigration by significantly raising their communication task supply by 0.33 percent for each 1 percentage-point increase in the foreign-born share of less-educated workers. At the same time, they decrease the supply of manual tasks by 0.04 percent for each percentage-point increase in the foreign-born share. Note that the magnitude of the communication task response is much bigger than that of the manual response for all specifications. The similarity of the coefficients in columns 1 to 4, and the fact that the point estimates are slightly larger in the 2SLS regressions, strengthens our conviction that the immigration shock was largely an exogenous shift in the relative supply of skills at the state level to which native workers responded.

Finally state-specific technology and sector-driven changes in task demand could confound the baseline results. The regressions in columns 5 and 6 of Table 2 augment specifications (3) and (4) by controlling for these factors. In particular, they include a variable measuring the share of workers who use a computer at work (to control for the diffusion of information technology across states) and an index of relative task demand based on the state's initial industrial composition and the measured task demand by industries nationwide.[29] While the technological control variables usually have a significant coefficient with the expected sign (not reported) the inclusion of these variables leaves the estimates of γ extremely significant and

---

[27] Table W3 in the Web Appendix reports the estimates of the same specifications as (3) and (4) using different subsets of instruments. The results are very similar to those reported here.

[28] The value reported in the second to last row is the χ^2 test statistic under the null hypothesis that none of the instruments appear in the second-stage regression. The degrees of freedom are given by the difference between the number of instruments and endogenous variables. We have eight degrees of freedom, one endogenous variable, and nine instruments (four distance-decade interactions, four border-decade interactions, and the imputed share of Mexican workers). The last row reports the probability of obtaining the observed value of the test statistic or higher under the null. We cannot reject the null at any level of significance, so the assumption of instrument exogeneity stands. See Jeffrey M. Wooldridge (2002).

[29] The construction of both variables is described in detail in Section IV of the Web Appendix.

slightly increased.[30] Including those controls, the native task specialization response to immigration is between 0.44 percent and 0.51 percent for a 1 percentage-point rise in the share of foreign-born labor. Also, as in the other specifications, the positive impact on the supply of interactive skills (0.43) is larger and more significant than the negative effect on physical ones (between -0.08 and 0.00).

Altogether, the results of this section provide robust evidence for the increasing task-specialization of less-educated natives as a consequence of the immigration of less-educated workers. The relative supply of communication versus manual skills among natives increased by roughly 0.40 percent for each one percentage-point increase in the foreign-born share of less-educated workers.

B. *Immigration and Total Task Supply*

The regression specification in (13) provides a test of the equilibrium condition in (11) which argues for a negative relationship between immigration and the aggregate relative supply of communication versus manual tasks in a state. If true, the parameter γ_{TOT} will be negative. (This is the mechanism that alters the relative compensation of tasks and induces the change in the relative supply among natives as shown above.) However, we can also test whether immigration affects the average amount of communication (c) and manual (m) tasks supplied in equilibrium by running two separate regressions with $\ln (c)_{st}$ and $\ln (m)_{st}$ as dependent variables. Analogous to the specifications in (16) and (17), we call these coefficients γ_{TOT}^C and γ_{TOT}^M. We obtain $(C/M)_{st}$ by aggregating the supply of physical and language skills, using the cleaned individual supply of tasks among natives and immigrants.[31]

The upper part of Table 3 (panel A) shows the estimates of γ_{TOT}, γ_{TOT}^C, and γ_{TOT}^M. Manual and communication tasks are measured using two sets of *O*NET* variables, with the basic-basic definitions represented in columns 1 and 3 and the basic-extended definition used in columns 2 and 4.[32] Both the WLS (columns 1 and 2) and 2SLS (columns 3 and 4) regressions exhibit negative and significant estimates of γ_{TOT} with similar point estimates ranging between -0.11 and -0.18. This confirms the prediction of our model. The point estimates of our preferred specification (column 3), in which the basic skill definitions are applied and all instruments are used, implies that a 1 percentage point rise in the foreign-born share increases the average supply of manual tasks in the state by 0.05 percent (γ_{TOT}^M), and decreases the average supply of communication tasks by 0.10 percent (γ_{TOT}^C). Both coefficients are significant, and they lend support to the idea that the inflow of new immigrants decreases the overall relative supply of communication tasks in a state.

---

[30] The estimated coefficient on the technological variables and alternative specifications are reported in Table W4 of the Web Appendix.

[31] As described above, we perform separate first-stage regressions for foreign-born and native workers to calculate skill supplies cleaned of demographic effects.

[32] Table W5 in the Web Appendix shows the estimated coefficients for all combinations of basic and extended definitions of manual and communication abilities.

TABLE 3—FOREIGN-BORN WORKERS, AGGREGATE SUPPLY OF TASKS AND
COMMUNICATION-MANUAL WAGE ELASTICITY
(Workers with a high school degree or less)

	(1)	(2)	(3)	(4)
Panel A: Explanatory variable: foreign-born share of workers with a high school degree or less				
Communication definition	Basic	Basic	Basic	Basic
Manual definition	Basic	Extended	Basic	Extended
Method of estimation	WLS		2SLS using imputed Mexican share, geographic variables as instruments	
Additional controls	State and year fixed effects		State and year fixed effects	
Dependent variables:				
Ln(C/M) γ_{TOT}	−0.18***	−0.13***	−0.15***	−0.11***
	(0.04)	(0.03)	(0.04)	(0.03)
Ln(c) γ_{TOT}^{C}	−0.12***	−0.12***	−0.10***	−0.09***
	(0.03)	(0.03)	(0.03)	(0.03)
Ln(m) γ_{TOT}^{M}	0.06***	0.01	0.05***	0.02
	(0.02)	(0.02)	(0.02)	(0.02)
First stage				
Joint F-test of the instruments	NA	NA	18.9	18.9
(p-value)			(0.00)	(0.00)
Panel B: Explanatory variable: Ln(C/M); dependent variable: Ln(w_C/w_M)				
Estimated relative wage elasticity:	−0.75**	−0.70	−1.58***	−1.36**
−1/θ_L	(0.37)	(0.39)	(0.26)	(0.32)
Implied elasticity of substitution	1.33	1.42	0.63	0.73
First stage				
Joint F-test of the instruments	NA	NA	11.4	11.4
(p-values)			(0.00)	(0.00)
Observations	255	255	255	255

Notes: Each cell contains estimates from separate regressions. In panel A, the dependent variable is indicated in the first column and the explanatory variable is the foreign-born share of workers with a high school degree or less. The average manual and communication skill supply by native and immigrant workers in a state-year are cleaned in a first-stage regression. They are then combined using hours worked by natives and immigrants as a weight to produce total skill supply at the state-year level. The explanatory variable is the foreign-born share of less-educated labor. Panel B implements the estimation of coefficient −1/θ_L from equation (14) in the main text. The dependent variable is the relative compensation to communication versus manual tasks. The explanatory variable is the aggregate communication relative to manual skill supply. In all regressions, the units of observation are US states in a census year (decennial panel of 50 states plus Washington DC from 1960–2000). All regressions include state and year fixed effects. Regressions use employment as an analytic weight for each observation, and the standard errors are heteroskedasticity-robust and clustered by state. Specifications (1) and (2) are estimated using least squares. Specifications (3)–(4) are estimated with 2SLS, using the imputed share of Mexicans (constructed as described in the main text), the distance between the center of gravity of the state and the Mexican border (interacted with decade dummies), and an indicator for states on the Mexican border (also interacted with decade dummies) as instruments.
  ***Significant at the 1 percent level.
  **Significant at the 5 percent level.

C. Immigration and Relative Task Compensation

The regression specification in equation (14) tests the last important prediction of our model (obtained from the relative demand for skills), which argues that by decreasing the relative supply of communication skills in a state, immigration increases their relative rate of return. The lower part of Table 3 (panel B) estimates the relative compensation response to a state's changing task composition. In particular, exogenous shifts in the overall relative supply of physical versus language skills across states identify the coefficient $1/\theta_L$, where θ_L represents the elasticity of substitution between the tasks. Since exogenous immigration changes will affect the aggregate relative supply of skills (as shown in Section IIIB), we employ the exogenous determinants of the foreign-born share of workers as instruments in the 2SLS specifications. We acquire estimates for compensation paid to communication $(\widehat{w_{M_{st}}})$ and manual $(\widehat{w_{C_{st}}})$ tasks by state and year according to the methodology in Section IIA and then substitute those values into equation (14) to estimate $-1/\theta_L$. Table 3 panel B reports the estimates of $-1/\theta_L$ as well as their implied elasticity of substitution measured using the basic-basic (columns 1 and 3) and basic-extended (columns 2 and 4) task variable definitions.[33] We estimate (14) first by weighted least squares (columns 1 and 2) and then with the imputed Mexicans and geographic variables as instruments (columns 3 and 4). The instruments are relatively powerful in predicting the explanatory variable $(\ln(C/M))$, with an F-statistic above 10. The WLS estimates of $-1/\theta_L$ are between -0.7 and -0.75 while the 2SLS estimates range between -1.36 and -1.58. Both the 2SLS estimates are statistically significant at the 1 percent level. These estimates imply that the share of foreign-born workers significantly increases the relative compensation paid to communication versus manual tasks, thus validating a key mechanism in our model. The results suggest that the elasticity of substitution ranges between 0.63 (2SLS estimates) and 1.42 (WLS estimates). Hence, manual and communication tasks have a significant degree of complementarity. These figures are comparable to commonly estimated values for the elasticity of substitution between labor and capital (usually near 1), or between workers of different education levels (σ, which falls between 1.5 and 2).[34]

D. *Specification Checks and Extensions*

Our model's prediction for the wages of less-educated native workers employs two implicit simplifying assumptions. First, we assume that highly-educated natives are imperfect substitutes with all less-educated workers, and that their relative task supply is not affected by the presence of less-educated immigrants. Second, we assume that long-term immigrants are similar to new immigrants and different from native workers in that, relative to natives, they also have a comparative advantage in manual tasks. This allows us to group new and long-term immigrants together in our empirical analysis. In this section, we test the validity of these two assumptions. Moreover, we assume a homogenous response among US-born workers with a high school education or less. Our approach, however, allows us to identify the effect of immigration on the task specialization of specific demographic groups of less educated native workers. If γ varies across these groups, then the wage implications of immigration on those groups will vary as well. We also explore this possibility.

---

[33] Estimates using different sets of instruments are reported in Table W6 of the Web Appendix.
[34] See Katz and Murphy (1992) or Angrist (1995).

VOL. 1 NO. 3   PERI AND SPARBER: TASK SPECIALIZATION, IMMIGRATION, AND WAGES   159

Impact on Highly-Educated Natives and Long-Term Immigrants.—Highly-educated workers (those with some college education) are not close substitutes for less-educated workers. Instead, they perform different production tasks (mostly analytical and cognitive) that are not affected by less-educated immigrants, and supply far fewer manual tasks than less-educated workers do. The average value of the manual supply index for workers with some college education is half of the average among those with a high school education or less, while the highly-educated supply of communication tasks is double that of less-educated workers. We also tested whether the average supply (by state and year) of tasks measured *among highly-educated natives* is affected by the *immigrant share of less educated workers* in the state and year.[35] While the standard errors are large, the regressions clearly indicate that there is no effect of less-educated immigration on the relative supply of communication and analytical tasks among highly-educated natives. The regressions also indicate that immigration does not affect the already small supply of manual tasks among highly-educated natives.

As for long-term immigrants, Figure 2 shows that they still supplied more manual versus communication tasks than natives throughout the 1970–2000 period. This similarity between new and long-term immigrants may be the reason that many authors find a larger effect of immigration on the wages of previous immigrants than on natives (see Card 2001; Ottaviano and Peri 2008; Cortes 2008). In the context of our model, the substitutability of skills among these groups implies that foreign-born workers will experience only a small (if any) reallocation of task supply in response to an inflow of new immigrants. They therefore experience more wage competition with new entrants. Column 1 of Table 4 compares estimates of γ, γ^C, and γ^M from regressions similar to (12), (16), and (17) where the dependent variable measures the task supply of less-educated workers, bifurcated between long-term immigrants (Group 1) and US natives (Group 2). The method of estimation is 2SLS using imputed Mexicans and geographic variables as instruments for the immigrant share of less educated workers.[36] The point-estimates show that long-term immigrants had a weaker tendency to respond to immigration by moving away from manual tasks and into communication tasks, relative to natives. Moreover the magnitude of the response is small for long-term immigrants ($\gamma = 0.24$ relative to 0.36 for natives), and the large standard errors imply that the estimates of γ for long-term immigrants are not significant at standard levels of confidence. Thus, the empirics concur with the predictions of our model. Though long-term immigrants are becoming more like natives in their skill use, their response to immigration is smaller and less significant, making them especially vulnerable to wage competition with new immigrants.

Impact across Demographic Groups.—The remaining columns of Table 4 compare estimates of γ, γ^C, and γ^M for groups of less-educated US natives, bifurcated by race (column 1), gender (column 2), age (column 3), and education (column 4). For each comparison, Group 1 represents those earning lower wages (blacks,

---

[35] The full set of estimates is reported in Table W7 in the Web Appendix.
[36] The full set of estimates using WLS and 2SLS methods of estimation with different sets of instruments is reported in Table W8 of the Web Appendix.

160   *AMERICAN ECONOMIC JOURNAL: APPLIED ECONOMICS*   *JULY 2009*

TABLE 4—IMPACT OF FOREIGN-BORN WORKERS ON THE SUPPLY OF TASKS AMONG
DIFFERENT DEMOGRAPHIC GROUPS
(Controlling for individual characteristics in the construction of aggregate skills)

Explanatory variable: foreign-born share among workers with a high school degree or less
Dependent variables: relative communication/manual skills for the group, basic definition

		Only US native workers are included in specifications (2) to (5)				
		(1)	(2)	(3)	(4)	(5)
Group 1		Long-term immigrants	Blacks	Women	Young (18–40)	High school dropout
Group 2		Natives	Nonblacks	Men	Old (41–65)	High school degree
Dependent variables						
Group 1, $\ln(C_1/M_1)$	γ	0.24 (0.28)	0.63** (0.11)	0.11** (0.05)	0.34*** (0.13)	0.34*** (0.07)
Group 1, $\ln(c_1)$	γ^C	0.13 (0.18)	0.50** (0.09)	0.10** (0.03)	0.25** (0.10)	0.28** (0.05)
Group 1, $\ln(m_1)$	γ^M	−0.11 (0.10)	−0.13** (0.03)	−0.01 (0.03)	−0.09** (0.04)	−0.06* (0.03)
Group 2, $\ln(C_2/M_2)$	γ	0.37** (0.05)	0.20** (0.10)	0.26** (0.11)	0.11 (0.08)	0.20 (0.14)
Group 2, $\ln(c_2)$	γ^C	0.33** (0.05)	0.15* (0.08)	0.20* (0.10)	0.09 (0.07)	0.15 (0.10)
Group 2, $\ln(m_2)$	γ^M	−0.04* (0.02)	−0.05 (0.03)	−0.06** (0.02)	−0.02 (0.02)	0.05 (0.04)
Observations		255	255	255	255	255

Notes: Each cell contains estimates from separate regressions. The dependent variable is calculated for specific demographic groups. Column 1 shows the estimates for immigrants and natives. Columns 2–5 include native workers only in each group. In each comparison, Group 1 earns lower wages than Group 2 does. The average manual m_i and communication c_i skill supply for each group i in a state-year are calculated by averaging individual supply using personal weight times hours worked as weights. The units of observation in each regression are US states in a census year (decennial panel of 50 states plus Washington, DC from 1960–2000) for a total of 255 observations. All regressions include state and year fixed effects. The method of estimation is 2SLS using imputed Mexican and geographic IV. Regressions use employment in the cell as an analytic weight for each observation, and the standard errors are heteroskedasticity-robust and clustered by state.
   ***Significant at the 1 percent level.
   **Significant at the 5 percent level.
   *Significant at the 10 percent level.

women, younger workers, and workers without a high school diploma). Except for women, individuals in Group 1 were also more specialized in manual than communication tasks, and more vulnerable to job competition with immigrants. The first three rows report the 2SLS estimates of γ, γ^C, and γ^M (using all instruments) for Group 1, and the remaining rows report the same coefficients for Group 2. Each of the eight native-born groups in Table 4 responds to immigration by shifting their specialization from manual tasks to communication tasks. The shift was significant in six cases, and the increase in supply of communication skills was more significant and larger than the decrease in supply of physical tasks for all eight groups. Interestingly, for each comparison, the native group that was more at risk to competition with immigrants (due to a larger reliance upon manual task performance) also exhibited a greater skill response. Men increased their relative skill supply by

0.26 percent for every percentage point increase in the foreign-born share, while women only increased theirs by 0.11 percent. Young workers and those without a high school diploma also significantly shifted their relative supply ($\gamma = 0.34$), while older workers, and those with a diploma, did not. This is not surprising since young workers have greater occupational mobility (older workers have very low rates of occupational change), and workers with extremely low educational attainment are potentially more threatened by immigrants. Most strikingly, black workers responded to immigration by changing their relative task specialization three times more than nonblack workers did ($\gamma = 0.63$ versus $\gamma = 0.20$). Blacks were much more specialized in manual tasks in comparison to nonblacks in 1960, and were more susceptible to competition with immigrants. The strong response among blacks in moving toward more language-intensive occupations should, at least in part, have shielded them from large negative wage effects.[37]

IV. Simulated Effects of Immigration on Real Wages, 1990–2000

Our empirical analysis suggests that to understand the wage implications of immigration, simulations must account for the adjustment in native-born task supply. Hence, we can use our model, production parameters (particularly σ), the estimated task complementarity (θ_L), and the effect of immigration on native-born task supply (γ) to simulate the full impact of immigration on the average wage of natives across US states.

We focus on the effect of immigration on wages paid to less-educated natives.[38] To do this, we must consider two channels. First, we need to obtain values for the percentage change in compensation to manual ($\Delta w_M/w_M$) and communication ($\Delta w_C/w_C$) tasks, and then weight those changes by the initial (pre-immigration) average task supply of natives (m_D and c_D).[39] Second, we need to account for the change in the effective supply of natives' manual and communication tasks due to immigration (Δm_D and Δc_D). The wage impact of this reallocation of tasks equals (Δm_D) w_M + (Δc_D) w_C. Altogether, equation (18) expresses the net effects of total immigration on average wages paid to native-born workers with little educational attainment, highlighting the contribution from these two channels.

(18) $$\frac{\Delta w_D}{w_D} = \underbrace{\frac{\Delta w_M}{w_M} \frac{w_M}{w_D} m_D + \frac{\Delta w_C}{w_C} \frac{w_C}{w_D} c_D}_{First\ Channel} + \underbrace{(\Delta m_D) \frac{w_M}{w_D} + (\Delta c_D) \frac{w_C}{w_D}}_{Second\ Channel}.$$

[37] We believe that the impact of immigration on subgroups of American workers, and blacks in particular, is worthy of further analysis. Borjas, Jeffrey Grogger, and Gordon H. Hanson (2006) present an alternative analysis of the effect of immigrants on black workers.

[38] The Appendix also shows the formula to obtain the effect of immigration on wages of highly educated workers.

[39] Equations (23) and (24) in the Appendix report the derived expressions for $\Delta w_M/w_M$ and $\Delta w_C/w_C$. The expressions are affected by inflows of both high and low education labor.

162   AMERICAN ECONOMIC JOURNAL: APPLIED ECONOMICS   JULY 2009

TABLE 5—THE SIMULATED EFFECTS OF IMMIGRATION ON TASK COMPENSATION AND AVERAGE NATIVE WAGE, 1990–2000

	Percentage change of highly-educated due to immigration (1)	Percentage change of less-educated due to immigration (2)	Percentage change in wage of less-educated, assuming perfect native-immigrant substitution (3)	Percentage change in wage of less-educated due to task complementarities and specialization (4)	Overall percent-age change of average wage paid to less-educated natives (3) + (4) (5)
Arizona	8	29	−8.2	2.5	−5.7
California	12	24	−4.5	2.3	−2.2
Nevada	16	34	−5.8	2.2	−3.6
New Jersey	13	10	1.6	1.3	2.9
New York	10	13	−0.7	1.6	0.9
Texas	8	22	−4.8	1.8	−3.0
United States	6	9	−1.2	0.9	−0.3

Notes: The variables and parameters used in the simulations reported above are described in the text. In particular, we assumed $\sigma = 1.75$ and $\theta_L = 1$. The six states chosen are those with the highest foreign-born employment shares among less-educated workers in 2000. The parameters used to estimate the change in supply of each task among native workers in response to immigration are the parameters in column 4 of Table 2, namely $\gamma^M = 0.33$ and $\gamma^C = -0.00$.

Importantly, there are two reasons why this model predicts a mitigated wage effect (that may even be positive) when compared to models that assume perfect substitution between natives and immigrants within education groups. First, while the impact on manual compensation $(\Delta w_M/w_M)$ due to the increased supply of manual skills from immigrants is negative, it is weighted by the manual task supply of the natives, which is smaller than the manual supply of the average individual because the average includes foreign-born workers. Similarly, the positive (or less negative) impact on language compensation $(\Delta w_C/w_C)$ is weighted by the language task supply of natives, which is larger than the average. Hence, the negative contribution from that term (labeled as "First Channel" in equation (18)) is smaller for less-educated natives than it is for the average less-educated worker. Second, the reallocation of tasks implies that $\Delta m_D < 0$ and $\Delta c_D > 0$, so that if the communication task supply response is larger than that of manual tasks, and if $w_M/w_D < w_C/w_D$ (both conditions are theoretically and empirically true), then the term labeled "Second Channel" in expression (18) would positively contribute to the average wage paid to domestic, less-educated workers. Hence, equation (18) reports the wage consequences of immigration on less-educated native workers, after accounting for task complementarity and for the reallocation of tasks by natives. That formula, combined with those in the Appendix (and plugging in the estimated parameters), allows us to simulate the effect of immigration on average wages paid to less-educated natives, once we feed in the percentage change in the supply of more- and less-educated workers due to immigration.

Table 5 reports such simulated effects of immigrant flows between 1990 and 2000 at the national level (last row) and for the six states with the highest immigrant share of less-educated labor in 2000 (listed alphabetically). The first two columns report the increase in foreign-born employment (as a percentage of 1990 total group employment) among workers with some college education ($\Delta H_F/H$), and those with a high school degree or less ($\Delta L_F/L$), respectively. While immigration of less-educated workers was larger than for more educated workers, flows were fairly balanced at the US level as the employment of more educated immigrant workers increased by 6 percent, while the employment of less educated immigrant workers increased by 9 percent.

Columns 3–5 simulate the wage consequences of immigration for less-educated native-born workers. In the simulations, we use a value of $\sigma = 1.75$, which is in the middle of the range of estimates usually found in the literature $(1.5 - 2.0)$,[40] and we set $\theta_L = 1$, a value close to the average of our estimates in panel B of Table 4. Since the inflow of more educated immigrants was usually smaller than the inflow of less educated ones, the simulated wage effect on workers with a high school education or less is usually negative. However, in order to emphasize the new insight of this paper, column (3) reports the effect on average wages before accounting for any shift in domestic task supply or for differences in the relative supply of tasks. That is, these figures are useful for identifying the counter-factual wage effects identified by models that assume perfect substitutability between native and foreign-born workers of similar educational attainment.[41] Column 5, by comparison, reports the wage effects for less-educated natives accounting for the complementarity and reallocation of tasks following immigration, according to equation (18).[42] Column 4 provides the difference between these values. Thus, this column illustrates the difference between the wage effects estimated in our model of comparative advantage versus a traditional model of homogeneous less-educated labor.

By specializing in language skill-intensive occupations, less-educated natives reduce wage losses due to immigration. At the national level, specialization causes a reduction in this loss of almost 1 percentage point, from -1.2 percent to an ultimate loss of just -0.3 percent. In states with large immigrant flows (such as California, Arizona, and Nevada), task reallocation reduces the wage loss by around 2.4 percentage points. In New York, specialization changes the effect of immigration on less-educated natives from negative to positive values. Let us reemphasize, again, that the wage effects presented in column 5 of Table 5 are the results of simulations. Their differences reflect the implementation of formula (18), using the same parameter estimates (θ_L and γ) on different inflows of more- and less-educated immigrants by state.

It is also interesting to note that the figures in column 3 of Table 5 represent the wage consequence for *any* less-educated worker who possesses skills that are perfectly substitutable with immigrants and who fails to respond to new labor flows

---

[40] See Katz and Murphy (1992), Johnson (1997), and Goldin and Katz (2007).

[41] Note that before accounting for the specialization adjustment, immigration would have caused a wage loss in the United States of 1.2 percent for less-educated workers. As emphasized repeatedly in Ottaviano and Peri (2008), this relatively moderate consequence is due to the roughly balanced flow of immigrants across education groups (after merging the highly substitutable workers with no degree and those with a high school diploma together).

[42] We compute the values of Δc_D and Δm_D by multiplying the change in the foreign-born share of each state between 1990 and 2000 by the average response of communication and manual task supply to immigration found in column 4 of Table 2 (respectively $+0.33$ and -0.00). The resulting values are elasticities that, when multiplied by the initial average values of task supply, equal Δc_D and Δm_D.

by changing occupations. Thus, column 3 also illustrates the change in wages paid to previously established immigrant workers.[43] By extension, column 4 can then be interpreted as the percentage change in the relative wage between less-educated natives and foreign-born workers. If we divide those values by the percentage change in relative hours worked (L_F/L_D), we can obtain the inverse elasticity of substitution between immigrant and native workers implied by our model. This provides a useful benchmark to compare with direct measures of this elasticity, such as those recently provided by Ottaviano and Peri (2008). The resulting inverse elasticity of substitution between natives and immigrants obtained with this method ranges between 0.021 and 0.051 with an average of 0.03, thus implying an elasticity between 20 and 47, with an average of 33. These values are similar to those estimated by Ottaviano and Peri (2008). In particular, their preferred specifications (pooling men and women) report values between 0.024 and 0.047 (significant at the 1 percent level). Hence, the mechanism illustrated in this paper can explain most of their estimated imperfect substitutability. On the surface, an average inverse elasticity of 0.03 looks small. Given that relative supply has changed by as much as 60–90 percent, however, our estimates suggest a 2–3 percent change in the relative native-immigrant wage that favors natives. This relative effect is large enough to significantly reduce the potential wage loss among natives, and it implies that less-educated foreign-born workers are the ones who experience most of the negative wage consequences of new immigration.

V. Conclusions

The effects of immigration on the wages paid to native-born workers with low levels of educational attainment depend upon two critical factors. The first is whether immigrants take jobs similar to those of native workers or, instead, take different jobs due to inherent comparative advantages between native and foreign-born employees in performing particular productive tasks. The second is whether US-born workers respond to immigration and adjust their occupation choices in order to shield themselves from competition with immigrant labor. This paper provides a simple theoretical framework, and new empirical evidence, to analyze these issues. We argue that production combines different labor skills. Immigrants with little educational attainment have a comparative advantage in manual and physical tasks, while natives of similar levels of education have a comparative advantage in communication- and language-intensive tasks. Native- and foreign-born workers specialize accordingly. When immigration generates large increases in manual task supply, the relative compensation paid to communication skills rises, thereby rewarding natives who progressively move to language-intensive jobs.

Our empirical analysis used *O*NET* data to measure the task content of occupations in the United States between 1960 and 2000. We find strong evidence supporting the implications of our theoretical model. On average, less educated immigrants supplied more manual tasks, relative to communication tasks, than

---

[43] This is because previous immigrants are similar to new immigrants in their task specialization and did not significantly change their task supply in response to immigration.

VOL. 1 NO. 3   PERI AND SPARBER: TASK SPECIALIZATION, IMMIGRATION, AND WAGES   165

did natives. In states with large immigrant inflows, native workers shifted to occupations more intensive in language skills and less intensive in physical skills. At the same time, immigrants more than compensated for the change in skill supply among natives, ensuring an overall increase in manual task supply and driving communication task-intensive occupations to earn higher wages in those states. As a consequence, immigration-induced wage losses among less-educated native workers are significantly smaller than the losses predicted by models in which less-educated native and foreign-born labor is perfectly substitutable. In particular, we estimate that immigration only reduced average real wages paid to less-educated US-born workers by 0.3 percent between 1990 and 2000. Without task specialization that loss would have been 1.2 percent.

$$\text{APPENDIX: DERIVATION OF } \frac{\Delta w_H}{w_H}, \frac{\Delta w_M}{w_M}, \frac{\Delta w_C}{w_C}, \text{ and } \frac{\Delta Y_L}{Y_L}$$

To isolate the effect of immigration on wages, first substitute (2) into the production function (1), and take the derivative with respect to the inputs M, C, and H to obtain their marginal products.

$$(19) \qquad w_M = (\beta_L \beta) Y^{\frac{1}{\sigma}} Y_L^{\left(\frac{1}{\theta_L} - \frac{1}{\sigma}\right)} M^{-\frac{1}{\theta_L}}.$$

$$(20) \qquad w_C = (1 - \beta_L)\beta Y^{\frac{1}{\sigma}} Y_L^{\left(\frac{1}{\theta_L} - \frac{1}{\sigma}\right)} C^{-\frac{1}{\theta_L}}.$$

$$(21) \qquad w_H = P_H = (1 - \beta) Y^{\frac{1}{\sigma}} Y_H^{-\frac{1}{\sigma}}.$$

Highly-educated workers earn the unit price of the intermediate good they produce. The logarithmic differential of (21) directly measures the change in wages paid to highly-educated workers (w_H) in response to immigration (among both high- and low-education workers), and can be expressed as in equation (22), where $\kappa_H = (w_H H/Y)$ is the income share paid to highly-educated labor, and $(1 - \kappa_H)$ is the share paid to less-educated labor.

$$(22) \qquad \frac{\Delta w_H}{w_H} = \frac{\Delta P_H}{P_H} = -\frac{1}{\sigma}\frac{\Delta H}{H} + \frac{1}{\sigma}\left(\kappa_H \frac{\Delta H}{H} + (1 - \kappa_H)\frac{\Delta Y_L}{Y_L}\right).$$

Wages paid to less-educated workers are divided into their task components. The first-order effect of immigration is equal to the percentage change in the intermediate good price P_L. Values for $(\Delta w_M/w_M)$ and $(\Delta w_C/w_C)$ in equations (23) and (24) are obtainable from logarithmic differentials of (19) and (20).

$$(23) \qquad \frac{\Delta w_M}{w_M} = \frac{1}{\sigma}\left(\kappa_H \frac{\Delta H}{H} + (1 - \kappa_H)\frac{\Delta Y_L}{Y_L}\right) + \left(\frac{1}{\theta_L} - \frac{1}{\sigma}\right)\frac{\Delta Y_L}{Y_L} - \frac{1}{\theta_L}\frac{\Delta M}{M}.$$

$$(24) \qquad \frac{\Delta w_C}{w_C} = \frac{1}{\sigma}\left(\kappa_H \frac{\Delta H}{H} + (1 - \kappa_H)\frac{\Delta Y_L}{Y_L}\right) + \left(\frac{1}{\theta_L} - \frac{1}{\sigma}\right)\frac{\Delta Y_L}{Y_L} - \frac{1}{\theta_L}\frac{\Delta C}{C}.$$

Using equations (23) and (24), we can express the wage effect for less-educated workers at constant specialization by substituting for $\Delta w_M/w_M$ and $\Delta w_C/w_C$, and simplifying to obtain equation (25).[44]

$$(25) \qquad \frac{\Delta w_L}{w_L} = \frac{\Delta w_M}{w_M} \frac{w_M}{w_L} m + \frac{\Delta w_C}{w_C} \frac{w_C}{w_L} c = \kappa_M \frac{\Delta w_M}{w_M} + (1 - \kappa_M) \frac{\Delta w_C}{w_C}.$$

Note that (25) represents the average manual and communication wage effects weighted by their respective initial supplies. The total effect of immigration on the average, native-born, less-educated worker, accounting for (25) as well as for the effect of changing specialization, is given by equation (18) in the main text.

To derive $\Delta Y_L/Y_L$, first note that, since Y_L is produced under perfect competition using services of less educated workers, we know the total income generated in sector Y_L will be distributed to less-educated workers as in equation (26).

$$(26) \qquad P_L Y_L = w_L L = w_M M + w_C C.$$

This allows us to relate changes in the production of Y_L to small changes in inputs M and C as in equation (30). The formal proof hinges only on constant returns to scale to M and C in (2). First, rewrite equation (30) by dividing by $P_L Y_L$. Then, take the total differential with respect to M and C to find equation (27).

$$(27) \qquad \frac{dY_L}{Y_L} = \frac{d(\frac{w_M}{P_L} \frac{M}{Y_L} + \frac{w_C}{P_L} \frac{C}{Y_L})}{dM} dM + \frac{d(\frac{w_M}{P_L} \frac{M}{Y_L} + \frac{w_C}{P_L} \frac{C}{Y_L})}{dC} dC.$$

From the definition of wages, we know that $w_M/P_L = dY_L/dM$ and $w_C/P_L = dY_L/dC$. Distributing the differentiation with respect to M and C, we can rewrite (27) as in (28).

$$(28) \qquad \frac{dY_L}{Y_L} = \frac{w_M M}{P_L Y_L} \frac{dM}{M} + \frac{w_C C}{P_L Y_L} \frac{dC}{C} + \left[\frac{d(\frac{dY_L}{dM})}{dM} \frac{M}{Y_L} + \frac{d(\frac{dY_L}{dC})}{dM} \frac{C}{Y_L} \right] dM$$

$$+ \left[\frac{d(\frac{dY_L}{dM})}{dC} \frac{M}{Y_L} + \frac{d(\frac{dY_L}{dC})}{dC} \frac{C}{Y_L} \right] dC.$$

Due to constant returns to scale of M and C in Y_L, the expression $(dY_L/dM) \times (M/Y_L) + (dY_L/dC) \times (C/Y_L)$ equals one (Euler Condition). Constant returns also imply that the second derivatives (with respect to M or C), multiplied by the shares M/Y_L and C/Y_L, sum to zero. Hence, the two terms in brackets equal zero so that (27) reduces to (29).

$$(29) \qquad \frac{dY_L}{Y_L} = \frac{w_M M}{P_L Y_L} \frac{dM}{M} + \frac{w_C C}{P_L Y_L} \frac{dC}{C}.$$

---

[44] This can be checked by taking the total logarithmic differential of $P_L = \beta Y^{1/\sigma} Y_L^{-1/\sigma}$ with respect to $\Delta Y_L/Y_L$ and $\Delta H/H$.

Finally, we label the term $w_M M / P_L Y_L = w_M M / w_L L$ as κ_M, and $w_C C / P_L Y_L = w_C C / w_L L$ as $(1 - \kappa_M)$. We then use Δ, rather than d, to indicate a small (rather than an infinitesimal) change to obtain equation (30)

$$(30) \qquad \frac{\Delta Y_L}{Y_L} = \frac{w_M \Delta M + w_C \Delta C}{P_L Y_L} = \kappa_M \frac{\Delta M}{M} + (1 - \kappa_M) \frac{\Delta C}{C}.$$

APPENDIX TABLE A1— SKILL TYPES, SUB-TYPES, AND VARIABLES FROM O*NET

Type of skill	Definition	Skill sub-type	O*NET variables
Manual (or physical) skills	Basic definition: movement and strength	Limb, hand, and finger dexterity	Arm-hand steadiness; manual dexterity; finger dexterity; control precision; multilimb coordination; response orientation; rate control; reaction time; wrist-finger speed; speed of limb movement
		Body coordination and flexibility	Extent flexibility; dynamic flexibility; gross body coordination; gross body equilibrium
		Strength	Static strength; explosive strength; dynamic strength; trunk strength; stamina
	Extended definition: movement and strength plus sensory-perception skills	General perception	Perceptual speed; spatial orientation; visualization; selective attention; time sharing
		Visual perception	Near vision; far vision; visual color discrimination; night vision; peripheral vision; depth perception; glare sensitivity
		Hearing perception	Hearing sensitivity; auditory attention; sound localization
Communication (or language) skills	Basic definition: oral and written	Oral	Oral comprehension; oral expression
		Written	Written comprehension; written expression
	Extended definition: oral and written plus cognitive, analytical, and vocal skills	Cognitive and analytical	Fluency of ideas; originality; problem sensitivity; category flexibility; mathematical reasoning; number facility; deductive reasoning; inductive reasoning; information ordering; memorization; speed of closure; flexibility of closure
		Vocal	Speech recognition; speech clarity

Note: O*NET variables are from the O*NET abilities survey available at http://www.onetcenter.org/.

TABLE A2—SUMMARY STATISTICS FOR THE ESTIMATED STATE-SPECIFIC COMPENSATION OF MANUAL AND COMMUNICATION TASKS, BASIC DEFINITIONS OF SKILLS

Year	Average W_M	Average W_C	R^2	Observations
1960	519	566	0.41	7738
1970	603	704	0.43	10591
1980	664	617	0.31	15880
1990	547	557	0.38	15607
2000	543	576	0.32	15142

Notes: The compensation paid to manual and communication tasks is in 2000 US dollars and corresponds to weekly returns. The R^2 are from Regression (15) when estimated with a constant term.

REFERENCES

Acemoglu, Daron. 1998. "Why Do New Technologies Complement Skills? Directed Technical Change and Wage Inequality." *Quarterly Journal of Economics*, 113(4): 1055–89.

Acemoglu, Daron. 2002. "Directed Technical Change." *Review of Economic Studies*, 69(4): 781–809.

Acemoglu, Daron, and Fabrizio Zilibotti. 2001. "Productivity Differences." *Quarterly Journal of Economics*, 116(2): 563–606.

Altonji, Joseph G., and David E. Card. 1991. "The Effects of Immigration on the Labor Market Outcomes of Less-Skilled Natives." In *Immigration, Trade, and the Labor Market,* ed. John M. Abowd and Richard B. Freeman, 201–34. Chicago: University of Chicago Press.

Angrist, Joshua D. 1995. "The Economic Returns to Schooling in the West Bank and Gaza Strip." *American Economic Review,* 85(5): 1065–87.

Autor, David H. 2007. "Inequality and Specialization: The Growth of Low-Skill Service Jobs in the United States." Massachusetts Institute of Technology August 2007.

Autor, David H., Frank Levy, and Richard Murnane. 2003. "The Skill Content of Recent Technological Change: An Empirical Exploration." *Quarterly Journal of Economics,* 118 (4): 1279–1333.

Borjas, George J. 1994. "The Economics of Immigration." *Journal of Economic Literature,* 32(4): 1667–1717.

Borjas, George J. 1995. "The Economic Benefits from Immigration." *Journal of Economic Perspectives,* 9(2): 3–22.

Borjas, George J. 1999. *Heaven's Door: Immigration Policy and the American Economy.* Princeton: Princeton University Press.

Borjas, George J. 2003. "The Labor Demand Curve is Downward Sloping: Reexamining the Impact of Immigration on the Labor Market." *Quarterly Journal of Economics,* 118(4): 1335–74.

Borjas, George J., Richard B. Freeman, and Larry F. Katz. 1997. "How Much Do Immigration and Trade Affect Labor Market Outcomes?" *Brookings Papers on Economic Activity,* (1): 1–67.

Borjas, George J., Jeffrey Grogger, and Gordon H. Hanson. 2006. "Immigration and African-American Employment Opportunities: The Response of Wages, Employment, and Incarceration to Labor Supply Shocks." National Bureau of Economic Research Working Paper 12518.

Borjas, George J., and Lawrence F. Katz. 2007. "The Evolution of the Mexican-Born Workforce in the United States." In *Mexican Immigration to the United States,* ed. George J. Borjas, 13–56. Chicago: University of Chicago Press.

Butcher, Kristin F., and David Card. 1991. "Immigration and Wages: Evidence from the 1980s." *American Economic Review,* 81(2): 292–96.

Card, David. 1990. "The Impact of the Mariel Boatlift on the Miami Labor Market." *Industrial and Labor Relations Review,* 43(2): 245–57.

Card, David. 2001. "Immigrant Inflows, Native Outflows, and the Local Labor Market Impacts of Higher Immigration." *Journal of Labor Economics,* 19(1): 22–64.

Card, David. 2007. "How Immigration Affects U.S. Cities." Centre for Research and Analysis of Migration Discussion Paper 11/07.

Card, David, and John E. DiNardo. 2000. "Do Immigrant Inflows Lead to Native Outflows?" National Bureau of Economic Research Working Paper 7578.

Card, David, and Thomas Lemieux. 2001. "Can Falling Supply Explain the Rising Return to College for Younger Men? A Cohort Based Analysis." *Quarterly Journal of Economics,* 116(2): 705–46.

Card, David, and Ethan G. Lewis. 2007. "The Diffusion of Mexican Immigrants During the 1990s: Explanations and Impacts." In *Mexican Immigration to the United States,* ed. George J. Borjas, 193–228. Chicago: University of Chicago Press.

Caselli, Francesco, and Wilbur John Coleman, II. 2006. "The World Technology Frontier." *American Economic Review,* 96(3): 499–522.

Chiswick, Barry R., and Paul W. Miller. 2007. "Occupational Language Requirements and the Value of English in the U.S. Labor Market." IZA Discussion Paper 2664.

Cortes, Patricia. 2008. "The Effect of Low-Skilled Immigration on U.S. Prices: Evidence from CPI Data." *Journal of Political Economy,* 116(3): 381–422.

D'Amuri, Francesco, Gianmarco I. P. Ottaviano, and Giovanni Peri. 2008. "The Labor Market Impact of Immigration in Western Germany in the 1990s." National Bureau of Economic Research Working Paper 13851.

Friedberg, Rachel M. 2001. "The Impact of Mass Migration on the Israeli Labor Market." *Quarterly Journal of Economics,* 116(4): 1373–1408.

Friedberg, Rachel M., and Jennifer Hunt. 1995. "The Impact of Immigrants on Host Country Wages, Employment and Growth." *Journal of Economic Perspectives,* 9(2): 23–44.

Goldin, Claudia, and Larry Katz. 2007. "The Race between Education and Technology: The Evolution of U.S. Educational Wage Differentials, 1980 to 2005." National Bureau of Economic Research Working Paper 12984.

Grossman, Gene M., and Esteban Rossi-Hansberg. 2008. "Trading Tasks: A Simple Theory of Offshoring." *American Economic Review*, 98(5): 1978–97.

Johnson, George E. 1997. "Changes in Earnings Inequality: The Role of Demand Shifts." *Journal of Economic Perspectives*, 11(2): 41–54.

Katz, Lawrence F., and Kevin M. Murphy. 1992. "Change in Relative Wages, 1963–1987: Supply and Demand Factors." *Quarterly Journal of Economics*, 107(1): 35–78.

Lewis, Ethan. 2005. "Immigration, Skill Mix, and the Choice of Technique." Federal Reserve Bank of Philadelphia Working Paper 05-8.

Manacorda, Marco, Alan Manning, and Jonathan Wadsworth. 2007. "The Impact of Immigration on the Structure of Male Wages: Theory and Evidence from Britain." Unpublished.

Ottaviano, Gianmarco I. P., and Giovanni Peri. 2006. "Rethinking the Effects of Immigration on Wages." National Bureau of Economic Research Working Paper 12497.

Ottaviano, Gianmarco I. P., and Giovanni Peri. 2007. "The Effects of Immigration on U.S. Wages and Rents: A General Equilibrium Approach." Centre for Research and Analysis of Migration Discussion Paper 13/07.

Ottaviano, Gianmarco I. P., and Giovanni Peri. 2008. "Immigration and National Wages: Clarifying the Theory and the Empirics." National Bureau of Economic Research Working Paper 14188.

Patel, Krishna, and Francis Vella. 2007. "Immigrant Networks and Their Implications for Occupational Choice and Wages." IZA Discussion Paper 3217.

Peri, Giovanni, and Chad Sparber. 2008a. "The Fallacy of Crowding-Out: A Note on Native Internal Migration and the Labor Market Impact of Immigration." Colgate University Economics Department Working Paper 2008–01.

Peri, Giovanni, and Chad Sparber. 2008b. "Highly-Educated Immigrants and Native Occupational Choice." Centre for Research and Analysis of Migration Discussion Paper 13/08.

Peri, Giovanni, and Chad Sparber. 2008c. "Task Specialization, Immigration, and Wages." Centre for Research and Analysis of Migration Discussion Paper 02/08.

Ruggles, Steven, Matthew Sobek, Trent Alexander, Catherine A. Fitch, Ronald Goeken, Patricia Kelly Hall, Miriam King, and Chad Ronnander. 2005. Integrated Public Use Microdata Series: Version 3.0. Minneapolis, MN: Minnesota Population Center. http://www.ipums.org.

Saiz, Albert. 2008. "Immigration and Housing Rents in American Cities." *Journal of Urban Economics*, 61(2): 345–71.

Smith, James P., and Barry Edmonston, ed. 1997. *The New Americans: Economic, Demographic, and Fiscal Effects of Immigration.* Washington, DC: National Academy Press.

Sparber, Chad. 2009. "Racial Diversity and Aggregate Productivity in US Industries: 1980–2000." *Southern Economic Journal*, 75(3): 829–56.

Wooldridge, Jeffrey M. 2002. *Econometric Analysis of Cross Section and Panel Data.* Cambridge, MA: MIT Press.

Immigration, Offshoring, and American Jobs†

By GIANMARCO I. P. OTTAVIANO, GIOVANNI PERI, AND GREG C. WRIGHT*

The relocation of jobs abroad by multinationals and the increased labor market competition due to immigrant workers are often credited with the demise of many manufacturing jobs once held by American citizens. While it is certainly true that manufacturing production and employment, as a percentage of the total economy, have declined over recent decades in the United States, measuring the impact of those two aspects of globalization on jobs has been difficult. This is due to the possible presence of two opposing effects. On the one hand, there is a direct "displacement effect": offshoring some production processes or hiring immigrants to perform them directly reduces the demand for native workers. On the other hand, there is an indirect "productivity effect": the cost savings associated with employing immigrant and offshore labor increases the efficiency of the production process, thus raising the demand for native workers—if not in the same tasks that are offshored or given to immigrant workers, then certainly in tasks that are complementary to them.

Several recent papers have emphasized the potential productivity effect of offshoring, arguing that this effect could offset or even reverse the displacement effect and thereby generate an overall non-negative effect on the wage or employment of native workers (Grossman and Rossi-Hansberg 2008; Costinot and Vogel 2010; Harrison and McMillan 2011; Wright 2012). These papers focus on the patterns of substitutability between native and offshore workers. Other papers have suggested that immigrants may generate an analogous productivity effect by increasing the demand for native workers, especially in production tasks that are complementary to those performed by immigrants (Ottaviano and Peri 2012; Peri 2012; Peri and Sparber 2009). These papers look at the patterns of substitutability between native and immigrant workers. Little attention has been paid so far to the simultaneous patterns of substitutability between native, immigrant and offshore workers.

In this paper we argue that the joint investigation of the interactions among these three groups of workers is useful in order to improve our understanding of the impact of globalization on the US labor market and, in particular, to answer two hotly debated questions. First, how do declines in offshoring and immigration costs affect the employment of native workers? Second, what kinds of jobs suffer, or benefit, the most from the competition created by offshore and immigrant workers?

*Ottaviano: Department of Economics, London School of Economics and Political Science, Houghton Street, London, WC2A 2AE, UK and Bocconi University (e-mail: g.i.ottaviano@lse.ac.uk); Peri: Department of Economics, UC Davis, One Shields Avenue, Davis, CA 95616 (e-mail: gperi@ucdavis.edu); Wright: Department of Economics, University of Essex, Wivenhoe Park, Colchester CO4 3SQ (e-mail: gcwright@essex.ac.uk). This paper was written as part of the project "Mobility of People and Mobility of Firms" coordinated by the Centro Studi Luca d'Agliano (LdA) and funded by the Fondazione CRT. We thank Daron Acemoglu, Giorgio Barba-Navaretti, Rosario Crinò, Gordon Hanson, Rob Feenstra, Gene Grossman, Alan Manning, John McLaren, Peter Neary, Esteban Rossi-Hansberg, Dan Trefler, and participants in several seminars and conferences for useful comments and suggestions.
† Go to http://dx.doi.org/10.1257/aer.103.5.1925 to visit the article page for additional materials and author disclosure statement(s).

1925

1926   THE AMERICAN ECONOMIC REVIEW   *AUGUST 2013*

At the core of our argument are two observations: first, that jobs ("tasks") vary in terms of the relative intensity of use of complex tasks and, second, that native, immigrant and offshore groups differ in their efficiency in performing complex tasks. Throughout the paper we consider the complexity of a task to be increasing in the intensity of use of communication and cognitive skills and decreasing in the manual content of the task. Communication skills may be important because the execution of complex tasks often requires a sophisticated dialogue between workers whereas, in contrast, manual tasks are much easier to describe and carry out in the absence of these skills. It is therefore natural to think that the cost of performing tasks in other countries (offshoring) or assigning these tasks to people with limited knowledge of the local language and culture (immigrants) increases with the complexity of the task. Efficiency gains can then be reaped by hiring these workers to perform tasks in which they have a comparative advantage, that is, in which they generate a lower cost per efficiency unit of labor,[1] while also giving native workers the opportunity to specialize in the tasks in which they exhibit their own comparative advantage. If strong enough, the productivity effect associated with this efficient pattern of task specialization may offset the displacement effect of immigration and offshoring on native workers' employment.

We develop this argument in three steps. First, we present some new facts on 58 industries, which together comprise the US manufacturing sector, from 2000 to 2007. We argue that these facts are consistent with a scenario in which: (i) there is stronger substitutability between immigrants and offshore workers than between immigrants and natives; (ii) immigrant, native and offshore workers are relatively specialized in tasks of different skill complexity; and, in particular, (iii) immigrants are relatively specialized in low complexity tasks, natives in high complexity tasks, and offshore workers in medium complexity tasks.[2] Unfortunately, the complexity of the tasks performed by offshore workers is not directly observable.

In the second step we build on Grossman and Rossi-Hansberg (2008) to design a partial equilibrium model of task assignment among heterogeneous native, immigrant and offshore workers within an industry that is consistent with the observed facts. We then use the model to draw systematic predictions of the effects of falling barriers to immigration and offshoring on the tasks, the employment share, and the employment level of native workers. An important assumption of the model, consistent with a series of facts that we present, is that offshore workers specialize in tasks of intermediate "complexity" between those of immigrants and natives. The model generates two main sets of predictions. First, borrowing the terminology of Costinot and Vogel (2010), a decline in immigration costs leads to "task upgrading" of immigrants as these workers are assigned some medium complexity tasks that were previously performed by offshore workers. Second, lower immigration costs have little impact on the task complexity of native workers, who are located at

---

[1] See Costinot and Vogel (2010) for the equivalence of the trade concept of "comparative advantage" and the matching concept of "log-supermodularity."

[2] The choice to focus on manufacturing and not include services reflects the research questions we have chosen to address. It is also forced on us by data availability as there is limited data on services offshoring. Moreover, the production function approach at the core of our analysis is much better understood in the context of manufacturing than in the context of services. Lastly, the range of skills spanned by tasks is richer in manufacturing than in services, leaving more room for gains due to their reallocation.

the high end of the task complexity spectrum. On the other hand, a decline in off-shoring costs simultaneously leads to task upgrading of natives and task downgrading of immigrants: offshore workers are assigned the most complex among the low complexity tasks previously performed by immigrants, as well as the least complex among the high complexity tasks previously performed by natives. In this case, the result is increased task polarization between immigrants and natives in the domestic labor market.

The other set of predictions concerns the response of industry employment following the reallocation of tasks described above. Employment shares move as dictated by the "displacement effect": a group of workers from which tasks are taken away sees its employment share fall; a group of workers to which new tasks are assigned sees its employment share increase. If the "productivity effect" is weak, employment levels move in the same direction as employment shares. On the other hand, when the efficiency gains from immigration or offshoring are strong enough, employment levels may increase for all groups of workers and not only for those whose employment shares go up. Intuitively, the changes in employment *shares* are determined by movements along the relative labor demand curves of the different groups of workers, as dictated by changes in their relative efficiency. The changes in employment *levels*, however, are also affected by the outward shifts in labor demand produced by the increase in the overall efficiency of the production process.

In the end, whether the employment of natives rises or falls when immigration and offshoring become easier, and whether the observed change is consistent with our story, is an empirical issue. By using employment data on immigrants and natives from the American Community Survey (ACS) and on offshore workers by US multinational affiliates from the Bureau of Economic Analysis (BEA), we indeed find that easier offshoring reduces the employment shares of both native and immigrant workers while easier immigration reduces the employment share of offshore workers only, with no impact on the employment share of natives. Nonetheless, when we look at employment levels (rather than shares), we find that easier offshoring does not have any significant effect whereas easier immigration has a positive and mildly significant impact on natives. This is consistent with the existence of positive productivity effects due to immigration and offshoring.

By matching occupation data from the ACS with the manual, communication and cognitive skill content of tasks performed in each occupation (from the US Department of Labor's O*NET abilities survey), we then assess the response of the "complexity" of those tasks to immigration and offshoring. Here we find that easier offshoring raises the average complexity of native tasks, increasing the gap between native and immigrant task complexity. In contrast, easier immigration has no effect on the average complexity of native tasks. Overall, our findings imply that immigrants do not compete directly with natives. We suggest that the reason for this is that immigrants and natives are concentrated at opposite ends of the task complexity spectrum. Offshore workers, instead, are specialized in tasks of intermediate complexity (though we do not directly observe this) generating some competition with both immigrants and natives, as revealed by the effect on employment shares and on task intensities of those two groups.

The rest of the paper is organized as follows. The next section describes the novel contributions of this paper in the context of the existing literature. Section II presents the data, highlighting some key facts that inform the subsequent analysis. Section III presents a theoretical model consistent with those facts, deriving predictions to be brought under econometric scrutiny. Section IV produces the econometric evidence on the predictions of the theoretical model. Section V concludes.

I. Related Literature

Several recent papers have analyzed the effect of offshoring on the demand for domestic labor and are relevant to the present analysis. On the theoretical front, Grossman and Rossi-Hansberg (2008) provide a simple model of trade in production tasks. This model will serve as the framework for our analysis, though we will focus on employment rather than on wage effects.[3] Recent and relevant empirical work includes Crinò (2010); Hummels et al. (2010); Harrison and McMillan (2011); and Wright (2012), each of which have tested some of the implications of existing theories with respect to the wage and employment effects of offshoring. Crinò (2010), who focuses on services offshoring, and Hummels et al. (2010), who focus on Denmark, both find positive wage and employment effects of offshoring for relatively skilled workers, especially for those performing more complex production tasks, but find that less skilled workers may suffer displacement. Wright (2012) finds a positive productivity effect of offshoring for domestic firms but, on net, an aggregate decline in low-skill employment. Harrison and McMillan (2011) find that a crucial distinction is between "horizontal" and "vertical" offshoring (the first aimed at locally serving foreign markets and the second aimed at producing intermediates that the multinational then re-imports to its domestic market), with the first hurting and the second stimulating domestic employment.

The present paper combines the above literature with the literature on the labor market effects of immigrants (e.g., Card 2001; Card 2009; Borjas 2003), proposing a common structure to think about offshoring and immigration within manufacturing industries. To do this, we extend the offshoring model by Grossman and Rossi-Hansberg (2008) to allow for immigration, which provides a simple, though still rich, way of thinking about these two phenomena within a unified framework. While the immigration literature has also analyzed the impact of immigrants on task allocation and productivity (e.g., Peri and Sparber 2009; Peri 2012; Chassamboulli and Palivos 2010), we expand on it by considering a multi-sector environment and an open economy.[4] What we find is that the joint analysis of immigration and offshoring indeed generates novel insights that get overlooked when considering each of those two phenomena in isolation.

---

[3] It is worth mentioning that this theory owes much to previous work on trade in intermediates, including seminal work by Jones and Kierzkowski (1990) and Feenstra and Hanson (1996, 1999), who present models in which trade in intermediate goods has consequences for labor demand much like those described in Grossman and Rossi-Hansberg (2008).

[4] Blinder (2007); Jensen and Kletzer (2007); Levy and Murnane (2006); and Becker, Ekholm, and Muendler (2009) find that tasks that intensively use cognitive-communication and non-routine skills are harder to offshore. Peri and Sparber (2009) find that immigrants have a comparative disadvantage (lower productivity) in performing communication-intensive tasks. None of these contributions, however, tackles the issue of the joint effects of offshoring and immigration on the employment shares, the employment levels and the task assignment of native, immigrant, and offshore workers as we do.

VOL. 103 NO. 5   OTTAVIANO ET AL.: IMMIGRATION, OFFSHORING, AND AMERICAN JOBS   1929

The only other papers we are aware of that tackle the analysis of immigration and offshoring in a joint framework are Olney (2012) and Barba Navaretti, Bertola, and Sembenelli (2008). The first paper assumes that immigrants are identical to natives and that their variation across US states and industries is exogenous. Moreover, native workers are assumed to be immobile across states and industries so that the impacts of immigration or offshoring manifest themselves entirely through wages. We think our model and its derived empirical implementation constitute a step forward from the reduced form approach of that study. The second paper presents a model of immigration and offshoring and tests its implications on firm-level data for Italy. It does not look, however, at the skill endowments of workers and the skill intensity of tasks nor at industry-level employment effects.

The importance of assortative matching between the skill requirements of tasks and the skill endowments of workers has been recently stressed by Costinot and Vogel (2010). By focusing on a Roy-like assignment model, in which a continuum of factors ("workers") are employed to produce a continuum of goods ("tasks"), they show that the comparative advantage of high skill workers in high complexity tasks provides sufficient conditions for rich comparative static predictions on the effects of various shocks to labor demand and supply. They explicitly analyze the consequences of easier offshoring, which they model as an increase in offshore labor productivity. Assuming that offshore workers have a comparative advantage in low complexity tasks, they conclude that easier offshoring induces task upgrading of all workers and rising wage inequality due to the increase in the effective supply of poorer low-skill workers. They do not consider immigration explicitly, but they discuss the effects of changes in the composition of labor supply. If one assumes that immigrants are relatively less skilled than natives, the impact of immigration is then similar to the impact of offshoring: task upgrading for all workers and increasing wage inequality. Since our model also features a Roy-like assignment problem, their tools and techniques can be used to generalize our theoretical results, with two important differences. First, our focus is on the employment effects rather than on the wage effects. Second, our joint consideration of immigration and offshoring uncovers a differential response of native employment to shocks to the cost of immigrating or offshoring workers.[5]

Finally, also related to our paper is work on the determinants of "job polarization," defined as rising employment shares in the highest and the lowest wage occupations (Autor, Katz, and Kearney 2006; Goos and Manning 2007). Three main explanations of job polarization have been put forth: the technological substitution of non-manual, routine jobs in the middle of the wage distribution (Katz and Autor 1999; Autor, Levy, and Murnane 2003); the offshoring of these jobs (Blinder 2007); or the "butlerization" or demand-driven explanation, whereby a rising income share at the top of the distribution leads to increased demand for low-skill services (Manning 2004). In summarizing the findings of this literature, Goos, Manning, and Salomons (2009) conclude that technical substitution of non-manual, routine jobs

---

[5] Costinot and Vogel (2010) are not the first to deal with assignment models in an international context. Applications to trade can be found, for instance, in Grossman and Maggi (2000); Grossman (2004); Yeaple (2005); Ohnsorge and Trefler (2007); Blanchard and Willmann (2011); Costinot (2009); Monte (2011); and Sly (2012). Examples of applications to offshoring are Kremer and Maskin (2006); Antràs, Garicano, and Rossi-Hansberg (2006); and Nocke and Yeaple (2008). None of these papers, however, deals jointly with offshoring and immigration.

1930   *THE AMERICAN ECONOMIC REVIEW*   *AUGUST 2013*

seems to be a better explanation of job polarization than offshoring and butlerization because of the pervasive effect of technology across sectors and countries. The present paper focuses on manufacturing jobs only, while also bringing immigration into the picture. We provide a somewhat different characterization of polarization in the US labor market, defined as the increasing difference in the types of jobs performed by immigrants relative to those performed by natives.

II. Data and Descriptive Statistics

In this section we present simple statistical evidence on US manufacturing industries that is consistent with a story of task specialization among native, immigrant, and offshore workers according to a specific pattern of comparative advantages. In particular, the data show that natives and immigrants have revealed comparative advantages in high and low complexity jobs, respectively. The revealed comparative advantage of offshore workers is not directly observable. However two related facts are observed. First, the cognitive and communication intensities of native jobs are higher (and the manual intensity lower) in manufacturing industries in which offshoring is relatively important. Second, within manufacturing the cognitive, communication and manual intensities of native jobs are not related to the relative importance of immigration. Third, a positive and significant relationship between immigration and the cognitive and communication intensities of native jobs exists in non-manufacturing industries where offshoring is negligible. These facts suggest that, in manufacturing industries, immigrants specialize in low complexity tasks, natives specialize in high complexity tasks and offshore workers specialize in intermediate complexity tasks. Specialization according to comparative advantages implies not only that immigration has a weaker "displacement effect" on natives relative to offshoring, but also that immigration and offshoring may generate a positive "productivity effect."[6] Again, it is important to note that throughout the paper we consider the complexity of a task to be increasing in the intensity of use of communication and cognitive skills and decreasing in the manual content of the task.

We formalize this story in Section III through a simple theoretical model. Section IV then brings these predictions to the data. It should be noted that, while the theoretical model is designed to be consistent with the descriptive evidence that we present, the econometric scrutiny will involve a more rigorous methodology and will test moments of the data different from those on which the assumptions of the model are based.

A. *Employment*

To measure the employment of native, immigrant, and offshore workers in each industry-year using a consistent and comparable industry classification, we merge data on multinational employment from the Bureau of Economic Analysis (BEA) with data on native and foreign-born workers from the IPUMS samples (Ruggles et al. 2008) of the Census and the American Community Survey (ACS). The only

---

[6]In non-manufacturing sectors offshoring tasks is relatively costly. Thus tasks are assigned primarily to natives or immigrants with a higher likelihood of substitution between them. The productivity effect may still exist, however.

VOL. 103 NO. 5   OTTAVIANO ET AL.: IMMIGRATION, OFFSHORING, AND AMERICAN JOBS   1931

years in which this merger can be consistently and reliably done are those from 2000 to 2007. We therefore take these eight years as our period of observation.

Information on offshore employment is obtained from the BEA US Direct Investment Abroad dataset, which collects data on the operations of US parent companies and their affiliates. From this dataset we obtain the total number of employees working abroad in foreign affiliates of US parent companies, by industry of the US parent.[7] These are jobs directly generated abroad by multinationals.[8] Data on native and immigrant workers come from the ACS and Census IPUMS samples for the period 2000–2007.[9] We add up all workers not living in group quarters, who worked at least one week during the year, weighting them by the sample weights assigned by the ACS in order to make the sample nationally representative. "Immigrants" are all foreign-born workers who were not citizens at birth. "Natives" are all other US workers. The relevant industry classification in the Census-ACS data 2000–2007 is the INDNAICS classification, which is based on the North American Industry Classification System (NAICS). Since the BEA industries are also associated with unique 4-digit NAICS industries, we are able to develop a straightforward concordance between the two datasets.

The 58 industries on which we have data and their BEA codes are reported in Table A1 in the online Appendix, while Figure A1 (also in the online Appendix) reports the evolution of the employment shares of immigrant and offshore workers across industries in each year with the connecting lines showing averages over time. From 2000 to 2007 there was only a fairly modest increase in the overall share of immigrant and offshore employment in total manufacturing (the former increased from 12.8 percent to 14 percent and the latter from 22.3 percent to 29.3 percent). The figure shows both that all industries hired some immigrant and offshore workers and, further, that the differences across industries are potentially large enough to allow for the identification of the differential effects of immigration and offshoring over the period.

While the employment shares of the different groups of workers vary across industries, there are interesting patterns of covariation. Panel A of Figure 1 depicts the correlations between native and immigrant employment shares over the period of observation. Panel B provides the same type of information for native and offshore workers and panel C shows employment shares for immigrant and offshore workers.

---

[7] As is standard in this literature, here we do not include in the definition of offshoring jobs that are subcontracted abroad by purely national firms.

[8] Jobs created by US multinational firms outsourcing production to unaffiliated foreign subcontractors, so-called *arm's length* offshoring (see, e.g. Antràs 2003) were not included in our analysis. We constructed a proxy for this variable, however. Assuming that a large part of the production output of these offshored jobs is subsequently imported as intermediate inputs by the US parent company, we calculated the ratio of imports of intermediates by the US parent coming from affiliates and employment in those affiliates. We then scaled the imports of the US parent coming from *non-affiliates* (data that are also available from the BEA) by this ratio to impute the employment in subcontracting companies. This procedure assumes that the labor content per unit of production of subcontracted intermediate inputs is the same as for production in US affiliates in the same industry. Adding the imputed employment increases offshore employment by 60–80 percent in most industries, confirming the importance of arm's length offshoring. The regression results using this measure of offshore employment are very similar to those presented in IV and we do not report them here. They can be found in a previous version of this paper (Ottaviano, Peri, and Wright 2010).

[9] For year 2000 we use the 5 percent Census sample. For 2001 we use the 1-in-232 national random sample. For 2002, we use the 1-in-261 national random sample. For 2003 we use the 1-in-236 national random sample. For 2004 we use the 1-in-239 national random sample. For 2005, 2006, and 2007 the 1-in-100 national random samples are used.

Panel A. Native and immigrant employment shares; Slope of the regression line:
0.05, standard error: 0.10

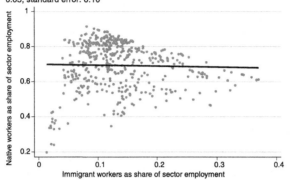

Panel B. Native and offshore employment shares; Slope of the regression line:
–0.80, standard error: 0.02

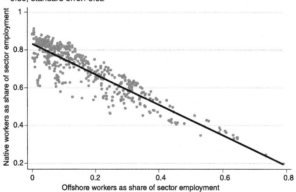

Panel C. Immigrants and offshore employment shares; Slope of the regression line:
–0.19, standard error: 0.02

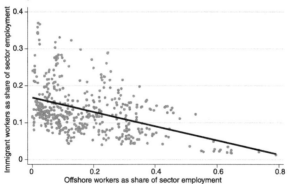

FIGURE 1. SHARES OF IMMIGRANT, NATIVE, AND OFFSHORE WORKERS
(58 *manufacturing sectors, 2000–2007*)

VOL. 103 NO. 5 *OTTAVIANO ET AL.: IMMIGRATION, OFFSHORING, AND AMERICAN JOBS* *1933*

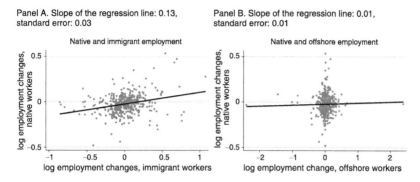

Panel A. Slope of the regression line: 0.13, standard error: 0.03

Panel B. Slope of the regression line: 0.01, standard error: 0.01

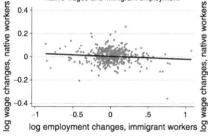
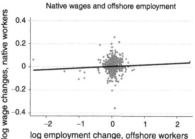

Panel C. Slope of the regression line: −0.02, standard error: 0.02

Panel D. Slope of the regression line 0.014, standard error: 0.012

FIGURE 2. GROWTH RATES OF EMPLOYMENT AND WAGES (*58 manufacturing sectors, yearly growth 2000–2007*)

The figure reveals a lack of correlation between the shares of immigrant and native workers. In contrast, it highlights a strong negative correlation between the shares of offshore and native workers, and a significant (but less strong) negative correlation between the share of immigrants and offshore workers. These correlations suggest that competition for jobs may be strongest between natives and offshore workers, intermediate between immigrant and offshore workers and weakest between natives and immigrants.

Figure 2 looks at yearly employment- and wage-growth rates across 58 manufacturing industries over eight years. Panel A reveals a positive correlation between the growth rates of employment of natives and immigrants whereas panel B shows no correlation between the growth of native and offshore workers. This is consistent with weaker native-immigrant employment competition relative to native-offshore worker competition in the presence of positive productivity effects due to both immigration and offshoring. Panels C and D look at the correlations between changes in native wages and changes in immigrant and offshore employment.[10] The two panels

---

[10] The wages of natives are constructed as follows. From the Census-ACS data we consider only US-born individuals who are employed (i.e., who have worked at least one week in the year and at least one hour in the week) and who have non-zero wage income, excluding the self-employed. We take yearly wage income deflated by the

do not suggest any significant correlation between changes in native wages and changes in immigrant and offshore employment across sectors. We interpret this as consistent with the equalization of native wages across manufacturing industries due to worker mobility between them, with the effect that the wage variation across sectors is random.[11]

B. *Tasks*

Data on the tasks performed by immigrants and natives is constructed using the US Department of Labor's (2012) O*NET abilities survey, which provides information on the characteristics of each occupation. Based on the Standard Occupation Classification (SOC), the dataset assigns numerical values to describe the importance of distinct abilities ("skills") required by different occupations ("tasks"). Each numerical value measures the intensity of a skill in a given task. Following Peri and Sparber (2009), we merge these task-specific values with individual workers in the 2000 Census, re-scaling each value so that it equals the percentile score in that year. This gives a measure of the relative importance of a given skill among US workers ranging between zero and one. For instance, a task with a score of 0.02 for some skill indicates that only 2 percent of workers in the United States in 2000 were supplying that skill less intensively. We then assign these O*NET percentile scores to individuals from 2000 to 2007 using the ACS variable *occ1990*, which provides an occupational crosswalk over time.

We focus on three skill indices: Cognitive Intensity, Communication Intensity, and Manual Intensity. These are constructed by averaging the relevant skill variables. Specifically, Cognitive Intensity includes ten variables classified as "cognitive and analytical" in O*NET. Communication Intensity includes four variables capturing written and oral expression and understanding. Manual Intensity includes nineteen variables capturing dexterity, strength, and coordination.[12] We have also calculated a synthetic Complexity index summarizing the intensity of a task in cognitive-communication skills *relative* to manual skills. This index is defined as: Complexity $= \ln((\text{Cognitive Intensity} + \text{Communication Intensity})/\text{Manual Intensity})$. It ranges between $-\infty$ and $+\infty$.

Overall, our sample consists of 295 occupations ("tasks") in the manufacturing sector over eight years, 2000–2007. This type of information is available for immigrants and natives but not for offshore workers. Absent direct information on the specific occupations of offshore workers, a crucial challenge for us is to indirectly assess the average complexity of offshore tasks. The four panels of Figure 3 plot the share of hours worked by immigrants relative to the total number of hours worked by immigrant and native workers as a function of Cognitive Intensity, Communication

---

consumption price index to constant 2005 dollars and average it at the industry level, weighting each individual by the corresponding sample weight in the Census.

[11] We also provide a more formal analysis of the correlation between offshore/immigrant employment and native wages in the online Appendix. Table A3 shows the estimated effects of log offshore employment and log immigrant employment on (log) native wages. The effects are estimated using 2SLS with tariffs as an instrument for offshoring and imputed immigration as an instrument for actual immigration (as described in Section IVA below). In all cases we obtain small and insignificant coefficients.

[12] The exact definition and list of the variables used for each index can be found in the online Appendix of this paper.

VOL. 103 NO. 5   OTTAVIANO ET AL.: IMMIGRATION, OFFSHORING, AND AMERICAN JOBS   1935

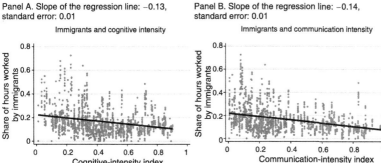

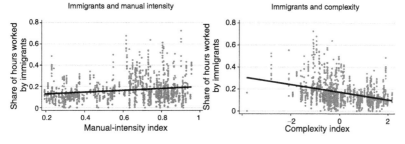

FIGURE 3. IMMIGRANTS AND TASK COMPLEXITY (across occupations)

Notes: Sample is 295 occupations over 2000–2007. Only occupations with over 5,000 workers are reported.

Intensity, Manual Intensity, and Complexity across occupation-years.[13] The figure clearly shows that immigrants are disproportionately represented in occupations characterized by low Cognitive Intensity, low Communication Intensity, high Manual Intensity, and low overall Complexity.[14]

While the complexity of offshored tasks is unobservable (because we do not observe offshore occupations), we can nonetheless gauge some indirect evidence from the way offshoring affects the complexity of native and immigrant tasks. Figure 4 reports this type of information in the case of all immigrants and natives. It plots the change in the Complexity of tasks performed by natives and immigrants against the change in the shares of offshore and immigrant employment, across manufacturing industries over the period 2000–2007. The figure conveys a clear

[13] A very similar picture would be obtained if we only considered workers with low educational attainment (i.e., workers with a high school diploma or less) This was shown in Ottaviano, Peri, and Wright (2010). Even within the low educated, immigrants are relatively specialized in tasks with low cognitive and communication content, low complexity and high manual content.

[14] This finding concurs with existing evidence. Peri and Sparber (2009) show that, due to their imperfect knowledge of language and local norms, immigrants have a relative advantage in tasks with high manual intensity and a relative disadvantage in tasks with high communication intensity.

128   *Immigrants and Labor Markets*

Panel A. Slope of the regression line: 0.35,
standard error: 0.14

Panel B. Slope of the regression line: −0.77,
standard error: 0.40

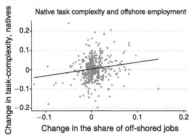

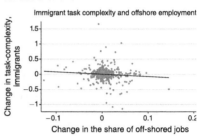

Panel C. Slope of the regression line: −0.05,
standard error: 0.14

Panel D. Slope of the regression line: 0.65,
standard error: 0.58

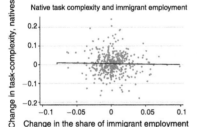

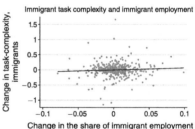

FIGURE 4. NATIVE COMPLEXITY, IMMIGRATION, AND OFFSHORING (*all workers*)

Notes: Sample from 58 manufacturing sectors of 295 occupations over 2000–2007. Only occupations with over 5,000 workers are reported.

message: increases in the share of offshore workers are associated with significant increases in the complexity of tasks performed by natives as well as decreases in the complexity of tasks performed by immigrants. In contrast, increases in the share of immigrants are not associated with any significant change in the complexity of native or immigrant tasks. Hence, a stronger presence of offshore workers is associated with a larger polarization in task complexity between natives and immigrants. Similar patterns arise when we focus on Cognitive Intensity, Communication Intensity, and Manual Intensity separately but we do not report them for conciseness.

The finding that changes in native complexity are not significantly correlated with changes in the share of immigrants may surprise readers familiar with Peri and Sparber (2009), as these authors find that native task complexity is sensitive to the share of immigrants. This can easily be explained in a manner that is consistent with our theory. In this study we focus on (mostly-tradable) manufacturing industries whereas Peri and Sparber (2009) consider all employment, most of which is in (non-tradable) services. Since offshoring was still negligible outside the manufacturing sector during our period of observation, we interpret this discrepancy as a signal that, when viable, offshore workers play an important role in weakening the

VOL. 103 NO. 5   OTTAVIANO ET AL.: IMMIGRATION, OFFSHORING, AND AMERICAN JOBS   1937

TABLE 1—COMPLEXITY OF NATIVE AND IMMIGRANT SHARE IN TRADABLE
VERSUS NON-TRADABLE INDUSTRIES

Dependent variable is the complexity index for natives	Complexity = $\ln[(\text{Cognitive} + \text{Communication})/\text{Manual}]$	
	Tradable sectors, 2000–2007 (1)	Non-tradable sectors, 2000–2007 (2)
Complexity index for the foreign-born	0.04** (0.02)	0.07** (0.01)
Share of foreign-born	−0.01 (0.09)	0.15** (0.07)
Industry effects	Yes	Yes
Observations	647	1,456

Notes: The estimation method is ordinary least squares including industry and time effects. Heteroskedasticity robust standard errors, clustered at the sector level are reported.
***Significant at the 1 percent level.
**Significant at the 5 percent level.
*Significant at the 10 percent level.

competition between immigrants and natives. Table 1 explores this interpretation by regressing native complexity on immigrants' complexity and employment share across industries and over time, distinguishing between manufacturing ("tradable") and non-manufacturing ("non-tradable") industries. All workers are included. The table shows significant positive correlation between native complexity and immigrant employment share within non-tradable industries (column 2), but no correlation is detected between native complexity and immigrant employment share in tradable industries (column 1).[15] This supports the idea that in non-tradable industries the competition between natives and immigrants is more direct and immigration pushes native workers to "upgrade" their jobs. In tradable industries this does not happen because offshore workers perform a large part of the intermediate-complex tasks and are therefore in direct competition with immigrants. While the results shown are not direct evidence of this, they are consistent with this explanation.

Our overall interpretation of the descriptive evidence presented in this section is that natives compete more directly with offshore workers relative to immigrant workers. This can be explained by a specific pattern of comparative advantages across the three groups of workers, with immigrants specializing in low complexity tasks, natives in high complexity tasks and offshore workers in intermediate complexity tasks.

III. A Labor Market Model of Task Allocation

A simple partial equilibrium model consistent with the descriptive evidence reported in the previous section can be designed following Grossman and Rossi-Hansberg (2008). Consider a small open economy that is active in several perfectly competitive sectors, indexed $s = 1, \dots, S$. We focus on one of these sectors

---

[15] In the regressions in Table 1 we also control for time and industry fixed effects.

1938   *THE AMERICAN ECONOMIC REVIEW*   *AUGUST 2013*

and leave both the sector index s and the time dependence of variables t implicit for ease of notation. We will make them explicit when we get to the empirics.

The sector employs two primary factors, workers with employment level N_L and a sector-specific factor with endowment H. To match the descriptive evidence on wages in Section II, the sector is small enough to face infinitely elastic labor supply at given wages.[16] All workers are endowed with one unit of labor each but differ in terms of productivity. They are employed in the production of intermediates ("tasks"), which are then assembled in a composite labor input L. This, in turn, is transformed into final output Y according to the following Cobb-Douglas production function:

$$(1) \qquad\qquad Y = AL^{\alpha} H^{1-\alpha},$$

where $A \in (0, \infty)$ and $\alpha \in (0, 1)$ are technological parameters. The price of final output p_Y is set in the international market.

Specifically, the composite labor input L is produced by assembling a fixed measure of differentiated tasks, indexed $i \in [0, 1]$ in increasing order of complexity, through the following CES technology:

$$(2) \qquad\qquad L = \left[\int_0^1 L(i)^{\frac{\sigma-1}{\sigma}} \, di \right]^{\frac{\sigma}{\sigma-1}},$$

where $L(i)$ is the input of task i and $\sigma > 0$ is the elasticity of substitution between tasks.[17]

A. Task Assignment

Each task can be managed in three modes: domestic production by native workers (D), domestic production by immigrant workers (M), and production abroad by offshore workers (O). The three groups of workers are perfect substitutes in the production of any task but differ in terms of their productivity as well as in terms of their wages, which we call w, $\tilde{w}$, and w^*, respectively. To allow for a "productivity effect" to arise from both immigration and offshoring, we assume that employers can discriminate between the three groups of workers so that w, $\tilde{w}$, and w^* may not be equal. We assume, however, that immigrant and offshore wages are linked, with a fixed gap between them determined by a differential "cost of hardship" that immigrants face with respect to their fellow countrymen who stay at home. In particular, if a foreign worker immigrates, she incurs a frictional cost $\delta \geq 1$ in terms of foregone productivity. In other words, an immigrant endowed with one unit of labor in her country of origin is able to provide only $1/\delta$ units of labor in the country of

---

[16]This leads to a crucial difference between our model and those by Grossman and Rossi-Hansberg (2008) and by Costinot and Vogel (2010). Both these models consider the general equilibrium effects of offshoring on wages under economy-wide full employment constraints. In the online Appendix we propose an extension of our model in which the assumption of perfectly elastic labor supply at given wages does not hold. There we show that, when the native wage is endogenous, immigration and offshoring generate wage effects, however the corresponding employment effects discussed in Section IIIB remain qualitatively the same.

[17]In Grossman and Rossi-Hansberg (2008) tasks are not substitutable. This corresponds to the limit case of $\sigma = 0$ where (2) becomes a Leontief production function.

destination. The migration decision therefore entails a choice between earning w^* in the country of origin or $\tilde{w}/\delta$ in the country of destination.[18] Positive supply of both immigrant and offshore workers then requires the migration indifference condition $\tilde{w} = w^*\delta$ to hold.[19]

In light of the descriptive evidence reported in Section II, we now introduce assumptions that ensure that immigrant, offshore, and native workers specialize in low, medium, and high complexity tasks, respectively. In so doing, we follow Grossman and Rossi-Hansberg (2008) and define tasks so that they all require the same unit labor requirement a_L when performed by native workers. Accordingly, the marginal cost of producing task i employing native workers is $c_D(i) = wa_L$. If task i is instead offshored, its unit input requirement is $\beta t(i)a_L$ with $\beta t(i) \geq 1$. This implies a marginal cost of producing task i employing offshore workers equal to $c_O(i) = w^*\beta t(i)a_L$. Lastly, if task i is assigned to immigrants, its unit input requirement is $\tau(i)a_L$ with $\tau(i) \geq 1$ so that the marginal cost of producing task i employing immigrants is $c_M(i) = \tilde{w}\tau(i)a_L = w^*\delta\tau(i)a_L$. Hence, in all tasks natives are more productive but, due to wage differences, not necessarily cheaper than immigrant and offshore workers. We interpret a lower value of the frictional parameter β as "easier offshoring" and a lower value of the frictional parameter δ as "easier immigration."

Since native, immigrant and offshore workers are perfectly substitutable, in equilibrium any task will be performed by only one type of worker: the one that entails the lowest marginal cost for that task.[20] Hence, a set of sufficient conditions for immigrant, offshore and native workers to specialize in low, medium and high complexity tasks can be stated as:

PROPOSITION 1: *Suppose*

$$(3) \qquad \frac{dt(i)}{di} > 0, \qquad \frac{w}{w^*t(1)} < \beta < \frac{w}{w^*t(0)}.$$

Then there exists a unique "marginal offshore task" $I_{NO} \in (0, 1)$ such that $c_O(I_{NO}) = c_D(I_{NO})$, $c_O(i) < c_D(i)$ for all $i \in [0, I_{NO})$ and $c_O(i) > c_D(i)$ for all $i \in (I_{NO}, 1]$. This task is implicitly defined by $w = w^*\beta t(I_{NO})$. Suppose in addition that

$$(4) \qquad \delta\frac{d\tau(i)}{di} > \beta\frac{dt(i)}{di}, \qquad \frac{\tau(0)}{t(0)} < \frac{\beta}{\delta} < \frac{\tau(I_{NO})}{t(I_{NO})}.$$

---

[18] For simplicity, in the theoretical model we consider only one country of origin for all immigrants.

[19] There is much empirical evidence that, for similar observable characteristics, immigrants are paid a lower wage than natives. Using data from the 2000 Census, Antecol, Cobb-Clark, and Trejo (2001); Butcher and DiNardo (2002); and Chiswick, Lee, and Miller (2005) all show that recent immigrants from non-English speaking countries earn on average 17 to 20 percent less than natives with identical observable characteristics. Our data provide estimates in the same ball park. Hendricks (2002) also shows that the immigrant-native wage differential, controlling for observable characteristics, is highly correlated with the wage differential between the United States and their country of origin. See, however, Section IIIB and the online Appendix for a detailed discussion of how the predictions of the model would change were firms assumed to be unable to discriminate between native and immigrant workers.

[20] If native, immigrant and offshore workers were imperfectly substitutable, each task could be performed by "teams" consisting of the three types of workers. Then, rather than full specialization of workers' types in different tasks, one would observe partial specialization, with the shares of the three types in each task inversely related to the corresponding marginal costs. In reality several tasks are indeed performed by a combination of different types of workers, nonetheless the intuition behind the key results of the model is better served by assuming perfect substitutability.

1940   THE AMERICAN ECONOMIC REVIEW   AUGUST 2013

Then there exists a unique "marginal immigrant task" $I_{MO} \in (0, I_{NO})$ such that $c_M(I_{MO}) = c_O(I_{MO})$, $c_M(i) < c_O(i)$ for all $i \in [0, I_{MO})$ and $c_M(i) > c_O(i)$ for all $i \in (I_{MO}, 1]$. This task is implicitly defined by $\beta t(I_{MO}) = \delta \tau(I_{MO})$.

See the Appendix for the proof. Intuitively, the first condition in (3) implies that the productivity of offshore workers relative to natives decreases with the complexity of tasks. The second condition in (3) requires offshoring frictions to be neither too large nor too small in order to generate a trade-off in the assignment of tasks between native and offshore workers. The first condition in (4) also implies that the productivity of immigrants falls with the complexity of tasks, and falls faster than in the case of offshore workers. The second condition in (4) requires offshoring frictions to be neither too large nor too small relative to migration frictions such that there is a trade-off in the assignment of tasks between immigrant and offshore workers. Conditions (3) and (4) together thus imply that tasks of complexity $0 \le i \le I_{MO}$ are assigned to immigrants, tasks of complexity $I_{MO} < i \le I_{NO}$ to offshore workers and tasks of complexity $I_{NO} < i \le 1$ to natives, where marginal tasks have been arbitrarily assigned to break the tie.[21]

The allocation of tasks among the three groups of workers is portrayed in Figure 5, where the task index i is measured along the horizontal axis and the production costs along the vertical axis. The flat line corresponds to c_D and the upward sloping curves correspond to $c_M(i)$ and $c_O(i)$, with the former starting from below but steeper than the latter. Since each task employs only the type of workers yielding the lowest marginal cost, tasks from 0 to I_{MO} are assigned to immigrants, tasks from I_{MO} to I_{NO} are offshored, and tasks from I_{NO} to 1 are assigned to natives.

B. Comparative Statics

We are interested in how tasks, employment shares, and employment levels, vary across the three types of workers when offshoring and migration costs change. The solution of our task assignment problem summarized in Proposition 1 implies that marginal tasks exhibit the following properties:

$$\frac{\partial I_{NO}}{\partial \beta} < 0, \qquad \frac{\partial I_{MO}}{\partial \beta} > 0$$

$$\frac{\partial I_{NO}}{\partial \delta} = 0, \qquad \frac{\partial I_{MO}}{\partial \delta} < 0.$$

---

[21] Readers familiar with Costinot and Vogel (2010) will recognize the log-supermodularity of this assignment problem in which, due to their different skills, native, immigrant, and offshore workers have a relative advantage in high, medium, and low skill intensity tasks. Indeed, the approach of Costinot and Vogel (2010) could be used to go beyond the stark view expressed in our theory by introducing skill heterogeneity among the three groups of workers. This could be achieved by matching the assumption that higher skill workers have a comparative advantage in more skill intensive tasks (see Costinot and Vogel 2010, Section IIIA) with the assumption that natives are more skilled relative to offshore and immigrant workers (see Costinot and Vogel 2010, Section VIIB).

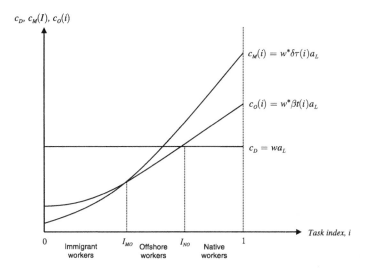

FIGURE 5. TASK ASSIGNMENT

These highlight the adjustments in employment occurring in terms of the number of tasks allocated to the three groups of workers. They can be readily understood using Figure 5. For example, a reduction in offshoring costs (lower β) shifts $c_O(i)$ downward, thus increasing the number of offshored tasks through a reduction in both the number of tasks assigned to immigrants $(\partial I_{MO}/\partial\beta > 0)$ and the number of tasks assigned to natives $(\partial I_{NO}/\partial\beta < 0)$. Analogously, a reduction in the migration costs (lower δ) shifts $c_M(i)$ downward, thus increasing the number of tasks assigned to immigrants through a decrease in the number of offshored tasks (higher I_{MO}).

While the theoretical model identifies the marginal tasks as cutoffs between tasks performed by different groups of workers, the distinction is not so stark in reality as workers are also heterogeneous within groups and some overlap among individuals belonging to different groups is possible along the complexity spectrum.[22] For the empirical analysis it is, therefore, also useful to characterize the "average task," I_M, I_O, or I_D, performed by each group, defined as the employment-weighted average across the corresponding is.[23] Average tasks exhibit the following properties:

(5) $$\frac{\partial I_D}{\partial \beta} < 0, \qquad \frac{\partial I_M}{\partial \beta} > 0$$

$$\frac{\partial I_D}{\partial \delta} = 0, \qquad \frac{\partial I_M}{\partial \delta} < 0.$$

[22] See the previous footnote on how the model could be extended to the case of within-group heterogeneity.
[23] See the Appendix for a formal definition of average tasks.

1942   *THE AMERICAN ECONOMIC REVIEW*   *AUGUST 2013*

These are driven by compositional changes due to adjustments both in the number of tasks allocated to the three groups and in the employment shares of the different tasks allocated to the three groups. Note that changes in migration costs also have a negative impact on the average offshored task $(\partial I_O/\partial \delta < 0)$. The impact of offshoring costs on the average offshore task $(\partial I_O/\partial \beta)$ is, instead, ambiguous. This is due to opposing adjustments in the allocation of tasks given that, when β falls, some of the additional offshore tasks have low i (i.e., I_{MO} falls) while others have high i (i.e., I_{NO} rises).

The impacts of declining β and δ on employment shares, s_M, s_O, and s_D, are all unambiguous.[24] By making offshore workers more productive and thus reducing the price index of offshore tasks P_O relative to the price index of all tasks P_L, a lower offshoring cost, β, reallocates tasks from immigrants and natives to offshore workers. By reducing the price index of immigrant tasks P_M relative to the price index of all tasks P_L, a lower migration cost, δ, moves tasks away from offshore and native workers toward immigrants:

$$(6) \qquad \frac{\partial s_M}{\partial \beta} > 0, \qquad \frac{\partial s_O}{\partial \beta} < 0, \qquad \frac{\partial s_D}{\partial \beta} > 0$$

$$\frac{\partial s_M}{\partial \delta} < 0, \qquad \frac{\partial s_O}{\partial \delta} > 0, \qquad \frac{\partial s_D}{\partial \delta} > 0.$$

These results capture the signs of the "displacement effects" for the three groups of workers.

Turning to the impact of declining β and δ on the employment levels N_M, N_O, and N_D, there is an additional effect beyond the substitution among groups of workers in terms of employment shares.[25] This is due to the fact that lower β and δ ultimately cause a fall in the price index of the labor composite P_L because, as a whole, workers become more productive. This is the "productivity effect" of offshoring and immigration. Specifically, a fall in the price index P_L of the labor composite has a positive impact on sectoral employment (due to the productivity effect), which is then distributed across groups depending on how the relative price indices of the three groups of workers P_M/P_L, P_O/P_L, and P_D/P_L vary (due to the displacement effects).

The impact of declining β and δ on employment levels can be signed only when the productivity effect and the displacement effects go in the same direction. In particular, since $\partial P_L/\partial \beta > 0$ and $\partial P_L/\partial \delta > 0$, we have

$$(7) \qquad \frac{\partial N_O}{\partial \beta} < 0, \qquad \frac{\partial N_M}{\partial \delta} < 0,$$

while the signs of $\partial N_M/\partial \beta$, $\partial N_D/\partial \beta$, $\partial N_O/\partial \delta$, and $\partial N_D/\partial \delta$ are generally ambiguous. In other words, whether the productivity effect is strong enough to offset the displacement effect for all groups of workers is an empirical question that we will

---

[24] See the Appendix for the expressions of employment shares and price indices.
[25] See the Appendix for the expressions of employment levels.

address in the next section. Lower β and δ certainly raise total sector employment $N_L = N_M + N_O + N_D$, as long as there is a non-zero productivity effect.

Results (5), (6), and (7) are the reduced form implications of the model that we will bring to the data in the next sections.[26]

IV. Empirical Specifications and Econometric Results

In this section we bring the predictions of our model to the data. We target the three sets of predictions highlighted in the previous section regarding the effects of easier immigration and easier offshoring on the employment shares, the employment levels and the average task assignments of natives and of the other groups of workers, as highlighted in (5), (6), and (7), respectively. The empirical specifications are derived from the theory but can be justified in a very general way. First, the impact of immigration or offshoring on the share of native employment allows us to infer the degree of direct competition (substitutability) between types of workers. Second, estimating the impact of immigration or offshoring on total employment allows us to quantify the productivity effects of those activities. Finally, the impact of immigration or offshoring on native task assignment tests whether the distribution of tasks across worker types according to task complexity is consistent with our hypothesis and with the estimated pattern of cross-substitution.

The predictions of the model have been derived for a single industry leaving industry and time indices implicit for notational convenience. Hence, in order to implement (5), (6), and (7) empirically we begin by identifying the parameters that vary across industries (to be indexed by s) and over time (to be indexed by t) and those that do not (and carry no index). First, the offshoring and immigration cost parameters vary across industries and over time, and thus we label them β_{st} and δ_{st}. We motivate this in Section IVA in which we present our empirical measures. Second, we consider the specific factor endowment H_s to be industry-specific but not time-varying. The same holds for the baseline sector-specific total factor productivity A_s. We allow, however, for random productivity shocks through a possibly serially correlated error term ε_{st}. Both H_s and A_s will be captured by an industry fixed effect. Finally, as wages have been assumed to be equalized across industries, we allow them to vary only over time, writing w_t and w_t^*, which calls for a time effect.

In sum, we will exploit differences in immigration and offshoring costs within industries over time in order to identify the impact on native and immigrant employment as well as on native and immigrant task specialization.

A. Costs of Immigration and Offshoring

Driving the shifts in β_{st} and δ_{st} are changes in the accessibility of offshore and immigrant workers. Since we do not observe industry-specific offshoring and

---

[26] Employers' ability to discriminate between natives and immigrants is crucial for the productivity effects of immigration to materialize. If employers were unable to discriminate, immigrants would always be paid native wages w earning rents $w - w^*\delta$. Thus, any reduction in δ would simply increase immigrants' rents with no impact on firms' costs. Note, however, that our assumption of perfect discrimination is not crucial to generate the productivity effect due to immigration since even partial discrimination generates rents for the firm. See the online Appendix for additional details.

immigration costs, we begin by using direct measures of the employment share of immigrant and offshore workers across industries and over time as explanatory variables. If the variation in costs, once we control for industry and time effects, were the main source of variation in immigration and offshoring within an industry, then the OLS regression would identify the effect on native outcomes of changes in the cost of immigration and offshoring. As we are aware that this is an heroic assumption, we instrument the share of immigrants and offshore workers with variables proxying their cross-industry costs and availability.

The assumption that offshoring costs vary across industries departs from Grossman and Rossi-Hansberg (2008), who suggest that this cost is more or less the same across industries. This is probably true if one wants to stress, as they do, the technological dimension of offshoring costs, which implies very little variation across similar tasks in different industries. Our focus is, instead, on the trade cost dimension of offshoring, which hampers the re-import of the output generated by offshored tasks and is affected by industry-specific characteristics. In this respect, in order to capture exogenous variation in offshoring costs and generate an instrument for offshore employment in an industry-year, we collect two types of US tariff data, each by year and product: Most Favored Nation (MFN) tariffs and Information Technology Agreement (ITA) tariffs.[27] These are then aggregated up to the BEA industry level for each year, weighting the tariffs by the value of imports in each detailed industry, where we obtain US imports from Feenstra, Romalis, and Schott (2002).[28] We call this variable $(Tariffs)_{st}$.

The instrument we use to proxy cost-driven immigration by industry and year extends the method first proposed by Altonji and Card (1991) and Card (2001) to identify cost-driven local shifts in immigrants. We exploit the fact that foreigners from different countries have increased or decreased their relative presence in the United States according to changes in the cost of migrating and to domestic conditions that are specific to their countries of origin. Differences in the initial presence of immigrants from different countries in an industry make that industry more or less subject to those shifts in origin-specific cost- and push-factors. Using these two facts we impute the population of each of 10 main groups of immigrants across industries over time.[29] Specifically, we use the share of immigrant workers, by origin-group, in each industry in year 2000 and we augment it by the aggregate growth rate of the specific immigrant group's population in the United States relative to the total US population. Then summing over origin-groups within an industry we obtain the imputed share of foreign-born in total employment. We call this measure $(Imputed\_s_M)_{st}$ and note that it varies across industries and over time.[30]

---

[27] These data come primarily from UNCTAD's TRAINS dataset, but were extended somewhat by Yingying Xu (2006) as part of her dissertation at UC Davis. The ITA data was added by the authors. ITA data is available via http://www.wto.org

[28] The MFN tariffs are mandated for all WTO signatories, while the ITA tariffs had been adopted by 43 countries at the end of our period (2007), covering 97 percent of world trade in technology products. The ITA covers a range of manufactured technology products (see the online Appendix for a full list of products and adopters) and, for our purposes, is an important source of time-series variation, as MFN tariffs do not change much within industries over our period.

[29] The ten countries/regions of origin are: Mexico, Rest of Latin America, Canada-Australia-New Zealand, Western Europe, Eastern Europe, China, India, Rest of Asia, Africa, and Other.

[30] This index is similar to the constructed shift-share instrument often used in studies of immigration in local labor markets (e.g., Card 2001; Card and DiNardo 2000; Peri and Sparber 2009), except that it exploits differences

Our identification approach is valid as long as industries, like localities, are important conduits for immigrant networks. This is likely to be more true for industries that are geographically concentrated. In Section IVE we focus exclusively on industries that are highly concentrated geographically. Because of localized ethnic networks (Bartel 1989), we would expect that the initial distribution of immigrants in such industries would be an even stronger predictor of future immigration flows.

B. Effects on Employment Shares

We begin by estimating the impact of variation in immigration and offshoring costs on the *shares* of native, immigrant, and offshore workers, thereby exploring the relative substitutability of these worker types through the extent to which they displace one another. In Section IVC we will then analyze the impact on the employment *levels* of these groups, which includes the productivity impact of the changing costs of immigration and offshoring. Finally, in Section IVD, we will explore the impact on the *task specialization* of natives and immigrants. Using the same notation as we used in the theoretical model but making industry and time indices explicit as discussed above, we implement (B4) empirically by estimating the following three regressions:

(8) $$s_{Dst} = \phi_s^D + \phi_t^D + b_{DO}(s_{Ost}) + b_{DM}(s_{Mst}) + \varepsilon_{st}^D$$

(9) $$s_{Mst} = \phi_s^M + \phi_t^M + b_{MO}(s_{Ost}) + \varepsilon_{st}^M$$

(10) $$s_{Ost} = \phi_s^O + \phi_t^O + b_{OM}(s_{Mst}) + \varepsilon_{st}^O,$$

where s_{Dst}, s_{Ost}, and s_{Mst} are the employment shares of domestic (native), offshore and immigrant workers in industry s at time t, the ϕ_ss are industry fixed effects, the ϕ_ts are time effects, and the ε_{st}s are (potentially) serially correlated errors. Estimation is based on 2SLS using the instruments $(Tariffs)_{st}$ for s_{Ost} and $(Imputed\_s_M)_{st}$ for s_{Mst} as described in Section IVA.

Equation (8) estimates the impact of variation in the offshoring and immigration share, driven by push and cost factors as captured by $(Tariffs)_{st}$ and $(Imputed\_s_M)_{st}$, on native workers' share of employment. By including industry effects we only exploit variation within industries over time. We also control for common-year effects and, as a result, any time-invariant difference in offshoring costs across industries and any common trend in offshoring costs over time will not contribute to the identification of the effect. Equation (9) estimates the effect of variation in offshoring costs on the immigrant share of employment and, conversely, equation (10) estimates the effect on the share of offshore workers due to a decrease in immigration costs.

Specifications (8) to (10) combine two desirable features. First, the coefficients can be easily interpreted as the percentage variation in native (immigrant/offshore)

---

in the presence of immigrant groups (from different countries) across industries, rather than across localities. There are some recent papers that document the existence of industry- and occupation-specific immigrant networks (e.g., Patel and Vella 2007), arising in part due to the geographic concentration of industries.

Immigrants and Labor Markets

TABLE 2—EFFECTS OF OFFSHORING AND IMMIGRATION ON EMPLOYMENT SHARES

	Native share of employment				Immigrant share of employment		Offshore share of employment	
	2SLS		OLS		2SLS	OLS	2SLS	OLS
Specifications	IV, One instrument (1)	IV, One instrument (2)	Direct OLS regression (3)	Direct OLS regression (4)	IV, One instrument (5)	Direct OLS regression (6)	IV, One instrument (7)	Direct OLS regression (8)
Immigrant share of employment		−0.46 (0.39)					−0.53 (0.39)	
Offshore share of employment	−0.79** (0.07)				−0.21** (0.07)			
Industry fixed effects	Yes	Yes	Yes	Yes	Yes	Yes	Yes	Yes
Year fixed effects	Yes	Yes	Yes	Yes	Yes	Yes	Yes	Yes
First stage:	Offshore share of employment	Immigrant share of employment			Offshore share of employment		Immigrant share of employment	
Imputed sector-specific share of immigrants		1.95** (0.55)		−0.91 (1.16)			1.90** (0.48)	−1.03 (0.94)
Sector-specific tariffs	−0.06** (0.01)		0.036* (0.022)		−0.06** (0.01)	0.01* (0.005)		
Observations	464	464	464	464	464	464	464	464
Wald F-stat of first stage	16.6	12.5	NA	NA	16.6	NA	12.5	NA

Notes: The dependent variable in each regression is specified at the top of the relative columns. The units of observations are industry by year. All regressions include industry and year effects. Heteroskedasticity-robust standard errors are reported in parenthesis. In the OLS regressions the standard errors are also clustered by industry.
*** Significant at the 1 percent level.
** Significant at the 5 percent level.
* Significant at the 10 percent level.

employment in response to a 1 percent change in immigrant/offshore employment. In addition, since we use $(Tariffs)_{st}$ and $(Imputed\_s_M)_{st}$ as instruments we only rely on variation driven by changes in the costs of immigration and offshoring. These will be our main specifications. Alternatively, we could regress employment shares directly on the constructed measures of offshoring costs $(Tariffs)_{st}$ and ease of immigration $(Imputed\_s_M)_{st}$. This is more consistent with the model, as we can interpret $(Tariffs)_{st}$ as a measure of β_{st} (cost of offshoring) and $(Imputed\_s_M)_{st}$ as an inverse measure of δ_{st} (cost of migration). However the quantitative interpretation of the coefficient will be less straightforward (because the constructed variables have a somewhat arbitrary scale). The significance and sign of the estimates, however, should be consistent. We will use this more direct regression as an alternative specification.

From Section IIIB the predictions of the model are as follows: $b_{DO} < 0$, $b_{DM} \approx 0$, $b_{MO} < 0$, and $b_{OM} < 0$. Table 2 reports the estimated effects. First, columns 1 and 2 show the 2SLS effects of increasing shares of immigrant and offshore workers on the share of native workers. Because the shares must sum to 1, the immigrant and offshore worker shares are collinear, and so we must estimate their effects separately (as the sole regressors in separate regressions). We therefore estimate each effect, with instrumental variables. In column 1 we use the tariff measure as an instrument for the offshore share of employment while in column 2 we use the imputed

VOL. 103 NO. 5   OTTAVIANO ET AL.: IMMIGRATION, OFFSHORING, AND AMERICAN JOBS   1947

immigration shares to instrument actual immigration.[31] The impact of the cost of offshoring (tariffs) and ease of immigration (imputed immigrants) on the explanatory variables, displayed in the first stage of the regressions, is quite significant and has the expected sign. Furthermore, the measures of ease of offshoring and migration are strong instruments, with a Wald F-statistic that is above the Stock and Yogo critical value (15 percent maximal IV size) equal to 8.96 (see last row of Table 2). Columns 3 and 4 show the coefficients from the corresponding "direct regressions." The native share of employment is regressed directly on the sector-specific tariff (column 3) and on the imputed immigration (specification 4). Columns 5 and 6 report the effects of variation in offshoring costs on the share of immigrants, first using the 2SLS specification and then the direct regression with tariffs as a measure of offshoring costs. Columns 7 and 8 show the effect of variation in immigration costs on the share of offshore workers either directly (specification 8) or using imputed migration as an instrument for the share of immigrants (specification 7). The standard errors reported in each regression are heteroskedasticity robust and, in the case of the OLS regressions, they are clustered at the industry level to account for potential serial correlation of errors.

The results are encouraging as the four predictions of the model are mostly matched by the estimates and the 2SLS and the direct OLS regressions provide the same qualitative evidence. Focussing on the 2SLS coefficients, and looking along the first row, we see that increased immigration in an industry has a non-significant effect on the share of native employment in that industry and a negative (but marginally non-significant, with a p-value of 0.18) effect on the share of offshore employment (recall that the model predicted no effect on natives and a negative effect on immigrants, respectively). Stronger results are obtained in the second row, which shows that there is a negative effect of offshore employment on the share of both native and immigrant workers in an industry, exactly as predicted in (6). Each of the estimates is significantly different from zero. Similarly, the direct regression coefficients show that an increase in the cost of offshoring (tariffs) has a positive and significant effect on the native and immigrant share of employment, while an increase in the ease of immigration has a negative (but non-significant) effect on the offshore share and a non-significant effect on the native share of employment.

These findings are in line with our model. More generally, they suggest that immigrants and natives compete more with offshore workers than with one another. This is consistent with a large part of the labor literature (e.g., Card 2001; or Ottaviano and Peri 2012) that does not find a significant negative impact of immigrants on native employment. Moreover, the decline in offshoring costs is shown to have a significant impact on the employment share of natives and immigrants, but one that is quantitatively larger for the first group. This suggests that over the eight years considered (2000–2007) the tasks that were offshored were more likely to be at the high end of the task spectrum for offshore workers.

---

[31] Using the definition of offshore employment that is inclusive of arm's length offshoring we obtain an effect of off-shoring on native share—in a specification as that in column 1—equal to −0.71, (with a standard error of 0.18). The estimated effect on the immigrant share—in a specification as that in column 5—is −0.29, (with a standard error of 0.18).

TABLE 3—EFFECTS OF OFFSHORING AND IMMIGRATION ON EMPLOYMENT LEVELS

	ln(native employment)				ln(immigrant employment)		ln(offshore employment)	
	2SLS		OLS		2SLS	OLS	2SLS	OLS
Specifications	IV, One instrument (1)	IV, One instrument (2)	Direct OLS regression (3)	Direct OLS regression (4)	IV, One instrument (5)	Direct OLS regression (6)	IV, One instrument (7)	Direct OLS regression (8)
ln(Immigrant employment)		0.41* (0.22)					0.15 (0.43)	
ln(Offshore employment)	−0.12 (0.12)				−0.23 (0.21)			
Industry fixed effects	Yes	Yes	Yes	Yes	Yes	Yes	Yes	Yes
Year fixed effects	Yes	Yes	Yes	Yes	Yes	Yes	Yes	Yes
First stage:	ln(Offshore employment)	ln(Immigrant employment)			ln(Offshore employment)		ln(Immigrant employment)	
Imputed sector-specific share of immigrants		14.07** (4.76)		5.83 (3.69)			14.07** (4.76)	2.07 (9.15)
Sector-specific tariffs	−0.032** (0.008)		0.004 (0.008)		−0.032** (0.007)	0.007 (0.010)		
Observations	464	464	464	464	464	464	464	464
Wald F-stat of first stage	17.2	8.7	NA	NA	17.2	NA	8.70	NA

Notes: The dependent variable in each regression is specified at the top of the relative columns. The units of observations are industry by year. All regressions include industry and year effects. Heteroskedasticity-robust standard errors are reported in parenthesis. In the OLS regressions the standard errors are also clustered by industry.
***Significant at the 1 percent level.
**Significant at the 5 percent level.
*Significant at the 10 percent level.

C. Effects on Employment Levels

Another important implication of our model, highlighted in Section IIIB, is the existence of a "productivity effect" that results from the cost decline associated with hiring immigrant and offshore workers. Such an effect leads to an increase in the aggregate demand for all worker types. This productivity effect, if significant, combined with the effect on shares described in the previous section, should imply a mitigated, or perhaps even positive effect of offshoring on native employment. Additionally, immigration should have a positive effect on native employment.

Table 3, which replicates the structure of Table 2, presents the estimated coefficients from the following four regressions:

$$(11) \qquad N_{Dst} = \phi_s^D + \phi_t^D + B_{DO}(N_{Ost}) + B_{DM}(N_{Mst}) + \varepsilon_{st}^D$$

$$(12) \qquad N_{Mst} = \phi_s^M + \phi_t^M + B_{MO}(N_{Ost}) + \varepsilon_{st}^M$$

$$(13) \qquad N_{Ost} = \phi_s^O + \phi_t^O + B_{OM}(N_{Mst}) + \varepsilon_{st}^O,$$

TABLE 4—EFFECTS OF OFFSHORING AND IMMIGRATION ON TOTAL EMPLOYMENT: THE PRODUCTIVITY EFFECT

	ln(total employment)			
	Method of estimation: 2SLS		Method of estimation: OLS	
Specifications	IV, one instrument (1)	IV, one instrument (2)	Direct OLS regression (3)	Direct OLS regression (4)
Immigrant share of employment		3.87** (1.87)		
Offshore share of employment	1.71** (0.57)			
Industry fixed effects	Yes	Yes	Yes	Yes
Year fixed effects	Yes	Yes	Yes	Yes
Observations	464	464	464	464
First stage:	Offshore share of employment	Immigrant share of employment		
Imputed sector-specific share of immigrants		1.94** (0.55)		7.53** (2.85)
Sector-specific tariffs	−0.06** (0.01)		−0.08 (0.05)	
F-test	16.6	12.5	NA	NA

Notes: The dependent variable in each regression is the logarithm of total (native+immigrant+offshore) employment in the sector. The units of observations are industry by year. All regressions include industry and year effects. Heteroskedasticity-robust standard errors are reported in parenthesis. In the OLS regressions the standard errors are also clustered by industry.

*** Significant at the 1 percent level.
** Significant at the 5 percent level.
* Significant at the 10 percent level.

where N_{Dst}, N_{Mst}, and N_{Ost} are the logarithm of the employment levels of native, immigrant and offshore workers, respectively. Similar to Table 2, columns 1 and 2 show the 2SLS estimates using the cost-driven offshoring and immigration instruments $(Tariffs)_{st}$ and $(Imputed\_s_M)_{st}$. In columns 3 and 4 we show the direct regressions. Similarly, columns 5 and 6 report the effect of offshoring costs on immigrant employment and columns 7 and 8 show the effect of ease of immigration on offshore employment. In Table 4 we then present the estimates for the aggregate employment regression:

$$(14) \qquad N_{Lst} = \phi_s^L + \phi_t^L + B_{LO}(s_{Ost}) + B_{LM}(s_{Mst}) + \varepsilon_{st}^L,$$

where N_{Lst} is the logarithm of aggregate employment in industry s and year t. Again we report the 2SLS estimates (columns 1 and 2) and then the direct regression results (columns 3 and 4). In all specifications the ϕ_ss are industry fixed effects, the ϕ_ts are time effects, and ε_{st}s are (possibly) serially correlated errors. The effects estimated in Table 3 combine the productivity effects with the displacement effects. Regression (14), instead, captures the pure productivity effects of offshoring and immigration at the industry level. A positive estimate of B_{LO} and B_{LM} would imply a positive overall productivity effect of a drop in offshoring and immigration costs. Heteroskedasticity-robust standard errors are reported and in the direct regression estimates we also cluster them by industry.

The results presented in Table 3 are in line with the predictions of the model. Firstly, it is important to note that the first-stage Wald F-Statistics are always above or close to the Stock and Yogo test critical value for weak instruments, equal to 8.96 (15 percent maximum IV size). They are slightly different from those in Table 2 because the explanatory variables are now employment levels (rather than employment shares) but their strength is similar. The employment estimates seem to reveal a positive and significant productivity effect of immigration, and an implied positive productivity effect of offshoring, on native-born workers. A decline of the costs of immigration associated with a 1 percent increase in immigrants produces a significant increase in the employment of natives equal to 0.42 percent (Table 3, column 2) and has no significant effect on the total employment of offshore workers (Table 3, column 7). The productivity effect of offshoring is revealed by the fact that, whereas offshoring unambiguously reduced the share of natives and immigrants in an industry (Table 2, columns 1 and 5), it has no significant effect on the aggregate employment of natives or immigrants (Table 3, columns 1 and 5). Thus, while offshore workers compete with natives and immigrants, their employment seems to generate productivity gains that increase the size of the pie, leading to an overall neutral impact on native and immigrant employment.

Table 4 shows the results from specification (14) which are informative on the size and significance of the productivity effects. The coefficients represent the impact of decreasing costs of offshoring and immigration on the overall size of the "employment pie" to be distributed across workers. As evidenced by the 2SLS results, both offshoring and immigration have positive productivity effects on an industry. The effect is quantitatively larger in the case of immigration.[32] Columns 1 and 2 in Table 4 show that an increase in the immigrant share equal to 1 percent increases aggregate employment by 3.9 percent, implying a significant expansion, again driven by the productivity effect. This is a substantial effect, particularly if we keep in mind that manufacturing employment actually declined over this period. At the same time an increase in the share of offshore employment by 1 percent is associated with an increase in aggregate employment of 1.7 percent. Columns 3 and 4 of Table 4 show the direct OLS regression of aggregate employment on the imputed share of immigrants and on sector-specific tariffs. The regression confirms that an increase in cost-driven availability of immigrants increases the employment of the sector. A decrease in offshoring costs, on the other hand, has a positive, but not significant, effect on employment. The presence of productivity effects due to immigration and offshoring implies that, even taken together, these two forms of globalization of labor have not harmed native employment in the industries most exposed to them. To the contrary, the cost savings obtained from the tasks performed by immigrants and offshore workers have promoted an expansion of these industries relative to others and have ultimately led to increased demand for native workers relative to a scenario in which all tasks were performed by natives.

---

[32] The results on offshoring are broadly consistent with Amiti and Wei (2005), who also find evidence of productivity effects by estimating conditional and unconditional labor demand functions.

D. Effects on Tasks

Finally, we test the model's predictions regarding the effects of offshoring and immigration costs on the complexity of the tasks performed by the three groups of workers. To see whether these predictions find support in the data, we focus on the average rather than the marginal task. Since in the data there is significant idiosyncratic heterogeneity across workers, there is, of course, a region of task overlap between workers of different types (native/offshore and immigrants). It is therefore impossible to define a marginal task in the clear and deterministic way suggested by the model. However, the predictions on average tasks also hold in a probabilistic environment where individual heterogeneity produces a less sharp and more continuous transition between the tasks performed by native, offshore, and immigrant workers. Therefore, we test the model's predictions in terms of average tasks. Formally, we compute the average task for each group by weighting the individual indices of complexity described in Section II by hours worked.

Given that complexity measures are only available for natives and immigrants, we implement (B5) empirically for these two groups by estimating the following two regressions:

$$(15) \qquad I_{Dst} = \phi_s^D + d_{DO}(s_{Ost}) + d_{DI}(s_{Mst}) + \varepsilon_{st}^D$$

$$(16) \qquad I_{Mst} = \phi_s^M + d_{MO}(s_{Ost}) + d_{MI}(s_{Mst}) + \varepsilon_{st}^M,$$

where the variables I_{Dst} and I_{Mst} in (15) and (16) are the average skill intensities of tasks assigned to natives and immigrants, respectively; s_{Ost} and s_{Mst} are the employment shares of offshore and immigrant workers in industry s at time t; and the ϕ_ss represent industry fixed effects. Finally the ε_{st}s are (possibly) serially correlated errors.

Table 5 shows the results from the 2SLS specifications (upper part of the Table) where we use, as always, the instruments $(Tariffs)_{st}$ and $(Imputed\_s_M)_{st}$ and from the direct OLS regressions (lower part of the table). We present the effects on the summary indices of Complexity, I_D and I_M (in columns 1 and 5, respectively), as well as the effect on Cognitive Intensity (column 2), Communication Intensity (column 3), and Non-Manual Intensity (the inverse of the Manual index, in column 4) separately. We focus on the 2SLS results, reported in the first and second row. The direct regression confirms those estimates. In this case the coefficients on offshoring and immigration are estimated in the same regression (since now we do not face the issue of collinearity of shares). The first stage F-Statistics are well above the critical value for the Stock and Yogo test (15 percent maximal IV size) which in the case of two endogenous variables and two instruments is 4.58. The first column of the upper part of Table 5 shows a positive and significant effect of offshoring and no effect of immigration on the Complexity of native tasks. The same holds true for their Communication Intensity, Cognitive Intensity, and Non-Manual Intensity. Again this is consistent with the predictions of the theoretical model. [33] Columns 5

---

[33] The lower part of Table 5 shows the corresponding direct regression coefficients. We see a significant effect of decreasing tariffs on native task complexity and no significant effect of migration. The magnitudes of the coefficients cannot be interpreted as the instruments have somewhat arbitrary scale.

TABLE 5—EFFECTS OF OFFSHORING AND IMMIGRATION ON THE SKILL INTENSITY OF NATIVE AND IMMIGRANT TASKS

Specification	Complexity index, natives (1)	Cognitive index, natives (2)	Communication index, natives (3)	Non-manual index, natives (4)	Complexity index, foreign-born (5)	Difference in complexity natives-foreign born (6)
Panel A. 2SLS estimates						
Immigrant share	0.04	0.04	0.12	0.01		
of employment	(0.66)	(0.43)	(0.510)	(0.22)		
Offshore share of	0.64*	0.38**	0.41*	0.26*	−0.10	0.75**
employment	(0.33)	(0.19)	(0.22)	(0.15)	(0.52)	(0.31)
First stage						
F-statistics	5.10	5.10	5.10	5.10	8.45	8.45
Panel B. Direct OLS estimate						
Imputed sector-	−0.73	−0.41	−0.37	−0.31		
specific share	(0.72)	(0.45)	(0.55)	(0.32)		
of immigrants						
Sector-specific	−0.028**	−0.017**	−0.019**	−0.011**	0.04	0.033
tariffs	(0.012)	(0.007)	(0.008)	(0.005)	(0.20)	(0.020)
Observations	464	464	464	464	464	464

Notes: Panel A shows the coefficients from the 2SLS estimation using imputed sector-specific share of immigrants and sector-specific tariffs as instrument. Panel B shows the results of a direct regression of the dependent variables on the instruments. The units of observations are industry by year. All regressions include industry fixed effects. Standard errors are heteroskedasticity robust and clustered at the sector level.

** Significant at the 5 percent level.
* Significant at the 10 percent level.

and 6 indicate that offshoring has little effect on the complexity of immigrant tasks but, at the same time, has a large positive impact on the gap between immigrant and native tasks $(I_D - I_M)$. This suggests that offshore workers affect native workers mainly by pushing them into more complex tasks, effectively hollowing out the task spectrum. This is consistent with the results found on employment shares (of natives and immigrants) in Table 2. These results are also consistent with Hummels et al. (2010) who find a positive effect of offshoring on the productivity of highly educated workers and with Harrison and McMillan (2011) who find that "vertical" offshoring has positive employment effects, mainly for the highly skilled. In summary we can say that offshoring leads to increased polarization in native and immigrant specialization, mainly by pushing natives toward more complex jobs. This effect is not negligible. Since the standard deviation across sectors in the share of offshore workers during the period is around 14 percent, when multiplied by the coefficient on the complexity index estimated in column 1 we find a difference in task complexity relative to natives of 9 percent. This is about half of the standard deviation of complexity across sectors, and also half of the average difference in complexity of tasks performed by immigrants and natives.

E. *Extensions and Checks*

Before concluding we briefly discuss the implications of three key assumptions of our theoretical framework. A more detailed discussion of these issues and details on the empirical results can be found in the online Appendix of the paper.

First, ours is a model of "vertical" offshoring. Namely, offshoring takes place in order to reduce costs and the intermediate tasks performed by offshore workers are combined to produce a good sold at home. Hence our implications on the impact of offshoring on native tasks should work better in industries that are engaged primarily in vertical offshoring. This is confirmed when we split the sample between industries that re-import a large share of their offshore production (vertical-offshoring) versus those that sell a larger share abroad (horizontal-offshoring). When running a specification as in (1) in Table 5, and focusing only on sectors doing vertical-offshoring, the impact of offshore employment on native complexity is large and significant (1.10 with standard error of 0.59). In contrast, the same regression run using the sample of sectors doing horizontal offshoring produces non-significant estimates (0.17 with standard error of 0.23).[34]

Second, whereas we assumed perfect mobility of workers, in the presence of imperfect mobility or barriers to transferring skills from one industry to another a portion of the industry-specific effects of immigration and offshoring could be captured by wage rather than employment differentials. In particular, while the US labor force is mobile geographically, as well as across industries, in the short run wages may not be perfectly equalized. We check directly whether industry wages are affected by offshoring and immigration by running a specification like (11), except using the average wage of natives instead of their employment as the dependent variable. The estimates (reported and described in online Appendix, Table A3) do not show any significant effect of offshoring and immigration on wages.

Finally, as discussed in Section IVA, imputed immigration, an instrument routinely used in the immigration literature, is usually constructed using variation across localities rather than industries. As a further check that industry-specific network effects are also driven, in part, by the geographic concentration of an industry, we re-run regression (11) focusing on industries that are particularly concentrated in space. Since our 2SLS approach relies on a strong relationship between the flow of immigrants from a particular country into an industry and the share of US immigrants from the same country already working in that industry, the first-stage regression should show increased power when we consider only highly geographically concentrated industries. Again, this is because new immigrants tend to favor destinations where there are ethnic networks created by previous immigrants (Card 2001; Card and DiNardo 2000; Peri and Sparber 2009). A recent paper by Patel and Vella (2007) also shows a concentration of immigrants by location and type of occupation.

In order to capture the degree to which an industry is concentrated within the United States, we calculate a geographic Gini coefficient for each industry using data on state and industry employment in 2000.[35] Interestingly, the manufacturing sector as a whole is significantly more concentrated than non-manufacturing, with an average Gini of 0.75 compared to 0.72, which bodes well for the validity of the instrument overall. In other words, an immigrant's decision regarding which industry to work in may overlap with their choice of location, strengthening the network effects underlying our IV approach. We therefore take the manufacturing average as our threshold and reproduce the first-stage regression using only

---

[34] The details of the empirical analysis and the exact definition of the variables are in the online Appendix.
[35] These employment data are available for download from the US Bureau of Labor Statistics website.

TABLE 6—EMPLOYMENT REGRESSIONS FOR GEOGRAPHICALLY CONCENTRATED INDUSTRIES

	ln(native employment)			
	Method of estimation: 2SLS		Method of estimation: OLS	
Specifications	IV, one instrument (1)	IV, one instrument (2)	Direct OLS regression (3)	Direct OLS regression (4)
ln(Immigrant employment)		0.49** (0.22)		
ln(Offshore employment)	−0.12 (0.08)			
Industry fixed effects	Yes	Yes	Yes	Yes
Year fixed effects	Yes	Yes	Yes	Yes
First stage:	ln(Offshore employment)	ln(Immigrant employment)		
Imputed sector-specific share of immigrants		20.96** (8.43)		10.37* (5.46)
Sector-specific tariffs	−0.06** (0.01)		0.08 (0.05)	
Observations	200	200	200	200
F-test of first stage	33.2	6.80	NA	NA

Notes: The dependent variable in each regression is the logarithm of native employment. We only include the manufacturing sectors with Gini coefficient of geographic concentration across states larger than 0.75, which is the average for the Gini in manufacturing. Heteroskedasticity-robust standard errors are reported. In specification (3) and (4) standard errors are also clustered at the industry level.
 *** Significant at the 1 percent level.
 ** Significant at the 5 percent level.
 * Significant at the 10 percent level.

those industries with a Gini larger than 0.75, a value that is near the median and so selects nearly 50 percent of the sample.

The corresponding findings are depicted in Table 6. Comparing the 2SLS results in columns 1 and 2 with the results for the entire sample (in columns 1 and 2 of Table 3), we see that restricting the sample to more concentrated industries increases the estimated, average impact of immigrants on native employment (from 0.42 to 0.50). This, combined with the relatively larger first-stage coefficient shown in column 2 (to be compared with column 2 in Table 3) constitutes evidence that our immigration instrument is somewhat stronger for spatially concentrated industries and, for these industries, the productivity effect of immigration is also somewhat stronger.

V. Concluding Remarks

We have analyzed the effects of easier offshoring and immigration on the employment share, employment level, and task specialization of native workers within the US manufacturing sector from 2000 to 2007. There are very few attempts to combine analyses of immigration and offshoring on labor markets. Analyzing each in isolation ignores the possibility that hiring immigrants or offshoring productive tasks are alternatives that are simultaneously available to producers and, in fact, may compete with one another or with hiring a native worker.

We have modeled and found empirical support for a scenario in which jobs ("tasks") vary in terms of their relative intensity of use of workers' complex skills, while native, immigrant and offshore workers differ systematically in their relative endowments of these skills. When only natives are available, producers will only employ them. When immigrant and offshore workers become increasingly employable, efficiency gains can be reaped by hiring them to perform tasks in which they have a comparative advantage, giving native workers the opportunity to specialize in the tasks in which they exhibit their own comparative advantage. If strong enough, the productivity effect associated with this improved task assignment may offset the displacement effect of immigration and offshoring on native workers' employment.

Despite the widely held belief that immigration and offshoring are reducing the job opportunities of US natives, we have found instead that, during our period of observation, manufacturing industries with a larger increase in global exposure (through offshoring and immigration) fared better than those with lagging exposure in terms of native employment growth.

Appendix A. Proof of Proposition 1

Sufficient conditions for the existence of $I_{NO} \in (0, 1)$ and $I_{MO} \in (0, I_{NO})$ such that

$$\min[c_D(i), c_M(i), c_O(i)] = \begin{cases} c_M(i), & 0 \leq i < I_{MO} \\ c_O(i), & I_{MO} < i < I_{NO} \\ c_D(i), & I_{NO} < i \leq 1 \end{cases}$$

are that, as i increases from 0 to 1, $c_O(i)$ crosses $c_D(i)$ once and only once and from below in the interval $i \in (0, 1)$ and $c_M(i)$ crosses $c_O(i)$ once and only once and from below in the interval $i \in (0, I_{NO})$. The first single-crossing condition holds if $c_O(0) < c_D(0)$, $c_O(1) > c_D(1)$, and $dc_O(i)/di > dc_D(i)/di = 0$. The "marginal offshore task" is then implicitly defined by $c_O(I_{NO}) = c_D(I_{NO})$. Substituting for $c_O(i) = w^*\beta t(i)a_L$ and $c_D(i) = wa_L$ gives (3) and $w = w^*\beta t(I_{NO})$. The second single-crossing condition holds if $c_M(0) < c_O(0), c_M(I_{NO}) > c_O(I_{NO})$ and $dc_M(i)/di > dc_O(i)/di$. The "marginal immigrant task" is then implicitly defined by $c_M(I_{MO}) = c_O(I_{MO})$. Substituting for $c_M(i) = w^*\delta\tau(i)a_L$ and $c_O(i) = w^*\beta t(i)a_L$ gives (4) and $\beta t(I_{MO}) = \delta\tau(I_{MO})$.

Appendix B.
Employment Levels, Employment Shares, and Average Tasks

Given the allocation of tasks in Proposition 1, marginal cost pricing under perfect competition implies that tasks are priced as follows

$$p(i) = \begin{cases} c_M(i) = w^*\delta\tau(i)a_L & 0 \leq i < I_{MO} \\ c_O(i) = w^*\beta t(i)a_L & I_{MO} \leq i < I_{NO} \cdot \\ c_D = wa_L & I_{NO} < i \leq 1 \end{cases}$$

Then, by (1) and (2), the demand for task i is

$$L(i) = \left[\frac{p(i)}{P_L}\right]^{-\sigma} (P_L)^{-\frac{1}{1-\alpha}} (\alpha p_Y A)^{\frac{1}{1-\alpha}} H,$$

where P_L is the exact price index of the labor composite, defined as

$$P_L = a_L \left\{ \int_0^{I_{MO}} [\delta\tau(i)w^*]^{1-\sigma} \, di + \int_{I_{MO}}^{I_{NO}} [\beta t(i)w^*]^{1-\sigma} \, di + (1 - I_{NO})w^{1-\sigma} \right\}^{\frac{1}{1-\sigma}}.$$

Since $i \in [0, 1]$, P_L is also the average price (and average marginal cost) of tasks. Given Proposition 1, we can rewrite this as $P_L = wa_L\Omega(I_{MO}, I_{NO})$ with

$$(B1) \quad \Omega(I_{MO}, I_{NO}) = \left\{ \int_0^{I_{MO}} \left[\frac{\delta\tau(i)}{\beta t(I_{NO})}\right]^{1-\sigma} di + \int_{I_{MO}}^{I_{NO}} \left[\frac{t(i)}{t(I_{NO})}\right]^{1-\sigma} di + (1 - I_{NO}) \right\}^{\frac{1}{1-\sigma}}.$$

This highlights the relationship between P_L and the bundling parameter Ω in Grossman and Rossi-Hansberg (2008), which we encompass as a limit case when σ goes to zero and δ goes to infinity—that is, when tasks are not substitutable and migration is prohibitively difficult. Expression (B1) shows that changes in the migration friction δ and the offshoring friction β that decrease $\Omega(I_{MO}, I_{NO})$ imply improved efficiency in labor usage. This is the source of the productivity effects of immigration and offshoring discussed in Section IIIB.

Taking into account the different marginal productivity of the three groups of workers, the amount of labor demanded to perform task i is

$$N(i) = \begin{cases} a_L\delta\tau(i)L(i) & 0 \le i < I_{MO} \\ a_L\beta t(i)L(i) & I_{MO} \le i < I_{NO} \\ a_L L(i) & I_{NO} < i \le 1 \end{cases},$$

so that immigrant, offshore, and native employment levels are given by

$$(B2) \qquad N_M = \int_0^{I_{MO}} N(i) \, di = \frac{1}{w^*}\left(\frac{P_M}{P_L}\right)^{1-\sigma} (P_L)^{-\frac{\alpha}{1-\alpha}} B$$

$$N_O = \int_{I_{MO}}^{I_{NO}} N(i) \, di = \frac{1}{w^*}\left(\frac{P_O}{P_L}\right)^{1-\sigma} (P_L)^{-\frac{\alpha}{1-\alpha}} B$$

$$N_D = \int_{I_{NO}}^{1} N(i) \, di = \frac{1}{w}\left(\frac{P_D}{P_L}\right)^{1-\sigma} (P_L)^{-\frac{\alpha}{1-\alpha}} B,$$

where $B = (\alpha p_Y A)^{\frac{1}{1-\alpha}} H > 0$ is a combination of parameters and exogenous variables, and the exact price indices of immigrant, offshore, and native tasks are given by

$$(B3) \quad P_M = a_L \left\{ \int_0^{I_{MO}} [\delta \tau(i) w^*]^{1-\sigma} \, di \right\}^{\frac{1}{1-\sigma}}, \quad P_O = a_L \left\{ \int_{I_{MO}}^{I_{NO}} [\beta t(i) w^*]^{1-\sigma} \, di \right\}^{\frac{1}{1-\sigma}},$$

$$P_D = a_L \{ (1 - I_{NO}) \, w^{1-\sigma} \}^{\frac{1}{1-\sigma}}.$$

Note that N_M is the number of immigrants employed whereas, due to the frictional migration cost, the corresponding number of units of immigrant labor is N_M / δ. Hence, sector employment is $N_L = N_M + N_O + N_D$. The shares of the three groups of workers in sectoral employment are thus

$$(B4) \quad s_M = \frac{(P_M)^{1-\sigma}}{(P_M)^{1-\sigma} + (P_O)^{1-\sigma} + (P_D)^{1-\sigma}(w^*/w)}$$

$$s_O = \frac{(P_O)^{1-\sigma}}{(P_M)^{1-\sigma} + (P_O)^{1-\sigma} + (P_D)^{1-\sigma}(w^*/w)}$$

$$s_D = \frac{(w^*/w)(P_D)^{1-\sigma}}{(P_M)^{1-\sigma} + (P_O)^{1-\sigma} + (P_D)^{1-\sigma}(w^*/w)}.$$

Finally, the "average task" performed by each group is defined as the employment-weighted average across the corresponding is:

$$(B5) \quad I_M = \frac{\int_0^{I_{MO}} i N(i) \, di}{N_M} = \frac{\int_0^{I_{MO}} i \tau(i)^{1-\sigma} \, di}{\int_0^{I_{MO}} \tau(i)^{1-\sigma} \, di}$$

$$I_O = I_{MO} + \frac{\int_{I_{MO}}^{I_{NO}} i N(i) \, di}{N_O} = I_{MO} + \frac{\int_{I_{MO}}^{I_{NO}} it(i)^{1-\sigma} \, di}{\int_{I_{MO}}^{I_{NO}} t(i)^{1-\sigma} \, di}$$

$$I_D = I_{NO} + \frac{\int_{I_{NO}}^{1} i N(i) \, di}{N_D} = \frac{I_{NO} + 1}{2}.$$

REFERENCES

Altonji, Joseph G., and David Card. 1991. "The Effects of Immigration on the Labor Market Outcomes of Less-Skilled Natives." In *Immigration, Trade, and the Labor Market*, edited by John M. Abowd and Richard B. Freeman, 201–34. Chicago: University of Chicago Press.

Amiti, Mary, and Shang-Jin Wei. 2005. "Fear of Service Outsourcing: Is It Justified?" *Economic Policy* 20 (42): 307–39.

Antecol, Heather, Deborah A. Cobb-Clark, and Stephen J. Trejo. 2001. "Immigration Policy and the Skills of Immigrants to Australia, Canada, and the United States." Claremont Colleges Working Paper 2001-26.

Antràs, Pol. 2003. "Firms, Contracts, and Trade Structure." *Quarterly Journal of Economics* 118 (4): 1375–1418.

Antràs, Pol, Luis Garicano, and Esteban Rossi-Hansberg. 2006. "Offshoring in a Knowledge Economy." *Quarterly Journal of Economics* 121 (1): 31–77.

Autor, David H., Lawrence F. Katz, and Melissa S. Kearney. 2006. "The Polarization of the US Labor Market." *American Economic Review* 96 (2): 189–94.

Autor, David H., Frank Levy, and Richard J. Murnane. 2003. "The Skill Content of Recent Technological Change: An Empirical Exploration." *Quarterly Journal of Economics* 118 (4): 1279–1333.

Barba Navaretti, Giorgio, Giuseppe Bertola, and Alessandro Sembenelli. 2008. "Offshoring and Immigrant Employment: Firm-Level Theory and Evidence." Centro Studi Luca d'Agliano Development Studies Working Paper 245.

Bartel, Ann P. 1989. "Where Do the New US Immigrants Live?" *Journal of Labor Economics* 7 (4): 371–91.

Becker, Sascha O., Karolina Ekholm, and Marc-Andreas Muendler. 2009. "Offshoring and the Onshore Composition of Tasks and Skills." Centre for Economic Policy Research Discussion Paper 7391.

Blanchard, Emily, and Gerald Willmann. 2011. "Trade, Education, and the Shrinking Middle Class." http://old-hha.asb.dk/nat/philipp/iei/2010/willmann.pdf.

Blinder, Alan S. 2007. "How many US Jobs might Be Offshorable?" Princeton University Center for Economic Policy Studies Working Paper 142.

Borjas, George J. 2003. "The Labor Demand Curve Is Downward Sloping: Reexamining the Impact of Immigration on the Labor Market." *Quarterly Journal of Economics* 118 (4): 1335–74.

Bureau of Economic Analysis. 2000–2007. "U.S. Direct Investment Abroad, Majority-Owned Nonbank Foreign Affiliates." http://www.bea.gov/ (accessed February 10, 2010).

Butcher, Kristin F., and John DiNardo. 2002. "The Immigrant and Native-Born Wage Distributions: Evidence from United States Censuses." *Industrial and Labor Relations Review* 56 (1): 97–121.

Card, David. 2001. "Immigrant Inflows, Native Outflows, and the Local Labor Market Impacts of Higher Immigration." *Journal of Labor Economics* 19 (1): 22–64.

Card, David. 2009. "Richard T. Ely Lecture: Immigration and Inequality." *American Economic Review* 99 (2): 1–21.

Card, David, and John DiNardo. 2000. "Do Immigrant Inflows Lead to Native Outflows?" *American Economic Review* 90 (2): 360–67.

Chassamboulli, Andri, and Theodore Palivos. 2010. "'Give Me Your Tired, Your Poor,' so I Can Prosper: Immigration in Search Equilibrium." http://mpra.ub.uni-muenchen.de/32379/1/12-10.pdf.

Chiswick, Barry R., Yew Liang Lee, and Paul W. Miller. 2005. "Immigrant Earnings: A Longitudinal Analysis." *Review of Income and Wealth* 51 (4): 485–503.

Costinot, Arnaud. 2009. "An Elementary Theory of Comparative Advantage." *Econometrica* 77 (4): 1165–92.

Costinot, Arnaud, and Jonathan Vogel. 2010. "Matching and Inequality in the World Economy." *Journal of Political Economy* 118 (4): 747–86.

Crinò, Rosario. 2010. "Service Offshoring and White-Collar Employment." *Review of Economic Studies* 77 (2): 595–632.

Feenstra, Robert C., and Gordon H. Hanson. 1996. "Foreign Investment, Outsourcing and Relative Wages." In *The Political Economy of Trade Policy: Papers in Honor of Jagdish Bhagwati*, edited by Robert Feenstra, Gene Grossman, and Douglas Irwin, 89–128. Cambridge, MA: MIT Press.

Feenstra, Robert C., and Gordon H. Hanson. 1999. "The Impact of Outsourcing and High-Technology Capital on Wages: Estimates for the United States, 1979–1990." *Quarterly Journal of Economics* 114 (3): 907–40.

Feenstra, Robert C., John Romalis, and Peter K. Schott. 2002. "US Imports, Exports and Tariff Data." Unpublished.

Goos, Maarten, and Alan Manning. 2007. "Lousy and Lovely Jobs: The Rising Polarization of Work in Britain." *Review of Economics and Statistics* 89 (1): 118–33.

Goos, Maarten, Alan Manning, and Anna Salomons. 2009. "Job Polarization in Europe." *American Economic Review* 99 (2): 58–63.

Grossman, Gene M. 2004. "The Distribution of Talent and the Pattern and Consequences of International Trade." *Journal of Political Economy* 112 (1): 209–39.

Grossman, Gene M., and Giovanni Maggi. 2000. "Diversity and Trade." *American Economic Review* 90 (5): 1255–75.

Grossman, Gene M., and Esteban Rossi-Hansberg. 2008. "Trading Tasks: A Simple Theory of Offshoring." *American Economic Review* 98 (5): 1978–97.

Harrison, Ann, and Margaret McMillan. 2011. "Offshoring Jobs? Multinationals and US Manufacturing Employment." *Review of Economics and Statistics* 93 (3): 857–75.

Hendricks, Lutz. 2002. "How Important Is Human Capital for Development? Evidence from Immigrant Earnings." *American Economic Review* 92 (1): 198–219.

Hummels, David, Rasmus Jorgenson, Jakob Munch, and Chong Xiang. 2011. "Wage and Employment Effects of Outsourcing: Evidence from Danish Matched Worker-Firm Data." National Bureau of Economic Research Working Paper 17496.

Jensen, Bradford J., and Lori G. Kletzer. 2007. "Measuring Tradable Services and the Task Content of Offshorable Services Jobs." http://www.irle-demo.berkeley.edu/events/fall08/kletzer/Kletzer_Job_task_content_080408.pdf (accessed February 14, 2010).

Jones, Ronald W., and Henryk Kierzkowski. 1990. "The Role of Services in Production and International Trade: A Theoretical Framework." In *The Political Economy of International Trade, Essays in Honor of Robert E. Baldwin,* edited by Ronald W. Jones and Anne O. Krueger, 31–48. New York: Basil Blackwell.

Katz, Lawrence F., and David H. Autor. 1999. "Changes in the Wage Structure and Earnings Inequality." In *Handbook of Labor Economics,* Vol. 3, Part A, edited by Orley C. Ashenfelter and David Card, 1463–1555. New York: Elsevier.

Kremer, Michael, and Eric Maskin. 2006. "Globalization and Inequality." Harvard University, Weatherhead Center for International Affairs Working Paper 2008-0087.

Levy, Frank, and Richard J. Murnane. 2006. "How Computerized Work and Globalization Shape Human Skill Demands." http://web.mit.edu/ipc/publications/pdf/05-006.pdf.

Manning, Alan. 2004. "We Can Work It Out: The Impact of Technological Change on the Demand for Low-Skill Workers." *Scottish Journal of Political Economy* 51 (5): 581–608.

Monte, Ferdinando. 2011. "Skill Bias, Trade, and Wage Dispersion." *Journal of International Economics* 83 (2): 202–18.

Nocke, Volker, and Stephen Yeaple. 2008. "An Assignment Theory of Foreign Direct Investment." *Review of Economic Studies* 75 (2): 529–57.

Ohnsorge, Franziska, and Daniel Trefler. 2007. "Sorting It Out: International Trade with Heterogeneous Workers." *Journal of Political Economy* 115 (5): 868–92.

Olney, William W. 2012. "Offshoring, Immigration, and the Native Wage Distribution." *Canadian Journal of Economics* 45 (3): 830–56.

Ottaviano, Gianmarco I. P., and Giovanni Peri. 2012. "Rethinking the Effect of Immigration on Wages." *Journal of the European Economic Association* 10 (1): 152–97.

Ottaviano, Gianmarco I. P., Giovanni Peri, and Greg C. Wright. 2010. "Immigration, Offshoring and American Jobs." National Bureau of Economic Research Working Paper 16439.

Ottaviano, Gianmarco I. P., Giovanni Peri, and Greg C. Wright. 2013. "Immigration, Offshoring, and American Jobs: Dataset." *American Economic Review.* http://dx.doi.org/10.1257/aer.103.5.1925.

Patel, Krishna, and Francis Vella. 2007. "Immigrant Networks and Their Implications for Occupational Choice and Wages." Institute for the Study of Labor Discussion Paper 3217.

Peri, Giovanni. 2012. "The Effect of Immigration on Productivity: Evidence from US States." *Review of Economics and Statistics* 94 (1): 348–58.

Peri, Giovanni, and Chad Sparber. 2009. "Task Specialization, Immigration, and Wages." *American Economic Journal: Applied Economics* 1 (3): 135–69.

Ruggles, Steven, Matthew Sobek, Trent Alexander, Catherine A. Fitch, Ronald Goeken, Patricia Kelly Hall, Miriam King, and Chad Ronnander. 2008. Integrated Public Use Microdata Series: Version 3.0 [Machine-readable database]. Minneapolis: MN: Minnesota Population Center [producer and distributor]. http://www.ipums.org.

Sly, Nicholas. 2012. "International Productivity Differences, Trade and the Distributions of Factor Endowments." *Review of International Economics* 20 (4): 740–57.

US Department of Labor. 2012. O*NET survey, version 11.0, http://www.onetcenter.org/ (accessed August 27, 2012).

Wright, Greg C. 2012. "Revisiting the Employment and Wage Impacts of Offshoring." http://gregcwright.weebly.com/uploads/8/2/7/5/8275912/wright_offemp_june.pdf (accessed July 18, 2009).

Xu, YingYing. 2006. "Global Tariff Database." PhD diss. University of California, Davis.

Yeaple, Stephen Ross. 2005. "A Simple Model of Firm Heterogeneity, International Trade, and Wages." *Journal of International Economics* 65 (1): 1–20.

IMMIGRATION, JOBS, AND EMPLOYMENT PROTECTION: EVIDENCE FROM EUROPE BEFORE AND DURING THE GREAT RECESSION

Francesco D'Amuri
Bank of Italy
and ISER, University of Essex

Giovanni Peri
University of California, Davis

Abstract
In this paper we analyze the impact of immigrants on the type and quantity of native jobs. We use data on 15 Western European countries during the 1996–2010 period. We find that immigrants, by taking manual-routine type of occupations pushed natives towards more "complex" (abstract and communication) jobs. This job upgrade was associated to a 0.7% increase in native wages for a doubling of the immigrants' share. These results are robust to the use of an IV strategy based on past settlement of immigrants across European countries. The job upgrade slowed but did not come to a halt during the Great Recession. We also document the labor market flows behind it: the complexity of jobs offered to new native hires was higher relative to the complexity of lost jobs. Finally, we find evidence that such reallocation was larger in countries with more flexible labor laws. (JEL: J24, J31, J61)

1. Introduction

The net flow of immigrants into Western Europe during the period 1996–2010 was very large. Considering the eleven countries for which we have a consistent time series[1] the percentage of foreign-born[2] nearly doubled from less than 8% of the population in 1996 to almost 14% in 2010. By comparison, in the United States, the presence of foreign-born increased by a smaller percentage, going from 10.6% of the population in 1998 to 12.9% in 2010.

Extensive literature has analyzed the labor market effect of immigrants in the United States and in other countries with large immigration flows, such as Canada and

---

The editor in charge of this paper was Stefano DellaVigna.

Acknowledgment: We are grateful to four anonymous referees for very useful comments. We thank Paul Gaggl for excellent assistance in research-PLXINSERT-, and editing. William Ambrosini, Corrado Giulietti, Michele Giuranno, Antonella Nocco, Chad Sparber-PLXINSERT-, and seminar participants at the Bank of Italy, European Central Bank, UC Berkeley, Bocconi-PLXINSERT-, and Lecce Universities provided helpful comments.

E-mail: francesco.damuri@gmail.com (D'Amuri); gperi@ucdavis.edu (Peri)

1. Namely Austria, Belgium, Denmark, Finland, France, Greece, Netherlands, Norway, Portugal, Spain, and Sweden. In the rest of the paper we also include: Ireland, Italy, Luxembourg, and the United Kingdom.
2. This is shown in Figure A.1 of the Online Appendix.

Australia.[3] With some disagreement, researchers have emphasized two facts. First, immigration is relatively large among workers with high education levels (college or higher).[4] These types of immigrants may compete with highly educated natives but have also positive productivity effects on the economy, so their overall wage impact on native workers is likely to be positive. Second, among workers in the intermediate-to-low range of education, immigrants tend to be concentrated among those with very low schooling levels. They also tend to take manual-intensive and routine-type occupations (e.g. in construction, agriculture, and personal-household sectors), which usually require manual and physical skills rather than communication and interactive abilities. This may generate strong competition for the least educated natives (e.g. Borjas 2003; Borjas and Katz 2007). However, the fact that natives are employed in larger numbers in occupations that are different from those taken by immigrants (Ottaviano and Peri 2012) and the fact that they tend to upgrade their job in response to immigration (Peri and Sparber 2009), taking on more complex and communication-intensive tasks and leaving manual tasks to immigrants, protects them from such competition. Hence, even for the group of less-educated native workers, several economists do not find significant wage effect of immigrants (e.g. Card 2009; Ottaviano and Peri 2012).

Considering European labor markets, economists have analyzed the impact of immigrants in specific countries (see for instance Dustmann, Frattini, and Preston (2013) for the United Kingdom, Glitz (2012) for Germany, and González and Ortega (2011) for Spain) using frameworks similar to those applied to the United States. Often those types of analyses are forced to use variation (of immigrants and labor market outcomes) across regions within a country. Hence, they are subject to the concern, put forward in several studies (e.g. Borjas, Freeman, and Katz 1996), of identifying an attenuated local wage effect relative to the possible national effect. With the notable exception of Angrist and Kugler (2003), we are not aware of any study that analyzes the impact of immigration on European labor markets considering evidence from all (or most) Western European economies. In this paper, we fill this gap by analyzing how immigration affects job specialization of natives and how these effects vary across E.U. countries. Besides a large variation in the inflow of immigrants across countries, the European case also provides significant variation in the institutional characteristics of their labor markets. These rich sources of additional variation allow us to address a host of novel questions: Are some countries better equipped to absorb immigrants? Is the response of native workers to immigrants, in terms of occupational mobility, stronger in countries with more flexible labor markets? Are these differences particularly relevant for some groups of workers? Do they vary with the conditions of the labor market? Did the recent deep recession affect how immigrants were absorbed in labor markets?

---

3. See for instance Longhi, Nijkamp, and Poot (2005) for a summary and meta-analysis of the literature on the wage effect of immigrants. Okkerse (2008) provides a survey of recent empirical evidence on the effect of immigration.

4. This is not only true for US immigrants but also for immigrants to European countries. See for instance Docquier, Özden, and Peri's (2010) data and empirical analysis that emphasize this fact.

The paper introduces two additional contributions to the literature on migration. First, we analyze some of the channels through which the impact of immigrants on hosts' labor markets operates. In particular, exploiting the recall questions present in our data, we recover labor market transitions of workers at yearly intervals and we inquire whether an increase in the number of migrants stimulates or depresses hiring and separations for natives, and the way it changes the skill content of such transitions. Second, we check whether the labor market adjustment to immigration changed significantly during the Great Recession (GR) years. A number of studies have analyzed the impact of the GR on European and US labor markets (Immervoll, Peichl, and Tatsiramos 2011; Elsby, Hobijn, and Sahin 2010, among others); there is instead little research on distinguishing the impact of immigration on the labor market of the host country along the business cycle. Exploiting the fact that the number of foreign born continued to rise during the recession years, although at a slower rate, we fill this gap in the literature and study whether there was a differential impact of immigration on native outcomes before and during the recent crisis.

In the broader picture, this paper also contributes to the understanding of the determinants of a shift in demand and supply of productive tasks in Europe. In the recent decades, an increase in the number of jobs requiring the use of complex and abstract skills, and a decrease in the number of manual-routine type of jobs has been documented for many developed countries. In particular, these phenomena have been observed in the United States (Acemoglu and Autor 2010) as well as in Europe (Goos, Manning, and Salomons 2009). In a search for common global tendencies that offer explanations for the aforementioned trends, most of the economic research (as summarized in Acemoglu and Autor 2010) has focused on two factors: the effect of technology and the effect of off-shoring. On the one hand, information and communication technologies have increased the productivity of complex-abstract jobs, while substituting for routine manual (and routine nonmanual) tasks. On the other hand, the internationalization of production has allowed the relocation of simple and manual phases of production abroad, but not (yet) the relocation of complex tasks. These two factors affected the demand for these tasks in developed countries.

In this paper we explore another dimension that may have produced a shift in the *supply* of tasks in rich countries: the increase in the immigrant labor force, especially from less-developed countries. Our hypothesis is that the inflow of these immigrants has increased the supply of manual-physical skills in rich economies, but also shifted native workers to more complex tasks. Hence, immigration has been an additional cause for the increase in employment in cognitive and complex tasks by native workers.

Our empirical strategy considers different skill cells (represented by combinations of education and age in each country) across European countries. Each of them, in the tradition of Borjas (2003) and Ottaviano and Peri (2012), is a differentiated labor market (mobility of natives across countries is small in Europe). Within each of them we consider a partition of productive tasks into "complex" tasks (abstract and cognitive) and "simple" tasks (routine and manual based). Such a partition follows the literature on the effect of information technology on the demand for productive tasks (e.g. Autor, Levy, and Murnane 2003) and the literature on "off-shorability" of tasks (e.g.

Crinò 2009; Blinder 2006). We consider this partition as relevant also in determining the relative specialization of native and immigrant workers. Jobs that can be easily codified, that are manual and repetitive in nature, are considered "simple" and may be easily taken by foreign-born workers who may have more limited native language skills and do not know the intricacy of the culture, social norms, and institutions of the host country. If this is the case, an inflow of immigrants in a cell (labor market) increases the supply of "simple" productive tasks in that cell. As we will show in a model of occupational choice, natives, who have a comparative advantage in communication-abstract tasks, would in response specialize in more "complex" tasks.

Using this structure we can then identify whether immigration has been a force promoting the specialization of native workers in Europe toward abstract-complex occupations and away from manual-routine ones. At the same time we can check whether such a shift in the occupational distribution of natives took place together with a variation of natives' employment rates, due to some crowding-out.

To establish whether the correlation between the inflow of immigrants in a labor-market cell and the increased specialization of natives captures a causal relationship between the first and the second variable we use two alternative instrumental variables, inspired to the approach of Altonji and Card (1991) and Card (2001). The presence of cell-specific demand shocks for complex tasks correlated with the inflow of immigrants and the measurement error in the inflow of immigrants could generate a biased estimate of the effect of immigration, using OLS. We use instruments based on the fact that the initial shares of foreign-born across country-skill cells in a year are good predictors of their subsequent flows. Assuming that the relative demand for manual and complex tasks taking place in Europe between 1996 and 2010 does not vary systematically with foreigners' initial settlements, the instruments are correlated with relative task supply only through their effect on the supply of immigrants. The difference between the two instruments is that in one case we use census data in 1991 and in the other Labor force survey data in 1996 to construct initial immigrant settlements.[5] We also control for factors that proxy shifts in the relative demand for complex-abstract tasks including country or skill-specific effects.

Our main empirical findings are four. First, according to results obtained using our preferred specification, higher immigration pushes natives to occupations with a stronger content of complex abilities. A doubling of the immigrants' share in a skill-country cell increases natives' relative specialization in complex skills by 5%–6%. This labour market adjustment takes place with no significant impact on natives' employment rates. Moreover it implies that, in the short run, a doubling of foreign-born share in the total population is associated with a 0.7% increase in native monthly wages. Second, we find mild evidence that such a positive reallocation takes place mainly through an increase in the average complexity of jobs offered to new hires. Hiring rates increase but not significantly. The separation margin is not much affected by immigration in the cell. Third, when we split countries in two groups, those with

---

5. In the case of Census data we distinguish immigrants by nationality. This is not possible in the Labor force data where we do not know the country of origin of immigrants.

strong Employment Protection Legislation (EPL) and those with weak employment protection, we find that the natives' positive reallocation towards complex jobs, caused by immigration, is more intense in less-protected markets. Moreover, in countries with low employment protection, the reallocation is stronger for workers with low levels of education. This is consistent with the hypothesis that in countries with high EPL, less-educated workers tend to remain in simple-manual occupations that suffer much more the wage competition of immigrants, while in low-EPL countries occupational upgrading moves less educated workers away from immigrants' wage competition. Finally, we test whether the positive job reallocation triggered by migration continued during the economic downturn taking place in 2007–2010. Testing for the differential labor market impact of immigration along the business cycle is not only interesting in itself, but it also provides an additional verification that our instrumental variable strategy works even in periods of negative labor demand shocks. We find that the previously described positive reallocation process slowed, but remained significant, during those years.

The rest of the paper is organized as follows. Sections 2 and 3 respectively define a theoretical model of immigration and natives' specialization and discuss the identification strategy. Section 4 describes the datasets and the task variables. Results of the empirical analysis of the effects of immigration on natives' specialization and employment rates are reported in Section 5. Section 6 analyzes the impact of immigrants separately on natives' hiring and separations, while Section 7 investigates how labor market institutions affect the extent of the occupational adjustment. Section 8 checks whether the impact of migration on the labor market changed in correspondence of the deep recession that affected Europe in the late part of the last decade. We then offer some simple calculations to quantify the effects of immigrants on native wages, through the previously illustrated occupational reallocation channel, in Section 9. Section 10 concludes the paper.

2. The Model

2.1. Relative Demand of Tasks

We consider that each labor market (country) is divided into cells of workers with differing observable skills, experience and education. Consistently with Katz and Murphy (1992), Ottaviano and Peri (2012) and Peri and Sparber (2009), we use a categorization that distinguishes between two education groups, those with secondary education or less and those with some tertiary education and more. These two groups are clearly differentiated for the type of jobs/production tasks that they perform. Within each group we consider five age sub-groups. As in Borjas (2003) and Ottaviano and Peri (2012), each of these skill groups provides labor services that are somewhat differentiated because they use different vintages of technology and have had different labor market experiences. Hence the structure of competition-substitutability within a schooling group is different from that across groups. We capture this production

structure by combining different skill cells in a multi-stage nested Constant Elasticity
of Substitution (CES) production function. In particular, output is produced using
capital and labor. Labor is a CES aggregate of labor services from workers in different
education groups and, in turn, each of those groups is a CES composite of labor
services of workers with different ages. Such a structure imposes specific restrictions
on the cross-cell elasticities. We follow the well established practice of grouping skills
that are harder to substitute into the outer groups, increasing substitutability as we
progress into the inner nests. Card (2009) and Goldin and Katz (2007) argue that
the split into two schooling groups is the one preferred by the data, and most of the
literature organizes the experience groups into bins of five or ten years. Our choice of
nesting structure follows their lead. Furthermore, the particular order of nesting does
not matter for our results as long as education-age cells are imperfectly substitutable
groups of workers. For each country c in year t we represent the production function
as follows:

$$Y_{ct} = A_{ct} N_{ct}^{\alpha} K_{ct}^{1-\alpha} \tag{1}$$

$$N_{ct} = \left[\sum_{edu} \theta_{edu,c,t} N_{edu,c,t}^{\frac{\sigma_{EDU}-1}{\sigma_{EDU}}} \right]^{\frac{\sigma_{EDU}}{\sigma_{EDU}-1}} \tag{2}$$

$$N_{edu,c,t} = \left[\sum_{age} \theta_{age,edu,t} N_{age,edu,c,t}^{\frac{\sigma_{AGE}-1}{\sigma_{AGE}}} \right]^{\frac{\sigma_{AGE}}{\sigma_{AGE}-1}} \quad \text{for each } edu, \tag{3}$$

where Y_{ct}, A_{ct}, K_{ct}, and N_{ct} are respectively output, total factor productivity, services
of physical capital, and the aggregate labor services in country c and year t. $N_{edu,c,t}$
is the composite labor input from workers with the same level of education "edu".
$N_{age,edu,c,t}$ is the composite input from workers of education "edu" and age "age".
The parameters θ capture the relative productivity of each skill group within the labor
composite. Notice that the relative productivity of education groups $\theta_{edu,c,t}$ is allowed
to vary across countries and over time and the relative productivity of age groups
$\theta_{age,edu,t}$ also varies by education and time. The elasticities σ_{EDU} and σ_{AGE} regulate
substitutability between labor services of workers with different education and age
level.

The observable characteristics are education and age of a worker. We use the index
j ($=edu, age$) to identify each education-age cell. We consider these characteristics
as given at a point in time. In each skill-cell j we separate the labor services supplied
as complex tasks (C) and those supplied as simple tasks (S) and consider those inputs
as imperfect substitutes, also combined in a CES:

$$N_{j,c,t} = \left[\beta_j S_{j,c,t}^{\frac{\sigma-1}{\sigma}} + (1-\beta_j) C_{j,c,t}^{\frac{\sigma-1}{\sigma}} \right]^{\frac{\sigma}{\sigma-1}} \quad \text{for each } j, c, t,$$

where $S_{j,c,t}$ and $C_{j,c,t}$ are the amount of "simple" (manual, routine) and "complex" (abstract, communication, mental) services supplied by the skill group j in country c and year t. The coefficient β_j determines the relative productivity of simple tasks in the cell and the elasticity σ determines the substitutability between the two types of tasks in the cell. We call w_C the compensation for one unit of service of complex work, and w_S the compensation for one unit of service of simple work. This allows us to derive the relative demand for complex and simple services in skill group j by equating the ratio of their marginal productivity to the ratio of their compensations:

$$\frac{C_{j,c,t}}{S_{j,c,t}} = \left(\frac{1 - \beta_{j,c,t}}{\beta_{j,c,t}}\right)^{\sigma} \left(\frac{w_C}{w_S}\right)^{-\sigma}_{jct}. \tag{4}$$

The relative supply, the relative compensation, and potentially the relative productivity of simple and complex services vary with skill, country, and year, hence the subscripts. Throughout the remainder of Section 2 we omit the $_{j,c,t}$ subscripts and we will reintroduce them when describing the empirical specification.

2.2. Relative Supply of Tasks

As in Peri and Sparber (2009), we assume that native and immigrant workers divide their labor endowment ($l = 1$) between simple and complex tasks in order to maximize their utility. Here, differently from Peri and Sparber (2009), we allow utility to depend positively on labor wage and negatively on a stigma associated with simple working tasks. Hence, individuals of similar skill j, if natives or immigrants, may have different productivity in simple and complex tasks as well as different degrees of "dislike" (stigma) for earning as simple manual-routine workers. The utility U_k for individuals of type k, with $k = D$ indicating domestic and $k = F$ denoting foreign-born workers, is given by the following expression:

$$U_k = \underbrace{\left(l_k\right)^{\delta} x_k w_S + \left(1 - l_k\right)^{\delta} \kappa_k w_C}_{\text{Wage Income}} - \underbrace{d_k \left(l_k\right)^{\delta} x_k w_S}_{\text{Stigma}}. \tag{5}$$

The first part is the wage income. Each individual of type k has some task-specific abilities κ_k and x_k and, by allocating l_k units of labor to simple tasks and $1 - l_k$ units to complex tasks, produces $s_k = \left(l_k\right)^{\delta} x_k$ units of simple service and $c_k = \left(1 - l_k\right)^{\delta}_D \kappa_k$ of complex service (with $\delta < 1$), compensated respectively at rate w_S and w_C per unit.[6] However, the part of income earned doing simple tasks does not convey the full utility of income as it may have some stigma, disutility, or penalty attached, represented by the last term in U_k. People may dislike doing manual jobs, or the status in society of these jobs may be low, or there may be some dislike of circumstances connected

---

6. The assumption of $\delta < 1$ implies an internal solution: all individuals do at least some of each tasks. This means that when a person spends almost the whole day doing only complex tasks (e.g. writing a complex paper) it is efficient to spend a little time doing simple tasks (such as cleaning up the desk).

with the manual part of the job (being outside, uncomfortable, etc.). We model this stigma-disutility as an "iceberg" cost on the part of the income that is earned doing the simple tasks, with d_k, between 0 and 1, as the parameter that captures the intensity of such psychological cost/dislike. The second part of the utility is essentially the equivalent amount of income that a person would give up in order to be able to do a "complex" rather than a "simple" job.

Maximizing equation (5) with respect to l_k we obtain the individual relative supply of tasks for type k:

$$\frac{c_k}{s_k} = \left(\frac{w_C}{w_S}\right)^{\frac{\delta}{1-\delta}} \left(\frac{1}{1-d_k}\right)^{\frac{\delta}{1-\delta}} \left(\frac{\kappa_k}{\varkappa_k}\right)^{\frac{1}{1-\delta}}. \tag{6}$$

In this simplified model each native supplies (c_D, s_D) task units and each immigrant supplies (c_F, s_F) so that members from each group will choose a common combination of tasks (empirically an occupation). Each group will choose a new combination of tasks if their relative compensation changes. The relative supply of complex tasks increases with the relative compensation w_C/w_S and it increases with the relative ability in complex tasks of the group, $\kappa_k/\varkappa_k$, as well as with its dislike for manual-routine services $1/(1-d_k)$. The aggregate task supply for native and foreign workers in skill j, country c and year t, will equal the product of individual task supply and total labor supply. This implies $c_{j,c,t}/s_{j,c,t} = C_{j,c,t}/S_{j,c,t}$ (by multiplying numerator and denominator by employment in the cell).

Finally, aggregating immigrants and natives we obtain the aggregate relative supply of tasks in cell j, c, t:

$$\frac{C}{S} = \frac{C_F + C_D}{S_F + S_D} = \phi\,(f)\,\frac{C_F}{S_F} + (1 - \phi\,(f))\frac{C_D}{S_D}. \tag{7}$$

The term $\phi\,(f) = S_F/(S_F + S_D) \in (0,1)$ is the share of simple tasks supplied by foreign-born workers, and is a simple monotonically increasing transformation of the foreign-born share of less-educated workers $f = L_F/(L_F + L_D)$.[7] Hence, the aggregate relative supply of tasks in the economy is a weighted average of each group's relative supply, and the weights are closely related to the share of each group in employment.

2.3. Equilibrium Results

Substituting equation (6) for natives and immigrants in equation (7) and equating relative supply with relative demand (expressed by equation (4)) one can solve for the

---

7.   Specifically, $\phi'(f) > 0$, $\phi(0) = 0$ and $\phi(1) = 1$.

equilibrium relative compensation of tasks:

$$\frac{w_C^*}{w_S^*} = \left(\frac{1-\beta}{\beta}\right)^{\frac{(1-\delta)\sigma}{(1-\delta)\sigma+\delta}} \left[\frac{\kappa}{x}\left(\underset{-}{f}, \underset{+}{\frac{\kappa_F}{x_F}}, \underset{+}{d_F}\right)\right]^{-\frac{1}{(1-\delta)\sigma+\delta}}. \tag{8}$$

The function $(\kappa/x)(f, \kappa_F/x_F, d_F)$ is a weighted average of the relative task abilities and of simple job aversion among natives and immigrants. More specifically,

$$\frac{\kappa}{x}\left(f, \frac{\kappa_F}{x_F}, d_F\right)$$

$$= \left[\phi(f)\cdot\left(\frac{\kappa_F}{x_F}\right)^{\frac{1}{1-\delta}}\left(\frac{1}{1-d_F}\right)^{\frac{\delta}{1-\delta}} + (1-\phi(f))\cdot\left(\frac{\kappa_D}{x_D}\right)^{\frac{1}{1-\delta}}\left(\frac{1}{1-d_D}\right)^{\frac{\delta}{1-\delta}}\right]^{(1-\delta)}.$$

The term $(\kappa/x)(f, \kappa_F/x_F, d_F)$ depends negatively on f and positively on κ_F/x_F and d_F, as indicated by the signs in equation (8).

By substituting the equilibrium wage into the aggregate relative supply for domestic workers, we find their equilibrium relative provision of tasks:

$$\frac{C_D^*}{S_D^*} = \left(\frac{1-\beta}{\beta}\right)^{\frac{\delta\sigma}{(1-\delta)\sigma+\delta}}\left(\frac{\kappa_D}{x_D}\right)^{\frac{1}{1-\delta}}\left(\frac{1}{1-d_D}\right)^{\frac{\delta}{1-\delta}}\left[\frac{\kappa}{x}\left(\underset{-}{f}, \underset{+}{\frac{\kappa_F}{x_F}}, \underset{+}{d_F}\right)\right]^{-\frac{1}{(1-\delta)\sigma+\delta}\frac{\delta}{1-\delta}} \tag{9}$$

The equilibrium expression (9) is the basis for the empirical analysis. In particular, based on the logarithmic derivative of (9), the model predicts a positive impact of the share of foreign-born f on the relative supply of complex tasks of natives, C_D^*/S_D^*.

3. Empirical Implications and Identifying Assumptions

Expression (9) holds for each skill-country-year cell; taking the logarithm of both sides of the equation and explicitly writing the subscripts in the variables for each skill-country-time group we approximate the equilibrium condition to the following empirically implementable condition:

$$\ln\left(\frac{C_D}{S_D}\right)_{j,c,t} = \gamma \ln(f_{j,c,t}) + d_{c,t} + d_{j,t} + \varepsilon_{j,c,t}. \tag{10}$$

The term C_D/S_D is the measure of relative complex versus simple tasks provided by home-born workers in the specific cell. This relative supply is responsive to the relative compensation of tasks, which in turn depends on the share of immigrants $\ln(f_{j,c,t})$ in the cell and $\gamma \equiv -\{1/[(1-\delta)\sigma+\delta]\}[\delta/(1-\delta)] \, [\partial \ln(\kappa/x)/\partial \ln f] > 0$.

The country by year effect $d_{c,t}$ captures the unobservable relative productivity and simple-job aversion for natives, $[1/(1-\delta)]\ln(\kappa_D/x_D)$ and $[\delta/(1-\delta)]$

$\ln[1/(1 - d_D)]$ and for immigrants, $-\{1/[(1 - \delta)\sigma + \delta]\}[\delta/(1 - \delta)]\{[\partial \ln (\kappa/\varkappa)]/ \partial d_F\}$ and $-\{1/[(1 - \delta)\sigma + \delta]\}[\delta/(1 - \delta)]\{[\partial \ln(\kappa/\varkappa)]/\partial(\kappa_F/\varkappa_F)\}$. These features of the native and immigrants population may vary across countries and year and hence we absorb them in a country by year effect. A certain country, due to its laws and institutions, selects immigrants with certain productivity and preference characteristics relative to natives. The skill by time effects $d_{j,t}$ absorb the variation of the relative productivity and efficiency term $\{\delta\sigma/[(1 - \delta)\sigma + \delta]\} \ln[(1 - \beta)/\beta]$. The relative productivity of simple and complex tasks may evolve over time. For instance, a common complex-biased technological progress that affects college-educated workers more than less-educated ones over the considered years would be captured by these effects. The term $\varepsilon_{j,c,t}$ is an idiosyncratic random shock (or measurement error) with average 0 and uncorrelated with the explanatory variables, while α is a constant. Our main interest is in estimating γ. Our model predicts a positive value of γ, as a larger share of immigrants would increase returns for complex tasks relative to simple tasks and hence push natives to specialize further into those tasks with potential productivity and wage gains. The magnitude of that effect is an empirical question.

3.1. Discussion of Endogeneity and Instruments

Once we control for the technological factors affecting skill demand (with the skill by year coefficients) and for country-specific time-varying shocks, we are assuming that the remaining variation over time in the share of immigrants across cells within country-year is driven by the exogenous variation of immigrant supply. In particular, in the OLS estimates we are assuming that, after controlling for the fixed effects, the whole variation of $f_{j,c,t}$ is exogenous. Residual correlation could still be present if, for example, skill upgrading is taking place among native workers of a particular skill cell and this increases the demand for immigrants. We deal with this potential issue of reverse causality/omitted variable bias in three ways.

First, and less important, in all specifications we define $f_{j,c,t}$ as the share of foreign-born individuals on total population (rather than employment) within each cell. Immigrant population is determined in large part by factors in the sending countries, the costs of migration, as well as immigration laws. Of course, employment opportunities (driven by labor demand conditions) affect immigration choices and hence the whole population in a cell may still depend on unobserved labor demand shocks. Still, population shares are less sensitive to labor demand shocks than employment shares.

Second, we address the potential omitted variable bias with two alternative instruments, both based on the strategy first developed by Altonji and Card (1991) and largely used in this literature. The underlying assumption is that while new immigrants tend to settle where existing immigrant communities already exist, in order to exploit ethnic networks and amenities, their historical presence is unrelated to current cell-specific changes in labor demand. Once we control for the fixed effects already described, current changes in labor demand have no correlation with the past presence of immigrants, which only affects the supply of labor and skills in that cell.

A first instrument (that we name IV1 throughout the paper) is developed using only information contained in the E.U. Labor Force Survey (EULFS) dataset. This is the main data source used in this study and it includes current data on native and immigrant workers.[8] In this case, we calculate immigrants' distribution across countries of destination and education-age cells for the first available year.[9] The instrument is then obtained by multiplying in each year the initial distribution (as shares of the total) by the total number of foreign-born present in the 15 E.U. countries analyzed in this study. As a consequence, the stock of immigrants imputed with this method depends on the *initial* distribution of immigrants across countries and skill groups, and on the evolution of the *total* number of foreign-born in Europe. The cell- and country-specific evolution of the number of migrants, that might be affected by local economic conditions, do not enter this imputation. For the second instrument (that we name IV2 throughout the paper), we combine EULFS data and external sources. From IPUMS-I (2010) we downloaded micro-data from national Censuses 1990–1991, for seven of the 15 countries included in the EULFS (Austria, France, Greece, Italy,[10] Portugal, Spain, United Kingdom). For that year, we computed the population of immigrants by area of origin (using nine large geographic groups)[11] in each country-education-age cell. We then use the data on aggregate yearly immigration flows from those nine areas of origin into the seven considered E.U. countries, available until 2009 only, and we construct the overall growth rates of each area-of-origin immigrant group.[12] We then multiply the initial (1991) number of immigrants in each country-education-age cell by the overall growth rate of that area-of-origin immigrant group. Finally, we aggregate across areas of origin within each education-age-country cell, in order to calculate the total imputed number of immigrants in the cell. This number is divided by the total (initial natives plus imputed migrants) population in the cell to obtain the imputed cell-specific migrants' share. This method implies that the variation in immigrant shares across cells and years is only driven by the initial cell composition of immigrants by area of origin and the variation in inflows in the aggregate area-of-origin groups over time. Suppose a country had a lot of young and highly educated Algerians in 1991, while another had young and less-educated Iranians. As Algerians turned out to increase their emigration rates more than Iranians in the considered period (due

---

8. See Section 4 for a description of the EULFS data.

9. For most countries 1996 is the first available year, see Table A.1 of the Online Appendix for a complete list of countries and years included in the analysis.

10. For Italy we used 2001 data, the first ones providing all necessary information. Nevertheless, for this country EULFS data are available starting with 2005 and not with 1996, so that the shares are still calculated according to the distribution of immigrants taking place four years before the estimation interval starts.

11. The groups of origin of immigrants are: North Africa, Other Africa, North America, Central and South America, Middle East and Central Asia, South and Eastern Asia, Eastern Europe, Western Europe, Oceania.

12. Data are described in detail in Ortega and Peri (2011); they were collected from several sources (OECD, UN) and report the total inflow of migrants from any country into OECD.

to push factors in the place of origin), the first country would obtain a larger group of educated young immigrants as of 2009 relative to the second. The advantage of the second instrument is that it uses 1991 as initial year, it employs the larger census sample and exploits the region of origin of immigrants. The disadvantage is that it does not cover all countries of the EULFS.

Both instruments turn out to be fairly strong and their first-stage statistics are reported in Table A.5. In particular, the first-stage coefficients always have the correct sign and the F-test for their exclusion is never below 23 for IV1 and 17 for IV2. Such strong correlation is a sign that the initial distribution across country-age-education cells combined with the subsequent total flows of foreign-born is a strong predictor of the increase in immigrants in a cell, consistently with the idea that the network of previous immigrants reduces costs of settling and finding a job for new immigrants.

Finally, as a check that positive labor demand shocks were not responsible for the positive correlation between immigration and native specialization changes, we test in Section 8 whether our results hold during the years of economic downturn starting with the onset of the GR (2007–2010). In that period, while the foreign-born's share in working age population continued to grow, labor demand fell dramatically.[13] If the estimated change in specialization of natives was due to labor demand (rather than to immigrants) we should observe a change in the sign of such estimates during this period.

3.2. Empirical Implementation

We analyze four alternative specifications for our main regressions. In the first two we estimate equation (10) using OLS and IV1, respectively, for all 15 countries included in the analysis. In the third and the fourth specification, we estimate the same equation by OLS and 2SLS restricting the sample to the seven countries for the years 1996–2009, due to the data limitation in the construction of the IV2 instrument. The main specifications are estimated with two sets of fixed effects (country by year and education by age by year), while standard errors are clustered alternatively at the country-skill (first entry) or at the country-year (second entry) level throughout the paper.[14]

Our empirical analysis consists of five parts. After a brief introduction of the data in Section 4, we begin by analyzing the impact of immigration on natives' relative skills based on equation (10) in Section 3. In the same section we also test whether immigration affects natives' employment rates. In the second part (Section 6), we investigate the labor market flows behind the potential task adjustment in response to

---

13.   Foreign-born's share over total working age population averaged 13.0% during the 2007–2010 period, 2.2 points higher than in the preceding four-year interval according to EULFS data.

14.   We performed estimates including other sets of fixed effects and clustering errors at alternative cell groups (country by age or country by education). The results are very similar to those reported and available upon request. Only when estimating very saturated models with country by education by age and country by time fixed effects (together explaining 97% of the variance of the main dependent variable in equation (10)) we find a nonsignificant effect of migration on native jobs relative complexity.

immigrant inflows. In particular, we inquire whether native workers' labor reallocation takes place through systematic changes in the hiring or separation margin.

In the third part (Section 7), we test whether country-level labor market policies, in particular employment protection laws, affected the native occupational reallocation in response to immigrants. The process we envision is a dynamic shift of native workers across occupations. Thus, the ease of transition between jobs within a particular country is potentially a crucial component in determining the strength of this channel. In Section 8 we check whether the impact of migration on the European labor market changed during the GR: the short-run effects of migration could be less favorable, or more adverse, during an economic downturn. Finally, we estimate the elasticities of individual wages to changes in the relative skill content of a job using European harmonized household survey data (EU-SILC) and we use them to calculate the impact of immigrants on native wages operating through the described reallocation towards jobs requiring more complex skills.

4. Data and Descriptive Statistics

The main dataset we use is the harmonized European Union Labour Force Survey (EULFS), which homogenizes country-specific labor force surveys at the European level (see EUROSTAT 2009). We restrict our analysis to the 1996–2010 period (before 1996 data on the place of birth of individuals are absent for most countries in the survey) and we consider the working age population (age 15–64) of Western European countries only.[15] The data include information on the occupation, working status, and demographic characteristics of the individuals. Unluckily, the EULFS does not include any information on wage levels. In 16 out of 225 (15 countries × 15 years) country-year cells one or more of the variables fundamental for our analysis[16] was completely missing and we had to drop it.[17]

In line with the previous literature, we classify as immigrants all individuals born in any country outside the considered one. In Figure A.1 we show the evolution of the share of foreign-born on the aggregate population of the sample countries during the 1996–2010 period analyzed here. In this figure, we pool data from all countries except Ireland, Italy, Luxembourg, and the United Kingdom, for which data are missing for one or more years. The share of foreign-born in the total population almost doubles from below 8% in 1996 to almost 14% in 2010.

In the empirical analysis, for each year between 1996 and 2010, we aggregate the individual data into cells, that we consider as proxies for labor markets. Cells are the

---

15. We include Austria, Belgium, Denmark, Finland, France, Greece, Ireland, Italy, Luxembourg, Netherlands, Norway, Portugal, Spain, Sweden, United Kingdom. We could not include Germany because main variables, including place of birth, were missing for most years.

16. Education, age, or country of birth.

17. See Table A.1 of the Online Appendix for the full list of country/years included in the empirical analysis. The table illustrates missing values as well as the subset of cells included in the IV2 specifications.

intersection of the 15 countries, two educational levels (upper secondary education or less and strictly more than upper secondary education) and five ten-year age-classes covering individuals between 15 and 64.

4.1. Task Variables

To test the key prediction of the model contained in condition (10) , we need indicators of the intensity of skills supplied in each job over time. Following Peri and Sparber (2009) and considering occupations as capturing the different types of jobs performed, we use the O^*NET data from the US Department of Labor (version 11, available at http://www.onetcenter.org/). This survey, started in 2000 (when it replaced the Dictionary of Occupational Titles, *DOT*), assigns values summarizing the importance of several different abilities to each of 339 Occupations (according to the Standard Occupation Classification, SOC). We use 78 of these tasks to construct our measures of skill-intensity for each occupation. As the scale of measurement for the task variables is arbitrary, we convert the values into the percentile of the task intensity in the 2000 distribution of occupations. We create five ability indicators: *communication, complex, mental, manual, and routine*. For example, skills used to construct the *communication* category include, among others, *oral comprehension, oral communication*, and *speech clarity*; *manual dexterity* and *reaction time* are among the skills used to construct the manual category; and so on. Table A.2 of the Online Appendix includes the full list of the skill/task measures employed to construct each of the indicators. We aggregate these categories into broad groups: *complex* and *simple*; the average of *communication, complex*, and *mental* skills constitutes the complex group, while average of *manual* and *routine* forms the simple one.

For each indicator, we merge occupation-specific values to individuals in the 2000 Census using the SOC codes. Then, using the Goos, Manning, and Salomons (2009) crosswalk, we collapse the more detailed SOC codes into 21 two-digit occupations classified according to the International Standard Classification of Occupations (ISCO) which is the classification used by the EULFS. We aggregate the scores (between 0 and 1) for each of the task intensity measures as a weighted average of the SOC occupations into the ISCO one. The weights used are the share of workers for each SOC occupation in the total of the ISCO grouping, according to the 2000 US Census. To give an idea of the indicators, a score of 0.79 in *communication skills* for the ISCO occupation *"corporate managers"* indicates that 79% of all workers in the US in 2000 were using *communication skills* less intensively than corporate managers. Table A.3 of the Online Appendix shows the score for each of the ability indices in the 21 occupations provided by the EULFS. For example, *Drivers and mobile plant operators* is the occupation with the highest *manual ability* intensity, while it is the second to last occupation when considering *complex abilities*. On the other hand, *Corporate managers* are highly ranked for *complex, mental*, and *communication* skills while being relatively less intensive in *manual* and *routine* abilities. Of course our way of quantifying the task intensities associated with each occupation has some drawbacks, mainly coming from the facts that (i) task intensities are measured for the United States and not Europe and (ii) we collapse 339 occupations surveyed by O*NET into the 21 ISCO ones provided by EULFS using as weights the distribution of workers of the 2000 US Census, which might be different from the one relevant for the E.U. countries considered here. These limitations could attenuate the estimated impact, because we can only measure changes in complexity associated with changes in broad occupations. On the other hand, their measurement error should not induce a bias in our results since we expect such an error to be uncorrelated with the share of migrants in the relevant cell[18] conditional on the number of controls we employ in our empirical analysis.

In Table A.4 of the Online Appendix we report simple correlations between each of the ability measures and some dummies that capture specific education- or age-level groups consistent with the cell partition employed in the empirical analysis. Two patterns emerge clearly in the correlations between observable skills and complex/simple tasks. First, there is a strong positive (negative) correlation between the high-education dummy and complex (simple) abilities. The schooling level affects the relative productivity in the two tasks and hence it is very important to control for it. Second, manual and routine abilities are positively correlated with young age dummies, while the opposite is true for more sophisticated skills such as complex, mental, and communication skills. Those skills exhibit a negative correlation with the lowest age level dummy (15–24), turning positive and then reaching a maximum with the age-dummy 35–44 to decrease afterward. Again, controlling for age effects would account for such systematic patterns.

Aggregate European data show patterns consistent with the idea that immigrants and natives specialize in different production tasks and this specialization increased over time. Figure 1, for instance, shows the evolution of the relative intensity of complex versus noncomplex tasks for the average European worker throughout the period 1996–2010, for native and foreign-born workers.[19] While the average native worker (as inferred from their occupational distribution) specialized increasingly in complex production tasks, the average immigrant workers' specialization remained almost unchanged. Such a pattern would be hard to explain as a consequence of a demand shock for tasks. In that case the trend should be common to the two types of workers. The divergent evolution, on the contrary, suggests that there is an increasing specialization, along the lines of comparative advantages, between the two groups. It also implies that recent immigrants have been taking much more manual-intensive jobs than natives, possibly because their schooling is lower or because their countries of origin have not provided them with complex skills. Figure A.2 in the Online Appendix illustrates additional stylized evidence supporting the main result of the

---

18.   The fact that the skill measures for an occupation are taken from the United States makes the presence of immigrants in Europe even less likely to contaminate it.

19.   Relative intensity of complex versus noncomplex tasks is the ratio of the two intensities, where the former is equal to the average intensity in complex, mental and communication tasks, while the latter is the average intensity in manual and routine tasks.

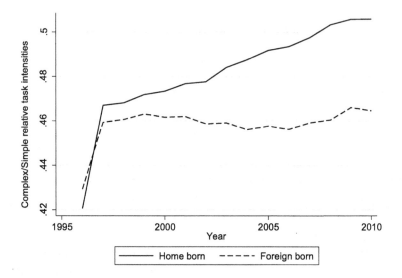

FIGURE 1. Relative complex/simple tasks, natives and foreign-born in Europe. Authors' calculations on EULFS data. Countries for which one or more years of data are missing (Ireland, Italy, Luxembourg, and the United Kingdom) are not included.

model in Section 2. It shows the correlation between the relative complex/noncomplex task specialization of *native workers* across labor markets (cells of age-education groups across EU countries) and the share of immigrants in those cells. The picture shows a positive and significant correlation between the share of immigrants and the specialization of natives in complex tasks. According to an OLS regression, an increase in the share of immigrants by 10% of the total population in the same labor market is associated with an increase of 4 percentage points in relative complex/noncomplex task intensity. This coefficient is significant at the 1% level with a standard error of 0.137.

5. Immigrants and Native Specialization

In this section we estimate the empirical implementation of the equilibrium derived in Section 2 (equation (10)). The coefficient of interest is γ, capturing the impact of the share of immigrants on natives' *relative* task supply, defined as the ratio between the average of complex skills (abstract, complex, and communication) and the average of noncomplex skills (manual and routine). In the first row of Table 1, we show a set of estimates for the average elasticity (variables are defined in logs), obtained introducing the most demanding specification including country by time and time by

TABLE 1. The effects of immigrants on relative task performance of natives.

Estimates	1 OLS	2 IV1	3 OLS2	4 IV2	5 IV1	6 IV2
Panel A $\ln(f_{j,c,t})$	0.058	0.06	0.069	0.074	0.104	0.076
	[0.018]***	[0.021]***	[0.022]***	[0.036]**	[0.011]***	[0.005]***
	[0.008]***	[0.007]***	[0.010]***	[0.016]***		
Panel B $\ln(f_{j,c,t})$ * Young	0.033	0.024	0.041	0.045		
	[0.022]	[0.056]	[0.028]	[0.096]		
	[0.012]***	[0.020]	[0.018]**	[0.054]		
$\ln(f_{j,c,t})$ * Old	0.062	0.06	0.074	0.074		
	[0.018]***	[0.022]***	[0.022]***	[0.035]**		
	[0.008]***	[0.008]***	[0.010]***	[0.015]***		
Panel C $\ln(f_{j,c,t})$ * Low edu	0.065	0.065	0.071	0.064		
	[0.017]***	[0.020]***	[0.022]***	[0.037]*		
	[0.008]***	[0.007]***	[0.010]***	[0.017]***		
$\ln(f_{j,c,t})$ * High edu	-0.002	-0.022	0.03	-0.012		
	[0.024]	[0.039]	[0.043]	[0.065]		
	[0.012]	[0.021]	[0.021]	[0.042]		
Observations	2,106	2,094	840	840	205	84
Controls:						
Year by country	Yes	Yes	Yes	Yes		
Year by age by education	Yes	Yes	Yes	Yes	Yes	Yes
Country and year					Yes	Yes

Notes: Dependent variable: log of relative skill intensity in the education-age cell. Units of observations are eight education-by-age cells in 15 E.U. countries in each year 1996–2010 (columns 1–4) and country/year cells (columns 5 and 6). The dependent variable is the logarithm of the relative task intensity (equation (10)). The main explanatory variable (row 1) is the log of the share of immigrants in the cell. In rows 2 and 3 it is interacted with Young/Old dummies, in rows 4 and 5 it is interacted with High/Low-education dummies. In square brackets we report the heteroskedasticity robust standard errors clustered respectively at the country-education-age level (first entry) or at the country-year level (second entry). Standard errors are not clustered in columns 5 and 6. OLS2 estimates are OLS estimates on the sample for which it was possible to compute the IV2 estimates. See Section 3.1 for details on the shift share instruments IV1 and IV2; first-stage statistics are reported in Table A.5 of the Online Appendix.
*** Significant at 1%; ** significant at 5%; * significant at 10%.

age by education fixed effects.[20] We adopt four different specifications (columns 1–4): OLS and IV1 on the whole sample, OLS and IV2 on the sub-sample for which IV2 is available. Point estimates range between 0.058 and 0.074; the estimates are strongly significant, both when clustering standard errors at the country-skill level (reported in the top brackets) and at the country-year level (reported in the bottom brackets). Native workers increase their supply of complex skills that are complementary to the manual-routine skills supplied by immigrants. As an additional test of the robustness of our results, we re-estimate (columns 5 and 6) equation (10) collapsing data into country-year cells and controlling for country and year fixed effects. This specification assumes that all workers in a country, independently of their education and age, compete within the same labor market and all that matters is the relative content of complex/noncomplex skills. We obtain a positive and strongly significant estimate for our parameter of interest, with our preferred 2SLS estimate for γ actually increasing to 0.10. This may imply that there is some actual complementarity across cells and that accounting for it further increases the response of natives to immigrants. As a final robustness check, we rerun all the specifications in levels instead of logarithms. Those estimates (not reported) confirm once again a positive and significant value for γ.[21]

In the following rows of Table 1 we move beyond average effects. We interact the main explanatory variable alternatively with age and education dummies. This allows us to estimate a different native response to immigration, depending on age and education levels. Estimates for γ are equal to 0.04 and 0.07 respectively for young and old workers, being nonsignificant for the former in most cases. When considering native workers differing in their educational level, we generally find higher elasticities for workers with low education. Let us emphasize that the task response of natives to immigration was first documented by Peri and Sparber (2009) for US workers. In that case the authors only considered less-educated workers and used an IV method. The coefficient they obtained should be compared with the one estimated in the fourth row, column 2 of Table 1. Interestingly, while the estimate is positive and significant in both cases, the magnitude of Peri and Sparber's (2009) coefficient (in the range of 0.30–0.35) is much larger than the one estimated in this paper (in the range of 0.06 to 0.07). Namely, the coefficient estimated using immigration across US states is 5 to 6 times larger than the one estimated using immigration across European Countries. The reason for such a difference can be the large differential in employment protection laws preventing the same amount of occupational mobility and adjustment in Europe. We will use cross-European differences in labor market institutions to emphasize this point in Section 7. Overall, the main result of this section is that, employing a number of specifications, differing in the estimating sample, the econometric technique and the controls included we find significant empirical support for the idea that an increase of the immigrants' share on the population pushes native workers to move to occupations requiring a relatively higher level of complexity.

---

20.   Results obtained with a less saturated specification including education by year, country by year and country by education controls are reported in Table A.6 of the Online Appendix.

21.   For brevity, we do not report these estimates in Table 1, but they are available upon request.

Does this positive reallocation take place at the expense of the total number of jobs available for natives? Namely, do immigrants only encourage specialization of natives or also crowd them out? The employment effects of immigration are relevant in themselves; furthermore, an increase in relative skill complexity in equation (10) could be driven by the destruction of "simple" jobs for a given number of "complex" ones. In that case, the set of workers losing their "simple" job (without getting a more "complex" one instead) would certainly suffer from immigration. To the contrary, if the increase in relative skill complexity takes place due to a genuine transition of natives from "simple" to "complex" jobs, the group of native workers could be collectively better off through this reallocation.

Considering different education-age skill cells in European countries as separate labor markets, we estimate the following equation:

$$\ln \left(\frac{empl_{j,c,t}}{pop_{j,c,t}} \right) = \delta \ln(f_{j,c,t}) + Controls + e_{j,c,t}, \qquad (11)$$

where $(empl_{j,c,t}/pop_{j,c,t})$ is the employment-population ratio *for natives* and $\ln(f_{j,c,t})$ is the logarithm of the share of foreign-born in the population of the education-age group j, in country c in year t; $e_{j,c,t}$ is an idiosyncratic random shock. Also in this case, we estimate four different OLS and 2SLS specifications including the same sets of fixed effects as in Table 1 (age by education by year, country by year).[22] Table 2 reports the estimates of the coefficient δ for different specifications of equation (11). We find no negative impact of immigration on employment rates. Usually we obtain estimates not significantly different from 0. Sometimes, when clustering standard errors at the country-year level, we find small but positive effects. When we collapse data at the country/year level and control for country and year fixed effects, we find a positive and significant estimate equal to 0.11. Looking at the other rows of Table 2 we find no negative impact of migration on employment rates also when differentiating among young/old workers and low/high educated ones.

What is relevant for our analysis is that the positive job reallocation described before did not take place together with a *decrease* in native workers' employment rates associated with immigration. Consistently with the literature for the United States (Card 2009; Peri and Sparber 2009), we find no detrimental impact of immigrants on native employment. Our results point to a null impact of immigration on natives' employment, and seem to rule out the possibility of negative employment effects of immigration.

6. Impact on Labor Market Flows

Our model is static and provides predictions on the task supply and on the employment of a representative agent. In this section we go beyond it. It is interesting and feasible

---

22. Results obtained with less saturated model including only country by education, country by year and education by year effects are reported in Table A.7 of the Online Appendix.

TABLE 2. The effect of immigrants on native employment.

Estimates	1 OLS	2 IV1	3 OLS2	4 IV2	5 IV1	6 IV2
Panel A $\ln(f_{j,c,t})$	0.015	0.044	0.028	0.096	0.11	0.134
	[0.078]	[0.099]	[0.095]	[0.156]	[0.018]***	[0.017]***
	[0.013]	[0.018]***	[0.015]*	[0.031]***		
Panel B $\ln(f_{j,c,t})$ * Young	0.134	0.341	0.153	0.181		
	[0.080]*	[0.208]	[0.089]*	[0.347]		
	[0.026]***	[0.071]***	[0.033]***	[0.102]*		
$\ln(f_{j,c,t})$ * Old	0.001	0.045	0.007	0.095		
	[0.078]	[0.098]	[0.097]	[0.154]		
	[0.015]	[0.023]*	[0.018]	[0.031]***		
Panel C $\ln(f_{j,c,t})$ * Low edu	0.017	0.047	0.031	0.081		
	[0.080]	[0.100]	[0.097]	[0.157]		
	[0.013]	[0.018]***	[0.016]*	[0.032]**		
$\ln(f_{j,c,t})$ * High edu	0.003	0.001	-0.025	-0.039		
	[0.073]	[0.110]	[0.105]	[0.219]		
	[0.015]	[0.031]	[0.024]	[0.065]		
Observations	2,106	2,094	840	840	205	84
Controls:						
Year by country	Yes	Yes	Yes	Yes		
Year by age by education	Yes	Yes	Yes	Yes		
Country and year					Yes	Yes

Notes: Dependent variable: log (employment rate) in the edu-age cell. Units of observations are eight education-by-age cells in 15 E.U. countries in each year (columns 1–4) and country/year cells (columns 5 and 6).
The dependent variable is the logarithm of Employment/Population for the native population in the cell (equation (10)). The main explanatory variable (row 1) is the log of the share of immigrants in the cell. In rows 2 and 3 it is interacted with Young/Old dummies, in rows 4 and 5 it is interacted with High/Low-education dummies. In squared bracket we report the heteroskedasticity robust standard errors clustered respectively at the country-education-age level (first entry) or at the country-year level (second entry). Standard bracket errors are not clustered in columns 5 and 6. OLS2 estimates are OLS estimates on the sample for which it was possible to compute the IV2 2SLS estimates. See Section 3.1 for details on the shift share instruments IV1 and IV2; first-stage statistics are reported in Table A.5 of the Online Appendix.
*** Significant at 1%; ** significant at 5%; * significant at 10%.

with our data to decompose the effect of immigrants on hiring, separations, and their complexity in producing the aggregate effect. The current economic literature on migration focuses only on the impact of immigration on the employment levels and/or wages of native workers. In this section, however, we depart somewhat from this literature as well as our model. In particular, we try to unveil the channels through which the labor reallocation found in the previous section takes place. The increase in the relative intensity of "complex" occupations of natives could take place through one or more of the following avenues:

  i) Immigration could generate more *hiring*, particularly concentrated in occupations requiring relatively complex skills;

 ii) Immigration could generate more *separations*, particularly in occupations requiring simple skills;

iii) Immigrants could induce more *job to job* transitions from less complex to more complex jobs.

With the dataset at hand, we are able to analyze the impact of immigration on the first two types of flows. This is because each respondent is asked about his/her labor market status and occupation a year before the survey and whether those have changed during the last year (from employed to non-employed or vice versa). This information allows us to define two binary variables, "hiring" and "separations". The "hiring" ("separations") variable is equal to one if the individual was not employed (was employed) in year $t - 1$ and is employed (is not employed) in year t, and zero otherwise. We then compute the hiring (separation) rate for each country-age-education-year cell as the ratio between the total number of hires (separations) and the population within the cell in each year. Moreover, as we know the occupation currently held by the individual (and the one previously held if the worker does not have a current job) we can also compute the average relative complexities of hiring and separations. One caveat to keep in mind is that these flows (and their skill content) are estimated on a relatively small number of individuals (those who change labor market state in a given year). Hence their measurement might be less precise at the country-age-education-year level than the measures of skill intensity used in Table 1. Moreover, the measures of job market transitions proposed here are subject to a certain degree of measurement error, being recovered from recall questions (among others see Poterba and Summers 1986). We estimate the impact of immigration on labor market flows in a set of four equations identical to equation (10), including, respectively, as dependent variables: hiring rates, separation rates, average complexity of hiring and average complexity of separations. As in the previous empirical analysis we estimate these equations both using OLS and IV1 on the 15 countries considered in this study (columns 1 and 2 of Table 3), or on the restricted sample of seven countries for which the shift-share IV2 instrument is available (columns 3 and 4).

An interesting pattern emerges across specifications and it is particularly clear when considering our preferred specification, namely the 2SLS estimation employing the IV2, reported in column 4. The pattern emerging, while not too strong, is as follows:

D'Amuri and Peri   Immigration, Jobs, and Employment Protection   453

TABLE 3. The effect of immigrants on the task intensity of employment flows.

| | 1 | 2 | 3 | 4 |
Estimates	OLS	IV1	OLS2	IV2
Hirings		Hirings rate		
	0.242	0.432	0.196	0.587
	[0.266]	[0.272]	[0.325]	[0.402]
	[0.121]**	[0.124]***	[0.158]	[0.147]***
		Hirings' relative complex/noncomplex skill intensity		
	0.085	0.108	0.088	0.152
	[0.020]***	[0.021]***	[0.025]***	[0.040]***
	[0.009]***	[0.009]***	[0.011]***	[0.018]***
Separations		Separations rate		
	0.028	0.031	0.066	–0.046
	[0.085]	[0.097]	[0.091]	[0.127]
	[0.025]	[0.031]	[0.028]**	[0.038]
		Separations' relative complex/noncomplex skill intensity		
	0.064	0.068	0.069	0.102
	[0.017]***	[0.020]***	[0.020]***	[0.029]***
	[0.008]***	[0.010]***	[0.009]***	[0.017]***
Observations	1,986	1,974	840	840
Controls:				
Country by education	Yes	Yes	Yes	Yes
Education by year	Yes	Yes	Yes	Yes
Country by year	Yes	Yes	Yes	Yes

Notes: Units of observations are eight education-by-age cells in 15 E.U. countries in each year, 1996–2010. Each coefficient in the table is estimated in a separate regression. The main explanatory variable is the log of the share of immigrants in the cell. In squared brackets we report the heteroskedasticity robust standard errors clustered respectively at the country-education-age level (first entry) or at the country-year level (second entry). OLS2 estimates are OLS estimates on the sample for which it was possible to compute the IV2 2SLS estimates. See Section 3.1 for details on the shift share instruments IV1 and IV2; first-stage statistics are reported in Table A.5 of the Online Appendix.
***Significant at 1%; **significant at 5%.

an increase in immigration alters the *quantity* and the *quality* of the transitions into and out of employment. In our 2SLS specification, we find a positive, but usually not very significant impact of foreign-born inflows in stimulating hiring and no impact at all on separation rates, as previously defined. Specifically, in our preferred estimate, an increase of immigrants by 1% of their share increases the hiring rate of native workers by 0.43%, significant when we cluster at the country/year level, while it has no impact at all on the separation rates for natives. Hence, in net, there is some evidence that immigration encourages new hires of natives. This effect is compatible with the positive (and only sometimes significant) effect of immigration on employment, shown in Table 2. At the same time, for a given size of the flows (into and out of employment) an increase in the number of immigrants within a cell is associated with an increase in the average relative complexity of jobs offered to new hires. The estimate for this elasticity is equal to 0.15 (significant at 1%) in our preferred 2SLS estimate based on IV2. When considering the separation margin, the effect of immigrants on the relative complexity of separations also has a positive sign. However, the elasticity estimates are 30% to 50% smaller compared to hiring (the elasticity is equal to 0.10 in the preferred estimates using IV2). These results, although somewhat sensitive to the specification used, are consistent with the overall labor reallocation process described in the previous section. Labor market flows into and out of employment are not very significantly affected by immigration. Instead, a substantial skill upgrading is obtained because the relative complexity of the new hires increases with immigration while the relative complexity of separations is less affected by immigration. Moreover, there could be a substantial degree of skill upgrading in job-to-job transition that we cannot observe in our data.

7. Differences Across Labor Market Institutions

Could the positive reallocation of natives towards more complex jobs be slowed by rigid labor markets and sluggish transitions? Labor markets with strong employment protection may reduce mobility in and out of employment, they may also keep workers within the boundaries of narrowly defined occupations (via collective contracts). Hence, labor market institutions can affect the occupational mobility margin of natives in response to immigrants. More flexible labor markets could facilitate immigrants' absorption, facilitating job upgrading and job creation, and thereby easing productive reallocation of natives (Angrist and Kugler 2003). As in any cross-country comparison, our results could be driven by the presence of confounders (such as the efficiency of the judiciary or the strictness of product market regulation); it is hard to disentangle their effects from the effect of labor market institutions, especially with a limited number of countries as in our sample. Nevertheless, after controlling for time-varying country level differences with country by time fixed effects, we expect labor market institutions in each country to be the main determinant of natives' labor dynamics associated with migration.

To check for this possibility, we re-estimate equation (10) interacting the main explanatory variable $\ln(f)$, the logarithm of the share of immigrants in the cell population, with two country-level indicators of the EPL. We construct a dummy (that we interact with $\ln(f)$) capturing whether the country has a high or low level of EPL. As a first measure of EPL we use an aggregate OECD indicator summarizing EPL in the 1990s based on averages of specific scores that classify countries along the following dimensions: (i) strictness of employment protection for regular employment, (ii) norms concerning temporary employment, and (iii) rules on collective dismissals.[23] We also consider an alternative measure of EPL based on an ad hoc employer survey conducted by the European Commission in 1989 (European Commission 1991). This last indicator is based on the share of employers stating that restrictions on hiring and firing were very important when surveyed. The two different indicators provide a robustness check for the results to the type of EPL index used and also to the countries included in the comparative analysis, since such indices are not available for some of

---

23. OECD (1999), for details see pp. 64–68.

the countries included in this study.[24] For each indicator, we define a country as a "high EPL" one when its strictness in the labor laws is higher than the weighted median of the countries included in the EPL ranking (see Table A.1, last two columns, for a list of countries by EPL levels). Similarly, "low EPL" corresponds to a value of the strictness index below the weighted median. We show the results of OLS and 2SLS estimation based on the IV1 instrument. We do not consider the IV2 instrument, since this would restrict the analysis to seven countries only, leaving little variability by EPL level.

In Table 4 we report the estimates of EPL-specific γ, finding two patterns. First, the positive reallocation of natives toward "complex" tasks is stronger in countries with low levels of EPL. In the preferred 2SLS estimates, using alternatively the EC89 index and the OECD aggregate one, we find that low EPL countries show coefficient estimates between 0.055 and 0.085 (always significant at the 1% confidence level), with these values increasing when using OLS. Again considering 2SLS estimates, the estimated coefficients are smaller (ranging between 0.019 and 0.047) for high EPL countries.[25] The difference in γ for high- and low-EPL countries is always significant at 1% when using the EC index, while it is not significant using the OECD one.

We also analyze whether the difference in the response due to the degree of employment protection across countries varies across skill groups defined alternatively by age or education. When interacting $\ln(f_s)$ with two age-specific dummies, we find patterns similar to the ones found at the aggregate level: estimated elasticities are greater for low EPL countries than for high EPL ones, both when considering young and old workers. According to our preferred 2SLS estimates, in countries with low EPL young and old workers alike respond to the inflow of immigrants with an elasticity of relocation to "complex" jobs ranging between 0.052 and 0.055. To the contrary, in countries with high EPL that elasticity is never larger than 0.04. Considering workers of different schooling levels it is interesting to note that the change in specialization in response to immigrants is strong in particular for less-educated workers in countries with low EPL. In our preferred 2SLS-IV1 estimate, the response of less-educated workers in flexible labor markets is 0.076% for each 1% increase in immigrants' shares, while in more rigid markets this value is equal to 0.054%. To the contrary, for highly educated workers the point estimates do not show a clear pattern between high- and low-EPL countries. The estimated elasticities for highly educated workers tend to be not different from zero at standard confidence levels both for high and low EPL countries. This is very interesting as it implies that strong employment protection laws hinder the ability of less-educated workers to change occupations in response to immigration. This deprives them of one of the most effective mechanisms to protect their job and wage from immigration.

As an additional check we explore the country-specific pattern of the native occupational response. We use a specification that interacts the log of the share of

---

24. European Commission indicators are not available for Austria, Denmark, Finland, Norway, and Sweden; Luxembourg is absent in OECD indices as well.

25. We also tried to distinguish labor market flows between low- and high-EPL countries following the analysis presented in Section 6, but the results became noisy and hard to interpret.

TABLE 4. The effects of immigrants on relative task performance of natives, by EPL levels.

			1	2	3	4
EPL indicator			OECD	OECD	EC89	EC89
Estimates			OLS	IV1	OLS	IV1
Panel A	$\ln(f_{j,c,t})$	*Low EPL	0.066	0.055	0.096	0.085
			[0.020]***	[0.021]***	[0.022]***	[0.024]***
			[0.005]***	[0.005]***	[0.007]***	[0.008]***
		*High EPL	0.053	0.047	0.028	0.019
			[0.021]**	[0.022]**	[0.010]***	[0.009]**
			[0.009]***	[0.010]***	[0.005]***	[0.005]***
Panel B	$\ln(f_{j,c,t}) *$ Young	*Low EPL	0.065	0.055	0.096	0.084
			[0.018]***	[0.020]***	[0.022]***	[0.024]***
			[0.004]***	[0.004]***	[0.007]***	[0.008]***
		*High EPL	0.049	0.043	0.04	0.034
			[0.024]**	[0.027]	[0.018]**	[0.019]*
			[0.010]***	[0.010]***	[0.007]***	[0.007]***
	$\ln(f_{j,c,t}) *$ Old	*Low EPL	0.062	0.052	0.102	0.09
			[0.017]***	[0.019]***	[0.024]***	[0.026]***
			[0.004]***	[0.005]***	[0.008]***	[0.009]***
		*High EPL	0.051	0.044	0.032	0.027
			[0.022]**	[0.023]*	[0.011]***	[0.012]**
			[0.009]***	[0.010]***	[0.006]***	[0.005]***
Panel C	$\ln(f_{j,c,t}) *$ Low edu	*Low EPL	0.076	0.06	0.109	0.096
			[0.019]***	[0.022]***	[0.022]***	[0.024]***
			[0.008]***	[0.008]***	[0.009]***	[0.010]***
		*High EPL	0.054	0.047	0.029	0.019
			[0.021]**	[0.022]**	[0.010]***	[0.009]**
			[0.009]***	[0.010]***	[0.005]***	[0.004]***
	$\ln(f_{j,c,t}) *$ High edu	*Low EPL	0.022	0.033	0.016	0.021
			[0.031]	[0.038]	[0.037]	[0.041]
			[0.014]	[0.016]**	[0.017]	[0.018]
		*High EPL	0.038	0.027	0.02	0.053
			[0.027]	[0.072]	[0.023]	[0.063]
			[0.010]***	[0.020]	[0.010]**	[0.026]**
Observations			1,947	1,935	1,220	1,220
Controls:						
Country by education			Yes	Yes	Yes	Yes
Education by year			Yes	Yes	Yes	Yes
Country by year			Yes	Yes	Yes	Yes

Notes: Units of observations are eight education-by-age cells in 15 E.U. countries in each year, 1996–2010. Dependent variable: log of relative complex/noncomplex skill intensity. Coefficients in each panel are estimated in a separate regression. The dependent variable is the logarithm of the relative task intensity (equation (10) of Section 3. The main explanatory variable (Panel A) is the log of the share of immigrants in the cell by 2 EPL levels. In Panel B it is further interacted with Young/Old dummies, in Panel C it is further interacted with High/Low-education dummies. In squared bracket we report the heteroskedasticity robust standard errors clustered respectively at the country-education-age level (first entry) or at the country-year level (second entry). OLS2 estimates are OLS estimates on the sample for which it was possible to compute the IV2, 2SLS, estimates. See Section 3.1 for details on the shift share instruments IV1 and IV2; first-stage statistics are reported in Table A.5 of the Online Appendix. Luxembourg is never included in EPL rankings. EC89 does not rank Austria, Denmark, Finland, Norway, and Sweden. See text (Section 7, Table A.1 of the Online Appendix, and OECD (1999, pp. 64–68) for details on the EPL indices.
***Significant at 1%; **significant at 5%; *significant at 10%.

Migration and relative skills

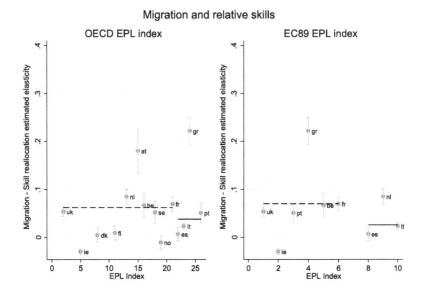

FIGURE 2. Job reallocation intensity, and EPL: Country by country IV1 estimates. Units of observations are eight education-by-age cells in each of the 15 E.U. countries in each year. The figure reports the results of the estimation of country-by-country regressions where the dependent variable is the logarithm of the log of skill intensity and the main explanatory variable is the log of the share of migrants in the cell. The regression includes education-by-year, country-by-education, and country-by-year fixed effects. Each point represents the point value country estimate, while the vertical bars identify 95% confidence intervals. The dashed (solid) horizontal line identifies the weighted average of the estimated γ for low (high) EPL countries. Luxembourg is never included in EPL rankings. EC89 does not rank Austria, Denmark, Finland, Sweden, or Norway. The specification adopted to estimate the skill reallocation elasticity on the y-axis is the one reported in column 2 of Table 1. See Section 3.1 for details on the shift share instrument IV1; first-stage statistics are reported in Table A.5 of the Online Appendix.

migrants in each cell with a full set of country specific dummies. This makes it possible to identify a country-specific coefficient and check whether the main results of this Section are due to the contribution of some outliers or if they follow a regular pattern across countries. In Figure 2 we show two graphs. On the horizontal axis we report the EPL indices (the OECD index in the left panel, and the EC in the right one) and on the vertical axis we report the country-specific estimates for γ together with 95% confidence intervals for those estimates. We also include two horizontal lines identifying the average values for γ estimated for the low- and the high-EPL countries. Due to the low number of observations there is not much precision in the country-by-country estimates but, on average, countries with a higher EPL level tend to have lower γ. We also see from the figure that Greece and Ireland (the country with highest and lowest estimated γ) are two outliers.

As a further robustness check, we rerun the previous regressions in which countries were grouped into high and low EPL levels (Table 4) excluding the countries for which we estimated the highest and the lowest γ (Greece and Ireland, respectively) in the country by country regressions. If anything, main results are reinforced in this case (Table A.9 of the Online Appendix), and once again show that the positive job reallocation of natives is stronger in countries with less-regulated labor markets.

The idea that labor market rigidities interact with shocks to produce inefficient labor market outcomes has been previously proposed in order to explain the high and persistent unemployment in Europe (vis-à-vis America) following the oil shocks of the 1970s (e.g. Blanchard and Justin 2000). We argue that another type of change to the economy, represented by the inflow of immigrants, has less-efficient effects in the presence of strong EPL. Moreover, these results confirm the analysis of Angrist and Kugler (2003), who find that low labor market flexibility can reduce gains from immigration and worsen its employment effects. Our model and explanation provide a reason for this. Countries in which native workers respond less to immigration forgo some of the efficiency gains as well as the positive complementarity effect of immigration. Moreover, less-educated workers, who are more vulnerable to foreigners, being specialized in manual-routine tasks, are those who can potentially gain the most from the positive job reallocation brought about by migration. Stricter EPL, preventing such a reallocation, is thus particularly harmful for them. Peri and Sparber (2009) find an even larger specialization response of natives to the inflow of immigrants that can be due to the very low levels of EPL in the United States.

8. Immigration During the Great Recession

The previous results were obtained using the 15-year interval 1996–2010. It is interesting to check whether the positive impact of immigration on native specialization continued after the onset of the GR that we can date with the collapse of Lehman Brothers in 2007. There are a number of studies on the impact of the GR on European and US labor markets.[26] There is no research, however,[27] analyzing the different impact of new immigrants on the labor markets along the business cycle. In this section we address this issue. We test whether there is evidence that immigrants had different effects on the European labor markets before and during the GR. In principle, the short-run effects of migration could be less favorable, or more adverse, during an economic downturn. At the same time, however, the net inflow of immigrants are reduced during periods of low labor demand and this may attenuate the effects.

Checking whether the job reallocation process outlined above was still at work during the crisis years is not only interesting in itself, but it also provides an additional check for our main results in a period of negative labor demand shocks. During a

---

26. Among others, see respectively Immervoll, Peichl, and Tatsiramos (2011) and Elsby, Hobijn, and Sahin (2010).

27. The policy study (Peri 2011) is the only attempt we know of, considering this issue.

period of low labor demand, in fact, the other determinants of immigration (ethnic networks, family reunification) are relatively stronger and produce a more clearly "supply-driven" change in immigrants. According to EULFS data, the foreign-born share of the working-age population continued to grow during the economic downturn, averaging 13.0% during the 2007–2010 period and hence 2.2 points higher than in the preceding four-year interval.

In our empirical analysis, we modify equation (10), interacting our main explanatory variable with binary variables, the first equal to one during the period before the GR (1996–2006) and zero otherwise, and the other one equal to one in the 2007–2010 period and zero otherwise. Results reported in Panel A of Table 5 show that the positive reallocation process described in the previous sections is at work even during the years of the GR. The parameter estimates for γ, the impact of immigration on skill complexity of native jobs is positive, significant and ranging between 0.038 and 0.05. Nevertheless, the values estimated for the pre-GR period are 50 to 70% higher, ranging between 0.059 and 0.08. In both cases the estimates are precise and statistically significant at the one percent level irrespective of the level adopted for standard errors' clustering. These patterns also emerge when we differentiate further between high- and low-EPL countries in Panel B of Table 5. The estimated values for γ are higher in countries where labor laws are more flexible, in particular during the GR.

In Panels C and D of Table 5, we also test for differential effects of the recession on the different margins of labor market flows. We find evidence that changes in migrants' shares have only a mild and barely significant positive effect on hiring and no effects on separation rates (before and during the GR). In specification 3 we find a slightly larger and barely significant effect of immigration on separation rates during the recession, but not before. However, this result seems weak and not confirmed in other specifications in which immigrants do not have effect on separations before or during the recession. Moreover, an exogenous increase in immigration stimulates the creation of jobs with a higher complexity, the larger is the inflow of immigrants, while the complexity of destroyed jobs relative to the created ones is not as high. This difference in complexity between jobs created and jobs destroyed decreases somewhat during the GR years. Overall, we estimate similar effects before and during the recession, confirming that the occupational upgrading of natives continued even during a period of weak labor demand.

9. Wage Simulations

In order to quantify the effect that the immigration-induced job reallocation has on wages, we first estimate the elasticity of individual wage to the complex/simple skill mix of the job using data from the E.U. Statistics on Income and Living Conditions (EU-SILC). The E.U. labor force data, used in the previous sections, do not contain information on wage levels. The EU-SILC data are gathered through household surveys conducted by E.U. member states and harmonized by EUROSTAT, the official statistical office of the European Union. The dataset is based on individual records,

TABLE 5. Immigrants and jobs, before and during the Great Recession.

Estimates	1 OLS	2 IV1	3 OLS2	4 IV2
Relative skill intensity				
Panel A $\ln(f_j, c, t)$ * Before GR	0.067	0.059	0.072	0.08
	[0.017]***	[0.019]***	[0.020]***	[0.026]***
	[0.008]***	[0.008]***	[0.010]***	[0.014]***
$\ln(f_{j,c,t})$ * GR	0.045	0.038	0.043	0.05
	[0.013]***	[0.012]***	[0.016]**	[0.025]**
	[0.008]***	[0.007]***	[0.012]***	[0.020]**
Panel B $\ln(f_{j,c,t})$ * BeforeGR * Low EPL	0.067	0.06		
	[0.021]***	[0.022]***		
	[0.005]***	[0.006]***		
$\ln(f_{j,c,t})$ * BeforeGR * High EPL	0.066	0.057		
	[0.027]**	[0.029]*		
	[0.015]***	[0.015]***		
$\ln(f_{j,c,t})$ * GR * Low EPL	0.064	0.044		
	[0.019]***	[0.019]**		
	[0.008]***	[0.005]***		
$\ln(f_{j,c,t})$ * GR * High EPL	0.034	0.034		
	[0.014]**	[0.015]**		
	[0.009]***	[0.010]***		
Hirings rate				
Panel C $\ln(f_{j,c,t})$ * Before GR	0.208	0.273	0.188	0.63
	[0.279]	[0.302]	[0.326]	[0.392]
	[0.154]	[0.172]	[0.181]	[0.162]***
$\ln(f_{j,c,t})$ * GR	0.298	0.668	0.218	0.445
	[0.258]	[0.225]***	[0.341]	[0.456]
	[0.188]	[0.144]***	[0.315]	[0.306]
Hirings' relative complex/noncomplex skill intensity				
Panel D $\ln(f_{j,c,t})$ * Before GR	0.092	0.104	0.098	0.16
	[0.023]***	[0.025]***	[0.027]***	[0.039]***
	[0.011]***	[0.012]***	[0.013]***	[0.019]***
$\ln(f_{j,c,t})$ * GR	0.074	0.114	0.063	0.125
	[0.020]***	[0.025]***	[0.024]***	[0.054]**
	[0.014]***	[0.015]***	[0.021]***	[0.048]**
Separations' rate				
Panel E $\ln(f_{j,c,t})$ * Before GR	0.018	0.034	0.038	−0.049
	[0.080]	[0.089]	[0.090]	[0.117]
	[0.025]	[0.032]	[0.027]	[0.039]
$\ln(f_{j,c,t})$ * GR	0.044	0.026	0.145	−0.037
	[0.111]	[0.127]	[0.105]	[0.182]
	[0.051]	[0.059]	[0.070]**	[0.087]
Separations' relative complex/noncomplex skill intensity				
Panel F $\ln(f_{j,c,t})$ * Before GR	0.066	0.074	0.083	0.107
	[0.020]***	[0.024]***	[0.023]***	[0.031]***
	[0.011]***	[0.015]***	[0.013]***	[0.021]***
$\ln(f_{j,c,t})$ * GR	0.061	0.062	0.038	0.088
	[0.020]***	[0.022]***	[0.016]**	[0.036]**
	[0.012]***	[0.012]***	[0.009]***	[0.019]***

(Continued)

TABLE 5. Continued.

Notes: Units of observations are eight education-by-age cells in 15 E.U. countries in each year, 1996–2010. Coefficients in each panel are estimated in a separate regression. The dependent variable is specified in the header. The main explanatory variable is the log of the share of immigrants in the cell interacted with GR/Before GR dummies. The GR (before GR) dummy is equal to one from year 2007 to 2010 (1996 to 2006) and zero otherwise. In Panel B, it is further interacted with High/Low EPL. Heteroskedasticity robust standard errors clustered respectively at the country-education-age level (first entry) or at the country-year level (second entry) are reported in squared brackets. OLS2 estimates are OLS estimates on the sample for which it was possible to compute the IV2 2SLS estimates (see Section 3.1 for details on the shift share instruments; first-stage statistics are reported in Table A.5 of the Online Appendix). Luxembourg is never included in EPL rankings. EC89 does not rank Austria, Denmark, Finland, Norway, and Sweden. See text (Section 7, Table A.1 of the Online Appendix, and OECD (1999, pp. 64–68) for details on the EPL indices.
*** Significant at 1%; ** significant at 5%; * significant at 10%.

being representative of the whole population of the surveyed countries. It provides information on occupational and migration status, as well as on total and labor income together with the main socio-demographic characteristics. The survey has been conducted every year since 2005, but we use only the three waves conducted in 2007, 2008, and 2009 (latest available), since in those years the data provide all the relevant information for each of the 15 countries included in the previous analysis.[28]

To estimate the elasticity of gross individual wages to the relative complexity of the job held we estimate the following wage regression:

$$\ln(wage_{i,t}) = \alpha + \beta * \ln\left(\frac{C_D}{S_D}\right)_{i,t} + d_{edu,c} + d_{edu,t} + d_{c,t} + \varepsilon_{i,t}, \qquad (12)$$

where $\ln(wage_{i,t})$ is the log of gross monthly average wage earned by native worker i in year t, $\ln(C/S)$ is the logarithm of the complex relative to simple skill intensity of her job and $d_{edu,c}$, $d_{edu,t}$, and $d_{c,t}$ are the usual education by country, education by year and country by year fixed effects. Expression (12) can be seen as a Mincerian regression at the individual level in which the return to the complex/simple skills are represented by β. The equilibrium condition in equation (9) determines the optimal $\ln(C_D/S_D)_{i,t}$ for natives which corresponds to an occupation. Hence β measures how the productivity and wage of the native worker will change as $\ln(C_D/S_D)_{i,t}$ changes in response to immigration.

When estimating equation (12) we cluster standard errors at the country-age-education level and alternatively at the country-year level. We estimate a wage/skill elasticity equal to 0.117 (Table 6), significant at the 1% level. This implies that an increase of 10% in the relative complex/simple skill mix of the job is associated with a 1.2% increase in gross monthly wages of natives in the same labor market. As a robustness check, we interact the main explanatory variable with binary dummies for each of the considered years, finding fairly stable estimates ranging between 0.117

---

28. An overview of EU-SILC data, together with national questionnaires, is available at circa.europa.eu/Public/irc/dsis/eusilc/library.

TABLE 6. Relative complex/simple intensity and wages, native workers.

	1 log(C/S)	log(C/S) × year 2007	2 log(C/S) × year 2008	log(C/S) × year 2009
	0.115	0.117	0.11	0.117
	[0.019]***	[0.019]***	[0.019]***	[0.021]***
	[0.009]***	[0.018]***	[0.012]***	[0.014]***
Observations	275,608	275,608		
Controls:				
Country by education	Yes	Yes	Yes	Yes
Education by year	Yes	Yes	Yes	Yes
Country by year	Yes	Yes	Yes	Yes

Notes: Elasticity: log of gross wage versus log of relative skill complexity: 2007–2009. Authors' calculations EU-SILC (2007, 2008 and 2009 waves); includes natives only. Coefficients in each column are estimated in a separate regression. Each regression is weighted with individual cross-sectional weights. The dependent variable is the log of gross monthly wage, the main explanatory variable is the log of the relative skill intensity for the individual (column 1). In column 2, the main explanatory variable is interacted by year. Heteroskedasticity robust standard errors clustered respectively at the country-education-age level (first entry) or at the country-year level (second entry) are reported in squared brackets.
***Significant at 1%.

(year 2007 and 2009) and 0.12 (year 2009), always significant at the 1% level. This effect on native wages is the one due only to the job upgrading estimated in this paper.[29]
Combining results from equation (12) with our favorite estimate of 0.06 for the migration/skill reallocation elasticity (Table 1, row 1, column 2), we can finally simulate the short-run impact of migration on wages, through job transition. We estimate that due to the reallocation of labor towards more complex tasks, triggered by migration, the doubling of the share of foreign-born which took place in the period 1996 to 2010 raised native workers wages by $100\%*0.06*0.12=0.7\%$. This effect is not large. However, (i) it is positive, (ii) it is a lower bound as only changes in broadly defined occupations are captured in the data, (iii) it takes place without any negative employment effect, and (iv) it is realized already in the short run, as our analysis uses yearly data.

10. Conclusions

In the last 15 years, the labor markets of most OECD countries have experienced a secular increase in the number of jobs requiring more abstract and complex skills relative to manual and routine skills. At the same time, Europe has experienced an unprecedented increase in its immigrant population. Most of the economics literature has focused on demand-side factors explaining shifts in task demand: technological change and the effects of off-shoring and trade (Acemoglu and Autor 2010). In this paper we have combined evidence on task changes and on immigration to analyze

---

29.   Immigrants will also have an effect on the return to complex and simple skills. This effect will also benefit natives as they specialize more intensely in complex type of jobs. Quantifying that effect would require the knowledge of wages for natives in each year, which we do not have.

a supply factor, namely the role of immigration, in determining such a change in the occupational structure of natives. Our idea is simple. Immigrants tend to be specialized in occupations requiring mainly noncomplex and routine skills, because their knowledge of local language and norms is lower than natives'. Immigrant inflows, thus, tend to reduce the supply of complex relative to simple skills in a labor market and increase the return to the first type of skills. This creates an incentive for native workers to move to occupations requiring relatively more abstract/complex skills. This intuition is confirmed by the empirical analysis conducted on European Labour Force Survey data. This result withstands a number of robustness checks, carried out using different skill indicators, estimation methods, sample definitions, and, most significantly, it is robust to the use of two sets of reasonable instrumental variables. We also document the labor market flows through which such a positive reallocation took place: immigration stimulated hiring, in jobs with relatively high complexity content. On the contrary, separations were not affected much by immigrants in the cell. We find evidence that this process slowed somewhat, but did not stop, during the economic downturn of 2007–2010. This positive reallocation process was stronger in relatively flexible labor markets, and in those markets it is particularly prominent for less-educated workers. By moving to complex jobs, natives protected their wages from immigrant competition and took advantage of the creation of those jobs that complement the manual tasks provided by immigrants. Letting this mechanism work may benefit less-educated natives, in particular through more hiring in those occupations. Strong protection of labor hurts this mechanism and reduces labor markets' ability to absorb immigrants through occupational upgrading of natives.

References

Acemoglu, A. and David Autor (2010). "Skills, Tasks and Technologies: Implications for Employment and Earnings." In *Handbook of Labor Economics*, edited by O. Ashenfelter and D. E. Card, Elsevier.

Altonji, Joseph G. and David Card (1991). "The Effects of Immigration on the Labor Market Outcomes of Less-skilled Natives." In *Immigration, Trade, and the Labor Market*, edited by J Abowd and R. B. Freeman, The University of Chicago Press.

Angrist, Joshua D. and Adriana D. Kugler (2003). "Protective or Counter-productive? Labour Market Institutions and the Effect of Immigration on EU Natives." *Economic Journal*, 113, F302–F331.

Autor, David H., Frank Levy, and Richard J. Murnane (2003). "The Skill Content Of Recent Technological Change: An Empirical Exploration." *The Quarterly Journal of Economics*, 118, 1279–1333.

Blanchard, Olivier and Wolfers Justin (2000). "The Role of Shocks and Institutions in the Rise of European Unemployment: The Aggregate Evidence." *Economic Journal*, 110, C1–33.

Blinder, Alan S. (2006). "Preparing America's Workforce: Are We Looking in the Rear-View Mirror?" Princeton University Working Paper No. 67.

Borjas, George J. (2003). "The Labor Demand Curve Is Downward Sloping: Reexamining The Impact Of Immigration On The Labor Market." *The Quarterly Journal of Economics*, 118, 1335–1374.

Borjas, George J. and Lawrence F. Katz (2007). "The Evolution of the Mexican-Born Workforce in the United States." In Mexican Immigration to the United States, NBER Chapters, pp. 13–56.

Borjas, George J., Richard B. Freeman, and Lawrence Katz (1996). "Searching for the Effect of Immigration on the Labor Market." *American Economic Review*, 86(2), 246–251.

Card, David (2001). "Immigrant Inflows, Native Outflows, and the Local Market Impacts of Higher Immigration." *Journal of Labor Economics*, 19, 22–64.

Card, David (2009). "Immigration and Inequality." *American Economic Review*, 99(2), 1–21.

Crinò, Rosario (2009). "Service Offshoring and the Skill Composition of Labor Demand." IAE Working Paper No. 802.

Docquier, Frédéric, Çaglar Özden, and Giovanni Peri (2010). "The Wage Effects of Immigration and Emigration." NBER Working Paper No. 16646.

Dustmann, Christian, Tommaso Frattini, and Ian Preston (2013). "The Effect of Immigration along the Distribution of Wages." *Review of Economic Studies*, 80, 145–173.

Elsby, Michael W., Bart Hobijn, and Aysegul Sahin (2010). "The Labor Market in the Great Recession." *Brookings Papers on Economic Activity*, 41, 1–69.

European Commission (1991). "European Economy", March.

EUROSTAT (2009). "EU Labour Force Survey database." *User guide*.

Glitz, Albrecht (2012). "The Labour Market Impact of Immigration: A Quasi-Experiment Exploiting Immigrant Location Rules in Germany." *Journal of Labor Economics, forthcoming*.

Goldin, Claudia and Lawrence F. Katz (2007). "The Race between Education and Technology: The Evolution of U.S. Educational Wage Differentials, 1890 to 2005." NBER Working Paper No. 12984.

González, Libertad and Francesc Ortega (2011). "How Do Very Open Economies Absorb Large Immigration Flows? Recent Evidence from Spanish Regions." *Labour Economics*, 18, 57–70.

Goos, Marteen, Alan Manning, and Anna Salomons (2009). "The Polarization of the European Labor Market." *American Economic Review Papers and Proceedings*, 99, 58–63.

Immervoll, Herwig, Andreas Peichl, and Konstantinos Tatsiramos (2011). "Who Loses in the Downturn? Economic Crisis, Employment and Income Distribution." In Research in Labor Economics, Vol. 32. Emerald Publishing.

IPUMS-I (2010). Integrated Public Use Microdata Series, International: Version 6.0. Minnesota Population Center, University of Minnesota.

Katz, Lawrence and Kevin M. Murphy (1992). "Change in Relative Wages 1963–1987: Supply or Demand Factors." *Quarterly Journal of Economics*, 107, 35–78.

Longhi, Simonetta, Peter Nijkamp, and Jacques Poot (2005). "A Meta-analytic Assessment of the Effect of Immigration on Wages." *Journal of Economic Surveys*, 19, 451–477.

OECD (1999). "Employment Protection and Labour Market Performance." *Employment Outlook—1999*.

Okkerse, Liesbet (2008). "How to Measure Labour Market Effects of Immigration: A Review." *Journal of Economic Surveys*, 22, 1–30.

Ortega, Francesc and Giovanni Peri (2011). "The Aggregate Effects of Trade and Migration: Evidence from OECD Countries." IZA Technical Report No. 5604.

Ottaviano, Gianmarco I. P. and Giovanni Peri (2012). "Rethinking the Effects of Immigration on Wages." *Journal of the European Economic Association*, 10, 152–197.

Peri, Giovanni (2011). "The Impact of Immigrants in Recession and Economic Expansion." Working paper, Migration Policy Institute.

Peri, Giovanni and Chad Sparber (2009). "Task Specialization, Immigration, and Wages." *American Economic Journal: Applied Economics*, 1, 135–169.

Poterba, James M. and Lawrence H. Summers (1986). "Reporting Errors and Labor Market Dynamics." *Econometrica*, 54, 1319–1338.

Supporting Information

Additional Supporting Information may be found in the online version of this article at the publisher's website:

Tables and Figures Online Appendix for IMMIGRATION, JOBS, AND EMPLOYMENT PROTECTION: EVIDENCE FROM EUROPE BEFORE AND DURING THE GREAT RECESSION.

THE LABOUR MARKET EFFECTS OF IMMIGRATION AND EMIGRATION IN OECD COUNTRIES*

Frédéric Docquier, Çağlar Ozden and Giovanni Peri

In this study, we quantify the labour market effects of migration flows in OECD countries during the 1990s based on a new global database on the bilateral stock of migrants, by education level. We simulate various outcomes using an aggregate model of labour markets, parameterised by a range of estimates from the literature. We find that immigration had a positive effect on the wages of less educated natives and it increased or left unchanged the average native wages. Emigration, instead, had a negative effect on the wages of less educated native workers and increased inequality within countries.

Immigration rates in OECD countries are larger than in the rest of the world and have increased significantly in the last 20 years.[1] The common portrayal of this process is a massive flow of uneducated individuals from poor countries who are trying to gain access to the labour markets and welfare systems of rich countries. This view also claims that immigration depresses wages and causes job losses for less educated native workers, a group that has under-performed in the labour markets during the last 20 years.

The available data (Docquier *et al.*, 2012), however, have uncovered different international migration patterns. First, a large portion of the labour movement is from other OECD countries. Foreign-born residents comprised 7.7% of OECD countries' population in 2000 and over half of those were from other OECD countries. Second, the share of college graduates among recent immigrants exceeded the share among natives virtually in all OECD countries.[2] In some cases, the share of college educated among recent immigrants is four to five times as large as their share among non-

---

* Corresponding author: Giovanni Peri, Department of Economics, UC Davis, One Shields Avenue, Davis, CA 95616, USA. Email: gperi@ucdavis.edu.

We thank four anonymous referees and the Editor in charge, for very helpful comments and suggestions. This study was funded by the project 'Brain drain, return migration and south–south migration: impact on labour markets and human capital' supported by the Austrian, German, Korean and Norwegian governments through the Multi-donor Trust Fund on Labour Markets, Job Creation and Economic Growth administered by the World Bank's Social Protection and Labour unit. The first author also acknowledges financial support from the Belgian French-speaking Community (convention ARC 09/14-019). We thank Massimo Anelli, Francesco D'Amuri, Paul Gaggl, Francesc Ortega, Kevin Shih and participants to seminars at Bocconi University, the OECD, the World Bank, Universitat Autonoma de Barcelona, Copenhagen Business School, University of Helsinki and IZA-World Bank conference in Mexico for valuable comments and suggestions. The findings, conclusions and views expressed are entirely those of the authors and should not be attributed to the World Bank, its executive directors or the countries they represent.

[1] According to Freeman (2006), in 2000, about 7.7% of the adult residents in OECD countries were born in another country, *versus* only 2.9% in the average world country. Since then, the number of foreign-born individuals has further increased. In 2009, about 10% of the OECD resident population was estimated to be foreign born (OECD, 2011).

[2] The total stock of immigrants exhibits lower educational attainment than the national labour force in some European countries such as France, Germany, Italy and the Netherlands. On the other hand, the total stock of immigrants, not just recent arrivals, is more educated than the natives in the UK, Spain and Portugal.

migrant natives. These patterns have clear implications for the potential labour market effects of immigration, especially on less educated native workers.

Most importantly, emigration from OECD countries to the rest of the world is routinely missing from the overall picture. Many studies have documented and explained the widespread presence of positive selection patterns in emigration (Docquier and Marfouk, 2006; Grogger and Hanson, 2011). Although positive selection on skills and education is particularly pronounced in the case of poor sending countries, it also characterises emigration from OECD countries. In particular, the emigration rates among college educated exceed the rates among less educated in almost all OECD countries in 2000.[3] Although there are many widely cited studies on the labour market effects of immigration in individual OECD countries, there are only a few articles investigating the effects of emigration.[4] These unbalanced views might lead to various misconceptions on the economic effects of overall migration patterns.

The goal of this study is to assess the impact of both immigration and emigration in the OECD countries in the 1990s on the employment and wage levels of natives who did not migrate. We first document the above migration patterns by using a new comprehensive database that provides bilateral migrant stocks by education level for 195 origin/destination countries for 1990 and 2000. The database is constructed by combining national census data from a large number of destination countries, which provides immigrant stocks from origin countries, complementing these data with imputed values for a small percentage of migrants. The database measures migration stocks for both college-educated and non–college-educated workers between every pair of the 195 countries in the world. We use it to construct net immigration and emigration flows by education level for all OECD countries in the 1990s. This is a substantial improvement over existing bilateral migration databases (Docquier and Marfouk, 2006; Docquier *et al.*, 2009), especially in the construction of emigration and net migration data numbers for OECD countries because we now have data for twice the number of destination countries. This study is the first to use this global data set to analyse labour market implications of migration.

Using these data and aggregate models of the national labour markets, we simulate the employment and wage effects of immigration and emigration on non-migrant natives in each OECD country. We use an aggregate production function model, which has become popular in the labour literature analysing the effects of immigration.[5] Macroeconomic studies of growth, productivity and skill premium have also used similar models.[6] This basic framework enables us to derive labour demand by skill group. We add a simple labour supply decision that generates an aggregate supply

---

[3] Emigration rates among the college-educated natives were more than twice as large of those among the less educated in 16 OECD countries. The highest ratios of college/non-college emigration rates were observed in Japan (5.0), Hungary (4.2), Poland (4.2), the Czech Republic (4.1) and the UK (3.3).

[4] The prevalence of the research focus on immigration is due to the absence of comprehensive emigration data and to the fact that countries can influence their immigration rates more easily than their emigration rates.

[5] Recent examples are Borjas (2003), D'Amuri *et al.* (2010), Ottaviano and Peri (2012) and Manacorda *et al.* (2012).

[6] Prominent examples are Acemoglu and Zilibotti (2001), Card and Lemieux (2001), Caselli and Coleman (2006) and Goldin and Katz (2008).

curve for each skill group. Equipped with this model, we calculate the wage and employment effect of migration on native workers.

The existing estimates of the labour market effects of immigration sometimes conflict with each other.[7] Most of the disagreement, however, is based on evidence from the US labour markets and limited to moderate differences on the wage impact of immigration on less educated workers. We take a different approach here and try to capture the extent of the disagreement within the literature by using different estimates of the fundamental parameters of the labour market. In particular, we produce different scenarios using different values for the elasticity of relative demand between college and non-college educated; the elasticity of relative demand between native and immigrant workers; the elasticity of human capital externalities and the elasticity of aggregate labour supply.

Different scenarios in our analysis span what can be interpreted as pessimistic or optimistic views on the labour market effects of migration as they emerged in the literature. Without taking any stand on the current debate, we present the range of resulting effects by varying the relevant parameter values within a reasonable spectrum established in the literature. Moreover, we do not aim to explain the determinants of immigration and emigration flows; we simply focus on the extent of the wage and employment response to these flows. On one hand, our exercise is somewhat limited as it simulates only the effect of migrations operating through the skill complementarity, the labour demand-supply and the human capital externality channels. On the other hand, we are assured that other confounding factors that would co-vary in the data (and affect the empirical estimates) are absent in this exercise. Our exercise captures the difference in wages and employment of natives during the 1990s between the scenario with actual migration flows and a counter-factual scenario with zero migration flows. The difference between the two scenarios is what we refer to as the effect of migration on native wage and employment.

Some general patterns emerge in our analysis, irrespective of the parameter choices. First, in general, immigration had a small positive or no effect on the average wages of non-migrant natives in all the OECD countries over the period 1990–2000. These effects, ranging from 0% to +4%, were usually positively correlated with the immigration rate of the country (the size of immigrant flow relative to the population). Canada, Australia and New Zealand (which implemented immigration policies with education-based preferences) had significant positive wage gains from immigration. In addition, countries which did not explicitly select their immigrants based on education, such as Luxembourg, Malta, Cyprus, the UK and Switzerland, also experienced positive average wage effects between 1% and 3%. Second, immigration had higher beneficial effects on wages of non–college-educated workers in OECD countries. These effects range between 0% and +6%. For some countries, such as Ireland, Canada, Australia, the UK and Switzerland, the effects are in the 2–4% range. Only Austria, Denmark, Italy, Japan and Greece show estimated effects on the wages of less educated (in the most pessimistic scenarios) that are close to 0. A corollary of this result is that immigration reduced the wage differential between more and less

[7] The estimates in Card (2001, 2009) and Borjas (2003) are considered as spanning the range between the more pessimistic and more optimistic views of the labour market effects of immigration.

2014]   LABOUR EFFECTS OF IMMIGRATION AND EMIGRATION   1109

educated natives. Third, emigration, to the contrary, had a negative and significant effect on the wages of less educated natives ranging between 0% and −7%. In countries like Cyprus, Ireland and New Zealand, less educated workers suffered a wage decline between 3% and 6% due to emigration of the highly skilled. Even in Portugal, the UK, South Korea, Latvia and Slovenia, the less educated suffered losses between 1% and 2% because of emigration.

All these results logically proceed from the nature of measured migrant flows. During the decade 1990–2000, OECD countries have experienced both immigration and emigration flows of workers who were more 'tertiary–education-intensive' than the corresponding non-migrant native labour force. Under these conditions, immigration was associated with average wage gains for less educated workers. Emigration, to the contrary, induces average wage losses for the same group of non-migrants.

The educational composition of migrants is crucial in determining our relative and average wage results, and thus we attempt to correct for the 'effective' skill content of immigrants in a series of checks. First, we use estimates of the extent of illegal immigration (from recent studies performed in several European countries) to correct for the inflows of low-skilled migrants as undocumented immigrants tend to be less educated. Second, we account for the potential 'downgrading' of immigrants' skills in the host countries' labour market, by using data on their occupational choices as of 2000. Third, we consider the full range of parameter estimates, including the standard error of those estimates. All these corrections reduce the share of 'effective' highly educated among all immigrants in OECD countries. However, those corrections do not reverse the general picture described above. Finally, we repeat the exercises for a subset of countries for which we have provisional net immigration data for the period 2000–7. These include some European countries that received large immigration flows (including Luxembourg, Spain and Greece) and the US. The data are from the EU Labour Force Survey and the American Community Survey respectively. They are based on smaller samples relative to the censuses and, hence, are subject to larger measurement errors. Even in this case, we find that the wage effects of the more recent immigration flows on less educated natives are above zero for all countries. For Luxembourg, the biggest recipient of immigrants in this period, the effects are as large as +6% for less educated. For Spain, usually considered as the country most affected by immigrants in the 2000s, the wage effect on less educated natives range between 0% and +2%.

The rest of the article is organised as follows. Section 1 presents the simple aggregate production and labour supply framework from which we derive wages and employment effects of exogenous immigration and emigration shocks. Section 2 describes the main sources and construction of our data set and provides simple summary statistics about the labour force and migrant data and their educational composition. Section 3 presents the basic results of the simulated wage effects of immigration and emigration using our model and the range of parameters available from the literature. Section 4 considers the wage effect of immigration when accounting for undocumented workers, for the downgrading of skills and using the preliminary data on net immigration in the 2000s. Section 5 concludes.

1. Model

We construct a simple aggregate model of an economy where the workers are differentiated by their place of birth (native *versus* foreign born) as well as their education (skill) levels.[8] This structure allows us to examine the wage and employment effects of immigration of foreign workers into the country and emigration of native workers to other countries. These movements change the relative composition of workers of different education levels in a country. The model shows that the main effects of migration patterns on employment and wages of non-migrant natives depend crucially on the size and educational composition of immigrants and emigrants relative to non-migrants, as well as on the parameters of the model.

1.1. *Aggregate Production Function*

The prevalent models in the literature (Borjas, 2003; Card, 2009; Ottaviano and Peri, 2012) are based on a production function where the labour aggregate is a nested constant elasticity of substitution (CES) aggregation of different types of workers. We assume that output (homogeneous, perfectly tradable and denoted by y) is produced with a constant-returns-to-scale production function f with two factors, physical capital (k) and a composite labour input (q):[9]

$$y = \tilde{A}f(k, q). \tag{1}$$

The term $\tilde{A}$ is the total factor productivity (TFP) parameter. Assuming that physical capital is internationally mobile (its supply is perfectly elastic) and that each single country is too small to affect global capital markets, returns to physical capital are equalised across countries. If R^* denotes the global net rate of return to capital, we can impose that marginal productivity of capital is equal to R^* and solve for the equilibrium k/q ratio.[10] Using the constant-return-to-scale property of the production function and substituting the equilibrium k/q ratio into (1), we obtain an expression of aggregate output as a linear function of the aggregate composite labour q:

$$y = Aq. \tag{2}$$

In this expression, we have $A \equiv \tilde{A}f[\tilde{f}'^{-1}(R^*/\tilde{A})]$, which depends on TFP and on the returns to capital. The function $\tilde{f}(k/q)$ in the expression is equal to $f(k/q,1)$. Expression (2) can be interpreted as the reduced long-run version of a production function with elastic capital.

Many articles in the labour (Katz and Murphy, 1992; Acemoglu and Zilibotti, 2001; Card and Lemieux, 2001; Card, 2009) and growth (Caselli and Coleman, 2006) literature assume that labour in efficiency units, denoted as q below, is a nested CES function of highly educated (q_h) and less educated workers (q_l):

---

[8] In this study, the terms high-skilled (low skilled) and highly educated (less educated) are used interchangeably. Tertiary education is the level defining high skills.

[9] All variables are relative to a specific country c and year t. We omit subscripts for compactness of notation.

[10] The condition above holds both in the short and the long run in a small open economy. In a closed economy, as in Ramsey (1928) or Solow (1956), Condition (2) holds on the long-run balanced growth path. R^* would be a function of the inter-temporal discount rate of individuals (or of the savings rate).

$$q = \left[\theta_q q_h^{\frac{\sigma_q-1}{\sigma_q}} + (1 - \theta_q) q_l^{\frac{\sigma_q-1}{\sigma_q}} \right]^{\frac{\sigma_q}{\sigma_q-1}}, \tag{3}$$

where θ_q and $1 - \theta_q$ are the productivity levels of highly educated workers (tertiary education or above) and less educated workers (less than tertiary education). The parameter σ_q is the elasticity of substitution between these two types of workers. This representation implies two types of simplifications. First, as there are more than two levels of schooling, we assume that the relevant split in terms of production abilities is between college and non-college-educated workers. This is consistent with Goldin and Katz (2008), Card (2009) and Ottaviano and Peri (2012) who find high substitutability between workers with no schooling and high school degree, but small substitutability between those and workers with college education. Second, we omit the further classification into age groups, considered as imperfectly substitutable skills (as in Borjas, 2003; Ottaviano and Peri, 2012). The simple reason is that we do not empirically observe the age distribution of migrants for all countries. This omission (as shown in Ottaviano and Peri, 2012) is not very relevant in predicting the wage effects on natives of different education groups, which is our goal in this study.

We distinguish between natives and immigrants within each education-specific labour aggregate, q_h and q_l. If native and immigrant workers of education level $i = (h, l)$ were perfectly substitutable, the economy-wide aggregate q_i would simply be equal to the sum of the native and immigrant labour supplies. However, native and immigrant workers with similar education levels may differ in several respects. First, immigrants have skills and preferences that may set them apart from natives. Second, in manual and intellectual work, they may have country-specific skills and limitations, such as inadequate knowledge of the language or culture of the host country. Third, immigrants tend to concentrate in sectors or occupations different from those mostly chosen by natives because of diaspora networks, information constraints and historical accidents (Beine *et al.*, 2011). In particular, new immigrants tend to cluster disproportionately in those sectors or occupations where previous migrant cohorts are already over-represented. Several articles (Card, 2009; D'Amuri *et al.*, 2010; Ottaviano and Peri, 2012; Manacorda *et al.*, 2012) find imperfect degrees of substitution between natives and immigrants. Hence, we assume that both highly educated (q_h) and less educated labour aggregates (q_l) are both nested CES functions of native and immigrant labour stocks with the respective education levels. This is represented as:

$$q_i = \left[\theta_n q_{i,n}^{\frac{\sigma_m-1}{\sigma_m}} + (1 - \theta_n) q_{i,f}^{\frac{\sigma_m-1}{\sigma_m}} \right]^{\frac{\sigma_m}{\sigma_m-1}} \quad \text{where } i = h, l, \tag{4}$$

where $q_{i,n}$ is the number of type-i native workers, $q_{i,f}$ is the number of type-i immigrant workers and σ_m is the elasticity of substitution between natives and immigrant workers. Finally, θ_n and $1 - \theta_n$ are the relative productivity levels of native and immigrant workers respectively.

1.2. *Schooling Externalities*

As physical capital is perfectly mobile across nations, the average wage effect of immigration on natives could not be negative in a standard model. When the educational composition of the immigrant population differs from that of the native population, natives benefit from a small immigration surplus. However, this is not true if the labour supply of natives is endogenous (see subsection 2.4) or if immigration affects the TFP. Both channels are at work in our model. We introduce the possibility of externalities from highly skilled workers in the same spirit as several recent articles (Acemoglu and Angrist, 2001; Moretti, 2004a, b; Ciccone and Peri, 2006; Iranzo and Peri, 2009). There is a large body of literature[11] that emphasises the role of human capital on technological progress, innovation and growth of GDP per capita. The main implication is that TFP could be an increasing function of the schooling level in the labour force. Following Moretti (2004a, b), we express the TFP of a country as follows:

$$A = A_0 e^{\lambda f_h}, \tag{5}$$

where A_0 captures the part of TFP that is independent of the human capital externality; $f_h \equiv (Q_{h,n} + Q_{h,f})/(Q_{h,n} + Q_{h,f} + Q_{l,n} + Q_{l,f})$ is the fraction of highly educated among working-age individuals (where $Q_{i,j}$ is the total number of working-age individuals with education i and nativity-status j) and λ is the semi-elasticity of the modified TFP to f_h. Throughout the article, upper case $Q_{i,j}$ denotes total working-age population for skill group i and nativity j, whereas lower case $q_{i,j}$ denotes employment of that group. Acemoglu and Angrist (2001) as well as Iranzo and Peri (2009) use a similar formulation to express economy-wide schooling externalities and we use their estimates for the value of the parameter λ.

1.3. Labour Demand

Each country is a single labour market. We derive the marginal productivity for native workers of both education levels ($w_{h,n}$ and $w_{l,n}$) by substituting (3) and (4) into (2) and taking the derivative with respect to the total quantity of labour $q_{h,n}$ and $q_{l,n}$ respectively. This yields the labour demand for each type of native worker:

$$w_{h,n} = A\theta_q \theta_n \left(\frac{q}{q_h}\right)^{\frac{1}{\sigma_q}}\left(\frac{q_h}{q_{h,n}}\right)^{\frac{1}{\sigma_m}}, \tag{6}$$

$$w_{l,n} = A(1 - \theta_q)\theta_n \left(\frac{q}{q_l}\right)^{\frac{1}{\sigma_q}}\left(\frac{q_l}{q_{l,n}}\right)^{\frac{1}{\sigma_m}}. \tag{7}$$

By taking the logarithm of the demand functions presented above and calculating the total differentials of each one of them with respect to variations (Δ) of the employment of each type of worker, we obtain the percentage change in marginal productivity in response to employment changes. For compactness, we define $\hat{x} = \Delta x / x$ as the percentage change in any variable x. Then, the percentage change in marginal productivity for native workers of education level $i = (h, l)$ in response to a percentage change in employment of immigrant ($\hat{q}_{h,f}$ and $\hat{q}_{l,f}$) and native ($\hat{q}_{h,n}$ and $\hat{q}_{l,n}$) workers can be written as follows:[12]

---

[11] This literature begins with Lucas (1988) and extends to Azariadis and Drazen (1990), Benhabib and Spiegel (2005), Vandenbussche et al. (2006) and Cohen and Soto (2007).
[12] The details of the derivation are fully developed in the online Appendices.

$$\hat{w}_{i,n} = \frac{1}{\sigma_q}\left(sh_{h,f}\hat{q}_{h,f} + sh_{l,f}\hat{q}_{l,f} + sh_{h,n}\hat{q}_{h,n} + sh_{l,n}\hat{q}_{l,n}\right)$$

$$+ \left(\frac{1}{\sigma_m} - \frac{1}{\sigma_q}\right)\left(\frac{sh_{i,f}}{sh_i}\hat{q}_{i,f} + \frac{sh_{i,n}}{sh_i}\hat{q}_{i,n}\right) - \frac{1}{\sigma_m}\hat{q}_{i,n} + \lambda\Delta f_h \text{ for } i = (h, l). \tag{8}$$

In (8), the term $sh_{i,j}$ represents the share of the wage bill going to workers of education level $i = (h, l)$ and place of origin $j = (n, f)$. The first term in brackets in the summation is the effect of changes in the employment of each group on the marginal productivity of natives of type $i = (h, l)$ through the term q in the wage equation. The second term, which depends only on the change in supply of workers of the same education type i, is the impact on marginal productivity of natives of type i through the terms q_i in the wage equation. The term $-(1/\sigma_m)\hat{q}_{i,n}$ captures the impact through the term $q_{i,n}$. The final term $\lambda\Delta f_h$ is the effect of a change in the share of the college educated in the working-age population through the TFP.

1.4. *Labour Supply*

A native worker of education level $i = (h, l)$ decides on how to split one unit of labour endowment between work l_i and leisure $1 - l_i$ to maximise an instant utility function,[13] which depends positively on consumption c_i and negatively on the amount of labour supplied l_i:

$$U_i = \theta_c c_i^\delta - \theta_l l_i^\eta. \tag{9}$$

The parameters θ_c, θ_l, δ and η ($\geq\delta$) can be specific to the education level i, but we consider them to be identical across groups for simplicity. We assume that individuals consume all their labour income which leads to the budget constraint $c_i = l_i w_{i,n}$. Substituting this constraint into the utility function and maximising with respect to l_i we obtain the labour supply for the individual worker of education level i:

$$l_i = \phi w_{i,n}^\gamma.$$

In this expression, $\phi = (\theta_c\delta/\theta_l\eta)^{\frac{1}{\eta-\delta}}$ is a constant and $\gamma = \delta/(\eta-\delta) \geq 0$ captures the elasticity of household labour supply. As there are $Q_{i,n}$ working-age individuals among all workers of education level i, the aggregate labour supply of type-i nationals is given by:

$$q_{i,n} = \phi Q_{i,n} w_{i,n}^\gamma \quad \text{for } i = (h, l). \tag{10}$$

As described above, $w_{i,n}$ is the wage paid to a native worker of schooling i; $Q_{i,n}$ (defined in Section 1.2) is the working-age population in group i; $\gamma \geq 0$ is the elasticity of labour supply and ϕ is a constant as defined above.

For immigrants, we make a further simplifying assumption that all working-age immigrants supply a constant amount of labour (call it $\phi_f > 0$) so that total employment of immigrants is given by $q_{i,f} = \phi_f Q_{i,f}$ for $i = (h, l)$. This implies that

---

[13] The model with savings and capital accumulation could be solved with the alternative utility function $U = [c^{1-\theta}\exp(-\zeta l) - 1]/(1 - \theta)$ as an inter-temporal optimisation model. In that case, which is illustrated in Barro and Sala-i-Martin (2003, pp. 422–5), the labour supply along a balanced growth path does not depend on wages. Consumption would be a constant fraction of income and, along a balanced growth path wages, would be growing at the rate of $\bar{A}$. Hence, it would be a special case with perfectly inelastic individual labour supply.

immigrant supply is rigid (i.e. $\gamma = 0$, which is not far from the measured elasticity for natives which is around $\gamma = 0.1$). Moreover, as we aim to analyse the effects of immigrants on native labour market outcomes, this assumption conveniently implies that a certain percentage change in immigrant population translates into the same percentage change in immigrant employment.

1.5. Equilibrium Effect of Immigration and Emigration

Changes in working-age immigrants ($\Delta Q_{h,f}$ and $\Delta Q_{l,f}$) and natives ($\Delta Q_{h,n}$ and $\Delta Q_{l,n}$) due to migration between countries are what we refer to as net immigration and net emigration. As discussed in Section 1.6, we consider those as 'given'. Our model analyses their implications on wages and employment of native non-migrants. In the new equilibrium, both labour markets (for highly educated and less educated native workers) respond to these given flows and adjust wage and employment levels to the new equilibrium.

We next consider a given immigration flow, represented by $\hat{Q}_{i,f}$ and a given emigration flow, given by $\hat{Q}_{i,n}$ for $i = (h,l)$. Building on (8) and (11), the following four conditions (i.e. two conditions for each worker type i) represent the response of native labour demand and supply in percentage changes in each labour market i:

$$\hat{w}_{i,n} = \frac{1}{\sigma_q}\left(sh_{h,f}\,\hat{Q}_{h,f} + sh_{l,f}\,\hat{Q}_{l,f} + sh_{h,n}\hat{q}_{h,n} + sh_{l,n}\hat{q}_{l,n}\right)$$

$$+ \left(\frac{1}{\sigma_m} - \frac{1}{\sigma_q}\right)\left(\frac{sh_{i,f}}{sh_i}\,\hat{Q}_{i,f} + \frac{sh_{i,n}}{sh_i}\,\hat{q}_{i,n}\right) - \frac{1}{\sigma_m}\hat{q}_{i,n} + \lambda\Delta f_h \quad \text{for } i = (h,l), \quad (11)$$

$$\hat{w}_{i,n} = \frac{1}{\gamma}(\hat{q}_{i,n} - \hat{Q}_{i,n}) \quad \text{for } i = (h,l). \tag{12}$$

The equilibrium response of native wage and employment for each skill group is obtained solving simultaneously the above system of four equations in four unknowns to find the following equilibrium native employment responses:

$$\hat{q}^*_{h,n} = \frac{\left(\frac{1}{\gamma} + d_l\right)\left(\widehat{mp}_{h,n} + \frac{1}{\gamma}\hat{Q}_{h,n}\right) + \frac{sh_{l,n}}{\sigma_q}\left(\widehat{mp}_{l,n} + \frac{1}{\gamma}\hat{Q}_{l,n}\right)}{\left(\frac{1}{\gamma} + d_l\right)\left(\frac{1}{\gamma} + d_h\right) - \frac{sh_{l,n}}{\sigma_q}\frac{sh_{h,n}}{\sigma_q}}, \tag{13}$$

$$\hat{q}^*_{l,n} = \frac{\left(\frac{1}{\gamma} + d_h\right)\left(\widehat{mp}_{l,n} + \frac{1}{\gamma}\hat{Q}_{l,n}\right) + \frac{sh_{h,n}}{\sigma_q}\left(\widehat{mp}_{h,n} + \frac{1}{\gamma}\hat{Q}_{h,n}\right)}{\left(\frac{1}{\gamma} + d_l\right)\left(\frac{1}{\gamma} + d_h\right) - \frac{sh_{l,n}}{\sigma_q}\frac{sh_{h,n}}{\sigma_q}}. \tag{14}$$

By substituting them into the supply functions, we obtain the equilibrium native wage response:

$$\hat{w}^*_{i,n} = \frac{1}{\gamma}(\hat{q}^*_{i,n} - \hat{Q}_{i,n}) \quad \text{for } i = (h,l). \tag{15}$$

In (13) and (14), the terms $\widehat{mp}_{i,n}$ (for $i = h,l$) are equal to

$$\widehat{mp}_{i,n} \equiv \frac{1}{\sigma_q}\left(sh_{h,f}\,\hat{Q}_{h,f} + sh_{l,f}\,\hat{Q}_{l,f}\right) + \left(\frac{1}{\sigma_m} - \frac{1}{\sigma_q}\right)\frac{sh_{i,f}}{sh_i}\,\hat{Q}_{i,f} + \lambda\Delta f_h, \tag{16}$$

and represent the impact of migration on the marginal productivity of native workers (n) of education level i for fixed native employment. The coefficients d_i ($i = h, l$) are equal to $1/\sigma_m - (1/\sigma_m - 1/\sigma_q)(sh_{i,n}/sh_i) - (sh_{i,n}/\sigma_q)$ and capture the absolute value of the slope of the logarithmic demand function for native workers of type i. The interactions between the two markets (h and l) and the need to solve simultaneously arise from the fact that a change in employment of workers with schooling level l affects the demand for workers of schooling level h through the term $(sh_{l,n}/\sigma_q)\hat{q}_{l,n}$ and, in turn, employment in the h market affects the demand for workers of type l through $(sh_{h,n}/\sigma_q)\hat{q}_{h,n}$ in the demand equation (11).

1.6. Simulations: Discussion and Caveats

Our goal is to quantify the impact of recent immigration and emigration flows on the wage and employment of non-migrant natives in OECD countries. Migration decisions are endogenous and depend, among other factors, on wage and employment disparities across countries. There are several models and studies analysing the determinants of migration.[14] This study, however, focuses on its consequences as do most studies of the labour market effects of immigration (Borjas, 2003; Card, 2009; D'Amuri *et al.*, 2010; Ottaviano and Peri, 2012) and emigration (Mishra, 2007; Elsner, 2011). The specific consequences we are interested in are the impact of immigration (or emigration respectively) on wages and employment outcomes of non-migrants in the host country (or source country respectively). We disregard indirect effects related to possible long-term education responses of natives or linkages between immigration and emigration, which are rarely considered and not very plausible in the cross-country literature. Rather than assessing the global effect of all migration flows in the world taken jointly, we isolate, by construction, the effect of migration on native wages and employment rates in each specific country without other potential confounding factors. In short, our model does not explain migration flows but it quantifies their effects, operating through labour market mechanisms, on native wage and employment. One interpretation of our results is that if the total migration flows of the 1990s were mainly driven by factors exogenous to the model (such as the opening of Eastern Europe to international mobility, the reduction in transportation costs or the relaxation of border controls between Western European Countries) then the model would produce the observed changes on native wage and employment caused by immigration, through labour markets. Alternatively, if migration flows in the 1990s were driven by factors endogenous to the model, such as an increase in a country's productivity (the term A_0 in (5)), then observed changes in native wages would combine the productivity effect and the labour market effect due to new immigration. In this case, an estimation approach would need to use exogenous variation from an instrument. Our simulation, instead, by keeping A_0 fixed, only accounts for the labour market effects of immigration. This is genuinely the 'effect' of immigration. It could not be observable separately in the actual wage data because of the simultaneity between productivity and immigration. Our model, however, isolates it.

---

[14] Recently Mayda (2010) and Grogger and Hanson (2011), among others, have tested empirically simple models of migration decisions.

Our simulation exercise consists of using (13, 14 and 15) to calculate the equilibrium responses of native wage and employment levels to immigration and emigration flows. We do this for each OECD country, for the decade 1990–2000. To perform the simulations, we need several sets of variables. The first is the share of the wage bill for each group by skill and country of origin, $sh_{i,j}$. Second, we need the percentage change in the population of each group caused by migration $\hat{Q}_{i,j}$. Finally, we also need the values for the key parameters, namely the elasticities $\sigma_q, \sigma_m, \lambda$ and γ. The variables that we use are country specific so that we can account for the skill distribution, the skill premium and migration flows by country. The model parameters, on the other hand, are assumed to be common across countries, and driven mainly by technology/preferences as is usually the case in cross-country studies (Hall and Jones, 1999; Caselli and Coleman, 2006). We are aware that this is a simplification, but we will allow for a range of parameter values that reflects differences in aggregate demand and supply elasticities possibly driven by differences in institutions, productivity levels and specialisation across countries. We describe in detail the construction of variables and the range of parameters in subsection 3.1 below.

2. Description of the New Data Set

This Section presents the database used to quantify net migration flows and the domestic labour force of OECD countries. We first describe the data sources and then discuss the main patterns observed for the period 1990–2000.

2.1. *Net Migration Data: Sources and Definitions*

The relevant migration data to be used in our analysis are net immigration and emigration flows for each OECD country between 1990 and 2000. Even though the description of the relevant migration data is simple, the construction was complicated and time consuming. There are several sources documenting yearly migration flows by receiving country (e.g. OECD International Migration Database, UN migration statistics). Quite problematically, these only include gross inflows of people from administrative records and do not correct for migrants who leave or return to their country of origin. Moreover, those records do not include undocumented migrants and often record immigrants when they achieve resident status rather than when they first enter the country. Most importantly for our purposes, these data do not have information on the education levels of migrants. Data by education level are available from national censuses. Those data are more representative, accurate and complete than other data sources. National censuses account for undocumented immigrants in some countries like the US and they categorise immigrants by place of birth (an immutable characteristic), rather than nationality (that may change). The net flow of immigrants to a country can be recovered by measuring the stock of foreign-born people in a destination country (from a certain origin country) at different points in time and then taking the difference. Finally, such direct data do not exist for emigration, which needs to be calculated from immigration data from all destination countries. For that purpose, the global bilateral matrices need to be complete.

Our database is described in greater detail in Docquier *et al.* (2012). It consists of bilateral immigrant and emigrant stocks for 195 countries in 1990 and 2000 for two skill/education levels. The starting point is the database assembled by Docquier *et al.* (2009) which includes the stock of foreign-born individuals in all OECD destination countries in 1990 and 2000, by country of origin and level of schooling (primary, secondary and tertiary), using censuses as primary data sources. The immigration data (and the analysis of its impact) is fully based on primary census data for those OECD countries. As far as emigration is concerned, the database does not quantify migration stocks to non-OECD destination countries. Hence, the OECD immigration data of Docquier *et al.* (2009) were supplemented with similar census data from the censuses of 70 and 31 additional destination countries in 2000 and 1990 respectively. For the rest of the destination countries with no available data, bilateral migrant stocks were predicted using a gravity framework as described in greater detail in Docquier *et al.* (2012). Table A1 in the online Appendix A shows that on average, imputed data account for a small proportion of the emigration stocks (only 5.9% in 2000) and emigration net flows (only 3.6% on the period 1990–2000) of OECD countries.[15] However, they represent a larger share of emigration in some countries (such as Israel, the Baltic States and France).

The database distinguishes between two schooling levels indexed by i. Highly educated people ($i = h$) are defined as tertiary education graduates whereas $i = l$ denotes individuals with secondary or lower education (referred to as less educated). The data set only includes people aged 25 years and over as a proxy of the working-age population. This choice maximises comparability between data on migration and on labour force for a given level of education. Furthermore, it excludes a large number of students who emigrate temporarily to complete their education or children who migrate with their families and are not yet active in the labour market.

We let $M_i^{ab}(t)$ denote the stock of migrants with education level i in year t working in country a and born in country b, i.e. an entry in the migration matrix. It is quite straightforward to calculate immigrant and emigrant stocks for any country once we have the complete migration matrix. The total immigrant stock in country a for education level i in year t is simply the sum of all bilateral immigrant stocks and it is given by $Q_{i,f}^a(t) \equiv \sum_{b \neq a} M_i^{ab}(t)$. Similarly, the stock of emigrants originally from country b is given by $E_i^b(t) \equiv \sum_{a \neq b} M_i^{ab}(t)$. The earlier databases allowed the calculation of total immigrant stocks for the OECD countries but had a limited set of destination countries. As some important destination countries (such as Russia, South Africa, Brazil, Argentina and Singapore) are outside the OECD, this new database ensures significantly better coverage of emigration from OECD countries relative to Docquier *et al.* (2009).

The last step is the construction of the immigration and emigration flows between 1990 and 2000 for each country and each skill level. We do this simply by taking the difference between the (immigrant or emigrant) stock in 2000 and 1990. For example, the flow of new immigrants with skill level i into country a is given by $\Delta Q_{i,f}^a = Q_{i,f}^a(2000) - Q_{i,f}^a(1990)$ and the emigrant flow is similarly defined.

---

[15] This pattern is also confirmed in Ozden *et al.* (2011) which presents global bilateral migration stocks.

The final data needed are the numbers of working-age residents in each country by level of education. The size of the adult population (i.e. population aged 25 years and over) is provided by the United Nations. Missing data in the case of several small countries can be estimated using several issues of the CIA world factbook.[16] Adult population data are then split across education groups using international indicators of educational attainment. We follow Docquier *et al.* (2009) in combining different data sets documenting the proportion of tertiary educated workers in the population aged 25 years and over. The main sources are De la Fuente and Domenech (2006) for OECD countries, and Cohen and Soto (2007) and Barro and Lee (2010) for non-OECD countries. In the remaining non-OECD countries where both Barro–Lee and Cohen–Soto are missing data (about 70 countries in 2000), we apply the educational proportion of the neighbouring country with the closest tertiary education enrolment rate and GDP per capita.

2.2. Description and General Trends

Table 1 shows the immigration patterns during the period 1990–2000 for all the countries considered in this study. These are member countries of the OECD as well as several non-OECD countries in Eastern Europe. Columns 1 and 2 show immigration rates in total population and among the college-educated population respectively. Columns 3 and 4 show immigration rates, considering only non-OECD countries of origin distinguished between total and college educated. Immigration rates, in column 1 of Table 1, are calculated as net inflow of immigrants (age 25 years and over) during the period 1990–2000, $\Delta Q_{h,f} + \Delta Q_{l,f}$, divided by the initial working-age population in 1990. For instance, during this time period, the net inflow of immigrants was equal to 14.35% of the 1990 population in Israel. This large value is a consequence of the removal of the migration restrictions in Soviet Union in the early 1990s.[17] Luxembourg, Austria and Ireland also received significant inflows of immigrants relative to their populations. Their total rates range between 7.6% and 12.5%. Three countries at the bottom of the table are also worth mentioning. The three Baltic countries (Estonia, Latvia and Lithuania), emerging after the break-up of the Soviet Union, experienced massive negative net immigration flows. This was a result of the return of many ethnic Russians (born in Russia) after having immigrated to these Baltic countries during the Soviet era. Several other Eastern European countries (e.g. Romania, Slovenia, Hungary and Poland) had similar experiences during this decade.

The second column of Table 1 presents the net immigration rates for college-educated workers, referred to as 'highly educated'. These are calculated as the net change (between 1990 and 2000) in the stock of college-educated foreign-born workers, $\Delta Q_{h,f}$, relative to the similarly educated resident population in 1990. An interesting pattern worth emphasising is that for all countries with positive net immigration rates (with the exception of Austria), the immigration rates of the college educated were larger than the rates for the total population. In some prominent

---

[16] See https://www.cia.gov/library/publications/the-world-factbook/index.html (accessed 13 June 2013).
[17] There are several studies analysing the economic impact of this episode on Israel's economy such as Friedberg (2001), Cohen-Goldner and Paserman (2011).

Table 1

Immigration Rates, 1990–2000 (Ranked by Total Immigration Rate)

Country	Total immigration rates from all countries (%)	College-educated immigration rates from all countries (%)	Total immigration rates from non-OECD countries (%)	College-educated immigration rates from non-OECD countries (%)
Israel	14.35	60.19	15.14	47.03
Luxembourg	12.53	16.47	3.03	2.17
Austria	9.35	7.87	3.42	2.11
Ireland	7.60	28.02	1.65	6.12
United States	5.71	6.50	3.40	4.71
New Zealand	5.61	7.61	4.79	8.11
Iceland	5.25	16.44	2.17	5.41
Canada	5.21	10.81	5.59	9.06
Cyprus	4.76	13.07	2.50	5.95
Australia	3.79	13.70	3.66	6.82
Spain	3.32	5.80	2.02	3.28
Malta	2.84	18.73	0.59	4.41
Sweden	2.66	6.63	2.59	4.29
Germany	2.64	3.91	0.90	1.65
Belgium	2.63	5.68	1.69	2.40
Denmark	2.54	2.95	1.82	1.57
Netherlands	2.39	6.60	1.77	3.16
United Kingdom	2.13	11.26	1.64	6.13
Finland	1.74	2.34	0.65	0.70
Switzerland	1.61	9.29	2.63	2.96
Portugal	1.55	2.99	1.23	1.76
Bulgaria	1.06	2.52	0.62	1.56
Italy	1.00	1.08	0.73	0.57
France	0.81	3.38	1.01	1.89
Turkey	0.71	7.10	0.06	1.27
Japan	0.46	0.78	0.39	0.54
Czech Republic	0.39	5.35	0.07	1.02
Slovakia	0.35	1.24	0.08	0.29
Greece	0.24	0.34	0.19	0.21
Chile	0.13	0.26	0.12	0.15
Mexico	0.11	1.09	0.03	0.36
Korea	0.00	0.15	0.00	0.11
Romania	−0.04	0.27	−0.02	0.13
Slovenia	−0.09	1.31	−0.08	0.84
Hungary	−0.12	0.17	−0.03	0.04
Poland	−1.14	−0.87	−0.77	−0.63
Lithuania	−2.96	0.36	−2.71	0.34
Latvia	−15.58	−17.93	−16.88	−19.79
Estonia	−16.73	−25.46	−16.60	−25.80

Note. Immigration rates are equal to the net change in the stock of immigrants within the group in the period 1990–2000 divided by the population of natives and immigrants within the group in 1990.

destinations, such as Israel, Ireland, Iceland, Canada, Australia and the UK, the immigration rates for college-educated workers were more than twice the overall immigration rates. Immigration, therefore, contributed to a considerable increase in the share of college-educated individuals in the labour forces for all countries in our sample (again with the exception of Austria). Latvia and Estonia had negative immigration rates, implying large returns of existing immigrants and even larger return rates for college-educated immigrants. Remarkably, columns 3 and 4 confirm the pattern of larger immigration rates for college-educated individuals, even when we consider only immigrants from non-OECD countries. Most countries have higher rates for college immigration than for total immigration even from non-OECD origin countries.

Table 2 presents the emigration rates for the countries in our sample where column 1 is the total emigration rate, calculated as the net outflow of natives (25 years and over) during the period 1990–2000, $(\Delta Q_{h,n} + \Delta Q_{l,n})$ relative to the total resident population (age 25 years and above) in 1990. Column 2 contains the net emigration rate of college-educated natives, $\Delta Q_{h,n}$, relative to the similarly educated resident

Table 2

Emigration Rates, Total and College Graduates, 1990–2000
(Ranked by College Emigration Rates)

Country	Total emigration rates (%)	College graduates emigration rates (%)
Cyprus	1.78	29.31
Malta	−1.77	27.99
Ireland	−4.23	23.30
Mexico	11.58	19.76
New Zealand	6.82	16.85
Portugal	3.09	12.57
Estonia	4.89	9.89
Romania	1.23	9.89
Latvia	2.42	9.17
Slovenia	4.90	9.15
Slovakia	1.04	8.74
Poland	0.49	8.32
Korea	1.76	8.20
Lithuania	0.76	7.51
Bulgaria	2.50	7.19
United Kingdom	0.40	6.36
Iceland	2.68	5.99
Turkey	2.43	5.57
Greece	0.25	4.57
Chile	1.24	4.05
Luxembourg	0.73	3.92
Switzerland	2.13	3.64
Finland	0.02	2.95
Netherlands	0.61	2.94
Spain	0.06	2.92
Belgium	0.51	2.91
Sweden	0.82	2.30
Denmark	0.30	2.22
Austria	0.32	2.03
Australia	1.07	1.70
Canada	0.17	1.65
Italy	−0.29	1.63
Czech Republic	0.74	1.48
Germany	0.20	1.37
France	0.44	1.31
Hungary	0.04	0.37
Japan	0.06	0.36
United States	0.10	0.23

Note. Emigration rates are equal to the net change in the stock of emigrants in the period 1990–2000 divided by the total population of natives and immigrant residents in 1990.

population in 1990. A negative emigration rate implies that the return rate of emigrants (natives who were abroad in 1990) was larger than the outflow of new emigrants during the period 1990–2000. Countries are ranked in decreasing order of their high-skilled emigration rates. A few observations are in order. First, as in the case of immigration, emigration rates are also larger for college-educated natives than on average (with the exception of Israel). For some small countries (Cyprus, Malta and Ireland), a large emigration rate for the college educated is associated with negative or very small overall emigration rates, implying large rates of return for non-college-educated natives from abroad. In some of these small countries, however, immigration of tertiary educated foreign-born workers compensated the emigration of the natives. Several Eastern European countries (such as Poland, Romania, Slovenia and Slovakia) and some Western European countries (Portugal and Greece) had significant college-educated emigration flows that were not compensated by similar immigration inflows. For those countries, emigration was a significant source of decrease in the relative supply of highly educated workers. Other European countries such as the UK, Luxembourg, Switzerland and the Netherlands had significant rates of college-educated emigration that were compensated with significant immigration from mostly non-OECD countries. The US, Canada and Australia were, as is widely known, main destination countries as the immigration rates (total and for highly educated) were much larger than the corresponding emigration rates of the natives. In summary, during the 1990s both the immigration and emigration flows were very skill intensive in most OECD countries. Less well known but clearly visible in our data, many OECD countries experienced emigration rates that were just as large as immigration rates.

3. Simulated Labour Market Effects

This Section presents the results of the simulated wage and employment effects of migration using our model. We first describe how parameters are combined in our scenarios. Then we discuss the effects of immigration and emigration.

3.1. *Parameterisation and Variable Measurement*

As one can see from (13, 14 and 15), we need three sets of variables for each country to simulate the labour market effects of immigration and emigration flows. The first is the share of the wage income that accrues to each of the four main groups in the labour force as of 1990. As mentioned in the previous section, these shares are denoted as $sh_{i,j}$, where i is the education level (high *versus* low) and j is the country of birth (immigrant *versus* native born). The second variable is the percentage change in employment among each of these four groups due to immigration and emigration during the decade 1990–2000. This is denoted by $\hat{Q}_{i,j}$. The last variable is the change in the ratio of college-educated individuals in the labour force due to immigration and emigration which we denote by Δf_H.

The shares of wage income accruing to different groups of workers depend on their employment levels (that we proxy with population in working age) and wages. As there is no comprehensive global database on wages of college educated and less educated, we proceed as follows. We take the estimated returns to a year of schooling in each country for the year as close as possible to 1990 from the Hendricks (2004) database.[18] We then calculate the average years of education for each of the two education groups (those with and without college degrees) using the Barro and Lee (2010) database. We multiply the return on education by the difference between average years of schooling of the two groups to identify the college wage premium in a given country. Table A2 in the online Appendix A shows the individual data and sources used for each country. Then, from several different sources (most of which are reviewed in Kerr and Kerr, 2009), we obtain the country-specific estimate of the native–foreign wage premium to adjust the wages of immigrants at each level of education. If any of the data are not available for a specific country, we use the estimate for the geographically closest country with the most similar income per capita.[19] We obtain the wage bill for that group by multiplying the group-specific employment level by the group-specific wage (standardised for the wage of less educated natives). This number provides the share $sh_{i,j}$[20] when divided by the total wage bill. These shares of wage income for each of the four groups in each country are reported in Table A4 in the online Appendix A. The percentage change in the employment of each group due to immigration and emigration during the period 1990–2000, as well as the change in the share of college educated, is calculated from the data set on stocks of migrants in 1990–2000 as described above.

The next critical step is the determination of the values of the four fundamental parameters of the model. σ_q is the elasticity of substitution between highly and less educated workers; σ_m is the elasticity of substitution between natives and immigrants with the same education level; λ is the intensity of college externalities and γ is the labour supply elasticity of more and less educated natives.

Table 3 presents the values of the parameters chosen in each of three scenarios considered in the main numerical simulations. The values are chosen to span the range found in the literature. There are several estimates in the literature for the parameter σ_q, the elasticity of substitution between more and less educated workers. Johnson (1970), Katz and Murphy (1992), Murphy *et al.* (1998) and Caselli and Coleman (2006) estimate values around 1.3–1.4 whereas Fallon and Layard (1975), Angrist (1995), Krusell *et al.* (2000) and Ciccone and Peri (2005) estimate values around 1.5–1.75 using data on the US, Canada or a cross section of world countries. Ottaviano and Peri (2012) estimate values around 2. Hence, the values

---

[18] If the estimate was not available for a country, we chose the estimate for the country sharing a border with the closest level of income per capita. We experimented with different imputation methods (countries with similar income or simply using the average return for all countries) and the differences are minuscule.
[19] The values used for the foreign/native wage ratios and their sources are reported in Table A3 of the online Appendix A. When we find more than one estimate for a country, we use the median value. Using different imputation methods for this variable does not change the results much. In fact, even imputing to all countries a fixed immigrant/native wage ratio at 0.99 (the average value in the sample) generates essentially identical simulated effects.
[20] This procedure assumes that the population in working age for each group approximates actual employment. While employment rates of immigrants can be different from those of natives, there is no systematic tendencies of being larger or smaller across countries and the differences are only by few percentage points. The largest part of the differences in wage shares is driven by differences in size of the population.

Table 3

Parameter Values

Parameters	Pessimistic scenario	Intermediate scenario	Optimistic scenario
σ_q: Elasticity of substitution between more and less educated	2.00	1.75	1.3
σ_m: Elasticity of substitution between immigrants and natives	Infinity	20	6
λ: Intensity of college externalities	0	0.45	0.75
γ: Elasticity of labour supply	0.2	0.1	0

Notes. The estimates used in each scenario are from the literature. The specific sources are specified in the text.

1.3, 1.75 and 2 span the entire range of estimates and we use them in the three main scenarios.

The elasticity of substitution between natives and immigrants, σ_m, has been the focus of many recent articles and has generated a certain level of debate. This parameter is important in determining the effect of immigration on the wages of non-migrant natives, and the value of this parameter influences the estimated wage effects of migration in many countries much more than other parameters. Peri (2011), Borjas *et al.* (2012), Ottaviano and Peri (2012) use the US data and Manacorda *et al.* (2012) use the UK data in their estimation of σ_m. The first study finds a value of infinity; the second and third articles estimate an elasticity between 10 and 20 and the article on the UK data finds a value of 6.[21] We use infinity, 20 and 6 as the three parameter values in the three main scenarios.

The parameter λ, measuring the externality generated by the share of the tertiary educated in the labour force, has been estimated using data from the US cities (Moretti, 2004*a*, *b*) or the US states (Acemoglu and Angrist, 2001; Iranzo and Peri, 2009). It is also subject to a certain level of debate as some studies find substantial schooling externalities ($\lambda = 0.75$ in Moretti, 2004*b*) while others do not ($\lambda = 0$ in Acemoglu and Angrist, 2001). These values define the range we use in our three scenarios (0, 0.45 and 0.75).

Finally, the estimates of the elasticity of labour supply γ (as summarised by Evers *et al.* (2008) for several European countries and the US) range from 0, in a study on the US by Flood and MaCurdy (1992), to 0.17, in a study on the Netherlands by van Soest *et al.* (1990).[22] One can argue that labour supply elasticity close to 0 (corresponding to rigid labour supply and maximum wage adjustment) would correspond more closely to the US, the UK and Canada. Several continental European countries, on the other hand, may exhibit a degree of wage rigidity captured by a supply elasticity of 0.20. As a result, we choose 0, 0.10 and 0.20 as the representative values for this parameter. We also show the effect of choosing a very high parameter value (i.e. 0.40) that is at the top of the

---

[21] Less known studies have also estimated this parameter value for Germany (D'Amuri *et al.*, 2010) and for Italy (Romiti, 2012). Those estimate all range between 12 and 20.

[22] Some studies found a negative and small elasticity of labour supply. We consider 0 as lower bound, as in the surveyed studies none of the negative estimates is significant.

95% confidence interval for the parameter estimates as presented in the literature (see panel (d) in Table 6).[23]

3.2. Wage and Employment Effects of Immigration

The percentage effects of immigration on the wages of less educated non-migrant native workers are shown in Figure 1 (a) and those on the average wages of all native workers are presented in Figure 1(b). Similarly, Figure 2(a, b) shows the percentage effects of immigration on employment of less educated and on overall employment of natives respectively. Our simulations compare the actual situation with one in which countries would have not allowed any immigration in the 1990s (everything else equal) and we identify the wage effect of immigration through this counter-factual experiment.

In addition to the average effects, we mainly discuss the implications for the less educated workers as that has been the main focus of the debate on immigration. Some academic studies (Borjas, 2003) and many public opinion pieces have argued that immigration is disruptive for less educated native workers. On the other hand, the average wage effect gives an idea about the overall impact of immigration on natives. Each figure reports the simulated values under three configurations of the parameters (shown in Table 3), which we refer to as the 'pessimistic', 'intermediate' and 'optimistic' scenarios reflecting their implications for the average wage of natives (from least to most positive).

The bold, solid and dashed lines connect the simulated values from the optimistic, intermediate and pessimistic scenarios respectively. Hence, the distance between the bold and the dashed lines encompasses the range of possible effects for each country, using the parameter ranges discussed in the previous Section. To show the effect of changes in each individual parameter on the estimated range of wage and employment outcomes, we also report the numerical values in Table 4. More specifically, the Table reports the effects for the top, median and bottom country (ranked according to the size of the overall effect) and it includes the effects on highly educated (not reported in the figures), less educated as well as the average worker. In the left-hand columns of Table 4, we report the value of each parameter, beginning with a baseline scenario in which all parameters take their baseline value and then separately vary each one, from the lowest to the highest value in the range. The last two rows show the 'optimistic' and the 'pessimistic' configuration and the relative simulated effects.[24]

The countries in Figures 1 and 2 are listed in decreasing order of their total immigration rate as defined in Table 1. A number of interesting features immediately

---

[23] Our simulations are 'long run' in the sense that we are assuming perfect elastic capital supply. In the previous version of this article (Docquier *et al.* 2010), we also simulated the short-run effect with sluggish capital adjustment which are available on request.

[24] In the Figures and Tables we drop Israel and the Baltic countries (Lithuania, Latvia and Estonia) from the sample. Israel's massive immigration experience, especially from Russia in the 1990s, makes it an outlier. Lithuania, Latvia and Estonia on the other hand experienced large negative net immigration rates, as discussed above in more detail, due to ethnic Russians returning after the disintegration of the Soviet Union. This really was more of an emigration phenomenon (return migration) in terms of the main characteristics and implications.

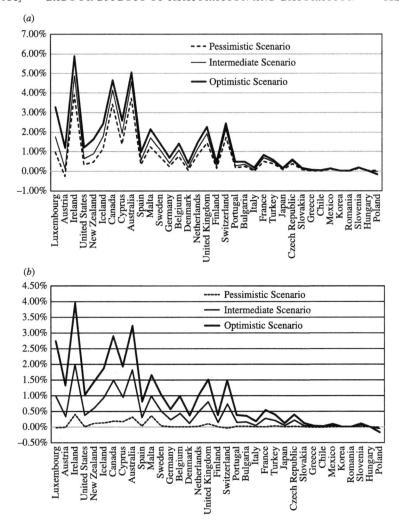

Fig. 1. *Wage Effects of Immigration on Native Workers, 1990–2000 (Countries Ranked Left to Right by Immigration Rate)*
Notes. (*a*) Percentage effects on less educated native wages. (*b*) Percentage effects on average native wages. Values on the vertical axis are the simulated wage effect (in percentage of the initial wage) of immigration on natives. We omit Israel, Lithuania, Latvia and Estonia from the chart as they are outliers (see online Appendix Table A4). The parameter values corresponding to the 'pessimistic', 'intermediate' and 'optimistic' scenarios are reported in Table 3.

become clear looking at Figures 1 and 2, and Table 4. First, all simulated wage effects on less educated natives (with the exception of the 'pessimistic' scenario for Austria) are positive. This indicates that in all countries and scenarios, less educated native

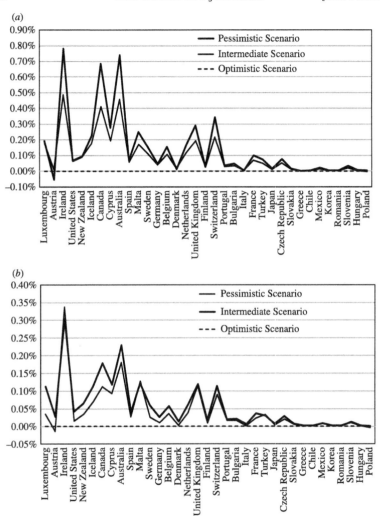

Fig. 2. *Employment Effects of Immigration on Native Workers, 1990–2000 (Countries Ranked Left to Right by Immigration Rate)*
Notes. (*a*) Percentage effects on employment of less educated natives. (*b*) Percentage effects on employment of all natives. Values on the vertical axis are the simulated aggregate employment effects (in percentage of the initial employment) of immigration on natives. We omit Israel, Lithuania, Latvia and Estonia from the chart as they are outliers (see online Appendix Table A5). The parameter values corresponding to the pessimistic, intermediate and optimistic scenario are reported in Table 3.

workers gain from the labour market effects of immigration. For some countries with high immigration rates, such as Ireland, Canada and Australia, the wage gains for less educated natives are quite significant and reach values as high as 6%. For other

Table 4

Simulated Effects of Immigration on Employment and Wage of Natives

Model	Parameter values σ_q σ_m λ		γ	Country rank, by size of the effect:	Percentage change in wages			Percentage change in employment		
					Less educated natives (%)	Overall natives (%)	More educated natives (%)	Less educated natives (%)	Overall natives (%)	More educated natives (%)
Basic	1.75	0.1		Top	4.8	2.0	1.0	0.5	0.3	0.1
	20			Median	0.5	0.2	−0.5	0.1	0.0	0.0
	0.45			Bottom	0.0	0.0	−8.2	0.0	0.0	−0.8
High σ_q	2.00	0.1		Top	4.4	1.9	0.9	0.4	0.3	0.1
	20			Median	0.4	0.2	−0.4	0.0	0.0	0.0
	0.45			Bottom	0.0	0.0	−6.9	0.0	0.0	−0.7
Low σ_q	1.3	0.1		Top	6.0	2.1	1.2	0.6	0.4	0.1
	20			Median	0.6	0.2	−0.8	0.0	0.0	−0.1
	0.45			Bottom	0.0	0.0	−11.8	0.0	0.0	−1.2
High σ_m	1.75	0.1		Top	4.6	1.6	0.6	0.5	0.3	0.1
	Infinity			Median	0.4	0.1	−0.7	0.0	0.0	−0.1
	0.45			Bottom	−0.3	−0.1	−9.8	0.0	0.0	−1.0
Low σ_m	1.75	0.1		Top	5.4	3.2	1.9	0.5	0.4	0.1
	6			Median	0.6	0.4	−0.2	0.0	0.0	0.0
	0.45			Bottom	−0.1	−0.1	−4.9	0.0	0.0	−0.5
High λ	1.75	0.1		Top	5.7	2.8	0.9	0.6	0.4	0.1
	20			Median	0.6	0.3	−0.5	0.1	0.0	0.0
	0.75			Bottom	0.0	0.0	−7.4	0.0	0.0	−0.7
Low λ	1.75	0.1		Top	3.6	0.8	1.1	0.4	0.2	0.1
	20			Median	0.3	0.1	−0.6	0.0	0.0	0.0
	0			Bottom	0.0	0.0	−9.5	0.0	0.0	−0.9
High γ	1.75		0.2	Top	4.8	2.0	1.0	1.0	0.1	0.2
	20			Median	0.5	0.2	−0.5	0.0	0.0	−0.1
	0.45			Bottom	0.0	0.0	−7.8	0.0	−0.06	−1.6
Low γ	1.75		0	Top	4.9	1.9	1.0	0.0	0.0	0.0
	20			Median	0.5	0.2	−0.6	0.0	0.0	0.0
	0.45			Bottom	0.0	0.0	−8.8	0.0	0.0	0.0
Optimistic	1.3		0	Top	7.5	4.0	2.1	0.0	0.0	0.0
	6			Median	0.8	0.5	−0.4	0.0	0.0	0.0
	0.75			Bottom	0.0	−0.1	−8.4	0.0	0.0	0.0
Pessimistic	2.0		0.2	Top	2.9	0.3	0.6	0.6	0.2	0.1
	Infinity			Median	0.2	0.0	−0.6	0.0	0.0	−0.1
	0			Bottom	−0.2	−0.1	−9.3	0.0	−0.06	−1.8

Notes. Each of the three rows corresponds to a simulation using the specified values of the parameters. We report the effects of immigration in the 1990s on wages and employment of native less educated, overall and more educated (respectively) in percentage changes. We show only the simulated effects for the countries with the highest (top), the median and lowest (bottom) values for each outcome.

countries with intermediate levels of immigration, such as Belgium, the UK and Switzerland, the effects are non-negligible and are between 1% and 2%. The median effect (Table 4, last two rows) on less educated workers ranges from 0.2% in the pessimistic scenario to 0.8% in the optimistic scenario. The effects on average native wages, in the optimistic scenario, are larger than 3% for countries like Canada, Ireland

and Australia. The effects on employment, reported in Figures 2(*a*, *b*), and in the last three columns of Table 4, have the same qualitative features as the wage changes but they are smaller in magnitude. They range between 0% and 0.5% in most of the countries in any scenario.

The inspection of different rows of Table 4 reveals the sensitivity of the simulated effects to each individual parameter. We clearly see that the effect on average native wages is strongly influenced by the parameters σ_m and λ. Moving from perfect substitution ($\sigma_m = \infty$) between natives and immigrants to a lower elasticity of substitution ($\sigma_m = 6$) increases the median effect from 0.1% to 0.4%. The wage effect on the top country rises from 1.6% to 3.2%. On the other hand, increasing the strength of human capital externalities (λ) from 0 to 0.75 increases the average wage effect of immigrants on the median country by 0.2 percentage points and on the top country by 2 percentage points. Changing the elasticity of substitution between more and less educated workers (σ_q) has no substantial effect on the average wage effects.

Focusing on the wage effect for less educated natives we see that imperfect substitution among different education categories, imperfect substitution between immigrants and natives as well as large human capital externalities all contribute in similar magnitudes. In the optimistic scenario, less educated workers gain 0.8% from immigration in the median country and up to 7.5% in the top country (Luxembourg). In the pessimistic scenario, less educated workers gain 0.2% in the median country and 2.9% in the top country. Changing the parameters σ_q, σ_m and λ one at the time (from the bottom to the top of the range) increases the median effect by 0.2 to 0.3 percentage points in each case.

The effect of immigration on the wages of highly educated natives is mostly negative. Especially in the scenarios with no externalities (seventh row of Table 4) and the one with low substitutability between more and less educated workers (third row), the effect on highly educated natives are −0.6 and −0.8%, respectively, in the median country considered. Finally, changing the elasticity of supply (γ) from 0 (in row 8) to 0.2 (in row 9) barely changes the wage effects. The employment effects, however, are increased with a top effect on less educated employment of 1% and a bottom effect on more educated employment equal to −1.6% in the case with highest elasticity of supply ($\gamma = 0.2$).

The magnitude of the wage effect of immigrants depends critically on the ratio of the highly educated to the less educated among the immigrants. Countries where laws explicitly favour more educated immigrants (such as Australia and Canada) experience larger positive effects for both the less educated natives and the total workforce. However, other countries without such explicit laws (such as Ireland, the UK and Switzerland) also enjoy significant positive effects as the composition of their immigrants was also tilted towards the highly educated. On the other hand, if the skill composition of immigration flows was not biased in favour of the educated, then the net wage effect on natives becomes quite small. The simulation results are fully determined by the composition and the size of the immigrant flows and by the chosen parameters. It is interesting to see how, within the reasonable parameter range, wage effects of immigrants are quite consistent. Immigration benefits less educated workers, through complementarities between high and low-skilled workers; it increases average productivity through schooling externalities and imperfect substitution with natives. These effects generate small positive wage effects on average and positive wage effects for less educated non-migrant native workers. For reasonable assumptions on the elasticity of labour supply, they have almost no effect on native employment. Finally, highly educated natives experience a wage decrease as a result of immigration. One group that we exclude from our analysis are the previous cohorts of immigrants who are more likely to experience a negative effect than natives from immigration due to closer substitutability.

3.3. Wage and Employment Effects of Emigration

We showed in Table 2 that net emigration rates for some of the OECD countries were even larger than net immigration rates during the period considered, 1990–2000. This was especially true for college-educated workers. While the literature almost exclusively focuses on the labour market effects of immigration, one original contribution of this article is the analysis of the labour market impact of emigration flows, modelling them as a decline in the supply of the relevant native worker group. In this case, our simulations compare the actual situation with one in which countries would allow no emigration[25] and identifies the effect of emigration through this counter-factual experiment.

Figure 3(a) shows the simulated effects of emigration on the wages of less educated non-migrant adults in their countries of origin. Figure 3(b) shows the same effect on average non-migrant wages. Figure 4(a, b) show the employment effects of emigration on less educated natives and natives overall respectively. We report the effects for the optimistic, the intermediate and the pessimistic scenarios. Notice that in this case the optimistic scenario is the one that produces the most negative effects of emigration (on wages and employment of non-migrants). This is because the parameter configuration that made skill-intensive immigration beneficial to the average non-migrant natives implies that skill-intensive emigration has a negative effect. The pessimistic scenario produces the smallest (negative) effects. In Figures 3 and 4, the countries are listed from left to right in decreasing order of college-educated emigration rates, as shown in Table 2. Table 5 shows the simulated values for the effects of emigration, including the wage and employment effect on the group of less educated, more educated and on average. As in Table 4, it includes only the effect on the median country and on the countries at the top and the bottom of the simulated range.

Focusing on Figure 3(a), the most striking fact is that the wage impact is opposite of what is seen in the previous Section on immigration. Net emigration involves a larger percentage decline in college-educated workers and, hence, it has a negative effect on less educated native workers. In countries with large emigration rates (left area of the graph, including countries such as Cyprus, Malta, Ireland, New Zealand and Portugal), the impact on wages of less educated natives is significantly negative. The range is between −1% (Portugal) and −6% (Ireland and Cyprus depending on the elasticity scenario). The effects on employment levels of less educated non-migrants are much smaller but still negative. Figure 4(a) shows

[25] Admittedly these type of policies are not literally implemented by democratic governments. However, increasing the cost of migrating or encouraging return migration can be considered as ways to achieve zero net emigration.

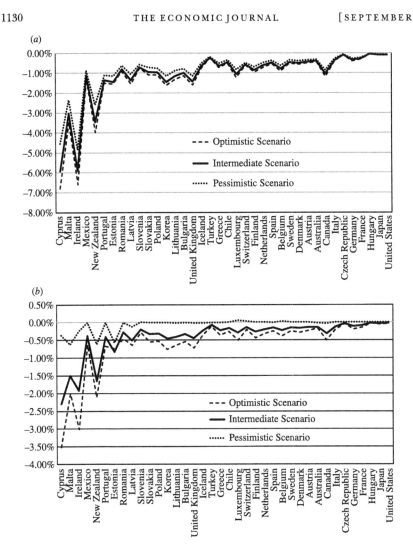

Fig. 3. *Wage Effects of Emigration on Native Workers, 1990–2000 (Countries Ranked Left to Right by Emigration Rate of College Educated)*

Notes. (*a*) Percentage effects on less educated native wages. (*b*) Percentage effects on average native wages. Values on the vertical axis are the simulated wage effects (in percentage of the initial wage). We omit Israel from the chart. The parameter values corresponding to the 'pessimistic', 'intermediate' and 'optimistic' scenarios are reported in Table 3.

that in countries such as Cyprus, Ireland and New Zealand, employment levels declined by 0.6 to 0.8% in the most optimistic scenario. Even at intermediate rates of emigration, some countries still experience negative wage effects on the less

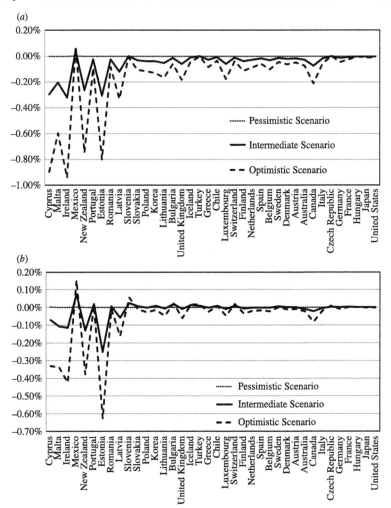

Fig. 4. *Employment Effects of Emigration on Native Workers, 1990–2000 (Countries Ranked Left to Right by Emigration Rate of College Educated)*

Notes. (*a*) Percentage effects on less educated native employment. (*b*) Percentage effects on average native employment. Values on the vertical axis are the simulated employment effects (in percentage of the initial employment) of emigration on native non-migrants. We omit Israel from the chart. The parameter values corresponding to the 'pessimistic', 'intermediate' and 'optimistic' scenarios are reported in Table 3.

educated workers of around −1% (e.g. Latvia, South Korea, the UK and Canada). The losses are due to the lost externalities from the departure of college-educated individuals. In particular, Table 5 shows that the median loss to less educated

Table 5
Simulated Effects of Emigration on Employment and Wage of Non-moving Natives

Model	Parameter values σ_q σ_m λ	γ	Country rank, by size of the effect:	Percentage change in wages of non-migrant natives			Percentage change in employment of non-migrant natives		
				Less educated natives (%)	Overall natives (%)	More educated natives (%)	Less educated natives (%)	Overall natives (%)	More educated natives (%)
Basic	1.75	0.1	Top	0.0	0.0	15.7	0.0	0.0	1.5
	20		Median	−0.7	−0.2	1.3	0.0	0.0	0.1
	0.45		Bottom	−5.9	−2.3	0.0	−0.3	−0.1	0.0
High σ_q	2.00	0.1	Top	0.0	0.0	13.7	0.0	0.1	1.3
	20		Median	−0.6	−0.2	1.2	0.0	0.0	0.1
	0.45		Bottom	−5.4	−2.3	0.0	−0.3	−0.3	0.0
Low σ_q	1.3	0.1	Top	0.0	0.0	21.3	0.1	0.1	2.0
	20		Median	−0.8	−0.2	1.9	0.0	0.0	0.2
	0.45		Bottom	−7.3	−2.4	0.1	−0.3	−0.1	0.0
High σ_m	1.75	0.1	Top	0.0	0.0	15.7	0.0	0.0	1.5
	Infinity		Median	−0.7	−0.2	1.3	0.0	0.0	0.1
	0.45		Bottom	−5.9	−2.3	0.0	−0.3	−0.1	0.0
Low σ_m	1.75	0.1	Top	0.0	0.0	15.7	0.0	0.0	1.5
	6		Median	−0.7	−0.2	1.3	0.0	0.0	0.1
	0.45		Bottom	−5.9	−2.3	0.0	−0.3	−0.1	0.0
High λ	1.75	0.1	Top	0.0	0.0	15.0	0.0	0.0	1.4
	20		Median	−0.8	−0.3	1.3	0.0	0.0	0.1
	0.75		Bottom	−7.3	−3.6	0.0	−0.4	−0.2	0.0
Low λ	1.75	0.1	Top	0.0	0.0	16.7	0.1	0.1	1.6
	20		Median	−0.4	0.0	1.5	0.0	0.0	0.1
	0		Bottom	−4.2	−0.5	0.0	−0.2	0.0	0.0
High γ	1.75	0.2	Top	0.0	0.0	15.7	0.1	0.1	2.9
	20		Median	−0.7	−0.2	1.3	0.0	0.0	0.2
	0.45		Bottom	−5.9	−2.3	0.0	−0.6	−0.3	0.0
Low γ	1.75	0	Top	0.0	0.0	15.7	0.0	0.0	0.0
	20		Median	−0.7	−0.2	1.4	0.0	0.0	0.0
	0.45		Bottom	−5.9	−2.3	0.0	0.0	0.0	0.0
Optimistic	1.3	0	Top	0.0	0.0	20.0	0.0	0.0	0.0
	6		Median	−1.0	−0.4	1.8	0.0	0.0	0.0
	0.75		Bottom	−8.6	−3.8	0.0	0.0	0.0	0.0
Pessimistic	2.0	0.2	Top	0.3	0.1	16.2	0.1	0.1	3.5
	Infinity		Median	0.0	0.0	1.3	0.0	0.0	0.3
	0		Bottom	−3.7	−0.3	0.0	−0.9	−0.5	0.0

Notes. Each of the three rows corresponds to one simulation using the specified values of the parameters. We report the effects of emigration in the 1990s on wages and employment of non-migrant native less educated, overall and more educated (respectively) in percentage changes. We show only the simulated effects for the countries with the highest (top), the median and lowest (Bottom) values for each outcome.

natives from emigration ranges from 0% to −1% (last two rows), where half of that difference is driven by the intensity of human capital externalities and the other half by the degree of substitutability between more and less educated. On the other hand, the median effect on average wages ranges from -0.3% to 0% and that variation is fully driven by the assumed intensity of human capital externalities (comparison of Rows 6 and 7).

Overall, the employment effects of emigration are very small on less educated workers as well as the average worker. Table 5 also shows that highly educated non-movers usually benefit from emigration. This is because competition is reduced, and skill-biased emigration makes highly educated more scarce in the labour force. While the effects are generally small, for some small countries with large 'brain drain' such as Cyprus or Ireland, the positive effect of emigration in the 1990s on the wages of highly educated could be as large as 15% to 20%.

Some of the countries that experience negative average effects from emigration (such as Ireland and the UK) offset these effects, partially or completely, with the positive effects of immigration. Others, however, such as Cyprus, Poland and Malta, fail to do so. The simulated effects of emigration, therefore, revealed some interesting patterns. First, in all scenarios and for all countries, emigration causes wage and (to a much smaller extent) employment levels of less educated natives to decrease. While the median loss is small (ranging between -0.4% and 0%), the less educated in some countries lose as much as 9%. Second, in most parameter configurations emigration decreases average native wages (and increases wages of more educated native non-movers). The aggregate effects of emigration on employment of non-migrants are usually very small and often negligible. The losses for less educated natives depend positively on the complementarity between more and less educated and on the intensity of human capital externalities. When those are set at the lowest level in the parameter range, the effects of emigration on wages of less educated are negligible. When they are set at their largest values, the losses are between 5% and 8% for some countries.

4. Extensions and Robustness Checks

The simulated wage and employment effects of immigration and emigration discussed in the previous Section are subject to caveats and possible measurement errors. The migration data are less than perfect. For example, emigration flows to some less developed countries are imputed; undocumented migrants are not fully measured among immigrants, and schooling is an imperfect measure of their human capital levels. Other issues may be due to the fact that the parameters used are estimated with error that should be accounted for. Finally, our exercise considers data from the 1990s which misses some recent large immigration flows from North Africa and the Middle East to Europe, and from Latin America to the US. These recent immigrant cohorts are also believed to be less educated which would influence our results. In this Section, we tackle all these issues in turn.[26]

---

[26] In the online Appendices we also set out a further extension: we calculate the effect of immigration when we limit it to people coming from 'poor' (i.e. non-OECD) countries. Most of the qualitative results are similar to those shown here for total immigration. We show these results as sometimes countries are particularly reluctant to open their borders to immigration from poor countries (see online Appendix Figures A1 and A2).

4.1. Actual Emigration Data Only

As described in detail in Section 2, we have census data on the stock of foreign-born migrants for a common set of 61 destination countries in 1990 and 2000, including all the OECD countries used in our analysis. However, for some of the remaining countries in the world, we use the existing data and the gravity-based imputations described in Section 2 to produce figures on their immigrant stocks. This implies that for the group of OECD countries in this article, the data on immigration are actual data from national censuses. However, the emigration data include a combination of actual and imputed data. Table A1 in online Appendix A shows what percentage of total emigration is imputed for each country. For most countries this is a very small or even negligible percentage, but for a few countries it is as large as 30%. To assess how the presence of the imputed data affect our results, in Figure 5(*a, b*) we show the wage effects of emigration, using only the actual data and removing the imputed portion of the emigration flows. Also panel (*a*) in Table 6 shows the range of the effects under the optimistic and pessimistic scenarios, when we include only the actual emigration data. The estimated effects are very similar to those of Table 5. For the countries that are most affected, because of the scale and selection of their emigration, the impact on the wages of less educated was between −6% and −8% in the optimistic scenario, whereas it was between −2% and −3% for the pessimistic scenario. For most countries, however, the negative effect on less educated native wages was much smaller in any scenario. The effect on the median country ranges between 0% and −1%. The effect on average wages is even smaller (in the range −0.4% to 0%) and also negative in most cases. The employment effects are all negligible. More importantly, these effects are very similar to those obtained when using all emigrant data (compare panel (*a*) of Table 6 with the last two rows of Table 5). The differences in the ranges of the effects and in specific effects for countries are usually as small as 0.1%.

4.2. Undocumented Immigrants and Skill Downgrading

The census data are the primary sources used to construct our immigration data for OECD countries. However, national censuses vary in their ability to properly measure undocumented immigration due to a variety of legal, economic and political constraints. In some countries, such as the US and Canada, the coverage of the resident population should be quite extensive and hence include the undocumented immigrant population (possibly with some small underestimates). In other countries, such as many in continental Europe, the censuses have a harder time in properly accounting for undocumented immigrants.

Several countries in Europe recently joined forces for the *Clandestino* study (European Union, 2010) which produced a picture of the undocumented population in 12 European countries for the years between 2000 and 2007. The study used several methods including surveys, data from regularisation laws and data on apprehension and expulsions of undocumented individuals, to produce estimates of the variable p_i, the fraction of undocumented in the total immigrant population of country i. We utilise these estimates, from around 2000 and we multiply the inflow of documented

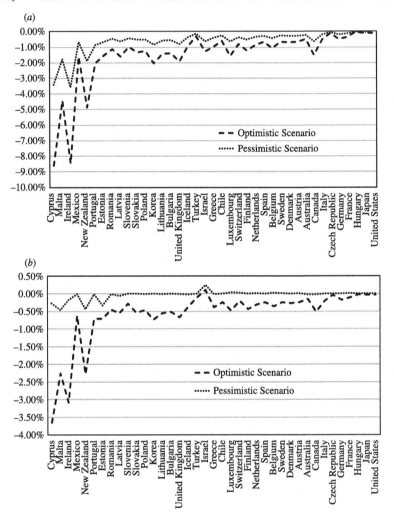

Fig. 5. *Wage Effects of Emigration Using Non-imputed Data Only, 1990–2000*
Notes. (*a*) Percentage effects on less educated native wages. (*b*) Percentage effects on average educated native wages. Values on the vertical axis are the simulated wage effects (in percentage of the initial wage) of emigration on native non-migrants. The parameter values corresponding to the 'pessimistic' and 'optimistic' scenarios are reported in Table 3.

(measured) immigrants over the period 1990–2000 by $p_i/(1 - p_i)$ to obtain a number of undocumented immigrants. Then, to maximise the possible impact of undocumented immigration on our estimates, we assume that all undocumented immigrants belong to the less educated category and we add these imputed numbers to the

Table 6
Robustness Checks

Model	σ_q	σ_m	λ	γ	Country rank by size of the effect:	Wages: Less educated natives (%)	Wages: Overall natives (%)	Wages: More educated natives (%)	Emp.: Less educated natives (%)	Emp.: Overall natives (%)	Emp.: More educated natives (%)
(a) Effects of emigration, using only non-imputed data											
Optimistic	1.3	6	0.75	0	Top	−0.1	0.0	22.1	0.1	0.0	0.0
					Median	−1.0	−0.4	1.71	0.0	0.0	0.0
					Bottom	−8.6	−3.6	0.0	0.0	0.0	0.0
Pessimistic	2.0	Infinity	0	0.2	Top	0.0	0.0	14.1	0.1	0.2	2.6
					Median	0.0	0.0	1.3	0.0	0.0	0.2
					Bottom	−3.6	−0.5	0.0	−0.2	0.0	0.0
(b) Effects of immigration including undocumented and skill downgrading											
Optimistic	1.3	6	0.75	0	Top	7.26	4.0	2.9	0.0	0.0	0.0
					Median	0.7	0.5	−0.1	0.0	0.0	0.0
					Bottom	−0.1	−0.2	−7.6	0.0	0.0	0.2
Pessimistic	2.0	Infinity	0	0.2	Top	2.7	0.2	1.2	0.5	0.2	−0.1
					Median	0.1	0.0	−0.5	0.0	0.0	0.0
					Bottom	−0.4	0.0	−8.7	0.0	0.0	−1.7
(c) Lower and upper bound of the 95% confidence interval											
Optimistic, 95% upper bound	1.01	3.03	1.10	−0.2	Top	11.2	6.6	3.8	0.0	0.0	2.0
					Median	1.3	0.9	−0.4	−0.2	−0.2	0.0
					Bottom	−0.3	−0.3	−10.6	−2.0	−1.6	−0.7
Pessimistic, 95% lower bound	10	Infinity	0	0.4	Top	0.6	0.0	0.1	0.2	0.1	0.0
					Median	0.0	0.0	−0.1	0.0	0.0	0.0
					Bottom	0.0	0.0	−1.9	0.0	0.0	−0.8
(d) Effects of immigration during the 2000s											
Optimistic	1.3	6	0.75	0	Top	7.9	4.7	1.9	0.0	0.0	0.0
					Median	0.7	0.6	0.2	0.0	0.0	0.0
					Bottom	0.3	0.2	−2.6	0.0	0.0	0.0
Pessimistic	2.0	0	infinity	0.2	Top	2.4	0.1	0.9	0.4	0.2	0.6
					Median	0.1	0.0	−0.4	0.0	0.0	−0.1
					Bottom	−0.3	0.0	−5.8	−0.1	0.0	−1.1

Notes. Each of the three rows corresponds to one simulation using the specified values of the parameters. We report the effects of immigration on wages and employment of native less educated, overall and more educated (respectively) in percentage changes. We show only the simulated effects for the countries with the highest (top), the median and lowest (bottom) values for each outcome.

corresponding groups in our database.[27] Only in Eastern European countries, Italy and Greece, do the upper-bound estimates of undocumented individuals reach values that are higher than 20% of the total immigrant population (e.g. 30% in Czech Republic, 37% in Poland, 23% in Greece and 33% in Italy). In all other European countries, the upper-bound estimates were lower than 10%. In particular, for the countries with the largest net inflows (Austria, Spain and Ireland), the estimates range between 3% and 10%.

A second reason that might cause under-estimation of the actual size of the unskilled immigrant population is 'skill downgrading'. As shown in several studies (such as Dustman *et al.* (2013) for the UK, Cohen-Goldner and Paserman (2011) for Israel as well as Mattoo *et al.* (2008) for the US), immigrants with intermediate and high education tend to find jobs in occupations typically staffed by natives with lower levels of schooling. Moreover, the quality of education abroad may not be as high as the quality in the receiving OECD countries. Hence, the actual 'human capital' supplied to the labour market might not correspond to what is indicated by their education levels, as reported in the census data. We might be over-estimating their contribution to the ratio of highly educated in the labour force by considering college-educated immigrants as fully equivalent to similarly educated natives. To correct for this bias, we use information on the occupations in which immigrants and natives are employed, by level of schooling in different countries (OECD, 2010) and we assign immigrants to high and low-education group based on their occupational distribution, relative to more and less educated natives.[28]

Figure 6(*a*, *b*) show the simulated wage effects on less educated and average native workers once we account for undocumented immigrants and downgrading of their education levels using the methods described above. Panel (*b*) in Table 6 shows the results of the same exercise for different parameter combinations. The thick solid line in Figure 6(*a*, *b*) connects the values obtained using the intermediate parameter configuration and accounting for downgrading and for the lower estimate for the share of undocumented workers. The thin solid line assumes the intermediate scenario and includes downgrading with high estimates of undocumented. The dashed line shows the pessimistic scenario with downgrading and high estimates of undocu-mented. The dashed line is really the most pessimistic scenario we can construct in accounting for undocumented migrants and skill downgrading: in it immigrants are perfect substitutes for natives; there are no externalities; undocumented immigrants are all counted as less educated and a part of highly educated immigrants are counted as low skilled because of their occupations. Despite these extreme assumptions, we still see positive effects on wages of less educated and on average in every country, with the exception of Austria. Less educated workers experience either no effect (such as the US, Denmark, Italy and Greece) or positive effects (as large as 3.5% in Ireland, Canada and Australia). Similarly, for average wages, the effect is zero (or very close) in most

---

[27] Table A5 in the online Appendix A shows the upper and lower estimates for p_i in all the countries. For the European countries not covered by the study, we assign the p_i of the closest country for which it is available. For non-European countries with a census system that covers all residents, we assume that undocumented individuals are included in our data. For Japan, South Korea and Chile, for which we have no information, we set the upper and lower bound of p_i to the average values in the sample.

[28] The detailed procedure used to convert immigrants into native skill groups using occupation is described in the online Appendix B.1.

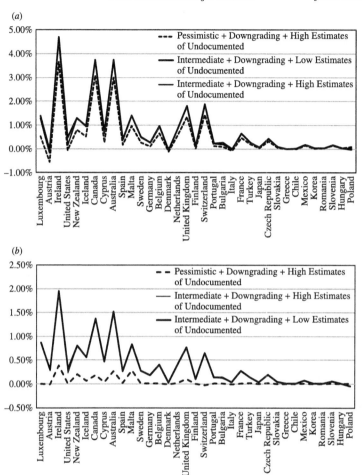

Fig. 6. *Wage Effects of Immigration Accounting for Undocumented and Downgrading, 1990–2000*
(Countries Ranked Left to Right by Immigration Rate)
Notes. (*a*) Percentage effects on less educated native wages. (*b*) Percentage effects on average native wages. Values on the vertical axis are the simulated wage effects (in percentage of the initial wage) of immigration on natives. We omit Israel, Lithuania, Latvia and Estonia from the chart as they are outliers. The parameter values corresponding to the 'pessimistic', 'intermediate' and 'optimistic' scenarios are reported in Table 3. The correction for undocumented is done using data from the European Union (2010) data set. The correction for downgrading uses occupational distribution of immigrants by schooling in each country from the OECD DIOC-E database.

countries in the worst-case scenario (dashed line). In the baseline and optimistic scenario, accounting for downgrading and undocumented still leaves average wage gains for natives in the order of 0 to 0.5%. These corrections attenuate the positive effects of the previous Section but in most cases they do not cancel, let alone reverse, them. A look at the ranges of simulated effects on employment of less educated and overall (panel (*b*) of Table 6) reveals that employment effects are still very small and positive ranging between 0% and 0.5%.

4.3. *Estimated Parameters' Confidence Intervals*

Another source of uncertainty in the simulated effects is due to the fact that, while we chose a large range in the parameter value, we did not account for the standard errors in their estimates. Are those errors so large that the estimated range is not very informative? In this section, we account for the estimation error in our simulations. In particular, panel (*c*) of Table 6, we show the lower bound of the 95% confidence interval for the pessimistic estimates and the upper bound for the 95% confidence interval for the optimistic scenario. We can be confident that the simulated effects are between these two bounds 95% of the time, no matter what scenario we choose, accounting for the sampling error of the parameter estimates. In particular, we consider, for each parameter estimate in the 'optimistic' scenario, the estimated standard error from the study that provides that estimate. Then we calculate the parameter values at the boundary of the 95% confidence interval.[29] We do this for all parameter and we report the largest effect. For the pessimistic scenario we do the same for all parameters and we report the lowest effect.[30] Panel (*c*) in Table 6 shows the parameter configuration at the 95% upper bound of the optimistic scenario, and at the 95% lower bound of the pessimistic one. Notice, interestingly, that the lower bound of the pessimistic scenario implies essentially zero effects for employment and wages of less educated natives in any country. Similarly, the effect on average wages at the lower bound of the pessimistic scenario is very close to zero for all countries. Having eliminated any source of complementarity and externality and making more and less educated as substitutable as possible we obtain a very small effect of immigration on average wages and on wages of less educated. At the other end of the spectrum, the upper bound of the optimistic estimates implies effects on wages of less educated and average natives that are quite high (+11% and +6.6%, respectively, for the most affected country). Notice in the case that the estimated elasticity of labour supply is negative, large increases in wages of less educated (and average) imply a slight decline in native employment, which decrease by as much as 1.6% for the most affected country. Overall, however, it is remarkable how even at the 95% boundaries, immigration is found to be either neutral or mildly positive in its effect on less educated and average wages. No parameter configuration implies a significant negative effect of immigration on less educated (or average) wages in any OECD country. This is a result of the significantly skill-biased composition of immigrants for all the considered countries.

4.4. *Effects of Immigration in the 2000s*

The data used so far cover migration patterns in the 1990s. Only with the collection and dissemination of data from the 2010 censuses, will an analysis of the last decade of

---

[29] We use, that is, the estimates equal to (average estimate) ±1.96 × (standard error).
[30] The details for the choice of parameters and standard errors to construct the lower and upper bound of the interval are reported in the online Appendices.

Table 7

*Immigration Rates for a Sample of EU Countries and the US, 1990–2000
and 2000–7*

Country	1990–2000 (%)	2000–2007 (%)
Cyprus	4.76	11.31
Spain	3.32	11.26
Luxembourg	12.53	8.46
Austria	9.35	5.06
United States	5.71	3.76
Sweden	2.66	3.66
Denmark	2.54	2.86
Portugal	1.55	2.81
Finland	1.74	2.68
Greece	0.24	2.46
France	0.81	1.26
Belgium	2.63	0.39
Netherlands	2.39	−0.45
Lithuania	−2.96	−1.71

Notes. The 2000–7 figures are obtained as our elaborations from the EULFS data
for the European countries, and using the ACS data for the US. The US rates are
relative to the 2000–9 period. The 1990–2000 figures are taken from Table 1.

migration be possible. The recent economic crisis, starting in 2007, reduced net
immigration rates to OECD countries drastically according to preliminary data
(Papademetriou *et al.*, 2011). During the 2000–7 period, some destination countries,
especially in Europe (mainly Spain, Italy, Greece and Ireland), experienced immigration rates even larger than the ones observed during the 1990s. Were these flows very
different from the previous ones? Was their composition less college intensive? Were
their effects on wages comparable to those of the 1990–2000 flows? To answer these
questions, we consider net immigration to 13 European countries for the period 2000–
7 plus immigration to the US during the 2000–9 period. The European data are from
the EU Labour Force surveys, that allow us to identify adults (older than 25 years) by
education level, separating natives from foreign-born immigrants.[31] For the US, we use
the American Community Survey data on the same definition of natives and
immigrants with different education levels. Table 7 shows the immigration rates for
the 2000–7[32] period for all the countries. We only included countries for which the
database includes the years 2000 as well as 2007 and for which the relevant
characteristics (age, education and place of birth) had fewer than 10% of missing
observations. This restriction excluded the UK, Italy and Ireland (among others). As
we see in Table 7, the country with a real boom, relative to the previous decade, was
Spain with an immigration rate of 11%. Luxembourg, Austria and the US, the other
countries with highest immigration rates, had lower rates than for the 1990s. As we are
excluding the crisis period (post-2007) for the European countries, most will end up
with even lower rates when the whole decade is considered. Figure 7(*a*, *b*) show the

[31] We thank Francesco D'Amuri for his help with the EULFS data.
[32] Immigration rates are calculated, as usual, as net immigrants during the period 2000–7 divided by total
residents in 2000.

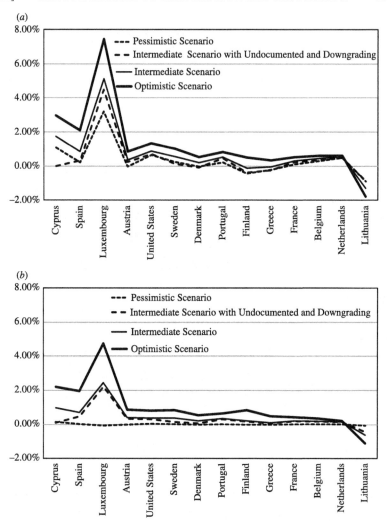

Fig. 7. *Wage Effects of Total Immigration on Native Workers, 2000–7 (Countries Ranked Left to Right by Immigration Rate – Sample for the US and EU Countries)*
Notes. (*a*) Percentage effects on less educated native wages. (*b*) Percentage effects on average native wages. The stock of immigrants and net immigration are calculated using EU Labour Force Survey data for European countries, and American Community Survey data for the US. The years considered are 2000 and 2007 for the European countries and 2000–9 for the US. We only include European countries with at least 80% of non-missing observations for age, schooling and country of birth.

simulated native wage effects (for less educated and for the average respectively) due to immigration 2000–7. Panel (*d*) in Table 6 shows the corresponding numerical values for the range of effects in 2000–7 using the most optimistic and most pessimistic parameter configurations. In Figure 7, the countries are listed in decreasing order of total immigration rates for the 2000–7 period. In most cases all specifications produce positive effects ranging from 0% to 2% in Figure 7(a) and between 0% and 1% in Figure 7(b). Exceptions are Luxembourg, with potentially large positive effects on less educated wages (between 3% and 7%). Only Lithuania, which experienced negative net immigration (hence emigration of foreign residents) suffered a 1–2% wage loss for the less educated. The other countries experienced average wage effects on natives between 0% and 4.7%, depending on the country and on the scenario. The effect on wages of less educated is almost always positive in all scenarios. One specification (intermediate dashed line) includes the corrections for undocumented and downgrading which somewhat reduce the gains but do not change the overall picture. Overall, the large immigration magnets of the 2000s (Spain, Austria and the US) experienced small-to-moderate positive effects for the wages of their less educated. The impact on employment was very small, in the order of few tenths of a percentage point.

5. Conclusions

Closing the borders to immigrants, restricting the inflow of people from poor countries and making their entry more costly are sometimes presented as a way of protecting employment and wages of domestic workers, especially those at the bottom of the income distribution. This study uses a new global data set on migration patterns and a simple aggregate model to show that immigration is likely to help native wages and employment. This is simply due to the fact that immigrants in OECD countries are more educated than non-migrant natives and college-educated workers are likely to create more opportunities for the receiving economy. We show that, in the long run, the wage and employment effects of immigration in the 1990s and in the 2000s were rather small and always positive for less educated workers of all OECD countries. Less educated workers in Canada, Australia, the US, Luxembourg, the UK and Switzerland, which were among the magnets of international migrants, all experienced positive long-run labour market effects from immigration, between 1% and 5%. Our most important and novel results are, however, on emigration, which entails the loss of talent and brains in much larger proportion than the loss of unskilled workers. Our results indicate that emigration poses a bigger threat for low-skilled workers left behind, even in some OECD countries. Less educated workers in Cyprus, Malta, Ireland, New Zealand and Portugal all lost between 1% and 6% of their wages because of the flight of highly educated emigrants. While net emigration, especially of college-educated individuals, may be a symptom of economic malaise and not its cause, it certainly directly contributes to lower productivity and wages of the remaining workers.

These results are striking. Hence, we undertake a series of robustness checks. We use estimates of the undocumented immigrants to correct for their flows. Second, we account for the actual occupations of highly educated immigrants to correct for skill downgrading. Third, we consider the largest 95% confidence interval for the effects. None of the corrections reverse (although some attenuate) the findings of positive long-run effects of immigrants on wage and employment of less educated workers in all OECD countries.

Université Catholique de Louvain
The World Bank
University of California, Davis

Submitted: 2 April 2012
Accepted: 14 June 2013

Additional Supporting Information may be found in the online version of this article:

Appendix A. Theory Derivations and Extensions.
Appendix B. Further Extensions and Robustness Checks.
Data S1.

References

Acemoglu, D., and Angrist, J. (2001). 'How large are human-capital externalities? Evidence from compulsory schooling laws', in (B. S. Bernanke and K. Rogoff, eds.), *NBER Macroeconomics Annual 2000, volume 15*, Cambridge, MA: MIT Press.

Acemoglu, D. and Zilibotti, F. (2001). 'Productivity differences', *Quarterly Journal of Economics*, vol. 116(2), pp. 563–606.

Angrist, J. (1995). 'The economic returns to schooling in the West Bank and Gaza Strip', *American Economic Review*, vol. 85(5), pp. 1065–87.

Azariadis, C. and Drazen, A. (1990). 'Threshold externalities in economic development', *Quarterly Journal of Economics*, vol. 105(2), pp. 501–26.

Barro, R.J. and Lee, J.W. (2010). 'A new data set of educational attainment in the world, 1950–2010', Working Paper 15902, National Bureau of Economic Research.

Barro, R.J. and Sala-i-Martin, X. (2003). *Economic Growth*, Cambridge, MA: MIT Press.

Beine, M., Docquier F. and Özden, Ç. (2011). 'Diasporas', *Journal of Development Economics*, vol. 95(1), pp. 30–41.

Benhabib, J. and Spiegel, M.M. (2005). 'Human capital and technology diffusion', in (P. Aghion and S. Durlauf, eds.), *Handbook of Economic Growth*, pp. 935–66, New York: American Elsevier Publishing Co.

Borjas, G.J. (2003). 'The labour demand curve is downward sloping: reexamining the impact of immigration on the labour market', *Quarterly Journal of Economics*, vol. 118(4), pp. 1335–74.

Borjas, G.J., Grogger, J. and Hanson, G.H. (2012). 'Comment: on estimating elasticities of substitution', *Journal of the European Economic Association*, vol. 10(1), pp. 198–210.

Card, D. (2001). 'Immigrant inflows, native outflows, and the local labour market impacts of higher immigration', *Journal of labour Economics*, vol. 19(1), pp. 22–64.

Card, D. (2009). 'Immigration and inequality', *American Economic Review*, vol. 99(2), pp. 1–21.

Card, D. and Lemieux, T. (2001). 'Can falling supply explain the rising returns to college for younger men? A cohort based analysis', *Quarterly Journal of Economics*, vol. 116(2), pp. 705–46.

Caselli, F. and Coleman, W. (2006). 'The world technology frontier', *American Economic Review*, vol. 96(3), pp. 499–522.

Ciccone, A. and Peri, G. (2005). 'Long-run substitutability between more and less educated workers: evidence from U.S. states 1950–1990', *Review of Economics and Statistics*, vol. 87(4), pp. 652–63.

Ciccone, A. and Peri, G. (2006). 'Identifying human capital externalities: theory with applications', *Review of Economic Studies*, vol. 73, pp. 381–412.

Cohen, D. and Soto, M. (2007). 'Growth and human capital: good data, good results', *Journal of Economic Growth*, vol. 12(1), pp. 51–76.

Cohen-Goldner, S. and Paserman, D. (2011). 'The dynamic impact of immigration on native's labour-market outcomes: evidence from Israel', *European Economics Review*, vol. 55(8), pp. 1027–45.

D'Amuri, F., Ottaviano, G.I.P. and Peri G. (2010). 'The labour market impact of immigration in Western Germany in the 1990s', *European Economic Review*, vol. 54(3), pp. 550–70.

De la Fuente, A. and Domenech, R. (2006). 'Human capital in growth regression: how much difference does quality data make?', *Journal of the European Economic Association*, vol. 4(1), pp. 1–36.

Docquier, F. and Marfouk, A. (2006). 'International migration by educational attainment (1990–2000)', in (C. Ozden and M. Schiff, eds.), *International Migration, Remittances and Development*, New York: Palgrave Macmillan.

Docquier, F., Lowell, B.L. and Marfouk, A. (2009). 'A gendered assessment of highly skilled emigration', *Population and Development Review*, vol. 35(2), pp. 297–321.

Docquier, F., Özden, Ç., Parsons, C.R. and Artuc, E. (2012). 'A global assessment of human capital mobility: the role of non-OECD destinations', Discussion Paper 2012-022, IRES. Available at http://sites.uclouvain.be/econ/DP/IRES/2012022.pdf.

Docquier, F., Özden, Ç. and Peri, G. (2010). 'The wage effects of immigration and emigration', Working Paper 16646, National Bureau of Economic Research.

Dustmann, C., Frattini, T. and Preston, I. (2013). 'The effect of immigration along the distribution of wages', *Review of Economic Studies*, vol. 80(1), pp. 145–73.

Elsner, B. (2011). 'Emigration and wages: the EU enlargement experiment', Trinity Economics Papers 1311, Trinity College Dublin.

European Union (2010). 'Clandestino project 2007–2009', available at http://clandestino.eliamep.gr/project-results/ (last accessed: 13 June 2013).

Evers, M., de Mooij, R. and van Vuuren, D. (2008). 'The wage elasticity of labour supply: a synthesis of empirical estimates', *De Economist*, vol. 156(1), pp. 25–43.

Fallon, P.R. and Layard, R. (1975). 'Capital-skill complementarity, income distribution, and output accounting', *Journal of Political Economy*, vol. 83(2), pp. 279–302.

Flood, L. and MaCurdy, T. (1992). 'Work disincentive effects of taxes: an empirical analysis of Swedish men', *Carnegie-Rochester Conference Series on Public Policy*, vol. 37(1), pp. 239–77.

Freeman, R.B. (2006). 'People flows in globalization', Working Paper 12315, National Bureau of Economics Research.

Friedberg, R. (2001). 'The impact of mass-migration on the Israeli labour market', *Quarterly Journal of Economics*, vol. 116(5), pp. 1373–408.

Goldin, C. and Katz, L. (2008). *The Race Between Education and Technology*, Cambridge, MA: Harvard University Press.

Grogger, J. and Hanson, G. (2011). 'Income maximization and the selection and sorting of international migrants', *Journal of Development Economics*, vol. 95(1), pp. 42–57.

Hall, R.E. and Jones, C.I. (1999). 'Why do some countries produce so much more output per worker than others?', *Quarterly Journal of Economics*, vol. 114(1), pp. 83–116.

Hendricks, L. (2004). 'A database of Mincerian earnings regressions', available at http://www.lhendricks.org/Mincer.htm (last accessed: 13 June 2013).

Iranzo, S. and Peri, G. (2009). 'Schooling externalities, technology and productivity: theory and evidence from US states', *Review of Economics and Statistics*, vol. 91(2), pp. 420–31.

Johnson, G.E. (1970). 'The demand for labour by educational category', *Southern Economic Journal*, vol. 37(2), pp. 190–203.

Katz, L. and Murphy, K. (1992). 'Changes in relative wages 1963–1987: supply and demand factors', *Quarterly Journal of Economics*, vol. 107(1), pp. 35–78.

Kerr, S.P. and Kerr, W. (2009). 'Economic impact of immigration: a survey', Working Paper 09-13, Harvard Business School.

Krusell, P., Ohanian, L.E., Rios-Rull, J.V. and Violante, G.L. (2000). 'Capital-skill complementarity and inequality: a macroeconomic analysis', *Econometrica*, vol. 68(5), pp. 1029–53.

Lucas, R.E.J. (1988). 'On the mechanics of economic development', *Journal of Monetary Economics*, vol. 22(1), pp. 3–42.

MaCurdy, T., Green, P. and Paarsch, H. (1990). 'Assessing empirical approaches for analyzing taxes and labour supply', *Journal of Human Resources*, vol. 25(3), pp. 415–90.

Manacorda, M., Manning, A. and Wadsworth, J. (2012). 'The impact of immigration on the structure of wages: theory and evidence from Britain', *Journal of the European Economic Association*, vol. 10(1), pp. 120–51.

Mattoo, A., Neagu, I.C. and Ozden, Ç. (2008). 'Brain waste? Educated immigrants in the US labour market', *Journal of Development Economics*, vol. 87(2), pp. 255–69.

Mayda, A.M. (2010). 'International migration: a panel data analysis of the determinants of bilateral flows', *Journal of Population Economics*, vol. 23(4), pp. 1249–74.

Mishra, P. (2007). 'Emigration and wages in source countries: evidence from Mexico', *Journal of Development Economics*, vol. 82(1), pp. 180–99.

Moretti, E. (2004a). 'Estimating the social return to higher education: evidence from longitudinal and repeated cross-sectional data', *Journal of Econometrics*, vol. 121(1), pp. 175–212.

Moretti, E. (2004b). 'Workers' education, spillovers and productivity: evidence from plant-level production functions', *American Economic Review*, vol. 94(3), pp. 656–90.

Murphy, K.M., Riddle, W.C. and Romer, P.M. (1998). 'Wages, skills and technology in the United States and Canada', in (E. Helpman, ed.), *General Purpose Technology and Economic Growth*, pp. 283–310, Cambridge, MA: MIT Press.

2014]   LABOUR EFFECTS OF IMMIGRATION AND EMIGRATION   1145

OECD (2010). 'Database on immigrants in OECD and non-OECD countries', available at http://www.oecd.org/document/33/0,3746,en_2649_37415_46561249_1_1_1_37415,00.html (last accessed: 13 June 2013).
OECD (2011). *Society at a Glance, 2011*, Paris: OECD Social Indicators.
Ottaviano, G.I.P. and Peri, G. (2012). 'Rethinking the effect of immigration on wages', *Journal of the European Economic Association*, vol. 10(1), pp. 152–97.
Ozden, Ç. and Neagu, I.C. (2008). 'Immigrant women's participation and performance in the US labour market', in (R. Morrison, M. Schiff and M. Sjöblom, eds.), *The International Migration of Women*, pp. 153–84, Washington, DC: World Bank and Palgrave Macmillan.
Ozden, Ç., Parsons, C.R., Schiff, M. and Walmsley, T. (2011). 'Where on Earth is everybody? The evolution of global bilateral migration 1960–2000', *World Bank Economic Review*, vol. 25(1), pp. 12–56.
Papademetriou, D.G., Sumption, M. and Terrazas, A. (2011). *Migration and the Great Recession. The Transatlantic Experience*, Washington, DC: Migration Policy Institution.
Peri, G. (2011). 'Rethinking the area approach: immigrants and the labour market in California, 1960–2005', *Journal of International Economics*, vol. 84(1), pp. 1–14.
Ramsey, F. (1928). 'A mathematical theory of saving', Economic Journal, vol. 38(152), pp. 543–59.
Romiti, A. (2012). 'Immigrants-native complementarieties in production: evidence from Italy', mimeo, University of Turin.
Solow, R. (1956). 'A contribution to the theory of economic growth', *Quarterly Journal of Economics*, vol. 70(1), pp. 65–94.
van Soest, A., Woittiez, I. and Kapteyn, A. (1990). 'Labour supply, income taxes, and hours restrictions in the Netherlands', *Journal of Human Resources*, vol. 25(3), pp. 517–58.
Vandenbussche, J., Aghion, P. and Meghir, C. (2006). 'Growth, distance to frontier and composition of human capital', *Journal of Economic Growth*, vol. 11(2), pp. 97–127.

II
IMMIGRANTS
AND PRODUCTIVITY

The economic value of cultural diversity: evidence from US cities

Gianmarco I.P. Ottaviano* and Giovanni Peri**

Abstract

What are the economic consequences to U.S. natives of the growing diversity of American cities? Is their productivity or utility affected by cultural diversity as measured by diversity of countries of birth of U.S. residents? We document in this paper a very robust correlation: US-born citizens living in metropolitan areas where the share of foreign-born increased between 1970 and 1990, experienced a significant increase in their wage and in the rental price of their housing. Such finding is economically significant and survives omitted variable bias and endogeneity bias. As people and firms are mobile across cities in the long run we argue that, in equilibrium, these correlations are consistent with a net positive effect of cultural diversity on the productivity of natives.

Keywords: cultural diversity, immigrants, productivity, local amenities, urban economics
JEL classifications: O4, R0, F1, O18
Date submitted: 7 September 2004 **Date accepted:** 20 April 2005

1. Introduction

Since the 1965 amendments to the Immigration and Nationality Act immigration into the United States has been on an upward surge. Indeed, immigration rates have been accelerating since the eighties. As a consequence, during the last thirty years foreign born residents in the United States have increased substantially as a share of both the total population and the labor force. In 1970 only 4.8% of the US residents were foreign-born; that percentage grew to 8% in 1990 and to 12.5% in the year 2000. Similarly, although to a lesser extent, other industrialized countries such as Europe and Australia have also recently experienced rising pressures from immigrants.[1] This phenomenon has spurred a heated policy debate and galvanized academic interest.

There is a large and growing body of empirical literature on the consequences of migration (see, among others Borjas 1994, 1995, 1999, 2003; Borjas et al., 1997; Boeri et al., 2002; Card 1990, 2001; Card and Di Nardo, 2000). This literature, however, has disproportionately focussed on one aspect of the subject: the impact of low-skilled immigrants on US wages. These studies typically treat labor markets for different skills as segmented, and focus on the consequences of wages for different skill-groups in the

* Department of Economics, University of Bologna, Strada Maggiore 45, 40125 Bologna, Italy, FEEM and CEPR.
email <ottavian@economia.unibo.it>
** Giovanni Peri, UCLA International Institute, 10266 Bunche Hall, UCLA, Los Angeles, CA 90024 USA, University of California, Davis and NBER.
email <gperi@international.ucla.edu>
1   See Peri (2005) for a comparison of immigration in the US and in the EU during the nineties.

10 • *Ottaviano and Peri*

short and medium run. Our work takes a different angle. Rather than study the short-run effects of new immigrants on the receiving country in a classic model of skill supply and demand, we consider a simple multi-city model of production and consumption in order to ask 'what is the economic value of "diversity" that the foreign born bring to each city'. The foreign born conceivably have different sets of skills and abilities than the US born, and therefore could serve as valuable factors in the production of differentiated goods and services. As different US cities attract very different shares of foreign-born we can learn about the value of such 'diversity' from the long-run equilibrium distribution of wages and prices across cities. For the rest of the paper, the term 'cultural diversity' will refer to the diversity of the workers' countries of birth (rather than ethnicity or ancestry characteristics) and will be measured by an index of 'plurality' of countries of origin.

Diversity over several dimensions has been considered by economists as valuable both in consumption and production. Jacobs (1969) attributes the prosperity of cities to their industrial diversity. Quigley (1998) and Glaeser et al. (2001) identify the diversity of available consumption goods and services as one of the attractive features of cities. Florida (2002a, 2002b) stresses the importance of the diversity of creative professions employed in research and development or high tech industries. More generally, Fujita et al. (1999) use the 'love of variety' in preferences and technology as the building block of their theory of spatial development: the production of a larger variety of goods and services in a particular location increases the productivity and utility of people living in that location.

Against this background, we conjecture that cultural diversity may very well be an important aspect of urban diversity, influencing local production and/or consumption.[2] The aim of this paper is to test this conjecture by quantifying the value of cultural diversity to US-born people. Who can deny that Italian restaurants, French beauty shops, German breweries, Belgian chocolate stores, Russian ballets, Chinese markets, and Indian tea houses all constitute valuable consumption amenities that would be inaccessible to Americans were it not for their foreign-born residents? Similarly the skills and abilities of foreign-born workers and thinkers may complement those of native workers and thus boost problem solving and efficiency in the workplace.[3] Cultural diversity, therefore, may increase consumption variety and improve the productivity of natives. On the other hand, natives may not enjoy living in a multi-cultural environment if they feel that their own cultural values are being endangered. Moreover, intercultural frictions may reduce productivity, particularly if natives associate increasing immigration with further job losses for the US born. Thus cultural diversity could possibly decrease both the utility and the productivity of natives.

We focus on 160 major metropolitan areas in the US, for which we can construct consistent data between 1970 and 1990. While these metropolitan areas do not cover

---

2   An economically oriented survey of the pros and cons of ethnic diversity is presented by Alesina and La Ferrara (2003).

3   The anedoctical evidence of the contribution of foreign born to 'big thinking' in the US is quite rich. One striking example is the following. In the last ten years, out of the 47 US-based Nobel laureates in Chemistry, Physics and Medicine, 25% (14 laureates) were not US-born. During the same time period the share of foreign-born in the general population was on average only 10%. From our perspective, such example is interesting because research in hard sciences is typically based on large team work.

The economic value of cultural diversity: evidence from US cities • 11

the whole US urban population, they include the largest and most important cities. More importantly, they span the whole range of 'diversity', for they include the most diverse cities (New York, Los Angeles, San Francisco) along with some of the least diverse. We use the 'index of fractionalization' (by the country of birth of each city resident) in order to measure cultural diversity across these 160 cities.[4] This index measures the probability that, in any one city, two individuals chosen at random were born in different countries. Cities entirely populated by US-born individuals would have an index of fractionalization equal to 0. Going to the other extreme, if each individual within a city was born in a different country, the index would equal one. US cities vary wildly by this measure, ranging from 0.02 (Cleveland) to 0.58 (Los Angeles). Since US-born people are highly mobile across US cities, following Roback (1982) we develop a model of 'open cities' that allows us to use the observed variations of wages and rents of US-born workers to identify the production and consumption gains associated with cultural diversity. In particular, we estimate two regressions in which cultural diversity, measured as 'fractionalization' (or the share of foreign-born residents) affects the average wage received and the average rent paid by US-born workers. Our main finding is that, on average, *cultural diversity has a net positive effect on the productivity of US-born citizens* because it is positively correlated with both the average wage received and the average rent paid by US-born individuals. This partial correlation survives the inclusion of many variables that proxy for productivity and amenity shocks across cities.

Two fundamental concerns arise when we attempt to interpret these correlations as *causal* effects of diversity on the wages and rents of natives, namely a potential endogeneity bias and the possibility of spatial selection of natives. Endogeneity works as follows. Cities may experience an increase in the average wage from a positive economic shock, disproportionately attracting immigrants and thus witnessing an increase in diversity (this hypothesis is often referred to as 'boom cities'). If this were the true story, the measured impact of diversity on wages and rents would be upwardly biased. To tackle this problem, we use instrumental variable estimations, a method widely used among economists that requires an 'auxiliary' variable whose exogenous variation affects diversity in a city (but not its productivity). Such a variable allows us to isolate that portion of the correlation between diversity and wages that is due to the causal effect of diversity on wages.

The spatial selection of native workers, on the other hand, is harder to deal with. In fact, if the presence of foreign-born people attracts a particular type of US born worker (call this group 'tolerant') and these workers also happen to be more productive, then the correlation between diversity and productivity of natives may be the effect of this selection rather than of complementarities or externalities with foreign-born. The best we can do is to control for observable characteristics of US-born residents and assume that their 'tolerance' is not highly correlated with the residual (unobserved) productivity. This issue, however, is certainly not settled with this paper and needs more research. We will come back to it in the final part of the paper.

The rest of the paper is organized as follows. Section 2 reviews the literature on the economic consequences of immigration and cultural diversity. In particular we

---

4   As an alternative and perhaps more intuitive measure of diversity in a city we also use, in several parts of the analysis, the share of foreign-born residents.

12 • *Ottaviano and Peri*

differentiate our work from (and reconcile it with) the common findings in labor economics that immigrants have negative or zero effects on the wages of US-born workers. Section 3 introduces our dataset and surveys the main stylized facts. Section 4 develops the theoretical model that is used to design and interpret our estimation strategy. Section 5 presents the results from the basic estimation, checks their robustness and tackles the issue of endogeneity. Section 6 discusses the results and provides some important caveats and qualifications to our conclusions.

2. Literature on diversity

Cultural diversity is a broad concept that has attracted the attention of both economists and social scientists. The applied 'labor' literature has analyzed ethnic diversity and ethnic 'segregation' in the US, as well as their impact on economic discrimination and the achievements of minorities.[5] The present paper does not focus on this aspect of cultural diversity even though we control for black-white composition issues.

More closely related to our analysis is the literature concerning the impact of immigration on the US labor market. Several contributions by George Borjas (notably Borjas, 1994, 1995, 1999, 2001 and 2003) focus on the issue of US immigration as a whole, and its effect on native workers. Similarly, important contributions by David Card (notably, Card, 1990; Butcher and Card, 1991; Card and Di Nardo, 2000; Card, 2001) analyze the wages and reactions of domestic workers to inflows of new immigrants by exploiting the geographic variation of immigration rates and wages across US states or US cities. These contributions do not achieve a consensus view either on the effect of new immigrants on the wages of domestic workers (which seems small except, possibly, for low skill levels) or on the effect of new immigrants on the migration behavior of domestic workers. Let us emphasize, however, that the negative (significant or small) effect that is found in this literature is merely a 'relative' effect. Immigrants bring down the relative wages of low-skilled workers (but raise the wages of intermediately-skilled workers) due to their composition (abundant in low skills and scarce in intermediate skills). This, however, does not comment on the overall (average) effect on US workers. In the presence of complementarities between the skills of immigrants and the skills of natives, or of externalities from highly skilled workers (who are also abundant among immigrants), the impact of immigration on the average wage of US born workers may very well be positive. While the labor literature estimates the relative effect of immigration within labor markets segmented by skills (such an effect would be negative if different skills are imperfect substitutes), we focus on the average effect of immigration that results from aggregating those effects with the positive complementarity-effects and the positive externality-effects.[6] This is a novel approach, and while we do not deny that a shift of relative wages (between skills) takes place as a consequence of immigration, we focus on the average overall effect on wages of US-born workers

---

5   Notable examples are Card and Krueger (1992, 1993), Cutler and Glaeser (1997), Eckstein and Wolpin (1999), Mason (2000).

6   While in the present paper we simplify these effects into an overall effect of diversity on the TFP of US-born workers, in Ottaviano and Peri (2005) we separately model and analyze the effects of complementarieties across skills. We find that the (positive) empirical effects of migration on the average wage of US-born workers are very close to the theoretically calculated effects from the diversity of skills generated by immigrants.

and find it significantly positive. Recently, evidence of a positive effect of immigrant inflows on rents in cities has been provided by Saiz (2003a, 2003b), although he interprets this as a consequence of increased demand in housing rather than an increased value of houses due to higher diversity and higher wages. To our knowledge this is the first work that looks at a general equilibrium effect of immigration (diversity) on wages, employment and rents of US born residents.

In short, the standard labor literature assumes that immigrants and domestic workers within a particular skill group are homogeneous, so that immigration will shift the labor supply and change local wages in that skill group, the extent of which will depend on the mobility of domestic workers. Our approach takes a rather different stand. We believe that 'place of birth' can be a feature that differentiates individuals in terms of their attributes, and that this differentiation may have positive or negative effects on the productivity (through complementarities and externalities) and the utility (through taste for variety) of US-born residents. Moreover, we consider equilibrium variations of wages and rents in the long-run, relying on the assumption of mobility of native workers and firms across cities.

Relevant to our work, several researchers in the social sciences have related diversity with urban agglomeration. The functioning and thriving of urban clusters relies on the variety of people, factors, goods and services within them. Examples abound in the urban studies literature. Jacobs (1969) views economic diversity as the key factor of a city's success. Sassen (1994) studies 'global cities' (such as London, Paris, New York, and Tokyo) and their strategic role in the development of activities that are central to world economic growth and innovation. A key feature of these cities is the cultural diversity of their populations. Similarly, Bairoch (1988) sees cities and their diversity as the engines of economic growth. Such diversity, however, has been seen mainly in terms of the diversified provision of consumer goods and services, as well as productive inputs (see, e.g. Quigley, 1998; Glaeser et al., 2001). In his work within the nexus of sociology and economics, Richard Florida (2002a, 2002b) argues that 'diverse' and tolerant cities are more likely to be populated by creative people, thus attracting industries such as high tech and research that heavily rely on creativity and innovative ability. The positive 'production value' of diversity has also been stressed in the literature on the organization and management of teams. Here the standard assumption is that higher diversity can lead to more innovation and creativity by increasing the number of ways groups frame problems, thus producing a richer set of alternative solutions and consequently better decisions. Lazear (1999) provides an attempt to model team interactions. He defines the 'global firm' as a team whose members come from different cultures or countries. Combining workers whose countries of origin have different cultures, legal systems, and languages imposes costs on the firm that would not be present if all the workers had similar backgrounds. However, complementarity between workers, in terms of skills, can more than offset the costs of cross-cultural interaction.[7]

Finally, several studies in political economics have looked at the historical effects of cultural and ethnic diversity on the formation and quality of institutions.

---

7   Berliant and Fujita (2004) model 'assimilation' as a result of team work: the very process of cooperative knowledge creation reduces the heterogeneity of team members through the accumulation of knowledge in common. In this respect, a perpetual reallocation of members across different teams may be necessary to keep creativity alive.

The traditional wisdom (confirmed by Easterly and Levine, 1997) had been that more fragmented (i.e. diverse) societies promote more conflicts and predatory behavior, stifling economic growth. However, recent studies have questioned that logic by showing that higher ethnic diversity is not necessarily harmful to economic development (see, e.g., Lian and Oneal, 1997). Collier (2001) finds that, as long as institutions are democratic, fractionalized societies perform better in the private sector than more homogenous ones. Framed within efficient institutions, diversity may serve as a valuable asset for society.

3. Cultural diversity, wages and rents

The questions we are interested in are the following. How does cultural diversity affect the US-born? Do they benefit or loose from the presence of foreign-born? How do we measure such benefits or costs?

We are able to extract interesting insights into these questions by analyzing the wage and rent distributions across cities, assuming that such distributions are the equilibrium outcomes of economically motivated choices. We assume that workers and firms are mobile across cities, and so can change their location in the long run if a productivity shock or a price differential were to arise. Since people can respond to changes in the local working and living environment of cities, the wage and rent variations that we observe in the long run should reflect a spatial equilibrium: workers and firms are indifferent among alternative locations as they have eliminated any systematic difference in indirect utility and profits through migration. Before formalizing these ideas in Section 4, we put our theoretical analysis into context by introducing our measure of cultural diversity (Section 3.1) and by establishing the main stylized facts about wages, rents and diversity in US cities (Section 3.3).

3.1. Data and diversity index

Data at the Metropolitan Statistical Area (MSA) level for the United States are available from different sources. We use mostly the Census Public Use Microdata Sample (PUMS) for the years 1970 and 1990 in order to calculate wages and rents for specific groups of citizens in each MSA. We use the 1/100 sample from the 15% PUMS of 1970 and the 5% PUMS for 1990. We also use data from the 'County and City Data Book' from several years in order to obtain some aggregate variables, such as employment, income, population and spending on local public goods. We consider 160 Standard MSA's that could be consistently identified in each census year. Our dataset contains around 1,200,000 individual observations for 1990, and 500,000 for 1970. We use these to construct aggregate variables and indices at the MSA level. The reasons for focusing on metropolitan areas are two-fold. First, urban areas constitute closely connected economic units within which interactions are intense. Second, they exhibit a higher degree of diversity than non-urban areas because immigrants traditionally settle in large cities. While it is possible to construct data only on 160 metropolitan areas (using 1970 and 1990 PUMS of the US Bureau of Census) those areas include the most important US cities, spanning a wide range of variation in terms of cultural diversity. Adding all the other metropolitan areas would simply amount to adding more observations characterized by low and similar levels of diversity. This would

The economic value of cultural diversity: evidence from US cities • 15

certainly add some noise, but probably would not help much in the identification of the effect of diversity on wages and rents.

We measure the average wage of native workers in an MSA using the yearly wage of white US-born male residents between 40 and 50 years of age. We denote by $\bar{w}_{US,c,t}$ the resulting average wage for city c in year t. This value is neither affected by composition effects nor distorted by potential discrimination factors (across genders or ethnicity) or life-cycle considerations. It can therefore serve as a good proxy for the average wage of US-born workers in the city, comparable across census years. The correlation between $\bar{w}_{US,c,t}$ and the degree of diversity of a city comes only through the equilibrium effect of diversity on the labor demand and supply of native workers. As a measure of the average land rent in an MSA we use the average monthly rent paid per room (i.e. the monthly rent divided by the number of rooms) by white US-born male residents of working age (16–65 year).[8] We denote this measure (for city c in year t) as $\bar{r}_{US,c,t}$. While this measure does not control for housing quality (beyond the number of rooms), there is no reason to think that housing quality is related to the percentage of foreign-born in a city, so this measure should not induce any relevant bias in the relation.

Turning to our key explanatory variable, our measure of cultural diversity considers the country of birth of people as defining their cultural identity. Foreign born residents have always been an important part of the US population, and their share of the population has only grown larger in the past decades. In 1970, they constituted 4.8% of the total population, while in 1990 they reached 8%, still continuing to grow afterwards. Our measure of cultural diversity is the so called 'index of fractionalization' (henceforth, simply 'diversity index'), routinely used in the political economics literature. This index has been popularized by cross-country studies by Mauro (1995) and has been widely used since. The index is simply the probability that two randomly selected individuals in a community belong to different groups. It accounts for the two main dimensions of diversity, i.e. 'richness' (number of groups) and 'evenness' (balanced distribution of individuals across groups).[9] Specifically, we use the variable CoB (Country of Birth of a person) to define the cultural identity of each group. The diversity index is defined as:

$$div_{ct} = 1 - \sum_{i=1}^{M}(CoB_i^c)_t^2 \qquad (1)$$

where $(CoB_i^c)_t$ is the share of people born in country i among the residents of city c in year t. This index is an increasing measure of both the cultural 'richness' of a city (i.e. the number of groups) and its cultural 'diversity' (i.e. the evenness of groups' sizes). It reaches its minimum value 0 when all individuals are born in the same country, and its maximum value 1 when there are no individuals born in the same country. Intuitively, when all individuals belong to the same group, the probability that two randomly selected individuals belong to different groups is 0, whereas it equals 1 when all individuals belong to

---

8 The housing market is less segmented by skills than the labor market. Therefore we use a larger age-range in order to calculate average rents.

9 Despite differences that may seem notable at first sight, most statistical measures of diversity are either formally equivalent or at least highly correlated when run on the same data set. See Maignan et al. (2003) for details.

16 • *Ottaviano and Peri*

Table 1. Foreign Born living in 160 U.S. metropolitan areas 15 Largest Groups 1970, 1990

Country of origin	Percentage of total foreign born 1970	Country of origin	Percentage of total foreign born 1990
Canada	9.0%	Mexico	20.0%
Italy	8.1%	Philippines	6.0%
Germany	7.8%	Cuba	4.2%
Mexico	7.3%	Germany	3.2%
Syria	7.0%	Canada	3.2%
Cuba	5.1%	China	2.8%
Poland	4.5%	India	2.8%
UK	4.4%	Viet-Nam	2.7%
Philippine	2.3%	El Salvador	2.6%
USSR	2.3%	Italy	2.4%
Ireland	2.3%	Korea	2.2%
China	2.3%	UK	2.2%
Yugoslavia	1.7%	Japan	1.8%
Greece	1.6%	Jamaica	1.7%
Hungary	1.6%	Colombia	1.6%
Foreign born as % of working age total population, 1970	8.0%	Foreign born as % of working age total population, 1990	11.9%

Source: Authors' elaborations on 1970 and 1990 PUMS census data.

different groups. On the other hand, for a given number of groups M (i.e. controlling for 'richness'), the index reaches its maximum at $(1 - 1/M)$ when individuals are uniformly distributed across groups.[10]

The 1970 and 1990 PUMS data report the country of birth of each individual. We count as separate groups the migrants of each country of origin contributing at least 0.5% of the total foreign-born population working in the US. Migrants from other countries of origin are gathered in a residual group. This choice implies that we consider 35 countries of origin both in 1970 and in 1990. These groups constitute 92% of all foreign-born immigrants; the remaining 8% are merged into a single group. The complete list of countries for each census year is reported in the data appendix, while the largest 15 of these groups are reported in Table 1. As the Table shows, between 1970 and 1990, the origin of immigrants has increasingly become Mexico; the share of foreign born, however, has increased as well, so that overall the diversity index has increased. As to the main countries of origin of immigrants, we note the well known shift from European countries towards Asian and Latin American countries.

3.2. Diversity across US cities

Table 2 shows the percentage of foreign-born and the diversity index for a representative group of metropolitan areas in the year 1990. To put into context the extent of

---

10 In our case as M, the number of groups, is 36 the maximum for the index is 0.972. See Maignan et al. (2003) for further details.

The economic value of cultural diversity: evidence from US cities • **17**

Table 2. Diversity in representative Metropolitan Areas, 1990

City	Share of foreign born	Country of origin of the five largest foreign groups	Diversity index
Atlanta, GA	5.8%	Germany, Mexico, India, England, Korea	0.11
Chicago, IL	15.2%	Mexico, Poland, Philippines, India, Germany	0.28
Cincinnati, OH-KY-IN	2.3%	Germany, England, India, Canada, Viet-Nam	0.057
Dallas, TX	10.6%	Mexico, Salvador, Viet-Nam, India, Germany	0.20
El Paso, TX	29%	Mexico, Japan, Korea, Canada, Panama	0.43
Indianapolis, IN	2.3%	Germany, England, Korea, Canada, Philippines	0.046
Las Vegas, NE	12%	Mexico, Philippines, Germany, Canada, Cuba	0.23
Los Angeles, CA	37%	Mexico, Salvador, Philippines, Guatemala, Korea	0.58
New York, NY	31%	Dominican Republic, China, Jamaica, Italy, Colombia	0.51
Oklahoma City, OK	4.1%	Mexico, Viet-Nam, Germany, England, Japan	0.08
Philadelphia, PA-NJ	5%	Germany, India, Italy, England, Philippines	0.10
Pittsburgh, PA	2.3%	Italy, Germany, India, England, Canada	0.04
Sacramento, CA	10.6%	Mexico, Philippines, Germany, China, Canada	0.19
San Francisco, CA	30.3%	Philippines, China, Mexico, Salvador, Hong Kong	0.50
Washington, DC-MD-VA-WV	14.8%	Salvador, Germany, India, Korea, Viet-Nam	0.27

Source: Authors' Elaborations on 1990 PUMS census data.

diversity across US cities, each diversity index can be compared with the cross-country value of the index of linguistic fractionalization reported by the Atlas Narodov Mira and published in Taylor and Hudson (1972) for the year 1960. These values have been largely used in the growth literature (see e.g. Easterly and Levine, 1997; Collier, 2001). Since foreign-born immigrants typically use their country's mother tongue at home, thus signalling their country's cultural identity, our diversity index captures cultural and linguistic fragmentation for different US cities much as that index does for different countries in the world. The comparison is instructive. Diversified cities, such as New York or Los Angeles, have diversity indices between 0.5 and 0.6, which are comparable to the values calculated for countries such as Rhodesia (0.54), which is often disrupted by ethnic wars, or Pakistan (0.62), which also features a problematic mix of conflicting cultures. More homogenous cities, such as Cincinnati and Pittsburgh, exhibit a degree of fractionalization of only 0.05, which is the same as that of very homogenous European countries, such as Norway or Denmark in the sixties. Between these two extremes, US cities span a range of diversity that is about two-thirds of the range spanned by the nations of the world.

Table 2 also shows that, even though people born in Mexico constitute an important group in many cities, the variety of countries of origin of residents of US cities is still remarkable. Finally we note that there is a very high correlation between the diversity index and the share of foreign born in a city. The main reason an American city is considered 'diverse' is because there is a large percentage of foreign born living there, not necessarily because there is a high degree of diversity within the foreign born.

3.3. Stylized facts

The key empirical finding of our paper is readily stated: *ceteris paribus, US-born workers living in cities with higher cultural diversity are paid, on average, higher wages, and pay higher rents, than those living in cities with lower cultural diversity.* In Section 5 we show that this correlation not only survives the inclusion of several other control variables, but it is likely to be the result of causation running from diversity to wages and rents.

We report in Figures 1 and 2, below, the correlation between the change of the diversity index for the 1970–1990 period, $\Delta(div_{c,t})$, and the percentage change in the wage of the US-born, $\Delta \ln(\bar{w}_{US,c})$, or the percentage change in rents paid by the US-born, $\Delta \ln(\bar{r}_{US,c})$ in 160 metropolitan areas. The effect of fixed city characteristics, such as location or geographic amenities, are eliminated by differencing. The figures show the scatter-plots of these partial correlations and report the OLS regression line. Cities whose diversity increased more than the average, during the 20 years considered (such as Jersey City, Los Angeles, San Francisco, and San Jose), have also experienced larger than average wage increases for their US-born residents. Similarly they also experienced a larger than average increase in rents. The OLS coefficient estimates imply that a city experiencing an increase of 0.09 in the diversity index (as Los Angeles did) would experience associated increases of 11 percentage points in the average wage and 17.7 percentage points in the average rent paid by US-born residents, relative to a city whose diversity index did not change at all (such as Cleveland).

4. Theoretical framework

4.1. The model

To structure and interpret our empirical investigation, we develop a stylized model in which 'diversity' affects both the productivity of firms and the satisfaction of consumers through a localized effect. Both the model and the identification procedure build on Roback (1982).[11]

We consider an open system of a large number N of non-overlapping cities, indexed by $c=1, \ldots, N$. There are two factors of production, labor and land. We assume that inter-city commuting costs are prohibitive, so that for all workers the city of work and residence coincides. We also ignore intra-city commuting costs, which allows us to focus on the inter-city allocation of workers.

The overall amount of labor available in the economy is equal to L. It is inelastically supplied by urban residents; without loss of generality, we choose units such that each resident supplies one unit of labor. Accordingly, we call L_c the number of workers who work and reside in city c. Workers are all identical in terms of attributes that are

---

11   Roback's (1982) framework has been extensively applied to measure the value of local amenities or local factors of production. Examples include Rauch (1993), Kahn (1995), and Dekle and Eaton (1999).

The economic value of cultural diversity: evidence from US cities • **19**

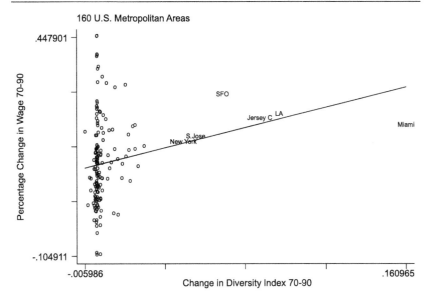

Figure 1. Wages of US-born and diversity.

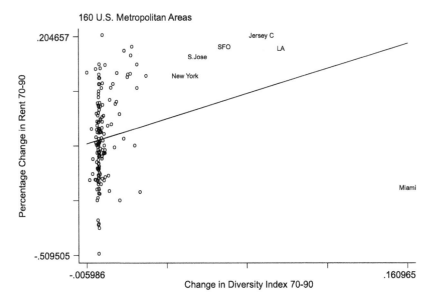

Figure 2. Rents of US-born and diversity.

20 • *Ottaviano and Peri*

relevant for market interactions. However, they differ in terms of non-market attributes, which exogenously classifies them into M different groups ('cultural identities') indexed by $i=1,\ldots,M$. Hence, calling L_i the overall number of workers belonging to group i, we have $\sum_{i=1}^{M} L_i = L$. In each city cultural diversity d_c, measured in terms of the number ('richness') and relative size L_{ic} ('evenness') of resident groups, enters both production and consumption as an effect that, in principle, can be positive or negative. To establish the existence and the sign of such effect is the final aim of the paper. While land is fixed among cities, it is nonetheless mobile between uses within the same city.[12] We call H_c the amount of land available in city c. As to land ownership, we assume that the land of a city is owned by locally resident landlords.[13]

Preferences are defined over the consumption of land H and a homogeneous good Y that is freely traded among cities. Specifically, the utility of a typical worker of group i in city c is given by:

$$U_{ic} = A_U(d_c) H_{ic}^{1-\mu} Y_{ic}^{\mu} \qquad (2)$$

with $0 < \mu < 1$. In equation (2) H_{ic} and Y_{ic} are land and good consumption respectively, while $A_u(d_c)$ captures the 'utility effect' associated with local diversity d_c. If the first derivative $A_u'(d_c)$ is positive, diversity can be seen as a local amenity; if negative as a local dis-amenity.

We assume that workers move to the city that offers them the highest indirect utility. Given equation (2), utility maximization yields:

$$r_c H_{ic} = (1 - \mu) E_{ic}, \quad p_c Y_{ic} = \mu E_{ic} \qquad (3)$$

which implies that the indirect utility of the typical worker of group i in city c is:

$$V_{ic} = (1 - \mu)^{1-\mu} \mu^{\mu} A_u(d_c) \frac{E_{ic}}{r_c^{1-\mu} p_c^{\mu}} \qquad (4)$$

where E_{ic} is her expenditures, while r_c and p_c are the local land rent and good price respectively.

As to production, good Y is supplied by perfectly competitive firms using both land and labor as inputs. The typical firm in city c produces according to the following technology:

$$Y_{jc} = A_Y(d_c) H_{jc}^{1-\alpha} L_{jc}^{\alpha} \qquad (5)$$

with $0 < \alpha < 1$. In equation (5) H_{jc} and L_{jc} are land and labor inputs respectively. $A_Y(d_c)$ captures the 'productivity effect' associated with local diversity d_c. It is convenient to treat the effect of diversity as a shift in total factor productivity, $A_Y'(d_c)$, that is

---

12   The assumption of exogenous and constant land area of a city is harmless. The same implications would follow under the more realistic assumption that expanding the land area of a city comes at a cost because of internal commuting costs and lower quality of the marginal land.

13   This assumption is made only for analytical convenience. What is crucial for what follows is that the rental income of workers, if any, is independent of location, and thus does not affect migration choice. The alternative assumptions of absentee landlords or balanced ownership of land across all cities would also serve that purpose.

The economic value of cultural diversity: evidence from US cities • **21**

---

common to all firms in city c. This shift could be positive or negative.[14] We should notice at this point that assuming identical effects of diversity on utility, $A_U(d_c)$, and productivity, $A_Y(d_c)$, across agents (i) and firms (j) is critical in order to use the model by Roback (1982) to characterize the average equilibrium rent and wage as a function of only diversity. If diversity were to affect firms and agents in different ways (say because some people like diversity more than others and some firms need diversity of workers more than others) then in equilibrium US-born agents would sort themselves across cities (see e.g. Combes et al., 2004). In this case the equilibrium wages and rents across cities would reflect not only different levels of diversity but also different evaluations of diversity by US-born individuals and firms. Such an equilibrium with heterogeneous agents would complicate the use of average wages and rents to infer the impact of diversity on productivity. The analysis of diversity assuming heterogeneous effects on US born agents is certainly an interesting issue that we leave for future research.

Given equation (5) and perfect competition, profit maximization yields:

$$r_c H_{jc} = (1 - \alpha)p_c Y_{jc}, \quad \omega_c L_{jc} = \alpha p_c Y_{jc} \tag{6}$$

which implies marginal cost pricing:

$$p_c = \frac{r_c^{1-\alpha}\omega_c^{\alpha}}{(1-\alpha)^{1-\alpha}\alpha^{\alpha}A_Y(d_c)} \tag{7}$$

so that firms make no profits in equilibrium. Given our assumption on land ownership, this implies that aggregate expenditures in the city equal local factor incomes and that workers' expenditures consist of wages only: $E_{ic} = \omega_c$. Since good Y is freely traded, its price is the same everywhere. We choose this good as numeraire, which allow us to write $p_c=1$.[15]

In a spatial equilibrium there exists a set of prices ($\omega_c, r_c, c = 1, \dots, N$) such that in all cities workers and landlords maximize their utilities given their budget constraints, firms maximize profits given their technological constraints, and factor and product markets clear. Moreover, no firm has an incentive to exit or enter. This is granted by equation (7) that, given our choice of numeraire, can be rewritten as:

$$r_c^{1-\alpha}\omega_c^{\alpha} = (1-\alpha)^{1-\alpha}\alpha^{\alpha}A_Y(d_c) \tag{8}$$

We will refer to equation (8) as the 'free entry condition'. Finally, in a spatial equilibrium no worker has an incentive to migrate. For an interior equilibrium (i.e. $L_c>0$ ∀ $c = 1, \dots, N$) this will be the case when workers are indifferent between alternative cities:

$$V_{ic} = V_{ik}, \quad \forall c,k = 0, \dots, N \tag{9}$$

We will refer to equation (9) as the 'free migration conditions'.

---

14 The contribution of diversity to total factor productivity could stem from imperfect substitutability of different groups as well as from pecuniary or learning externalities. For instance, Ottaviano and Peri (2004a) derive a production function similar to equation (5) with non-tradable intermediates and taste for variety.

15 Anticipating the empirical implementation of the model, by setting $p_c = 1$ for all cities we are requiring the law-of-one-price to hold for tradable goods and non-tradable goods prices to be reasonably proxied by land rents. This is supported by the large positive correlation between local price indices and land rents at the SMSA level.

To complete the equilibrium analysis we have to determine the spatial allocation of workers L_{ic}. This is achieved by evaluating the implications of market clearing for factor prices. Specifically, given $L_c = \sum_j L_{jc}$ and $Y_c = \sum_j Y_{jc}$, equation (6) implies $\omega_c L_c = \alpha p_c Y_c$. Given $H_c = \sum_j H_{jc} + \sum_i H_{ic}$, equation (6) and (3) imply $\mu r_c H_c = (1-\alpha\,\mu)$ $p_c\, Y_c$. Together with $E_{ic} = \omega_c$ and $p_c = 1$, these results can be plugged into equation (4) to obtain:

$$V_{ic} = \mu \left(\frac{1-\mu}{1-\alpha\mu}\right)^{1-\mu} \left(\frac{H_c}{L_c}\right)^{1-\alpha\mu} A_U(d_c)[A_Y(d_c)]^\mu \qquad (10)$$

Equation (10) shows that the indirect utility of a person is higher, *ceteris paribus*, in a city with low population density, L_c/H_c, (because of the lower price of housing) and is affected by diversity through its impact on productivity, $A_Y(d_c)$, which determines wages, and its direct effect on utility $A_U(d_c)$. Substituting equation (10) into equation (9) generates a system of equations that can be solved for the equilibrium spatial allocation of workers. In particular, substitution gives $M(N-1)$ free migration conditions that, together with the M group-wise full-employment conditions $\sum_{c=1}^{N} L_{ic} = L_i$, assign L_{ic} mobile workers of each group $i = 1, \ldots, M$ to each city $c = 1, \ldots, N$. Constant returns to scale and fixed land ensure that the spatial equilibrium is unique and has a positive number of workers in every city ('no ghost town'). Then, the composition of the urban community depends on the net impact of diversity on utility and productivity.

4.2. Identification: wage and rent equations

To prepare the model for empirical investigation, it is useful to evaluate wages and land rents at the equilibrium allocation. This is achieved by solving together the logarithmic versions of the free entry condition as in equation (8) and the free migration conditions in equation (9) that take equation (4) into account. Specifically, call v the equilibrium value of indirect utility. Due to the free mobility of US-born individuals, this value is common among cities and, due to the large number of cities, is unaffected by city-level idiosyncratic shocks. Then, solving equations (8) and (9) for factor prices gives the 'rent equation':

$$\ln r_c = \frac{\eta_Y + \alpha\eta_U}{1 - \alpha\mu} + \frac{1}{1 - \alpha\mu}\ln\left(A_Y(d_c)[A_U(d_c)]^\alpha\right) \qquad (11)$$

and the 'wage equation':

$$\ln w_c = \frac{(1 - \mu)\eta_Y - (1 - \alpha)\eta_U}{1 - \alpha\mu} + \frac{1}{1 - \alpha\mu}\ln\left(\frac{[A_Y(d_c)]^{1-\mu}}{[A_U(d_c)]^{1-\alpha}}\right) \qquad (12)$$

where $\eta_Y \equiv \ln(1-\alpha)^{1-\alpha}\,\alpha^\alpha$ and $\eta_U \equiv (1 - \mu)^{1-\mu}\,\mu^\mu/v$.

Equations (11) and (12) constitute the theoretical foundation of our empirical analysis. They capture the equilibrium relationship between diversity and factor prices. In light of Roback (1982), the two equations must be estimated together in order to identify the effects of diversity on productivity and utility. Consider, for instance, equation (11) in isolation. A positive correlation between d_c and r_c is consistent either with a positive effect of diversity on utility ($A'_U(d_c) > 0$) or a positive effect of diversity on productivity ($A'_Y(d_c) > 0$). Analogously, if one considers equation (12) in isolation, a

The economic value of cultural diversity: evidence from US cities • **23**

---

positive correlation between d_c and w_c is consistent either with a negative utility effect $(A'_U(d_c) < 0)$ or a positive productivity effect $(A'_Y(d_c) > 0)$ from diversity. Only the joint estimation of equations (11) and (12) allows one to establish which effect indeed dominates. Specifically:

$$\frac{\partial r_c}{\partial d_c} > 0 \text{ and } \frac{\partial w_c}{\partial d_c} > 0 \quad \textit{iff dominant positive productivity effect } (A'_Y(d_c) > 0)$$

$$\frac{\partial r_c}{\partial d_c} > 0 \text{ and } \frac{\partial w_c}{\partial d_c} < 0 \quad \textit{iff dominant positive utility effect } (A'_U(d_c) > 0)$$

$$\frac{\partial r_c}{\partial d_c} < 0 \text{ and } \frac{\partial w_c}{\partial d_c} < 0 \quad \textit{iff dominant negative productivity effect } (A'_Y(d_c) < 0)$$

$$\frac{\partial r_c}{\partial d_c} < 0 \text{ and } \frac{\partial w_c}{\partial d_c} > 0 \quad \textit{iff dominant negative utility effect } (A'_U(d_c) < 0)$$

(13)

Figure 3 provides a graphical intuition of the proposed identification. In the Figure w_c and r_c are measured along the horizontal and vertical axes respectively. Given the utility level v and diversity d_c, the free entry condition in equation (8) is met along the downward sloping curve, while the free migration condition in equation (9) holds along the upward sloping curve. The equilibrium factor prices for city c are found at the intersection of the two curves. Diversity d_c acts as a shift parameter on the two curves: any shock to diversity shifts both curves. An increase in d_c shifts equation (8) up (down) if diversity has a positive (negative) productivity effect and it shifts equation (9) up (down) if diversity has a positive (negative) utility effect. Thus, by looking at the impact of a diversity shock on the equilibrium wage and rent, we are able to identify the dominant effect of diversity. For example, consider the initial equilibrium A and the new equilibrium A' that prevails after a shock to diversity. In A' both w_c and r_c have risen. Our identification argument states that both factor prices rise if and only if an

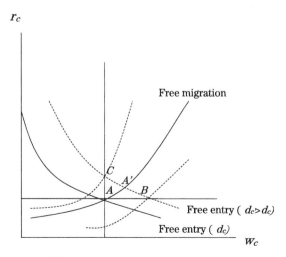

Figure 3. The spatial equilibrium.

upward shift of equation (8) dwarfs any shift of equation (9); i.e. the positive productivity effect dominates.

5. Wage and rent regressions

5.1. Basic specifications

The theoretical model above provides us with a consistent framework to structure our empirical analysis. In particular it suggests how to use wage and rent regressions to identify the effects of diversity, a characteristic particular to each city, on the productivity and utility of US natives. Our units of observation are the 160 Metropolitan Statistical Areas (MSA's) listed in the Appendix. The years of observation are 1970 and 1990. As an empirical implementation of the wage equation (12), we run the following basic regression:

$$\ln(\bar{w}_{US,c,t}) = \beta_1(Controls_{c,t}) + \beta_2(div_{c,t}) + e_c + e_t + e_{c,t} \qquad (14)$$

The average wage of natives in city c in year t, $\bar{w}_{US,c,t}$, is defined as described in Section 3.1. The focal independent variable is $div_{c,t}$, which is the diversity index defined in equation (1). The other independent variable, $Controls_{c,t}$, capture other controls. Specifically we always include among the controls some measure of the average education of workers in city c at time t (either the average schooling or the share of education groups) while in Section 5.2 we include several other alternative variables which may potentially affect the productivity and the share of foreign-born in a city. We also include 160 city fixed effects e_c and common time-effects e_t. Finally, $e_{c,t}$ is a zero-mean random error term independent from the other regressors.

Under these assumptions, the coefficient β_2 captures the equilibrium effect of a change in cultural diversity on wages. However, as discussed in subsection 4.2, the sign of β_2 cannot be directly interpreted as evidence of any positive effect of diversity on production. Identification thus requires us to estimate the following parallel rent regression:

$$\ln(\bar{r}_{US,c,t}) = \gamma_1(Controls_{c,t}) + \gamma_2 div_{c,t} + \varepsilon_c + \varepsilon_t + \varepsilon_{ct} \qquad (15)$$

Our definition of the average rent per room of natives $\bar{r}_{US,c,t}$ in city c in year t is described in Section 3.1. The focal independent variable is again the diversity index $div_{c,t}$. The other independent variables, $Controls_{c,t}$, capture other controls. We add these to check that the correlation of interest is robust to the inclusion of other variables, and thus is not spurious. Further we control for city fixed effects ε_c, include a year dummy ε_t, and assume that $\varepsilon_{c,t}$ is a zero-mean random error uncorrelated with the regressors. The coefficient γ_2 captures the equilibrium effect of a change in cultural diversity on average city rents. By merging the information on the signs of β_2 and γ_2, we are able to identify the net effect of diversity. We begin by estimating the two basic regressions using least squares, including further controls and using different estimation methods later on as we proceed.

The least squares estimates of the regressions (14) and (15) are reported in specifications I and VII of Table 3. Specification I shows the basic estimates for the wage equation, when we only include, besides state and year fixed effects, the average schooling of the considered group of white US-born males 40–50 years of age as a control. Specification VII considers the rent equation with only state and year fixed effects as controls. The estimated coefficients β_2 and γ_2 are both positive and statistically and

The economic value of cultural diversity: evidence from US cities • **25**

Table 3. Basic Wage and Rent Specifications

Dependent variable Specification:	Average log wage for US-born workers						Average log rent for US-born residents		
	I Base 1 wage	II 4 school groups	III Polynomial school	IV Base 1, Pop. weighted	V Include empl.	VI Base 2 wage	VII Base 1 rent	VIII With population and income	XI Base 2 rent
Average schooling	0.11** (0.01)			0.11* (0.01)	0.11** (0.01)	0.10** (0.01)			
4 School groups		Yes							
Quartic in schooling			Yes						
ln(income per capita)								0.67** (0.08)	
ln(employment)					0.02 (0.02)				
ln(population)								0.03 (0.04)	
Diversity index	1.27** (0.30)	1.17** (0.36)	1.29** (0.30)	1.37** (0.23)	1.29** (0.29)		1.90* (0.60)	0.95** (0.50)	
Share of foreign born						0.57** (0.11)			1.13** (0.24)
Diversity index among foreign born						0.14* (0.08)			0.12 (0.16)
City fixed effects	Yes	Yes	Yes	Yes	Yes	Yes	Yes	Yes	Yes
Time fixed effects	Yes	Yes	Yes	Yes	Yes	Yes	Yes	Yes	Yes
R^2 (excluding city and time fixed effects)	0.10	0.14	0.12	0.11	0.10	0.12	0.30	0.30	0.31
Observations	320	320	320	320	320	320	320	320	320

Specification I–VI: Dependent variable is logged average yearly wage of white, US-born, males 40–50 years expressed in 1990 US$.
Specification VII–IX: Dependent variable is logged average monthly rent per room paid by white, US born 16–65 years of age, expressed in 1990 US$.
**Significant at 5%, * significant at 10%.
In parenthesis: heteroskedasticity-robust standard errors.

26 • *Ottaviano and Peri*

economically significant. An increase in the diversity index by 0.1 (roughly the increase experienced by Los Angeles during the 1970–1990 period) is associated with a 13% increase in the average real wage of US natives and with a 19% increase in real rents.

Similarly specifications VI and IX of Table 3 use the same controls as specification I and VII and decompose the effect of diversity (on wages and rents) into two parts. Specifically the diversity index can be expressed as the contribution of two factors. First, a city is more diverse if the overall group of foreign-born people is larger. Second, a city is more diverse if the foreign-born group is made up of a wider variety of groups. The diversity index can thus be written as a (non-linear) function of the share of foreign-born, or a diversity index can be calculated considering only the foreign born. We enter these two factors separately in specifications VI and IX in order to analyze their impact on wages and rents, respectively. Let us note that the share of foreign born is, by far, the most important component in determining the variation of the diversity index across cities. It explains, by itself, almost 90% of the index variation. It is not a surprise, therefore, to find that the share of foreigners is the most important contributor to the effect on wages and rents. An increase in the share of foreign born by 0.25 (experienced by Los Angeles during the considered period) is associated with a 14.5% increase in wages of US natives and a 28% increase in rents. The effect of the diversity of foreigners, on the other hand, has a positive but hardly significant impact.

The intermediate specifications (II to V for the wage equations and VIII for the rent equation) in Table 3 include alternative controls in order to check wether the correlation is robust to potential omitted variables. Specification II of the wage regression controls for the schooling of the group of US-born by including the shares of three groups (high school graduates, college dropouts and college graduates) among the total employed in each city, rather than simply the average years of schooling. Specification III includes a quartic polynomial in average schooling. While non-linear effects at different schooling levels may be relevant, here we see that the coefficient on diversity changes only marginally when we use different methods to control for education. We also run a specification (not reported) controlling for individual years of schooling in the construction of $\ln(\bar{w}_{US,c,t})$, rather than at the second stage. Doing this reduces the coefficient on diversity somewhat to 1.00 (standard error equal to 0.32). All in all how we control for education does not seem to have a relevant effect on the coefficient on diversity. Specification IV weighs each observation (city) by its population. This control allows us to under-emphasize the role of small cities. The effect of diversity does not change much with this amendment; in fact it increases a bit (the coefficient is now equal to 1.37), which is a consequence of the fact that cities in which diversity has the largest impact (as seen in Figure 1 and 2) are indeed the largest cities, such as Los Angeles and New York. Specification V includes the log of employment as an additional control. On the one hand, if there are effects of employment density on productivity (as suggested by Ciccone and Hall, 1996) it may be relevant to control for employment; on the other hand employment (along with wages and rents) is determined endogenously as an equilibrium outcome in our model. As a consequence, including an endogenous variable as a control may bias the estimates of all coefficients. Fortunately we find that employment is not significantly correlated to wages (coefficient equal to 0.02 with standard error equal to 0.02), and its inclusion does not change the coefficient on diversity much. Omitting employment, therefore, is theoretically justified and empirically sound. These specifications reassure us that our basic specification captures both the correct sign and magnitude of the correlation between diversity and wages.

As for the rent regression, column VIII includes the average log income and log population of each city as controls. In reality, these variables may depend on several exogenous factors and may affect the value of housing. They are, however, endogenously determined in the equilibrium described in Section (4). In fact wages are the main determinant of income, while population is affected by internal migration. The two channels through which diversity can affect rents, described by our model, are either by increasing productivity (which pushes up income and rents), or by increasing the desirability of a city. When controlling for income and population, a residual positive effect of diversity would imply that people do value diversity per se, and are willing to bid up rents more than what would be implied only by higher income and higher population. The problem, however, is that including these two endogenous variables may induce a bias in the estimates of the coefficients of regression in equation (15). The estimated coefficients in specification VIII show that including income and population reduces the effect of diversity by half. In particular income per capita is a main determinant of rents and enters the regression with a very significant coefficient. Even controlling for this effect through income, however, diversity still plays a very important role in determining rents (coefficient equal to 0.90). While we take this as a potential sign that diversity has a positive amenity value (it actually shifts the free migration condition in Figure 3 to the left) we are concerned with the endogeneity of the income and population variables, and so we omit them in the rest of the analysis. To summarize, diversity has *positive and highly significant correlations* with both wages ($\beta_2 > 0$) and land rents ($\gamma_2 > 0$). These positive correlations can be interpreted as consistent with a dominant and positive effect of diversity on productivity.

Finally, as we have mentioned that employment and population are endogenous variables in the equilibrium of our model, let us consider another correlation that reinforces our interpretation of a dominant positive effect of diversity on productivity. The theoretical model makes clear (see equation (6)) that, in the presence of a positive productivity effect, the increase of diversity in a certain city shifts the local labor demand up, thus raising not only local wages but also local total employment. In contrast, a negative utility effect would be associated with higher wages but lower native employment. Table 4 reports the correlation between changes in diversity and changes in employment as well as the population of US cities between 1970 and 1990. If the labor supply curve had shifted up and the labor demand curve remained fixed, we should observe an increase in wages but a decrease in total employment caused by the outflow of US-born workers. The Table rather shows positive effects of diversity on both employment and population, consistent with the idea that there was no outflow of natives counterbalancing immigration. This is consistent with a dominant upward shift of labor demand as expected in the presence of a dominant positive productivity effect.

5.2. Checks of robustness

Our basic specifications for the wage (I and VI in Table 3) and rent (VII and IX in Table 3) regressions omit several variables that, in principle, could simultaneously affect local diversity, wages, and rents, thus creating spurious correlation. In so far as they change over time, the impacts of such omitted variables are not captured by city fixed effects. We have already discussed the potential roles of employment, income and population in the previous section. This section is devoted to testing whether the estimated

28 • *Ottaviano and Peri*

Table 4. Correlation between growth in diversity and in employment/population

Dependent variable:	Index of diversity	City fixed effects	Time fixed effects	R^2	Observations
Ln (employment)	0.72 (1.12)	Yes	Yes	0.97	320
Ln (population)	1.70* (1.02)	Yes	Yes	0.97	320

**Significant at 5%, *significant at 10%.
Heteroskedasticity-robust standard errors are reported in parentheses.

effects of diversity are robust to the inclusion of other omitted exogenous variables. While our list of potential controls can not be considered exhaustive, we do include some important ones for which we can think of plausible stories that could generate spurious correlation. Table 5 reports the estimated effects of the diversity index (and its components) in the wage equation as we include additional controls. Table 6 presents analogous results for the rent regression. The coefficients in each row of Tables 5 and 6 arise from separate regressions. While it may be informative to discuss each regression in detail, we prefer simply to focus on the coefficients of interest; thus for the sake of brevity we comment only briefly on each specification. This section is meant to give the reader a general impression of the robustness of our estimates to a very ample range of controls, rather than to analyze in detail any one of the alternative specifications proposed.[16]

The positive effect of diversity on the wage of the US-born may simply be a result of the foreigners' measurable average education. Specifications (2) in Tables 5 and 6 include the average years of schooling of the foreign-born workers as an additional control variable in the wage and rent regressions respectively. While analyzing human capital externalities using average schooling has been a common practice (Rauch, 1993; Moretti, 2004), if workers with different schooling levels are imperfect substitutes, or if the distribution of their skills matters, then average schooling may not be a sufficient statistic to capture the presence of complementarity or externalities. The estimated effects of diversity on wages and rents remain significant and positive when we include this control. Interestingly, the effect of the average schooling of the foreign-born on the wages of the US-born (not reported) is not significant, while it is small and positive on the rents of the US-born. This result tells us that the simple average schooling of the foreign-born does not fully capture their true 'value.' Not only might the skill distribution of the foreign-born matter, but their abilities may be differentiated from (and complementary to) those of natives, even at the same schooling level. When we decompose the overall diversity (column 2 and 3 in the Tables) by including separately the share of foreign born and their diversity, we still find a significant and positive effect of the share of foreign born on both rents and wages, while the diversity of foreigners has a significant positive impact on wages but not on rents.

Another plausible (but spurious) reason for positive correlations between diversity and wages-rents may be that immigration responds to productivity and amenity shocks.

---

16 If the reader is interested in the details of each regression and in a more thorough discussion of each specification we suggest reading the working paper Ottaviano and Peri (2004b).

The economic value of cultural diversity: evidence from US cities • **29**

Table 5. Wage regression: robustness checks

Specification	1 Coefficient on the diversity index	2 Coefficient on the share of foreign born	3 Coefficient on diversity index among foreign born
Specification:			
(1) Basic	1.27**	0.57**	0.14*
	(0.30)	(0.11)	(0.08)
(2) Including schooling	1.26**	0.56**	0.14*
of foreign born	(0.38)	(0.16)	(0.09)
(3) Including share of out of	1.35**	0.58**	0.09
state born	(0.38)	(0.15)	(0.11)
(4) Including share of non whites	1.39**	0.66**	0.12
	(0.40)	(0.17)	(0.10)
(5) Including public spending	1.28**	0.63**	0.14*
on local services per capita	(0.38)	(0.17)	(0.09)
(6) Including public spending in	1.27**	0.65**	0.13
education per capita	(0.38)	(0.16)	(0.09)
(7) Including employment of	1.32**	0.67**	0.14
white-US born males 40–50.	(0.39)	(0.16)	(0.10)
(8) Including all of the above	1.43**	0.75**	0.10
	(0.40)	(0.18)	(0.08)
(9) Basic without CA, FL, NY	0.96**	0.23	0.21**
	(0.49)	(0.27)	(0.12)
(10) In changes 1990–1970 with	0.85**	0.64**	0.02
state-fixed effects	(0.31)	(0.17)	(0.12)
(11) Using wage of white-US born	1.20*	0.69*	0.04
males 30–40 as dep. variable	(0.37)	(0.14)	(0.10)

Dependent variable: ln average yearly wage to white, US born, males 40–50 years old expressed in 1990 US$. The coefficients in column 1 correspond to different regressions in each row. The coefficients in column 2 and 3 correspond to different regressions for each row.
(1) Basic: specification from Table 3 column I (for coefficient 1) and Column VI (for coefficients 2 and 3).
(2) Includes average years of schooling of foreign born.
(3) Includes the share of US-born outside the state in which they live.
(4) Includes the share of non-white people in working age.
(5) Include the spending per capita on local government services.
(6) Includes the spending in education per capita.
(7) Includes ln(Employment) of the group US-born, white males 40–50 years old.
(8) Includes all the variables in (1)–(7) together as controls.
(9) Excluding from the regression MSAs in the biggest immigrations states: CA, FL, NY.
(10) Regression in changes including 49-state fixed-effects.
(11) Uses the wage of the group white, US, born, males, 30–40 years old as dependent variable.
**Significant at 5%, *significant at 10%.
Heteroskedasticity-robust standard errors are reported in parentheses.s

In so far as we do not observe these shocks, we are potentially omitting the common underlying cause of changes in wages, rents and diversity. To address this issue we use two strategies. The first strategy, which we postpone implementing until Section 3, attempts to identify a variable correlated (or at least more correlated) with the share of foreign born and not otherwise correlated (or at least less correlated) with shocks to productivity or amenities. Then, it uses this variable as an instrument in the estimation. The second strategy, pursued here, exploits the fact that productivity shocks which attract workers into a city should attract the US-born and the

30 • *Ottaviano and Peri*

Table 6. Rent regression: robustness checks

Specification	1 Coefficient on the diversity index	2 Coefficient on the share of foreign born	3 Coefficient on diversity index among foreign born
Specification:			
(1) Basic	1.90**	1.13**	0.12
	(0.50)	(0.20)	(0.13)
(2) Including schooling of	2.00**	1.24**	0.14
foreign born	(0.59)	(0.23)	(0.15)
(3) Including share of out	1.98**	1.03*	0.22
of state born	(0.59)	(0.24)	(0.17)
(4) Including share of non	1.50**	0.96**	0.09
whites	(0.62)	(0.26)	(0.16)
(5) Including Public spending	1.93**	0.98**	0.22
on local services per capita	(0.59)	(0.25)	(0.16)
(6) Including public spending	1.92**	0.98**	0.22
in education per capita	(0.58)	(0.25)	(0.16)
(7) Including population of	1.50**	0.96**	0.08
white US-born males	(0.62)	(0.26)	(0.16)
(8) Including All of the above	1.69**	1.12**	0.07
	(0.60)	(0.27)	(0.16)
(9) Basic without CA, FL, NY	4.70*	1.23*	0.24*
	(1.20)	(0.27)	(0.16)
(10) 1990–1970	0.15	0.21	0.14
with state-fixed effects	(0.64)	(0.31)	(0.20)

Dependent variable: ln average monthly rent paid by white, US born, expressed in 1990 US$. The coefficients in column 1 correspond to different regressions in each row. The coefficients in column 2 and 3 correspond to different regressions for each row.
(1) Basic: specification from Table 4 column VII (for coefficient 1) and column IX (for coefficients 2 and 3).
(2) Includes average years of schooling of foreign born.
(3) Includes the share of US born outside the state in which they live.
(4) Includes the share of non-white people in working age.
(5) Include the Spending per capita on local government services.
(6) Includes the Spending in education per capita.
(7) Includes the ln(population) of white US-born males.
(8) Includes all the variables in (1)–(7) together as controls.
(9) Excluding from the regression MSAs in the biggest immigrations states (CA, FL, NY).
(10) Regression in changes including 49 state fixed-effects.
**Significant at 5%, *significant at 10%.
Heteroskedasticity-robust standard errors are reported in parentheses.

foreign-born by the same degree. Therefore, the share of US-born citizens in each city coming from out of state (i.e. born in a different state) is a variable that should be correlated with the same local productivity and amenities shocks that attract foreigners.[17] Accordingly, its inclusion in the wage and rent regressions should

17   It may be the case, however, as argued by Borjas (2001), that the US-born move away from cities in which immigrants go because they look for different amenities or better wages. However, both our results shown in Table 4 (population increases where diversity increases) as well as recent studies by Card (2001) and Card and Di Nardo (2000) do not find evidence of this 'displacement effect'.

The economic value of cultural diversity: evidence from US cities • **31**

---

significantly decrease the estimated coefficients β_2 and γ_2. Moreover, we should find a significant positive correlation between this share and the wage-rents of US-born citizens. Specification (3) in Tables 5 and 6 include the share of US-born citizens who were born out of state. Its coefficient (not reported) is not significant in either regression, while the effects of diversity and the share of foreign born on wages and rents are still significantly positive and virtually unchanged. These results suggest that the presence of the foreign born does not simply signal that cities have experienced an unobserved positive shock, since that would have attracted both foreign and US-born workers. Interestingly, they also imply that their presence does not simply reveal that boom cities have attracted more talented people, since people of similar talent should respond similarly to the same shock.

Some sociologists have advanced the hypothesis that environments which are tolerant towards diversity are more productive and more pleasant to live in. Along similar lines, Richard Florida (2002a, 2002b) has argued that cities with larger numbers of artists and bohemian professionals are more innovative in high tech sectors. It is likely that part of our correlations may actually depend on this positive attitude of cities towards diversity. However, to show that there is something specific to the presence of foreign-born, we include in specification (4) of Tables 5 and 6 the share of US-born people identifying themselves as 'non-white.' Since we consider only US-born people, this index essentially captures the white-black composition of a city. The coefficients on this variable (not reported) turn out to be positive in the wage regression (0.20) and negative in the rent regression (-0.22). We may interpret these results as (weak) evidence of the aversion white US-born individuals feel living close to large non-white (US-born) communities. The standard errors however (in both cases around 0.2), render the estimated coefficients insignificant. As to the coefficients of the diversity index, they are still positive, significant (except in one case for the rent regression), and similar to previous estimates. Thus, in spite of the more ambiguous effect of ethnic diversity, diversity in terms of the country of birth maintains its importance.

Several public services in US cities are supplied by local governments. Public schools, public health care, and public security are all desirable local services. Therefore, cities whose quality of public services has improved in our period of observation may have experienced both an increase in the share of foreign born (possibly because they are larger users of these services) and a rise in property values. From the County and City Databook we have gathered data on the spending of local government services per person in a city and on its breakdown across different categories, particularly in education. Specification (5) of Tables 5 and 6 includes overall spending by local government, whereas specification (6) includes spending on just education, a very important determinant of the quality of schools. The effect of public spending per person on rents (not reported) is positive in both specifications; however, its inclusion does not change the effects of diversity.

If different groups of workers are imperfect substitutes, then even among US natives the average wage of white males 40–50 years of age may be affected by their relative supply. While there is no clear reason to believe that the relative size of this group is correlated with the diversity of a city, it may be appropriate to control for the (log) employment of this group, and not just for total employment. The corresponding results are reported in specification (7) of Table 5, which shows that the coefficient of the diversity index is still equal to 1.32. Specification (7) of Table 6 considers instead the group of white US-born males as potentially competing for similar housing, and

32 • *Ottaviano and Peri*

---

therefore includes the log of their population together with that of total population. This specification is very similar to specification (4), which includes the share of non-whites and produces similar estimates: 1.50 for the coefficient on diversity and 0.96 for the coefficient on the share of foreign born.

The most conservative check is specification (8), which includes together all the controls that are included separately in specifications (2) to (7). Reassuringly, the coefficient on the share of foreign-born is still positive, very stable, and significant in both regressions. The coefficient on the diversity index is also positive, very stable, and significant in the wage regression, while it turns out not significant in the rent regression.[18]

Specifications (9) and (10) of Tables 5 and 6 push our data as far as they can go. Specification (9) estimates the wage and rent regressions excluding the three states with the highest shares of foreign-born, namely California, New York and Florida. The aim is to check whether a few highly diverse cities in those states generate the correlations of diversity with wages and rents. This turns out not to be the case. In the wage regression the coefficient on diversity decreases somewhat but remains both positive and significant. In the rent equation the coefficient on diversity grows larger but also becomes less precisely estimated. In general, however, there is no evidence that in the long run the effect of diversity is different for high immigration states than low immigration states.

In Specification (10), rather than use city and year dummies, we use the differences of the basic variables between 1990 and 1970. We also include state fixed effects to control for differences in the state-specific growth rates of wages and rents. In so doing we identify the effects of diversity on wages and rents through the variation across cities within states. This is an extremely demanding specification as we are probably eliminating most of the variation needed to identify the results by estimating 48 dummies using 160 observations. Remarkably, the positive effect of diversity on productivity still stands, and its point estimate is similar to those of previous specifications. The effect of diversity on rents, however, while still positive, is no longer significant.

We perform one more check in specification (11) of Table 5 in order to verify that our results survive when we consider groups that are more mobile across cities than 40 to 50 year-old workers. We estimate the wage equation using the average wage of white US-born males between 30 and 40 years of age. The coefficients on diversity and the share of foreign born are still significantly positive, equal to 1.20 and 0.69, respectively.

Finally, since our theoretical model shows that in equilibrium wages and rents are simultaneously determined (see equations (11) and (12)), thus implying correlation between the unobservable idiosyncratic shocks to wages $\varepsilon_{c,t}$ and rents $e_{c,t}$, we can increase the efficiency of our estimates by explicitly accounting for such correlation, and estimate a seemingly unrelated regression (SUR). While OLS estimates are still consistent and unbiased even when $\varepsilon_{c,t}$ and $e_{c,t}$ are correlated, SUR estimates are more efficient. The estimated coefficients are virtually identical to those estimated in Table 5 and 6. For sake of brevity we do not report the results here.[19]

---

18 Some authors (see e.g. Sivitanidou and Wheaton, 1992) have argued that the institutional constraints on land use ('zoning') can affect land values. Thus, higher property values may be associated with more efficient institutional constraints in the presence of market failures. This effect, however, should be captured by our local public goods measures.

19 The results of SUR estimations are available in Ottaviano and Peri (2004b).

In summary, most wage and rent regressions yield positive and significant coefficients for both the diversity index and the share of foreign born. The diversity of the foreign born also has a positive effect but this effect is less often significant. We do not find any specification such that the coefficients on the diversity variable are simultaneously not significant in both the wage and the rent regressions. Moreover, each single estimate delivers positive estimates of diversity on wages and rents of natives. Therefore, our identification (13) allows us to conclude that *no specification contradicts the hypothesis of a positive productivity effect of diversity*.

5.3. Endogeneity and instrumental variables

Short of a randomized experiment in which diversity across cities is changed randomly, we cannot rest assured that our correlations reveal any causal link from diversity to wages and rents. Nonetheless, some steps towards tackling the endogeneity problem can be taken using instrumental variables (IV) estimation. Our instruments should be correlated with the change in the diversity of cities between 1970 and 1990, and not otherwise correlated with changes in wages and rents. We construct our main instrument building on the fact that foreigners tend to settle in 'enclaves' where other people from their country of origin already live (Winters et al., 2001; Munshi, 2003). Following Card (2002) and Saiz (2003b) we construct the 'predicted' change in the number of immigrants from each country in each city during the observed period. The predicted change is based on the actual shares of people from each country in each city at the beginning of the period, and the total immigration rate from each country of origin to the US during the whole period. By construction the 'predicted' change does not depend on any city-specific shock during the observed period. We then observe that the stocks and flows of immigrants tend to be larger in cities that are closer to important 'gateways' into the US. By contrast, the stocks of the native born and their changes over time are much less dependent on their proximity to these gateways. Therefore, as additional instruments, we also add the distance of a city from the main gateways into the US after having tested for the exogeneity of these instruments. The inclusion of more instruments, as long as they are exogenous, should improve our estimates while still correcting for the potential endogeneity bias. We now describe the instruments and the estimation results in the following two sections.

5.3.1. Shift-Share methodology

We construct our main instrument by adopting the 'shift-share methodology,' used by Card (2001) and more recently by Saiz (2003b), to migration in MSA's. Immigrants tend to settle, at least initially, where other immigrants from the same country already reside (immigration enclaves). Therefore, we can use the share of residents of an MSA in 1970 for each country of birth, and attribute to each group the growth rate of that group within the whole US population in the 1970–1990 time period. In so doing we compute the predicted composition of the city based on its 1970 composition and attribute to each group the average growth rate of its share in the US population. Once we have constructed these 'predicted' shares for 1990 we can calculate a 'predicted' diversity index for each city in 1990.

Let us use the notation introduced in Section 3.1, where $\left(CoB_i^c\right)_t$ denotes the share of people born in country i among the residents of city c in year t. Hence,

34 • *Ottaviano and Peri*

$(CoB_i)_t = \sum_c (CoB_i^c)_t$ is the share of people born in country i among US residents in year t. Between 1970 and 1990 its growth rate is:

$$(g_i)_{1970-90} = [(CoB_i)_{1990} - (CoB_i)_{1970}]/(CoB_i)_{1970} \qquad (16)$$

This allows us to calculate the 'attributed' share of people born in country j and residing in city c in 1990 as:

$$(\widehat{CoB_i^c})_{1990} = (CoB_i^c)_{1970}[1 + (g_i)_{1970-90}] \qquad (17)$$

The attributed share of foreign born and the attributed diversity index can be evaluated accordingly. In particular, the latter equals:

$$\widehat{div}_{c,1990} = 1 - \sum_i (\widehat{CoB_i^c})^2_{1990} \qquad (18)$$

As the attributed diversity for each city in 1990 is built using the city's share in 1970 and the 1970–1990 national growth rates of each group, this value is independent from any city-specific shock during the period.

Tables 7 and 8 present the results of the IV estimation of the wage and rent regressions. Relative to previous regressions, some adjustments in the grouping of countries of birth are needed. This is because as we input the shares in 1990 based on the initial shares in 1970, we need to identify the same countries of origin across census years. This is achieved by allocating more than one country of birth to the same group, as some countries have disappeared or changed during the period. In so doing, we follow the classification adopted by Card (2001) and described in the data appendix.

In Tables 7 and 8, column 1 reports the OLS estimates of the basic specification in which we control for schooling using the change in average years of schooling in the city (Δ schooling). The point estimates of the OLS specification are very similar to our previous estimates (Table 3, columns I and VII), confirming that the reclassification

Table 7. Wage regression. IV estimation, instrument: shift-share imputed diversity

Dependent variable : Δln(wage)	1 OLS in differences	2 Controlling for initial average wage	3 IV	4 IV without CA-FL-NY
ΔSchooling	0.11**	0.11**	0.11**	0.10**
	(0.01)	(0.01)	(0.01)	(0.01)
Δ(diversity)	1.27**	1.43**	0.98**	0.99*
	(0.38)	(0.39)	(0.50)	(0.60)
R^2	0.34	0.36	0.35	0.33
Observations	160	160	160	145
		First stage regression		
Shift-share constructed diversity	n.a.	n.a.	0.51**	0.21**
			(0.05)	(0.04)
Partial R^2	n.a.	n.a.	0.31	0.17

Dependent variable: change between 1970 and 1990 in ln average yearly wage of white, US born, males, 40–50 years, expressed in 1990 US $.
Instrumental variable: imputed change in diversity index and share of foreign born, using the shift-share method described in the text.
**Significant at 5%, *significant at 10%.
Heteroskedasticity-robust standard errors are reported in parentheses.

The economic value of cultural diversity: evidence from US cities • **35**

Table 8. Rent regression. IV estimation, instrument: shift-share imputed diversity

Dependent variable : Δln(rent)	1 OLS in differences	2 Controlling for initial average rent	3 IV	4 IV, Without CA-FL-NY
Δ(diversity)	1.97**	2.07**	2.60**	3.29**
	(0.60)	(0.65)	(0.96)	(1.50)
R²	0.07	0.12	0.10	0.12
Observations	160	160	160	145
		First stage regression		
Shift-share constructed	n.a.	n.a.	0.51**	0.21**
diversity			(0.05)	(0.04)
Partial R²	n.a.	n.a.	0.23	0.11

Dependent variable: Change between 1970 and 1990 in logged average yearly rent of white, US-born, aged 16–65, expressed in 1990 US$.
Instrumental variable: imputed change in diversity index and share of foreign born, using the shift-share method, described in the text.
**Significant at 5%, *significant at 10%.
Heteroskedasticity-robust standard errors are reported in parentheses.

by country groups has only small effects. In column 2, as we are running the specifications in differences (rather than in levels with fixed effects), we also check that the implicit treatment of long-run effects as equilibrium effects is appropriate. In particular we include the initial values of average wages and rents (coefficients on those variables are not reported), in order to control for the possibility that cities were not at a long-run equilibrium at the beginning of the period (1970), so that their dynamic behavior exhibits 'conditional convergence'. The estimated effects of diversity do not change much, and are statistically not different from the previous estimates.

As for the IV estimates of columns 3 and 4, we notice that the first stage regressions (of the endogenous measure of diversity on the instrument) imply that the imputed diversity indices are good predictors of the actual ones, explaining 31% of their variation (orthogonal to the other regressors) when all states are included. The exclusion of large immigration states, however, reduces significantly the partial R² of the first stage regression to 17%.

The estimated effect of diversity on wages is reported in column 3 of Table 7. Its value (0.98) is close to the OLS estimate and significantly positive. When we exclude the high-immigration states (column 4 of Table 7), the effect of diversity is estimated to be positive but significant only at the 10% confidence level. However, the main problem encountered when we exclude California, Florida and New York is that, as just mentioned, the instruments lose much of their explanatory power (the partial R² of the excluded instruments drops to 0.17). Therefore, insignificance is mostly driven by large standard errors, rather than by evidence of any endogeneity bias (i.e., changes in point estimates).

Columns 3 and 4 in Table 8 show that the rent regression exhibits a similar qualitative pattern but sharper results. Using the shift-share instruments, the diversity index has a positive and significant effect in each specification. Including all states, the IV estimates are 30% higher than the OLS estimates (although, due to the large standard error we cannot reject the hypothesis that they are equal). When we exclude California, Florida, and New York (specification 4 of Table 8), both the estimate and the standard

36 • *Ottaviano and Peri*

---

error increase significantly. The point estimates of the effect of diversity are still firmly in the positive range. Somewhat surprising (possibly driven by the exclusion of some 'perverse' outliers such as Miami, see Figure 2) is the very large (and imprecisely estimated) effect of diversity on rents in this specification.

5.3.2. Gateways into the US

We can increase the set of instruments by noting the fact that immigrants tend to enter the US through a few 'gateways,' or through the border. As a consequence, the total number of foreign born in city c at time t, F_{ct}, as well as the total increase in foreign born in city c, ΔF_{ct}, depend negatively on the distance from the closest gateway. As long as the total number of US-born residents in a city, N_{ct}, does not depend (or depends to a lesser extent) on that distance, we have that both the share of foreign born, $F_{ct}/(F_{ct}+N_{ct})$, and its change are negatively correlated with the distance from the immigration gateways into the US.

Each year the US Office of Tourism publishes the percentage of inbound travellers by point of entry. Looking at this data for the eighties, we see that the three main gateways were New York, Miami, and Los Angeles. About 30% of foreign (immigrant and non-immigrant) travellers entered the US through the airports and ports of these cities. Moreover, due to the benefits of networks, the costs of travelling, and the costs of spreading information, immigrants were more likely to settle in cities closer to these gateways. A similar argument can be made for Canadian and Mexican immigrants. For them, it seems reasonable to assume that the US borders with their own countries constitute the natural place of entry into the US. Thus, as before, cities closer to these borders were more likely to receive Canadian or Mexican immigrants during the 1970–1990 period.

These considerations suggest the use of the overall distance of a city from the main gateways into the US (New York, Miami, Los Angeles, and the US borders with Canada and Mexico) to instrument for its diversity index (heavily dependent on the share of foreign-born). This distance should be negatively correlated with diversity but not with shocks to wages and rents.

This strategy is certainly open to criticism. If the three main gateways (New York, Miami, and Los Angeles) or the region of the US-Mexican border experienced above average growth during the time period considered, then positive spillover effects on nearby cities could attract foreigners. As a result, the distance of a city from these gateways would be negatively correlated with the increases in wages and rents because of a 'boom city' effect rather than a positive effect from diversity. This criticism, however, does not apply to the 'predicted diversity' constructed in the previous section. As we are confident of the 'exogeneity' of one instrument (the 'predicted diversity'), when using additional instruments (distance from gateways) we can test for their exogeneity[20]. We find that the variables that do not fail the exogeneity test jointly are 'predicted diversity', distance from NY, distance from LA and distance from Miami. We had to drop the distance from the border variable, as it failed this exogeneity test.

---

20   The exact form of our test of exogeneity can be find in Woolridge (2001), 124–125. Intuitively the test checks wether the restriction that excludes the extra-instruments from the second-stage regression is rejected or not by the data. If it is not rejected the assumption of exogeneity stands.

The economic value of cultural diversity: evidence from US cities • **37**

Table 9. Wage regression. IV estimation, instruments are distance from 'Gateways' and imputed diversity

Dependent variable : Δln(wage)	1 IV	2 IV with state effects	3 IV, without CA-FL-NY
ΔSchooling	0.11**	0.11**	0.11**
	(0.01)	(0.02)	(0.01)
Δ(Diversity)	1.50**	0.68**	1.91**
	(0.39)	(0.33)	(0.54)
State fixed effects	No	Yes	No
R^2	0.35	0.63	0.30
Observations	160	160	144
	First stage regression		
Shift-share constructed	0.44**	0.44**	0.30**
diversity	(0.04)	(0.04)	(0.04)
Ln(distance from LA)	−0.01**	−0.01**	−0.01**
	(0.001)	(0.001)	(0.002)
Ln(distance from NY)	−0.005**	−0.005**	−0.006**
	(0.0008)	(0.0008)	(0.0007)
Ln(distance from Miami)	−0.01**	−0.01**	−0.004**
	(0.001)	(0.001)	(0.002)
Partial R^2	0.71	0.51	0.46

Dependent variable: change between 1970 and 1990 in ln average yearly wage of white, US-born, males, 40–50 years, expressed in 1990 US$.
**Significant at 5%, *significant at 10%
Heteroskedasticity-robust standard errors are reported in parentheses.
Test of over-identifying restrictions, from Woolridge (2001) pp. 124–125, cannot reject the joint exogeneity of instruments at the 5% confidence level. The value of the test statistic is 3.2 for the first specification, 4.5 for the second and 3.7 for the third. The statistic is distributed as a chi-square with 3 degrees of freedom under the null hypothesis of no Instrument included in the second stage equation.

Tables 9 and 10 report the first and second stage estimates of the described IV regressions using wages and rents, respectively, as the dependent variable. Column 1 of Table 9 shows the basic specification of the wage regression; column 2 includes 48 state fixed-effects; column 3 excludes the biggest immigration states. Similarly column 1 of Table 10 includes the basic specification while column 2 and 3 exclude from the regression coastal cities and cities in California, Florida and New York as a check for potential outliers driving the results. The first stage regressions confirm that our excluded instruments are excellent: in the first stage they explain about 70% of the variation in diversity that is orthogonal to the other regressors. Even including state effects, more than 50% of the residual variation in diversity is still explained by the instruments. This increases the power of instrument, relative to Table 7 and 8 and may result in more precise estimates.

The estimates of specification 1 (Table 9 and 10) confirm that the effects of diversity on wages and rents are positive and large. The estimated coefficient is significant and very large for wages (1.50) as well as for rents (1.48). Moreover, the IV estimates of the effect on wages are somewhat higher than the OLS ones; hence we are reassured that no significant (endogeneity-driven) downward OLS bias exists. For the wage regressions we obtain a positive and significant effect of diversity when controlling for 48 state fixed effects (specification 2 of Table 9) and when eliminating coastal cities (specifications 3 of Table 9). The last specification has quite large standard errors, but it certainly

38 • *Ottaviano and Peri*

Table 10. Rent regression. IV estimation, instruments are distance from 'Gateways' and imputed diversity.

Dependent variable : Δln (rent)	1 IV	2 IV non-coastal cities	3 IV, without CA-FL-NY
Δ(Diversity)	1.48**	5.50**	4.70**
	(0.61)	(2.31)	(1.04)
State fixed effects	No	No	No
R^2	0.13	0.10	0.12
Observations	160	160	144
	First stage regression		
Shift-share constructed diversity	0.44**	0.23**	0.30**
	(0.04)	(0.05)	(0.04)
Ln(distance from LA)	−0.01**	−0.005**	−0.01**
	(0.001)	(0.001)	(0.002)
Ln(distance from NY)	−0.005**	−0.004**	−0.006**
	(0.0008)	(0.0008)	(0.0007)
Ln(distance from Miami)	−0.01**	−0.01**	−0.004**
	(0.001)	(0.001)	(0.002)
Partial R^2	0.71	0.38	0.46

Dependent variable: change between 1970 and 1990 in ln average monthly rent paid by white, US-born, expressed in 1990 US$.
**Significant at 5%, *significant at 10%.
Heteroskedasticity-robust standard errors are reported in parentheses.
Test of over-identifying restrictions, from Woolridge (2001) pp. 124–125, cannot reject the joint exogeneity of instruments at the 5% confidence level. The value of the test statistic is 4.8 for the first specification, 7.2 for the second and 4.5 for the third. The statistic is distributed as a chi-square with 3 degrees of freedom under the null hypothesis of no instrument included in the second stage equation.

reinforces our thesis that the foreign-born have a positive effect in non-coastal cities as well. As for the rent regressions, the share of foreigners once again has a positive and significant effect in specifications 2 and 3 of Table 10 (excluding coastal cities and excluding the largest immigration states). Again, somewhat oddly, and probably due to the elimination of some outliers, the estimated effect on rents increases significantly in specifications 2 and 3.

All in all the results using shift-share instruments seem to confirm very strongly the positive effect of diversity on wages and rents of natives. In particular, considering all the IV regressions, we find no specification in which the coefficients of diversity are not significant in either the wage or rent equations. Moreover the point estimates are always robustly positive (although sometimes they are not very precise due to instrument weakness). Thus, on the basis of the discussion in subsection 2, we can conclude that our data support the hypothesis of a positive productivity effect of diversity with *causation running from diversity to productivity of US workers*.

6. Discussion and conclusions

We have looked at US metropolitan areas as a system of open cities in which cultural diversity can affect the productivity and utility of natives. In principle, the effects of diversity can be positive or negative. We have considered a simple model that handles all possible cases (i.e. positive or negative effects on productivity and utility), and we have designed a simple identification procedure to figure out which case receives empirical support based on cross-city wage and rent variations. We have showed that higher wages and higher rents for US natives are significantly correlated with higher diversity. This result has survived several robustness checks against possible alternative explanations based on omitted variables and instrumental variables estimation.

Given our identification procedure, these findings are consistent with a dominant positive effect of diversity on productivity: *a more multicultural urban environment makes US-born citizens more productive*. To the best of our knowledge, in terms of both data and identification procedure, our results are new. We need to add two caveats, however, to these conclusions. First, while we are confident that the identified positive correlation between diversity and wage-rents is a robust feature of the data, our interpretation of a positive effect of diversity on productivity is not the only possible one. A plausible, and not less interesting one, is that spatial selection of US born residents in cities with high or low diversity may reflect some of their characteristics. For instance, people with higher education, higher international experience, and higher exposure to culture and news may be more appreciative of diversity. They may also be different from other US natives in several characteristics that are related to productivity. If this is true, 'tolerant' cities are more productive due to the characteristics of US-born residents rather than to the 'diversity' of these cities. Our current and future research is proceeding in the direction of analyzing this selection effect better and trying to determine which factor (diversity or tolerance) is more relevant for productivity (in fact both effects are likely to play important roles).

Secondly, even assuming the existence of a positive effect of foreign-born residents on the productivity of US natives, we have not yet opened the 'black box' to analyze theoretically and empirically what the channels are through which that effect works. The complementarity of skills between the US and foreign born seems a very promising avenue of research. Even at the same level of education, problem solving, creativity and adaptability may differ between native and foreign-born workers so that reciprocal learning may take place. Another promising avenue is that foreign-born workers may provide services that are not perfectly substitutable with those of natives. An Italian stylist, a Mexican cook and a Russian dancer simply provide different services that their US-born counterparts cannot. Because of a taste for variety, this may increase the value of total production. We need to analyze more closely the effects in different sectors and on different skill groups in order to gain a better understanding of these channels. Overall our findings look plausible and encouraging, leaving to future research the important goal of pursuing further the analysis of the mechanisms through which foreign-born residents affect the US economy.

Acknowledgements

We are grateful to Gilles Duranton, Michael Storper and two anonymous referees for very helpful comments and suggestions. We also thank Alberto Alesina, Richard Arnott, David Card, Masa Fujita, Ed Glaeser, Vernon Henderson, Eliana LaFerrara, David Levine, Doug Miller, Enrico Moretti, Dino Pinelli, Matt Turner as well as workshop participants at FEEM Milan, RSAI Philadelphia, UBC Vancouver, UC Berkeley and UCLA International Institute for helpful discussions and suggestions. We thank Elena Bellini for outstanding research assistance. Ahmed Rahman provided extremely competent assistance with the editing of the article. Ottaviano gratefully acknowledges financial support from Bocconi University and FEEM. Peri gratefully acknowledge financial support form UCLA International Institute. Errors are ours.

References

Alesina, A., La Ferrara, E. (2003) Ethnic diversity and economic performance. Working Paper 10313, NBER, Cambridge, MA.

Bairoch, P. (1988) *Cities and Economic Development: from the Dawn of History to the Present.* Oxford: Oxford University Press.

Berliant, M., Fujita, M. (2004) Knowledge creation as a square dance on the Hilbert Cube. Working Paper Washington University at Saint Louis, Department of Economics.

Boeri, T., Hanson G., McCormick, B. (2002) *Immigration Policy and the Welfare System.* Oxford: Oxford University Press.

Borjas, G. (1994) The economics of immigration. *Journal of Economic Literature*, 32: 1667–1717.

Borjas, G. (1995) The economic benefits of immigration. *Journal of Economic Perspectives*, 9: 3–22.

Borjas, G. (1999) *Heaven's Doors*. Princeton: Princeton University Press.

Borjas, G. (2001) Does Immigration Grease the Wheels of the Labor Market? *Brookings Papers on Economic Activity*, 1: 69–119.

Borjas, G. (2003) The labor demand curve is downward sloping: Re-examining the impact of immigration on the labor market. *Quarterly Journal of Economics*, 118: 1335–1374.

Borjas, G., Freeman, R., Katz, L. (1997) How much do immigration and trade affect labor market outcomes? *Brookings Papers on Economic Activity*, 1: 1–90.

Butcher, K., Card, D. (1991) Immigration and wages, evidence from the 1980's. *American Economic Review*, 81, *Papers and Proceedings of the Hundred and Third Annual Meeting of the American Economic Association*, 292–296.

Card, D. (1990) The impact of the Mariel Boatlift on the Miami labor market. *Industrial and Labor Relations Review*, 43: 245–257.

Card, D. (2001) Immigrant inflows, native outflows and the local labor market impacts of higher immigration, *Journal of Labor Economics*, 19, 22–61.

Card, D., Di Nardo, J. (2000) Do immigrant inflows lead to native outflows? *American Economic Review*, 90: 360–367.

Card, D., Krueger, A. (1992) School quality and black-white relative earnings: A direct assessment. *Quarterly Journal of Economics*, 107: 151–200.

Card, D., Krueger, A. (1993) Trends in relative black-white earnings revisited. *American Economic Review, Papers and Proceedings*, 83: 85–91.

Ciccone, A, Hall, R. (1996) Productivity and the Density of Economic Activity. *American Economic Review*, 86: 54–70.

Collier, P. (2001) Implications of ethnic diversity, *Economic Policy: a European Forum*, 0: 127–55.

Combes, P. P., Duranton, G., Gobillon, L. (2004) Spatial wage disparities: Sorting matters!, Discussion Paper, 4240, CEPR, London UK.

Cutler, D., Glaeser, D. (1997) Are ghettos good or bad? *Quarterly Journal of Economics*, 112: 827–72.

Dekle, R., Eaton, J. (1999) Agglomeration and Land Rents: Evidence from the Prefectures. *Journal of Urban Economics*, 46(2): 200–214.

Easterly, W., Levine, R. (1997) Africa's growth tragedy: Policies and ethnic division. *Quarterly Journal of Economics*, 112: 1203–50.

Eckstein, Z., Wolpin, K. (1999) Estimating the effect of racial discrimination on first job wage offers. *Review of Economics and Statistics*, 81: 384–392.

Florida, R. (2002a) Bohemia and economic geography. *Journal of Economic Geography*, 2: 55–71.

Florida, R. (2002b) *The Rise of the Creative Class*. Basic Books, New York.

Fujita, M., Krugman, P., Venables, A. (1999) *The Spatial Economy. Cities, regions and international trade*. Cambridge MA: MIT Press.

Glaeser, E., Kolko, J., Saiz, A. (2001) Consumer city. *Journal of Economic Geography*, 1: 27–50.

Jacobs, J. (1969) *The Economy of Cities*. New York: Random House.

Kahn, M. E. (1995), A revealed preference approach to ranking city quality of life. *Journal of Urban Economics*, 38: 221–235.

Lazear, E. (1999) Globalization and the market for team-mates. *Economic Journal*, 109: C15–C40.

Lian, B., Oneal J. (1997) Cultural diversity and economic development: a cross-national study of 98 Countries. 1960–1985. *Economic Development and Cultural Change*, 46: 61–77.

Maignan, C., Ottaviano, G., Pinelli, D., Rullani, F. (2003) Bio-Ecological Diversity vs Socio-Economic Diversity: A Comparison of Existing Measures. Working Paper n.13 Fondazione Enrico Mattei, Venice.

Mason, P. (2000) Persistent discrimination: racial disparity in the United States, 1967–1998, *American Economic Review*, 90: 312–16.

Mauro, P. (1995) Corruption and growth. *Quarterly Journal of Economics*, 110: 681–712.

Moretti, E. (2004) Workers' education, spillovers and productivity: evidence from plant-level production functions. *American Economic Review*, 94: 656–690.

Munshi, K. (2003) Networks in the modern economy: Mexican migrants in the US labor market. *Quarterly Journal of Economics*, 118: 549–599.

Ottaviano, G., Peri, G. (2004a) Cities and Cultures. Discussion Paper, 4438 CEPR London, UK.

Ottaviano, G., Peri, G. (2004b) The economic value of cultural diversity: evidence from US Cities. CESifo Working Paper 1117, Munich, Germany.

Ottaviano, G., Peri, G. (2005) Gains from "Diversity": Theory and Evidence from Immigration in US Cities. Manuscript, Department of Economics UCLA, January 2005.

Park, J. (1994) Estimation of sheepskin effects and returns to schooling using the old and new CPS measures of educational attainment. Princeton University Industrial Relation Section, Working Paper No. 338.

Peri, G. (2005) Skills and Talent of Immigrants: A Comparison between the European Union and the United States, Institute of European Studies (UC Berkeley) Working Paper, March 2005.

Quigley, J. (1998) Urban diversity and economic growth. *Journal of Economic Perspectives*, 12: 127–138.

Rauch, J. (1993) Productivity gains from geographic concentration in cities. *Journal of Urban Economics*, 34: 380–400.

Roback, J. (1982) Wages, rents and the quality of life. *Journal of Political Economy*, 90: 1257–78.

Saiz, A. (2003a) Room in the kitchen for the melting pot: immigration and rental prices, *Review of Economics and Statistics*, 85(3): 502–521.

Saiz, A. (2003b) Immigration and housing rents in American cities. Working Paper No. 03–12, Federal Reserve Bank of Philadelphia.

Sassen, S. (1994) *Cities in a World Economy*. Thousand Oaks: Pine Forge Press.

Sivitanidou, R., Wheaton, S. (1992) Wage and rent capitalization in the commercial real estate market, *Journal of Urban Economics*, Vol, 31: 206–229.

Taylor, C., Hudson, M. (1972) *World Handbook of Political and Social Indicators*. Second edition, New Haven: Yale University Press.

Winters, P., de Janvry, A., Sadoulet, E. (2001) Family and community networks on Mexico-US migration. *Journal of Human Resources*, 36: 159–184.

Woolridge, J. L. (2001) Econometric Analysis of Cross Section and Panel Data, MIT Press, Boston MA.

A. Data Appendix

A.1 Data for MSA's

The data on cultural diversity and foreign-born are obtained from the 1970–1990 Public Use Microdata Sample (PUMS) of the US Census. We selected all people in working age (16–65 year) in each year and we identified the city where they lived using the SMSA code for 1990, while in 1970 we used the county group code to identify the metropolitan area. We used the variable 'Place of Birth' in order to identify the country of origin of the person. We considered only the countries of origin in which was born at least 0.5 % of the foreign-born working age population. We obtained 35 groups for 1970 as well as for 1990.

We used the Variable 'Salary and Wage' to measure the yearly wage income of each person. We transformed the wage in real 1990 US$ by deflating it with the national GDP deflator. The years of schooling for individuals are measured using the variable 'higrad' for the 1970 census, which indicates the highest grade attended, while for 1990 the variable 'grade completed' is converted into years of schooling using Park's (1994) correspondence Table 4. Average rents are calculated using gross monthly rent per room (i.e. rent divided by number of rooms) expressed in real 1990 US$ terms. The data on total city employment, total local public spending, and public spending in education are from the County and City Databook.

The list of metropolitan areas used in our study is reported in the following table.

A.2 Grouping by country of birth

In Tables from 1 to 8 we consider the diversity index constructed using 35 countries of origin of immigrants which top the list of all countries of origin plus a residual group called 'others'. These account for more than 90 % of all foreign-born, both in 1970 and 1990, and a country that is not in this list supplies at most 0.5 % of all foreign-born living in the US. Here is the list of the non-residual countries, in alphabetical order. For year 1970 the countries are: Argentina, Australia, Canada, Czechoslovakia, China, Colombia, Cuba, Dominican Republic, England, France, Germany, Greece, Hungary, India, Ireland, Italy, Jamaica, Japan, Korea, Latvia, Lithuania, Mexico, Netherlands, Norway, Philippines, Poland, Portugal, Romania, Scotland, Sweden, Syria, Ukraine, USSR, Yugoslavia, Others. For 1990 the countries are: Argentina, Canada, China, Colombia, Cuba, Dominican Republic, Ecuador, England, France, Germany, Greece, Guyana, Haiti, Honduras, Hong-Kong, India, Iran, Ireland, Italy, Jamaica, Japan, Korea, Mexico, Nicaragua, Panama, Peru, Philippines, Poland, Portugal, El Salvador, Taiwan, Trinidad and Tobago, USSR, Vietnam, Yugoslavia.

In Tables 9 and 10, in order to have the same groups in 1970 and 1990, we allocate more than one non-residual country to the same group based on geographical proximity. Our fifteen groups are almost the same as those defined and used in Card (2001). This is the list: Mexico, Caribbean Countries, Central America, China-Hong-Kong-Singapore, South America, South East Asia, Korea and Japan, Philippines, Australia-New Zealand-Canada-UK, India and Pakistan, Russia and Central Europe, Turkey, North Africa and Middle East, Northwestern Europe and Israel, South-western Europe, Sub-Saharan Africa, Cuba.

The economic value of cultural diversity: evidence from US cities • **43**

Table A1. Name and state of the cities used

Abilene, TX	Dayton-Springfield, OH	Lexington, KY	Rockford, IL
Akron, OH	Decatur, IL	Lima, OH	Sacramento, CA
Albany-Schenectady-Troy, NY	Denver, CO	Lincoln, NE	Saginaw-Bay City-Midland, MI
Albuquerque, NM	Des Moines, IA	Little Rock-North Little Rock, AR	St. Louis, MO-IL
Allentown-Bethlehem-Easton, PA	Detroit, MI	Los Angeles-Long Beach, CA	Salem, OR
Altoona, PA	Duluth-Superior, MN-WI	Louisville, KY-IN	Salinas, CA
Amarillo, TX	El Paso, TX	Lubbock, TX	Salt Lake City-Ogden, UT
Appleton-Oshkosh-Neenah, WI	Erie, PA	Macon, GA	San Antonio, TX
Atlanta, GA	Eugene-Springfield, OR	Madison, WI	San Diego, CA
Atlantic-Cape May, NJ	Fayetteville, NC	Mansfield, OH	San Francisco, CA
Augusta-Aiken, GA-SC	Flint, MI	Memphis, TN-AR-MS	San Jose, CA
Austin-San Marcos, TX	Fort Lauderdale, FL	Miami, FL	Santa Barbara-Santa Maria- Lompoc, CA
Bakersfield, CA	Fort Wayne, IN	Milwaukee-Waukesha, WI	Santa Rosa, CA
Baltimore, MD	Fresno, CA	Minneapolis-St. Paul, MN-WI	Seattle-Bellevue-Everett, WA
Baton Rouge, LA	Gainesville, FL	Modesto, CA	Shreveport-Bossier City, LA
Beaumont-Port Arthur, TX	Gary, IN	Monroe, LA	South Bend, IN
Billings, MT	Grand Rapids-Muskegon-Holland, MI	Montgomery, AL	Spokane, WA
Biloxi-Gulfport-Pascagoula, MS	Green Bay, WI	Muncie, IN	Springfield, MO
Binghamton, NY	Greensboro–Winston-Salem-High Point, NC	Nashville, TN	Stockton-Lodi, CA
Birmingham, AL	Greenville-Spartanburg-Anderson, SC	New Orleans, LA	Syracuse, NY
Bloomington-Normal, IL	Hamilton-Middletown, OH	New York, NY	Tacoma, WA
Boise City, ID	Harrisburg-Lebanon-Carlisle, PA	Newark, NJ	Tampa-St. Petersburg-Clearwater, FL
Brownsville-Harlingen-San Benito, TX	Honolulu, HI	Norfolk-Virginia Beach-Newport News, VA-NC	Terre Haute, IN
Buffalo-Niagara Falls, NY	Houston, TX	Odessa-Midland, TX	Toledo, OH
Canton-Massillon, OH	Huntington-Ashland, WV-KY-OH	Oklahoma City, OK	Trenton, NJ
Cedar Rapids, IA	Indianapolis, IN	Omaha, NE-IA	Tucson, AZ
Champaign-Urbana, IL	Jackson, MI	Orlando, FL	Tulsa, OK
Charleston-North Charleston, SC	Jackson, MS	Pensacola, FL	Tuscaloosa, AL
Charlotte-Gastonia-Rock Hill, NC-SC	Jacksonville, FL	Peoria-Pekin, IL	Tyler, TX
Chattanooga, TN-GA	Jersey City, NJ	Philadelphia, PA-NJ	Utica-Rome, NY
Chicago, IL	Johnstown, PA	Phoenix-Mesa, AZ	Vallejo-Fairfield-Napa, CA
Cincinnati, OH-KY-IN	Kalamazoo-Battle Creek, MI	Pittsburgh, PA	Waco, TX

44 • *Ottaviano and Peri*

Table A1. *Continued*

Cleveland-Lorain-Elyria, OH	Kansas City, MO-KS	Portland-Vancouver, OR-WA	Washington, DC-MD-VA-WV
Colorado Springs, CO	Kenosha, WI	Raleigh-Durham-Chapel Hill, NC	Waterloo-Cedar Falls, IA
Columbia, MO	Knoxville, TN	Reading, PA	West Palm Beach-Boca Raton, FL
Columbia, SC	Lafayette, LA	Reno, NV	Wichita, KS
Columbus, OH	Lafayette, IN	Richmond-Petersburg, VA	Wilmington-Newark, DE-MD
Corpus Christi, TX	Lancaster, PA	Riverside-San Bernardino, CA	Wilmington, NC
Dallas, TX	Lansing-East Lansing, MI	Roanoke, VA	York, PA
Davenport-Moline-Rock Island, IA-IL	Las Vegas, NV-AZ	Rochester, NY	Youngstown-Warren, OH

THE EFFECT OF IMMIGRATION ON PRODUCTIVITY: EVIDENCE FROM U.S. STATES

Giovanni Peri*

Abstract—In this paper we analyze the long-run impact of immigration on employment, productivity, and its skill bias. We use the existence of immigrant communities across U.S. states before 1960 and the distance from the Mexican border as instruments for immigration flows. We find no evidence that immigrants crowded out employment. At the same time, we find that immigration had a strong, positive association with total factor productivity and a negative association with the high skill bias of production technologies. The results are consistent with the idea that immigrants promoted efficient task specialization, thus increasing TFP, and also promoted the adoption of unskilled-efficient technologies.

I. Introduction

IMMIGRATION during the 1990s and the 2000s has significantly increased the presence of foreign-born workers in the United States. This increase has been very large on average and very unequal across states. Several studies analyzed how such differential inflows of immigrants have affected different aspects of state economies such as labor markets (Borjas 2006; Card, 2001, 2007, 2009; Peri & Sparber, 2009), industrial specialization (Card & Lewis, 2007), and innovative capacity (Gauthier-Loiselle & Hunt, 2008).

In this paper we use a production-function representation of the economies of U.S. states to analyze the impact of immigration on the inputs to production, on productivity, and, through these, on income per worker. While a large literature has analyzed the effects of immigration on native employment, hours worked, and wages, using labor market data, our contribution is to identify the impact of immigration on total factor productivity and the skill bias of aggregate productivity using national accounting data combined with Census data.[1] As for the difficulty of establishing a causal link between immigration and economic outcomes due to simultaneity and omitted variable biases, we take a two-pronged approach. First, we identify some state characteristics more likely to be related to immigration and less to other determinants of productivity. Following Peri and Sparber (2009), we use two sets of variables as instruments: the distance from the Mexican border (interacted with decade dummies) that is correlated with the inflow of Mexicans and the imputed number of immigrants inferred from the prior presence of immigrant communities as revealed by the 1960 Census. These variables together provide variation that is a strong predictor of immigrant inflow over the period, but a priori (as they are essentially geography based) much less correlated

Received for publication July 14, 2008. Revision accepted for publication July 22, 2010.

* University of California, Davis, and NBER.

I thank Gregory Wright and Will Ambrosini for outstanding research assistance. I thank the editor in charge and two anonymous referees for very helpful comments on previous drafts of this paper. Participants to several seminars provided useful suggestions.

An online supplement is available at http://www.mitpressjournals.org/doi/suppl/10.1162/REST_a_00137.

[1] Card (2007, 2009) discuss the status of this literature.

with other productivity shocks. Second, we introduce proxies for some of the relevant causes of productivity growth in the past few decades. Treating these as potentially endogenous and using the same instruments, we isolate the features of geography that are uncorrelated with those factors while still correlated with immigration and use them as predictors of immigrant inflows. The factors that we explicitly control for are the intensity of R&D, the adoption of computers, the openness to international trade as measured by the export intensity, and the sector composition of the state as measured by the productivity, employment, and gross product growth imputed to a state on the basis of its sector composition. Both the positive and significant effects of immigration on total factor productivity and the large, negative, and significant effects of immigration on the skill bias of productivity survive the instrumental variable strategy and the inclusion of these controls. However, we need to be cautious in interpreting the results causally because some lingering correlation, due to omitted variables, may remain. In particular, while the positive association between immigrants and productivity growth survives the inclusion of several controls, the estimated standard errors are large. Moreover, the inclusion of all controls simultaneously reduces much of the power of the instruments and eliminates the statistical significance of the relation between immigrants and productivity. Our estimates are consistent with the interpretation that more immigrants in a state stimulate its productivity growth, but it is hard to rule out a spurious correlation driven by unobserved productivity shocks.

We also show that a measure of task specialization of native workers induced by immigrants explains one-third to one-half of the positive productivity effect, while the effect on unskilled-biased technological adoption survives all controls. This is consistent with a state-level choice of skill-directed technology as first pointed out by Lewis (2005) and then by Beaudry, Doms, and Lewis (2006). These results suggest that these productivity gains may be associated with the efficient allocation of skills to tasks, as immigrants are allocated to manual-intensive jobs, pushing natives to perform communication-intensive tasks more efficiently. Hence, the efficiency gains that we measure are likely to come from specialization, competition, and the choice of appropriate techniques in traditional sectors.

The rest of the paper is as follows. Section II introduces the production-function approach that we use to decompose the effects of immigration on inputs and productivity. Section III describes how each state-level variable is constructed and presents summary statistics for the period 1960 to 2006. Section IV shows the OLS and 2SLS estimates of the effect of immigration on inputs, total factor productivity, and productivity skill bias and performs several robustness checks with respect to the effect of immigration on productivity. Section V provides some concluding remarks.

II. Production Function and Accounting Framework

We consider each U.S. state s in year t as producing a homogeneous, perfectly tradeable output, using the following production function,

$$Y_{st} = K_{st}^{\alpha}[X_{st}A_{st}\phi(h_{st})]^{(1-\alpha)}. \tag{1}$$

In expression (1), Y_{st} indicates total production of the numeraire good; K_{st} measures aggregate physical capital; X_{st} measures aggregate hours worked; $A_{st}^{(1-\alpha)}$ captures total factor productivity; and $\phi(h_{st})$ is an index of skill intensity defined by the following formula:

$$\phi(h_{st}) = \left[(\beta_{st}h_{st})^{\frac{\sigma-1}{\sigma}} + ((1-\beta_{st})(1-h_{st}))^{\frac{\sigma-1}{\sigma}}\right]^{\frac{\sigma}{\sigma-1}}, \tag{2}$$

where $h_{st} = H_{st}/X_{st}$ is the share of total hours worked (X_{st}) supplied by highly educated workers (H_{st}) and $(1 - h_{st}) = L_{st}/X_{st}$ is the share of total hours worked supplied by less educated workers (L_{st}).[2] The parameter β_{st} captures the degree of skill bias of the productivity used in state s and year t.[3] In such a production function, more and less educated workers combine their labor inputs in a constant elasticity of substitution (CES) function, where the elasticity of substitution is $\sigma > 0$. In order to decompose the growth rate of output per worker, it is convenient to rewrite equation (1) in terms of output per worker, $y_{st} = Y_{st}/N_{st}$ (where N_{st} is total employment in state s and year t) as follows:

$$y_{st} = \left(\frac{K_{st}}{Y_{st}}\right)^{\frac{\alpha}{1-\alpha}}[x_{st}A_{st}\phi(h_{st})]. \tag{3}$$

In equation (3) $x_{st} = X_{st}/N_{st}$ captures average hours worked per person, and $\frac{K_{st}}{Y_{st}}$ is the capital-output ratio.[4] Taking the logarithmic derivative over time (growth rate) of both sides of equation (3) and expressing them with a ^ we get[5]

$$\widehat{Y}_{st} = \widehat{N}_{st} + \widehat{y}_{st} = \widehat{N}_{st} + \left(\frac{\alpha}{1-\alpha}\right)\widehat{\frac{K_{st}}{Y_{st}}} + \widehat{A}_{st} + \widehat{x}_{st} + \widehat{\phi}_{st}. \tag{4}$$

Expression (4) is the basis of our empirical decomposition. It says that total output in a state increases as a consequence of increased employment ($\widehat{N}_{st}$) and of increased output per

worker ($\widehat{y}_{st}$), which in turn increases due to the contribution of four factors: (a) capital intensity $\widehat{\frac{K_{st}}{Y_{st}}}$, (b) total factor productivity $\widehat{A}_{st}$, (c) average hours worked $\widehat{x}_{st}$, and (d) the productivity-weighted skill-intensity index, $\widehat{\phi}_{st}$. The neoclassical growth model predicts that in the long run (balanced growth path), output per worker, y_{st}, grows only because of total factor productivity growth ($\widehat{A}_{st} > 0$) while the other terms ($\frac{K_{st}}{Y_{st}}$, x_{st} and ϕ_{st}) are constant. Hence, a simple exogenous increase in employment, as immigration is often considered, would only increase $\widehat{N}_{st}$, with no long-run effect on any other variable or on y_{st}. However, immigration can be more than a simple inflow of people. On the positive side, differences in skills, increased competition, changes in the specialization of natives, and directed technical change can promote increases in productivity and capital intensity. On the negative side, crowding of fixed factors and incomplete capital adjustment can produce decreases in productivity and capital intensity. With our approach, we can analyze the impact of immigration on each of the five terms on the right-hand side of equation (4).

Our empirical approach entails estimating the impact of immigration on each term on the right-hand side of equation (4). First, using measures of gross state product (GSP), capital stocks, hours worked, employment, and relative wages of more and less educated workers, we can calculate each term on the right-hand side of equation (4). Then, if we can identify an inflow of immigrants exogenous to the receiving-state economies (driven, that is, by factors that are not correlated with productivity, employment, or physical capital), we can estimate the elasticities η_b from the following type of regression,

$$\widehat{b}_{st} = d_t + d_s + \eta_b \frac{\Delta N_{st}^F}{N_{st}} + \varepsilon_{st}, \tag{5}$$

where b_{st} is alternatively the total employment (L_{st}), the capital-output ratio $\frac{K_{st}}{Y_{st}}$, total factor productivity A_{st}, average hours worked x_{st} or the index of skill intensity ϕ_{st}. The explanatory variable $\frac{\Delta N_{st}^F}{N_{st}}$ is the percentage change in employment due to immigrants (N_{st}^F), and d_t, d_s, and ε_{st} are, respectively, year fixed effects, state fixed effects, and zero-mean random shocks. These regressions produce estimates that can then be aggregated to obtain the effect on total income and on income per worker.[6] Clearly, identifying an exogenous inflow of immigrants and ensuring that immigration, and not

---

[2] The definitions imply that $L_{st} + H_{st} = X_{st}$.

[3] In equation (1), if we carry the terms X_{st} and A_{st} inside the index $f(h_{st})$ and call $A_{st}^H = \beta_{st}A_{st}$ and $A_{st}^L = (1-\beta_{st})A_{st}$ we obtain a common production function used in several studies of aggregate labor markets (Katz & Murphy, 1992; Card & Lemieux, 2001), income distribution (Krusell et al. 2000), and technological growth (Acemoglu, 1998; Caselli & Coleman, 2006).

[4] In the balanced growth path of any neoclassical model, the capital output ratio is constant due to the linearity of the physical capital accumulation equation in K_{st} and Y_{st} (see, for instance, Barro & Sala i Martin, 2004, p. 99).

[5] For any variable b, $d \ln b/dt = \widehat{b}$.

[6] If immigration has some effect on productivity or capital intensity, then differential immigration can drive differences in productivity and wages across states. Because of worker mobility, these differences will push all workers into states with higher productivity. To avoid this, we assume that while in terms of production prices (in units of the numeraire), permanent differences in income per person could arise, these are absorbed by corresponding differences in the average price index across states. This is compatible with an equilibrium where workers are mobile. The large literature that documents a strong, positive effect of immigration on housing prices (such as Saiz, 2003, 2007; Ottaviano & Peri, 2006; Gonzales & Ortega, 2009) confirms that this adjustment mechanism, through land prices and local price indices, is plausible.

other unobservable shocks, is driving the estimated elasticity is crucial to our goal. For these reasons, we discuss the instrumental variable strategy and the validity of the instruments at length and introduce controls for other long-run technological and specialization trends in section IV.

III.   Construction of Variables and Summary Statistics

We consider as the units of analysis fifty U.S. states plus Washington, DC, in each Census year between 1960 and 2000 and in 2006. We use three main data sources. For data on aggregate employment and hours worked, including the distinction between more and less educated workers and natives and immigrant workers, we use the public use microdata samples (IPUMS) of the U.S. Decennial Census and the American Community Survey (Ruggles et al., 2008). For data on GSP, we use the series available from the U.S. Bureau of Economic Analysis (2008b). Finally, to calculate state physical capital, we use data from the National Economic Accounts, obtained from the U.S. Bureau of Economic Analysis (2008a). We now describe the construction of each variable in detail.

To construct employment and hours worked,[7] we use Census data.[8] Since they are all weighted samples, we use the variable personal weight ($PERWT$) to produce the aggregate statistics. We divide workers into two education groups: H (those with some college education or more) and L (those with high school education or less). The "foreign-born" status used to identify native and immigrant workers is given to workers who are noncitizens or naturalized citizens.[9]

The hours of labor supplied by each worker are calculated by multiplying hours worked in a week by weeks worked in a year, and individual hours are multiplied by the individual weight and aggregated within each education-state group. This measure of hours worked by education group and state is the basic measure of labor supply. We call H_{st}^D and H_{st}^F the hours worked, respectively, of domestic (native) and foreign-born highly educated workers in state s and year t so that $H_{st} = H_{st}^D + H_{st}^F$ is the total hours worked by highly educated workers in state s and year t. Similarly, we call L_{st}^D and L_{st}^F the hours worked, respectively, by domestic (native) and foreign-born less educated workers in state s and year t so that $L_{st} = L_{st}^D + L_{st}^F$ is the total of hours worked by less educated workers in state s and year t. Finally, consistent with the model below, we call $X_{st} = X_{st}^D + X_{st}^F$ the total hours supplied by workers of both education levels (sum of H and L) in state s and year t; $N_{st} = N_{st}^D + N_{st}^F$ denotes the total employment (sum of natives and foreign born) in state s and year t.

[7] The details on variable definition, construction, and data are contained in the appendix in the online supplement.
[8] Specifically, we use the general 1% sample for Census 1960, the 1% State Sample, Form 1, for Census 1970, the 1% State Sample for Censuses 1980 and 1990, the 1% Census Sample for the year 2000, and the 1% sample of the American Community Survey (ACS) for the year 2006.
[9] To identify foreign born, we use the variable $CITIZEN$ beginning in 1970 and $BPLD$ in 1960.

We measure gross product at the state level Y_{st} using data on GSP available from the U.S. Bureau of Economic Analysis (BEA; 2008a). The BEA produces figures on GSP in current dollars. The currently available series covers the period 1963 to 2006. We use that series and convert it to constant 2000 dollars using the implicit price deflators for gross domestic product available from the BEA (2008b). Finally, we extend the series backward to 1960 using the state-specific real growth rates of GSP averaged over the 1963–1970 period in order to impute growth between 1960 and 1963. We use data relative only to 1960, 1970, 1980, 1990, 2000, and 2006 for the fifty states plus Washington, DC. The variable y_{st}, output per worker, is then constructed by dividing the real GSP Y_{st} by total employment in the state, N_{st}.

The construction of physical capital K_{st} is a bit more cumbersome. The National Economic Accounts estimates only the stock of physical capital by industry at the national level.[10] Following Garofalo and Yamarik (2002), we use the national estimates of the capital stock over the period 1963 to 2006 for nineteen industries (listed in appendix 2 of the online supplement). We then distribute the national capital stock in a year for each industry across states in proportion to the value added in that industry that is generated in each state. This assumes that industries operate at the same capital-output (and capital-labor) ratios across states; hence, deviation of the capital stock from its long-run level for an industry is similar across states because capital mobility across states ensures equalization of capital returns by industry. Essentially the state composition across industries and the adjustment of the capital-labor ratio at the industry level determine in our data the adjustment of state capital-labor ratios. We then deflate the value of the capital stocks using the implicit capital stock price deflator available from the Bureau of Economic Analysis (2008b) and we extend the stock backward for each state to 1960, applying the average growth rate between 1963 and 1970 to the period 1960 to 1962. This procedure gives us the panel of real capital stock values by state K_{st}. Capital per worker ($k_{st} = K_{st}/N_{st}$) is calculated by dividing the capital stock by total employment in the state and year. Hence, in total, we can obtain direct measures of the variables $Y_{st}, N_{st}, X_{st}, H_{st}, L_{st}$ and of the ratios y_{st}, x_{st}, and h_{st}.

The variables A_{st} and β_{st} are not observed directly. However, we can use the production function expression in equation (1) and the condition that the average hourly wage of more and less educated (w_{st}^H and w_{st}^L) equals the marginal productivity of H_{st} and L_{st}, respectively, to obtain two equations in two unknowns and solve them. In particular, setting the ratio of the hourly wages of H_{st} to L_{st} equal to the ratio of their marginal productivity gives

$$\frac{w_{st}^H}{w_{st}^L} = \left(\frac{\beta_{st}}{1-\beta_{st}}\right)^{\frac{\sigma-1}{\sigma}} \left(\frac{h_{st}}{1-h_{st}}\right)^{-\frac{1}{\sigma}}. \tag{6}$$

[10] See the Appendix in the online supplement for a detailed description.

Solving equation (6) for the parameter β, we obtain the following expression:

$$\beta_{st} = \frac{\left(w_{st}^H\right)^{\frac{\sigma}{\sigma-1}} h_{st}^{\frac{1}{\sigma-1}}}{\left(w_{st}^H\right)^{\frac{\sigma}{\sigma-1}} h_{st}^{\frac{1}{\sigma-1}} + \left(w_{st}^L\right)^{\frac{\sigma}{\sigma-1}} (1-h_{st})^{\frac{1}{\sigma-1}}}. \quad (7)$$

Substituting equation (7) into equation (1) and solving explicitly for A_{st} we obtain

$$A_{st} = \left(\frac{Y_{st}^{\frac{1}{1-\alpha}} K_{st}^{-\frac{\alpha}{1-\alpha}}}{X_{st}}\right)$$

$$\times \frac{\left(w_{st}^H\right)^{\frac{1}{\sigma-1}} h_{st}^{\frac{1}{\sigma-1}} + \left(w_{st}^L\right)^{\frac{1}{\sigma-1}} (1-h_{st})^{\frac{1}{\sigma-1}}}{\left[w_{st}^H h_{st} + w_{st}^L (1-h_{st})\right]^{\frac{\sigma}{\sigma-1}}}. \quad (8)$$

The only new variables required to calculate β_{st} and A_{st}, besides those described above, are the hourly wages for more and less educated workers, w_{st}^H and w_{st}^L. We obtain these from the IPUMS data by averaging hourly wages by state and year separately for individuals with some college education or more, w_{st}^H, and for those with high school education or less, w_{st}^L.[11] Finally, in order to implement equations (7) and (8), we need a value for the parameter σ, the elasticity of substitution in production between more and less educated workers, and for the parameter α, the elasticity of output to capital. Because there are several estimates of σ in the literature, most of which cluster between 1.5 and 2.0 (see Ciccone & Peri, 2005, a recent estimate and a survey of previous ones), we choose the median value of 1.75 for σ and check the robustness of our most relevant results to a value of 1.5 and of 2.0. As for α, we consider the value of 0.33 that is commonly used in exercises of growth accounting and is based on the value of 1 minus the share of income to labor (usually estimated around 0.67; Gollin, 2002).

The average growth rates by decade of all the variables described above are reported in table A1 in the online supplement. Some well-known tendencies are evident in the data. The progressive increase in the inflow of immigrants as a share of employment during the 1970s and again during the 1990s is noticeable. We also see the slowdown in total factor productivity during the 1970s and 1980s and the reacceleration during the 2000–2006 period. Employment and working hours per person experienced sustained growth over the entire 1970–2000 period, with a reduction only in the 2000–2006 period. The last two rows of table A1 show that both the skill bias of technology, β_{st}, and the share of highly educated workers, h_{st}, increased constantly and significantly over the whole period, in particular during the 1970s and 1980s. The literature on wage dispersion across education groups (Katz & Murphy 1992; Autor, Katz, & Kearney, 2008) has emphasized this finding, attributing it to directed skill-biased technological change. Reassured by the behavior of our measured and

[11] The exact procedure used to calculate individual hourly wages is described in the appendix in the online supplement.

TABLE 1.—OLS ESTIMATES OF THE IMPACT OF IMMIGRATION ON THE COMPONENTS OF GROSS STATE PRODUCT GROWTH

Dependent Variable	(1) Basic OLS	(2) 1970–2006	(3) 1960–2000	(4) Including Lagged Dependent Variable	(5) 2SLS Estimates Population Change as Instrument
$\hat{N}$	1.76*	2.06**	2.32**	2.15**	1.73*
	(0.80)	(0.95)	(0.71)	(0.91)	
$\hat{y}$	0.62	0.54	0.93*	0.55	0.51
	(0.43)	(0.47)	(0.50)	(0.36)	(0.50)
Components of $\hat{y}$					
$\left(\frac{\alpha}{1-\alpha}\right)(\hat{K}-\hat{Y})$	−0.13	−0.21	0.07	−0.18	−0.22
	(0.12)	(0.15)	(0.22)	(0.12)	(0.17)
$\hat{A}$	0.80**	0.88*	0.68	0.82**	1.08**
	(0.39)	(0.43)	(0.48)	(0.39)	(0.32)
$\hat{x}$	0.15**	0.09	0.29**	0.14*	0.14**
	(0.05)	(0.05)	(0.09)	(0.07)	(0.05)
$\hat{\phi}$	−0.20**	−0.22**	−0.11**	−0.26**	−0.19**
	(0.05)	(0.05)	(0.05)	(0.05)	(0.06)
Components of $\hat{\phi}$					
$\hat{h}$	−0.75**	−0.56**	−0.92**	−0.52**	−0.73**
	(0.15)	(0.15)	(0.24)	(0.17)	(0.18)
$\hat{\beta}$	−0.92**	−0.68**	−1.19**	−0.62**	−0.89**
	(0.20)	(0.19)	(0.34)	(0.19)	(0.24)
Observations	255	204	204	204	255

The explanatory variable is immigration as a percentage of initial employment. Each cell is the result of a separate regression. The explanatory variable is the net inflow of immigrant workers over an intercensus period as a percentage of the initial employment. The units of observations are U.S. states (plus DC) in each decade 1960–2000 plus 2000–2006. Each regression includes time fixed effects and state fixed effects. The method of estimation is least squares with observations weighted by the employment of the state. Errors in parentheses are heteroskedasticity robust and clustered by state. The calculated variables use the assumption that $\sigma = 1.75$ and $\alpha = 0.33$. **Significant 5%, *10%.

constructed variables, which match some important trends emphasized in the literature, we proceed to the empirical analysis.

IV. Estimates of the Effects of Immigrants

A. OLS Estimates

Our main empirical strategy is to estimate equations like equation (5), using, alternatively, the growth rate of different variables in lieu of the placeholder $\hat{b}_{st}$. The dependent variables used in the regressions are shown in the first column of tables 1 and 2, and the estimated elasticity (η_b) is reported in the cells of those tables. As introductory results, table 1 reports the OLS estimates of equation (5) using a panel of fifty U.S. states (plus Washington, DC) using intercensus changes between 1960 and 2000 and the 2000–2006 change. Each cell reports the result of a different regression that includes time and state fixed effects, weights each cell by the total employment in it, and reports the heteroskedasticity-robust standard errors clustered by state to account for potential correlation of the residuals over time. The first two rows of table 1 decompose the effect of immigration on total income into its effect on total employment ($\widehat{N_{st}}$) and on output (gross state product) per worker ($\hat{y}_{st}$). The following four rows decompose the effect on output per worker into the contributions due to the capital intensity $\left(\frac{\alpha}{1-\alpha}\right)\frac{\widehat{K_{st}}}{Y_{st}}$, total factor productivity $\widehat{A}_{st}$, average hours worked $\hat{x}_{st}$, and the skill

TABLE 2.—2SLS ESTIMATES OF THE IMPACT OF IMMIGRATION ON THE COMPONENTS OF GROSS STATE PRODUCT GROWTH

	(1)	(2)	(3)	(4)	(5)
				2SLS, Including Lagged	Border
Dependent Variable	Basic 2SLS	1970–2006	1960–2000	Dependent Variable	Instrument Only
$\hat{N}$	1.09**	1.39**	1.23**	1.94**	1.11**
	(0.45)	(0.55)	(0.25)	(0.69)	(0.46)
$\hat{y}$	0.88**	0.71*	1.47**	0.22	1.03**
	(0.25)	(0.35)	(0.30)	(0.27)	(0.34)
Components of $\hat{y}$					
$\left(\frac{\alpha}{1-\alpha}\right)(\hat{K}-\hat{Y})$	−0.08	−0.13	0.27	−0.10	−0.08
	(0.13)	(0.13)	(0.23)	(0.14)	(0.09)
$\hat{A}$	1.37**	1.11**	0.97**	0.61**	1.15**
	(0.27)	(0.36)	(0.36)	(0.24)	(0.30)
$\hat{x}$	0.28**	0.17	0.61**	0.27**	0.24**
	(0.11)	(0.09)	(0.19)	(0.10)	(0.08)
$\hat{\phi}$	−0.26**	−0.29**	−0.14	−0.38**	−0.27**
	(0.07)	(0.08)	(0.11)	(0.08)	(0.07)
Components of $\hat{\phi}$					
$\hat{h}$	−1.16**	−0.90**	−1.58**	−0.89**	−1.14**
	(0.25)	(0.23)	(0.36)	(0.20)	(0.27)
$\hat{\beta}$	−1.14**	−0.84**	−1.74**	−0.49**	−1.08**
	(0.15)	(0.13)	(0.25)	(0.18)	(0.15)
First-stage F-test	17.42	7.48	17.99	17.42	13.11
Observations	255	204	204	204	255

The explanatory variable is immigration as a percentage of initial employment. Each cell is the result of a separate regression. The explanatory variable is the net inflow of immigrant workers over an intercensus period as a percentage of the initial employment. The units of observations are U.S. states (plus DC) in each decade 1960–2000 plus 2000–2006. Each regression includes state fixed effects and year fixed effects. The method of estimation is 2SLS with imputed immigrants and distance from border interacted with decade dummies as instruments. The errors in parentheses are heteroskedasticity robust and clustered by state. The calculated variables use the assumption that $\sigma = 1.75$ and $\alpha = 0.33$. **Significant at 5%, *10%.

intensity index $\widehat{\phi}_{st}$. Those four effects add up to the total effect on $\hat{y}_{st}$.[12] Finally, the last two rows show the effect of immigration on the share of educated workers $\hat{h}_{st}$ and the skill bias of productivity $\hat{\beta}_{st}$, both of which enter the expression for the skill-intensity index $\widehat{\phi}_{st}$. Estimating the effect by OLS, including time and state fixed effects, accounts for common U.S. cycles specific to each decade and for state-specific trends in income and immigration. However, these estimates are still potentially subject to endogeneity and omitted variable biases. We propose an estimation strategy that addresses those issues in the next sections.

Nevertheless, table 1 shows some evidence of stable and significant correlations between net immigration and some of the relevant growth rates. In particular, we also check whether the correlations depend on the period considered (in column 2 we drop the 1960s, and in column 3 we drop the 2000s) and whether including the lagged dependent variable in order to capture autocorrelation over time (column 4) or instrumenting immigrant employment changes with immigrant population changes (column 5) affects the estimates.

The estimates are quite stable across specifications, so we can simply comment on the general features of these correlations.[13] First, the elasticity of total employment to immigrants is always larger than 1 (sometimes as large as 2) and never

[12] This is true, by construction, for the OLS estimates of table 1 but not for the 2SLS estimates of table 2.

[13] The specification that produces estimates further from the others is the one including the lagged dependent variable in column 4. As we include

significantly different from 1. This confirms previous studies, such as Card (2001, 2005), Ottaviano and Peri (2006), and Peri and Sparber (2009), that report no evidence of crowding out of native employment by immigrants using correlation across local labor markets.[14] The estimates are often much larger than 1, potentially suggesting the existence of a demand-driven bias. Second, the coefficients in the second row show a positive and sometimes significant correlation between income per worker and immigration. This positive correlation results from the combination of a large, positive, and significant correlation between immigration and total factor productivity (fourth row of table 1) and a small, negative, and insignificant correlation between immigration and capital intensity (third row of Table 1). The positive correlation of immigrants with average hours worked (ranging from +0.09 to 0.29) and their negative correlation with the average skill index $\widehat{\phi}_{st}$ (between −0.11 and −0.26) compensate for each other in terms of income per worker.

Finally, we find a significant negative correlation between the immigration rate in employment and both the share of more educated workers and the skill bias of technology, both with an elasticity within (or close to) the range −0.7/−1.0. States with larger-than-average inflows of immigrants over the period 1960 to 2006 were therefore associated with a more than one-for-one increase in employment, a larger growth of income per worker (entirely due to larger TFP growth), while at the same time the skill intensity and the skill bias of production grew at a slower rate.

B. Instruments and 2SLS

Our instrumental variable approach combines the instruments based on the past settlement of immigrants (augmented by their national rate of growth) drawn from Card (2001), and then used in several other studies (including Card, 2009, and Peri & Sparber, 2009), with a purely geographical instrument based on the distance from the border between Mexico and the United States. Specifically, the imputed growth of immigrants as a share of the working-age population was calculated as follows. We first identify from the Census foreign-born workers from ten different areas.[15] For each nationality of origin and each state, the total number of people of working age (16–65) in Census 1960 is augmented in 1970 to 2006 by applying the decade national growth rate of the population from that nationality in the whole United States. This allows us to impute the immigrant population from each nationality of origin in each state that we then

fixed effects, these panel estimates are subject to the bias emphasized by Nickell (1981).

[14] Given the way we constructed our variables, a coefficient of 1 on $\hat{N}_{st}$ implies that one immigrant worker produced an increase in total employment of 1; hence, it produces no change in native employment.

[15] The nationality of origin that we consider are the following: Mexico, rest of Latin America, Canada-Australia-New Zealand, western Europe, eastern Europe and Russia, China, India, rest of Asia, Africa, and others.

add up across nationalities within a state to construct the imputed decennial growth of working-age population due to imputed immigrants. The variation of this measure across states depends only on the initial presence of immigrants (as of 1960) and their national composition and is independent of any subsequent state-specific economic factor. We use this measure as an instrument for the growth in employment due to immigrants in each state and decade, $\frac{\Delta N_{it}^F}{N_{st}}$.

The U.S.-Mexico border (for Mexican immigrants) is the main point of entry to the United States. The distance of each state's center of gravity from the border is first calculated. We then interact the logarithmic distance variables with five decade dummies (1960s, 1970s, 1980s, 1990s, and 2000–2006). This captures the fact that distance from the border had a larger effect in predicting the inflow of immigrants in decades with larger Mexican immigration.[16]

The imputed immigrants and time-interacted border-distance have significant power in predicting immigration. Their F-test in the samples is usually around 17 when used jointly (see the second-to-last row in table 2). Even the border-distance instruments by themselves have significant power (F-test of 13, as reported in the last column of table 2). The imputed immigrants by themselves, however, have only a weak power (F-test of 6.77), and hence we cannot use that instrument by itself. Importantly, the instruments, when used jointly, pass the test of overidentifying restrictions, and one cannot reject the assumption of exogeneity of instruments at the 1%, 5%, or 10% confidence level.[17] Surveying the results across specifications, again using different samples (omitting 1960 in specification 2 and 2006 in specification 3), controlling for past lagged values (specification 4), and using only the set of instruments based on the Mexican border distance (specification 5), we obtain a rather consistent picture. First, the impact on total employment is now estimated to be close to 1 and never statistically different from 1. This confirms the idea that some reverse causality may bias the OLS estimates of the employment effects up. The effect on the growth of income per worker is similar than in the OLS case and significant except for specification (4) and mostly between 0.7 and 1. The standard errors, always clustered by state to account for potential autocorrelation of the errors over time, are sometimes large enough to make the estimates only marginally significant. Decomposing this effect, one sees that the positive elasticity of income per workers to immigration results mainly from the positive effect on TFP. The estimated effects on capital intensity (usually insignificant) on average

hours worked (usually positive) and on the skill index (usually negative) roughly balance each other.

As in the estimates of table 1, the negative coefficient of immigration on the skill index $\widehat{\phi}_{st}$ is roughly balanced by the positive effect on hours worked, and so those two terms contribute very little to output per worker. The negative effects of immigration on the share of highly educated workers and on the skill bias of technology are strongly confirmed by the 2SLS estimates, and in both cases the elasticity is around -1. One should still be very careful in interpreting the coefficient as causal, as the instruments could be correlated with economic factors affecting productivity and growth in a state-decade.[18] The estimates, however, are consistent with three effects of immigration: one is well known, but two have not been clearly identified by the existing literature. First, immigration mechanically increases employment and reduces its share of highly educated workers, and it does not crowd out native employment. These are well-known effects already emphasized by Card (2007) and Card and Lewis (2007). Second, immigration promotes production techniques that are more unskilled-efficient (as suggested by Lewis, 2005, and consistent with the idea of directed technological choice). Finally, immigration is also associated with faster growth in overall factor-neutral productivity.

The most interesting estimates are those regarding total factor productivity and its skill bias. The first is responsible for the significant net positive effect of immigrants on output per worker, and the second is a direct test of directed technical adoption. Hence, we devote section IVC to testing their robustness to the inclusion of several controls. Before doing that, we remind readers that the 0 effect of immigration on capital intensity (capital-output ratio) in the long run (ten-year intervals) is consistent with the idea that U.S. states have been growing along their balanced growth path: increased employment and higher productivity were matched by investments to guarantee a constant capital output intensity. This is what is predicted by a simple neoclassical growth model.

C. The Effects on Productivity and Skill Bias

The most remarkable and novel effects estimated in table 2 are the positive and significant effect of immigration on total factor productivity ($\widehat{A}$) and the negative and significant effect on the skill bias of technology ($\widehat{\beta}$). Both effects are quite large, and while they are not estimated extremely precisely, they are usually significant. The concern is that the geographic location of a state used in constructing the instrument in the 2SLS estimation, while certainly affecting the immigration rates and exogenous with respect to technological changes, may be correlated with other features that have affected productivity growth and its skill intensity. For these reasons, while keeping the border distance and the imputed immigration as instruments (we need both of them for sufficiently powerful instruments), we include in the regression several variables

---

[16] A detailed description of how these instruments are constructed can be found in Peri (2009).

[17] The test statistic, under the null hypothesis that none of the instruments appears in the second-stage regression, is distributed as a chi square with degrees of freedom given by the difference between the number of instruments and the endogenous variables (five in our case). The test statistics equals 7.65. The corresponding p-value for the relevant chi square distribution, with 5 degrees of freedom, is 0.18, and hence the null hypothesis of exogenous instruments stands at 10% confidence. See Wooldridge (2002) for the details of the test.

[18] We control for several of these state-specific factors in section IVC.

TABLE 3.—ESTIMATED IMPACT OF IMMIGRATION ON TOTAL FACTOR PRODUCTIVITY ($\hat{A}$)

Dependent Variable: $\hat{A}$	(1) Basic (1960–2006)	(2) Controlling for R&D per Worker (1970–2006)	(3) Controlling for Computer Adoption	(4) Controlling for Trade (1980–2006)	(5) Controlling for TFP Growth Based on Sector Composition (1960–2006)
OLS	0.80**	0.90**	0.70**	1.05**	0.50
	(0.39)	(0.37)	(0.38)	(0.53)	(0.35)
2SLS	1.37**	1.02**	0.88**	1.17**	0.82**
	(0.27)	(0.31)	(0.26)	(0.49)	(0.31)
2SLS	0.77*	0.73**	0.59*	0.94*	0.56*
TFP calculated as standard	(0.41)	(0.35)	(0.29)	(0.54)	(0.30)
Solow residual (σ = ∞)					
2SLS	1.72**	1.81**	1.70**	1.78**	1.53**
$\hat{A}$ *constructed with σ = 1.5*	(0.44)	(0.29)	(0.28)	(0.43)	(0.36)
2SLS	0.80*	0.75**	0.62**	0.94*	0.59*
$\hat{A}$ *constructed with σ = 2*	(0.41)	(0.34)	(0.29)	(0.53)	(0.31)
Explanatory variables	Task Specialization Channel: Dependent Variable $\hat{A}$				
Change in employment due to immigration	0.90	0.51	0.69	0.51	0.13
	(0.94)	(0.58)	(0.67)	(0.79)	(0.62)
Change in communication-manual specialization of natives	1.30*	1.63	2.70**	1.20	0.67
	(1.30)	(1.68)	(1.16)	(1.00)	(1.20)
Observations	255	204	255	153	255

Explanatory variables: Immigrants as a share of employment. Each cell in rows 1 to 5 is the coefficient of the regression of $\hat{A}$ on the change in employment due to immigrants, estimated including time and state fixed effects. The baseline estimate (row 1) is OLS with TFP constructed using the assumption that σ = 1.75. In the second row, we use 2SLS with imputed immigrants and border distance interacted with decade dummies as instruments. In the third row, we calculate the TFP as simply a Solow residual without accounting for the imperfect substitution of the more and the less educated. In the fourth and fifth rows, total factor productivity is constructed under the assumption that σ, the elasticity of substitution between the more and the less educated, is 1.5 or 2. In the last two rows, we report the coefficient of a regression of A simultaneously on the immigration rate and the change in task specialization of less educated natives. The units of observations are fifty U.S. states plus DC in each decade 1960–2000 plus 2000–2006. The errors in parentheses are heteroskedasticity robust and clustered by state. **Significant at 5%, *10%.

TABLE 4.—ESTIMATED IMPACT OF IMMIGRATION ON SKILL BIAS ($\hat{\beta}$)

Dependent Variable: $\hat{\beta}$	(1) Basic	(2) Controlling for R&D per Worker	(3) Controlling for Computer Adoption	(4) Controlling for Trade	(5) Controlling for TFP Growth Based on Sector Composition (1960–2006)
OLS	−0.98**	−0.72**	−0.91**	−0.85**	−0.94**
	(0.17)	(0.17)	(0.17)	(0.19)	(0.17)
2SLS	−1.10**	−0.84**	−1.01	−0.89**	−1.11**
	(0.34)	(0.14)	(0.18)	(0.18)	(0.16)
$\hat{\beta}$ *constructed with σ = 1.5*	−2.34**	−2.04**	−2.30**	−1.90**	−2.40**
	(0.45)	(0.31)	(0.37)	(0.35)	(0.35)
$\hat{\beta}$ *constructed with σ = 2*	−0.59*	−0.36**	−0.48**	−0.45**	−0.60**
	(0.30)	(0.10)	(0.10)	(0.14)	(0.10)
Explanatory variables	Task Specialization Channel: Dependent Variable $\hat{\beta}$				
Change in employment due to immigration	−1.12**	−0.65**	−1.02**	−0.78**	−0.96**
	(0.38)	(0.20)	(0.17)	(0.25)	(0.13)
Change in communication-manual specialization of natives	−0.06	−0.29	−0.11	−0.58	0.39
	(0.35)	(0.44)	(0.36)	(0.43)	(0.52)
Observations	255	204	255	153	255

Explanatory variables: Immigrants as a share of employment. Each cell in rows 1 to 4 is the coefficient of the regression of $\hat{\beta}$ on the change in employment due to immigrants, estimated including time and state fixed effects. The baseline estimate (row 1) is OLS with TFP constructed using the assumption that σ = 1.75. In the second row, we use 2SLS with imputed immigrants and border distance interacted with decade dummies as instruments. In the third and fourth rows, the method of estimation is 2SLS, and skill-biased productivity is constructed under the assumption that σ, the elasticity of substitution between the more and the less educated, is 1.5 or 2. In the last two rows, we report the coefficient of a regression of $\hat{\beta}$ simultaneously on the immigration rate and the change in task specialization of natives. The units of observations are 50 U.S. states plus D.C. in each decade 1960–2000 plus 2000–2006. The errors in parentheses are heteroskedasticity robust and clustered by state. **Significant at 5%, *10%.

that are aimed at capturing other influences on the productivity and technology of U.S. states. We include each of them, one by one, considering them as potentially endogenous and therefore using the border distance and imputed immigrant instruments to predict them.

The coefficients on the control variables are sometimes estimated imprecisely (and we do not report them in tables 3 and 4); however, what we care about is the coefficient on the immigration rate, estimated using the instruments. The inclusion of the controls implies that we are using the variation in the instruments that is orthogonal to the controlled factor (and hence independent from it) to predict the immigration rate and estimate its effect on productivity. We include the controls one at the time. Including them all together and treating them as potentially endogenous reduces the power of the instrument drastically, producing very large standard errors. Table 3 shows the estimated coefficients on the immigration rates in regressions based on equation (5), using $\hat{A}_{st}$ as the dependent variable. Table 4 shows the coefficients of similar regressions with $\hat{\beta}_{st}$ as the dependent variable. Proceeding from top to bottom, tables 3 and 4 show estimates obtained using OLS (first row) or 2SLS estimation methods (rows 2–5). Moreover, to check how robust the results are to the choice of the parameter σ (the substitutability between more and less educated workers) in the construction of $\hat{A}_{st}$ and $\hat{\beta}_{st}$, we report the estimates using two alternative values of that parameter (equal to 1.5 and 2, respectively). We also report in the third row of table 3 the results obtained when using the more standard formula for the Solow[19] residual in order to compute $\hat{A}_{st}$.[20] The last two rows of tables 3 and 4 report results from a specification that we discuss in section D.

Considering the different specifications (columns) in table 3 (and table 4), we first report the basic estimates obtained from a regression that controls only for time and state fixed effects; then column 2 controls for the average real yearly R&D spending per worker in each state in the 1970s, 1980s, 1990s, and 2000s.[21] We obtain the variable by dividing the aggregate state expenditures by state employment. The estimated effect of the R&D variable on TFP changes (not reported) corresponding to the second row of specification (2) is 0.10 (with a standard error equal to 0.09), while its effect on $\hat{\beta}_{st}$ is 0.04 (with standard error 0.10). So the R&D variable positively affects both productivity and skill bias, which is expected. More important for our purposes, the inclusion of R&D as a control does not much affect the estimated effect of immigration on TFP (with an elasticity of 1.02 in the 2SLS specification) and on the skill bias (an elasticity of −0.84).

The third column of tables 3 and 4 introduces computer use as a control. The adoption of computer technology was a major technological innovation leading to increased productivity, and since its diffusion varied by sector and location, we can control for it. To do this, we include the change in share of workers using the computer (computer adoption) in specification (3).[22] The estimated coefficient of the computer adoption variable on $\hat{A}_{st}$ (not reported) is 2.10 (standard error 0.90), while on $\hat{\beta}_{st}$, it is 0.21 (standard error 0.16).[23] As expected, computer adoption has a positive and skill-biased effect on productivity across states. More interesting for us is

that the effect of immigration on $\hat{A}_{st}$ is still positive and significant (but reduced by about 40% from its basic estimate to an elasticity of 0.88), and the effect on the skill bias is essentially unchanged in its magnitude (−1.01) and significance (standard error equal to 0.18).

The geographic location of an economy is an important determinant of its trade with the rest of the world. Being close to a major port, to the coast, and its distance from other countries all affect trade costs and hence trade volumes. Moreover, during the decades between 1980 and 2006, the United States significantly increased its trade with the rest of the world. Since trade may increase productivity (promoting competition, inducing specialization, reducing costs of inputs), we control for trade as a share of GSP in order to account for this effect.[24] We calculate exports as a share of GSP in 1987–1989 and attribute this value to the entire decade of the 1980s and then calculate the average export/GSP value by state in the 1990s and in the 2000–2006 period. We include these values in the regression as a proxy for the access of a state to international trade in each decade. Two things are important to notice. First, proximity to the Mexican border is not a very good predictor of increase in trade (the *F*-test of the border distance instrument in predicting trade over the considered decades is only 2.56). Second, trade with Asia, Europe, and Canada has been much larger (in value) than trade with Mexico. Hence, while the geographic location of a state affected its trade, the specific distance from the Mexican border did not have much correlation with trade growth. The coefficient obtained for the effect of trade on productivity (not reported) is negative (−0.15) and not significant (s.e. = 0.20) while the effect on the skill bias is also negative and not significant. When trade is included as a control (column 4) immigration maintains a positive and very significant effect on productivity (+1.17 reported in table 3), as well as a negative and largely unchanged effect on the productivity bias (−0.89 as reported in table 4).

Finally, the last column of tables 3 and 4 introduces a control that accounts for the sector composition of each state and its effect on productivity. In particular, we construct and include in the regression the sector-driven productivity growth by averaging the national growth rate of total factor productivity in each of fourteen sectors,[25] each weighted by the initial (1960) share of that sector in the state value added (BEA, 2009).[26]

[19] As it is described in Solow (1957).
[20] Formula (8) reduces to that of the Solow residual when σ = ∞.
[21] The data are from the National Science Foundation (1998) and include total (private and federal) funds for industrial R&D in constant 2000 U.S. dollars. The data are available every year for the period 1975 to 2006. We calculate the average yearly expenditure in a state between 1975 and 1977 and impute it over the 1970s. In the following periods we use the average yearly expenditure during the period.
[22] The original (individual) data are from the March supplement of the Current Population Survey and are available for the years 1984, 1997, and 2001. Assuming that in 1960 and 1970 no worker used a computer, since the PC was introduced in 1980, we interpolate linearly the three data points and impute the shares of workers using computers in 1980, 1990, 2000, and 2006 for each state.
[23] In both cases, these are the coefficients from the basic 2SLS specification in the second row.

[24] The data on exports of manufactured goods by state of origin are from the Origin of Movement data available from the U.S. Census and for purchase on CD-ROM (at www.gtis.com). These data are the total value, in current dollars, of exports from each state from 1987 to 2006.
[25] These sectors are agriculture, agricultural services, mining, construction, manufacturing of durable goods, manufacturing of nondurable goods, transportation, utilities, wholesale trade, retail trade, F.I.R.E., other services, and government.
[26] The data on sector-specific TFP are calculated using data on value added and capital stocks from BEA (2008b), deflated to 2000 US$ using the GDP and investment price deflator, respectively, and employment by industry also obtained from BEA (2008b) (merging the SIC codes before 1997 and the NAICS codes from 1998). We apply a simple growth accounting method to construct the Solow residual in each industry using a share of labor equal to 0.66.

This control accounts for the fact that different states had different sector structures in 1960, and this might be correlated with the presence of immigrants back in 1960 (or with the geographic location of the state) invalidating the exclusion restriction. The inclusion of this sector-based productivity growth (whose coefficient on TFP is positive and very significant) does not modify much the effect of immigration on $\tilde{A}_{st}$ and on $\tilde{\beta}_{st}$. The impact of immigrants on $\tilde{A}_{st}$ including this control is 0.82 (s.e. $= 0.31$; see column 5 of table 3) and the impact on the skill-bias of technology is -1.11 (with a standard error of 0.16); see column 5 of table 4. The (unskilled-biased) productivity effect of immigrants is quite robust to the inclusion of several controls.

D. The Task-Specialization Hypothesis and Robustness Checks

Two mechanisms proposed and studied in the previous literature can jointly explain the positive productivity effect of immigrants and its skill bias. Lewis and Card (2007) find that in markets with an increase in less educated immigrants, a large proportion of all sectors shows a higher intensity of unskilled workers. Furthermore, Lewis (2005) documents that in those labor markets, there is a slower adoption of skill-intensive techniques. This is in accordance with the theory of directed technological change or appropriate technological adoption (Acemoglu, 2002) in which the availability of a production factor pushes firms to adopt technologies that are more efficient and intensive in the use of that factor. More recently, in a paper with Chad Sparber (Peri & Sparber 2009), we show that in states with large inflows of immigrants, natives with lower education tend to specialize in more communication-intensive production tasks, leaving more manual-intensive tasks to immigrants. This produces increased task specialization following comparative advantages and results in efficiency gains, especially among less educated workers. In the last two rows of table 3, we analyze whether the reorganization of production around the efficient specialization of natives (and immigrants) can explain part of the measured productivity gains.

We include in the regression a measure of the change in relative specialization of less educated natives between communication and manual tasks at the state level. The variable is constructed (as described in Peri & Sparber 2009) by attributing the intensity of physical manual tasks (M_i) and of communication-interactive (C_i) tasks to each worker, i, based on occupation, using the average of 52 ability variables collected in the U.S. Department of Labor's O*NET data set.[27] Then we calculate the average of the ratio of these two task intensities for less educated native workers in each state s and year t, C_{st}/M_{st}. The percentage change in this variable measures the change in task specialization of natives and is then included in the regression. The idea is that if immigrants

affect the efficiency of production in a state by reallocating natives toward communication tasks and undertaking manual tasks, leading to an overall productivity improvement, we should observe the productivity effect of immigrants mostly through the task reallocation of natives. Hence, when this task reallocation is controlled for, the productivity impact of immigrants should decrease. Moreover, the instruments used to predict immigrant flows should also be good instruments for the endogenous task reallocation. This is what we observe in the last two rows of table 3, where we report the coefficients on the immigration variable and on the native specialization change, estimated by 2SLS and also including the other controls.

Two patterns emerge. First, the estimated coefficient on the change in specialization is positive and sometimes significant—in other words, the specialization change instrumented by geography has a positive effect on productivity.[28] Second, the coefficient on the immigration variable, while still positive, is reduced significantly, often to half of its original estimate (considering as reference the 2SLS estimates without a control for specialization). It also loses its significance in all cases. Hence, the effect of controlling for the change in specialization on the estimated coefficient of immigration on TFP is much more drastic than the effect of introducing any other control. This is evidence that at least part of the effect of immigrants on productivity comes from the reallocation of natives and immigrants across production tasks. Table 4 shows that the effect of controlling for task reallocation on the skill bias regression is much smaller (the coefficient is reduced by 5% to 10% in absolute value). Reallocation is likely to enhance overall efficiency. However, controlling for task reallocation, states with a large inflows of immigrants are still likely to choose relatively unskilled-intensive (and perhaps manual-intensive) techniques.

Finally, table 5 shows the robustness of the main estimated coefficients (on $\bar{N}_{st}, \hat{y}_{st}, \tilde{A}_{st}$, and $\tilde{\beta}_{st}$) to further controls and sample restrictions. First, especially for GSP and productivity, one may suspect that convergence across states may bias the estimates if immigrants tend to flow into states that are catching up with the economic frontier. Hence, growth rates may depend on the initial level of the variable. Including the initial value of the dependent variable to account for convergence and omitting fixed state effects[29] (column 2 of table 5) does not change any qualitative result; it only increases the estimated positive impact of immigration on employment, while it decreases somewhat the effect on GSP per worker and productivity.

If we eliminate the Mexican border states in specification (3), the explanatory power of the instruments is reduced,

---

[27] For a list and classification of abilities into manual and communication skills, see table A1 of Peri and Sparber (2009).

[28] If we include only the change in task specialization of natives and not the share of foreign born as explanatory variable and use the same set of instruments, the coefficient on that variable turns out to be always significant.

[29] We omit fixed effects in order to avoid the bias emphasized in Nickell (1981).

TABLE 5.—FURTHER ROBUSTNESS CHECKS OF THE MAIN EFFECTS OF NET IMMIGRATION

Dependent Variable	(1) Basic	(2) Controlling for Initial Value of Dependent Variable: No State Effects	(3) Without Border States (CA, AZ, NM, TX)	(4) Without the Largest States (CA, NY, TX)	(5) 1980–2006	(6) Controlling for Growth of Dependent Variable Imputed from the Sector Composition
$\hat{N}$	1.09**	1.76**	3.20**	2.90**	0.79**	1.11**
	(0.45)	(0.43)	(0.87)	(1.10)	(0.27)	(0.47)
$\hat{y}$	0.88**	0.60**	2.41**	2.77**	0.64	0.75**
	(0.25)	(0.15)	(1.12)	(1.20)	(0.47)	(0.25)
$\hat{A}$	1.37**	0.76**	2.33**	2.59*	1.06**	0.82**
	(0.27)	(0.18)	(1.16)	(1.39)	(0.39)	(0.15)
$\hat{\beta}$	−1.14**	−0.44**	−1.73**	−1.05**	−0.97**	−1.11**
	(0.15)	(0.09)	(0.63)	(0.47)	(0.16)	(0.16)
Observations	255	255	235	240	153	255

Explanatory variable is immigration as a percentage of initial employment. Each cell is the result of a separate regression. The explanatory variable is the net inflow of immigrant workers over an intercensus period as a percentage of the initial employment. The units of observations are U.S. states (plus DC) in each decade 1960–2000 plus 2000–2006. The method of estimation is 2SLS with imputed immigrants and distance from border interacted with decade dummies as instruments. Each regression includes state and decade dummies unless otherwise specified. The errors in parentheses are heteroskedasticity robust and clustered by state. The calculated variables use the assumption that σ = 1.75 and α = 0.33. **Significant at 5%; *10%.

as is evident in the larger standard errors. However, all the effects, though very imprecise, are positive, significant, and much larger than in the basic sample. The standard errors and the point estimates also increase when we eliminate the largest state economies (California, Texas, and New York), which are also the largest receivers of immigrants (specification 4). Restricting the sample to the three most recent decades that experienced by far the largest aggregate inflow of immigrants (specification 5), does not change the results. Finally, including the sector-based imputed growth of the dependent variable ($\widehat{N_{st}}, \widehat{y_{st}}, \widehat{A_{st}}$ or $\widehat{\beta_{st}}$) constructed using the national growth rate of the relevant variable in thirteen industries and then weighting those growth rates by the 1960 share of that industry in state value added[30] (specification 6) does not change the estimate much either.

V. Conclusion

This paper uses an aggregate accounting approach to analyze the relation between immigration and employment and the productivity of U.S. state economies. While the aggregate nature of the data and the impossibility of identifying a genuinely random variation in immigration flows call for caution in the causal interpretation of our estimates, we present three interesting findings, two of them new in this literature. First, we confirm that there is no evidence that immigrants crowd out employment of (or hours worked by) natives. Second, we find that immigration is significantly associated with total factor productivity growth. Third, such efficiency gains are unskilled biased—larger, that is, for less educated workers. These correlations are robust to including several control variables individually (such as R&D spending, technological adoption, sector composition, openness to international

trade, or sector composition), and they are not explained by productivity convergence across states or driven by a few states or particular decades. We conjecture that at least part of the positive productivity effects are due to an efficient specialization of immigrants and natives in manual-intensive and communication-intensive tasks, respectively (in which each group has a comparative advantage), resulting in a gain in overall efficiency. Preliminary empirical evidence supports this claim. The positive coefficient from the 2SLS estimates implies that the net inflow of immigrants, even those driven by their historical location and proximity to the border, is associated with significant productivity gains for the receiving states.

REFERENCES

Acemoglu, Daron, "Why Do New Technologies Complement Skills? Directed Technical Change and Wage Inequality," *Quarterly Journal of Economics* 113 (1998), 1055–1090.
——— "Directed Technical Change," *Review of Economic Studies* 69:4 (2002), 781–810.
Autor, David H. Lawrence F. Katz, and Melissa S. Kearney, "Trends in U.S. Wage Inequality: Revising the Revisionists," this REVIEW 90:2 (2008), 300–322.
Barro, Robert J., and Xavier Sala-i-Martin, *Economic Growth*, 2nd ed. (Cambridge, MA: MIT Press, 2004).
Beaudry, Paul, Mark Doms, and Ethan Lewis, "Endogenous Skill Bias in Technology Adoption: City-Level Evidence from the IT Revolution," NBER working papers no. 12521 (2006).
Borjas, George, "Native Internal Migration and the Labor Market Impact of Immigration," *Journal of Human Resources* 41 (2006), 221–258.
Card, David, "Immigrant Inflows, Native Outflows, and the Local Labor Market Impacts of Higher Immigration," *Journal of Labor Economics* 19 (2001), 22–64.
——— "Is the New Immigration Really So Bad?" *Economic Journal* 115 (2005), 300–323.
——— "How Immigrants Affects U.S. Cities" CReAM discussion paper no. 11/07 (2007).
——— "Immigration and Inequality," *American Economic Review, Papers and Proceedings* 99:2 (2009), 1–21.
Card, David, and Thomas Lemieux, "Can Falling Supply Explain the Rising Returns to College for Younger Men? A Cohort Based Analysis," *Quarterly Journal of Economics* 116 (2001), 705–746.
Card, David, and Ethan Lewis, "The Diffusion of Mexican Immigrants during the 1990s: Explanations and Impacts," in George J. Borjas (Ed.), *Mexican Immigration to the United States* (Chicago: University of Chicago Press, 2007).

[30] The sector-based imputed growth of the dependent variables included in these regressions is the analog of those included for TFP and for skill bias in columns 5 of tables 3 and 4. In the regressions of the first row, we include imputed employment growth as a control. In the regressions of the second row, we include imputed GSP growth as a control. In the regressions of the third and fourth rows, we include the imputed TFP growth as a control.

Caselli, Francesco, and John W. Coleman, "The World Technology Frontier," *American Economic Review* 96:3 (2006), 499–522.

Ciccone, Antonio, and Giovanni Peri, "Long-Run Substitutability between More and Less Educated Workers: Evidence from U.S. States, 1950–1990," this REVIEW 87:4 (2005), 652–663.

Garofalo, Gasper A., and Steven Yamarik, "Regional Convergence: Evidence from a New State-by-State Capital Stock Series," this REVIEW 84:2 (2002), 316–323.

Gauthier-Loiselle, Marjolaine, and Jennifer Hunt, "How Much Does Immigration Boost Innovation?" NBER working paper no. 14312 (2008).

Gonzales, Libertad, and Francesc Ortega, "Immigration and Housing Booms: Evidence from Spain," IZA discussion papers no. 4333 (2009).

Gollin, Douglas, "Getting Income Shares Right," *Journal of Political Economy* 100 (2002), 458–474.

Katz, Lawrence F., and Kevin M. Murphy, "Changes in Relative Wages 1963–1987: Supply and Demand Factors," *Quarterly Journal of Economics* 107:1 (1992), 35–78.

Krusell, P. L. Ohanian, V. Rios-Rull, and G. Violante, "Capital-Skill Complementarity and Inequality: A Macroeconomic Analysis," *Econometrica* 68 (2000), 1029–1053.

Lewis, Ethan, "Immigration, Skill Mix, and the Choice of Technique," Federal Reserve Bank of Philadelphia working paper no. 05-08 (2005).

National Science Foundation, *Survey of Industrial Research and Development* (Washington, DC: Division of Science Resource Studies, 1998).

Nickell, Stephen J., "Biases in Dynamic Models with Fixed Effects," *Econometrica* 49 (1981), 1417–1426.

Ottaviano, Gianmarco, and Giovanni Peri, "The Economic Value of Cultural Diversity: Evidence from U.S. Cities," *Journal of Economic Geography* 6:1 (2006), 9–44.

Peri, Giovanni, "The Effect of Immigration on Productivity: Evidence from US States," NBER working paper no. 15507 (2009).

Peri, Giovanni, and Chad Sparber, "Task Specialization, Immigration and Wages," *American Economic Journal: Applied Economics* 1:3 (2009), 135–169.

Ruggles, Steven, Matthew Sobek, Trent Alexander, Catherine A. Fitch, Ronald Goeken, Patricia Kelly Hall, Miriam King, and Chad Ronnander, *Integrated Public Use Microdata Series: Version 3.0* [Machine-readable database] (Minneapolis, MN: Minnesota Population Center, 2008). http://www.ipums.org.

Saiz, Albert, "Room in the Kitchen for the Melting Pot: Immigration and Rental Prices," this REVIEW 85:3 (2003), 502–521.

—— "Immigration and Housing Rents in American Cities," *Journal of Urban Economics* 61 (2007), 345–371.

Solow, Robert, "Technical Change and the Aggregate Production Function," this REVIEW 39 (1957), 312–320.

U.S. Bureau of Economic Analysis, *Gross Domestic Product by State* (2008a), http://www.bea.gov/regional/gsp/default.cfm?series=SIC.

—— *Interactive NIPA Tables and Interactive Fixed Assets Tables* (2008b), http://www.bea.gov/bea/dn/home/gdp.htm.

—— *Gross Domestic Product by Industry Data* (2009), http://bea.gov/industry/gdpbyind_data.htm.

Wooldridge J. L., *Econometric Analysis of Cross Section and Panel Data* (Cambridge, MA: MIT Press, 2002).

STEM Workers, H-1B Visas, and Productivity in US Cities

Giovanni Peri, *University of California, Davis*

Kevin Shih, *University of California, Davis*

Chad Sparber, *Colgate University*

Science, technology, engineering, and mathematics (STEM) workers are fundamental inputs for innovation, the main driver of productivity growth. We identify the long-run effect of STEM employment growth on outcomes for native workers across 219 US cities from 1990 to 2010. We use the 1980 distribution of foreign-born STEM workers and variation in the H-1B visa program to identify supply-driven STEM increases across cities. Increases in STEM workers are associated with significant wage gains for college-educated natives. Gains for non-college-educated natives are smaller but still significant. Our results imply that foreign STEM increased total factor productivity growth in US cities.

I. Introduction

Science, technology, engineering, and mathematics (STEM) workers are the primary contributors to the creation and adoption of technological in-

We thank Nick Bloom, Hilary Hoynes, William Kerr, Enrico Moretti, Sarah Turner, and seminar participants at the University of California, Davis and Berkeley, Université Catholique del Louvain, Institute for the Study of Labor (IZA), and the National Bureau of Economic Research for helpful comments and suggestions. Peri gratefully acknowledges an Interdisciplinary Frontiers in the Humanities and Arts grant from the University of California, Davis, for partially funding this project. Sparber gratefully acknowledges a Major grant from Colgate University for funding his research. Contact the corresponding author, Giovanni Peri, at

[*Journal of Labor Economics*, 2015, vol. 33, no. 3, pt. 2]
Submitted January 31, 2013; Accepted May 7, 2014; Electronically published June 29, 2015

novation, the fundamental driver of sustained economic growth. The importance of STEM innovations has long been recognized by growth economists. Griliches (1992) and Jones (1995), for example, have used measures of scientists and engineers to identify research and development (R&D) contributions to idea production, with the latter study arguing that scientists and engineers are responsible for 50% of long-run US productivity growth. A related literature (e.g., Katz and Murphy 1992; Acemoglu 2002; Autor, Katz, and Kearney 2006) has noted that technological innovation during the past 30 years has not increased the productivity of all workers equally. The development of new technologies—especially information and communication technologies (ICT)—significantly increased the productivity and wages of college-educated workers. They had a much smaller effect on the demand for non-college-educated workers, which has remained rather stagnant.

Importantly, while technological and scientific knowledge is footloose and spreads across regions and countries, STEM workers are less mobile. Tacit knowledge and face-to-face interactions influence the speed with which new ideas are locally adopted. Several studies (e.g., Moretti 2004a, 2004b; Iranzo and Peri 2009) have illustrated that concentrations of college-educated workers spur local productivity. Others have shown the tendency for innovation- and idea-intensive industries to agglomerate (Ellison and Glaeser 1999; Glaeser 2011; Moretti 2012) and for ideas to remain local generators of virtuous innovation cycles (Jaffe, Trajtenberg, and Henderson 1993; Saxenian 2002).

This article sits at the intersection of these literatures. We quantify the long-run effect of increased city-level STEM employment on labor market outcomes for STEM, college-educated, and non-college-educated native-born workers. Sections II and III describe our empirical specification and data. The challenge of the exercise is to identify variation in the growth of STEM workers across US metropolitan statistical areas (MSAs, or cities) that is supply driven and hence exogenous to other factors that affect local wages, employment, and productivity. We do this by exploiting the introduction of the H-1B visa in 1990 and the differential effect that these visas had in bringing foreign-born college-educated workers (mostly STEM workers) to 219 US cities from 1990 to 2010. The H-1B policy changes were national in scope but had differentiated local effects because foreign STEM workers were unevenly distributed across US cities before the inception of the H-1B visa program. Migrant preferences and the availability of information spread by ethnic networks led subsequent inflows of H-1B workers to concentrate in areas with a large preexisting foreign STEM presence.

---

gperi@ucdavis.edu. Information concerning access to the data used in this article is available as supplementary material online.

Our identification strategy is rooted in methods used by Altonji and Card (1991), Card (2001), and Kerr and Lincoln (2010). First, we measure foreign STEM workers as a share of employment in each MSA in 1980. This share exhibits large variation. Next, we predict the number of new foreign STEM workers in each city by allocating the H-1B visas to 14 foreign nationality groups in proportion to their city-level presence in 1980. This H-1B-driven imputation of future foreign STEM is a good predictor of the actual increase of both foreign STEM and overall STEM workers in a city over subsequent decades. Thus, we use this prediction as an instrument for the actual growth of foreign STEM workers in order to obtain causal estimates of the impact of STEM growth on the wages and employment of college-educated and non-college-educated native-born workers.

The 1980 distribution of foreign STEM and the overall inflow of H-1B workers between 1990 and 2010 could be correlated with unobservable city-specific shocks that affect employment and wage growth, so Section IV explores the power and validity of our instrumental variable strategy. We check that the initial industrial structure of the metropolitan area, the 1980 distribution of other types of foreign-born workers (e.g., less educated and manual workers), and the subsequent inflow of non-STEM immigrants do not predict foreign STEM employment growth. We also show that the trends of native outcomes prior to the inception of the H-1B program (1970–80) were uncorrelated with the H-1B-driven growth in STEM workers from 1990 to 2010. Finally, our demanding regression specifications always include both city and period fixed effects while relying on changes in growth rates of H-1B-driven STEM workers within MSAs over time for identification.

The main regression estimates are in Section V. Our preferred specifications reveal that a rise in foreign STEM growth by 1 percentage point of total employment increases wage growth of college-educated natives by 7–8 percentage points. The same change had a smaller but usually significant effect on non-college-educated native wage growth equal to 3–4 percentage points. We find no statistically significant effects for native employment growth.

Section VI closes the analysis by introducing a simple model of city-level production and combining it with our estimated parameters to simulate the effect of STEM on total factor productivity and skill-biased productivity. When we aggregate at the national level, inflows of foreign STEM workers explain between 30% and 50% of the aggregate productivity growth that took place in the United States between 1990 and 2010. This range is consistent with Jones's (2002) analysis of science and engineering contributions to productivity growth. We also find that foreign STEM inflows account for a more modest 4%–8% of US skill-biased technological change.

II. Empirical Framework

Our empirical analysis uses variation in foreign-born STEM workers across US cities (c) and time periods (t) to estimate their impact on native wages and employment. We discuss identification and its challenges in Section IV. The basic specifications we estimate in Section V take the form

$$y_{ct}^{\text{Native},X} = \phi_t + \phi_c + b_{y,X} \cdot \frac{\Delta\text{STEM}_{ct}^{\text{Foreign}}}{E_{ct}} + b_3 \cdot \text{Controls}_{ct}^X + \varepsilon_{ct}. \quad (1)$$

The variable $y_{ct}^{\text{Native},X}$ is the period change in outcome y (either employment or average weekly wages) for the subgroup of natives with skill X (either STEM workers, college-educated workers, or non-college-educated workers), standardized by the initial year outcome level. The term ϕ_t captures period fixed effects, while ϕ_c captures city fixed effects. The variable $\Delta\text{STEM}_{ct}^{\text{Foreign}}/E_{ct}$ is the change of foreign STEM over a period, standardized by a city's initial total employment (E_{ct}). The term Controls_{ct}^X includes other city-specific controls, and ε_{ct} is a zero mean idiosyncratic random error. The specification implies that identification relies on variation in the growth of foreign STEM workers within cities over time periods.

Our analysis spans 1990–2010, and we choose to partition these two decades into three specific time periods: 1990–2000, 2000–2005, and 2005–10. This enables us to exploit the large variation in national H-1B policy that occurred between 2000 and 2005 relative to the other periods. Additionally, this facilitates (unreported) robustness checks that remove the 2005–10 period to avoid influence from the Great Recession.[1]

The coefficient $b_{y,X}$ captures the elasticity of outcome y, for worker group X, to an exogenous increase in STEM workers. Interpreting these estimates as causal requires changes in $\text{STEM}_{ct}^{\text{Foreign}}$ that are exogenous to productivity shocks and other unobservable determinants of city-level wage and employment changes. Before turning attention to this challenge, we describe our data, STEM employment measures, the construction of the H-1B-driven foreign STEM instrument, and our instrument's power.

III. Data: STEM Workers in US Cities

We develop two separate methods of defining STEM occupations. Each method also uses both a more inclusive and a more restrictive STEM identification criterion, resulting in four possible STEM definitions. The first method is based on skills that workers use in their occupations. We use the US Department of Labor's (2012) O*NET database, which measures the occupation-specific importance of several dozen skills required

---

[1] Estimates are robust to removing the Great Recession. Similarly, they remain robust when constructing variables over 1990–2000 and 2000–2010. Results are available on request.

to perform the job. We select four O*NET skills that involve STEM use, namely, mathematics in problem solving, science in problem solving, technology design, and programming. We then compute the average score of each occupation across the four skills and rank the 331 occupations consistently identified in the 1980–2010 census according to the average STEM skill value defined above.[2] We classify STEM occupations as those employing the top 4% (strict definition) or 8% (broad definition) of workers in that ranking in the year 2010; O*NET 4% (or 8%) STEM workers are the individuals with these occupations.

Our second method for identifying STEM occupations is based on the skills workers possess before employment—the college majors found among workers within occupations. The US State Department recognizes a list of STEM majors for the purpose of granting foreign students extended time to work under the Optional Practical Training (OPT) program.[3] We rank occupations on the basis of the 2010 ACS share of individuals with a college degree in a STEM major. We then classify STEM occupations as those employing the top 4% (strict) or 8% (broad) of workers following that ranking in 2010. Major-based 4% (or 8%) STEM workers are the individuals within those occupations. Both the O*NET and major-based strict definitions include mainly census occupations with "scientist" or "engineer" in the title. Major-based STEM occupations largely coincide with O*NET STEM occupations.

A. H-1B Visa Policy Changes

Our analysis exploits large shifts in national H-1B visa policy between 1990 and 2010 as an exogenous source of variation in the inflow of foreign STEM workers across US cities to identify the effect of STEM workers on the wages and employment of native-born workers. The H-1B visa, introduced in 1990, provides temporary permits for college-educated foreign "specialty" workers. The visa has been a crucial channel of admission for many college-educated foreign-born workers employed in STEM occupations.[4] Set initially at 65,000 H-1B visas annually, the cap rose to 115,000 for

---

[2] We make small refinements to the census occupational classification in order to ensure complete time consistency in the availability of occupations over the 1980–2010 period. A detailed description of both of our STEM definitions, as well as the refinement of occupations, is available in the online appendix.

[3] There is no direct crosswalk between majors listed under the OPT STEM classification and major categories in the 2010 American Community Survey (ACS). Thus, our list is consistent with, but not identical to, OPT STEM degree fields.

[4] Lowell (2000) notes that 70% of H-1B visas have been awarded to people employed as computer analysts, programmers, electrical engineers, university professors, accountants, other engineers, and architects. Similarly, US Citizenship and Immigration Services (various years) reports that for all years between 2004 and 2011, more than 85% of new H-1B visa holders worked in computer science, health science, accounting, architecture, engineering, and mathematics.

fiscal years 1999 and 2000 and then to 195,000 per year for 2001, 2002, and 2003. It reverted to the original 65,000 beginning in 2004. Though the limit officially remains at 65,000, the first 20,000 H-1B visas issued to individuals who have obtained a graduate degree in the United States became exempt from H-1B limits beginning in 2005, effectively raising the cap to 85,000.[5]

Not only has the size of the H-1B program varied greatly since its inception, but the ensuing inflow of foreign STEM workers has been heterogeneously distributed across US cities as well. Part of these cross-city differences was certainly due to varying economic conditions, industrial structures, and labor demand influencing wage and employment growth. Importantly, however, a portion of this variation was due to persistent immigrant preferences to locate in cities with historical communities of past immigration. The 1980 distribution of STEM workers by nationality proxies for these historical settlements. Our analysis needs to capture only the heterogeneity in foreign STEM created by this differential initial presence (in 1980) of foreign enclaves by nationality that are exogenous to other determinants of future city-level native wage and employment growth. To do this we construct an H-1B-driven instrument that retains only the portion of growth in foreign STEM attributable to national policy fluctuations, and our regressions account for city-specific factors that may have attracted foreign STEM and native workers alike.

B. The H-1B-Driven Increase in STEM

Our data on the occupations, employment, wages, age, and education of individuals come from the Ruggles et al. (2010) Integrated Public Use Microdata Series (IPUMS) 5% census files for 1980, 1990, and 2000; the 1% ACS sample for 2005; and the 2008–10 3% merged ACS sample for 2010. We use data only on 219 MSAs consistently identified from 1980 through 2010. These span a range of US metropolitan sizes, including all the largest cities in the United States down to MSAs with close to 200,000 people (Danville, VA, Decatur, IL, Sharon, PA, Waterbury, CT, Muncie, IN, and Alexandria, PA, are the six smallest). Data on aggregate H-1B flows by nationality and year are publicly available from the US Department of State (2012).

We construct our H-1B-driven increase in STEM workers variable for each city between 1990 and 2010. This captures supply-driven variation in the growth of foreign STEM workers, which we use as an instrumental variable to estimate equation (1). To create this instrument, we first impute the number of foreign STEM workers in city c and year t:

$$\widehat{\text{STEM}}_{ct}^{\text{FOR}} = \sum_{n=1}^{14} \text{STEM}_{c1980}^{\text{FOR}_n} \left(\frac{\widehat{\text{STEM}}_t^{\text{FOR}_n}}{\text{STEM}_{1980}^{\text{FOR}_n}} \right). \tag{2}$$

---

[5] Kerr and Lincoln (2010) and Kato and Sparber (2013) provide more discussion on the H-1B visa and its economic effects.

The term $STEM_{c1980}^{FOR_n}$ is the number of foreign STEM workers of national-ity n in city c in 1980.[6] The growth factor of all foreign STEM workers for each nationality in the United States between 1980 and year t is repre-sented by $STEM_{t}^{FOR_n}/STEM_{1980}^{FOR_n}$. This is calculated by adding the inflow of STEM workers from each nationality between 1980 and t to its initial 1980 level. For the period 1980–90, we simply add the net increase in STEM workers from nationality n as recorded in the US census ($\Delta STEM_{1980-90}^{FOR_n}$). For later periods we use the cumulative H-1B visas allocated to each na-tionality ($\# \text{ of } H1B_{1990-t}^{FOR_n}$).[7] The imputed growth factor for STEM workers for each foreign nationality in year t is therefore

$$\frac{\widehat{STEM}_{t}^{FOR_n}}{STEM_{1980}^{FOR_n}} = \frac{STEM_{1980}^{FOR_n} + \Delta STEM_{1980-90}^{FOR_n} + \# \text{ of } H1B_{1990-t}^{FOR_n}}{STEM_{1980}^{FOR_n}}. \quad (3)$$

The H-1B-driven change in foreign STEM workers that we use as our instrument is the time period change in $STEM_{ct}^{FOR}$ standardized by the ini-tial imputed city employment $(\widehat{E}_{ct})$.[8]

Our identification strategy is closely related to those used by Altonji and Card (1991) and Card (2001), who exploit the initial distribution of foreign workers across US cities. We use the initial distribution of foreign STEM workers across cities rather than all immigrants. In this regard, our

[6] We aggregate to 14 nationality groups: Canada, Mexico, rest of the Americas (excluding the United States), western Europe, eastern Europe, China, Japan, Korea, Philippines, India, rest of Asia, Africa, Oceania, and other. We choose 1980 as the base year in the imputation of foreign STEM for three reasons. First, it is the earliest census that allows the identification of 219 metropolitan areas. Second, it occurs well before the creation of the H-1B visa and hence does not reflect the distribution of foreign STEM workers affected by the policy. Third, it predates most of the ICT revolution so that the distribution of STEM workers was hardly affected by the geographic location of the computer and software industries.

[7] Data on visas issued by nationality begin in 1997. While we know the total number of H-1B visas issued in each year from 1990, we must estimate the total number of visas issued by nationality between 1990 and 1996 as

$$\# \text{ of } \widehat{H1B}_{n,1990-t} = \# \text{ of } H1B_{1990-t} \left(\frac{\# \text{ of } H1B_{n,1997-2010}}{\# \text{ of } H1B_{1997-2010}} \right),$$

where $\# \text{ of } H1B_{n,1997-2010}/\# \text{ of } H1B_{1997-2010}$ is the share of visas issued to nationality group n among the total visas issued from 1997 to 2010. For t larger than 1997, we have the actual number of yearly visas by nationality.

[8] To avoid endogenous changes in total employment at the city level, we also im-pute city employment by augmenting employment by nativity and skill level in 1980 by the corresponding growth factor in total national employment. Hence, $\widehat{E}_{ct}^x = E_{c1980}^x \times (E_t^x/E_{1980}^x)$, where x is native college-educated workers, native non-college-educated workers, foreign college-educated workers, and foreign non-college-educated workers. Thus, $\widehat{E}_{ct} = \Sigma_x \widehat{E}^x$, and the instrument is $\Delta \widehat{STEM}_{ct}^{FOR}/\widehat{E}_{ct}$.

methodology is more similar to Kerr and Lincoln's (2010) examination of the impact of H-1B flows on innovation. We distinguish our approach by using the foreign STEM presence in 1980, rather than in 1990, and by further differentiating immigrant groups by nationality, instead of using aggregate immigrants. We also use a more demanding panel specification, measuring variables in growth rates while including both city and time period effects. Before discussing the validity of our instrumental variables approach in detail, we present descriptive statistics that illustrate the significance of foreign-born STEM workers and the importance of the H-1B program in transforming the US STEM workforce.

C. Foreign STEM Summary Statistics

Foreign-born individuals have been persistently overrepresented in STEM occupations and have contributed substantially to the aggregate growth of STEM jobs in the United States.[9] Table 1 displays the foreign-born share of four different employment groups. Columns 1–4 represent the foreign-born percentage among total employment, college-educated workers, STEM occupations, and college-educated STEM workers—all calculated for the aggregate of 219 MSAs that we analyze. While foreign-born individuals represented about 16% of total US employment in 2010, they counted for more than 27% of college-educated STEM workers in the MSAs we analyze. This percentage has more than doubled since 1980.

Columns 1 and 2 of table 2 show that college-educated STEM workers have increased from 1.7% of total employment in 1980 to 3.2% in 2010. The share of college-educated foreign STEM workers has grown from 0.2% to 0.87%. Of the 0.78 point increase in college-educated STEM as a percentage of employment between 1990 and 2010, 0.53 percentage points (two-thirds of the total) were due to foreigners.

Columns 3–5 display changes in STEM employment and H-1B visas between periods. Column 3 reports the net total increase in college-educated STEM workers in the United States over the periods, and column 4 displays the rise in college-educated foreign STEM workers. While only one-fifth of the net increase in STEM workers between 1980 and 1990 was driven by foreigners, they were responsible for 77% of the net STEM growth between 1990 and 2000 and for more than the total growth from 2000 to 2010. Column 5 displays the cumulative number of H-1B visas issued between periods. It is clear that enough H-1B visas were issued to cover the whole growth in college-educated foreign STEM workers in the United States. Remarkably, H-1B issuances were three to four times as large as the net increase in college-educated STEM between 2000–2005 and 2005–10. This implies that many foreign STEM workers,

---

[9] In the summary statistics and in the empirical analysis we mainly use the O*NET 4% STEM definition unless we note otherwise.

STEM Workers, H-1B Visas, Productivity in US Cities   S233

Table 1
Summary Statistics: Percentage of Foreign-Born by Group, 219 MSAs

	Total Employment (%) (1)	College-Educated Employment (%) (2)	Employment in STEM Occupations (%) (3)	College-Educated Employment in STEM Occupations (%) (4)
1980	6.15	6.81	8.14	11.09
1990	8.82	8.95	10.98	14.24
2000	13.31	12.80	17.47	22.69
2005	15.37	14.81	20.03	25.76
2010	16.37	15.46	21.19	27.15

NOTE.—The figures are obtained by the authors' calculations using IPUMS census data from 1980–2010. The relevant population includes only noninstitutionalized individuals between ages 18 and 65 who have worked at least 1 week in the previous year and report identified occupations. The statistics exclude those with unknown, unreported, or military occupations and individuals without a clearly identified birthplace who do not possess US citizenship through parents with US citizenship. STEM occupations are defined according to the O*NET 4% definition. College-educated workers have a bachelor degree or higher. The sample comprises 219 consistently identified MSAs from 1980–2010.

Table 2
Shares and Absolute Net Changes in STEM Employment, 219 MSAs

	Share of Employment (%)		Net Absolute Change from Previous Period (1,000s)			
Period	College-Educated Total STEM (1)	College-Educated Foreign STEM (2)	College-Educated Total STEM (3)	College-Educated Foreign STEM (4)	H-1B Visas Issued (5)
1980	1.76	.19			
1990	2.42	.34	915	218	0
2000	2.99	.68	670	518	574
2005	3.01	.77	109	208	659
2010	3.20	.87	164	146	653

NOTE.—The figures in cols. 1–4 are obtained by the authors' calculations on data from 219 consistently identified MSAs in IPUMS census data from 1980–2010. The relevant population includes only noninstitutionalized individuals between ages 18 and 65 who have worked at least 1 week in the previous year and report identified occupations. The statistics exclude those with unknown, unreported, or military occupations and individuals without a clearly identified birthplace who do not possess US citizenship through parents with US citizenship. STEM occupations are defined according to the O*NET 4% definition. College-educated workers have a bachelor degree or higher. Data on the total number of H-1B and TN visas issued (col. 5) are from the Department of State (2012). H-1B numbers also include TN visas and are relative to the whole United States.

including H-1B recipients, have left the United States.[10] Overall, table 2 highlights the importance of foreign workers within STEM jobs and confirms that the scope of the H-1B program was large enough to substantially contribute toward foreign STEM growth since 1990.

[10] Depew, Norlander, and Sorensen (2013) provide a detailed analysis of quit and return rates for temporary skilled employees of six large Indian ICT firms. During the course of the survey period (2003–11), 29% of their sample returned to India.

IV. Identification: Power and Validity of the Instruments

Our identification strategy relies on the H-1B supply-driven instrument. Its validity is based, in large part, on the assumption that the 1980 employment share of foreign STEM workers varied across cities because of factors related to the persistent agglomeration of foreign communities in some localities. These historical differences—after controlling for an array of other city characteristics and shocks—affected the change in the supply of foreign STEM workers but were unrelated to shocks affecting city-level native wage and employment growth. Though our modeling choices aim to reduce the risk of correlation between the instrument and unobserved determinants of wage and employment growth, such confounding factors are of great concern. For example, the initial distribution of foreign STEM may be correlated with persistent city factors that influenced future labor market outcomes, resulting in omitted variables bias. Alternatively, aggregate inflows of H-1B workers might have been driven by a few specific cities. The presence of measurement error, more likely in cities with small populations, could lead to attenuation bias. This section tests our instrument's validity and addresses key challenges to our identification strategy.

The following first-stage regression provides a framework to explore these issues:

$$\frac{\Delta \text{STEM}_{ct}^{\text{FOR}}}{E_{ct}} = \phi_t + \phi_c + \beta \cdot \frac{\widehat{\Delta \text{STEM}_{ct}^{\text{FOR}}}}{\widehat{E_{ct}}} + \varepsilon_{ct}. \qquad (4)$$

The coefficient β measures the impact of H-1B-driven STEM inflows—our instrument—on the measured increase in foreign STEM workers, the explanatory variable in our second-stage regression (1). This coefficient and its power are the main objects of interest for causal interpretation. The terms ϕ_t and ϕ_c capture period and MSA fixed effects. Changes refer to the periods 1990–2000, 2000–2005, and 2005–10. The zero-mean random error (ε_{ct}) is uncorrelated with the explanatory variable.

A. Basic Specifications and Checks

We tackle several threats to the identification assumptions and begin by showing that the 1980 presence of foreign STEM workers in cities did not always mirror the presence of native STEM workers. Table 3 shows the estimated coefficient (β) and the partial F-statistic from first-stage regression equation (4). The coefficients reported in the first and the second rows are the β and the F-statistics of the instrument when using the O*NET STEM definition for both the endogenous variable and the instrument. Those in the third and fourth rows are the corresponding statistics when using the major-based STEM definition.

Column 1 includes period effects, state effects, and the 1980 employment share of native STEM. Imputed H-1B-driven STEM growth has a

Table 3
First Stage: Power and Validity of H-1B-Driven STEM as an Instrumental Variable

Explanatory Variable	Strict (4%) Definition of STEM (with State Fixed Effects) (1)	Baseline: Strict (4%) Definition of STEM (with City Fixed Effects) (2)	Broad (8%) Definition of STEM for Both Endogenous Variable and Instrument (3)	As Col. 2, Excluding the 5 Cities with Largest Number of STEM Workers (4)	As Col. 2, Excluding STEM from India (5)	As Col. 2, Imputation Using Aggregate H-1B Visas (Not by Nationality) (6)	As Col. 2, Excluding Cities with Population ≤400,000 (7)	As Col. 2, Controlling for Imputed Non-College-Educated Immigrants (8)	As Col. 8, Controlling for Bartik Employment and Wage Growth (9)
H-1B-driven growth in foreign STEM, O*Net:									
Coefficient	.48***	2.56***	4.06***	1.82**	3.53***	3.02***	3.22***	2.48***	2.34***
	(.18)	(.88)	(1.29)	(.83)	(.91)	(.75)	(.86)	(.90)	(.92)
F-statistic	6.57	8.51	9.95	4.86	15.09	16.43	14.04	7.59	6.46
H-1B-driven growth in foreign STEM, major-based:									
Coefficient	.44***	2.83***	4.23***	2.13***	3.59***	3.26***	3.34***	2.79***	2.42**
	(.16)	(.84)	(.93)	(.63)	(1.00)	(1.04)	(1.08)	(.86)	(.88)
F-statistic	7.73	11.32	20.53	11.27	12.91	9.86	9.48	10.64	7.50
Fixed effects	State and period	City and period	City and period	City and period	City and period	City and period	City and period	City and period	City and period
Observations	657	657	657	642	657	657	354	657	657
Metro areas	219	219	219	214	219	219	118	219	219

NOTE.—Each cell shows the coefficient from a different regression. The dependent variable is the growth in foreign STEM as a percentage of the labor force. The units of observations are 219 US metropolitan areas over the periods 1990–2000, 2000–2005, and 2005–10. The explanatory variable is the H-1B-driven growth of foreign STEM jobs, as a percentage of initial employment. The top 2 rows use the O*NET-based definition of STEM occupations. The third and fourth rows use major-based STEM definitions. Baseline models use the narrow (4%) definition of STEM. Column 1 also controls for a city's native STEM employment in 1980. Standard errors (in parentheses) are always clustered at the metro area level.
* Significant at the 10% level.
** Significant at the 5% level.
*** Significant at the 1% level.

highly significant impact on foreign STEM growth. This implies that even controlling for the initial native STEM share, the foreign STEM share has significant explanatory power.[11]

The next two columns introduce MSA fixed effects to control for all other initial city-specific conditions so that our identification relies only on deviations in MSA growth rates from MSA-specific trends. We include city fixed effects in all subsequent specifications. Column 2 uses the narrow 4% (STEM or major-based) definitions for both the endogenous variable and the instrument, whereas column 3 uses the broader 8% definitions. The power of the instrument in these specifications is stronger than in column 1. The F-statistics are close to or above 10, emphasizing that our H-1B-based instrument is good at capturing changes in the inflow of STEM workers within cities over time. Moreover, we find that the two definitions of STEM produce similar results, though some small differences exist.

Columns 4 and 5 of table 3 address two important concerns. The first is that the correlation between the instrument and the actual change in foreign STEM could be driven by the large high-tech boom in a few large MSAs rather than by the exogenous initial distribution of immigrants. If large metropolitan areas drove most of the country's R&D and produced a large increase in demand for foreign H-1B visas and STEM workers, the instrument and the endogenous variable for large R&D-intensive cities could be spuriously correlated. Alternatively, the presence of a few particular industries (e.g., the ICT sector) might have attracted particular types of immigrants whose growth simply proxies for the success of those industries. The current population of foreign STEM workers from India, for example, is strongly associated with information technology since most of them are employed in computer, software, and electrical engineering occupations. Moreover, Indians have always accounted for at least 40% of H-1B visas.

Column 4 excludes the five metro areas with the largest number of STEM workers in 1980.[12] Column 5 excludes Indian STEM workers from the calculations of the instrument. The coefficients are still highly significant (although somewhat reduced in col. 4 for O*NET STEM), indicating that the correlation between H-1B-driven STEM growth and a city's actual foreign STEM growth is not driven by top STEM cities or by a specific nationality group.

An alternative way to ensure that the predictive power of our instrument is not driven by individual nationality groups—whose location preferences

---

[11] One reason for the power of foreign STEM after controlling for native STEM is that cities with large native STEM shares in 1980 were associated with traditional sectors that attracted scientists and engineers in the 1970s but did not predict the presence of information technology and computer sectors that dominated R&D in the 1990s and 2000s.

[12] New York, Los Angeles, Chicago, San Jose, and San Francisco account for 24% of STEM workers in our sample.

may be affected by specific industries—is to remove the nationality dimension. We construct an instrument similar to the one used by Kerr and Lincoln (2010) by exploiting only variation in the aggregate number of H-1B visas over time, interacted with the initial overall presence of foreign STEM workers. First-stage results using this instrument are shown in column 6. The estimates remain similar, and F-statistics confirm that the instrument retains its power.

Column 7 accounts for another potential weakness of our instrument. The use of 1%–5% population samples may introduce measurement error. Aydemir and Borjas (2011) show how measurement error can produce attenuation bias when estimating the causal effect of immigrants on native outcomes. Small census and ACS samples might fail to record small foreign STEM communities in small cities. In order to see whether this measurement error affects the power of our instrument, column 7 shows the first-stage estimates when eliminating all metropolitan areas with fewer than 400,000 people. This cutoff eliminates all cities from our sample that have a measured zero foreign STEM (or imputed foreign STEM) employment share. Although we retain only 118 of the 219 cities, the coefficient estimates remain significant and stable, while the instrument is still reasonably powerful (more so for the O*NET STEM definition). While we will discuss the potential impact of measurement error on attenuation bias when presenting the second-stage estimates (in table 5 below), it is reassuring that the exclusion of the cities in which measurement error is most likely hardly affects the power of the instrument and the first-stage coefficient estimate.

B. Confounding Shocks

Two types of shocks at the MSA level might be correlated with the inflow of STEM workers, wages, and employment, thereby creating omitted variable bias. The first is a change in the skill distribution of workers related to the inflow of non-STEM immigrants. The second is an industry-driven change in productivity affecting native employment and wages. Directly controlling for such shocks would introduce endogeneity. Instead, we include predicted values formed by interacting the 1980 immigrant and industry distributions with national immigrant and industry shocks, respectively.

As STEM immigrants usually earned a college degree, we introduce a control for the imputed number of non-college-educated immigrants ($\text{NoColl}_{ct}^{\text{FOR}}$) based on their 1980 distribution, by nationality, across metropolitan areas ($\text{NoColl}_{c1980}^{\text{FOR}_n}$) and their subsequent aggregate growth in the United States ($\text{NoColl}_{t}^{\text{FOR}_n}/\text{NoColl}_{1980}^{\text{FOR}_n}$). Using notation similar to (2), we use equation (5) to calculate $\text{NoColl}_{ct}^{\text{FOR}}$ and then construct our control by taking the change over time relative to total initial imputed employment ($\Delta\widehat{\text{NoColl}}_{ct}^{\text{FOR}}/\widehat{E}_{ct}$):

$$\widehat{\mathrm{NoColl}}_{ct}^{\mathrm{FOR}} = \sum_{n=1,14} \mathrm{NoColl}_{c1980}^{\mathrm{FOR}_n} \left(\frac{\mathrm{NoColl}_t^{\mathrm{FOR}_n}}{\mathrm{NoColl}_{1980}^{\mathrm{FOR}_n}} \right). \tag{5}$$

To control for shocks driven by a city's industrial structure, we construct Bartik instruments (from Bartik [1991]) that predict the wage and employment growth of college- and non-college-educated workers based on each city's industrial composition in 1980. Specifically, let $s_{ic,1980}$ denote the share of total city employment in each three-digit census industry classification sector ($i = 1, 2, \ldots, 212$) in 1980. Then let $\Delta y_t^{i,X}/y_t^{i,X}$ be the real growth of $y = \{\text{Wage, Employment}\}$ over the decade for group $X = \{\text{College, NoCollege}\}$ in sector i. We define our sector-driven Bartik variables as

$$\left(\frac{\Delta y^X}{y^X} \right)_{ct}^{\mathrm{Sector\text{-}Driven}} = \sum_{s=1}^{212} \left(s_{ic,1980} \frac{\Delta y_t^{i,X}}{y_t^{i,X}} \right). \tag{6}$$

Column 8 of table 3 adds the imputed growth of non-college-educated immigrants to the basic first-stage regression of column 2. Cities with large communities of less educated immigrants might also have large communities of highly educated immigrants, although usually from different nationalities. Controlling for these flows will also be important to account for complementarities between college- and non-college-educated workers and their possible effect on wages in the second-stage regressions. Nonetheless, the imputed H-1B-driven instrument retains its power when controlling for the imputed number of non-college-educated immigrants. Column 9 further adds the employment and the wage Bartik instruments. This still leaves the H-1B imputed STEM growth instrument with significant, albeit somewhat reduced, explanatory power, especially when using the O*NET definition.

C. Falsification and Extensions

Our instrument is predicated on two assumptions. First, from the perspective of each metropolitan area, the H-1B visa policy significantly and exogenously affected the inflow of foreign STEM workers to the United States from 1990 to 2010. Second, the initial distribution of foreign STEM was crucial in determining the subsequent city-level inflow of H-1B immigrants and was uncorrelated with other city-level shocks affecting native wages and employment. Columns 1–4 of table 4 test these assumptions.

The aggregate inflow of H-1B workers in the United States could simply be a proxy for aggregate labor demand growth and not policy-driven supply changes. This could induce a positive correlation between the instrument and the explanatory variable even in the presence of city and period effects. Note, however, that this scenario would also imply a positive correlation between the explanatory variable and a falsified instrument constructed by substituting non-H-1B immigrant flows (or non-college-educated immigrant flows) for H-1B flows. Columns 1 and 2 show that the first-stage point estimates are insignificant and close to zero when we impute foreign STEM growth by interacting the 1980 distribution of foreign STEM with subsequent noncollege immigrant flows (col. 1) or with aggregate immigrant flows net of H-1B flows (col. 2). Hence, the aggregate variation of H-1B visas over time is crucial for predicting subsequent STEM variation across cities. The two "falsified instruments" used in these specifications, therefore, do not covary with foreign STEM changes because they do not incorporate the variation in H-1B aggregate visas. Column 3 similarly finds no evidence of correlation when we substitute the initial presence of foreign workers in manual-intensive jobs (rather than in STEM) across metropolitan areas in the construction of the instrument. Therefore, less skilled immigration—though possibly correlated with STEM immigration—did not drive the explanatory power of the instrument. These results reassure that our preferred policy-driven instrument is not simply reflecting aggregate labor demand or aggregate migration.[13]

Column 4 tests the correlation between the instrument—calculated for the 1990–2000 decade—and the preexisting growth in native college wages from 1970 to 1980. Reassuringly, there is no correlation between the H-1B imputed STEM growth after 1980 and pre-1980 native wage growth despite, as will be seen in Section V, the strong relationship between increased STEM during the 1990s and 2000s and concurrent wage growth. This test ensures that the pre-H-1B (pre-1980) outcomes across MSAs were not correlated with the post-1990 H-1B-driven STEM growth.

As a final check in this section, we explore how H-1B policy affects the total number of STEM workers and, specifically, whether metropolitan areas with large foreign STEM inflows substitute foreign STEM for native STEM or instead increase the overall STEM labor force. If the latter is true, we can consider the H-1B policy as an exogenous shock to assess the impact of total STEM on native wages, employment, and productivity. Columns 5 and 6 examine this by regressing native plus foreign STEM worker growth on the H-1B-predicted inflow of foreign STEM (the instrument). The estimated coefficient is even larger than in the basic specification, implying, as we will see below, a positive response of native STEM to foreign inflows. In column 5, we use the stricter 4% STEM definition (based on O*NET in the top rows and on college major in the two lower rows) for both the endogenous and instrumental variables. In column 6, we use the broader 8% definition of STEM for the endogenous and instrumental variables. The power of the instrument is relatively strong in most cases.

Overall, the specifications and falsifications shown in this section demonstrate that our H-1B imputed instrument has significant power in

---

[13] The online appendix details the construction of these falsified instruments.

Table 4
First Stage: Falsification and Extensions

Explanatory Variable	Falsification: Endogenous Variable			Dependent Variable		
	Growth of Foreign STEM O*NET 4% (1)	Growth of Foreign STEM O*NET 4% (2)	Growth of Foreign STEM Major-Based 4% (3)	1970–80 College-Educated Native Wages; Explanatory Variable, 1990–2000 (4)	Total STEM Growth (Native + Immigrant), 4% STEM Definition (5)	Total STEM Growth, 8% STEM Definition (6)
Predicted Foreign STEM, O*NET definition:						
Coefficient				1.66	5.03***	8.50**
				(1.02)	(1.81)	(4.40)
F-statistic				2.62	7.70	3.65
Predicted foreign STEM, major-based definition:						
Coefficient				1.12	5.29***	9.63***
				(1.10)	(1.71)	(2.56)
F-statistic				1.05	9.54	14.05

	Falsification: Endogenous Variable			Dependent Variable		
Predicted growth in foreign STEM using flows of noncollege immigrants:						
Coefficient	.04					
	(.03)					
F-statistic	2.24					
Predicted growth in foreign STEM using flows of total immigrants minus H-1B:						
Coefficient		.043				
		(.024)				
F-statistic		3.08				
Predicted growth in foreign STEM using 1980 distribution of manual immigrants:						
Coefficient			.41			
			(.27)			
F-statistic			2.42			
Observations	657	657	657	116	657	657
Metro areas	219	219	219	116	219	219

Note.—Each cell shows the coefficient from a different regression and below it the F-test of significance. The units of observations are 219 US metropolitan areas over the periods 1990–2000, 2000–2005, and 2005–10. The dependent variable is the growth in foreign STEM in cols. 1–3; the growth in native college-educated wages, 1970–80, in col. 4; and total STEM growth in cols. 5 and 6. The explanatory variables are described at the beginning of the row. Standard errors (in parentheses) are always clustered at the metro area level.

* Significant at the 10% level.
** Significant at the 5% level.
*** Significant at the 1% level.

predicting foreign STEM and total STEM growth, which is not driven by top cities, one ethnic group, or labor demand and survives the inclusion of city effects and controls for industrial composition and low-skilled immigration. The instrument's predictive power is crucially driven by the H-1B program and by the initial distribution of STEM immigrants across cities.

V. The Effect of STEM on Native Outcomes

A. Basic Results

The empirical specifications estimated in this section follow the regression described in equation (1) to identify the impact of STEM workers on native labor market outcomes ($y_{ct}^{\text{Native},X}$) by group X (STEM, college-educated, or non-college-educated) in city c. Outcomes measure growth either in average weekly wages or in employment. The explanatory variable in each regression is the change in foreign STEM relative to the initial level of total employment, $\Delta\text{STEM}_{ct}^{\text{Foreign}}/E_{ct}$. All two-stage least-squares (2SLS) regressions use the H-1B-driven change in foreign STEM relative to initial imputed employment ($\widehat{\Delta\text{STEM}_{ct}^{\text{FOR}}/E_{ct}}$) as an instrument for the actual change.

Each of the six columns of table 5 reports the $b_{y,X}$ coefficient of interest, as defined in equation (1), corresponding to the differing outcome variables. The basic specification includes time period effects, 219 MSA fixed effects, and the Bartik instruments for the relevant wage and employment changes. We always cluster standard errors at the MSA level.

In columns 1–3, the dependent variable is the percentage change of the weekly wage ($\Delta w_X^{\text{Native}}/w_X^{\text{Native}}$) paid to STEM, college-educated, and non-college-educated native-born workers, respectively.[14] We define college-educated workers as individuals who completed 4 years of college, while non-college-educated are those who did not. Columns 4–6 show the effect of STEM on the employment change of these native-born groups as a percentage of total city employment (respectively, $\Delta\text{STEM}_{ct}^{\text{Native}}/E_{ct}$, $\Delta H_{ct}^{\text{Native}}/E_{ct}$, and $\Delta L_{ct}^{\text{Native}}/E_{ct}$).

The different rows of table 5 represent different specifications to test the robustness of the estimates, mirroring in large part the first stage in table 3. Row 1, the baseline specification, shows the results when the O*NET 4% definition of STEM workers is used for both the explanatory variable and the instrument. Row 2 instead uses the major-based 4% definition of

---

[14] Weekly wages are defined as yearly wage income divided by the number of weeks worked. Employment includes all individuals between 18 and 65 years old who have worked at least 1 week during the previous year and do not live in group quarters. We convert all wages to current 2010 prices using the Bureau of Labor Statistics Inflation Calculator. See the online appendix for full details on the sample selection process.

Table 5
The Effects of Foreign STEM on Native Wages and Employment

Explanatory Variable: Growth Rate of Foreign STEM	Weekly Wage, Native STEM (1)	Weekly Wage, Native College-Educated (2)	Weekly Wage, Native Non-College-Educated (3)	Employment, Native STEM (4)	Employment, Native College-Educated (5)	Employment, Native Non-College-Educated (6)
1. Baseline 2SLS; O*NET 4% definition	6.65	8.03***	3.78**	.53	2.48	5.17
	(4.53)	(3.03)	(1.75)	(.56)	(4.69)	(4.20)
2. 2SLS; major-based 4% definition	6.64	10.95**	3.22**	.60	1.05	7.82
	(5.08)	(4.34)	(1.67)	(.63)	(3.99)	(4.90)
3. 2SLS; O*NET 8% definition	7.23**	5.64***	2.55**	.53	1.85	4.14
	(3.52)	(1.95)	(1.08)	(.75)	(3.21)	(3.32)
4. Omitting top 5 STEM cities	11.35	12.78***	5.03	1.65***	8.46	2.51
	(8.63)	(4.99)	(3.42)	(.53)	(7.04)	(7.46)
5. Controlling for imputed noncollege immigrants	7.94	7.00**	4.95**	.76	3.29	3.39
	(5.38)	(2.98)	(2.09)	(.61)	(4.85)	(4.15)
6. Dropping small cities (population <400,000)	5.70	7.18***	4.28***	.34	-.60	5.20
	(3.51)	(2.61)	(1.45)	(.58)	(1.51)	(3.18)
7. Dropping Indians	3.48	9.38**	3.46*	.47	1.31	6.44*
	(5.07)	(4.37)	(2.08)	(.51)	(3.61)	(3.54)
8. Aggregate H-1B IV	5.76	6.04**	4.13***	.31	1.64	5.56
	(4.05)	(2.75)	(1.34)	(.48)	(4.20)	(3.63)
9. Controlling for imputed college natives	2.72	7.58**	2.39	-.32	-.62	7.29
	(4.68)	(3.78)	(2.00)	(.47)	(4.19)	(5.15)
10. OLS version of specification 5	3.32	4.10***	1.16	.92**	4.97	2.11
	(2.99)	(1.86)	(1.24)	(.34)	(3.69)	(2.51)

NOTE.—The instrument is the H-1B imputed growth of foreign STEM. Each cell shows the estimate of the coefficient on the growth in foreign STEM (relative to employment) when the dependent variable is the one described at the top of the column. Each regression includes period effects, metropolitan area effects, and the Bartik for employment or wage of the relevant group. Rows 1 and 4–8 are 2SLS regressions using the O*NET 4% definition of STEM. Rows 2 and 3 use alternative definitions of STEM. Row 10 shows the OLS estimates. Standard errors (in parentheses) are clustered at the metro area level. Units of observations are 219 metro areas over three periods: 1990–2000, 2000–2005, and 2005–10.
* Significant at the 10% level.
** Significant at the 5% level.
*** Significant at the 1% level.

STEM workers, and row 3 uses the broader O*NET 8% definition. Row 4 omits the top five metropolitan areas in terms of STEM employment but is otherwise identical to the specification in row 1. Row 5 adds the growth of imputed non-college-educated immigrants, defined in (5), as a control to the baseline specification. Row 6 excludes MSAs with populations below 400,000. Row 7 excludes Indian STEM workers from the construction of the instrument. Row 8 uses the instrument constructed using aggregate H-1B flows and the initial foreign STEM distribution, thus removing the nationality dimension. Row 9 controls for growth in native college-educated employment by including a shift share instrument for the growth of college-educated natives, constructed by interacting the 1980 number of college-educated natives in each city with the national growth of college-educated natives. Finally, row 10 shows the ordinary least squares (OLS) estimates of the basic specification.

The main results are relatively consistent across specifications. First, there is a large, positive, and significant effect of foreign STEM workers on wages paid to college-educated natives. The estimated effect is significantly different from zero at the 5% significance level in all specifications and is significant at the 1% level in most. The point estimates from the 2SLS specifications are mostly between 5.6 and 9.3, with some larger values. This implies that a rise in foreign STEM growth by 1 percentage point of initial employment increases college-educated native wage growth between 5.6 and 9.3 percentage points.[15]

Second, the estimates of the effects on native STEM wages are comparable to, but less precisely estimated than, the effects on native college-educated wages. While we can never rule out the hypothesis that the estimated effects for the two groups are equal, the native STEM wage effect is only occasionally different from zero at the 5% significance level.[16] As there are fewer STEM natives (about 4% of employment) than college-educated natives (about 25% of employment), measurement error in the average wage of the first group reduces the precision of the estimates.

The third regularity of table 5 is that foreign STEM workers had a positive and usually significant effect on wages paid to non-college-educated natives. Point estimates are mostly between 2.4 and 4.3—results that are both smaller and less significant than those for college-educated natives. This implies that STEM workers generate a productivity effect that is skill

[15] Note that 1 percentage point of employment is a very large increase of STEM workers, comparable to the increase over the whole 1990–2010 period, as shown in table 2.

[16] For instance, a formal test that the estimated coefficient on STEM wages in row 1 is equal to 8.03 (the point estimate for the effect on the college-educated) has a p-value of .76. At no level of confidence can we reject the hypothesis that they are equal. Similarly for the other specifications, we can never reject the hypothesis of equality at the 10% confidence level.

biased. Foreign STEM workers are closer substitutes for college-educated natives than for non-college-educated natives, yet they generate a larger increase in the wages paid to college-educated natives.

Fourth, the inflow of STEM workers did not significantly affect the employment of any native group. The point estimates are mainly positive for native STEM and college-educated workers and mainly negative for non-college-educated natives. However, they are usually not significant, even at the 10% level. Given the mobility of college-educated natives and their city-level wage gain from STEM flows, this weak employment response is somewhat surprising and suggests the potential existence of additional adjustment mechanisms for college-educated workers at the metropolitan area level. In section 5.4 of the working paper version of this study (Peri, Shih, and Sparber 2014), we argue that STEM flows are also associated with increased housing rents for college-educated natives and that this increase in nontradables prices might absorb up to 50% of the college-educated native wage gain. This might help explain the small employment response while cautioning against interpreting the wage gains of table 5 as full increases in total purchasing power.

B. Robustness Checks

We now comment on the robustness checks performed in table 5. To mitigate endogeneity concerns discussed earlier, row 4 omits the top five STEM-dependent cities and row 7 removes Indian workers. The estimated effects of STEM on native wages remain stable and even increase in some cases, albeit at the cost of larger standard errors. On one hand, this suggests that the fixed effects, instrumental variable strategy, and Bartik controls in the baseline model largely address endogeneity bias. On the other hand, the increase in standard errors indicates that the omitted cities, when included in regressions, afford precision in the estimates due to larger data variation.

Row 5 adds a control for imputed low-skilled immigrants. As above, this also results in minimal changes in the coefficient estimates when compared to row 1. The estimated STEM effect on college-educated wages is somewhat smaller (down to 7.00 from 8.03), and the coefficient for non-college-educated wages is somewhat larger (up to 4.95 from 3.78). This could indicate that the inflow of less educated immigrants, as predicted by the 1980 MSA distribution, was slightly correlated with foreign STEM and that less educated labor inflows complemented college-educated natives but substituted for non-college-educated ones. Explicitly controlling for such imputed inflows helps to isolate the effect of STEM and identifies more balanced productivity effects for college- and non-college-educated natives.

Similarly, a large initial share of foreign STEM in a city might proxy for high initial education levels. If such cities also experienced wage and employment growth during periods of sizable foreign STEM inflows, it would generate spurious regression results. Row 9 includes a shift share predictor of college-educated native growth to help address this issue. The estimated STEM impact on wages paid to college-educated natives remains quantitatively similar to baseline estimates and is still statistically significant.

Row 6 omits small cities to examine measurement error issues. The point estimates are similar to those in row 5, but the standard errors decrease. Hence, measurement error does not seem to bias the coefficients, but the focus on large MSAs reduces measurement error and improves precision.

Finally, it is worth commenting on the difference between the OLS estimates in row 10 and the corresponding 2SLS results in row 5. Interestingly, while the estimated employment effects have an upward bias in OLS relative to 2SLS, the wage effects have a downward bias. This may be due to the correlation between unobserved shocks and the inflow of foreign STEM. It is likely that foreign STEM inflows are positively correlated with employment growth and a city's openness to new workers. Hence, the cities endogenously attracting foreign STEM workers could be those with fast inflows of workers in general, which could moderate wage growth. Thus, the correlation between STEM growth and omitted employment determinants could be positive, and the correlation between openness and wage growth could be negative, thereby resulting in the observed biases.

Before extending the findings, we provide a sense of the magnitude of the estimated effects. Foreign STEM growth, measured as a percentage of total initial employment in aggregate, was only about 0.53% between 1990 and 2010. Applying the 7.00 2SLS estimates of row 5 to the national growth in foreign STEM implies that the foreign-driven net growth in STEM increased real wages of college-educated natives by around 3.71 percentage points ($= 7.00 \times 0.53$) during this period. For reference, census data suggest that the cumulative growth of college-educated wages in this period equaled about 13 percentage points. Thus, almost one-third of that growth can be attributed to the increased presence of foreign STEM workers. We return to these implications in Section VI when we analyze the implied productivity and skill-bias effects of STEM.

C. Extensions

As shown in the first-stage results in columns 5 and 6 of table 4, our H-1B-driven increase in the STEM instrument raises overall STEM employment, not just foreign STEM. Table 6 generalizes the main second-stage results by replacing the foreign STEM growth explanatory variable with total STEM growth. The estimates confirm that STEM workers generate wage gains for college-educated and non-college-educated natives. More specifically, using the estimates in row 1 of table 6, a 1 percentage point increase in STEM as a share of employment caused a 4 percentage point

STEM Workers, H-1B Visas, Productivity in US Cities   S247

Table 6
The Effects of Total STEM on Native Wages and Employment

Explanatory Variable: Growth Rate of Total STEM	Weekly Wage, Native STEM (1)	Weekly Wage, Native College-Educated (2)	Weekly Wage, Native Non-College-Educated (3)	Employment, Native College-Educated (4)	Employment, Native Non-College-Educated (5)
1. 2SLS; O*NET	4.50	3.97***	2.44**	1.86	−1.67
4% definition	(2.94)	(1.42)	(1.02)	(2.31)	(2.34)
2. 2SLS; major-based	4.90	5.68**	2.40**	1.15	−2.92
4% definition	(3.41)	(2.42)	(1.00)	(2.10)	(2.82)
3. 2SLS; O*NET,	4.55	2.64*	1.67**	1.46	−1.23
8% definition	(3.01)	(1.43)	(.76)	(1.25)	(1.79)
4. Same as row 1 but	4.50	4.03**	1.97*	3.23	−.28
omitting top 5 STEM cities	(3.39)	(1.74)	(1.12)	(2.38)	(2.33)
5. OLS; O*NET	.37	.73	.75*	2.72***	4.60***
4% definition	(1.08)	(.54)	(.40)	(.77)	(.79)

NOTE.—Each cell shows the estimate of the coefficient on the growth in total STEM (relative to employment) when the dependent variable is the one described at the top of the column and the instrument is the H-1B driven STEM growth. Each regression includes period effects, metropolitan area effects, the Bartik for employment and wage of the relevant group, and the imputed growth of non-college-educated immigrants. Standard errors (in parentheses) are clustered at the metro area level. Units of observations are 219 metro areas over three periods: 1990–2000, 2000–2005, and 2005–10.
* Significant at the 10% level.
** Significant at the 5% level.
*** Significant at the 1% level.

increase in college-educated native wage growth and about a 2.4 percentage point wage growth for non-college-educated natives. There is no evidence that either group experiences an employment effect.

These results are robust to using the major-based definition of STEM (row 2), using the broad (8%) definition of STEM (row 3), and omitting top STEM cities (row 4). Also, the OLS estimates continue to exhibit a positive bias (relative to the 2SLS results) for employment effects and a negative one for wage effects. Overall, our estimates confirm that STEM workers raise the demand for college-educated and non-college-educated natives, with a smaller effect for the latter group.

A lot of heterogeneity exists among non-college-educated workers. Table 7 explores whether the wage and employment effects of foreign STEM workers are different for natives without a high school diploma (high school dropouts) and those with a high school diploma (high school graduates). The table presents foreign STEM effects for wages (cols. 1 and 2) and employment (cols. 3 and 4). Rows 1–4 present several specifications of the 2SLS regression mirroring those in the corresponding rows of tables 5 and 6. Row 5 reports the coefficients when using total STEM as the explanatory variable.

Table 7
The Effect of Foreign STEM on Non-College-Educated Natives

Explanatory Variable: Growth Rate of Total STEM	Weekly Wage, Native High School Graduates (1)	Weekly Wage, Native High School Dropouts (2)	Employment, Native High School Graduates (3)	Employment, Native High School Dropouts (4)
1. 2SLS; O*NET	5.54**	3.30	3.36	−.03
4% definition	(2.33)	(4.26)	(3.72)	(.55)
2. 2SLS; major-based	4.87**	5.97	5.12	−.50
4% definition	(2.10)	(4.67)	(4.08)	(.66)
3. 2SLS; O*NET	4.10**	2.45	2.48	−.02
8% definition	(1.70)	(3.01)	(2.88)	(.40)
4. Same as row 1	7.05*	6.28	1.38	.50
but dropping	(4.29)	(7.58)	(6.65)	(.96)
top 5 STEM cities				
5. Explanatory variable:	2.73**	1.63	1.65	−.02
total STEM,	(1.15)	(1.99)	(2.12)	(.27)
O*NET 4%				

NOTE.—Each cell in rows 1–4 shows the estimate of the coefficient on the growth in foreign STEM (relative to employment) when the dependent variable is the one described at the top of the column. Row 5 shows the estimate of the coefficient on the growth in total STEM (relative to employment) as the explanatory variable, still instrumented with H-1B imputed growth of foreign STEM. Each regression includes period effects, metropolitan area effects, the Bartik for employment and wage of the relevant group, and the imputed growth of non-college-educated immigrants. Standard errors (in parentheses) are clustered at the metro area level. Units of observations are 219 metro areas over three periods: 1990–2000, 2000–2005, and 2005–10.
* Significant at the 10% level.
** Significant at the 5% level.
*** Significant at the 1% level.

By separating high school graduates from high school dropouts, we can check whether these two groups exhibit different complementarities with foreign STEM labor. On the one hand, STEM-generated innovation could be skill biased, complementing educational attainment (see Acemoglu 1998, 2002). If so, then foreign STEM would generate the largest positive effects for college-educated workers, followed by high school graduates and, finally, by high school dropouts. On the other hand, it could be polarizing, substituting for intermediate skills but complementing low- and high-end skills (see Autor et al. 2006; Autor 2010). If so, then foreign STEM would generate the largest positive effects at the high and low ends of the educational spectrum at the expense of intermediate-level levels of schooling.

Table 7 shows that STEM effects are significant only for high school graduates, while point estimates for dropouts are smaller but insignificant. Neither group had significant employment effects. The basic specification in row 1 shows that each percentage point increase in foreign STEM employment raised native high school graduate wage growth by 5.54 percentage points. This can be interpreted as evidence that STEM-driven technological progress has been skill (or schooling) biased rather than polarizing.

The difference between the effects on high school graduates and dropouts is not usually significant, however, because of the lack of precision in estimating the effects for dropouts.

VI. Simulated Productivity and Skill Bias Effects

We close our analysis by estimating the long-run effect of STEM on total factor productivity (TFP) and skill-biased productivity (SBP). More specifically, we assume a basic structural model of production and substitute parameter values from our analysis, observed data, and other sources, and then we simulate the TFP and SBP effects that can be explained by growth in foreign STEM workers. The advantage of this approach is that we have an intuitive and standard definition of TFP and SBP based on a city-specific production function. The limitation is its dependence on the assumed nature of productive interactions between different types of labor inherent to the specific production structure.

A full model and derivation are available in the online appendix. Here, we provide just a simple production function and the intuition of the exercise. Suppose that a city (c) produces a homogeneous, tradable, numeraire product (Q_{ct}) in year t. The economy employs three types of labor: non-college-educated (L_{ct}); college-educated, non-STEM (H_{ct}); and STEM workers (ST_c). Production occurs according to the long-run production function in (7):

$$Q_{ct} = (A(ST_{ct})\{\beta(ST_{ct})K_{ct}^{(\sigma_H-1)/\sigma_H} + [1 - \beta(ST_{ct})]L_{ct}^{(\sigma_H-1)/\sigma_H}\})^{\sigma_H/(\sigma_H-1)}. \quad (7)$$

Input K is a composite factor combining college-educated and STEM workers such that

$$K_{ct} = [ST_{ct}^{(\sigma_S-1)/\sigma_S} + H_{ct}^{(\sigma_S-1)/\sigma_S}]^{\sigma_S/(\sigma_S-1)}. \quad (8)$$

The parameter $\sigma_H > 1$ captures the elasticity of substitution between non-college- and college-educated labor. Similarly, $\sigma_S > 1$ is the elasticity of substitution between college-educated and STEM workers.

A long literature has recognized STEM workers as the key inputs in developing and adopting new technologies. Equation (7) captures this by allowing the level of TFP, $A(ST_{ct})^{\sigma_H/(\sigma_H-1)} > 0$, to be an increasing function of the number of STEM workers in a city. It also allows for STEM workers to potentially raise SBP, $\beta(ST_{ct}) \in [0, 1]$. Note that our model assumes that STEM workers are uniquely capable of generating ideas, innovation, and externalities that benefit productivity even if STEM and college-educated workers are close substitutes in production itself (i.e., if $\sigma_S \approx \infty$).

We assume that labor is paid its marginal product and then calculate the total logarithmic (percentage) change in wages for each group in response to a change in the supply of STEM workers. After normalizing the resulting demand conditions by the exogenous change of STEM workers expressed as a percentage of total employment, we derive three linear conditions relating the elasticity of each group's wage and employment to STEM (i.e., the $b_{y,x}$ coefficients estimated from eq. [1]). Remaining parameters in the demand functions (including σ_H, σ_s, and wage and employment shares) come from prior studies, our analysis, or census data. By combining them, we can estimate our values of interest: $\phi_A = (\Delta A/A)/(\Delta ST/E)$, the elasticity of TFP to changes in STEM (relative to initial employment), and $\phi_\beta = (\Delta \beta/\beta)/(\Delta ST/E)$, the analogous elasticity of SBP.[17]

    Table 8 displays the simulated TFP (col. 1) and SBP (col. 2) changes from 1990 to 2010. We set $\sigma_S = \infty$ since our regression estimates of $1/\sigma_S$ are never significantly different from zero and the elasticity of college-educated wages and STEM wages to STEM supply are always very close to each other (implying high substitutability). Ciccone and Peri's (2005) review of σ_H estimates suggests a value between 1.5 and 2.5. We assume a σ_H value of 2 in our basic simulation and use values of 1.75 and 2.25 in robustness checks. US census data on wages and employment imply a β value equal to 0.57, a share of STEM workers equal to 0.05 in total employment and 0.09 in the total wage bill, and a college-educated share of the wage bill equal to 0.46. Fernald (2009) measures annual TFP growth equal to 0.89%. Our census calculations measure annual SBP growth equal to 1.75%. Foreign STEM increased by 0.04% of total employment each year.

    Values for the elasticity of outcome y for group X to STEM workers come from our regression estimates. The first row of table 8 reports the simulated effects when we use coefficients from the basic specification in table 5, row 1. Row 2 uses the estimates from table 5, row 6, in which we control for imputed unskilled immigrants and reduce the attenuation bias by including only large cities in the regression. We label this row conservative estimates because the underlying regression leads to somewhat smaller estimates of the STEM effect on native wages. Row 3 uses the estimates from table 6, row 1, that adopt total STEM as the explanatory variable. These tend to be 40%–50% smaller than those obtained with foreign STEM.[18] Rows 4 and 5 are the same as row 1 but illustrate the robustness of the simulations to changes in values of the parameter σ_H.

    Our simulations imply that foreign STEM growth explained only a modest 5%–8% of SBP growth from 1990 to 2010. In contrast, foreign STEM growth explained between one-third and one-half of the average TFP

---

[17] Note that we can calculate these effects without specifying the labor supply side of the model as long as we have the table 5 and table 6 equilibrium employment elasticity estimates for each factor.

[18] We also use the elasticity of college-educated wages (3.96) for STEM since the model implies that the elasticity of college-educated wages to foreign STEM cannot be smaller than that of native STEM wages.

Table 8
Simulated Foreign STEM Effects on Yearly Average TFP Growth and SBP Change

	Simulated Foreign STEM Effect on TFP Growth (%) (1)	Simulated Foreign STEM Effect on Skill-Biased Growth (%) (2)	Average US TFP Growth 1990–2010 (%) (3)	Average Change in Skill-Biased Productivity 1990–2010 (%) (4)	TFP Growth Explained by Foreign STEM (Col. 3/Col. 1) (5)	Skill-Biased Growth Explained by Foreign STEM (Col. 4/Col. 2) (6)
1. Basic estimates	.47	.13	.89	1.75	.53	.07
2. Conservative estimates	.41	.08	.89	1.75	.47	.05
3. Based on total STEM	.27	.04	.89	1.75	.30	.04
4. $\sigma_H = 1.75$	.54	.13	.89	1.75	.61	.08
5. $\sigma_H = 2.25$	.43	.12	.89	1.75	.48	.7

NOTE.—The table uses the formulas in the online appendix to calculate the implied elasticity ϕ_A and ϕ_B. We then use the growth of US foreign STEM workers as a share of employment to calculate the implied effects on TFP. The average TFP growth 1990–2010 is taken from Fernald (2009) and the average skill-biased growth is calculated using the average US values for the wages and employment (in hours) of college-educated and non-college-educated workers from the 1990 and 2010 censuses. Unless otherwise noted, the elasticity of substitution between college- and non-college-educated workers is $\sigma_H = 2$. The STEM share of employment is 0.05, the STEM share of wages is 0.09, and the college-educated share of wages is 0.46. These values are calculated from the 2000 US census.

growth during the period. While this result might appear to be very high, it is more plausible when assessed in context with two additional figures. First, foreign labor accounted for about-two thirds of the net growth in STEM workers in our data set. Second, STEM workers are the primary source of sustained economic growth. Jones (2002), for example, argued that 50% of long-run US productivity growth in recent decades is attributable to growth in scientists and engineers as a share of employment. The 33% TFP growth implied by combining Jones's figure with our calculation of the foreign contribution to STEM growth aligns with the simulated results presented in table 8.

In income terms, the average annual TFP effect in table 8, column 1, translates to about 0.47 percentage points per year, implying that native income per capita in 2010 was 9.8% larger than it would have been without the growth contributions from foreign STEM. This would be impossible to justify on the basis of the foreign-born increase in skilled labor supply alone; but when considered as a source of technological innovation, foreign STEM workers may credibly generate large productivity and wage increases. Nonetheless, we concede that our simulated results are based on strong assumptions. In particular, we apply parameters that were estimated across cities to simulate national foreign STEM effects. This will overstate productivity effects if the wage coefficients from the underlying regressions are related to the selection of natives. On the other hand, since our regressions capture only within-city productivity effects and ignore spillovers to other cities, we could also be underestimating national productivity gains.

VII. Conclusions

This article uses the inflow of foreign science, technology, engineering, and mathematics (STEM) workers, made possible by the H-1B visa program, to estimate the impact of STEM workers on the productivity of college- and non-college-educated American workers between 1990 and 2010. The uneven distribution of foreign STEM workers across cities in 1980—a decade before the introduction of the H-1B visa—and the high correlation between the preexisting presence of foreign-born workers and subsequent immigration flows allow us to use the variation in foreign STEM as a supply-driven increase in STEM workers across metropolitan areas.

We find that a 1 percentage point increase in the foreign STEM share of a city's total employment increased the wage growth of native college-educated labor by about 7–8 percentage points and the wage growth of non-college-educated natives by 3–4 percentage points. We find insignificant effects on the employment of those two groups. These results indicate that STEM workers spur economic growth by increasing productivity, especially that of college-educated workers.

The Economics of International Migration 305

STEM Workers, H-1B Visas, Productivity in US Cities S253

References

Acemoglu, Daron. 1998. Why do new technologies complement skills? Directed technical change and wage inequality. *Quarterly Journal of Economics* 113, no. 4:1055–89.

———. 2002. Technical change, inequality and the labor market. *Journal of Economic Literature* 40, no. 1:7–72.

Altonji, Joseph G., and David Card. 1991. The effects of immigration on the labor market outcomes of less-skilled natives. In *Immigration, trade, and the labor market*, ed. John M. Abowd and Richard B. Freeman. Chicago: University of Chicago Press.

Autor, David H. 2010. The polarization of job opportunities in the U.S. labor market: Implications for employment and earnings. Hamilton Project, Washington, DC, April.

Autor, David H., Lawrence F. Katz, and Melissa S. Kearney. 2006. The polarization of the U.S. labor market. *American Economic Review* 96, no. 2:189–94.

Aydemir, Abdurrahman, and George J. Borjas. 2011. Attenuation bias in measuring the wage impact of immigration. *Journal of Labor Economics* 29, no. 1:69–113.

Bartik, Timothy J. 1991. *Who benefits from state and local economic development policies?* Kalamazoo, MI: W. E. Upjohn Institute for Employment Research.

Card, David. 2001. Immigrant inflows, native outflows, and the local labor market impacts of higher immigration. *Journal of Labor Economics* 19, no. 1:22–64.

Ciccone, Antonio, and Giovanni Peri. 2005. Long-run substitutability between more and less educated workers: Evidence from U.S. states 1950–1990. *Review of Economics and Statistics* 87, no. 4:652–63.

Depew, Briggs, Peter Norlander, and Todd A. Sorensen. 2013. Flight of the H-1B: Inter-firm mobility and return migration patterns for skilled guest workers. IZA Discussion Paper no. 7456, Institute for the Study of Labor, Bonn.

Ellison, Glenn, and Edward L. Glaeser. 1999. The geographic concentration of industry: Does natural advantage explain agglomeration? *American Economic Review* 89, no. 2:311–16.

Fernald, John. 2009. A quarterly, utilization-adjusted series on total factor productivity. Unpublished manuscript, Federal Reserve Bank of San Francisco.

Glaeser, Edward L. 2011. *The triumph of the city: How our greatest invention makes us richer, smarter, greener, healthier, and happier.* New York: Penguin.

Griliches, Zvi. 1992. The search for R&D spillovers. *Scandinavian Journal of Economics* 94:S29–S47.

306 *Immigrants and Productivity*

S254 Peri et al.

Iranzo, Susana, and Giovanni Peri. 2009. Schooling externalities, technology, and productivity: Theory and evidence from U.S. states. *Review of Economics and Statistics* 91, no. 2:420–31.

Jaffe, Adam B., Manuel Trajtenberg, and Rebecca Henderson. 1993. Geographic localization of knowledge spillovers as evidenced by patent citations. *Quarterly Journal of Economics* 108, no. 3:577–98.

Jones, Charles I. 1995. Time series tests of endogenous growth models. *Quarterly Journal of Economics* 110, no. 2:495–525.

———. 2002. Sources of U.S. economic growth in a world of ideas. *American Economic Review* 92, no. 1:220–39.

Kato, Takao, and Chad Sparber. 2013. Quotas and quality: The effect of H-1B visa restrictions on the pool of prospective undergraduate students from abroad. *Review of Economics and Statistics* 95, no. 1:109–26.

Katz, Lawrence F., and Kevin M. Murphy. 1992. Changes in relative wages, 1963–1987: Supply and demand factors. *Quarterly Journal of Economics* 107, no. 1:35–78.

Kerr, William, and William F. Lincoln. 2010. The supply side of innovation: H-1B visa reforms and U.S. ethnic invention. *Journal of Labor Economics* 28, no. 3:473–508.

Lowell, Lindsay. 2000. H-1B temporary workers: Estimating the population. Working Paper no. 12, Center for Comparative Immigration Studies, University of California, San Diego.

Moretti, Enrico. 2004a. Estimating the social return to higher education: Evidence from longitudinal and repeated cross-sectional data. *Journal of Econometrics* 121, no. 1:175–212.

———. 2004b. Workers' education, spillovers and productivity: Evidence from plant-level production functions. *American Economic Review* 94, no. 3:656–90.

———. 2012. *The new geography of jobs*. New York: Houghton Mifflin Harcourt.

Peri, Giovanni, Kevin Shih, and Chad Sparber. 2014. Foreign STEM workers and native wages and employment in US cities. Working Paper no. 20093, National Bureau of Economic Research, Cambridge, MA.

Ruggles, Steven J., Trent Alexander, Katie Genadek, Ronald Goeken, Matthew B. Schroeder, and Matthew Sobek. 2010. Integrated Public Use Microdata Series: Version 5.0 [machine-readable database]. Minneapolis: University of Minnesota.

Saxenian, Anna Lee. 2002. Silicon Valley's new immigrant high growth entrepreneurs. *Economic Development Quarterly* 16, no. 1:20–31.

US Citizenship and Immigration Services. Various years. *Characteristics of specialty occupation workers (H-1B) annual reports*. http://www.uscis.gov/tools/reports-studies/reports-and-studies.

STEM Workers, H-1B Visas, Productivity in US Cities   S255

US Department of Labor. National O*NET Consortium. 2012. O*NET 17.0 database. http://www.onetcenter.org/db_releases.html. Accessed July 8, 2013.
US Department of State. 2012. Nonimmigrant visa issuances by visa class and by nationality: FY1997–2011 NIV detail table. http://travel.state.gov/content/visas/english/law-and-policy/statistics/non-immigrant-visas.html. Accessed August 23, 2012.

Openness and income: The roles of trade and migration [☆]

Francesc Ortega [a], Giovanni Peri [b,c,*]

[a] Economics Department, Queens College, City University of New York, Powdermaker Hall, 65-30 Kissena Blvd, Flushing, New York 11367, United States
[b] University of California, Davis, One Shields Avenue, Davis, CA 95616, United States
[c] NBER, United States

ARTICLE INFO

Article history:
Received 16 September 2012
Received in revised form 14 November 2013
Accepted 23 November 2013
Available online 6 December 2013

JEL classification:
F22
J61
O4

Keywords:
International migration
Trade
Income per person
Geography
Institutions
Diversity

ABSTRACT

This paper explores the relationship between openness to trade, immigration, and income per person across countries. To address endogeneity concerns we extend the instrumental-variables strategy introduced by Frankel and Romer (1999). We build predictors of openness to immigration and to trade for each country by using information on bilateral geographical and cultural distance (while controlling for country size). Since geography may affect income through other channels, we also control for climate, disease environment, natural resources, and colonial origins. Most importantly, we also account for the roles of institutions and early development. Our instrumental-variables estimates provide evidence of a robust, positive effect of openness to immigration on long-run income per capita. In contrast, we are unable to establish an effect of trade openness on income. We also show that the effect of migration operates through an increase in total factor productivity, which appears to reflect increased diversity in productive skills and, to some extent, a higher rate of innovation.

© 2014 International Monetary Fund. Published by Elsevier B.V. All rights reserved.

1. Introduction

Interactions with other countries can be a powerful engine of economic development and technological change, especially for small countries (Alesina et al., 2000, 2005; Frankel and Romer, 1999). For several decades economists have focused on a country's openness to trade, measured by policies (as in Sachs and Warner, 1995; Lucas, 2009), or by trade flows as a share of GDP (as in Frankel and Romer, 1999; Rodrik, 2000; Alcalá and Ciccone, 2004) to quantify the importance of cross-country interactions on income. They realized early on, however, that openness to trade could be a consequence, as much as a cause, of high income per person across countries. To address this endogeneity, Frankel and Romer (1999) (FR from now on) proposed using cross-country variation in trade flows arising from bilateral geography in order to identify the causal effects of trade openness on income per capita. Subsequent works by Rodriguez and Rodrik (2001) and others

have pointed out that the exclusion restriction behind this identification approach is likely to be violated unless one controls for other channels through which geography is likely to affect income per capita, such as natural endowments, climate, disease environment, colonization history, and so on. Rodrik et al. (2004) further argued that once one controls for institutional quality, neither geography nor trade matter much in determining a country's income per person.

There is yet another potential problem with the approach proposed by FR. Trade openness is correlated with openness to migration.[1] Furthermore bilateral migration flows are well explained by a gravity relationship, just like trade flows (Mayda, 2007; Clark et al., 2007; Grogger and Hanson, 2011). Hence, the original specification used by FR may also suffer from a potential omitted-variables problem. Geographical proximity and accessibility also affect other forms of bilateral interactions between countries such as flows of ideas, technology and investments. However, unless these interactions are perfectly disembodied (and hence hard to measure), such flows would be

[☆] The authors thank two anonymous referees for very helpful comments. Antonio Ciccone, John Devereux, Jesus Fernandez-Huertas, Andrei Levchenko, Joan Llull, Petra Moeser, Enrico Moretti, Jonathan Portes, Kevin Shih, Ryuichi Tanaka and Nico Voigtlaender provided helpful discussions. We also benefitted from comments from seminar participants at GRIPS (Tokyo), Collegio Carlo Alberto, UC Berkeley, University of Colorado, UC Santa Cruz, Harvard University, Queens College CUNY, and All UC History Conference.
* Corresponding author at: University of California, Davis, One Shields Avenue, Davis, CA 95616, United States.
E-mail addresses: fortega@qc.cuny.edu (F. Ortega), gperi@ucdavis.edu (G. Peri).

[1] Fig. 1 reports the partial correlation between trade as a share of GDP and the foreign-born share across the 146 countries included in the Frankel and Romer (1999) sample. Each variable is a residual, after we control for country size (measured by the logarithms of population and area) to purge its effect on openness to trade and migration. The Figure illustrates a clear positive and significant (but far from perfect) correlation between openness to trade and to migration.

232   F. Ortega, G. Peri / Journal of International Economics 92 (2014) 231–251

Note: The data are relative to 147 countries in year 2000. We plot the residuals after adjusting by log population and log area. The sources and construction of the trade as share of GDP and of the foreign-born share are described in the text.

Fig. 1. Migration share and trade share. Note: The data are relative to 147 countries in year 2000. We plot the residuals after adjusting by log population and log area. The sources and construction of the trade as share of GDP and of the foreign-born share are described in the text.

reflected in the mobility of goods (including capital goods) and of people. Thus we focus our analysis on these two vehicles of globalization.

This paper extends the approach proposed by FR using a new global immigration dataset and estimates the effects of economic openness, jointly considering migration and trade, on income per person. The first step in the analysis is to produce gravity-based predictors for both trade and migration. Our predictors are based on bilateral regressions that separately fit migration and trade flows on the basis of proxies for bilateral geographical and cultural distance. By examining jointly the roles played by these two dimensions of globalization, our work extends the recent analysis of the effect of trade and it connects with the research by economic historians on the First Globalization era.[2]

We also recognize that a country's geographic location may have a direct effect on income per capita (besides its effect through the channels of trade and migration), which threatens our instrumental-variables strategy. While it is infeasible to perfectly control for all possible channels in a cross-sectional setting, we consider the most plausible suspects and directly control for them in our econometric specifications. Namely, we explicitly account for the roles of climate, natural resources, disease environment, colonial origin, early development and, perhaps most importantly, the quality of institutions. In a series of influential papers, Hall and Jones (1999), Acemoglu et al. (2001), Rodrik et al. (2004) and many others, have argued that institutions are the main factor accounting for cross-country disparities in income per capita.

Our analysis produces the following main findings. First, our gravity-based predictors appear to be highly relevant when appropriate controls for the direct effect of geography are included in the specification. Even though the predictor for the share of immigrants performs better than the predictor for the trade share, we are able to identify fairly well the roles of both trade and migration on income per capita. Second, our two-stage least-squares estimates imply that the share of immigrants in the population has a significant and robust estimated effect on long-run income per capita, although there is substantial uncertainty around its exact magnitude. On the basis of our point estimates, we find a qualitatively large effect: a 10 percentage-point difference in the share

of foreign born in the population, which is close to the standard deviation in our sample, is associated with differences in income per person by a factor close to 2. If we attach a causal interpretation to this coefficient it would imply that Japan, with a foreign-born share below 1% in year 2000, adopted a degree of openness to immigration equal to that of the US (about 11% of foreign born in 2000) its long-run income per capita would double. To the contrary, we do not find a robust effect of trade openness once we control for other effects of migration. We also show that our finding of the positive effect of migration is clearly distinct from the effects of early development and institutional quality, which we also document.

Then we empirically investigate the mechanism behind our main finding. First, we show that the estimated effect of migration on income operates mainly by increasing total factor productivity (TFP). Next, we show that underlying this finding there is a positive diversity effect. Namely, we show that the degree of diversity by country of origin within the immigrant population has an additional positive effect on income per person. Our interpretation is that diverse immigration expands the set of differentiated skills in the labor force. Finally, we also provide some suggestive evidence indicating that immigration appears to increase innovation activity, as measured by patents. This may also account for a part of the TFP effect that we uncovered. It may also imply that immigrants bring new ideas to a country, along with a wider set of skills.

While our results are consistent with immigration playing an important role in increasing productivity, two important caveats are in order. First, our cross-sectional approach is unable to control for persistent country-specific unobserved characteristics that may affect income. Short of longitudinal data, we cannot fully rule out the possibility of omitted-variable bias.[3] Second, disembodied flows of knowledge may affect productivity and are also influenced by geography may bias our estimates of the effect of migration (and trade). While we interpret our instrumental-variables estimates throughout the paper as uncovering causal effects, these two caveats should always be kept in mind.

There is a vast theoretical literature linking several aspects of openness (or globalization) to income levels and growth.[4] Some authors emphasize the role of openness to trade in promoting innovation, technological diffusion and catch-up (Grossman and Helpman, 1991 Rivera-Batiz and Romer, 1994; Eaton and Kortum, 1996; Lucas, 2009 to name a few). Others have focused on the effect of market size via trade on innovation and growth. Acemoglu (2003) has argued that the size of the market can affect the speed (as well as the direction) of technological adoption. Matsuyama (1992) and Galor and Mountford (2008) have argued that market size may encourage specialization and learning by doing. Finally, Weil (2005) has focused on the efficiency gains experienced by firms subject to international competition.

More closely related to this paper are empirical studies that estimate the effects of openness to trade on income per capita. We have already discussed the important contribution by FR, extended by Alcalá and Ciccone (2004), Noguer and Siscart (2005), and others, and the critiques by Rodrik (2000), Rodriguez and Rodrik (2001), and Rodrik et al. (2004).[5] As summarized earlier, the literature is inconclusive. Several authors have reported positive and significant effects of trade openness on income while others have raised concerns about the robustness of those findings. Two important recent contributions to this debate provide evidence based on longitudinal data. Feyrer (2009a) provides within-country estimates of the effect of trade on income that exploit the rising importance of international trade carried by air, particularly for country pairs that are connected by relatively short air routes

---

[2] Economic historians have argued that migration was an important vehicle for economic convergence in terms of factor prices and income levels between the 1870s and World War I, the so-called First Globalization era (Taylor and Williamson, 1997; Taylor, 1997a, 1997b). The sustained increase in international migration flows since the early 1990s has rekindled the interest in the role of migration in accounting for cross-country differences on income per capita. Recently, Putterman and Weil (2010) have argued that migration played an important role in the early economic development of many countries and that its effects have been extremely persistent.

[3] Feyrer (2009a, 2009b) shows that longitudinal data is very important to identify the effects of trade on income. These papers are reviewed below.

[4] For excellent textbook treatments of openness and economic growth, see Acemoglu (2009) chapters 18 and 19, on the roles of knowledge diffusion and trade; Barro and Sala i Martin (2004) chapter 8, discuss technology diffusion and endogenous growth. Weil (2005), chapter 11, describes the relationship between economic growth and openness

[5] An influential early contribution was Sachs and Warner (1995) who analyzed the effect of trade policies (over the period 1965–1990) on economic growth.

F. Ortega, G. Peri / Journal of International Economics 92 (2014) 231–251   233

relative to the corresponding sea routes. Feyrer (2009b) exploits the closing of the Suez canal as a natural experiment to try to identify the causal effects of distance on trade, and trade on income. Both papers find evidence of a positive causal effect, with some disagreement regarding the exact magnitude. On the basis of these findings Feyrer argues that longitudinal variation is crucial for identifying the effect of trade. We largely agree with this view. Our results suggest a limited ability of cross-sectional data to identify the effect of trade on income while controlling for the direct effect of geography. Nevertheless, our findings also suggest that the cross-sectional approach is much more informative regarding the effect of migration on income.

This paper is also related to several studies that analyze the determinants of bilateral migration flows using a gravity equation (such as Adsera and Pytlikova, 2012; Beine et al., 2011; Bertoli and Fernandez-Huertas, 2013; Clark et al., 2007; Grogger and Hanson, 2011; Llull, 2011; Mayda, 2007, 2010; Pedersen et al., 2006, to name a few). Much more scant is the literature that employs cross-country variation to attempt to identify the causal effects of migration on income per person.[6] The closest paper to ours is Andersen and Dalgaard (2011). The main goals of this paper are similar to ours. However, these authors measure openness to migration on the basis of data on short-run cross-border movements of people (travel). As most travel is driven by tourism and business, it is strongly correlated with trade flows.[7] Still, they are able to find a positive effect of travel on income per person while controlling for trade openness. Our estimates for openness to migration and the role of institutions are robust to more demanding empirical specifications than those used in Andersen and Dalgaard (2011). Our interpretation is that the foreign-born share in a country's population may better capture the channels through which immigration affects long-run income.

Our paper is also related to the recent work of diversity on economic development. Ashraf and Galor (forthcoming) argue that there is a hump-shaped effect of genetic diversity on country-level productivity. High diversity leads to a wider spectrum of genetic traits, which makes a society more adaptable to a changing technological environment. On the other hand, high genetic diversity may undermine trust. They provide empirical evidence for this non-monotonic relationship and argue that the current levels of diversity in the US are close to the optimum implied by their estimates. Recently, Alesina et al. (2013) have analyzed the impact of birthplace diversity on economic development. These authors build diversity indicators for a large set of countries for years 1990 and 2000, disaggregated by education and nativity. Using these data they estimate a positive effect of birthplace diversity on income per capita, which appears to be larger for college-educated migrants and high-income receiving countries.

Finally, our work is also related to the strand of literature studying the role of institutions and early development on economic growth. According to Hall and Jones (1999) and Acemoglu et al. (2001, 2002), the main reason why geography appears to be a crucial determinant of cross-country differences in income per capita is that geography decisively shaped a country's history of colonization, cementing the foundations for the existing institutional arrangements. In particular, good early institutions may have allowed for policies aimed at sustaining free markets, democracy, checks and balances and well-functioning legal and judicial systems. Current cross-country income differences are also closely related to differences in development several centuries earlier (Diamond, 1997; Comin et al., 2010). Putterman and Weil (2010) show that existing measures of a country's early development substantially increase their explanatory power over current income

differences when we take into account the countries of origin of the *ancestors* of the current population. Thus they argue that a country's immigration history is a crucial determinant of its current level of development. We will discuss in Section 6 the role of a country's immigration history relative to the role of its current immigrant population.

The rest of the paper is organized as follows. In Section 2 we present our empirical strategy. Section 3 presents the data and descriptive statistics. In Section 4 we reproduce the analysis of the effect of trade openness on income per person. Section 5 focuses on the effect of openness to migration on income. Section 6 analyzes the roles of institutions and ancestors. Section 7 explores the role of diversity as a channel that can account for our empirical results. Section 8 concludes. The Appendix A contains some additional material.

2. Empirical approach

2.1. Specification

Our empirical specification can be seen as a natural extension of the specification proposed by FR. We postulate that the log of income per capita in country c (y_c) is given by:

$$lny_c = \beta_0 + \beta_T TSH_c + \beta_M MSH_c + \beta_S lnS_c + \beta_C \textbf{Controls}_c + u_c, \qquad (1)$$

where TSH_c represents total trade (import plus export) as a share of GDP, MSH_c is the migration share in the population, S_c controls for country size, X_c collects all other regressors, and u_c accounts for unobserved determinants of log income per capita. To better explain the rationale behind this empirical model we present (in the Appendix A) a simple multi-country model that features trade and migration flows both across country borders and across regions within the same country. The presence of within-country flows necessitates controlling for country size. The model is based on Alesina et al. (2000) and has two main features. In the style of Armington (1969), each region is endowed with a differentiated good and a differentiated type of labor. Secondly, international trade and migration costs are higher than the analogous costs across regions within the same country (normalized to zero). Moreover, these costs are not perfectly observable. The model can be used to derive the following equilibrium relationship between (the log of) income per worker and the theoretical measures of international trade and migration openness, θ_c^T and θ_c^M, which are, respectively, inverse measures of trade and migration costs:

$$lny_c = \beta_0 + \beta_1 \theta_c^T + \beta_2 \theta_c^M + \beta_3 lnS_c + \beta_4 \textbf{X}_c + \varepsilon_c. \qquad (2)$$

Coefficients β_1 and β_2 represent the long-run semi-elasticity of income per person to trade and to migration openness, respectively. S_c is a measure of country size. X_c is a vector that includes other determinants of long-run output per person, such as the quality of institutions, natural resources, climate, and so on. The zero-mean term ε_c allows for idiosyncratic deviations of $ln y_c$ from its steady state and is uncorrelated with the other explanatory variables X_c. Eq. (2) cannot be directly estimated because we do not observe the latent openness of trade and migration (θ_c^T and θ_c^M), which depend on physical, cultural and policy factors. We do observe, however, the volume of trade and migration flows. Specifically, we have data on the migration shares, defined as the share of immigrants (foreign-born) in the total population, MSH_c, and the international trade flows (export plus imports) as a share of the country's GDP, TSH_c. Within our theoretical model (in the Appendix A), we derive the following relationships between the (unobserved) ideal measures of trade and migration openness and their empirical counterparts:

$$MSH_c = \Upsilon + a_1 \theta_c^M - a_2 S_c + \textbf{a} \Xi_c^M \qquad (3)$$

$$TSH_c = \Psi + b_1 \theta_c^T - b_2 S_c + \textbf{b} \Xi_c^T. \qquad (4)$$

---

[6] Peri (2012) looks at the long-run effect of immigration on productivity and income per person across US states.

[7] Their main measure is based on arrivals and departures of people traveling to, and staying in, places outside their usual place of residence, normalized by the size of the workforce. These are short-term stays (no more than one consecutive year) and include business as well as leisure travel.

As one would expect, international trade and migration openness (an inverse function of the respective international trade and migration costs) affect the equilibrium trade and migration shares. In addition, country size enters these equations. The reason is that larger countries enjoy greater domestic variety in terms of goods and factors. Since domestic trade and migration flows are less costly than international ones, larger countries will display lower trade and lower migration (in terms of TSH and MSH) than comparable countries of smaller size. Terms Ξ_c^M and Ξ_c^T collect other determinants of these shares, such as labor demand shocks or exchange rate volatility. We assume that some of those factors are not observable to the econometrician. Combining Eqs. (3) and (4) with Eq. (2) we obtain Eq. (1).[8] It is important to note that the unobserved terms in Ξ_c^M and Ξ_c^T are now housed in the error term of Eq. (1). Some of those may affect output per worker directly and are certainly correlated with MSH_c and TSH_c. Hence, OLS estimates of Eq. (1) will suffer from some degree of omitted-variable bias. Other unobserved terms in Ξ_c^M and Ξ_c^T, uncorrelated with output per worker will act as classical measurement error.

2.2. Gravity-based instruments

Recognizing the econometric concerns discussed above, FR proposed an instrumental-variables strategy based on exploiting cross-country differences in trade and migration openness arising from the geography-based trade and migration costs. These costs are proxied by bilateral geographic and cultural characteristics. The implicit assumption is that these costs only determine output per worker by affecting access to international trade and migration.

We begin by building a predictor for bilateral trade and migration shares of country c:

$$lnx_{cj} = \gamma_1 ln(Dist)_{cj} + \gamma_2 ln(Pop)_c + \gamma_3 ln(Pop)_j + \gamma_4 ln(Area)_c + \gamma_5 ln(Area)_j$$
$$+ \gamma_6 (Landlocked)_c + \gamma_7 (Border)_{cj} + \gamma_8 (ComLang)_{cj} + \gamma_9 (Colony)_{cj}$$
$$+ \gamma_{10} ln(Dist)_{cj}(Border)_{cj} + \gamma_{11} ln(Pop)_c (Border)_{cj} + \gamma_{12} ln(Pop)_j (Border)_{cj}$$
$$+ \gamma_{13} ln(Area)_c (Border)_{cj} + \gamma_{14} ln(Area)_j (Border)_{cj}$$
$$+ \gamma_{15} ln(Landlocked)_j (Border)_{cj} + u_{cj}. \qquad (5)$$

The dependent variable x_{cj} is either MSH_{cj}, the stock of immigrants from country j to country c relative to the population of country c, or TSH_c, the value of trade (export + imports) between country c and j divided by the GDP of country c. The explanatory variables are the distance between the two countries, the population and area of each country, the number of countries in the pair that is landlocked, a dummy for whether country c and j share a border, a dummy for speaking a common language and a dummy for shared colonial past.[9] The interactions of the border dummies with the distance, population area, and landlocked dummies are also included to increase the predictive power of the regression. In one specification we include origin and destination dummy variables, which absorb the origin-specific and the destination-specific regressors. In that case we omit area, population and the landlocked dummies that only vary by origin or destination.

Once we have estimated the gravity regressions (5) we aggregate them across destinations j to obtain the predicted trade and migration shares for each country c. More specifically, define Z_{cj} to be the vector of explanatory variables included in Eq. (5) and γ_M to be the vector

coefficients in the regression for migration flows, while γ_T is the vector of coefficients in the bilateral trade regression. Then we define the trade share predicted by bilateral costs for country c as:

$$\widehat{TSH}_c = \sum_{j \neq c} exp\left(\hat{\gamma}_T Z_{cj}\right). \qquad (6)$$

Similarly we define the migration share predicted by bilateral costs in country c as:

$$\widehat{MSH}_c = \sum_{j \neq c} exp\left(\hat{\gamma}_M Z_{cj}\right). \qquad (7)$$

These predictors reflect the variation in bilateral trade and migration flows driven by bilateral costs and partners' size. Hence, once we control for country size, variations in the predicted values of $\widehat{TSH}_c$ and $\widehat{MSH}_c$ will be driven solely by the relative position of a country in terms of its geographic and cultural coordinates. We note that the right-hand side of the gravity regressions is identical for migration and trade flows. How can then one hope to obtain two distinct predictors for openness to trade and migration from these regressions? What is crucial here is that we allow the data to assign potentially different coefficients to these explanatory variables for trade and migration flows and this will generate different predictions when interacted with the partner country characteristics. The degree of correlation between the two resulting predictors is an empirical issue, however, that needs to be examined below. The trade and migration literature have estimated gravity equations like Eq. (5) repeatedly. Our goal is not to have a structural interpretation of the coefficients $\hat{\gamma}_T$ and $\hat{\gamma}_M$ but rather to use the predictors (6) and (7) as instruments for the trade and migration shares.[10] We also note that our strategy here is in the same spirit as Do and Levchenko (2007) and di Giovanni and Levchenko (2009) who estimate a set of similar bilateral trade models at the sector level. Variation in their sector-level predictors is also based on the different sensitivity across sectors to the same determinants of cultural and geographic distance.

2.3. Identification strategy

As discussed earlier our main estimating equation is given by

$$ln y_c = \beta_0 + \beta_T TSH_c + \beta_M MSH_c + \beta_S lnS_c + \beta_C \textbf{Controls}_c + u_c.$$

Compared to the original FR specification, we account for migration and trade jointly. More importantly, we take seriously the criticism by Rodriguez and Rodrik (2001) and address the threats to the validity of the instrumental variables by explicitly accounting for the main channels through which trade and geographical and cultural features may directly affect income per capita. On the basis of the empirical economic growth literature these channels are the effects of geography on early political economic development (Putterman and Weil, 2010), on colonization

[8] In Eq. (1) β_T is equal to β_1/a_1, β_M is equal to β_2/a_2, and $\beta_S = \beta_1/b_1 + \beta_2/b_2 + \beta_3$. Term $\beta_S \Xi_c$ is a linear combination of the residual determinants of trade, $\textbf{b}\Xi_{T,c}$, and immigration, $\textbf{a}\Xi_{M,c}$.
[9] The role of language in shaping international migration flows has been firmly established by Adsera and Pytlikova (2012). Their findings also show that sharing a common language matters more for non-English-speaking destinations. One may be tempted to include as regressors measures of immigration policy, which have been shown to be important determinants of migration flows, Bertoli et al. (2011, 2013), and so on. However, immigration policies may not be exogenous with respect to economic conditions in the country, as emphasized in political-economy models of immigration, such as Benhabib (1996) or Ortega (2005, 2010).

[10] Nevertheless, we note that the more recent model-based implementations of the gravity equation to predict trade (e.g. Anderson and van Wincoop, 2003) and migration (e.g. Ortega and Peri, 2009, 2012) include a full set of country of origin and of country of destination fixed effects. These are needed to capture the effect of "multilateral resistance" and not including them may introduce omitted-variable bias. Hence, in one empirical implementation we estimate Eq. (5) augmented by a set of country of origin and country of destination fixed effects, which naturally greatly increases the goodness of fit of the regression. Obviously, this is because the country dummies absorb all the country-specific factors that account for the bilateral flows. This includes the roles of country size (population and area) but also expected income levels at destination. The latter is the source of the endogeneity bias that we are trying to purge. Hence, when we build the predictors for migration (and trade) we do not include the estimated coefficients associated with these country dummies. The resulting predictors are more credibly exogenous but, naturally, their ability to predict the migration flows in the data is greatly diminished. One promising intermediate step is to build the fixed-effects gravity predictor using the estimated source country fixed-effects but leaving out the destination fixed-effects. Since in our particular application this did not make much of a difference we opted for the simpler and more clearly exogenous predictor that does not use any of the estimated country fixed effects.

F. Ortega, G. Peri / Journal of International Economics 92 (2014) 231–251   235

and institutional quality (Hall and Jones, 1999; Acemoglu et al., 2001), on climate and the disease environment (Weil, 2007), and on agricultural productivity and availability of natural resources (Comin et al., 2010).

In order to deal with these concerns we use two approaches. Our first approach is to include an extensive vector of control variables aiming at accounting for all the main potential channels through which geography can affect income. In this way the exogeneity assumptions required for the validity of the instruments are weakened substantially. Specifically, we include distance from the equator and regional dummy variables (sub-Saharan Africa, Latin America, and East Asia) to deal with differences in culture, and type of colonization history, we include the percent of land in the tropics, a measure of soil quality, a landlocked dummy, average distance to the coast, average temperature and average humidity to control for agricultural productivity, measures of general accessibility to the country, and characteristics of its climate and measure of oil resources. We also include morbidity variables (incidence of malaria and yellow fever) that may affect health and human capital and colonial-history controls (former French colony, former English colony) that may affect the legal origin of a country (La Porta et al., 1999).

Our second approach is more ambitious, since we also attempt to provide causal estimates for the role of institutions, in addition to the role of trade and migration shares. The reason to do this is twofold. First, it is another route to relax the exclusion restrictions behind our instrumental-variables approach. Good institutions, such as protection of property rights, granting balance of powers and ensuring economic freedom, are certainly a key determinant of a country's current productivity. Moreover, institutional quality is extremely persistent over time and can be traced back to a country's colonization history, which was shaped by geographic factors (Acemoglu et al., 2001). So failing to include the quality of institutions as a regressor in Eq. (1) requires the rather heroic assumption of no correlation between our gravity-based predictors for trade and migration and the (omitted) quality of institutions. A second reason to include institutional quality as a regressor is that we will be able to compare our estimated effects of trade and migration on income to the effect of institutional quality, which has often been considered as the most important factor accounting for cross-country differences in income per capita. Clearly, this approach requires estimating a regression model with more than one endogenous regressor. Following Hall and Jones (1999) and Alcalá and Ciccone (2004), we exploit distance from the equator, that proxies for European settlement, as a source of exogenous variation for a country's current institutional quality.

In our analysis we also pay attention to the recent work by Putterman and Weil (2010). These authors have argued that the origin countries of our ancestors played an important role in shaping early political institutions. Due to the extreme persistence of institutional quality over the centuries a country's migration history is an important determinant of present-day cross-country differences in income. Controlling for it is important to isolate the effect of more recent mobility on income. Finally, we also note that the trade and migration shares we employ are imperfect proxies for the underlying theoretical openness of movements of goods and people. Our instrumental-variables estimates will also help address the resulting measurement error.

3. Data and summary statistics

Our bilateral trade data is from the NBER-UN dataset (Feenstra et al., 2005). This database uses National Accounts in order to obtain bilateral trade data and checks the importing as well as the exporting country statistics in order to improve on accuracy. We also cross-examined these data with the International Trade database (BACI) available at CEPII.[11] The UN-NBER database has slightly larger coverage, filling

some missing values, especially for smaller bilateral trade values. This dataset has information on imports for over thirty thousand bilateral pairs for the year 2000. We then replace missing values with zeros.[12] The bilateral migration data are from Docquier et al. (2010) and are described there in greater detail. They measure the number of people (older than 25) born in each of 194 world countries and residing in any of these countries in 2000. The original sources of these data are national censuses conducted around the year 2000. Specifically, for 194 countries we have their working-age population broken down by country of birth and level of education (with or without college education). There are 38,031 bilateral cells, none of which have missing values, however a large fraction contain zeros, corresponding to the fact that there are no migrants between many country pairs. We complement the bilateral dataset with data on geography (bilateral distance, a dummy for sharing a border, and the number of landlocked countries in the pair), country size (in terms of population and area), language (common languages), and colonial ties. These data are from the BACI dataset, provided by CEPII and described in Head et al. (2010). The resulting dataset has over 33,000 bilateral observations for trade and migration flows, around 24,000 of which have nonzero observations for trade flows, and 8000 have nonzero observations for migration flows (see the number of observations in Table 2). In comparison FR had only 3220 bilateral trade flows and Noguer and Siscart (2005) had 8906. Hence the coverage of our trade data is significantly larger than in the previous studies and the migration data are completely new.

We now turn to our country-level dataset, which spans 188 countries, 146 of which were present in the FR dataset. To maintain comparability we estimate our main models on this sub-sample. The remaining 42 countries tend to be low-income and small in size, which raises some issues about the quality of their data. However, we made a significant effort to extend the coverage for most variables, and thus we also present results for the full sample.[13] Our main variables of interest are real GDP per person (PPP-adjusted), a measure of income inequality (Gini coefficient), the trade share in GDP (defined as imports plus exports over PPP-adjusted GDP), real trade openness (as in Alcalá and Ciccone, 2004), the foreign-born share (both in terms of population and of human capital), an index of institutional quality and a measure of patents per person. The GDP and trade shares are from the Penn World Tables (version 7.0), the foreign-born share is calculated using the Docquier et al. (2010) data. Along the lines of Hall and Jones (1999) and Alcalá and Ciccone (2004) we build a measure of institutional quality. Our index of institutional quality is based on data in Acemoglu et al. (2001) and is built as a simple average of an index of average protection against expropriation risk and an index of constraints on the executive (around year 1990).[14] Acemoglu et al. (2001) is also our source for several additional variables that measure absolute geography, disease environment, natural resources, climate, institutional characteristics and cultural traits. We use the database from Alesina and La Ferrara (2005) for ethnic, linguistic and religious fractionalization.

Table 1 reports some basic descriptive statistics and the source for the main variables of the paper. The mean real GDP per person is $10,682, with a standard deviation that is 20% larger than the mean. The mean Gini coefficient (from the UNU-WIDER dataset) is 41.53 (standard deviation 11.04). The mean trade share is 90%, with a standard deviation of 50 percentage points.[15] The average degree of real

---

[11] The correlation coefficient with the CEPII bilateral trade data for year 2000 is 0.99 when restricting to the same country pairs. These data can be downloaded at http://www.cepii.fr/anglaisgraph/bdd/baci.htm.

[12] We note that this will have no effect on our linear-in-logs predictors since the zero values will be dropped anyway. However, it will allow us to increase the number of observations in the non-linear estimation (Poisson pseudo-maximum likelihood). We build the trade flow for each country pair by adding imports and exports.

[13] We have also performed most of the regressions on the full dataset, with very similar findings (available upon request).

[14] For more details see page 1397 in Acemoglu et al. (2001).

[15] As small countries have very large degree of trade openness, if one weights each country by its GDP the average trade share is 54%.

Table 1
Descriptive statistics and data sources for the main variables.

Variable	Obs	Mean	Std. Dev.	Min	Max	Source
Dummy Frankel and Romer sample	188	0.78				Frankel and Romer (1999)
Real GDP per person in 2000 (PPP, chain-weighted 2005 USD)	184	10,682	12,881	117	74,162	PWT, 7.2
TSH = trade flows/GDP	184	0.9	0.5	0.02	3.78	PWT, 7.2
Real TSH	184	0.5	0.42	0.01	2.72	Aicalá and Ciccone (2004), PWT 7.2
MSH = foreign-born/resident pop.	188	0.04	0.08	0	0.52	Docquier et al. (2010)
Emigrated/resident population	188	0.06	0.09	0	0.49	Docquier et al. (2010)
MSH in terms of human capital	175	0.09	0.15	0	0.8	Docquier et al. (2010)
Institutional quality index	157	5.45	2.01	1	8.5	Acemoglu et al. (2001)
Diversity index immigration	168	0.7	0.22	0.02	0.96	Own calculations
Diversity index trade flows	168	0.87	0.1	0.39	0.96	Own calculations
Logarithm of population	183	1.71	2.01	−3.12	7.14	PWT, 7.2
Logarithm of area	186	11.34	2.68	3.22	16.65	BACI dataset
Distance to equator	187	25.07	17	0	67.47	BACI dataset
Share of tropical land	153	0.49	0.48	0	1	BACI dataset
Pct. Euro. descent in 1900	153	28.38	40.97	0	100	Acemoglu et al. (2001)
PW share of foreign ancestors	188	0.24	0.32	0	1	Putterman and Weil (2010)
PW early political dev. (Statehist)	160	0.48	0.23	0	0.96	Putterman and Weil (2010)
Pct. population speaking a European Language in 1975	149	31.01	43.01	0	100	Acemoglu et al. (2001)
Gini coefficient	130	41.53	11.04	21.8	76.6	UNU-WIDER
90–10 income ratio	71	11.57	11.21	3.16	67.58	UNU-WIDER
Predicted TSH (FR specification)	188	0.16	0.11	0	0.69	Own calculations
Predicted TSH (linear specification)	188	0.27	0.3	0	2.43	Own calculations
Predicted TSH (non-linear spec.)	188	0.85	0.42	0	2.14	Own calculations
Predicted TSH (linear FE)	188	0	0	0	0.01	Own calculations
Predicted MSH (FR specification)	188	0.01	0.01	0	0.04	Own calculations
Predicted MSH (linear specification)	188	0.01	0.01	0	0.06	Own calculations
Predicted MSH (non-linear spec.)	188	0.04	0.03	0	0.16	Own calculations
Predicted MSH (linear FE)	188	0.01	0.01	0	0.03	Own calculations

trade openness is 0.50 (with a standard deviation of 0.42).[16] The correlation coefficient between the two variables is 0.76. The foreign-born share, defined as the foreign-born population over the total population in the country has a mean of 0.04 (standard deviation 0.08) and ranges from virtually zero to 0.52. When we build the migration share in terms of human capital (as opposed to population), we rely on estimates of Mincerian returns and the share of college-educated. The resulting migration share (in terms of human capital) is 0.09 on average (standard deviation 0.15), and ranges from zero to 0.80. These figures reflect the fact that immigrants are more educated than natives in many countries. As one would expect, the correlation coefficient between the two definitions of the migration share is very high (0.96).

Among the remaining variables let us comment on two important control variables from Putterman and Weil (2010). The first is an index of early political development (the so-called *Statehist* variable). This index characterizes the level of sophistication of the sociopolitical institutions in the countries of origin of the ancestors around year 1500 of the current population for each country. This index is available for 160 of the countries in our sample. We also use their data, specifically their bilateral matrix of ancestry, to compute the share of the current population (year 2000) in each country whose ancestors in year 1500 lived in a different country. This is a measure of openness to international migration over the very long run. The average value is 0.24, with a large standard deviation (0.32), and ranges from zero to 1. In addition the Table reports descriptive statistics on some of our main control variables (population, area, percent of the population speaking European languages), measures of income inequality (used as dependent variables later in the analysis), and a series of variations on our gravity-based predictors for the trade share (*TSH*) and migration share (*MSH*), which are the core of our instrumental-variables strategy. We discuss their construction in detail below.

---

[16] Following footnote 4 in Aicalá and Ciccone (2004), real trade openness is defined as (nominal) openness times the price level, which undoes the dependence on relative nontradeable goods prices.

4. Preface: Trade and income

We preface our empirical analysis by briefly presenting the estimates of the gravity models for bilateral trade flows, and reproducing the results of the previous literature that focused only on the effect of trade openness on income.

4.1. Gravity estimates for trade flows

Table 2 (specifications 1 to 3) reports the estimates of the gravity model for bilateral trade flows, based on Eq. (5). The dependent variable is the log of the bilateral trade share. Column 1 reports the estimates of a linear-in-logs model. Column 2 reports the estimates of a similar model that includes country of origin and country of destination dummy variables. This specification will be helpful in assessing if the coefficients estimated with the standard predictor (column 1) suffer from omitted-variable bias. Moreover the fixed-effects specification is better motivated theoretically (see Anderson and van Wincoop, 2003 regarding trade flows, and Ortega and Peri, 2009; Bertoli and Fernandez-Huertas, 2013 in the context of international migration).[17] In column 3, we follow Silva and Tenreyro (2006) and adopt a non-linear estimation method (Poisson pseudo-maximum likelihood). As argued by these authors, the latter estimation method addresses important heteroskedasticity issues and also boosts the sample size because it can naturally accommodate observations with zero bilateral values.[18]

Qualitatively, the point estimates are similar across the three columns and have the expected signs: geographical distance is associated with lower bilateral trade shares, while sharing a common language and having colonial ties are all associated to larger bilateral trade shares. In particular, we note that the coefficient on log distance is very similar

---

[17] It is important to keep in mind that our goal here is not to identify the structural parameters of the underlying model for trade and migration flows. Our aim is to build predictors for those flows that can be considered plausibly exogenous. For an instance of convincing identification of the effects of distance on trade flows see Feyrer (2009b).
[18] To reduce the computational burden we do not include country fixed effects in the non-linear model.

F. Ortega, G. Peri / Journal of International Economics 92 (2014) 231–251

Table 2
Gravity models for bilateral trade share (TSH) and migration share (MSH).

Estimation	OLS	FE	Poisson	OLS	FE	Poisson
Dep. Var.	Ln bil. TSH	Ln bil. TSH	Ln bil. TSH	Ln bil. MSH	Ln bil. MSH	Ln bil. MSH
	(1)	(2)	(3)	(4)	(5)	(6)
Ln distance	−1.82***	−1.71***	−0.87***	−1.38***	−1.37***	−1.46***
	(0.04)	(0.03)	(0.08)	(0.04)	(0.04)	(0.08)
Ln pop. dest	0.02		−0.21***	−0.40***		−0.30***
	(0.01)		(0.03)	(0.02)		(0.04)
Ln pop. origin	1.08***		0.83***	0.63***		0.74***
	(0.01)		(0.04)	(0.02)		(0.07)
Ln area origin	−0.07***		0.04	0.20***		0.15***
	(0.01)		(0.03)	(0.02)		(0.04)
Ln area dest.	−0.25***		−0.21***	−0.08***		−0.08
	(0.01)		(0.05)	(0.02)		(0.05)
Sum landlocked	−0.82***	0.05	−0.64***	−0.25***	−2.50***	−0.67***
	(0.03)	(0.45)	(0.07)	(0.05)	(0.95)	(0.14)
Border	−4.71***	−7.64***	−1.95	−1.01	−1.45	−2.49**
	(1.00)	(0.95)	(1.25)	(0.94)	(1.09)	(1.19)
Border * (ln dist.)	0.69***	−0.04	0.23	−0.07	0.11	0.97***
	(0.21)	(0.20)	(0.39)	(0.23)	(0.24)	(0.36)
Border * (ln pop origin)	−0.32***	−0.49***	0.01	−0.21**	−0.06	−0.08
	(0.08)	(0.07)	(0.09)	(0.09)	(0.10)	(0.11)
Border * (ln pop dest.)	−0.34***	−0.54***	−0.28***	−0.25***	−0.35***	−0.58***
	(0.08)	(0.07)	(0.10)	(0.09)	(0.09)	(0.12)
Border * (ln area origin)	0.05	0.41***	−0.11	−0.06	−0.04	−0.34***
	(0.09)	(0.08)	(0.13)	(0.10)	(0.11)	(0.12)
Border * (ln area dest.)	0.11	0.45***	0.21	0.31***	0.25**	0.20
	(0.09)	(0.08)	(0.22)	(0.10)	(0.10)	(0.15)
Border * landlocked	0.81***	0.80***	0.83***	0.32**	0.06	0.49**
	(0.11)	(0.11)	(0.14)	(0.13)	(0.14)	(0.20)
Common language	0.60***	0.21***	1.00***	0.88***	0.50***	0.85***
	(0.08)	(0.07)	(0.26)	(0.10)	(0.10)	(0.19)
Common official lang.	0.01	0.69***	−0.38	0.47***	0.64***	0.13
	(0.08)	(0.07)	(0.27)	(0.10)	(0.09)	(0.20)
Time zone diff.	0.13***	0.01	0.02	0.09***	0.02*	0.02
	(0.01)	(0.01)	(0.03)	(0.01)	(0.01)	(0.03)
Colonial ties	3.09***	0.94***	1.43***	1.27***	1.49***	1.02***
	(0.13)	(0.09)	(0.13)	(0.17)	(0.11)	(0.22)
Origin hegemon	−2.23***		−1.78***	1.02***		0.53*
	(0.18)		(0.23)	(0.22)		(0.30)
Observations R-squared	24,627	24,627	33,108	8022	8022	34,782
	0.4	0.71	0.22	0.42	0.70	0.23
Country fixed effects	No	Yes	No	No	Yes	No

Note: All models contain an intercept (not shown here). The trade share (TSH) is defined as the sum of bilateral imports and exports over GDP of the receiving country, the migration share (MSH) is the number of foreign-born in the country over the total population. The fixed-effects estimator includes a full set of origin and destination dummy variables (not reported). The estimated fixed effects are not used in building the predictors for TSH and MSH. In parenthesis we report the heteroskedasticity-robust standard errors. *, **, and *** significant at 10%, 5% and 1% confidence level.

in the first two columns. This suggests that the vector of explanatory variables included in the first column is large enough to help identify the crucial role of bilateral distance in determining trade flows.[19] We also note that the point estimates of destination population are much smaller (even negative) than the corresponding origin coefficients. This reflects the construction of trade shares where the denominator is the destination GDP. The goodness of fit is obviously substantially higher in the specification including fixed effects (column 2). Compared to the original exercise performed by FR, our gravity model includes information on past colonial ties, along the lines of Head et al. (2010), which increases the explanatory power of the model and the resulting strength of the predictor for the trade share.

As explained earlier, we use our estimates of the vector of coefficients γ_T, obtained from specifications (Acemoglu, 2003, 2009; Acemoglu et al., 2001) in Table 2, to build predicted values for all bilateral country pairs (not just those pairs used in the estimation). We then aggregate these predicted values following Eq. (6) to obtain the

predicted trade share for each country. The right panel of the Table reports the estimates for the migration gravity regressions. For now it suffices to note that the overall pattern of coefficient signs is similar to that obtained for bilateral trade flows. We will return to the migration gravity regressions in Section 5 below.

4.2. Replication of the literature

In order to assess our contribution we show briefly that we can replicate the finding by FR. The benchmark of our replication is the initial work of FR, and a more updated version of the same exercise by Noguer and Siscart (2005). Following these authors, we estimate the following model:

$$lny_c = \beta_0 + \beta_T TSH_c + \beta_P lnPop_c + \beta_A lnArea_c + \beta_C \textbf{Controls} + u_c. \quad (8)$$

In Eq. (8) the dependent variable is the log of income per person in country c measured in 2000 US Dollars, corrected for PPP as in the Penn World Tables. We include as explanatory variables the logarithm of area ($lnArea_c$) and population ($lnPop_c$) to capture the effect of country size. As an instrument for the trade share we use the gravity-based predictor proposed by FR and constructed using the estimates of Table 2

---

[19] The same is true regarding bilateral migration flows (the right panel). We note though that the coefficient on log distance in column 6 is very similar to those in columns 4 and 5, while this is not the case for trade flows (column 3). This suggests that our estimates for migration flows may be more robust than the estimates for trade flows.

238 F. Ortega, G. Peri / Journal of International Economics 92 (2014) 231–251

Table 3
The effects of openness to trade, 2SLS estimates.

Specification	FR sample	Full sample	Dist. to equator	Controls	OLS
	(1)	(2)	(3)	(4)	(5)
TSH	3.03***	3.49***	−0.33	−0.19	0.33
	(1.14)	(1.35)	(0.68)	(0.72)	(0.22)
ln population	0.10	0.11	0.03	−0.18*	−0.13*
	(0.13)	(0.14)	(0.08)	(0.09)	(0.07)
ln area	0.17	0.14	−0.23**	0.05	0.07
	(0.19)	(0.17)	(0.11)	(0.08)	(0.07)
Dist. to equator			0.05***	0.03***	0.02***
			(0.01)	(0.01)	(0.01)
Pct. Land tropics				0.39	
				(0.46)	
Observations	146	181	146	122	122
Controls					
Region	No	No	No	Yes	Yes
Geo/climate/disease/oil	No	No	No	Yes	Yes
Colonial origin	No	No	No	Yes	Yes
First-stage regression					
Instruments	Pred. TSH	Pred. TSH	Pred. TSH	Pred. TSH	
KP weak identif. F test	6.71	6.25	5.04	7.85	

Note: The dependent variable is the log of income per capita. All regressions include an intercept. Regional dummies for sub-Saharan Africa, East Asia, and Latin America. Geography, climate and disease controls include the percentage of land in the tropics, a landlocked dummy, average distance to the coast, average yearly temperature, average yearly humidity, an index of soil quality, an index of the incidence of malaria, and an index of the incidence of yellow fever. Colonial origin controls include dummy variables for former French colony, former English colony, and a dummy for the 4 rich 'young' countries (US, Canada, Australia and New Zealand), and the share of 1900 population of European origin. For columns 1 through 4 (one endogenous variable and one excluded instrument) the Stock and Yogo (2005) critical values (maximal IV size) range from 5.53 to 16.38, respectively, from the less stringent to the most stringent test (the 25% to 15% maximal IV size). Predictors based on fixed-effects gravity regression, but not using the estimated country fixed effects. In parenthesis we report the heteroskedasticity-robust standard errors. *, **, and *** significant at 10%, 5% and 1% confidence level. The KP weak identification test is the Kleibergen–Paap rk Wald F statistic. In the case of one endogenous regressor, as here, it coincides with the Angrist and Pischke (2009) test.

(column 1) described above. Table 3 reports the two-stage least-squares estimates for Eq. (8) and heteroskedasticity-robust standard errors. Columns 1 and 2 of Table 3 report the estimates of the basic model, which includes only controls for country size (logs of area and population). Our main sample is the one used by FR and contains 146 countries. We also report results with the largest sample we could assemble (181 countries, in column 2). Column 1 reproduces the finding in FR, where the trade share appears to have a positive and significant effect on income per person. Specifically, the point estimate is around 3, implying that a one percentage point increase in the trade is associated with a 2.5% increase in long-run income per person. These estimates are close to those found by FR, who report estimates between 1.97 and 2.96, and also hold in a larger sample of countries (column 2). Columns 3 and 4 include further controls, and represent the essence of the Rodriguez and Rodrik (2001) critique: the direct effect of geography on income overshadows the effect of the trade share. Column 3 includes distance from the equator as an additional control. This variable is highly significant, confirming the results in Hall and Jones (1999). Importantly, the coefficient on the trade share falls dramatically (by an order of magnitude) and becomes statistically insignificant. Column 4 includes three continental dummies (sub-Saharan Africa, East Asia and Latin America) and additional variables to control for geography, climate, soil quality, disease environment, and the colonial past. The point estimate of the trade share coefficient remains very small and insignificant.[20] The lack of a significance could be due to a problem of

weak instruments, revealing little or no correlation between the trade share and its predictor. At the bottom of column 4 we report the Kleibergen–Paap F-statistic for weak identification. We obtain a value of 7.8. This value is higher than the least demanding critical values (5.53) reported by Stock and Yogo (2005) although lies below the highest ones (16.38). We take this as indicating that while there may be a concern about weak instruments, the problem does not seem to be extremely severe. We shall conduct a more systematic analysis of non- and weak identification in the next section. Perhaps more informative are the results reported in column 5, which report the OLS estimates of the model that includes the geography and colonial controls. Interestingly, the partial correlation between the trade share and income appears to be very small and, in fact, we cannot reject a value of zero.[21]

5. Openness to migration

The empirical growth literature has almost exclusively focused on trade data to measure overall economic openness.[22] This viewpoint neglects the well established fact that migration has played a very important role historically in disseminating ideas across the globe.[23] Research on the economic effects of immigration, instead, has taken a narrower focus, stressing the identification of labor market effects. As argued by Hanson (2009), a more general approach is needed to carry out a comprehensive analysis of the aggregate economic effects of migration.

It is certainly plausible that openness to migration may play an important role in accounting for cross-country differences in income per capita. Fig. 2 shows that there exists a robust positive partial correlation between the migration share and the logarithm of income per person across countries, after controlling for country size (population and area).[24] Naturally, these correlations may be driven by the confounding effect of trade, by reverse causality or by other dimensions of openness. To address this point we examine the joint effects of openness to trade and migration on income in a more formal regression setting. Building on the basic FR specification, Table 4 includes openness to migration (measured by the share of immigrants in the population) as an additional explanatory variable. We estimate Eq. (1), treating both the trade and migration shares as *endogenous* regressors and use the respective gravity-based predictors as instrumental variables.

Table 2 reports the estimates of the coefficients in the gravity migration model. The signs of the coefficients are largely as expected. As was the case with trade flows, bilateral distance reduces migration, while sharing a common language and colonial ties appear to significantly increase migration. While not dramatic, there are some noticeable and intuitive differences between the marginal roles played by some variables in accounting for trade and migration flows.[25] Consider, for instance, the simplest model (linear in logs

_____

[20] We also run specifications (not reported) using the non-linear and the fixed-effect gravity predictors for trade as instruments. The estimates are less precise but the results are similar: the coefficient on the trade share is significant only if we do not include any control for geography.

[21] Our results differ from those of Noguer and Siscart (2005), who find that the positive effect of trade openness on income is robust to the inclusion of the geographic controls. We use different (more complete and updated) data, which accounts for the disparity in results. At minimum our results suggest that the effect of trade openness uncovered by these authors using the Frankel and Romer methodology is sensitive to the data used in the estimation. It is also possible that over time the trade to GDP ratio has become an increasingly worse proxy of openness to trade.

[22] See, for instance, the review in the textbook by Weil (2007).

[23] See, for instance, Acemoglu et al. (2001), Comin et al. (2010), Diamond (1997), and more recently, Putterman and Weil (2010).

[24] Fig. 2A plots log income per person against the foreign-born share in the country. The associated regression coefficient is 6.5 with a standard error of 1.18. Fig. 2B plots the gravity-predicted migration share (after partialling out population and area) and income per capita. The regression coefficient is 15.7 with a standard error of 3.95. In both cases the correlation is robust to dropping outliers. It is also not driven by the US, Canada, or Australia—countries that are both highly economically developed and have a high foreign-born share. This is particularly clear for the predicted migration share (Fig. 2B) since the large size and relative remoteness of these countries lead to relatively low predicted immigration shares.

[25] The point estimates display some variation across estimation methods. For comparison see the estimates provided by Ortega and Peri (2013) who emphasize the role of immigration policies.

F. Ortega, G. Peri / Journal of International Economics 92 (2014) 231–251   239

A) MSH and GDP per person

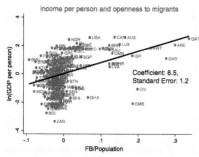

income per person and openness to migrants

Coefficient: 6.5,
Standard Error: 1.2

B) Gravity-predicted MSH and GDP per person

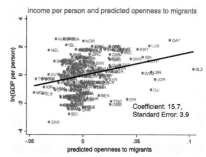

income per person and predicted openness to migrants

Coefficient: 15.7,
Standard Error: 3.9

Note: The scatterplot shows each variable after adjusting for logarithm of population and area. The predictor for immigration share used is the linear gravity predictor.

Fig. 2. Openness to immigration (MSH) and GDP per person, adjusted for country size. A: MSH and GDP per person. B: Gravity-predicted MSH and GDP per person. Note: The scatterplot shows each variable after adjusting for logarithm of population and area. The predictor for immigration share used is the linear gravity predictor.

and estimated by OLS) displayed in columns 1 and 4. Bilateral distance seems to affect trade flows much more than migration flows. On the contrary, sharing a common language appears to be much more important in accounting for migration than for trade flows. Colonial ties instead seem to affect trade more than migration. It is useful to examine the relationship between actual and predicted trade and migration shares. Fig. 3 displays the corresponding scatterplots. Clearly, the predicted migration share is strongly correlated with the actual data (as seen in Fig. 3A). This correlation is large, statistically significant, and not driven by outliers (as shown in Fig. 3B). This is in clear contrast with the ability of the predicted trade share to account for the actual data (Fig. 3C and D). In this case the positive correlation between predicted and actual values depends strongly on a few influential observations. When the observations for Ireland, Luxembourg and Singapore are omitted, the correlation is weakened substantially and loses its statistical significance.[26] While the gravity-based predictors are successful in explaining both bilateral trade and migration, when aggregating to obtain the total openness of a country, the gravity predictor works noticeably better for migration.

It is also interesting to note that while the raw data exhibits a strong positive relationship between immigration shares and income per person across countries, the correlation between *predicted* immigration shares and income per person is still positive but diminished.[27] The reason for the weakening of the relationship between income per person and immigration shares is clear. Our gravity-based predictors do not incorporate in any direct way the fact that rich countries tend to attract more immigrants, as this is precisely the endogeneity bias we are trying to eliminate. The moderate remaining positive relationship arises from the fact that small, easily accessible countries (of any income level) near large populous countries are more likely to receive large immigration flows relative to their population.

5.1. Trade and migration jointly

Table 4 reports the 2SLS joint estimates of the coefficients of trade and migration openness on income per person.[28] In column 1 we only control for country size (area and population). Here only the trade share appears to be statistically significant. Specifications 2 through 5 control for distance to the equator, the key geographic control identified by Rodriguez and Rodrik (2001) on the basis of its role in determining the history of a country's institutions. The coefficient on the trade share falls dramatically and becomes statistically insignificant whereas the migration share has a large and significant effect. Column 3 reports estimates based on the full sample, column 4 uses a predictor for the migration share based on the fixed-effects gravity regression (but not using the estimated fixed effects to form the predictions, as mentioned above). Column 5 includes a comprehensive set of control variables to account for the effects of geography, disease environment, natural resources, climate, and colonial past on income.[29] Throughout, the point estimate on the MSH remains very robust.

Let us provide at this point a thorough analysis of the power of our instruments or, more formally, let us test the hypothesis of weak identification of the parameters of interest. The bottom of the table reports information regarding the performance of the instrumental variables we are using. For each regression model we report the Kleibergen–Paap F test (KP), which allows us to test the null of jointly weak instruments.[30] While in several specifications we are not able to reject the null of weak instruments, in our most preferred specifications, columns 5 and 8, we can reject the null. Specifically, for column 5 (specification with all the controls) the statistic is 5.92, which lies above all the Stock and Yogo critical values except for the most demanding one (7.03).

---

[26] The role of influential observations in the prediction power of the gravity-based trade shares had already been noticed in the previous literature (see Fig. 1 and following discussion in Frankel and Romer, 1999).

[27] When we compute the country-level predicted immigration shares we find that the ratio for the average rich country (income per person above 10,000 dollars) to the average poor country is 1.11, much smaller than the 3.67 ratio in the raw data. So, in practice, our gravity-based predictor predicts moderately larger immigration shares for high income countries.

---

[28] On the basis of these estimates we experiment to find the version of the aggregated predictors for country-level openness to trade and migration that perform better. We find that the strongest predictions for the actual shares are obtained by the linear-in-logs OLS estimation for the trade share and the non-linear estimation for the migration share. Most of our two-stage least-squares estimates are based on this vector of instruments.

[29] The controls included are the same as those in specification 4 of Table 3 and they are listed in the footnote to Table 4.

[30] This is the KP test for weak identification (not underidentification). The Stock and Yogo (2005) critical values we report are only strictly appropriate under homoskedasticity. We report heteroskedasticity-robust standard errors, which in our application tend to be higher than those obtained under the assumption of homoskedasticity. See the discussion in Baum et al. (2007).

240   F. Ortega, G. Peri / Journal of International Economics 92 (2014) 231–251

Table 4
The effects of openness to migration. 2SLS estimates.

Specification	(1)	(2)	(3)	(4)	(5)	(6)	(7)	(8)	(9)
	FR sample	Dist. equator	Full sample	FE pred. MSH	Controls	Reduced form	OLS	Only MSH	VATSH
MSH	5.06	6.09***	8.51***	13.24***	7.32***		6.34***	7.30***	10.14**
	[3.43]	[2.18]	[2.18]	[4.54]	[2.05]		[1.22]	[2.15]	[5.13]
TSH	2.80**	−0.29	−0.11	0.05	−0.01		0.29*		−1.22
	[1.15]	[0.57]	[0.96]	[1.22]	[0.56]		[0.17]		[1.62]
Dist. equator		0.05***	0.04***	0.03***	0.03***	0.03***	0.03***	0.03***	0.02
		[0.01]	[0.01]	[0.01]	[0.01]	[0.01]	[0.01]	[0.01]	[0.01]
Pred. MSH						10.92**			
						[5.19]			
Pred. TSH						−0.24			
						[0.27]			
Observations	146	146	181	181	119	119	119	119	69
Controls									
Region dummies	No	No	No	No	Yes	Yes	Yes	Yes	Yes
Geo/climate/disease/oil	No	No	No	No	Yes	Yes	Yes	Yes	Yes
Colonial origin	No	No	No	No	Yes	Yes	Yes	Yes	Yes
First stage reg.									
K–P weak identif. F-test	3.7	2.47	1.69	1.41	5.92	.	.	12.27	2.26
Angrist–Pischke. F-test for MSH	11.46	12.14	12.82	5.28	11.43	.	.	12.27	8.65
Angrist–Pischke F-test for TSH	6.6	4.9	3.2	3.25	10.2	.	.	.	6.8
Instruments:	Pred. TSH	Pred. TSH	Pred. TSH	Pred. TSH	Pred. TSH	.	.		Pred. TSH
	Pred. MSH	Pred. MSH	Pred. MSH	Pred. MSH fe	Pred. MSH	.	.	Pred. MSH	Pred. MSH
SY 10% max IV size	7.03	7.03	7.03	7.03	7.03	.	.	16.38	7.03
SY 25% max IV size	3.63	3.63	3.63	3.63	3.63	.	.	5.53	3.63

Note: The dependent variable is the log of income per capita. Unless noted otherwise the predicted TSH is based on the OLS gravity estimates and the predicted MSH is based on the non-linear estimation. All regressions include an intercept, log population, log area, and the percent of land in the tropics. Regional dummies for sub-Saharan Africa, East Asia, and Latin America. Geography, climate and disease controls include the percentage of land in the tropics, a landlocked dummy, average distance to the coast, average yearly temperature, average yearly humidity, an index of soil quality, an index of the incidence of malaria, and a measure for oil reserves; colonial controls include dummy variables for former French colony, former English colony, and a dummy for the 4 rich "young" countries (US, Canada, Australia and New Zealand). Predictors based on fixed-effects gravity regression do not use the estimated fixed effects. In parenthesis we report the heteroskedasticity-robust standard errors. *, **, and *** significant at 10%, 5% and 1% confidence level. The KP weak identification test is the Kleibergen–Paap rk Wald F statistic. The AP weak identification test is the Angrist and Pischke (2009) test for weak identification of individual regressors. The reported critical values are those provided by Stock and Yogo (2005) under the assumption of IID errors.

We also report the Angrist and Pischke (2009) F-statistic (AP) for the migration share and for the trade share, separately. This test is very useful in the context of our application since it evaluates whether each individual endogenous regressor, in our case the migration share or the trade share, is well identified separately, after partialling out the other endogenous regressor. A strong AP statistics for one of the endogenous regressors is an indication that we can perform inference on that coefficient, even if the other endogenous regressor is weakly identified. Across the majority of specifications we can reject the null that MSH is weakly identified for most of the Stock and Yogo critical values. In particular, for our preferred specification (column 5) we can reject the null for all but the most demanding critical value. As for the TSH, the AP F-statistic is uniformly lower. In columns 3 and 4 we cannot reject the null even at the lowest critical value. However, when we add the controls and focus on our preferred specification (columns 5), the coefficient becomes better identified. The AP F-statistic takes the value 10.2, which again is above all but the most demanding critical value (and above the "rule of thumb" of 10). On the basis of these tests we conclude that neither of our two coefficients suffer from severe weak identification in the preferred specification, provided the controls for geography, climate, and colonial past are included in the specification.[31]

As further check that weak instrument bias is not a severe concern, we report the reduced-form regression in column 6, where we include the geography-predicted trade and migration as explanatory variables. Here the power of the first stage is not an issue, as the instruments appear directly in the regression. Even in this specification the migration share predictor is positively and significantly correlated with income per person, while the trade predictor is not. This indicates that when including our extensive set of controls there does not appear to be a cross-sectional correlation between the trade share and income per capita. Column 7 reports the OLS estimates of the model with all the controls. Of course, these estimates should not be interpreted causally. Nevertheless, it is worth noting that there is a strong association between income and the migration share in the cross-section, even after controlling for many other variables.[32] In contrast, this is not the case for the trade share, which has a small point estimate (compared to the FR estimate) and is only marginally significant. Finally, column 8 presents a model that omits the TSH from the regression but includes all the controls. The point estimate of the migration share is hardly affected, which suggests the two are not strongly correlated after controlling for all other regressors.[33] Column 9 reports estimates based on a model where we have defined openness to trade on the basis of value added, following Johnson and Noguera (2012).[34] Such definition makes the trade share measure more internally consistent as only the value added of trade is divided by GDP, which is itself measured as value added. We note that the sample size falls almost by half in this case. This reduces the

---

[31] There is some disagreement on what critical values to use for the tests of weak instruments reported here. The Stock and Yogo critical values are only strictly appropriate when errors are IID. In the presence of heteroskedasticity, it is common practice to use these critical values as well but only as a rough guideline. It is also common to use the rule of thumb of a value of 10. In this context we choose to be cautious and we also perform a series of tests that are robust to weak instruments (and to heteroskedasticity). Specifically, we have conducted three such tests for the null hypothesis that the coefficients on the MSH and the TSH are jointly equal to zero, namely, the Anderson–Rubin chi-square and F tests, and the Stock and Wright S test. In two cases we reject the null of no joint effect at the 10% significance level and, in the third case the p-value is 0.11. This provides additional evidence of a significant effect of our regressors on income per person.

[32] We also note that the OLS estimate for the effect of migration is similar to the corresponding instrumental-variables estimate (column 5). This suggests that endogeneity and measurement error OLS biases may be of similar magnitude.

[33] We have also performed the weak-instrument robust inference on the coefficient of the MSH in specification 8. The resulting confidence set is [1.77, 11.47], which does not contain the zero value. The interval is rather wide, thus there is a fair amount of uncertainty regarding the exact magnitude of the effect.

[34] Recent studies such as Bems et al. (2010) and Johnson and Noguera (2012) have emphasized that with the increasing fragmentation of production across countries, (gross) trade flows may be much larger than the value added content of trade, especially for those countries doing a lot of processing trade.

F. Ortega, G. Peri / Journal of International Economics 92 (2014) 231–251   241

A) Fit of the predicted migration share, adjusted for country size

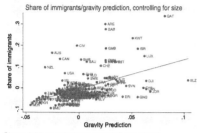

Slope: 1.37, standard error: 0.30 F-stat: 20.56

B) Excluding 2 outliers

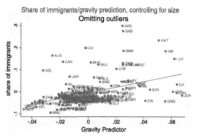

Slope: 1.28, standard error: 0.26 F-stat: 22.90

C) Fit of the predicted trade share, adjusted for country size

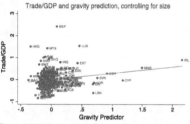

Slope: 0.29 std. error 0.09, F-test 9.39

D) Excluding 4 outliers

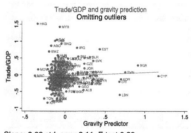

Slope: 0.09 std. error 0.11, F-test 0.39

Fig. 3. A: Fit of the predicted migration share, adjusted for country size. B: Excluding 2 outliers. C: Fit of the predicted trade share, adjusted for country size. D: Excluding 4 outliers.

precision of the estimates. Nevertheless, we still find a positive and significant effect of the migration share and no evidence of an effect of openness to trade. Finally, we observe a stronger first stage in column 8, when only one endogenous regressor is present in the regression model. The F-statistic of the first stage is now above 12.

Let us illustrate here the magnitude of the effect of openness of immigration on income per person using a point estimate of 7.32 (the median estimate in Table 4). Assuming a causal interpretation of our estimates, if country A has a migration (foreign-born) share that is 10 percentage points larger than country B, we would expect it to have a long-run level of income per capita that is about twice the level of country B.[35] Ten percentage points in the migration share is the difference between the migration shares of the tenth and ninetieth percentiles in the country distribution by income per capita. By way of comparison, Hall and Jones (1999) reported that cross-country differences in schooling levels would account for income per capita differences between these two groups of countries by a factor or 3. Before concluding this section we conduct three important robustness exercises on our measure of openness to migration.

5.2. Human capital

Thus far our analysis has ignored educational differences among natives and immigrants by measuring openness to migration as the

migrant (foreign-born) share in the population. Here we take into account that the human capital content of immigration flows, relative to natives, varies across countries. It is possible that migrants with high education generate a larger contribution to income than those with lower education levels. On the other hand, several authors have argued that migrants' formal education is only a rough measure of the productive skills of immigrants (Dustmann et al. (2013)). To investigate this question we distinguish between individuals with a college degree and those without, and we compute the share in the human capital of a country that is accounted for by its foreign-born population.

Specifically, we assume that the average college-educated worker has higher efficiency units of labor than the average non-college educated worker. These efficiency units are assessed following a simple Mincerian approach as in Hall and Jones (1999). We assume that the return to each additional year of education is 6.8% in terms of wages across all countries in our sample. Assuming that the average gap in years of schooling between college educated and non-college educated workers is 6 years, we obtain that the efficiency units of skilled workers are 1.503 times the units for unskilled workers.[36]

Column 1 in Table 5 reports estimates for the main specification (that is, column 8 in Table 4, which includes all the controls) but using now the migration share in terms of human capital, rather than in

---

[35] Since $e^{0.1 \times \beta} = e^{0.1 \times 7.3} = 2.08$.

[36] We define country c's stock of human capital as $H_c = U_c + 1.503 \cdot S_c$, where S_c and U_c denote the number of college graduates and non-college graduates in the population, respectively.

Table 5
Human capital, net migration and heterogeneous effects, 2SLS estimates.

Specification	Human capital (1)	Emigration (2)	Net immig. (3)	TSH (4)	Human capital (5)
MSH		7.75*** (2.11)			
MSH HK	3.60*** (1.17)				
Emig./Pop.		1.38** (0.63)			
Imm. − Emig./Pop			5.50** (2.15)		
MSH • High				7.50*** (1.85)	8.08*** (1.86)
MSH • Low				6.31** (3.05)	3.52 (4.71)
Observations	119	119	119	118	118
R-squared	0.82	0.84	0.77	0.85	0.86
Controls					
Region dummies	Yes	Yes	Yes	Yes	Yes
Geo/climate/disease/oil	Yes	Yes	Yes	Yes	Yes
Colonial origin	Yes	Yes	Yes	Yes	Yes
First stage regression					
KP weak ident. F test	19.06	12.02	9.75	4.51	2.61
Instruments:	Pred. MSH	Pred. MSH	Pred. MSH	Pred. MSH • High Pred. MSH • Low	Pred. MSH • High Pred. MSH • Low
SY 10% max IV size	16.38	16.38	16.38	7.03	7.03
SY 25% max IV size	5.53	5.53	5.53	3.63	3.63

Note: The dependent variable in all these specifications is the log of income per capita. Predicted values for the Migration share are based on the non-linear gravity estimates. All regressions include an intercept, log population, log area, and distance to the equator. For columns 4–5 countries are classified as having a high (low) value if they are above (below) the median along the respective dimension. The instruments are the gravity-predictor of share of foreign-born interacted with the dummy "high" and "low" for the considered dimension. Regional dummies for sub-Saharan Africa, East Asia, and Latin America. Other geography, climate and disease controls include the percentage of land in the tropics, a landlocked dummy, average distance to the coast, average yearly temperature, average yearly humidity, an index of soil quality, an index of the incidence of malaria, and an index of the incidence of yellow fever, and a measure for oil reserves. Colonial Controls includes dummy variables for former French colony, former English colony, and a dummy for the group of 4 young, rich countries (US, Canada, Australia and New Zealand), and the share of 1900 population of European origin. In parenthesis we report the heteroskedasticity-robust standard errors. *, **, and *** = significant at 10%, 5% and 1% confidence level. The KP weak identification test is the Kleibergen–Paap rk Wald F statistic. The reported critical values are those provided by Stock and Yogo (2005) under the assumption of IID errors.

terms of population. The estimates confirm our previous finding: the migration share has a positive and very significant effect on income per capita. Compared to the estimates in column 8 in Table 4, both the point estimate and the associated standard errors have been cut in half. The scale of the coefficient is smaller because the range of variation of the human capital migration share is larger (almost twice as large) than the analogous measure in terms of population. However, the implications in terms of accounting for cross-country disparities in income per capita remain essentially unchanged.

5.3. Net migration

Our measure of openness to migration is based on *gross* immigration. Namely, it is the foreign-born share in the country, which does not take into account the magnitude of emigration flows of natives to the rest of the world. Next we examine whether *emigration* has an additional effect on income, and whether the implications for net immigration, defined as immigration minus emigration, differ from those of gross migration. Let us first focus on the emigration share. It is possible that emigration has negative effects on income per capita by depriving a country of valuable skills (brain drain). However, the converse may also be true since remittances, human capital gains from return migration, and the transfer of knowledge through the diaspora may compensate for the loss of workers (Stark et al., 1997; Beine et al., 2008).[37]

Column 2 in Table 5 estimates a regression model that features both the immigration share (based on gross immigration) and the emigration share, defined as the number of emigrants over the country's total population, besides the extensive set of controls used in the previous table. We note that the point estimate for the immigration share remains

largely unaffected and the coefficient on the emigration share is positive and significant. We also note that here we are treating the emigration share as an exogenous regressor.[38] Since it is very likely that this regressor is correlated with unobserved determinants of income per person we do not wish to draw any strong conclusions from this estimate. Nevertheless, one may argue the estimated coefficient should be seen as a lower bound for the true effect (as higher income should be correlated with lower emigration).[39] Column 3 in this table presents a possibly more interesting set of estimates. The key regressor here is the net immigration share, defined as stock of immigrants minus the stock of emigrants divided by the country's total population. We treat this as an endogenous regressor and we still instrument it with the gravity-based predictor for the (gross) immigration share. We find that the net immigrant share has a positive effect on income. The coefficient is only slightly lower than the one we found using MSH as the main regressor (5.50 versus 7.75), and we cannot reject equality. Hence, this provides an important robustness check on our main finding.

5.4. Heterogeneous effects

Next we explore whether the effects of immigration on income per capita differ across host countries in any systematic way. For example, it is possible that countries that are more open to international trade or that have a more educated labor force, benefit to a larger extent from openness to immigration.

To address this question we classify countries between those that have high and low levels of openness to trade and of average human

---

[37] di Giovanni et al. (2012) argue that the gains from remittances more than compensate for the loss of labor associated to emigration.

[38] We tried to instrument the emigration share of a country with the gravity-predicted emigration, but this turns out to be a very weak instrument when including both emigration and immigration as endogenous variables.

[39] It is also worth noting that emigration data are typically of poorer quality than immigration data so there is potentially more measurement error.

F. Ortega, G. Peri / Journal of International Economics 92 (2014) 231–251   243

capital per person. Then we estimate an augmented model where we allow for the effect of immigration on income to differ for these two sets of countries. Specifically, we interact MSH with dummy variables for "high" (above the median) and "low" (below the median) values along each one of these dimensions. Analogously, we expand the vector of instruments by including interactions of the predicted migration share with the same dummy variables. The resulting estimates are reported in columns 4 and 5 in Table 5. On the basis of column 4, we find that immigration appears to have similar effects on all countries, regardless of their openness to trade. The point estimate is slightly lower for low-trade-openness countries but we cannot reject equality of the two coefficients. Turning now to column 5, the estimates here reveal a positive and significant effect of migration on countries with above-median levels of human capital in their labor force. With regard to low human capital host countries, the point estimate is still positive, but much smaller (3.5 versus 8.1) and not statistically significant. This suggests that countries with a highly educated domestic labor force benefit more from immigration. This result is reminiscent of research finding that countries endowed with higher human capital are better at absorbing knowledge created abroad. This will be the case, for instance, if immigrants are vehicles of knowledge and ideas.

6. Institutions and ancestors

In our previous empirical model we included a fairly complete set of controls to address the Rodriguez and Rodrik critique. According to Hall and Jones (1999), Acemoglu et al. (2001) and Rodrik et al. (2004), the main reason why geographical variables are relevant (latitude, in particular) is that geography was decisive in determining a country's history of colonization. They argue that those initially less-developed countries that were colonized by a Western European power through long-term settlements were endowed with good institutions. Since good institutions beget good institutions, those countries are likely to enjoy high institutional quality today in the form of well-functioning markets, protection of property rights, and constraints on the power of government which contributed substantially to their economic success. On the contrary, countries that were colonized but not settled by Europeans experienced "exploitative" early institutions, which became a persistent burden on their economic development, lacking checks and balances and furthering concentration of power.

It is also plausible that good early institutions may have led to sustained openness to international trade and migration. Since our predictors for the trade and migration shares are based on geography, which influenced a country's history of colonization and its resulting institutions, it is important to attempt to separately identify the roles of economic openness and good institutions on income. Our measure of institutional quality follows Acemoglu et al. (2001) and is the average between their indices for "protection against expropriation risk" and "constraints on the executive". Both are measured over the period 1975–85. These indices capture some fundamental aspects of protection of private property rights and the limitation of the power of government, which have been found to be crucial for an institutional setting conducive to economic growth.[40] Of course, institutional quality is likely to be endogenous to economic development. Following Hall and Jones (1999) and Alcalá and Ciccone (2004), we complement the gravity-based predictors for openness (to trade and migration) with plausibly exogenous determinants of early institutions. Namely, distance from the equator and the share of the population of European descent measured in 1975. The former has been shown to affect the odds of having been settled by a European power. The latter provides a measure of the degree of social, economic and cultural influence from Europe, and is likely a good proxy for the size of historical European settlements in the country.

Table 6 reports the 2SLS estimates. Column 1 considers the roles played by the share of immigrants and our index of institutional quality on income per person, considering both as endogenous regressors. We include regional dummies and controls for the whole set of geography, climate, disease environment, and natural resource variables. Note that, unlike in the previous section, here we do not control for distance to the equator (as it is used as an excluded instrument) or dummies for the colonial past of a country (as its influence is mainly through institutions). Both the migration share and institutional quality are highly significant, with coefficients of 8.4 and 0.4, respectively and t-statistics of 4 and 5. In our sample the difference in the institutional quality index between the 90th and 10th income percentiles is around 6. Based on our point estimate, the resulting income difference explained by institutions is equal to a factor of 14.[41] In comparison, the migration share accounts for a factor of about 2 in the income gap between countries in the 90–10 percentiles. Hence, while institutions still appear to be the main determinant of income per capita disparities, openness to immigrants also has a sizable and distinct contribution. The total difference in income per capita between the 10th and the 90th percentile is a factor of 38, so institutions and migration together explain a substantial part of that gap (14 ∗ 2 = 28).

While the vector of instruments is not strikingly strong, we do reject the null of weak instruments at the less stringent critical values using the Stock and Yogo statistic. The second column reports the estimates when we include the exogenous predictors of institutions (distance from the equator and share of population of European descent) directly as regressors, rather than using them as instruments. The positive and very significant effect of the migration share on income per capita hardly changes. In column 3 we perform a joint estimation of the effects of migration, trade and institutions, treating all of them as endogenous regressors. The trade share is not significant and including it hardly affects the point estimates of the migration share and institutional quality.

Next we examine another channel that may mediate the relationship between migration and development. Putterman and Weil (2010) argue that the birthplace of a country's ancestors has highly persistent economic effects. In particular, countries whose ancestors originated from countries with high early socioeconomic development, as measured by political and administrative institutions around year 1500, have higher income per capita in year 2000.[42] This finding suggests that historical migration played a crucial role as a vehicle for the dissemination of institutions. While related, this argument differs from ours. Their channel is fundamentally based on the countries of origin of the ancestors of today's *native* population and operates through the quality of institutions. In contrast, our MSH variable is the share of *immigrants* (foreign-born) in the current population and it is significant in a regression model where we control for institutional quality. In a way they focus on the effects of historical migration while our emphasis is on the effect of current migration flows.

We distinguish the two mechanisms in the following way. First, we use the data by Putterman and Weil (2010) to directly control for the long-run effect of migration through institutions. Namely, we introduce the ancestor-adjusted quality of political institutions before year 1500 (the so-called *Statehist* variable) and the share of the current population whose ancestors lived in a foreign country circa 1500.[43]

In columns 4 through 6 of Table 6 we introduce these two controls. As we see in column 4, the 'Statehist' variable is positive and significant,

---

[40] The value of this index ranges between 0 and 8.

[41] This is calculated as exp(0.4 ∗ 6).

[42] Putterman and Weil (2010) also offer suggestive evidence indicating that greater variety in the composition by origin of ancestors may have had an additional positive effect. We return to this point later on.

[43] The raw *Statehist* variable is an index, ranging between 0 and 1, capturing the (discounted) length of time prior to year 1500 since the country had developed a supratribal government. The ancestor-adjusted variable, say for the US, is a weighted average of *Statehist* across all countries in the world, where the weights correspond to the shares by country of origin of the ancestors of the current US population around year 1500. The exact definition can be found in pages 1640 and 1641 of Putterman and Weil (2010).

244   F. Ortega, G. Peri / Journal of International Economics 92 (2014) 231–251

Table 6
Institutions and early development, 2SLS estimates.

Specification	Main	Exog. Instit.	TSH, MSH, IQ	Putt.–Weil	PW	PW	PW	AC	AC
Dep. Var.	Ln GDP/pop	Ln GDP/pop	Ln GDP/pop	Ln GDP/pop	Ln GDP/pop	Ln GDP/pop	Inst. Qual.	Ln GDP/emp	Ln GDP/emp
	(1)	(2)	(3)	(4)	(5)	(6)	(7)	(8)	(9)
MSH	8.39***	7.07***	7.54***	12.18***	9.77***	6.17**	−3.11		5.18***
	(2.09)	(2.08)	(1.84)	(3.28)	(2.74)	(2.51)	(3.64)		(1.55)
Institution quality	0.45***		0.44***		0.48***			0.23	0.26***
	(0.09)		(0.09)		(0.11)			(0.15)	(0.09)
TSH			0.27						
			(0.47)						
Ln real TSH								2.09***	0.33
								(0.71)	(0.34)
PW statehist.				2.54***	0.05	0.02	0.08		
				(0.50)	(0.44)	(0.37)	(0.82)		
PW sh. foreign ancestors				−0.05	−0.56	0.81**	2.13***		
				(0.33)	(0.50)	(0.35)	(0.57)		
Dist. equator		0.01*				0.03***	0.08***		
		(0.01)				(0.01)	(0.02)		
Sh. Euro. descent 1975		0.01***							
		(0.00)							
Observations	117	119	117		114	116		128	117
R-squared	0.78	0.84	0.80		0.75	0.84		0.21	0.83
Controls									
Region dummies	Yes	Yes	Yes	No	Yes	Yes	Yes	No	Yes
Geo/climate/disease/oil	Yes	Yes	Yes	No	Yes	Yes	Yes	No	Yes
Colonial origin	No	No	No	No	No	No	Yes	No	No
First stage regression									
KP weak ident. F test	8.99	9.32	4.65	8.68	6.24	7.32	16.67	2.12	3.7
AP weak ident. F-test for MSH	7.09	9.32	8.74	8.68	6.29	7.32	16.67		7.95
Instruments:	Pred. MSH	Pred. MSH	Pred. MSH	Pred. MSH	Pred. MSH	Pred. MSH			Pred. MSH
		EUdes75	EUdes75		EUdes75			EUdes75	EUdes75
		Dist. Equa.	Dist. Equa.		Dist. Equa.			Dist. Equa.	Ln pred. TSH
			Pred. TSH					Ln pred. TSH	
SY 10% max IV size	13.43	16.38		16.38	13.43	16.38	16.38	13.43	
SY 25% max IV size	5.45	5.53		5.53	5.45	5.53	5.53	5.45	

Note: The dependent variable is the log of income per capita or the log of income over employment. Unless noted otherwise the predicted TSH is based on the linear-in-logs gravity estimates and the predicted MSH is based on the non-linear estimation. All regressions include an intercept, log population, log size, and the percent of land in US states. PW refers to Putterman and Weil (2010). We use two variables from their study: "Statehist" and the share of foreign ancestors around year 1500. AC refers to Alcalá and Ciccone (2010). EDES75 refers to the share of European descendents in 1975. Regional dummies for sub-Saharan Africa, East Asia, and Latin America. Geography, climate, and disease controls include the percentage of land in the tropics, a landlocked dummy, average distance to the coast, average yearly temperature, average yearly humidity, an index of soil quality, an index of the incidence of malaria, an index of the incidence of yellow fever, and a measure for oil reserves. Predictors based on fixed-effects gravity regression do not use the estimated fixed effects. In parenthesis we report the heteroskedasticity-robust standard errors. *, **, and *** significant at 10%, 5% and 1% confidence level. The KP weak identification test is the Kleibergen–Paap rk Wald F statistic. The AP weak identification test is the Angrist and Pischke (2009) test for weak identification of individual regressors. The reported critical values are those provided by Stock and Yogo (2005) under the assumption of IID errors.

confirming the finding by Putterman and Weil (2010).[44] At the same time the coefficient on the immigration share, capturing current mobility, is still extremely significant and large. In column 5 we include institutional quality plus an extensive vector of controls. In this case neither of the two early history variables appears to be significant. Still the positive effects of the migration share and institutional quality remain fairly unaffected. This is not surprising since the mechanism emphasized by Putterman and Weil (2010) operates through the role of institutions and, hence, controlling for that diminishes its effect. When we do not control for the current quality of institutions (column 6), one of the Putterman and Weil variables does feature a positive and significant point estimate. To strengthen this point column 7 reports the estimates of a regression model with *institutional quality* as the dependent variable. Both of the Putterman and Weil variables are now highly significant even though we are including a very demanding set of controls. The current migration share, instead, is not a determinant of the quality of institutions. Hence, the historical mobility variables of Putterman and Weil (2010) affect income through their effect on institutional quality. The current migration share, proxying for recent cross-border mobility, seems to affect income per capita above and beyond the effect of institutions.

Finally, we address an interesting measurement issue regarding trade openness. Alcalá and Ciccone (2004) argue that because the prices of

tradable goods are similar across countries while the prices of non-tradable goods are not, it is more appropriate to build the trade share by dividing total trade by PPP income, rather than by income in US dollars. They call this measure *real openness*. Column 8 reports the estimates of a specification analogous to the one they use in their study. The estimate for the (log of) real openness is positive, highly significant and similar to theirs. However, when we introduce our controls we are unable to reject the null of a zero effect (not shown here) on real openness. Column 9 includes also the migration share, institutional quality and controls for region, geography, climate, disease environment, and oil resources. The estimates show that the non-significant effect of trade openness that we find does not depend on measuring the trade share in nominal or real terms.

Our findings confirm that a country's history of migration had a historically important role in economic development by shaping its institutions, as first noted by Putterman and Weil (2010). However, in addition to this, contemporary levels of migration appear to increase income through channels other than institutions. In the remainder of the paper we discuss a potential explanation for that positive effect.

7. The channel: gains from diversity

The previous sections have provided evidence consistent with a large, positive effect of the immigration share on income per capita. We have also shown that the estimated effect is distinct from those of the current quality of institutions and a country's early migration

---

[44] Note that we are only controlling for country size and the current migration share. When we control for distance to the equator and regional dummies the Putterman and Weil regressors lose significance.

F. Ortega, G. Peri / Journal of International Economics 92 (2014) 231–251 245

Table 7
Channels. The Hall and Jones, 1999 Decomposition, 2SLS Estimates.

Dep. Var.	ln Y/L	$(\alpha/1 - \alpha) * \ln K/Y$	ln H/L	ln TFP	ln Y/L	ln TFP	Gini coeff.	P90/P10
	(1)	(2)	(3)	(4)	(5)	(6)	(7)	(8)
MSH	7.52***	1.01	1.29	5.22**	9.01***	6.77***	−0.38	−82.56
	(2.49)	(1.00)	(0.80)	(2.58)	(2.48)	(2.34)	(0.42)	(54.99)
Instit. quality					0.48***	0.53***		
					(0.12)	(0.13)		
Observations	99	99	99	99	99	99	103	59
R-squared	0.84	0.31	0.77	0.77	0.79	0.65	0.59	0.53
Controls								
Region dummies	Yes	Yes	Yes	Yes	Yes	Yes	Yes	Yes
Geo/climate/disease/oil	Yes	Yes	Yes	Yes	Yes	Yes	Yes	Yes
Colonial origin	Yes	Yes	Yes	Yes	Yes	Yes	Yes	Yes
First-stage regression								
AP weak ident. F-test for MSH	8.47	8.47	8.47	8.47	4.94	4.94	10.74	7.15
KP weak ident. F-test	8.47	8.47	8.47	8.47	6.29	6.29	10.74	7.15
Instruments:	Pred. MSH	Pred. MSH	Pred. MSH	Pred. MSH	Pred. MSH	Pred. MSH	Pred. MSH	Pred. MSH
SY 10% max IV size	16.38	16.38	16.38	16.38	13.43	13.43	16.38	16.38
SY 25% max IV size	5.53	5.53	5.53	5.53	5.45	5.45	5.53	5.53

Note: Dependent variables for columns 1–6 are normalized by the US value. Coefficient alpha is the capital share in the Cobb–Douglas production function underlying this decomposition (Hall and Jones, 1999). We have assumed alpha equal to 0.33. In columns 7 and 8 the dependent variables are the Gini coefficient and the 90–01 income percentile ratios. All regression models include an intercept and control for log population and log area, and distance to the equator (except for the last two columns where we treat institutional quality as an endogenous regressor and distance to the equator is part of the vector of instruments). Regional dummies for sub-Saharan Africa, East Asia, and Latin America. Geography, climate and disease controls include the percentage of land in the tropics, a landlocked dummy, average distance to the coast, average yearly temperature, average yearly humidity, an index of soil quality, an index of the incidence of malaria, an index of the incidence of yellow fever, and a measure of the country's oil reserves. Colonial controls include dummy variables for former French colony, former English colony, and a dummy for the 4 rich "young" countries (US, Canada, Australia and New Zealand), and the share of 1900 population of European origin. The predicted migration share is based on the non-linear Poisson pseudo-ML estimator. In parenthesis we report the heteroskedasticity-robust standard errors. *, **, and *** significant at 10%, 5% and 1% confidence level. The KP weak identification test is the Kleibergen–Paap rk Wald F statistic. The AP weak identification test is the Angrist and Pischke (2009) test for weak identification of individual regressors. The reported critical values are those provided by Stock and Yogo (2005) under the assumption of IID errors.

history, both of which have been emphasized as key factors in accounting for cross-country income disparities. The goal of this section is to provide a potential explanation for the channel that mediates the estimated effects of openness to migration on income. In particular we investigate a hypothesis based on gains from diversity. We postulate that countries may benefit from a more diverse immigrant population because this increases the available variety of skills, abilities and ideas, which may, in turn, increase average labor productivity in the long-run.

7.1. Decomposing the effect

Following Hall and Jones (1999) and Alcalá and Ciccone (2004), we postulate a simple Cobb–Douglas aggregate production function in which output is produced using human capital and physical capital. Income per worker (rather than per person) can be decomposed into: physical capital intensity, human capital intensity, and total factor productivity. Specifically,

$$\ln y_c = \frac{\alpha}{1-\alpha} \ln \frac{K_c}{Y_c} + \ln h_c + \ln TFP_c, \qquad (9)$$

where α is the labor share in income, which we set equal to 0.33, K_c/Y_c is the capital–output ratio, $h_c = \exp(\gamma S_c)$ is the average human capital per worker, calculated as the exponential of average years of schooling times its Mincerian return. Finally, TFP_c is the total factor productivity, calculated as a Solow residual. The data on physical capital and output per worker are obtained from the Penn World Tables while the data on average schooling are from the Barro and Lee (2011) and the Cohen and Soto (2007) databases.[45]

Table 7 reports the 2SLS estimates for a series of models where the dependent variables are, in turn, the log of income per worker, and the terms on the right hand side of Eq. (9): the log of the capital–output ratio, the log of human capital per person, and the log of TFP (columns 1 through 4). Our main regressor of interest is the migration share and we include the same extensive set of controls as in the previous tables. A clear pattern emerges from these estimates: the migration share has a positive and high significant effect on income per worker, which operates through total factor productivity. We find no evidence of an effect of immigration on capital intensity, consistent with the prediction of the neoclassical growth model stating that changes in the size of the labor force will not affect capital per worker in steady state. Likewise we do not find an effect on the level of human capital per person in the receiving economy. Columns 5 and 6 reproduce the specifications in columns 1 and 4, respectively, but we now include institutional quality as an endogenous regressor. This does not affect the finding that the main reason why immigration increases income per capita is its positive effect on total factor productivity.

The last two columns of Table 7 examine whether immigration affects the degree of income inequality in the country.[46] We consider two measures of inequality, the Gini coefficient and the 90–10 ratio of income percentiles. In neither case we find evidence of an effect. This is consistent with the previous findings that immigration alters neither the physical capital intensity nor the human capital intensity of the receiving economy. Those channels could alter the relative wage between more and less educated individuals or the return to capital relative to labor and lead to distributional effects on income. To the contrary an effect through TFP does not need to generate inequality. Recent studies have examined other mechanisms that may account for the mitigated effect of immigration on the wage structure (Manacorda et al., 2012; Ottaviano and Peri, 2012; Lewis, 2003; Gonzalez and Ortega, 2010, among many others).[47] The lack of an effect of immigration on the income distribution (beyond its effect on the mean) is consistent with the diversity channel that we focus on next.

---

[45] Where available the data on years of schooling have been obtained from the most recent version of the Barro and Lee (2011) database. For a dozen countries for which the information is not available in that database we rely on Cohen and Soto's (2007) data, available at their personal website. Following Hall and Jones (1999) all dependent variables have been normalized by the US value.

[46] There is an abundance of papers on the effects of international trade on income inequality. The debate has been reignited by the rise of trade flows with China and the public debate on the pros and cons of globalization. See Richardson (1995) for a survey and the recent studies by Autor et al. (2012) and Levchenko and Zhang (2012).

[47] For a good review of the literature see Raphael and Ronconi (2007). Few studies have examined the role of both international trade and migration. One influential contribution using US data is Borjas et al. (1992, 1997) and the response by DiNardo and Abowd to the 1997 article.

7.2. Diversity in skills

One way in which immigration may increase TFP and labor productivity is by increasing the diversity of skills and ideas in the labor force. The simplest way to conceptualize this is to consider that workers of different origin are differentiated factors of production, in the fashion of the Armington (1969) model of international trade.[48] For instance, this may reflect differences across countries in their social norms, language, cultural values, social prestige attached to science or the arts, and so on. In the context of trade flows, Broda and Weinstein (2006) find productivity gains arising from trading a wider variety of goods differentiated by country of origin. In the context of migration, Ottaviano and Peri (2006) find that U.S. cities with more diverse immigrant population (by country of origin) have higher productivity. Peri and Sparber (2009) find that immigration affects the supply of differentiated tasks and induces task-specialization that produces efficiency gains through deepening comparative advantage.[49] In related research Alesina et al. (2013) emphasize the role of birthplace diversity as a source of productivity gains.[50]

We construct our *immigrant diversity index* by country of origin as follows.[51] The starting point is a breakdown of the foreign-born population in each (host) country according to birthplace. Consistent with the notation that we used in our bilateral migration regressions, we denote by MSH_{jc} is the share of individuals born in country j in the total foreign-born population residing in country c. Then we compute the following index:

$$DivM_c = 1 - \sum_{j \neq c} \left(MSH_{jc} \right)^2, \qquad (10)$$

where the summation range spans all countries in the world (with available data), except for host country c. A value of the index equal to zero indicates that one single origin country accounts for all foreign-born population, hence minimum diversity. This would be the case, for instance, if all immigrants in the US were born in Mexico. Higher values of the index correspond to a more balanced distribution of immigrants by country of origin. When all countries of origin have similar shares, the index reaches its highest value, $1-1/N$ representing maximum diversity. We also build an analogous diversity index for trade flows using the share of trade with a specific country relative to total trade. Before turning to the analysis, let us comment briefly on some features of the diversity index in our data. The value for the US is 0.91, which will be a useful benchmark. This value indicates that migration flows into the US are fairly diverse. Mexico plays a clearly dominant role in US immigration, however it is important to note that the US also hosts immigrants originating in all other countries in the world, and the shares of these countries in the total immigrant population in the US are fairly balanced. Several countries attain higher values: Israel (0.94), Spain (0.94), the UK (0.96), Denmark (0.96), and Canada (0.96), to name just a few. Many countries display much lower values: Bangladesh (0.06), Pakistan (0.09), India (0.60), and among OECD countries, Greece (0.70), or Japan (0.75).[52]

We now turn to the formal analysis. Table 8 reports two-stage least-squares estimates of models that include the diversity index. The first column simply reproduces the basic specification from Column 5 in Table 4: the migration share has a positive and significant effect on income, while the point estimate of the trade share is low and statistically insignificant. Column 2 adds the migration diversity index as a control. The coefficient for this variable is positive and highly significant and it reduces by almost 50% the point estimate for the effect of the immigration share. This suggests that the effect of immigration on income operates, at least in part, through the diversity channel. Column 3 adds the diversity index for trade. The point estimates for the migration share and the migration diversity index remain largely unaffected, although now the coefficient on MSH is marginally significant, and the point estimate for diversity in trade flows is in fact negative and marginally significant.

Before reading too much into these estimates we note that the diversity indices may be correlated with other determinants of income and certainly contain substantial measurement error. Ideally, one would like to treat them as endogenous regressors. In practice though the gravity predictors for the diversity indices perform poorly, thus hindering attempts at estimation by instrumental variables. To address this shortcoming we adopt a direct-regression approach and we use the gravity predictors for the diversity indices directly in the regression, rather than as instruments, while the trade and migration shares are still considered as endogenous and instrumented for. This is our preferred set of estimates and we report them in column 4. The migration share displays a positive and very significant effect, falling slightly from a coefficient of 7.3 down to 6.7. Furthermore, immigrant diversity has an additional positive and significant effect on income per capita. To the contrary diversity of trade flows continues to have a negative effect on income per person.[53] The income effect of immigrant diversity is large. An increase in the diversity of migrants from 0.05 (the value for Sri Lanka whose immigrants are essentially all from India) to 0.96 (the value for the UK) implies a corresponding increase in output per person by a factor of 3.5. Beyond the positive effect of immigration, these results suggest that a diverse immigrant population has an additional positive effect on income per capita.

7.3. Ethnic fractionalization

The previous results suggest that large and diverse migration flows increase long-run income per capita. However, there may also be negative by-products associated with large and diverse migration flows. In particular, it may lead to ethnic or linguistic fractionalization, which has been related to conflict and under-provision of public goods.[54] Alesina et al. (1999) provide evidence indicating that ethnic or linguistic fractionalization increases conflict and reduces solidarity, leading to a reduction in the provision of public goods.[55] However, Alesina et al. (2003) examine the consequences of different types of fractionalization (ethnic, linguistic and religious) for economic growth and several other economic outcomes. While they find effects of ethnic and linguistic fractionalization on some economic outcomes (corruption, political rights) they report that these effects appear to be sensitive to the specification used, and they find much weaker and not consistent effects on economic growth.

[48] This idea is formalized in a simple model in the Appendix A.
[49] Amuedo-Dorantes and de la Rica (2011) largely confirm these findings using data for Spain, which experienced a very large immigration wave over the last decade.
[50] Alesina et al. (2013) argue that diversity among skilled immigrants has a larger productivity effect, particularly for rich host countries.
[51] Here we define the index for migration but we also build an analogous measure for trade flows. This index corresponds to one minus the Herfindahl–Hirschman concentration index.
[52] Here are some observations regarding the diversity of trade flows, denoted by *DivT*. We again use the US as the benchmark (value of 0.92). Several rich countries have more diverse trade flows, such as France (0.93), the UK (0.94), or Germany (0.95), reflecting the low trade costs within Europe. However, the countries with the highest values tend to be low income (Pakistan, India, Kenya or Tanzania are all in the top 10). At the other extreme, Mexico (0.39) and Canada (0.43) display very low values of the trade diversity index, reflecting the dominant position of the US as their main trading partner.

[53] We have also estimated a specification where we treat migration diversity as an endogenous regressor, instrumented with its gravity predictor and we omit the migration share from the regression. In that case (not reported in the table) we obtain a point estimate for migration diversity equal to 3.87, significant at the 10% level.
[54] See Alesina and La Ferrara (2005) for a review. Alesina et al. (2013) revisit this question.
[55] Garcia-Montalvo and Reynal-Querol (2005a, 2005b) argue that it is more appropriate to use polarization, as opposed to fractionalization measures. They find evidence of increased conflict and lower economic development.

F. Ortega, G. Peri / Journal of International Economics 92 (2014) 231–251 247

Table 8
Diversity and fractionalization, 2SLS estimates.

Dep. var.	ln GDP/pop	ln GDP/pop	ln GDP/pop	ln GDP/pop	Ethnic Frac.	Ling. Frac.	ln GDP/pop
	(1)	(2)	(3)	(4)	(5)	(6)	(7)
MSH	7.32***	4.01	4.34*	6.66***	2.04***	2.61***	9.81***
	(2.05)	(2.45)	(2.31)	(1.83)	(0.68)	(1.00)	(2.46)
TSH	−0.01	−0.07	−0.07	−0.02	−0.01	−0.04	
	(0.56)	(0.61)	(0.60)	(0.54)	(0.14)	(0.14)	
Diversity M.		1.30***	1.25***				
		(0.39)	(0.38)				
Diversity T.			−1.35*				
			(0.73)				
Pred. Div. M.				1.29**			
				(0.57)			
Pred. Div. T.				−1.76***			
				(0.44)			
Ethnic Frac.							0.61*
Ling. Frac.							−0.65**
Catholic 1980							0.00**
Muslim 1980							−0.01**
Protest. 1980							0.01***
Observations	119	117	117	117	118	115	113
R-squared	0.84	0.85	0.86	0.86	0.55	0.49	0.86
Controls							
Region dummies	Yes	Yes	Yes	Yes	Yes	Yes	Yes
Geo/climate/disease/oil	Yes	Yes	Yes	Yes	Yes	Yes	Yes
Colonial origin	Yes	Yes	Yes	Yes	Yes	Yes	Yes
Instruments:	NL pred. MSH	NL pred. MSH	NL pred. MSH	NL pred. MSH	NL pred. MSH	NL pred. MSH	NL pred. MSH
	pred. TSH	pred. TSH	pred. TSH	pred. TSH	pred. TSH	pred. TSH	

Note: The predicted TSH is based on the linear in logs gravity estimates and the predicted MSH is based on the non-linear Poisson-ML. Predicted values for the TSH and the diversity (fractionalization) index for trade flows are based on the linear-in-logs gravity estimates and the analogous variables for Migration are based on the non-linear gravity estimates. All regressions include an intercept, log population, log area, and distance to the equator (not shown). Regional dummies for sub-Saharan Africa, East Asia, and Latin America. Other geography, climate and disease controls include the percentage of land in the tropics, a landlocked dummy, average distance to the coast, average yearly temperature, average yearly humidity, an index of soil quality, oil reserves, an index of the incidence of malaria, and an index of the incidence of yellow fever. Colonial controls include dummy variables for former French colony, former English colony, and a dummy for the group of 4 young, rich countries (US, Canada, Australia and New Zealand). Standard errors for some control variables have been omitted for lack of space. In parenthesis we report the heteroskedasticity-robust standard errors. *, **, and *** = significant at 10%, 5% and 1% confidence level.

We examine if immigration affects observed measures of fractionalization (taken from Alesina et al., 2003). Columns 5 and 6 in Table 8 estimate models using ethnic and linguistic fractionalization, respectively, as dependent variables. As one would expect, we find that immigration significantly increases both dimensions of fractionalization.[56] The increase in fractionalization and potential ethnic conflict may offset the aggregate productivity gains from greater variety in terms of skills and ideas. This begs an important question. Does increased ethnic and linguistic fractionalization lead to lower long-run income levels? We address this question as follows. Column 7 in Table 8 reports the estimates of a specification where we explicitly control for ethnic, linguistic, and religious fractionalization. The point estimate associated to linguistic fractionalization is negative and significant. In addition the point estimate for the coefficient on the migration share is 9.8, which is larger than the 7.3 point estimate in the baseline specification (column 1). While we cannot reject the null of equal coefficients across the two models, this suggests that, on average, the negative effects of fractionalization are more than offset by the gains arising from a more diverse labor force. The net effect of immigration on income per person estimated in column 1, in fact, includes the attenuation effect due to the indirect influence of ethnic and linguistic fractionalization, and is still significantly positive.

7.4. Diversity and idea creation

Another channel through which immigration might affect total factor productivity in the long-run is its effect on the rate of innovation of a country. Cross-country differences in their scientific and technological histories and in the structure of their research and academic institutions may shape the way talent is allocated across disciplines or the cognitive or non-cognitive abilities emphasized in the schooling system. As a result, individuals originating from a specific country may be more likely to innovate in some fields than in others. International migration exposes a country to the creative ideas of different people and may result in more innovation. We use data on patenting to measure innovation. While not all innovations are patented and while the patenting rate of innovations depends on the field and sector of discovery, statistics on patents have long been used as a measure of innovation.[57] Here we follow this approach by using patenting data, which is directly related to this question and widely available.

We are not the first in examining the relationship between immigration and their direct effect on innovation and entrepreneurship. Important contributions to this literature are Kerr and Lincoln (2010), Gauthier-Loiselle and Hunt (2010) and Hunt (2011). These studies provide evidence of high rates of patenting activity among the immigrant population in the U.S., compared to natives with similar educational attainment. Similarly, some recent studies link openness to trade to technology adoption and innovation (Bloom et al., 2011). Our data is from the World Intellectual Property Organization (WIPO), which collects data on patents granted by any patent office in the world to inventors residing in 108 countries between 1995 and 2010.[58] We construct the average yearly number of patents per million of inhabitants. In our data, the cross-country mean is 91 patents per year and per million of inhabitants, and ranges from 0.01 to 227.

Consistently with our treatment of other outcomes we consider the log of patents per capita as the relevant measure of innovation per

---

[56] We have also estimated an analogous specification where the dependent variable is an index of religious fractionalization but did not find a significant effect of migration.

[57] See for instance the book by Jaffe and Trajtenberg (2002).

[58] The data are available at the website http://www.wipo.int/ipstats/en/statistics/patents/.

248   F. Ortega, G. Peri / Journal of International Economics 92 (2014) 231–251

Table 9
Patenting rates, 2SLS estimates.

Dep. Var.	Ln patents/pop	Ln patents/pop	Ln patents/pop
	(1)	(2)	(3)
MSH	13.37**	9.28*	
	(6.34)	(5.47)	
Instit. Qual.		1.31***	1.33***
		(0.31)	(0.34)
TSH			1.97
			(1.75)
Observations	105	103	103
R-squared	0.76	0.70	0.70
Controls			
Region dummies	Yes	Yes	Yes
Geo/climate/disease/oil	Yes	Yes	Yes
Colonial origin	Yes	No	No
Instruments:	NL pred. MSH	NL pred. MSH	Pred. TSH
		Dist. equator	Dist. equator
		Euro. descent 1975	Euro. descent 1975

Notes: The dependent variables in this table are the average annual patents per million people over the period 1995–2010 granted to applicants residing in the country by any patent office in the world, the log of the previous variable, and the log of the total number of patents. All regressions include an intercept, log population, log area, and distance to the equator. Regional dummies for sub-Saharan Africa, East Asia, and Latin America. Other geography, climate and disease controls include the percentage of land in the tropics, a landlocked dummy, average distance to the coast, average yearly temperature, average yearly humidity, an index of soil quality, an index of the incidence of malaria, an index of the incidence of yellow fever, and a measure of oil reserves. Colonial controls includes dummy variables for former French colony, former English colony, and a dummy for the group of 4 young, rich countries (US, Canada, Australia and New Zealand), and the share of 1900 population of European origin. In parenthesis we report the heteroskedasticity-robust standard errors. *, **, and *** are significant at 10%, 5% and 1% confidence level.

person in a country.[59] The key explanatory variable is the migration share. Table 9 reports our findings. The first column shows a positive estimated effect, significant at the 5% level, of the share of immigrants on log patenting per person, after controlling for the usual geographic and colonial variables. Column 2 includes in the regression the measure of institutional quality (treated as endogenous), and finds a strongly significant effect of institutions on innovative intensity. The point estimate on the immigrant share is reduced somewhat but remains significant at the 10% level. In contrast, the trade share, included in column 3, does not seem to play any role. Acknowledging the relatively high standard errors, these findings provide suggestive evidence that one of the channels through which immigration increases labor productivity in the long run may be by contributing to higher rates of innovation across the world. It is also worth noting that our findings do not necessarily imply that the immigrants themselves produce the whole increase in innovation. Combining different and complementary ideas can also make natives more innovative.

8. Discussion and conclusions

Our empirical findings support the idea that openness to migration, by increasing the range of skills and ideas in the host country, plays a role in accounting for cross-country differences in income per capita, beyond the important roles played by geography, history, and institutions. In our data the ratio between the income per person of the countries in the 90 and 10 percentiles is about 38. Approximately, this corresponds to Ireland and Uganda, respectively. On the basis of our estimates, if Uganda were to adopt immigration policies that equalized its immigration share to that of Ireland, its income per capita in the long run would increase by 70%. In comparison, if Uganda's institutional

[59] One may argue that if ideas are public goods the log of total patents in a country might be more appropriate. We are, however, more interested on the effect on the innovation rate, defined as innovations per person. At any rate, the results obtained using log of total patents as outcome (not reported) are consistent with those reported in the Table.

quality were brought to Irish levels, its long-run income per person would increase by a factor of 8.[60]

Our cross-sectional analysis is not able to uncover a significant role of trade openness on income. Even though we have been able to reproduce the positive effect found by Frankel and Romer (1999), the size and significance of this effect were sharply reduced when including geographical controls, confirming the critique by Rodriguez and Rodrik (2001). Ironically, the technique developed by Frankel and Romer appears to be more successful in identifying the effect of migration on income that turns out to be positive and significant.

In recent work Feyrer (2009a, 2009b) argues that longitudinal (or quasi-experimental) data substantially help identifying the effects of trade openness on income. His point estimates are not directly comparable to ours or to those reported by Frankel and Romer (1999). Feyrer's regression estimates the effect of the log of the total trade volume, not the trade to GDP ratio, on the log of income per capita. Let us denote this trade-income elasticity by b. Let also Y, y, and T denote, GDP, GDP per person, and total trade volume. Straightforward manipulation of Feyrer's regression model delivers the following relationship between income per capita ratios and trade to GDP ratios between two periods 0 and 1:

$$\frac{y_1}{y_0} = \left(\frac{T_1/y_1}{T_0/y_0}\right)^{\frac{b}{1-b}} = \left(\frac{T_1/Y_1}{T_0/Y_0}\right)^{\frac{b}{1-b}},$$

where we have assumed that the population is not affected by the increase in trade flows. Note that the expression above takes into account a feedback effect: an increase in the volume of trade increases income (per capita) which enter the expression of trade share. Now suppose that there is a one percentage point increase in the trade share so that $T_1/Y_1 = T_0/Y_0 + 0.01$. Using Feyrer's preferred point estimate $b = 0.58$ (Table 5, Column 1) and evaluating the expression at the median trade share in year 2000 (0.80) the previous equation simplifies to

$$\frac{y_1}{y_0} = \left(\frac{0.81}{0.80}\right)^{\frac{0.58}{1-0.58}} = 1.017.$$

Hence, Feyrer's estimates imply that a one percentage point increase in the trade share (evaluated at the median trade share in the sample) leads to a 1.7% increase in income per capita.[61] This estimate is very similar to the original estimates reported by FR (about 2%).

In comparison, our estimates of the effect of migration (as share of the population) imply that a one percentage point increase in the immigration share in the population increases income per person by about 6%. A direct comparison of the semi-elasticities for these measures of trade and migration openness should be done cautiously.[62] However this comparison emphasizes the quantitative relevance of immigration for productivity and hence our study calls for more research and more rigorous thinking about that relationship between openness to immigration and long-run economic growth. This is likely to be particularly relevant for policies, because international migration remains highly regulated when compared to trade flows, implying large unrealized efficiency gains, as recently emphasized by Clemens (2011).

[60] Equalizing the levels of the residual factors, other than the share of immigrants in the population and institutional quality, would increase Uganda's income per capita by a factor close to 3.

[61] Another interesting statistic derived from Feyrer's estimate is the following elasticity, the percentage increase in income per capita associated to a 1% increase in the trade share equals $1.01^{\frac{b}{1-b}} - 1 = 0.014$, or 1.4%. Unlike the previous semi-elasticity, this elasticity does not depend on the level of trade share.

[62] Migration shares are lower and less variable across countries than trade shares. In addition, as discussed earlier, trade to GDP ratios are inflated because the numerator is based on gross, rather than value-added, flows.

F. Ortega, G. Peri / Journal of International Economics 92 (2014) 231–251   249

Appendix A. A theoretical framework

We present a simple model to justify our main empirical specifications for the effect of openness to international trade and migration on income per person, namely Eqs. (2), (4) and (3). The model is a minor extension of Alesina et al. (2000).[63] Consider N regions in the world, indexed by $i = 1,2,...,N$. These regions are partitioned into C countries. The size of each country, S_i, is given by the number of regions it encompasses. Each region i is endowed with human capital (workers) H_i and physical capital K_i. Each region's capital stock is used to produce a differentiated intermediate good, one unit for one unit. Human capital is also differentiated by country of origin. All regions produce a common final good (used as numeraire) by means of the following aggregate production function:

$$Y_i = A_i \left(\sum_{j=1}^{N} H_{ij}^{\alpha} \right) \left(\sum_{j=1}^{N} X_{ij}^{1-\alpha} \right), \tag{11}$$

where $0 < \alpha < 1$. Expression (11) implies that producers in any region i have access to a full range of varieties for intermediate goods and human capital. H_{ij} denotes the units of human capital of variety j used in production of good i. Likewise, X_{ij} denotes the units of intermediate good j used in region i.

Intermediate goods and workers are geographically mobile but subject to iceberg-type costs. Intermediate goods are shipped costlessly across regions within the same country. However, when Z^X units of intermediate good X are shipped to a foreign region only $(1 - \gamma^X)Z^X$ units reach the destination, where $0 \leq \gamma^X \leq 1$ denotes the cost of shipping internationally as share of the goods' value. We denote by p^i the price charged by the producer of intermediate good i to ship one unit. The shipping costs (zero for domestic shipments) are paid by the buyer. Likewise, there are costs associated to hiring a foreign-born worker. These costs can be thought of as the additional costs of recruiting abroad, sponsoring an immigrant or training costs paid by the employer to help adapt foreign skills to the host economy. When Z^H foreign workers are hired by a firm, only $(1 - \gamma^H)Z^H$ units are available for production of the final good, where $0 \leq \gamma^H \leq 1$ is the immigration cost per unit of human capital. Factors are paid their marginal products. For tractability we impose the following symmetry assumptions: $A_i = A$, $K_i = K$, and $H_i = H$, for all regions $i = 1, 2, ..., N$. We also assume that all countries have the same number of regions, $S_i = S$, which guarantees the existence of a symmetric equilibrium.

Let us now characterize the demand for domestic and foreign factors of production for a given region i. The marginal product of a unit of intermediate good purchased from a domestic producer from region j in the same country is

$$\frac{\partial Y_i}{\partial Z_{ij}^X} = A(1-\alpha) \left(Z_{ij}^X \right)^{-\alpha} \left(\sum_{k=1}^{N} H_{ik}^{\alpha} \right). \tag{12}$$

Let us now compute the marginal product of a unit of intermediate good purchased from *foreign* producer j', keeping in mind that only $X_{ij} = (1 - \gamma^X)Z_{ij}^X$ units are available for production when Z_{ij} units are purchased. Then

$$\frac{\partial Y_i}{\partial Z_{ij}^X} = A(1-\alpha)\left(1 - \gamma^X\right)^{(1-\alpha)} \left(Z_{ij}^X \right)^{-\alpha} \left(\sum_{k=1}^{N} H_{ik}^{\alpha} \right). \tag{13}$$

In a symmetric equilibrium all producers charge equal prices to all destinations (net of shipping costs), that is, $p_j = p_{j'}$. As a result each region purchases equal amounts of all domestically produced varieties (Z_D^X) and equal amounts of all foreign varieties (Z_F^X). Equal prices (net of shipping costs) and profit maximization imply that the marginal products of domestic and imported intermediate capital goods will be equalized:

$$Z_F^X = \theta^T Z_D^X \tag{14}$$

where $\theta^T = (1 - \gamma^X)^{1 - \alpha/\alpha}$[64]

In similar fashion, wages (net of migration costs) will be equal across regions in a symmetric equilibrium. Thus profit maximization will lead to equalization of the marginal products of domestic (Z_D^H) and foreign workers (Z_F^H). Thus

$$Z_F^H = \theta^M Z_D^H \tag{15}$$

where $\theta^M = (1 - \gamma^H)^{\alpha/(1 - \alpha)}$. Let us now turn to the resource constraints for intermediate goods and workers. The stock of capital in a region is used to produce its own variety of intermediate good. Then Z_D^X units are shipped to each region within the same country and Z_F^X are shipped to each region in another country. Similarly, Z_D^H workers will migrate to each domestic region and Z_F^H will migrate to each foreign region. The resulting resource constraints for each variety of human capital and intermediate input satisfy

$$SZ_D^X + (N-S)Z_F^X = K \tag{16}$$

$$SZ_D^H + (N-S)Z_F^H = H. \tag{17}$$

We can use these equations to derive closed-form solutions:

$$Z_D^X = \frac{K}{S + (N-S)\theta^X} \tag{18}$$

$$Z_D^H = \frac{H}{S + (N-S)\theta^H} \tag{19}$$

plus $Z_F^X = \theta^T Z_D^X$, and $Z_F^H = \theta^M Z_D^H$.

Let us now use these expressions to derive the measures of openness to international trade and migration that we will employ in the empirical section. Let us define the trade to GDP ratio, for short, the *trade share* (TSH) as the sum of exports plus imports as a share of GDP in country i[65]:

$$TSH_i = 2(1-\alpha)\frac{Z_F^X(N-S)}{Z_F^X(N-S) + Z_D^X S} = 2(1-\alpha)\frac{\theta^T(N-S)}{\theta^T(N-S) + S}. \tag{20}$$

Clearly, given country size, an increase in trade openness, θ^T, would increase the trade share. And an increase in the size of the country, S, for a given degree of trade openness (as long as $\theta^T < 1$), will reduce the trade share.[66] Expression (20) shows that the trade share also depends on the elasticity of final output to intermediates $(1 - \alpha)$ and on the overall size of the world economy N. Similarly, we define the

---

[63] As these authors show, this static model can be interpreted as the steady state of a growth model. Hence, we stress that our predictions relate openness to long-run income per capita levels across countries.

[64] Note that $Z_F^X < Z_D^X$ as long as $\gamma^X > 0$.

[65] Imports are equal to exports in this model. In symmetric allocations the price of intermediate goods is the same (net of shipping costs) for all regions. Hence, the value of imports plus exports relative to the total value of intermediate goods is equal to twice the ratio of exported quantities relative to total quantities. Coefficient $(1 - \alpha)$ is the share of capital in total income in symmetric allocations.

[66] As the model is symmetric across countries, an increase in the country size S should be thought of as an increase in the size of each country (in number of regions), and consequently also as a reduction in the number of countries in the world.

migration share (*MSH*) as the foreign-born share in the population.[67] That is, for country *i*,

$$MSH_i = \frac{Z_F^H(N-S)}{Z_D^H S + Z_F^H(N-S)} = \frac{\theta^M(N-S)}{S + \theta^M(N-S)}. \tag{21}$$

It is easy to see that, for a given country size *S*, the migration share depends positively on openness to immigration. Conversely, for given openness θ^M, the migration share depends negatively on the size of the country. Log linearizing expressions (20) and (21) we obtain expressions (3) and (4) in the text. Finally, substituting Eqs. (18) and (19) into Eq. (11), we can express real GDP in country *c*, which is constant across regions within a country, as:

$$Y = A\left[S\left(1-\left(\theta^T\right)^{1-\alpha}\right) + N\left(\theta^T\right)^{1-\alpha}\right]\left[S\left(1-\left(\theta^M\right)^\alpha\right) + N\left(\theta^M\right)^\alpha\right]^\alpha H^\alpha K^{1-\alpha}. \tag{22}$$

Dividing by the initial population in the region, H_c, we can now compute GDP per capita:

$$y_c = TFP\left(A_c, \theta_c^M, \theta_c^T, S_c\right)\left(\frac{K_c}{H_c}\right)^{1-\alpha}, \tag{23}$$

where we have reintroduced the country subindices for all variables. The first term collects all the determinants of total factor productivity in this model and the second is the factor intensity (capital-labor ratio). The previous expressions make clear that openness to migration θ^M and openness to trade θ^T affect positively TFP and income per person.[68] Similarly, for a given degree of openness, an increase in the size of the country, *S*, also increases productivity. We note also that this expression allows other factors to also affect TFP, such as government policies, institutions or social norms, which are absorbed in the term A_c. Taking a log-linear approximation if 23 we obtain 2 in the text.

References

Acemoglu, D., 2003. Patterns of skill premia. Rev. Econ. Stud. 70 (2), 199–230.
Acemoglu, D., 2009. Modern Economic Growth. Princeton University Press, Princeton, NJ.
Acemoglu, D., Johnson, S., Robinson, J., 2001. The colonial origins of comparative development: an empirical investigation. Am. Econ. Rev. 91, 1369–1401.
Acemoglu, D., Johnson, S., Robinson, J., 2002. Reversal of fortunes: geography and institutions in the making of the modern world income distribution. Q. J. Econ. 117 (4), 1231–1294.
Adsera, A., Pytlikova, M., 2012. The role of language in shaping international migration. IZA Working Paper 6333.
Alcalá, F., Ciccone, A., 2004. Trade and productivity. Q. J. Econ. 119 (2), 612–645.
Alesina, A., La Ferrara, E., 2005. Ethnic diversity and economic performance. J. Econ. Lit. 43 (3), 762–800.
Alesina, A., Baqir, R., Easterly, W., 1999. Public goods and ethnic divisions. Q. J. Econ. 114 (4), 1243–1284.
Alesina, A., Spolaore, E., Wacziarg, R., 2000. Economic integration and political disintegration. Am. Econ. Rev. 90 (5), 1276–1296.
Alesina, A., Devleeschauwer, A., Easterly, W., Kurlat, S., Wacziarg, R., 2003. Fractionalization. J. Econ. Growth 8 (2), 155–194.
Alesina, A., Spolaore, E., Wacziarg, R., 2005. Trade, growth and the size of countries. In: Aghion, P., Durlauf, S. (Eds.), 1st ed. Handbook of Economic Growth, vol. 1, pp. 1499–1542 (Ch. 23).
Alesina, A., Harnoss, J., Rapoport, H., 2013. Birthplace Diversity and Economic Prosperity. Working Paper 18699. National Bureau of Economic Research.
Amuedo-Dorantes, C., de la Rica, S., 2011. Complements or substitutes? Task specialization by gender and nativity in Spain. Labour Econ. 18 (5), 697–707.
Andersen, T.B., Dalgaard, C.J., 2011. Flows of people, flows of ideas, and the inequality of nations. J. Econ. Growth 16 (1), 1–32.
Anderson, J.E., van Wincoop, E., 2003. Gravity with gravitas: a solution to the border puzzle. Am. Econ. Rev. 93 (1), 170–192.
Angrist, J., Pischke, S., 2009. Mostly Harmless Econometrics: An Empiricist's Companion. Princeton University Press.
Armington, P.S., 1969. A theory of demand for products distinguished by place of production. Staff Pap. Int. Monet. Fund 16 (1), 159–178.

Ashraf, Q., Galor, O., 2013. The "Out of Africa" hypothesis, human genetic diversity, and comparative economic development. Am. Econ. Rev. (forthcoming).
Autor, D., Dorn, D., Hanson, G.H., 2012. The China Syndrome: Local Labor Market Effects of Import Competition in the United States. Working Paper 18054. National Bureau of Economic Research.
Barro, R., Lee, J.W., 2011. Educational attainment dataset. http://www.barrolee.com/.
Barro, R., Sala i Martin, X., 2004. Economic Growth, 2nd ed. MIT Press, Cambridge, MA.
Baum, C., Schaffer, M., Stillman, S., 2007. Enhanced routines for instrumental variables/GMM estimation and testing. Boston College Working Papers in Economics, 667. Boston College Department of Economics.
Beine, M., Docquier, F., Rapoport, H., 2008. Brain drain and human capital formation in developing countries: winners and losers. Econ. J. 118 (528), 631–652.
Beine, M., Docquier, F., Özden, Ç., 2011. Diasporas. J. Dev. Econ. 95 (1), 30–41.
Bems, R., Johnson, R., Yi, K.M., 2010. The role of vertical linkages in the propagation of the global downturn of 2008. IMF Econ. Rev. 58 (2), 295–326.
Benhabib, J., 1996. On the political economy of immigration. Eur. Econ. Rev. 40 (9) 1737–1743.
Bertoli, S., Fernández-Huertas Moraga, J., 2013. Multilateral resistance to migration. J. Dev. Econ. 102 (C), 79–100.
Bertoli, S., Fernández-Huertas, J., Ortega, F., 2011. Immigration policies and the Ecuadorian exodus. World Bank Econ. Rev. 25 (1), 55–76.
Bertoli, S., Fernández-Huertas, J., Ortega, F., 2013. Crossing the border: self-selection, earnings, and individual migration decisions. J. Dev. Econ. 101, 75–91.
Bloom, N., Draca, M., van Reenen, J., 2011. Trade induced technical change? The impact of Chinese imports on innovation and information technology. CEP Discussion Paper No. 1000.
Borjas, G.J., Freeman, R.B., Katz, L.F., 1992. On the labor market effects of immigration and trade. In: Borjas, G.J., Freeman, R.B. (Eds.), Immigration and the Workforce: Economic Consequences for the United States and Source Areas. National Bureau of Economic Research, pp. 213–244.
Borjas, G.J., Freeman, R.B., Katz, L.F., 1997. How much do immigration and trade affect labor market outcomes? Brook. Pap. Econ. Act. 1997 (1), 1–90.
Broda, C., Weinstein, D.E., 2006. Globalization and the gains from variety. Q. J. Econ. 121 (2), 541–585.
Clark, X., Hatton, T.J., Williamson, J., 2007. Explaining U.S. immigration 1971–1998. Rev. Econ. Stat. 89 (2), 359–373.
Clemens, M., 2011. Economics and emigration: trillion-dollar bills on the sidewalk? J. Econ. Perspect. 25 (3), 83–106.
Cohen, D., Soto, M., 2007. Growth and human capital: good data, good results. J. Econ. Growth 12 (1), 51–76.
Comin, D.A., Easterly, W., Gong, E., 2010. Was the wealth of nations determined in 1000 BC? Am. Econ. J. Macroecon. 2 (3), 65–97.
di Giovanni, Julian, Levchenko, Andrei A., 2009. Trade openness and volatility. The Review of Economics and Statistics, 91(3). MIT Press, pp. 558–585.
di Giovanni, J., Levchenko, A., Ortega, F., 2012. A global view of cross-border migration. CReAM Discussion Paper Series 1218.
Diamond, J., 1997. Guns, Germs and Steel: The Fates of Human Societies. WW Norton & Company, NY 14.
Do, Q., Levchenko, A., 2007. Comparative advantage, demand for external finance, and financial development. J. Financ. Econ. 86 (3), 796–834 (December).
Docquier, F., Özden, Ç., Peri, G., 2010. The Wage Effects of Immigration and Emigration. Working Paper 16646. National Bureau of Economic Research.
Dustmann, C., Frattini, T., Preston, I.P., 2013. The effect of immigration along the distribution of wages. Rev. Econ. Stud. 80 (1), 145–173.
Eaton, J., Kortum, S., 1996. Trade in ideas: patenting and productivity in the OECD. J. Int. Econ. 40 (3), 251–278.
Feenstra, R.C., Lipsey, R.E., Deng, H., Ma, A.C., Mo, H.Y., 2005. World Trade Flows: 1962–2000. Working Paper 11040. National Bureau of Economic Research.
Feyrer, J., 2009a. Trade and income—exploiting time series in geography. Working Paper 14910. National Bureau of Economic Research.
Feyrer, J., 2009b. Distance, trade, and income—the 1967 to 1975 closing of the Suez Canal as a natural experiment. National Bureau of Economic Research Working Paper 15557.
Frankel, J.A., Romer, D., 1999. Does trade cause growth? Am. Econ. Rev. 89 (3), 379–399.
Galor, O., Mountford, A., 2008. Trading population for productivity: theory and evidence. Rev. Econ. Stud. 75 (4), 1143–1179.
Garcia-Montalvo, J., Reynal-Querol, M., 2005a. Ethnic diversity and economic development. J. Dev. Econ. 76 (2), 293–323 (April).
Garcia-Montalvo, J., Reynal-Querol, M., 2005b. Ethnic polarization, potential conflict and civil war. Am. Econ. Rev. 95 (3), 796–816 (June).
Gauthier-Loiselle, M., Hunt, J., 2010. How much does immigration boost innovation? Am. Econ. J. Macroecon. 2 (2), 31–56.
Gonzalez, L., Ortega, F., 2010. How do very open economies absorb large immigration flows? Evidence from Spanish regions. Labour Econ. 18 (1), 57–70.
Grogger, J., Hanson, G.H., 2011. Income maximization and the selection and sorting of international migrants. J. Dev. Econ. 95 (1), 42–57.
Grossman, G.M., Helpman, E., 1991. Trade, knowledge spillovers, and growth. Eur. Econ. Rev. 35 (2), 517–526.
Hall, R.E., Jones, C.I., 1999. Why do some countries produce so much more output per worker than others? Q. J. Econ. 114 (1), 83–116.
Hanson, G.H., 2009. The economic consequences of the international migration of labor. Ann. Rev. Econ. 1 (1), 179–208.
Head, K., Mayer, T., Ries, J., 2010. The erosion of colonial trade linkages after independence. J. Int. Econ. 81 (1), 1–14.
Hunt, J., 2011. Which immigrants are most innovative and entrepreneurial? Distinction by entry visa. J. Labor Econ. 29 (3), 417–457.

---

[67] Note that the TSH and MSH are the same across regions within a country.
[68] Recall that *N*, the number of regions in the world, is obviously larger than *S*, the number of regions in a given country.

F. Ortega, G. Peri / Journal of International Economics 92 (2014) 231–251   251

Jaffe, A., Trajtenberg, M., 2002. Patents, Citations and Innovations: A Window on the Knowledge Economy. MIT Press, Cambridge, MA.

Johnson, R., Noguera, G., 2012. Accounting for intermediates: production sharing and trade in value added. J. Int. Econ. 86 (2), 224–236.

Kerr, W., Lincoln, W.F., 2010. The supply side of innovation: H-1B visa reforms and U.S. ethnic invention. J. Labor Econ. 28 (3), 473–508.

La Porta, R., Lopez-de-Silanes, F., Shleifer, A., Vishny, R., 1999. The quality of government. J. Law Econ. Org. 15 (1), 222–279.

Levchenko, A., Zhang, J., 2012. Comparative advantage and the welfare impact of European integration. National Bureau of Economic Research Working Paper 18061.

Lewis, E., 2003. Local, open economies within the US: how do industries respond to immigration? Federal Reserve Bank of Philadelphia Working Paper 04-01.

Llull, J., 2011. Understanding international migration: evidence from a new dataset of bilateral stocks (1960–2000). Manuscript .

Lucas, R.E., 2009. Trade and the diffusion of the industrial revolution. Am. Econ. J. Macroecon. 1 (1), 1–25.

Manacorda, M., Manning, A., Wadsworth, J., 2012. The impact of immigration on the structure of wages: theory and evidence from Britain. J. Eur. Econ. Assoc. 10 (1), 120–151.

Matsuyama, K., 1992. A simple model of sectoral adjustment. Rev. Econ. Stud. 59 (2), 375–388.

Mayda, A.M., 2007. International Migration Flows: An Analysis of the Forces and Constraints at Work. Manuscript Georgetown University.

Mayda, A.M., 2010. International migration: a panel data analysis of the determinants of bilateral flows. J. Popul. Econ. 23 (4), 1249–1274.

Noguer, M., Siscart, M., 2005. Trade raises income: a precise and robust result. J. Int. Econ. 65 (2), 447–460.

Ortega, F., 2005. Immigration policy and skill upgrading. J. Public Econ. 89 (9), 1841–1863.

Ortega, F., 2010. Immigration, citizenship, and the size of government. B.E. J. Econ. Anal. Policy 10 (1).

Ortega, F., Peri, G., 2009. The causes and effects of international migrations: evidence from OECD countries 1980–2005. National Bureau of Economic Research Working Paper 14833.

Ortega, F., Peri, G., 2012. The role of income and immigration policies in attracting international migrants. IZA Discussion Paper 6655.

Ortega, F., Peri, G., 2013. The effect of income and immigration policies on international migration. Migr. Stud. 1, 1–28.

Ottaviano, G.I.P., Peri, G., 2006. The economic value of cultural diversity: evidence from US cities. J. Econ. Geogr. 6 (1), 9–44.

Ottaviano, G.I.P., Peri, G., 2012. Rethinking the effects of immigration on wages. J. Eur. Econ. Assoc. 10 (1), 152–197.

Pedersen, P.J., Pytlikova, M., Smith, N., 2006. Migration into OECD countries 1990–2000. In: Parson, C.A., Smeeding, T.M. (Eds.), Immigration and the Transformation of Europe. Cambridge University Press.

Peri, G., 2012. The effect of immigration on productivity: evidence from U.S. states. Rev. Econ. Stat. 94 (1), 348–358.

Peri, G., Sparber, C., 2009. Task specialization, immigration, and wages. Am. Econ. J. Appl. Econ. 1 (3), 135–169.

Putterman, L., Weil, D.N., 2010. Post-1500 population flows and the long-run determinants of economic growth and inequality. Q. J. Econ. 125 (4), 1627–1682.

Raphael, S., Ronconi, L., 2007. The effect of labor market competition with immigrants on the wages and employment of natives: what does existing research tell us?. Manuscript available at http://gsppi.berkeley.edu/faculty/sraphael/du-bois-review-january-2007.pdf.

Richardson, D.J., 1995. Income inequality and trade: how to think, what to conclude. J. Econ. Perspect. 9 (3), 33–55.

Rivera-Batiz, L., Romer, P.M., 1994. Economic integration and endogenous growth: an addendum. Q. J. Econ. 109 (1), 307–308.

Rodriguez, F., Rodrik, D., 2001. Trade policy and economic growth: a skeptic's guide to the cross-national evidence. NBER Macroeconomics Annual 2000, vol. 15, pp. 261–338.

Rodrik, D., 2000. How far will international economic integration go? J. Econ. Perspect. 14 (1), 177–186.

Rodrik, D., Subramanian, A., Trebbi, F., 2004. Institutions rule: the primacy of institutions over geography and integration in economic development. J. Econ. Growth 9, 131–165.

Sachs, J.D., Warner, A., 1995. Economic reform and the process of global integration. Brook. Pap. Econ. Act. 1995 (1), 1–118.

Silva, J.M.C.S., Tenreyro, S., 2006. The log of gravity. Rev. Econ. Stat. 88 (4), 641–658.

Stark, O., Helmenstein, C., Prskawetz, A., 1997. A brain gain with a brain drain. Econ. Lett. 55 (2), 227–234.

Stock, J.H., Yogo, M., 2005. Testing for weak instruments in linear IV regression. In: Stock, J.H., Andrews, D.W.K. (Eds.), Identification and Inference for Econometric Models: Essays in Honor of Thomas J. Rothenberg, Chapter 5. Cambridge University Press.

Taylor, A.M., 1997a. Peopling the pampa: on the impact of mass migration to the River Plate, 1870–1914. Explor. Econ. Hist. 34 (1), 100–132.

Taylor, A.M., 1997b. Growth and convergence in the Asia-Pacific region: on the role of openness, trade and migration. In: Lloyd, P.J., Williams, L.S. (Eds.), International Trade and Migration in the APEC Region. Oxford University Press, Oxford.

Taylor, A.M., Williamson, J.G., 1997. Convergence in the age of mass migration. Eur. Rev. Econ. Hist. 1 (1), 27–63.

Weil, D.N., 2005. Economic Growth. Pearson Addison, Wesley, New York.

Weil, D.N., 2007. Accounting for the effect of health on economic growth. Q. J. Econ. 122 (3), 1265–1306.

III
IMMIGRATION POLICIES AND MIGRANT MOBILITY

MIGRATION STUDIES   VOLUME 1 • NUMBER 1 • 2013 • 47–74

The effect of income and immigration policies on international migration

Francesc Ortega[†] and Giovanni Peri*

[†]Economics Department, City University of New York, Queens College, Flushing, New York, 11365, USA.
*Corresponding author: Economics Department, University of California, Davis, California, 95616, USA.
Email: gperi@ucdavis.edu

Abstract

This article makes two contributions to the literature on the determinants of international migration flows. First, we compile a new dataset on annual bilateral migration flows covering 15 OECD destination countries and 120 sending countries for the period 1980–2006. The dataset also contains data on time-varying immigration policies that regulate the entry of immigrants in our destination countries over this period. Second, we present an empirical model of migration choice across multiple destinations that allows for unobserved individual heterogeneity and derive a structural estimating equation. Our estimates show that international migration flows are highly responsive to income per capita at destination. This elasticity is twice as high for within-European Union (EU) migration, reflecting the higher degree of labor mobility within the EU. We also find that tightening of laws regulating immigrant entry reduce rapidly and significantly their flow.

Keywords: international migration, labor movements, immigration policies

1. Introduction

The first decade of the new millennium has witnessed growing international mobility, especially towards OECD countries. Economic factors, and in particular the large income differentials between countries, are likely to play a very important role in determining migration flows. Other factors affecting the cost of migration are also fundamental in shaping those flows. A particularly interesting question is to what extent and how rapidly immigration policies enacted by receiving countries affect these flows. While some studies (Clark et al. 2007; Mayda 2010) have considered the role of immigration policies on migration flows, the limitation of data on both flows and policies has severely constrained these analyses.

In this article, we make two contributions to the literature on the determinants of international migration flows. The first contribution is in terms of data. Building on

Mayda (2010), we extend the existing dataset on bilateral migration flows by including a larger number of receiving (fifteen OECD destinations) and sending countries (120 countries of origin) and years (1980–2006). More importantly, we also build a new quantitative measure of immigration policy restrictions to new immigration flows summarizing the effects of quotas and admission requirements.[1] Following some mechanical rules and carefully reading the content of hundreds of laws, we classify them based on whether they tightened or relaxed the requirements for *entry*.[2]

Secondly, we extend the empirical model of utility-maximizing migration choices in Grogger and Hanson (2011) by allowing for unobserved individual heterogeneity between migrants and non-migrants.[3] Specifically, our model can be cast into the nested logit model by McFadden (1978). Under some distributional assumptions on the unobserved heterogeneity of individuals, we then derive an empirical specification that can be estimated using aggregate-level data on bilateral migration flows, provided a rich set of fixed effects are included in the estimation. In such a model the aggregate number of migrants from a given origin into a particular destination is a function of income per capita at destination, the cost of migration, and a set of origin-specific factors. As proxies for overall immigration costs we use a number of measures of geographic and cultural distance between countries, plus our measure of policy-driven tightness of entry for immigrants. We estimate the model on a bilateral panel containing information on migration flows and immigration policies over time.

Our main findings are as follows. First, confirming previous literature (such as Mayda 2010 and Grogger and Hanson 2011), we show that destination income per capita is a key determinant of migration choices. A 10 per cent increase in income per capita at a particular destination is associated to a 7.6 per cent increase in immigration flows. This elasticity doubles for intra-EU migration flows, reflecting the higher integration within the European Union. We also find that when a typical (non-European) immigrant destination, such as the USA, Canada, or Australia, tightens its entry laws immigration flows already fall after one year. Specifically, the introduction of a new law that tightens entry of immigrants for these countries reduces immigration by 6 per cent within the same year. Within the European Union the key laws affecting immigration flows are the treaties regulating the free movement of people within the Union.

Our paper is also related to the literature on the determinants of international flows of goods and people. Gravity regressions have become very popular in analyzing trade flows (e.g. Anderson and van Wincoop 2003; Chaney 2008; Helpman et al. 2008) primarily because they can be derived from an equilibrium model with optimizing firms. However, the literature on international migration flows has lagged behind. A large part of the literature on migration flows estimated similar models but often focusing on a single destination (and many origins) and using reduced-form models not well justified by a rational choice framework (Karemera et al. 2000; Pedersen et al. 2004; Garcia-Gomez and Lopez-Casasnovas 2006; Clark et al. 2007 among others). As a result, the empirical estimates, while informative and interesting, lacked a theoretical foundation. Recent work in this area includes Adsera and Pytlikova (2012) who focus on the role of linguistic distance, Beine et al. (2011) who focus on the role of networks in shaping international migration flows, and McKenzie et al. (2012), who exploit a unique dataset for migration out of the Philippines.[4] Our emphasis on the role of immigration policies on regulating inflows is inspired by the studies on the role of restrictions in ending the First Great Migration (Hatton and Williamson 2005; Hatton 2010).[5]

In a more structural fashion Grogger and Hanson (2011) analyzed the scale, selection, and sorting across destinations of migrants with different education levels using a model based on optimal migration choices. In econometric terms, their model is an application of the logit model by McFadden (1974). Their specification for the 'scale' of migration uses the difference between the log of the odds of migrating to a specific country and the log of the odds of not migrating at all as the dependent variable. In comparison, our model features only one type of labor (aggregated across education groups), but accommodates unobserved individual heterogeneity. Moreover, our model has a panel dimension that allows us to include a much richer set of fixed effects that control for origin-specific variables which are often not available or very imprecisely measured (as the countries of origin are many and often poor).[6] Our work is also related to the work by Bertocchi and Strozzi (2010) and Mayda (2010) on the evolution of immigration laws and citizenship, and their consequences for migration flows.[7]

The rest of the article is organized as follows. Section 2 describes the data. Section 3 presents the theoretical model of migration choices and derives the estimating equation. Section 4 presents the results and Section 5 concludes.

2. Data

Our data spans 15 countries of destination and 120 countries of origin over the period 1980–2006.[8] While the period we consider is dictated in large part by the availability of reliable and comparable data across most destination countries, there is also a logic in ending the period in 2006. Beginning in 2007 the onset of the great recession in several countries significantly disrupted migration flows, especially in Europe. Moreover the immigration policies that we are considering for Europe (the Maastricht Treaty and the Schengen Agreement) likely produced most of their effects by that date, while some more recent policies that we do not consider (the accession to the EU of some Eastern European countries) affected migration mainly post 2006. In Section 2.1 we describe in detail the construction and source of the immigration data. In Section 2.2 we present the sources and construction of the variables capturing the tightness of entry laws.

2.1 Migration flows

Our immigration data measure the yearly inflow of foreign citizens who intend to be residents in the receiving countries. This definition implies that we measure all foreign-born (or in some cases foreign nationals) who come to the country to reside there and not for temporary tourism, study, or business reasons.[9] To span the whole period of analysis we merged bilateral immigration data from three sources. The first source is Mayda (2010). That paper uses the original OECD series on flows of migrants that were discontinued in 1994 and extends them up to 2005. The second source is United Nations (2005), which reports very long time series but only for a subset of fifteen destination countries. This source goes back to the 1960s for some countries, but ends in the early

2000s for all of them. The third source is the International Migration Database (IMD) gathered by the OECD and available up to 2007.[10] The latter has the most extensive coverage in terms of destination and sending countries, but it only begins in 1998, and for some destinations it only has a few countries as sources. We have made sure that the definitions of immigrant are consistent across databases for each receiving country. All datasets use as primary sources the original data released by the statistical offices of each receiving country, which try to maintain internal consistency over time. In our checks we often find an exact coincidence of the figures in overlapping periods. Occasionally there are slight differences introducing discontinuities as we merge two series from different sources. The national data are based on population registers or residence permits. In both cases these are considered to be accurate measures of the entry of *legal* foreign nationals. Table A.1 in the Appendix summarizes the availability from each data source by destination country. To construct the final migration flows, starting with the UN migration data, we have filled in missing origin-destination-year observations using the IMD data. For the remaining cells we have used the data from Mayda (2010). In a small number of cases we have also interpolated observations to fill in missing values in intermediate years. We did this only when a data point for a bilateral migration flow was missing and both the previous and following years were available. While the OECD has made an effort (especially since 1995) to maintain a consistent definition of immigrants across countries, there are some differences between destination country definitions. An important one is that some countries define immigrants on the basis of the place of birth, and others on the basis of nationality. While this inconsistency can make a pure cross-country comparison inaccurate, our analysis focuses on changes within destination countries over time. While our gathering and organizing effort has produced what we think is a significant improvement on existing data, several limitations still exist. First of all only a limited number of receiving countries is covered, second we miss most of the outflows of migrants due to return migrants (who are often poorly recorded), third the timing of recording may not be the same as the time of entry. In view of these limitations, while our results are new and interesting, we certainly ought to take them with caution. Further empirical analysis and continued effort in data gathering will be crucial to reach a consensus on the proposed findings.

Figure 1 plots the total immigration rates in our data, defined as the total annual inflows into each destination country (aggregating across all origins), relative to the resident population in the country at the beginning of the year. A few observations are worth noting. First, immigration rates exhibit an upward trend in many countries: Belgium, Denmark, Italy, Norway, and New Zealand. Second, immigration flows were higher during the 1990s than in the 2000s for a group of countries. For example, annual inflows into Germany and Sweden peaked in the first half of the 1990s, reflecting the fall of the Iron Curtain and the Yugoslavian war, with the subsequent westward migration. Over our period of study, Spain has experienced a striking migration episode. Immigration flows into Spain during the 1980s were practically zero and, in fact, Spain exhibited net outflows during this decade. From the mid-1990s Spain received a spectacular immigration wave, with annual immigration rates much higher than all other countries in our sample (up to 1.5 per cent per year).[11] The main reason behind this immigration wave is the robust economic growth displayed by the Spanish economy starting in the mid-1980s and extending over two decades. It is also worth noting that housing and tourism were the main engines of economic

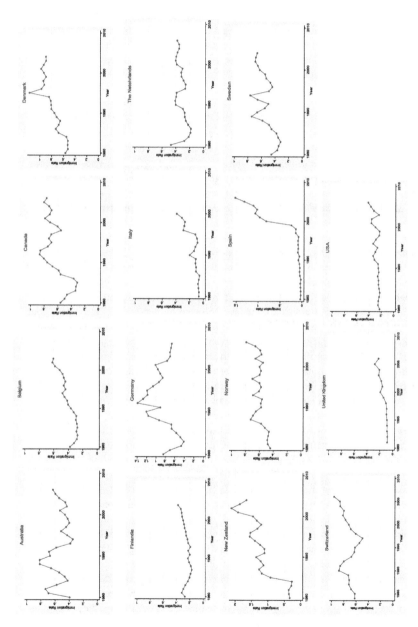

Figure 1. Yearly immigration flows as percentage of resident population; fifteen OECD countries.

growth, and both sectors have employed a very large fraction of immigrants (Gonzalez and Ortega (forthcoming)). At the same time the deep economic crises experienced by Argentina and Ecuador during this period, together with the tightened entry requirements into the USA, increased the relative attractiveness of Spain as an immigrant destination. Our empirical model is able to accommodate this large country heterogeneity in the relevant factors behind migration flows.

2.2 Immigration laws

Immigration policy has become very salient in many countries. The issue of allowing in (or trying to keep out) and absorbing existing immigrants is very contentious. The growing immigration pressure has driven some countries to adopt substantial reforms of their immigration laws, aiming at controlling immigration flows. On the other hand the need for the labor provided by some of these immigrants (particularly in agriculture, construction, and personal services) has pushed governments to create specific favored-entry categories or to be lenient ex-post with those who entered illegally, by passing amnesties. Among economists there has been a growing interest on the study of the determinants of immigration policy since the seminal paper by Benhabib (1996).[12] It remains unclear to what extent entry restrictions are able to control immigration flows.

An important contribution of this paper is the creation of a database and a classification for tightness of entry of immigration laws for the main OECD immigration countries categorized. Our starting points are the laws collected by Mayda and Patel (2004) and the Social Reforms database of the Fondazione Rodolfo DeBenedetti (FRDB, 2007). Mayda and Patel (2004) documented the main characteristics of the migration policies of several OECD countries between 1980 and 2000 and the changes in their legislations over time. The FRDB Social Reforms Database collects information about social reforms in the EU15 countries (except Luxembourg) over the period 1987–2005. We merged and updated these two datasets obtaining the complete set of immigration reforms in the period 1980–2006 for twelve of our fifteen OECD countries.[13] The resulting dataset includes more than 240 laws that we analyzed and classified. The list of immigration laws by country and year and a brief description of each of them can be found in the online appendix to the paper.[14]

We then constructed an index that captures the direction of the change in *entry tightness* associated to any major immigration law. Specifically, we initialize each country at zero in the first year. If no relevant policy changes occur, the variable remains constant. In the year when an immigration law is passed that entails a tightening of entry conditions the variable increases its value by one. On the contrary, relaxation of entry conditions reduces the degree of tightness by one. A reform is considered as tightening of entry laws if (i) it introduces or decreases quotas for entry, or (ii) it increases the requirements, fees, or documents for entry, or (iii) it increases requirements or the waiting time to obtain residence or work permits. There are several reforms that may indirectly affect ease of entry but do not explicitly fit any of the categories above. In those cases we classified them as loosening or tightening, or no change, by scrutinizing the content of each regulation.

Admittedly, this variable captures only one specific dimension of immigration policies, namely how numerically restricted and costly the process of admission to a country is.

Besides entry laws, other laws may also be relevant to migration decisions: integration and citizenship, access to public services and employment, and so on. We believe our narrow focus allows us to build a more precise measure that is closely linked to immigration flows.[15]

Figure 2 plots our index variable for *tightness of entry laws*. Recall that the initial value for each country has been set to 0. Hence only the within-country variation over time is meaningful and not the cross-country variation. Given that in all our regressions we include fixed receiving country effects, and hence, we identify the impact of explanatory variables on the within-country variation over time, this feature of the index does not affect our findings. A quick glance at the evolution of entry tightness over time reveals several episodes of substantial loosening of entry laws. For instance Canada and Germany relaxed their entry requirements since 1990, Sweden since the mid-1990s, and the USA between 1980 and the end of the 1990s. We can also identify episodes of tightening of entry laws: Denmark in the 2000s, and the USA beginning in year 2000 (essentially after the events of 11 September 2001). Overall there are more countries that have loosened their entry requirements than countries that have tightened them. However, many countries passed measures in opposite directions, ending up without a clear trend toward tightening or loosening, such as Spain or Belgium.

As several of the countries in our sample are in Europe we also build three additional policy variables that account for the evolution of the European integration process. We build destination–year indicator variables for the adoption of the Maastricht and Schengen treaties, and an origin–destination–year indicator for sharing a common currency. The Maastricht Treaty dummy takes a value of one after 1992 (year of the ratification of the treaty) for countries within the EU-15. For countries that joined the EU later it takes a value of one from the year of adhesion onward (across all origins). The Schengen Agreement, adopted in different years by different European countries, regulates and coordinates immigration and border policies among the signatory countries. While it eases intra-EU movement for citizens of the signatory countries, the Agreement also implies more restrictive border controls to enter the Schengen area. The corresponding dummy takes a value of one for destination countries participating in the Agreement only in the years in which the Agreement is in place and zero otherwise (across all origins). It is worth recalling that significant changes in migration laws were also produced by the enlargement of the European Union first in May 2004 (with the accession of Poland, Czech Republic, Slovakia, Hungary, and other Eastern European countries) and then in 2007 (with the accession of Bulgaria and Romania). These events, however, took place either at the very end or after the ending date of our data coverage and hence their consequences are not analyzed in this study. We leave the analysis of their impact to future research.

Data on income per capita is from the Penn World Tables (version 7.0), expressed in constant year 2000 US dollars at purchasing power parity. The other control variables are the logarithm of the inter-country distance, a dummy for sharing a contiguous border, a dummy for sharing a common language (not necessarily the official one) by large shares of the population, a dummy for having colonial ties, one for sharing legal origin and one for sharing a common currency. The latter variable is time-varying and even though it mostly reflects the creation and adoption of the European common currency, there are several other instances of countries sharing currency, as we discuss below. These variables are from Glick and Rose (2002) and Head et al. (2010).

54   •   FRANCESC ORTEGA AND GIOVANNI PERI

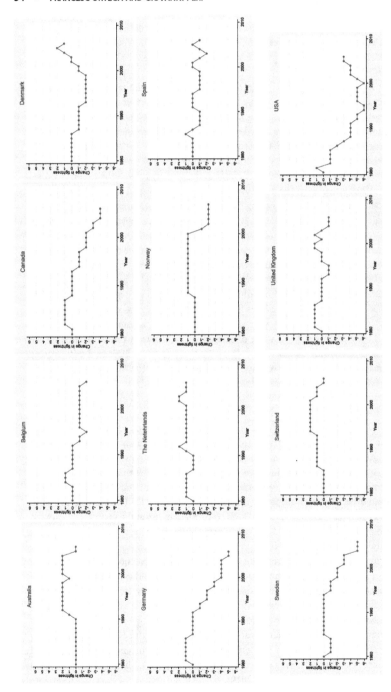

Figure 2. Changes in tightness of immigration entry laws over time; twelve OECD countries.

3. Determinants of international migration flows

This section presents a model of migration choice across multiple locations and derives an estimating equation. Our specification is consistent both with a simple logit model (McFadden 1974) as well as with a nested logit model (McFadden 1978). Our migration model extends Grogger and Hanson (2011) by allowing for unobserved individual heterogeneity between migrants and non-migrants. It is plausible that migrants systematically differ from non-migrants along important dimensions that are hard to measure, such as ability, risk aversion, and the psychological costs of living far from home. An additional attractive feature of our empirical specification is that it is reminiscent of a generalized gravity equation in which the logarithm of bilateral migration flows is a function of origin- and destination-country fixed effects and overall bilateral migration costs.

3.1 Migration model

We study the problem of the migration choice across multiple destinations: $d \in D = \{1, \ldots, N_D\}$. Agent i, born in country of origin $o \in D$, decides whether to stay in o or to migrate to any other country. We denote by $D_o = D, \{o\}$ the set of potential destinations for individuals born in country o, by excluding the country of origin.

The utility from staying at the origin is given by:

$$U_{ooi} = V_{oo} + \nu_{ooi}, \tag{1}$$

where the V_{oo} is deterministic and country-of-origin specific and ν_{ooi} is stochastic and individual specific. The first term captures the average utility of staying in country o while the second is an idiosyncratic individual-specific term. Analogously, the utility from migrating to destination $d \in D_o$ is

$$U_{odi} = V_{od} + \nu_{odi}. \tag{2}$$

In this case the deterministic component of the utility varies by origin and destination pair so as to allow for bilateral costs of migration. Specifically, we shall assume that $V_{od} = W_d - C_{od}$, where W_d is the present value of the expected earnings at destination and C_{od} encompasses the deterministic component of the costs of migrating to country d from origin o. The stochastic terms ν_{ooi} and ν_{odi} in these equations capture unobserved components of the individual utility associated with each choice. Grogger and Hanson (2011) adopt the standard logit assumption, namely, that all stochastic terms are identically and independently distributed as type-I extreme value. While highly tractable, the logit model imposes very strong assumptions on substitution patterns.[16]

We wish to consider a more general stochastic specification. The reason is that it is highly plausible that migrants may differ systematically from non-movers in aspects that are very hard to measure, such as talent, risk-aversion, or the psychological cost of living abroad. That is to say, there may be individual unobserved factors that induce correlations across the disturbance terms of equations (1) and (2). Specifically, we assume that the stochastic term of the stay option is simply $\nu_{ooi} = \varepsilon_{ooi}$ while for each destination $d \in D_o$ we have $\nu_{odi} = \zeta_i + \varepsilon_{odi}$ where ζ_i is drawn from a probability distribution with mean zero and is uncorrelated with ε_{odi}. These individual random effects, however, are allowed to be correlated. In particular, we allow migrants to have correlated utility within a destination. This implies that migrants could be a selected group and our structure takes care of this selection, correlated within destination countries. The random variables ε_{ooi} and ε_{odi} are all identically and independently distributed as type-I extreme value. These assumptions on the stochastic components of the model give rise to the nested-logit model (McFadden 1978), which allows for more general substitution patterns while still remaining analytically tractable.[17] In particular, it allows for closed-form solutions for the choice probabilities of staying in the country of origin (P_o) or migrating to destination $d \in D_o, P_o$:

$$P_o = \frac{e^{V_{oo}}}{e^{V_{oo}} + \left(\sum_{j \in D_o} e^{V_{od}/\tau}\right)^{\tau}} \tag{3}$$

$$P_d = \frac{\left(\sum_{j \in D_o} e^{V_{oj}/\tau}\right)^{\tau}}{e^{V_{oo}} + \left(\sum_{j \in D_o} e^{V_{oj}/\tau}\right)^{\tau}} \cdot \frac{e^{V_{od}/\tau}}{\sum_{j \in D_o} e^{V_{oj}/\tau}} \cdot \tag{4}$$

Simple algebra delivers the following *log odds ratios*:[18]

$$\ln \frac{P_d}{P_o} = \left(\frac{V_{od}}{\tau} - V_{oo}\right) - (1 - \tau)\left(\ln \sum_{j \in D_o} e^{V_{oj}/\tau}\right) \text{ for } d \in D_o \tag{5}$$

$$\ln \frac{P_d}{P_f} = \frac{V_{od}}{V_{of}} \text{ for } d, f \in D_o. \tag{6}$$

As in the logit model, the odds ratio between two destinations depends only on the relative attractiveness between those two destinations (equation (6)). However, the odds ratio between the origin and any given destination (equation (5)) contains an additional term, which corrects for the correlation across destinations induced by the individual-specific unobserved characteristics (selection).[19]

The probability that an individual chooses one location approximately coincides in the aggregate population with the share of individuals born in country o that choose that particular location.[20] Thus $P_d = n_{od}/\sum_{j=1}^{D} n_{oj}$ where n_{oj} denotes the number of individuals born in country o that choose location j. Hence, expression (5) can be written as

$$\ln n_{od} = \ln n_{oo} + \left(\frac{V_{od}}{\tau} - V_{oo}\right) - (1 - \tau)\left(\ln \sum_{j \in D_o} e^{V_{oj}/\tau}\right). \tag{7}$$

It is important to note that except for V_{od} all terms in the right-hand side of the equation are constant across destinations and only vary by country of origin.[21] Over time different locations will experience different levels of income and wages, which will affect their relative attractiveness and, hence, the shares of migrants that they will receive. By considering a period-specific choice we derive the multi-period version of the previous relationship:

$$\ln n_{od}^t = \ln n_{oo}^t + \left(\frac{V_{od}^t}{\tau} - V_{oo}^t\right) - (1 - \tau)\left(\ln \sum_{j \in D_o} e^{V_{oj}^t/\tau}\right), \qquad (8)$$

for any destination $d \in D_o$ in time period t.

3.2 Estimating equation

Let us consider how we can estimate the relationship we just derived on the basis of panel data on bilateral migration flows.[22] Equation (8) can be rewritten as

$$\ln n_{odt} = \alpha_{ot} + \beta V_{odt} + \epsilon_{odt} , \qquad (9)$$

which features origin-by-year fixed effects (α_{ot}) capturing all time-varying terms that are constant across destinations $d \in D_o$ and only vary by year and country of origin, namely the first and third term in the right-hand side of expression (8). The term ϵ_{odt} accounts for measurement error due to the fact that we approximate probabilities with frequencies in the finite sample.

Now we can be more specific about the variables that determine the average attractiveness of a particular destination for all individuals. We assume that V_{odt} is as follows:

$$V_{odt} = \beta W_{dt} + \alpha_d + \pi T_{dt} + \gamma_2 X_{od}. \qquad (10)$$

For a particular destination d, the term W_{dt} denotes the expected earnings at that destination in year t, which we shall proxy with income per capita. α_d represents a destination country fixed effect that accounts for time-invariant characteristics of the receiving country that also influence migration decisions, such as institutions, culture, and attitudes toward immigration that vary a lot across countries, but very slowly within countries over time. The variable T_{dt} which varies over time and across countries, stands for the *tightness of entry laws* described above. Presumably, when a particular destination tightens its entry requirements, the cost of choosing that destination increases (and the utility falls) as it becomes more costly to enter the country. Finally the term X_{od} accounts for country-pair-specific variables that affect the cost of migration from a given origin to a particular destination. This cost is a function of bilateral geographical distance, cultural distance (measured by a common language), past colonial ties between the two countries, whether the two countries share a common currency, and so on.

4. Results

4.1 Descriptive statistics

Table 1 reports descriptive statistics for the main variables used in the analysis. Specifically, this table reports averages across years and country pairs. The observations span the period 1980–2006 annually, with missing values for some countries. The average bilateral

Table 1. Summary statistics for the main variables

Variable	Observations	Mean	SD	Min	Max
Bilateral migration flow	45,565	1,498.21	7,239.56	0	455,075
GDP/Pop in destination	41,515	23,990.49	9,750.22	4,354.15	66,964.37
GDP/Pop in origin	38,877	6,560.86	9,833.51	62.95	89,563.63
Migration costs					
Distance	41,515	7,366.26	4,402.26	160.93	19,516.56
Contiguous	41,515	0.02	0.14	0	1
Common language	41,515	0.19	0.40	0	1
Common currency	41,515	0.02	0.13	0	1
Common legislation	41,515	0.22	0.42	0	1
Colonial ties	41,515	0.04	0.21	0	1
Tightness of entry laws	35,805	−0.90	1.99	−6	2
Maastricht	35,805	0.25	0.43	0	1
Schengen	35,805	0.21	0.41	0	1

Note: the sources for each variable are described in the text. Common language takes a value of one if a substantial share of the population in the two countries shares a common language. We constructed the variables on tightness of entry, Maastricht and Schengen.

migration flow is 1,498 individuals, with a very large standard deviation. Several country pairs have zero migration flows between them. The largest flows, experienced between Mexico and the USA in the years around 2000 and between Poland and Germany in the years around 1990, were as large as 300,000 people per year. As one would expect, the average income (GDP) per person at destination is much larger than the average GDP per capita among countries of origin (by a factor of almost four). We proxy for migration costs using bilateral distance and dummy variables for contiguous countries, common language, common legal origin, colonial ties (the countries were in the same colonial empire), and a common currency.[23] Finally, we also have three policy variables. The average of the entry tightness variable takes on a negative value which indicates that across years and countries, entry laws were loosened more often than they were tightened. We also include Maastricht and Schengen indicator variables. On average, these indicators take the value of one for 21–25 per cent of the origin–destination–year observations.

Table 2 reports destination country averages across years. Column 1 reports the average yearly flow of immigrants (across years) for the average bilateral pair involving each specific destination country and all origins. Germany and the USA report the highest average bilateral migration flows. Column 2 reports the average population size (in millions) in the country of destination and Column 3 shows the average population in the country of origin for that destination. Similarly, Columns 4 and 5 report GDP per person for the destination country and for the average country of origin for that destination. Clearly, income per person is several times larger in the destination country than in the average of the countries of origin. These ratios range from 1.5 (for destination New Zealand) to 5.7 (destination Norway), as reported in Column 6. The average across all destinations is 3.8.

Table 2. Main variables in destination country: average over the considered period

Destination country	(1) Yearly average bilateral flow of immigrants	(2) Population in destination	(3) Population in origin	(4) GDP/ population destination	(5) GDP/ population origin	(4)/(5)
Australia	737	18.1	34.1	21,305	6,068	3.5
Belgium	1,023	10.1	49.2	21,498	7,208	3.0
Canada	1,002	28.6	28.7	20,105	5,541	3.6
Denmark	300	5.2	35.6	27,541	5,510	5.0
Finland	102	5.0	32.2	22,132	5,402	4.1
Germany	5,019	80.6	32.4	22,430	5,540	4.0
Italy	1,443	57.0	29.6	17,945	5,279	3.4
Netherlands	781	15.3	30.0	22,335	5,578	4.0
New Zealand	727	3.7	73.4	15,114	10,317	1.5
Norway	169	4.3	29.2	31,486	5,496	5.7
Spain	2,028	39.6	33.3	13,087	5,504	2.4
Sweden	309	8.7	30.1	25,096	5,370	4.7
Switzerland	2,747	7.0	54.4	36,427	8,277	4.4
UK	1,223	59.0	46.9	25,445	8,368	3.0
USA	3,991	261.2	27.4	26,421	5,505	4.8

Note: The period considered for all countries is 1980–2006, however, some countries have missing data in the early part of the sample. Columns 2 and 3 are in millions of individuals. Columns 4 and 5 are in PPP year-2000 US Dollars.

4.2 Income per capita and bilateral costs as determinants of migration flows

We now estimate our main migration model in equation (9). Mainly, the dependent variable is the log of annual migration flows (plus one) between a particular country pair. This allows us to maintain the exact logarithmic specification, obtained from our model, and at the same time keep the information from the zero-migration pairs. Our main hypothesis is that income per capita at destination has a positive effect on migration flows, given income per capita at the origin. Variables that proxy for higher costs of migration (such as geographical or cultural distance) are expected to have a negative effect while having colonial ties or a common currency is likely to facilitate migration between a given pair of countries.[24]

Let us emphasize that, relative to the existing literature, which mainly uses cross-sectional data (such as Grogger and Hanson 2011) or data relative to only one destination country (such as Clark et al. 2007), this paper uses a full panel specification with multiple origins, multiple destinations, and several years. This allows us to control much more carefully for origin and destination country-specific factors, identifying the effects of income and immigration policies based solely on within-destination-country variation over time.

Table 3 presents the results from estimating specification (9). The explanatory variables are the logs of income per person at destination and origin (lagged one year), the log of distance, and dummy variables for sharing a border, sharing a common language, having a common currency, or having colonial ties.[25] In general, the sign and significance of bilateral variables is as expected. Distance significantly decreases migration flows, while sharing a border, sharing the official language, sharing legal origins, and having been part of the same colonial empire all significantly increase the size of bilateral migration.[26] Across specifications we vary the sets of fixed effects that we include (in the form of dummy variables). In the theoretically justified specification (Columns 4 and beyond), we include a full vector of origin-year dummy variables. They capture factors, including the unobserved heterogeneity between migrants and non-migrants, that vary across origin and year but not destination. Column 1 does not include any fixed effects and Column 2 includes only destination fixed effects. In these two sets of specifications, the point estimates of the income coefficients are not as expected (the sign of the destination income is negative), suggesting the presence of origin–year specific confounding effects. Column 3 includes both origin fixed effects and destination fixed effects. This specification, which is closer to what our theoretical model implies, delivers the expected signs: income per capita at destination is positively associated with migration flows, while income per capita at origin appears to have a negative effect. A 1 per cent increase in income per capita at destination is associated with a 0.54 per cent increase in migration flows from each origin country. Likewise a 1 per cent increase in income per capita at the origin appears to reduce migration flows to each destination by about 0.33 per cent. Previous estimates found, sometimes, an ambiguous effect of income per capita in the country of origin on migration. Some have argued that income may affect emigration positively up to a certain income level (by reducing the poverty trap and relaxing the budget constraint for migrants) and then, once potential migrants become richer, further increase in income may affect migration negatively. However, in our case, in which we control for country fixed effects, splitting countries between those with income below the World median and those above gives very similar coefficients on the country of origin income. In a specification as 3 in Table 3 the coefficients on income per person in the country of origin, allowing for different effects (not reported in the table), is estimated at −0.31 for origin countries below the World median income and −0.32 for those above.

Column 4 is the first column including the whole vector of origin–year fixed effects, besides destination fixed effects and hence is the one *consistent with our model*. In this case, note that the effect of income per capita in the country of origin is absorbed by the origin–year fixed effects and hence we do not have an estimate of it. As expected, income per capita in the destination country has a positive and significant effect on migration flows. The effect is estimated precisely (at around 0.6), and the results are very robust. Hence this specification reveals that it is very important to use panel data and to control for unobserved shocks and heterogeneity in order to obtain the correct estimates of the effect of income on migration flows. While the model is a very simplified representation of migration decisions and, as acknowledged above, the data have limitations, it is very encouraging to see that the preferred model has the flexibility needed to obtain reasonable results. The signs of the control variables are also all as expected and significant. Geographic distance reduces migration flows while common language, currency, legislation, or a shared colonial past all

Table 3. Income per capita, bilateral costs, and migration flows

Specification: Dep. variable: ln(1 + migration)	(1)	(2)	(3)	(4)	(5)	(6)	(7)	(8)	(9)	(10)
Lagged Ln(GDP/Pop) destination	-0.14***	0.62***	0.54***	0.63***	1.82***	0.57***	0.78***	0.56***	0.38***	0.41***
	(0.05)	(0.10)	(0.06)	(0.06)	(0.17)	(0.14)	(0.07)	(0.07)	(0.04)	(0.13)
Lagged Ln GDP/Pop origin	0.22***	0.21***	-0.33***							
	(0.01)	(0.01)	(0.02)							
Ln distance	-0.56***	-0.76***	-0.99***	-0.98***	-0.52***	-1.61***	-0.89***	-0.99***		-1.03***
	(0.02)	(0.02)	(0.01)	(0.01)	(0.06)	(0.03)	(0.02)	(0.01)		(0.03)
Contiguous	1.39***	0.89***	0	-0.04	0.65***	-0.79***	0.49***	-0.06		-0.12
	(0.09)	(0.08)	(0.05)	(0.05)	(0.06)	(0.16)	(0.07)	(0.05)		(0.12)
Common language	1.04***	0.27***	0.54***	0.58***	-0.37***	1.01***	0.82***	0.58***		0.62***
	(0.04)	(0.03)	(0.03)	(0.03)	(0.08)	(0.04)	(0.03)	(0.03)		(0.06)
Common currency	0.29***	0.03	0.53***	0.96***	0.27***	0.94***	0.71***	0.91***	0.53***	0.86***
	(0.10)	(0.09)	(0.06)	(0.06)	(0.07)	(0.12)	(0.08)	(0.06)	(0.05)	(0.13)
Common legislation	0.36***	0.19***	0.38***	0.33***	0.78***		0.27***	0.34***		0.30***
	(0.03)	(0.03)	(0.02)	(0.02)	(0.05)		(0.02)	(0.02)		(0.05)
Colonial ties	0.80***	1.31***	1.37***	1.48***	0.57***	0.30***	1.46***	1.52***		1.47***
	(0.06)	(0.06)	(0.04)	(0.04)	(0.10)	(0.09)	(0.05)	(0.04)		(0.09)
Observations	37852	37852	37852	40307	4,374	14,643	59314	34610	40,307	7,540
R-squared	0.16	0.37	0.77	0.79	0.79	0.88	0.67	0.8	0.94	0.80
Fixed effects										
Year	Yes	Yes	Yes	Yes	Yes	Yes	Yes	Yes	Yes	Yes
Destination	No	Yes	Yes	Yes	Yes	Yes	Yes	Yes	Yes	Yes
Origin	No	No	Yes	Yes	Yes	Yes	Yes	Yes	Yes	Yes
Origin-year	No	No	No	Yes	Yes	Yes	Yes	Yes	Yes	Yes
Origin-destination	No	No	No	No	No	No	No	No	Yes	No
Sample	All	All	All	All	Europe	non-Europe	All - Zeros	1985-2005	All	All (5-year)

Note: All models include an intercept. Column 5 includes only European country pairs. Column 6 includes only non-European destinations (and all origins). Column 10 uses only data for years 1985, 1990, 1995, 2000, and 2005. Standard errors in parenthesis are heteroskedasticity robust and clustered by country-pair. ***, **, *significant at 1%, 5%, 10% level.

increase bilateral migration flows.[27] In Column 5, we restrict the analysis to the subsample of European origin and European destination country pairs. We notice a large increase in the point estimate of per capita income at destination as a determinant of the flows. The estimated coefficient suggests an elasticity of destination income per capita of 1.82. At the same time most of the controls now exhibit much lower point estimates (in absolute value). This suggests that, within Europe, barriers to migration are much less important, and migration is much more sensitive to economic conditions at destination, once we control for income per capita and other time-varying factors at the origin. Column 6 reports the estimates when we restrict the analysis to the subsample of non-European destinations (and all origins). These estimates are very similar to those obtained in Column 4 using the whole sample (elasticity 0.57).

Columns 7–10 perform several robustness checks. In Column 7 we replace all missing values for bilateral migration flows by zeros, which increases the sample size by about 50 per cent. This is because in many instances some countries do not report small bilateral flows. Hence a reasonable approximation is to replace those entries with a zero value. The estimated coefficient for the income variable is only slightly larger (0.78) than that shown in Column 4. Column 8 restricts the estimation to the subsample of 1985–2005, for which we have relatively fewer missing values than for the whole sample period (1980– 2006). Again, the point estimate (0.56) is essentially unaffected. Column 9 includes a full set of origin–destination dummy variables, which absorb all time-invariant bilateral variables that affect migration flows.[28] This is a very demanding specification as we absorb all bilateral-specific factors as well as all origin by time factors. Still, we obtain that the destination income per capita plays a highly significant role in determining migration flows, with a slightly lower elasticity of 0.38.[29] Finally, Column 10 reports the estimates obtained on a subsample where only five-year periods are considered (1985, 1990, 1995, 2000, and 2005). Short-term confounding factors and reverse causality of immigration on income are arguably less of a concern with longer time lags in the explanatory variables. Moreover a five-year interval allows a fuller response of migration flows to variation of income and of other variables. The estimated elasticity of migration to income per person at destination is 0.41, very significant and quantitatively close to our preferred estimate (0.63).

Although we need caution in interpreting the results due to the highly stylized nature of the model and to data limitations, Table 3 provides evidence that the empirical specification implemented in regressions (4–10) delivers plausible and fairly robust estimates. Income per person in the destination country is a very important determinant of migration, particularly among countries with low barriers to migration (such as within Europe).[30] Changes in income per person have significant short-run (one year) as well as medium-run (five years) effects on immigration flows.

4.3 The role of immigration restrictions

In this section we extend the previous regression model by including a vector of time-varying immigration policies. Policy makers and researchers are interested in evaluating the effectiveness of immigration restrictions in controlling immigration flows. Historically, restrictions have played a crucial role but it is unclear whether the same is true in the current context with lower transportation and communication costs and stronger economic incentives to migrate between poor and rich countries.[31] Specifically, we consider our measure of *tightness of entry laws*. This is an indicator that records the introduction of immigration laws and their direction in tightening or loosening ease of entry. We also include two more indicator variables to account for the increasing degree of economic interaction within Europe, namely indicators for the presence of the Maastricht and Schengen treaties, and bilateral dummies for having a common currency.[32]

The Maastricht Treaty, formally known as the Treaty of the European Union, was signed in February 1992 and became operative from 1993. It ushered in the first major step from a common market toward greater economic and political ties among its member countries. The Treaty led to the creation of the Euro and reorganized the main institutions of the European Union. For our purposes it is worth noting that the Maastricht Treaty increased cooperation in asylum, immigration, and foreign policy, but it had no major implications for immigration from outside the European Union. The Treaty also restated the principle of an internal market, characterized by the free movement of goods, persons, services, and capital. It also lifted the remaining restrictions on migration from Spain and Portugal to other EU countries, while citizens of the other EU Member States were already free to move and work within the EU.

The Schengen Agreement was signed in June 1985 and implemented ten years later. Initially, only five countries signed the Agreement but over time the number of countries signing in has increased. Its main goal was to create a large area with free internal labor mobility and a common external frontier. Specifically, this Treaty laid the guidelines for harmonization of entry and short stays by non-EU citizens, asylum matters, and police and judicial cooperation among the country members. The Schengen Agreement can be interpreted as a tightening of the EU border vis-à-vis the rest of the world. For instance, the harmonization mandated by the Agreement forced some countries to severe some ties with former colonies. Spain was asked to eliminate its visa waiver programs with some former colonies (e.g. Colombia in 2001 and Ecuador in 2003). The Agreement also led to the swift removal of border posts, which despite its strong symbolism, did not add much to the existing effective free internal mobility of European workers within the European Union.[33]

Before presenting the results we need to add some caveats. All variables, and especially the indicator of *tightness of entry laws,* are rather coarse proxies for capturing the stance of immigration laws. The fact that we consider only the introduction of laws, and not details about their implementation, the fact that we cannot quantify how 'significant' the law is and that we only include laws explicitly affecting entry all contribute to make our measure imperfect. Nevertheless as we are pioneering the introduction of variables capturing specific immigration laws, and given the significant effort involved in collecting those laws, it is still very interesting to measure their impact on migration. With this in mind we move to presenting the empirical results.

On the basis of their content we would expect a positive effect of the Maastricht Treaty on subsequent migration flows. Specifically, it probably enhanced migration flows within the European Union, leaving inflows from outside unaffected. Regarding the Schengen Agreement we expect a negative effect on migration flows since it increased migration requirements (and, implicitly, migration costs) for non-EU migrants, while probably not having an effect on internal migration. Of course, the two variables are highly correlated, however, the correlation coefficient is well below one (0.70). Countries differed in their timing of accession to the EU. In addition, some countries have opted out of one of the treaties. In particular, the UK signed the Maastricht Treaty (in 1993) but opted out of the Schengen Agreement, as well as Ireland. In addition, some non-EU members also participated in the Schengen Agreement (Iceland, Norway, Liechtenstein, and Switzerland).

Table 4 reports our estimates of specification (9) including the immigration policy variables. As in the previous table, the dependent variable is the log of annual migration flows (plus one). Besides lagged income per capita at destination and the same set of control variables and fixed effects as in specification 4 of Table 3, we now include the time-varying immigration policy variables. Columns 1 and 2 include the entry policy variable either measured in the same year as the immigration flows (specification 1) or lagged one period (specification 2). The policies should affect migration flows from the very first year that they become law. However, some implementation delay may generate stronger effects with some lag. The coefficient on income per capita are slightly larger than in the previous table (0.78–0.79 as opposed to 0.63 in Column 4 in the previous table), and highly significant. The degree of tightness of entry laws has a significant negative effect, indicating that as countries tighten their entry conditions immigration flows already fall within the same year and (even more) the following year. The Maastricht and Schengen indicator variables are introduced in Column 3 and also have the expected signs: the former is associated with an increase in total migration flows while the latter had a negative effect. Sharing a common currency also appears to have a significant and positive effect on the size of migration flows.

In Column 4 we restrict the analysis to European country pairs. Two points are worth noting. First, the coefficient on income doubles, suggesting a much larger elasticity of migration flows to income per capita within the European economic area, as was the case in the previous table as well. Second, the coefficient of the Maastricht Treaty takes on a larger positive value, reflecting the large effect that the process of European economic integration has on within-Europe migration flows. The Schengen Agreement now is not statistically significant, supporting our expectation that its main effect was to reduce inflows from outside the European Union. The coefficient on entry tightness now appears to be positive and significant. This reflects the tightening of entry laws by European countries *vis-à-vis non-EU immigrants* at the same time as internal restrictions to worker mobility were being eliminated. Column 5 reports the estimates for the subsample of non-European destination countries (and all origins). As expected, the point estimate on income per capita at destination is now lower (0.42), but still highly significant. Also the coefficient on entry tightness is still negative and significant, and much larger in absolute value (-0.06 versus -0.02 earlier).

In order to allow for a differential effect of entry laws on migration from within the European Union, we include an interaction of entry tightness and a European origin country indicator variable. As expected, in Columns 6 through 9 we find a negative effect of entry tightness on inflows from outside the European Union, while negligible effects on within-Europe migration flows (that is, the sum of the two coefficients), which are mostly affected by accession to the EU and the subsequent adoption of the Maastricht Treaty. Column 6 shows that the results are robust to dropping the observations for the first few years and for the last year, which feature more missing values.

Column 8 reports the estimates for a specification that replaces the origin–year dummies by an origin-specific cubic time trend. Of course, this is less flexible than the whole set of

Table 4. The role of immigration policy: tightness of entry laws

Dep. variable: ln(1+migration)	1 Basic	2 Lag(policy)	3 EU policies	4 Europe only	5 Non-Europe	6 With Interaction	7 1985–2000	8 Polyn-trend	9 Linear trend	10 Long-diff
Lagged Ln GDP/Pop dest.	0.78***	0.79***	0.76***	1.90***	0.42***	0.76***	0.71***	0.54***	0.50***	0.71**
	(0.07)	(0.07)	(0.08)	(0.22)	(0.14)	(0.08)	(0.09)	(0.05)	(0.04)	(0.33)
Entry tightness	−0.02***	−0.03***	−0.02***	0.07***	−0.06***	−0.03***	−0.04***	−0.02***	−0.02***	−0.05***
	(0.01)	(0.01)	(0.01)	(0.02)	(0.01)	(0.01)	(0.01)	(0.01)	(0.01)	(0.02)
Entry tightness *European origin						0.04***	0.05***	0.04***	0.04***	
						(0.01)	(0.01)	(0.01)	(0.01)	
Maastricht			0.10***	0.29***		0.10***	0.14***	−0.00	−0.00	
			(0.04)	(0.08)		(0.04)	(0.04)	(0.03)	(0.03)	
Schengen			−0.11***	0.05		−0.11***	−0.11***	−0.03	−0.03	
			(0.03)	(0.07)		(0.03)	(0.03)	(0.03)	(0.03)	
Common currency	1.02***	1.02***	1.02***	0.10	1.04***	1.02***	0.96***	1.02***	1.01***	0.86***
	(0.06)	(0.06)	(0.06)	(0.08)	(0.11)	(0.06)	(0.07)	(0.06)	(0.06)	(0.26)
Ln Distance	−0.98***	−0.98***	−0.98***	−0.64***	−1.52***	−0.98***	−0.98***	−0.98***	−0.98***	−1.59***
	(0.02)	(0.02)	(0.02)	(0.07)	(0.03)	(0.02)	(0.02)	(0.01)	(0.01)	(0.07)
Contiguous	−0.08	−0.08	−0.08	0.53***	−0.53***	−0.07	−0.09	−0.07	−0.08	−0.69*
	(0.06)	(0.06)	(0.06)	(0.07)	(0.17)	(0.06)	(0.06)	(0.05)	(0.05)	(0.37)
Common language	0.67***	0.66***	0.67***	−0.46***	1.06***	0.66***	0.67***	0.67***	0.67***	1.08***
	(0.03)	(0.03)	(0.03)	(0.08)	(0.04)	(0.03)	(0.03)	(0.03)	(0.03)	(0.09)

(continued)

Table 4. Continued

Dep. variable: ln(1+migration)	1 Basic	2 Lag(policy)	3 EU policies	4 Europe only	5 Non-Europe	6 With Interaction	7 1985-2000	8 Polyn-trend	9 Linear trend	10 Long-diff
Common legislation	0.25***	0.25***	0.25***	0.84***		0.25***	0.25***	0.25***	0.25***	
	(0.02)	(0.02)	(0.02)	(0.05)		(0.02)	(0.02)	(0.02)	(0.02)	
Colony	1.42***	1.41***	1.42***	0.15	-0.17*	1.43***	1.51***	1.43***	1.43***	-0.15
	(0.04)	(0.04)	(0.04)	(0.12)	(0.10)	(0.04)	(0.04)	(0.04)	(0.04)	(0.23)
Observations	34,749	34,749	34,749	3,620	13,469	34,749	29,746	34,749	34,749	2,537
R-squared	0.80	0.80	0.80	0.79	0.90	0.80	0.80	0.79	0.78	0.91
Fixed effects										
Destination	Yes	Yes	Yes	Yes	Yes	Yes	Yes	Yes	Yes	Yes
Origin-year	Yes	Yes	Yes	Yes	Yes	Yes	Yes	No	No	Yes
Origin-time trend	No	No	No	No	No	No	No	Cubic	Linear	No
Sample	All	All	All	Europe	Non-Europe	All	1985-2005	All	All	Non-Europe (5-year)

Note: All specifications include destination and origin-year fixed effects. Column 4 includes only European country pairs. Column 5 includes only non-European destinations (and all origins). The sample in Column 10 is analogous to Column 1 but uses only data for years 1980, 1985, 1990, 1995, 2000, and 2005. Standard errors in parenthesis are heteroskedasticity robust and clustered by country-pair. ***, **, *significant at 1%, 5%, 10% level.

origin–year dummies but it is much faster to implement.[34] As we can see, the coefficient on income per capita at destination falls slightly (from 0.76 in Column 5 to 0.54) but retains its significance. The effect on tightening entry laws remains largely unchanged. Column 9 employs a more simplistic origin-specific linear time trend, with very similar results. On the basis of these findings, we conclude that origin-specific polynomial time trends are able to replace the large set of origin–year dummies reasonably well and hence can be used instead of the more demanding model with country-by-year effects in shorter panels.

Column 10 reports an important robustness check, where we employ long (five-year) differences, as we did already in the last column of Table 3. The number of observations is drastically reduced as we only consider five-year differences. The results, however, confirm the findings in Column 4, with a positive and significant effect of destination income per capita and a negative and significant effect of entry tightness. While five years may not be long enough for all the immigration laws to produce their effect it is certainly a significant step towards the long-run. It appears, in fact, that in the medium run the impact of immigration laws tightening entry conditions is stronger than in the short run. This is very reasonable as immigrant inflow may take some time to respond to the immigration laws of a country.

Let us emphasize that these estimates are based on a very demanding specification, featuring hundreds of fixed effects. As a result, the identifying variation behind our estimates is very specific: within-destination variation over time, after controlling for origin–year variation. We are not aware of any previous analysis that provided estimates of the roles of per capita income and immigration restrictions based on such a demanding specification.

In conclusion, the estimates in Table 4 deliver a preferred elasticity of migration flows to destination per capita income of 0.76 (Column 2). However, this estimate averages the very high elasticity for within-Europe migration flows (1.90, Column 3) and a lower value (0.42, Column 4) for migration flows to non-European destinations. Analogously, legislation that tightens entry laws is associated with reductions in migration flows (about 2 percentage points for the typical restrictive law) but this effect largely arises from non-European destinations. For European country pairs, the treaties governing the European integration process are the fundamental aspects of immigration policy. The Maastricht Treaty increased significantly the intra-European mobility, while the Schengen Agreement has reduced immigration flows from outside the European Union. Our results suggest that as barriers to internal labor mobility within the EU have fallen there has been a tightening of entry laws vis-à-vis immigration from the rest of the world. Let us emphasize, in concluding this section, that the limitations of the existing immigration data (measurement error, potential heterogeneity of sources) and of the variables measuring immigration policy call for some caution in interpreting the results. While our estimates deliver rather robust and plausible implications, further work is needed in order to understand the effects of immigration policy on immigration flows.

5. Conclusions

This article takes two important steps in the direction of establishing and implementing a common framework to analyze the economic and policy determinants of international migration flows, guided by the more developed empirical literature on international trade flows. First, we propose a discrete-choice migration model with unobserved heterogeneity at the individual level that incorporates a rich structure for migration costs. We exploit the nesting structure that arises from our model to derive an estimating equation for aggregate bilateral migration flows, which we estimate using a large annual panel of origin–destination countries over time. This provides a stronger identification for the roles of income and migration policies in determining migration flows. Second, we gather a new dataset containing information on immigration policies (tightness of entry laws and economic integration within Europe) over time for the main immigrant destinations.

We find several interesting results. First, a 1 per cent increase in income per capita at a given destination is associated with a 0.76 per cent increase in immigration flows. This elasticity is twice as large for intra-EU migration flows, reflecting the higher degree of mobility within the European Union. Second, when a typical (non-European) immigrant destination, such as the USA, Canada, or Australia, tightens its entry laws, immigration flows fall by about 6 per cent. Third, in Europe the Maastricht Treaty has significantly increased internal migration by around 10 per cent, while the Schengen Treaty has decreased immigration from outside the EU.

Overall, our results suggest that the existing large income per capita differences between rich and poor countries will continue to generate large international worker mobility. However, national immigration policies also play a large role in determining the size of these flows, as had already been the case in the past (Hatton and Williamson 2005). We also find that regional European economic integration has had a large effect on the size and pattern of migration flows for European destinations. Ultimately, these policies reflect voters' views of the socioeconomic effects of immigration on the receiving countries. Immigration researchers should therefore continue to make progress in the study of the channels through which economies absorb immigrants, particularly in the current context of increasing economic interdependence.[35]

We conclude by suggesting avenues for future research. We think that more work is needed to understand the microfoundations of aggregate migration flows. In particular, we need a better understanding of the nature of migration costs and how immigration policies shape these costs. More research should also be directed to understanding migration decisions in response to macroeconomic shocks, particularly in the current context of highly asymmetric shocks among European countries. In terms of data the priority should be on assembling large homogeneous individual-level data (from national censuses) that provide information on migration decisions, and on coordinating efforts across all social sciences to produce more comprehensive and sophisticated quantitative measures of immigration policies.

Supplementary data

Supplementary data is available at *Migration Studies* online.

Acknowledgements

We are thankful to Greg Wright and Tommaso Colussi for their research assistance. Simone Bertoli and Jesus Fernandez-Huertas provided very helpful comments on an early draft of the paper.

Conflict of interest statement. None declared.

Notes

1. In this article we do not address policies regarding asylum seekers. For an important reference in the European context, see Hatton (2005).
2. While our dataset improves upon existing data, we note that it is likely that measurement error is still pervasive: the definition of migrant remains somewhat different across countries, flows of undocumented are not appropriately measured, and there may be lags in reporting. Moreover, classifying changes in immigration laws simply as discrete steps that 'tighten' or 'loosen' the entry of immigrants is a very rough and imperfect proxy for the resulting implications regarding immigration flows. In particular, there may be differences in implementation across countries and over time in phasing-in and phasing-out of such laws. Hence the results need to be interpreted with some caution.
3. Grogger and Hanson (2011) disaggregate migration flows by education but we do not.
4. Borjas (1987) studies the selection of migrants on the basis of the Roy model.
5. See Chiswick and Hatton (2003) for an even longer term perspective on international migration.
6. Bertoli et al. (2011) examine more general multilateral migration models.
7. See also Bertocchi and Strozzi (2008) for a historical analysis of the effects of institutions on migration flows for a reduced number of countries.
8. Table 2 reports the full list of destination countries.
9. Typically these statistics exclude people entering on non-immigrant temporary visas.
10. Downloadable at http://stats.oecd.org/Index.aspx?DataSetCode=MIG, accessed 19 September 2012.
11. With the Great Recession net immigration into Spain became practically zero in 2010 and negative in 2011.
12. For more recent work on the political economy of immigration see: Dolmas and Huffman (2004), Ortega (2005, 2010), Bertocchi and Strozzi (2010), Facchini et al. (2011), or Facchini and Steinhardt (2011). In these models immigration policy is largely a reflection of voters' attitudes toward immigration. Some recent empirical contributions to this literature are Mayda (2006), Facchini and Mayda (2009), and Ortega and Polavieja (2012) in the European context. Hatton and Williamson (2005) provide evidence of the role of political economy forces as an important driver of the immigration restrictions in the USA around 1920.
13. For France, Japan, and Luxembourg we constructed the immigration law variable but their immigration data were very inconsistent and we did not use them in the analysis. For Italy, Finland, and New Zealand we were unable to construct the measure of entry laws in a reliable manner.
14. http://www.econ.ucdavis.edu/faculty/gperi/data_codes/immigration_laws_appendix/immigration_laws_June_2012.xls, accessed 19 September 2012.
15. In a previous version of this paper (Ortega and Peri 2009) we explored the role of some of these more general aspects of immigration laws. The results were not very robust and we decided to limit our attention to laws affecting entry. At any rate, the web appendix

contains a brief description of the amendments to immigration laws concerning entry conditions for all destination countries in our sample. The reader can use them to alter the criteria used to build our specific measure of the tightness of entry laws.

16. This is the well-known property of *independence of irrelevant alternatives*.

17. For a given origin country, the first *nest* contains only the location of origin and the second *nest* contains all other possible locations. See Berry (1994) for a detailed discussion of the nested logit model and its relationship to other random-utility models.

18. Parameter τ is known as the dissimilarity parameter and governs the degree of correlation across the stochastic terms in the destination equations. Setting $\tau = 1$.corresponds to zero correlation, which delivers the familiar expression for the log odds ratio of the logit model. Under our assumptions, there will be non-negative correlation among the disturbance terms of the destination equations. This implies that $0 < \tau < 1$.

19. A similar term arises generally in gravity models of trade and migration and is usually referred to as *multilateral resistance* (Anderson and van Wincoop 2003). This term accounts for the influence of third countries in determining the flows between a given pair of countries. See Bertoli et al. (2011) for a general discussion in the context of migration flows.

20. This is an application of the law of large numbers.

21. Bertoli et al. (2010) use micro-data to estimate a similar model, which allows them to identify coefficient τ. Bertoli et al. (2011) explore some important policy implications.

22. See Berry (1994) for an analogous exercise where data on aggregate market shares is used to estimate the structural parameters of a consumer's problem consisting in choosing among alternative products.

23. We point out that the latter is time-varying.

24. These variables have been known to play an important role in determining migration decisions since Taylor (1994).

25. The set of controls that we include in the bilateral regression contains those variables commonly used in the trade and migration literature as proxy for migration costs. Far from being an exhaustive list of variables affecting the geographic and cultural distance between countries they however capture the most important differences. The goal of this article is to identify the effect of income and immigration policies and not the role of each cultural trait on international migration.

26. We have also performed different specifications. For instance if countries were still in the same colonial empire after 1945, then the effect on migration flows is 0.85, while if the colonial tie ended in 1945 it is only 0.77. Similarly we tried with nonlinear specification of log distance, but the coefficient on a quadratic and cubic term was not significant.

27. Our main goal is to include controls for the cost of bilateral migrations that capture the main determinants of those and allow us to estimate consistently the effect of income and immigration laws. We enter those variables as linear control (we experimented with nonlinear specifications without finding much evidence of quadratic and cubic terms), and we limit ourselves to the most commonly used variables.

28. Sharing a common currency is a time-varying variable.

29. The reason that we do not report a specification with a destination by year effect is that such effect would absorb any impact of the receiving-country income and of receiving

country's immigration policies. This would render impossible to estimate the effects of the variables that constitute the focus of this article.

30. On a similar note, Llull (2012) finds that the income elasticity of migration flows is a function of geographical distance.

31. See Taylor's (1994) account of the reasons behind the sharp drop in international migration in the interwar period.

32. The latter is fundamentally about the creation and adoption of the Euro, but not exclusively. For example, some country pairs that shared a currency in 1995 follow: Australia and Tuvalu, Belgium and Luxembourg, Denmark and Greenland, Spain and Andorra, or the USA and Panama.

33. For more details see http://europa.eu/legislation_summaries.

34. It also allows for the estimation of more computationally demanding nonlinear models within a short amount of time.

35. Some recent contributions that emphasize the role of trade openness in mediating the economic effects of immigration are Iranzo and Peri (2009), di Giovanni et al. (2012), and Ortega and Peri (2012).

References

Adsera, A. and Pytlikova, M. (2012), *The Role of Language in Shaping International Migration.* IZA Working Paper 6333, Institute for the Study of Labor (IZA).

Anderson, J. E. and van Wincoop, E. (2003) 'Gravity with Gravitas: A Solution to the Border Puzzle', *American Economic Review*, 93/1: 170–92.

Beine, M., Docquier, F. and Ozden, C. (2011), *Dissecting Network Externalities in International Migration*, Discussion Papers (IRES—Institut de Recherches Economiques et Sociales) 2011022, Universite' Catholique de Louvain.

Benhabib, J. (1996) 'On the Political Economy of Immigration', *European Economic Review*, 40/9: 1737–3.

Berry, S. T. (1994) 'Estimating Discrete Choice models of Product Differentiation', *RAND Journal of Economics*, 25/2: 242–62.

Bertocchi, G. and Strozzi, C. (2008) 'International Migration and the Role of Institutions', *Public Choice*, 137/1: 81–102.

—— (2010) 'The Evolution of Citizenship: Economic and Institutional Determinants', *Journal of Law and Economics*, 53/1: 95–136.

Bertoli, S., Fernandez-Huertas Moraga, J. and Ortega, F. (2010), *Crossing the Border: Self-Selection, Earnings and Individual Migration Decisions*, IZA Discussion Papers 4957, Institute for the Study of Labor (IZA).

—— & —— and Francesc, O. (2011) 'Immigration Policies and the Ecuadorian Exodus', *World Bank Economic Review*, 25/1: 57–76.

Borjas, G. (1987) 'Self Selection and the Earnings of Immigrants', *American Economic Review*, 77/4: 531–53.

Chaney, T. (2008) 'Distorted Gravity: The Intensive and Extensive Margin of International Trade', *American Economic Review*, 98/4: 1707–172.

Chiswick, B. R. and Hatton, T. J. (2003) 'International Migration and the Integration of Labor Markets', in Bordo, M., Taylor, A. and Williamson, J. (eds), *Globalization in Historical Perspective*, pp. 65–119, NBER Conference Report, University of Chicago Press.

Clark, X., Hatton, T. J. and Williamson, J. (2007) 'Explaining U.S. Immigration 1971–1998', *Review of Economics and Statistics*, 89/2: 359–73.

di Giovanni, J., Levchenko, A. and Ortega, F. (2012), *A Global View of Cross-border Migration*, CReAM Discussion Paper 18/12, Center for Research and Analysis of Migration, University College London.

Dolmas, J. and Huffman, G. (2004) 'On the Political Economy of Immigration and Income Redistribution', *International Economic Review*, 45/4: 1129–68.

Facchini, G. and Mayda, A. M. (2009) 'Does the Welfare State Affect Individual Attitudes toward Immigrants? Evidence across Countries', *The Review of Economics and Statistics*, 91/2: 295–314.

—— & —— and Mishra, P. (2011) 'Do Interest Groups Affect US Immigration Policy?' *Journal of International Economics*, 85/1: 114–28.

—— and Steinhardt, M. (2011) 'What Drives U.S. Immigration Policy? Evidence from Congressional Roll Call Votes', *Journal of Public Economics*, 95/7: 734–43.

Fondazione Rodolfo DeBenedetti (2007) 'Social Reform Database', <http://www.frdb.org/language/eng/topic/data-sources/dataset/international-data/doc_pk/11028> accessed 19 September 2012.

Garcia-Gomez, P. and Lopez-Casasnovas, G. (2006) 'Hypotheses on Immigration and Welfare' (in Spanish), *Moneda y Credito*, 222: 79–123.

Glick, R. and Rose, A. (2002) 'Does a Currency Union Affect Trade? The Time-Series Evidence', *European Economic Review*, 46/6: 1125–51.

Gonzalez, L. and Ortega, F. (forthcoming) 'Immigration and Housing Booms: Evidence from Spain', *Journal of Regional Science*.

Grogger, J. and Hanson, G. H. (2011) 'Income Maximization and the Selection and Sorting of International Migrants', *Journal of Development Economics*, 95/1: 42–57.

Hatton, T. (2005) 'European Asylum Policy', *National Institute Economic Review*, 194/1: 106–19.

Hatton, T. J. (2010) 'The Cliometrics of International Migration: A Survey', *Journal of Economic Surveys*, 24/5: 941–69.

—— and Williamson, J. G. (2005) 'International Migration in the Long-Run: Positive Selection, Negative Selection and Policy', in Foders, F. and Langhammer, R. F. (eds), *Labour Mobility and the World Economy*. Springer: Kiel.

Head, K., Mayer, T. and Ries, J. (2010) 'The Erosion of Colonial Trade Linkages after Independence', *Journal of International Economics*, 81/1: 1–14.

Helpman, E., Melitz, M. and Rubinstein, Y. (2008) 'Estimating Trade Flows: Trading Partners and Trading Volumes', *The Quarterly Journal of Economics*, 123/2: 441–87.

Iranzo, S. and Peri, G. (2009) 'Migration and Trade: Theory with an Application to the Eastern-Western European integration', *Journal of International Economics*, 79/1: 1–19.

Karemera, D., Oguledo, V. I. and Davis, B. (2000) 'A Gravity Model Analysis of International Migration to North America', *Applied Economics*, 32: 1745–55.

Llull, J. (2011), *Understanding International Migration: Evidence from a New Dataset of Bilateral Stocks (1960–2000)*, Manuscript Universitat Autonoma Barcelona.

Mayda, A. M. (2006) 'Who Is Against Immigration? A Cross-Country Investigation of Individual Attitudes toward Immigrants', *The Review of Economics and Statistics*, 88/3: 510–30.

—— (2010) 'International Migrations: A Panel Data Analysis of the Determinants of Bilateral Flows', *Journal of Population Economics*, 23/4: 1249–74.

—— and Krishna, P. (2004) 'OECD Countries Migration Policy Changes', Appendix to Mayda (2010) <http://www9.georgetown.edu/faculty/amm223/policychanges Appendix.pdf> accessed 19 September 2012.

McFadden, D. (1974) 'Conditional logit Analysis of Qualitative Choice Behavior', in Zarembka, P. (ed.), *Frontiers in Econometrics*. New York: Academic Press.

—— (1978) 'Modelling the Choice of Residential Location', in Karlgvist, A. *et al.* (eds), *Spatial Interaction Theories and Models*. Amsterdam: North Holland.

McKenzie, D., Theoharides, C. and Yang, D. (2012), *Distortions in the International Migrant Labor Market: Evidence from Filipino Migration and Wage Responses to Destination Country Economic Shocks*. Mimeo.

OECD (2001) 'OECD Social Expenditure Database', *Public Expenditures*, 2001, Release 01.

Ortega, F. (2005) 'Immigration Policy and Skill Upgrading', *Journal of Public Economics*, 89: 1841–63.

—— (2010) 'Immigration, Citizenship, and the Size of Government', *The B.E. Journal of Economic Analysis and Policy*, 10/1: 1–26.

—— and Peri, G. (2009), *The Causes and Effects of International Migrations: Evidence from OECD Countries 1980–2005*; NBER Working Paper 14833. National Bureau of Economic Analysis.

—— (2012) *The Effect of Trade and Migration on Income*, NBER Working Paper 18193, National Bureau of Economic Analysis.

—— and Polavieja, J. (2012) 'Labor-market Exposure as a Determinant of Attitudes toward Immigration', *Labour Economics*, 19: 298–311.

Pedersen, P. J., Pytlikova, M. and Smith, N. (2006) 'Migration into OECD countries 1990–2006', in Parson, C. and Smeeding, T. (eds), *Immigration and the Transformation of Europe*. Cambridge: Cambridge University Press, pp. 43–84.

Taylor, A. M. (1994) 'Mass Migration to Distant Southern Shores: Argentina and Australia', in Hatton, T. J. and Williamson, J. G. (eds), *Migration and the International Labor Market*. London: Routledge, pp. 1850–939.

United Nations (2005) *International Migration Flows to and From Selected Countries*, Revision 2005, Population Division, the Department of Economic and Social Affairs, Washington, DC.

Appendix

Table A.1. Sources of the immigration data

Sources of the data: country	Mayda (2010) Years covered	United Nations Years covered	International migration database Years covered
Australia	1983–2005	1960–2004	1998–2006
Belgium	1984–2005	1960–2003	1998–2006
Canada	1980–2005	1961–2004	1998–2006
Denmark	1990–2004	1980–2004	1998–2006
Finland	NA	1980–2004	1998–2006
Germany	1984–2005	1965–2004	1998–2006
Italy	NA	1980–2000	1998–2006
Netherlands	1984–2005	1960–2004	1998–2006
New Zealand	NA	1950–2004	1998–2006
Norway	1984–2005	1980–2003	1998–2006
Spain	NA	1980–2004	1998–2006
Sweden	1980–2005	1960–2004	1998–2006
Switzerland	1984–2005	NA	1998–2006
UK	1982–2006	1964–2003	1998–2001
USA	1980–2006	1946–2004	1998–2006

Note: This table summarizes the source for migration data for each receiving country. The main sources are Mayda (2010), United Nations, and IMD. For each country the specific database covers a certain year range, which is indicated in the table above.

The Cross-country Determinants of Potential and Actual Migration[1]

Frédéric Docquier
FNRS, Fonds National de la Recherche Scientifique and IRES, Université Catholique de Louvain

Giovanni Peri
University of California, Davis

Ilse Ruyssen
IRES, Université Catholique de Louvain and SHERPPA, Ghent University

In this study, we use cross-country bilateral data to quantify a two-step process of international migration and its aggregate determinants. We first analyze which country-specific factors affect the probability that individuals join the pool of potential (aspiring) migrants. Then, we consider the bilateral and destination country factors that affect the frequency at which potential migrants turn into actual migrants. Using information on potential migrants from World Gallup surveys and on actual migrants from national censuses for 138 origin countries and 30 major destinations between 2000 and 2010, we analyze economic, policy, cultural, and network determinants of each step. We find that the size of the network of previous migrants and the average income per person at destination are crucial determinants of the size of the pool of potential migrants. Economic growth in the destination country, on the other hand, is the main economic generator of migration opportunities for a given pool of potential migrants. We also find that college-educated exhibit greater actual emigration rates mainly because of better chances in realizing their immigration potentials, rather than because of higher willingness to migrate.

[1]We thank the editors and three referees for their helpful remarks and suggestions. We acknowledge financial support from the ARC convention on "Geographical Mobility of Factors" (convention 09/14-019). We also gratefully thank Robert Manchin and the Gallup-initiated Institute for Advanced Behavioural Studies for allowing us access to the data for research purposes.

INTRODUCTION

Migrating from a country of origin to a country of destination involves several steps, not all of them observable and measurable (Paul, 2011). This paper relates to the existing literature by considering the migration process as comprised of two main steps. We first analyze the macrodeterminants of the aggregate probabilities of becoming potential migrants (first step), and then, we look at the factors determining what fraction of potential become actual (second step) migrants. A tradition in the migration literature identifies a clear first step in the decision of looking for migration opportunities. "Aspiring" migrants are those who express an intention/desire to emigrate (Carling, 2002; van Dalen *et al.*, 2005a; van Dalen *et al.*, 2005b; Jónsson, 2008; Becerra, 2012; Creighton, 2013). Several studies have used survey questions to elicit this information and have thoroughly analyzed specific cases, often focused on one country of origin or one migration corridor, such as Mexico–U.S. These studies have been focused on uncovering detailed motivations of potential migrants and on individual level analysis, but are hard to compare with each other or across countries and to generalize into quantifiable tendencies.

From an economist's perspective, deciding to be in the pool of potential migrants is explained as a rational decision. Individuals evaluate how desirable it would be to migrate to a foreign country relative to staying in the country of origin. An implicit comparison of the utility (benefits minus costs) of staying with the utility of migrating to different potential countries is made by individuals. "Potential" migrants are those who state a preference for migrating (arguably because perceived benefits of migrating are larger than perceived costs). Those benefits and costs depend on the presence of family members abroad, on individual characteristics and on economic and social conditions, among other things. Hence, a large part of the sociological literature, relating those factors to the intention of migrating (both by individuals and families), can be interpreted in this framework (*e.g.* Yang, 2000; Papapanagos and Sanfey, 2001; Wood *et al.*, 2010).

The second step of the migration process takes place when some *searchers* in the pool of potential migrants find *opportunities* to migrate – such as a job offer, a temporary visa, a study opportunity or a family permit – and migrate. The interactions between potential migrants and migration opportunities determine the flow of actual migrants (Carling,

2002). From an economic perspective, it can be considered as somewhat similar to a matching process: Heterogeneous individuals who are willing to migrate find – through a slow and costly process – potential migration opportunities. Pissarides (2000) popularized the use of search and matching in labor market studies. Some of the underlying features of those models can be used in the analysis of how potential migrants (searchers) and migration opportunities are matched and produce the flow of actual migrants.

In the present study, we implement a simple two-stage empirical analysis to illustrate the role of aggregate determinants of migration flows. First, we analyze empirically what country-specific and bilateral factors determine the size (and composition between education groups) of the pool of potential migrants. The latter is defined as those who have revealed being willing to migrate by positively answering the question "Ideally, if you had the opportunity, would you like to move permanently or temporarily to another country, or would you prefer to continue living in this country?." Most of them have, then, indicated a preferred country in the follow-up question "To which country would you like to move?." In the second step, we analyze how these potential migrants combine with factors determining migration opportunities and generate actual migration flows.

The answers to the questions described above were obtained from representative Gallup polls (described in detail in Gallup, 2012) and available for 138 countries – representing 97% of the world population – between 2007 and 2013. After organizing, cleaning, and aggregating these data by origin–destination pairs, we merged them with data on actual bilateral net migration flows for the 2000–2010 period from 138 countries to 30 major migrant-receiving countries. Bilateral net migrations are measured as the difference in the stock of migrants from an origin to a specific destination between 2000 and 2010. Hence, they are good estimates of the long-term flows of permanent migrants. Dividing by native population in the country of origin, we construct net migration rates and potential migration rates between country pairs over the 2000–2010 decade. With these bilateral data, we analyze in a simple econometric framework how the pool of potential migrants and migration opportunities (stemming among others from economic growth, policies in the receiving country, the presence of networks) determine the net migration rates. In doing so, we learn (1) which factors affect migration by changing the share of potential migrants in the population and (2) which factors affect the actual migration rate, given the pool of potential migrants.

Throughout our analysis, we distinguish between individuals with at least some college education (that we call college-educated) and those without (sometimes called "less educated" or non-college-educated).[2] Their increasingly different labor market performance in most developed countries (Autor *et al.*, 2008; Goldin and Katz, 2008; Moretti, 2012), and – even more importantly – their different degree of national and international mobility (Grogger and Hanson, 2011; Artuç *et al.*, forthcoming) calls for a separate analysis to better understand their differences. Are college-educated individuals more mobile because they are more likely to be potential migrants in response to perceived economic opportunities? Or are they more mobile because within the pool of *potential migrants*, they have a greater probability of finding opportunities? As most receiving countries' immigration policies, either directly or covertly, favor highly educated immigrants, differences in the rate of realization of migration opportunities between college-educated and non-college-educated are likely to depend on immigration policies. Alternatively, college-educated may be able to navigate through foreign labor markets more easily and acquire knowledge of more opportunities.

Several interesting results emerge from our analysis. First, supporting the cost–benefit model used as the basis of economic studies of migration, we find that the average income at destination and the presence of networks of previous migrants are robust and quantitatively significant determinants of potential migration rates. Interestingly college-educated and non-college-educated respond to destination income and networks *in a broadly similar way* when it comes to willingness to migrate. On average, the less educated are only somewhat less likely to be willing to migrate, and their willingness to migrate responds to economic incentives with similar elasticities as college-educated. Yet, college-educated have a three to four times larger probability of actually migrating, once in the pool of potential migrants. This is the main factor determining skill-biased emigration. Third, growth in gross domestic product (GDP) per capita in the receiving country is the only economic factor that we find positively correlated with migration rates once we control for the pool of potential

[2]In the two datasets used in this paper, the definition of college-educated is slightly different. In the data on actual migration, college-educated are defined as described here. In the Gallup poll, only individuals with a college degree are defined as college-educated. (We do not have information on individuals who attended college without graduating.) Hence, we use the desired migration rates for college graduates and apply them to the population of all college-educated.

migrants, and such correlation is stronger for non-college-educated. Fourth, policies allowing free mobility of labor across borders (such as within the European Union), which are the closest to having open borders, had a small (and sometimes statistically insignificant) effect in translating potential into actual migrants among non-college-educated. They had no effect on the mobility of college-educated in 2000–2010. Similarly, the presence of visa waiver agreement between countries has a positive but small correlation with actual migration flows of the less educated, for given potential. One has to keep in mind, however, that free migration policies only exist between rather similar countries within Europe. Likewise, visa waiving agreements exist between countries with similar levels of development and democracy, mainly the rich Western countries (Neumayer, 2006). Finally, we find that economic growth in the destination countries had a proportionally stronger effect on migration opportunities from sending countries where the pool of potential migrants to that destination was larger. Networks in the destination country, income differentials, and geographical and cultural proximity had only a minor impact on migration rates once we control for the pool of potential searchers.

The rest of the paper is organized as follows. First, we review the existing literature on the determinants of migration, focusing on the empirical aggregate approach we use that derives from the economics literature. In the following section, we present the data on potential and on actual migrants and show some descriptive statistics and general trends. Subsequently, we provide the framework for the empirical analysis. In the empirical section, we first estimate the impact of economic characteristics, policy variables, and network size on the pool of searchers, among college- and non-college-educated. Then, we analyze how the pool of potential migrants and receiving-country opportunities determine actual migration rates of college- and non-college-educated. We end with a brief summary and some conclusions.

LITERATURE REVIEW

The classical way economists look at migration has been by founding the decision to migrate in an individual cost–benefit analysis (utility maximization). By aggregating heterogeneous individuals, this framework has allowed scholars to analyze the determinants of aggregate migration flows and the selection of migrants (along the skill dimension). Examples of this approach can be found in Borjas (1987), Clark *et al.* (2007), Grogger and Hanson (2011), Hatton (2005), Roy (1951), and Sjaastad (1962). In this paper, we use this aggregate empirical perspective based on an individual cost–benefit analysis. However, we incorporate it in a two-step process by analyzing first the aspiration and then the realization of migration potentials in sequence. This approach draws inspiration from a framework that has long been applied in other social sciences. As mentioned in the introduction, several studies (*e.g.* De Jong, 2000; Carling, 2002; van Dalen *et al.*, 2005a van Dalen *et al.*, 2005b; Hagen-Zanker *et al.*, 2009; Becerra, 2012; Creighton, 2013; Czaika and Vothknecht, 2014) have recognized the importance of analyzing the factors influencing the aspiration to migrate in specific countries and contexts. Some of these studies have explicitly taken a two-step approach, analyzing (1) aspirations and (2) ability to migrate (Carling, 2002). Our analysis extends this approach by drawing upon additional economic theory and using a uniquely extensive dataset. Our two-step analysis is loosely based on utility maximization in the first step and "matching" of potential migrants and migration opportunities in the second.

Empirically, the specifications we use to analyze the "first step" are similar to the bilateral gravity-like regressions grounded on theoretical microfoundations and used in several previous studies (*e.g.* Karemera *et al.*, 2000; Hatton and Williamson, 2005; Clark *et al.*, 2007; Bahna, 2008; Hooghe *et al.*, 2008; Pedersen *et al.*, 2008; Mayda, 2010; Ruyssen *et al.*, 2014). Several recent papers have refined the economic analysis of the determinants of migration, framing the empirical estimates within a more rigorous multicountry choice, random utility maximization model derived from McFadden (1974). Grogger and Hanson (2011), Beine *et al.* (2011), and Ortega and Peri (2013), for instance, analyze bilateral migration as the result of a multinomial choice among alternative locations, driven by utility maximization determined by a comparison of costs and benefits. They relate the migrant/non-migrant ratios to economic and policy factors. Recently, Bertoli and Fernández-Huertas Moraga (2013) extended this framework to more general decision structures and implemented more complex, yet more general, econometric analyses. More generally, Beine *et al.* (forthcoming) discuss the methodological challenges that are implied by the use of bilateral data for the analysis of international migration. These papers are closely related to ours in that they also use aggregate bilateral cross-country data to identify determinants of migration flows.

In the first step, we analyze the role of several factors that previous researchers have found to be important in affecting costs and benefits of migration: first of all income and job availability at destination, but also geographical, cultural, and institutional distance and social linkages (networks) between countries. Fawcett (1989), Bauer and Zimmerman (1997), Hooghe *et al.* (2008), Pedersen *et al.* (2008), Mayda (2010), Beine *et al.* (2011), and Ruyssen *et al.* (2014) are examples analyzing the impact of some of these factors directly on migration. Differently from these studies, however, we first focus on the impact of those factors on potential (rather than actual) migration.

The second part of our analysis looks at the process of combining potential migrants with factors that produce migration opportunities. In this respect, the combination of potential migrants and potential opportunities in receiving countries can be described in the context of a "matching" function (as in Pissarides and Petrongolo, 2001; Petrongolo and Pissarides, 2006; or Gregg and Petrongolo, 2005 among others) that summarizes the slow and uncertain process through which potential migrants realize migration opportunities. This is a somewhat new way of looking at the second stage of the migration process in which potential migrants become actual migrants. By including policy, cultural, geographical, and other determinants of the likelihood of migration among potential migrants, we want to identify all factors (economic and not) that affect the probability that a potential migrant turns into an actual migrant.

There is a small but growing literature analyzing migration opportunities in a search and matching framework. Chassamboulli and Peri (2014), for instance, used such a framework to investigate the effect of the U.S. immigration policy on illegal immigration from Mexico. Ortega (2000), on the other hand, theoretically showed that multiplicity of equilibria can arise from the interaction of searching firms' and migrants' optimizing behavior due to search and job creation externalities. Whereas those are search and matching models of migration for labor reasons, this paper uses the matching framework in a broader sense. In particular, we use bilateral data to statistically describe the process of matching potential migrants with "migration opportunities." It is worth noticing that we do not directly observe "migration opportunities" (namely the number of jobs, permits, or visas available to foreigners) in receiving countries. We can identify, however, some receiving-country factors (such as productivity growth and policies) that could affect the availability of those opportunities and the probability of matching them with potential migrants.

Immigration Policies and Migrant Mobility

As the Gallup data on willingness to migrate are new, the literature relying on these data to capture potential migration is very limited. There are several studies analyzing the willingness (aspiration) to migrate using country-specific surveys–for instance, in Mexico (Becerra *et al.*, 2010; Becerra, 2012; Creighton, 2013), in Cape Verde (Carling, 2002), in North Africa (van Dalen 2005a; van Dalen 2005b), and in China (Yang, 2000), just to cite a few. The fact that our database, on the other hand, covers all countries in the world makes it exceptional. A recent report by the International Migration Organization (Esipova *et al.*, 2011) presents detailed descriptive statistics on the willingness to migrate across countries based on these data. A very recent working paper by Manchin *et al.* (2014), in addition, analyzes the importance of individual satisfaction on the desire to migrate using individual data from the same Gallup Poll, disregarding the bilateral dimension.

DATA ON MIGRATION AND WILLINGNESS TO MIGRATE

Our database includes 138 countries of origin for which data on both actual and desired emigration are available toward 30 major destination countries.[3] The set of destinations includes all major OECD countries as well as Persian Gulf countries, the Russian Federation, and South Africa. According to the United Nations database, our set of destination countries accounts for 66.3% of the worldwide stock of international migrants in 2010 (and 63.4% of the stock in 2000). Throughout our analysis, we always separate college-educated individuals (denoted as *h*) who attended some tertiary education and less (or non-college) educated individuals (denoted with *l*) who did not attend any tertiary education. These two groups are very different in terms of wage, job type, and mobility. During the recent decades, their economic differences, especially in developed countries, have grown (*see* Autor *et al.*, 2008; Moretti, 2012). We compare statistics and findings for the two groups. Our set of 30 destination countries accounted, respectively, for 82.5% and 57.8% of the stock of highly and less educated adult migrants in the year 2000.

We focus on bilateral migration flows over the period 2000–2010. The actual migration rate from country of origin *o* to destination country

---

[3]In the Appendix, we describe in greater detail the methodology and the original data used to construct actual and desired migration rates. We also show in Table A3 the summary statistics for all 138 countries of origin.

d is calculated as the net migration flow (obtained as the difference between the 2010 and the 2000 stocks of people born in *o* residing in country *d*), normalized by the native non-migrant population of country *o* in 2000. These bilateral rates are denoted by $m^b_{o,d}$ and $m^l_{o,d}$ for college- and non-college- educated, respectively. While net migration rates over 10 years imperfectly capture short-term gross migration,[4] they represent more closely the change in permanent migrants. Moreover, net measures of migration, as they are derived from census data (rather than from registers of entry), are much more reliable and include non-documented migrants in several countries.

We then define the "desired" (though unrealized) migration rate from country *o* to country *d* as the share among native non-migrants in country *o*, interviewed by the Gallup Poll between 2007 and 2013, who said that they would be willing to migrate (permanently or temporarily) to country *d* if they had an opportunity, but who are still in the country of origin. Whereas most respondents indicated a specific country of desired migration, some individuals only demonstrate a willingness to migrate but no specific desired destination. We considered all those who indicated a preference for migrating as "willing" and allocated those who did not express a country preference in proportion of the preferences expressed by those who did.[5] We denote these bilateral rates as $w^b_{o,d}$ and $w^l_{o,d}$ (for "willingness"), respectively, for college- and non-college-educated. The population of reference, encompassing all people who could, in principle, migrate, is always the initial population of natives in country *o* as of the year 2000, denoted by N^b_o and N^l_o, respectively, for college- and non-college-educated. The rates *m* and *w* are both expressed relative to this initial population of natives in 2000. The sum of those two rates, therefore, gives the "potential" emigration rate. It combines those who emigrated (between 2000–2010) and those who are willing to migrate but were still in the country of origin by 2010. Hence, potential migration

[4]*See* Smith and Swanson (1998) and Rogers (1990) for a discussion of the pros and cons in the use of net and gross migration rates.
[5]It could be argued that individuals are willing to migrate to many different destinations and decide which country to move to only once an opportunity arises. In this case, the only meaningful distinction would be between willing and non-willing, making the bilateral preferences irrelevant. We will describe and analyze overall emigration rates (rather than bilateral) as well. Their responses to economic and network variables are similar to the response of bilateral rates implying that we are not distorting the choice too much by analyzing potential migration as bilateral preferences.

rates are denoted by $p_{o,d}^h = m_{o,d}^h + w_{o,d}^h$ and $p_{o,d}^l = m_{o,d}^l + w_{o,d}^l$. To capture some key characteristics of potential and actual migrants, let us consider some summary statistics and aggregate features of migration rates from the origin and destination countries' perspectives.

General Overview

Table 1 shows the values for emigration rates of college-educated and the less educated (without college degree), averaging 138 countries of origin in the upper part of the table. In the second row, we show the actual net emigration rate, and in the third row, the "desired" emigration rate as defined above. In the first row, for comparison, we show the stock of emigrants relative to the native population as of 2000. The first two columns of the table show the values averaged across countries of origin, weighted by their native population. The percentages correspond to those in the aggregate native population. The third and fourth columns, on the other hand, show the simple average rates counting each country as one, so that small countries have the same weight as large countries in the summary statistics. The much larger values in columns 3 and 4 are due to the fact that emigration rates (both actual and desired) are larger in small countries.

    Three interesting facts emerge from these aggregate statistics. Focusing on the weighted figures, actual emigration rates between 2000 and 2010 as a share of the world population were fairly small. Only 0.4 percentage points of the native non-migrant population without college education migrated between 2000 and 2010, compared to 3.9 percentage points of those with college education. Desired emigration rates were larger. About 8.5% of non-college-educated and 16.2% of college-educated said that they were willing to migrate (if they had an opportunity), but they did not do so in the considered period. Most strikingly, there was a much larger difference between non-college- and college-educated in actual rates (ratio of almost 10 to 1) than in desired rates (ratio of 1.9 to 1). This is even more notable when we consider the simple averages in columns 3 and 4. This fact suggests that the low migration rates of non-college-educated may not be due to a difference in perceived benefits/costs of migrating, but may rather be explained by the fact that those searching for migration opportunities without a college degree have a much harder time finding them. An additional interesting implication of the simple averages is that if all people who say that, ideally, they are willing to

TABLE 1
Aggregate Statistics on Actual and Desired Migration Rates (2000–2010), As Percentage of the Population in 2000

	Aggregate Population-weighted Less educated	Aggregate Population-weighted College educated	Average Non-weighted Less educated	Average Non-weighted College educated
Actual and desired emigration rates, as percentage of the country-of-origin, native population				
Stock of emigrants/Native population 2000	1.8	5.8	6.4	34.9
Actual emigration rate: Net emigrants 2000-2010 relative to native population in the country of origin, 2000	0.4	3.9	1.1	30.3
Desired rate: Willing to Migrate 2000-2010, still in the country, relative to native population in the country of origin, 2000	8.5	16.2	14.2	21.4
Actual and desired immigration rates, as percentage of the country-of-destination, native population				
Stock of immigrants/Native population 2000	9.4	10.9	20.9	30.0
Actual immigration rate: Net immigrants 2000-2010 relative to native population in the country of destination, 2000	2.4	6.0	11.0	35.0
Desired rate: Willing to Migrate 2000-2010, still in the country, relative to native population in the country of destination, 2000	42.0	26.0	87.0	93.0

The stock of migrants and native population in 2000 are calculated using data from Arruç *et al*, (forthcoming) and Brücker *et al*. (2013). Net migration rates in the period 2000–2010 are calculated as the difference in bilateral stocks of migrants 2010–2000, aggregated by country of origin or destination. Willingness to migrate is calculated as the share of people, among those interviewed by Gallup between 2007 and 2013, who have expressed a desire to migrate, if an opportunity arises. We consider 138 countries of origin and 30 destinations.

migrate would do so, the migration rate of college-educated would still exceed that of non-college-educated, but emigration rates of the two groups would be much closer. However, we should be cautious in considering the desired (potential) migration rate as realizable under any circumstances. Our results below show that even free labor mobility policies do not seem to move potential and actual migration rates any closer together. While "potential migration" is an interesting concept to identify migration *searchers*, the frictions and hurdles preventing its translation into actual migration could be pervasive and hard to reduce, at least within the plausible range of policies and institutions.

The lower part of Table 1 shows, instead, summary statistics on actual and desired migration rates from the perspective of the receiving country. The actual and desired flows (and stocks in 2000) of migrants are aggregated by country of destination (or desired destination) and divided by the native resident population of the *destination* country. Hence, those two rows show actual and desired "immigration" rates for the 30 destinations considered, averaged either by weighting by the destination country population (columns 1 and 2) or without weights (columns 3 and 4).

As stated above, the considered 30 destination countries receive about two-thirds of the actual, worldwide migration stock, and 82.5% of the worldwide stock of high-skilled migrants. Yet, they include less than 20% of the world population so that the immigration rates for these countries are much greater than the emigration rates for the origins in our sample. During the 2000–2010 period, immigration of non-college-educated into the considered destination countries corresponded to 2.4% of their aggregate non-college-educated population as of 2000, compared to 6% for college-educated. Desired immigration among non-college-educated, that is, the size of the inflow of all "willing" migrants, would amount to 42% of the native non-college-educated population. For college-educated, desired immigration equals 26% of the receiving-country population. In this case, there are more potential non-college-educated migrants to our destination countries than there are college-educated. The reason is that, while the emigration rate from almost any country is larger for college-educated, there are many more non-college-educated in the sending than in the receiving countries so that – from the destination point of view – the flow in percentage of non-college-educated would be much larger. Hence, if all people who are willing to migrate would follow on their desire, the inflow of immigrants into the considered receiving countries would be much less skill intensive than it is today. For most countries, it would still be college intensive, but in some countries (such as the U.S.), the inflow would become much larger and non-college intensive. Let us emphasize, before moving to the analysis of individual countries, that the data used to construct desired *emigration* rates only use the information about people's willingness to migrate. On the other hand, those used to calculate desired *immigration* rates use also the information on the most preferred country of migration. In as much as potential migrants are willing to migrate to other (less preferred) countries, or do not know exactly which country they would like to migrate to, there would be significantly more imprecision in the second measure than in the first. Countries that do not top the lists of most preferred but could still be desirable destinations, in particular, could receive significantly more immigrants than these figures suggest, if they unilaterally opened their borders.

Sending and Receiving Countries

Desired and hence, potential migration rates are significantly larger than actual migration rates. Here, we show preliminary evidence that they are also correlated with those. Table 2 shows the actual net immigration rates and the desired immigration rates – desired from the point of view of migrants – for each of the 30 considered receiving countries. First, note that the actual net immigration rate for non-college-educated is usually below 10% and sometimes quite small (or even negative in the presence of return migration). In contrast, the immigration rate of college-educated is found to be usually quite large, on average it is 35.8%. The United Arab Emirates form a clear outlier, attracting immigrants in much larger numbers than the native population both among more and less educated. The labor force of professionals and workers in these countries has typically been built by attracting immigrants. Australia, Canada, Ireland, and the United Kingdom, on the other hand, attracted a large inflow of college-educated and had a very skill-intensive immigration in the 2000–2010 period. These data confirm previous studies (Docquier *et al.*, 2014; Artuç *et al.*, forthcoming) in finding that, for essentially all migration-receiving countries, the flow of recent immigrants was college-educated intensive relative to the native population. The third column defines immigration as "skilled" ("unskilled") if the net immigration rate between 2000 and 2010 was larger for college (non-college)-educated. All but two countries in our sample (U.S. and New Zealand) were characterized by skilled immigration in the 2000s. The remaining columns calculate the desired immigration rate for the same set of receiving countries 2000–

TABLE 2

ACTUAL AND DESIRED IMMIGRATION RATES OF COLLEGE-EDUCATED AND THE LESS EDUCATED BY DESTINATION COUNTRY

Destination	Net rates 2000–2010 Less educated	Net rates 2000–2010 College-educated	Skill Intensity	Desired rates Less educated	Desired rates College-educated	Skill Intensity
Australia	−0.6	33.5	Skilled	148.6	245.4	Skilled
Austria	3.1	11.7	Skilled	37.7	72.9	Skilled
Belgium	2.0	11.8	Skilled	24.1	16.4	Unskilled
Canada	−0.8	71.2	Skilled	142.3	240.7	Skilled
Chile	16.7	20.8	Skilled	6.0	9.3	Skilled
Denmark	2.9	8.6	Skilled	30.5	62.9	Skilled
Finland	2.4	5.6	Skilled	15.1	78.3	Skilled
France	1.8	7.3	Skilled	41.7	71.3	Skilled
Germany	0.8	0.9	Skilled	26.0	44.2	Skilled
Greece	7.1	23.1	Skilled	20.5	34.1	Skilled
Ireland	6.1	30.4	Skilled	63.1	88.7	Skilled
Israel	−18.7	2.3	Skilled	35.8	38.0	Skilled
Italy	1.3	7.5	Skilled	24.4	67.7	Skilled
Japan	0.2	0.7	Skilled	12.8	9.3	Unskilled
Luxembourg	10.5	23.6	Skilled	119.5	118.6	Unskilled
Mexico	0.1	1.3	Skilled	3.8	8.5	Skilled
Netherlands	−4.3	−0.9	Skilled	24.6	23.4	Unskilled
New Zealand	9.1	8.7	Unskilled	212.4	154.6	Unskilled
Norway	5.2	14.1	Skilled	48.0	78.5	Skilled
Poland	−0.9	1.0	Skilled	1.2	3.8	Skilled
Portugal	6.7	21.4	Skilled	23.9	50.0	Skilled
Russian Federation	−2.7	1.0	Skilled	8.3	1.5	Unskilled
Saudi Arabia	20.4	121.5	Skilled	300.0	173.4	Unskilled
South Africa	2.8	18.4	Skilled	19.0	8.5	Unskilled
Spain	10.6	20.0	Skilled	58.6	58.8	Skilled
Sweden	4.7	15.4	Skilled	62.0	79.8	Skilled
Switzerland	3.0	3.7	Skilled	119.9	295.5	Skilled
United Arab Emirates	248.4	587.2	Skilled	937.7	622.4	Unskilled
United Kingdom	0.9	26.3	Skilled	50.6	117.8	Skilled
United States	6.3	3.9	Unskilled	92.8	12.9	Unskilled
Average	11.1	35.8	Skilled	87.6	93.6	Skilled

2010. While both rates are much larger than the actual ones, non-college-educated desired immigration is eight times as large as actual, while the ratio for college-educated is less than three. As a result, while the majority of countries would still be facing skilled desired immigration, ten countries would switch to primarily low-skilled immigration if all those who are willing to migrate were to do so leading to a much smaller overrepresentation of college-educated among immigrants. The U.S. exhibits desired immigration rates heavily biased in favor of unskilled, mainly because it is the most popular migration destination for most people in the world and because, on average, there are many more non-college-educated than college-educated in the world.

Preliminary evidence also shows high correlation between potential migration and actual emigration rates in Figures I and II. These figures report scatterplots of actual and potential emigration rates from the 138 sending countries and the OLS regression lines describing their correlation separately for non-college- and college-educated. By aggregating all destinations, we are reducing also the error in assigning potential migrants to one or another destination. We observe a positive and very significant correlation for both college- and non-college-educated. The regression line for the college-educated, however, has a slope of 0.93, and potential

Figure I.   **Potential and Actual Emigration Rates of the Less Educated (138 countries of origin).**

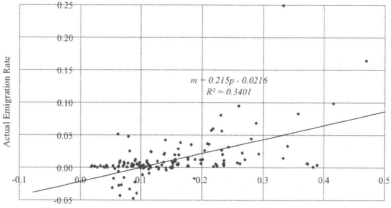

$$m = 0.215p - 0.0216$$
$$R^2 = 0.3401$$

Potential Emigration Rate

Notes: Actual and potential emigration rates are calculated as described in the text. They are aggregated by country of origin. Each point shows the total actual and potential migration rate from one origin to all destinations.

Figure II.   **Potential and Actual Emigration Rates of College-educated (138 Countries of Origin).**

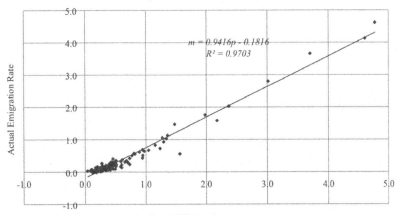

Notes: Actual and potential emigration rates are calculated as described in the text. They are aggregated by country of origin. Each point shows the total actual and potential migration rate from one origin to all destinations.

migration rates explain most of the variation of actual rates (R^2 =0.969). For non-college-educated, the slope is only 0.24, though still very significant (R^2=0.378). We can summarize this stylized fact by saying that countries with a very large net emigration rate of college-educated are those where many college-educated want to emigrate. To the contrary, for less educated, the percentage of people willing to emigrate is always much larger than (and less correlated to) the percentage of actual migrants. This is a clear sign that desiring to emigrate is far less effective in realizing emigration for non-college-educated than for college-educated.

Figures III and IV show similar scatterplots for immigration rates in the 30 destination countries. The scatterplots are more noisy implying that our data about willingness to migrate to a specific country may be less precise than in capturing a general willingness to migrate, as mentioned above. Nevertheless, potential immigration rates have a significant and positive effect on actual immigration rates. Yet, for each increase in the potential immigration rate of non-college-educated by one percentage point of the native population, only 0.05 percentage points of actual immigrants would materialize. For each percentage point of potential college-educated, instead, the country would receive almost 0.2 percentage points of actual immigrants. This difference between college and non-college in the percentages of potential migrants turning into actual migrants will

Figure III.   Potential and Actual Immigration Rates of the Less Educated (30 Countries of Destination).

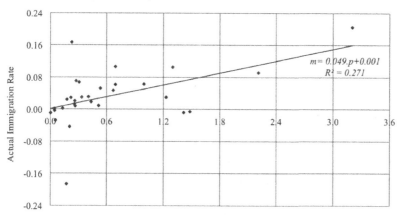

Notes: Actual and potential immigration rates are calculated by dividing the number of net migrants and potential migrants (2000–2010) by the native population in the destination country in 2000. They are aggregated by country of destination. Each point shows the total actual and potential migration rate from all origin countries to one destination.

Figure IV.   Potential and Actual Immigration Rates of College-educated (30 Countries of Destination).

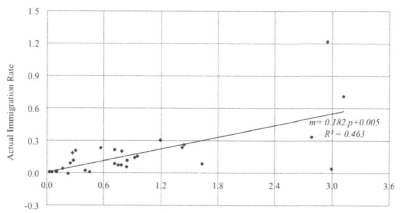

Notes: Actual and potential immigration rates are calculated by dividing the number of net migrants and potential migrants (2000–2010) by the native population in the destination country in 2000. They are aggregated by country of destination. Each point shows the total actual and potential migration rate from all origin countries to one destination.

prove to be a very pervasive feature of international migration. It survives the inclusion of many controls, it is present both in aggregate and bilateral rates, and it is common to poor and not so poor countries of origin.

FRAMEWORK

As described above, we organize our data into aggregate groups by country of origin o, destination d, and education categories: h (college-educated) and l (non-college or less educated). The native population of reference is defined as the total number of individuals aged 25 and over, born and residing in country o in the year 2000 (the first year of our sample). We call these groups N_o^h and N_o^l, respectively, for more and less educated. The desired migration rates, $w_{o,d}^h$ and $w_{o,d}^l$, then capture those who revealed themselves as willing to migrate to country d yet who were still residing in o between 2007 and 2013, expressed as shares of N_o^h and N_o^l. The net migration rates $m_{o,d}^h$ and $m_{o,d}^l$ then equal the net flows of actual migrants from country o to country d in the period 2000–2010, relative to the initial population in 2000. The sum of these two groups constitutes the total of potential migrants, that is, $P_{o,d}^h$ and $P_{o,d}^l$, which, standardized by the initial population, correspond to the potential migration rates denoted by $p_{o,d}^h$ and $p_{o,d}^l$.

Potential migrants should have higher utility (accounting for migration costs and gains) from living/working in country d than in their country of birth o. This is the group identified by migration scholars as "aspiring" or "intended" migrants. Our main specification considers the revealed migration preference for a specific destination country d. This may be a strong assumption (De Jong *et al.*, 1996; De Jong, 2000) which is relaxed when we analyze the overall migration potential (rather than bilateral) by aggregating all potential migrants in a country of origin. Allowing for heterogeneity in preferences across individuals, but assuming that all individuals (1) value income from higher wages and higher probability of employment and (2) incur higher costs when moving farther and to more different countries, implies that – after controlling for country-of-origin characteristics – the share of people who would potentially migrate from o to d among all individuals, $p_{o,d}^s$, depends positively on the returns and negatively on the costs of migrating from o to d (*see* Borjas, 1987; or Grogger and Hanson, 2011 for a similar framework). So we assume that people account for all perceived costs and benefits of migration when revealing whether they would like to migrate or not and to which country. Also, the willingness to move to a country shows that individuals know about the opportunities in that country, and therefore, the availability of information about that country can be a crucial determinant of willingness to move there. In general, we can write:

$$p_{o,d}^s = f(\text{Returns}_d, \text{Costs}_{o,d}, \text{Info}_{o,d}) \qquad (1)$$

We then consider a linear approximation of (1) which expresses the potential migration rate, $p_{o,d}^s$, as a linear function of factors affecting the returns in a specific destination, the bilateral cost of migrating, and the flow of information from country d.[6] Following the economic literature (as in Borjas, 1987; Hatton, 2005; Mayda, 2010), we consider wages (approximated by income per person) and employment opportunities (approximated by employment/population ratio) in country d as the main determinants of the economic returns to migration. Following the economic and anthropological literature (*e.g.* Spolaore and Wacziarg, 2009; Putterman and Weil, 2010), we include measures of distance and proximity in geographic, language, genetic, and cultural space to capture migration costs. Finally, we consider the size of the destination country and the presence of a pre-existing diaspora of migrants from country o as the main sources of information about the country. The diaspora presence can also directly reduce migration costs by providing easier assimilation. We can therefore write relation (1) as a linear specification of the following form (for $s = h, l$):

$$p_{o,d}^s = \alpha_o^s + a_1^s y_{d,2000} + a_2^s e_{d,2000} + a_3^s \text{Dist}_{o,d} + a_4^s \ln \text{Pop}_d + a_5^s \text{Netw}_{o,d} + \epsilon_{o,d}^s$$
$$(2)$$

In equation (2), α_o^s is a set of 138 country-of-origin dummies that capture heterogeneity of people and preferences and economic conditions across origins. The term $y_{d,2000}$ captures per capita income (GDP) in the destination country in PPP US \$ as of the year 2000. The term $e_{d,2000}$ is the ratio of employment to population in working age as of 2000 in the destination country. These variables proxy (imperfectly) for the expected

---

[6]A random utility maximization model with (1) individuals with heterogeneous preferences, maximizing utility that depends on the same arguments as function f above, and (2) errors following a Gumbel distribution, would produce a linear relation between the logarithm of $p_{o,d}^s$, the odds ratio of migrating or not, and the arguments of the function f. This simpler form can be considered a linear approximation of the former.

income and employment probability of a migrant and determine the economic attractiveness of a destination. Their cross-sectional differences are very large, and one can plausibly assume that individual decisions on long-term migration are informed by these differences. $Dist_{o,d}$ is a set of bilateral variables capturing geographical distance, such as common border, language or colonial origin, and measures of genetic, religious, and legal distance across countries. Those factors affect the transferability of skills, cultural barriers, and moving costs, hence influencing costs and benefits from migration. The term $\ln Pop_d$ captures the size of the receiving country which affects its "visibility" to potential migrants. $Netw_{o,d}$ finally, is a measure of the size of the stock of existing migrants from o in d in 2000 expressed as percentage of the population in the origin country. This is a first approximation of the connection with the country of destination, which can affect information and reduce costs of settling and hence could affect potential migration. The term $\epsilon_{o,d}^s$ captures measurement error.

Specification equation (2) is similar to what is usually estimated in the economic literature using *actual migration data* (Grogger and Hanson, 2011; Beine *et al.*, 2011; Ortega and Peri, 2013). Our data allow us to go one step further. The actual migration "action" requires that "a migration opportunity" becomes available to potential migrants. This could be the opportunity of a visa or a migration permit, or it may involve a study, working or career opportunity. A successful migration episode, in other words, involves the matching of a migration opportunity at destination d and a potential migrant from country o, from the pool $p_{o,d}^s$. Hence, we express actual migration, $m_{o,d}^s$, as the number of successful potential migrant–opportunity matches, which depends positively on the size of the population willing to migrate to d, $p_{o,d}^s$, and on the opportunities for migrants arising in the 2000–2010 period in the destination country, v_d^s. Those viable opportunities (hence the letter v) are usually not specific to people in country o; hence, we only have a subscript d, but in practice, some bilateral factors could improve the availability of those opportunities to some specific countries of origin. In general, we write:

$$m_{o,d}^s = m(\underset{+}{p_{o,d}^s}, \underset{+}{v_d^s}) \qquad (3)$$

The superscript s permits differentiating between college- and non-college-educated. This framework allows us to explore whether economic growth (captured by real income per capita growth, gy_d^{00-10}) or employment growth (captured by the growth of employment relative to the population, ge_d^{00-10}) in the period 2000–2010 in the destination countries contributed to actual migration, once we account for the pool of potential migrants for that country. Fast growth of income per capita or growth of employment is driven by productivity growth, which would increase demand for labor in a destination country, creating opportunities (jobs, study, business) for immigrants. These vacancies could be matched to potential migrants willing to move to that country. Potential migrants are a stock (share of those who would migrate) measured at a specific point in time. This is why their size depends on a static comparison of income per person, capturing long-run present discounted values. Actual migrants, on the other hand, are a flow (the subset that realize migration potential within a period). Hence, the creation of opportunities to migrate which affects the flow is correlated to GDP and employment growth at destination. Such flows, however, may have a different impact on sending countries depending on the stock of potential migrants. New jobs and growth of productivity are needed to produce new opportunities for an existing stock of potential immigrants. We will test the premise that income levels (rather than growth) affect potential immigrants while income growth (rather than levels) affect net migration for given potential immigrants.

Potentially important in translating potential into actual migrants are also the policies in the destination country. We analyze the role of some specific policies (Policy$_{o,d}$). In particular, we consider visa waiver policies that regulate access to a country for all foreigners as well as free mobility of labor which is the closest policy to open borders. It is worth noticing that these two policy variables only affect entry conditions and not the conditions of stay in the destination countries (*e.g.* employment, taxation, etc.). Clearly, the details and nuances of immigration policies are large and very different across countries (for more sophisticated indices, *see* Ortega and Peri, 2013; Helbling and Vink, 2013), and our simple indicators may not be capturing important aspects of those policies. Finally, we can analyze whether the pool of potential migrants and economic and policy variables interacted with each other to increase the matching rate, and hence the realized migration rate. Linearizing the matching function given in equation (3), including country-of-origin fixed effects β_o^s and substituting the potential determinants of opportunities of migration, v_d^s, we have:

$$m_{o,d}^s = \beta_o^s + b_1^s p_{o,d}^s + b_2^s gy_d^{00-10} + b_3^s ge_d^{00-10} + b_4^s \text{Policy}_{o,d} + \varepsilon_{o,d}^s \quad (4)$$

where $\varepsilon_{o,d}^s$ is the residual term.

While we consider economic growth and receiving-country policies as the key determinants of migration opportunities for potential migrants in the empirical analysis, we will also include bilateral cost variables, network variables, and other economic variables as controls. In our empirical analysis, we will estimate the basic equations (2) and (4) in order to determine which factors affect the size of the pool of potential migrants and which factors affect their matching with migration opportunities.

DETERMINANTS OF POTENTIAL MIGRATION RATES

We first estimate several versions of equation (2) to analyze the determinants of potential migration rates, including a progressively larger set of determinants and controls. The dependent variable is the potential emigration rate for each skill group s from country o to country d in the period 2000–2010, $p_{o,d}^s$. As some values of the actual net emigration rate, $m_{o,d}^s$, are negative (due to return migration or migrants' mortality), we set them to zero before calculating the potential rate and, similarly, we censor the observations on bilateral migration at a value equal to the average plus five standard deviations as some of them are relative to very small countries and hence excessively noisy. Let us emphasize that, while customary in this literature, the identification of causal effects using a cross-sectional estimation has to be taken with caution. While controlling for country-of-origin-specific factors and for important bilateral factors, there are still unobserved bilateral and destination-specific factors that may bias the coefficients. While we will sometimes use a causal language referring to the explanatory variables as "determinants of potential migration," we are well aware that our estimates mainly identify correlates of potential migration and migration flows.

Table 3 shows summary statistics for the migration variables, net emigration rates, and potential emigration rates and for the stock of migrants, divided by the native population and for the share of natives with at least one member of the household who migrated abroad during the previous five years.[7] The potential bilateral migration rate for

---

[7]The variable is constructed as the share of the resident population answering yes to the question: "Have any members of your household gone to live in a foreign country permanently or temporarily in the past five years?"

TABLE 3
SUMMARY STATISTICS: ACTUAL AND POTENTIAL MIGRATION RATES, AND MEASURES OF MIGRATION NET-
WORKS. AS PERCENTAGE OF THE NATIVE POPULATION AT ORIGIN IN 2000

	Observations	Mean	Standard deviation
Net emigration rate 2000–2010, Less educated	5,654	0.05	0.28
Net emigration rate 2000–2010, College-educated	4,239	0.21	0.62
Potential emigration rate 2000–2010, Less educated	4,239	0.49	1.67
Potential emigration rate 2000–2010, College-educated	4,100	0.71	1.72
Stock of migrants relative to native population, 2000	5,654	0.28	1.78
Share of residents with at least one member of household abroad in the last 5 years, non-college-educated	3,929	0.10	0.80
Share of residents with at least one member of household abroad in the last 5 years , college-educated	3,929	0.07	0.30

The unit of observation is a country of origin–country of destination pair. The average and standard deviation are calculated including all observations without weighting them. The definition of the actual and potential migration rates is given in the text.

non-college-educated has an unweighted average value equal to 0.49%, compared to 0.71% for college-educated.[8] The actual bilateral migration rate for non-college-educated was on average 0.05%, while for college-educated the average bilateral rate amounted to 0.21%. These rates are small but capture bilateral (not aggregate) migration net flows (not stocks) of migrants. Each country of origin has 30 destinations. Hence, average bilateral rates of 0.05% and 0.21% imply migration rates of 1.5% and 6% of the native population in total over the 2000–2010 period.[9]

Tables 4 and 5 display estimation results for non-college- and college-educated, respectively. They show the coefficients on economic, network, and policy variables in regressions whose dependent variable is the potential emigration rate for the two skill groups separately. In each regression, we include a set of 138 country-of-origin fixed effects to

[8]The total number of observations for actual migration from 143 origins into 30 destinations is 5,673. However, we are missing desired migration data for some countries of origin (mainly small developing countries) that therefore are dropped, leaving us with 4,247 observations. Eliminating observations five times larger than the standard deviation, we are left with 4,162 valid observations.

[9]The remaining summary, statistics for the other control and explanatory variables are reported in Table A1 in the appendix.

TABLE 4

DETERMINANTS OF POTENTIAL MIGRATION RATES ($p \times 100$) OF NON-COLLEGE-EDUCATED. ONE HUNDRED AND THIRTY EIGHT SENDING COUNTRIES TO OUR 30 DESTINATION COUNTRIES, 2000–2010

Explanatory Variable	(1) Basic, non-negative rates	(2) All rates	(3) Basic geography and culture	(4) Extended geography and culture	(5) Including contemporaneous growth rate	(6) Policies	(7) Only migrants from Asia–Africa–Latin America
Stock migrants/ population in 2000	0.83*** (0.31)	0.46 (0.32)	0.77*** (0.31)	0.73** (0.31)	0.77** (0.31)	0.77** (0.31)	0.95* (0.52)
Stock people with household member abroad/ population	0.91** (0.44)	0.97** (0.45)	0.89** (0.43)	0.87** (0.42)	0.89** (0.43)	0.89** (0.43)	0.83* (0.44)
Real GDP per person (1,000 $ PPP), destination in 2000	0.02*** (0.003)	0.02*** (0.03)	0.02*** (0.003)	0.02*** (0.003)	0.02*** (0.003)	0.02*** (0.003)	0.02** (0.004)
Empl/Pop 15+, destination in 2000	0.005** (0.002)	0.005** (0.002)	0.004** (0.002)	0.004** (0.002)	0.004** (0.002)	0.004*** (0.002)	0.007*** (0.001)
Free labor movement dummy in 2000						0.046 (0.124)	
Visa waiver dummy in 2000						−0.016 (0.085)	−0.001 (0.001)
Growth of GDP per person 2000-2010					−0.001 (0.001)	−0.001 (0.001)	
Standard controls	Origin FE, ln(Pop_d)	Origin FE, ln(Pop_d)	Origin FE, ln(Pop_d)	Origin FE, ln(Pop_d)	Origin FE, ln(Pop_d)	Origin FE, ln(Pop_d)	Origin FE, ln(Pop_d)
Geographical and cultural controls	None	None	ln(distance), border, common lang.	ln(distance), border, common lang, colony, legal origin, currency, landlocked, religious prox., genetic distance	ln(distance), border, common lang	ln(distance), border, common lang	ln(distance), border, common lang

The dependent variable is the potential emigration rate from country of origin to country of destination, calculated as the sum of total 2000–2010 net migrants plus those that indicated willingness to migrate from origin to destination, divided by the population of natives in the country of origin as of 2000. Only individuals without college education are included. An observation is a country of origin–destination pair, for 138 origins and 30 (mainly OECD) destinations. All regressions include country-of-origin fixed effects and the size of the population at destination. The observations are weighted by the country-of-origin population without college education, and we drop migration rates smaller than 0 and larger than the 99th percentile of the distribution. Standard errors are clustered by country of origin. ***, **, and * imply significance at 1%, 5%, and 10% level.

TABLE 5

DETERMINANTS OF POTENTIAL MIGRATION RATES ($p \times 100$) OF COLLEGE-EDUCATED. ONE HUNDRED AND THIRTY EIGHT SENDING COUNTRIES TO OUR 30 DESTINATION COUNTRIES, 2000–2010

Explanatory Variable	(1) Basic, non-negative rates	(2) All rates	(3) Basic geography and culture	(4) Extended geography and culture	(5) Including contemporaneous growth rate	(6) Policies	(7) Only migrants from Asia–Africa–Latin America
Stock migrants/ population in 2000	1.03*** (0.33)	0.94*** (0.30)	0.98*** (0.27)	0.80*** (0.25)	0.99*** (0.27)	0.964*** (0.27)	1.90 (1.23)
Stock people with household member abroad /population	2.17*** (0.35)	2.17*** (0.35)	2.01*** (0.32)	2.01*** (0.32)	2.01*** (0.32)	1.9823*** (0.332)	1.70*** (0.34)
Real GDP per person (1,000 $ PPP), destination in 2000	0.03*** (0.002)	0.03*** (0.002)	0.03*** (0.003)	0.03*** (0.002)	0.03*** (0.003)	0.035*** (0.004)	0.03*** (0.006)
Empl/Pop 15+, destination in 2000	0.009* (0.005)	0.009* (0.005)	0.01** (0.005)	0.01** (0.004)	0.01** (0.04)	0.011** (0.005)	0.02*** (0.005)
Free labor movement dummy in 2000						0.207 (0.155)	
Visa waiver dummy						0.112 (0.078)	
Growth of GDP per person 2000-2010					−0.001 (0.001)	−0.001 (0.001)	−0.001 (0.001)
Standard controls	Origin FE, ln(Pop$_d$)	Origin FE, ln(Pop$_d$)	Origin FE, ln(Pop$_d$)	Origin FE, ln(Pop$_d$)	Origin FE, ln(Pop$_d$)	Origin FE, ln(Pop$_d$)	Origin FE, ln(Pop$_d$)
Geographical and cultural controls	None	None	ln(distance), border, common lang.	ln(distance), border, common lang, colony, legal origin, currency, landlocked, religious prox., genetic distance	ln(distance), border, common lang	ln(distance), border, common lang	ln(distance), border, common lang

The dependent variable is the potential emigration rate from country of origin to country of destination, calculated as the sum of total 2000–2010 net migrants plus those that indicated willingness to migrate from origin to destination, divided by the population of natives in the country of origin as of 2000. Only individuals with college education are included. An observation is a country of origin–destination pair, for 138 origins and 30 (mainly OECD) destinations. All regressions include country-of-origin fixed effects and the size of the population at destination. The observations are weighted by the country-of-origin population with college education, and we drop migration rates smaller than 0 and larger than the 99th percentile of the distribution. Standard errors are clustered by country of origin. ***,**, and * imply significance at 1%, 5%, and 10% level.

account for heterogeneity in characteristics and conditions in the countries of origin. We also include the logarithm of population at destination to account for the size of the destination country, which could affect the potential to migrate there if people are more likely to know of larger countries' opportunities relative to smaller ones. We also cluster the standard errors at the country of origin level to allow residuals to be correlated among individuals in the same country of origin. We progressively include more controls from column 1 to 6. In column 1, we only include the measures of migrant networks (i.e., the stock of natives from country o residing in country d as of 2000, in percentage of the native population and the percentage of the native population with a household member abroad), income per person (thousands of 2000 US \$ in PPP), and the employment rate in the destination country. In column 2, we allow the dependent variable to have negative values (i.e., the negative net migration rates were not set to zero). In column 3, we add some basic geographical and cultural distance controls: the logarithm of bilateral distance, a common border dummy, and a dummy for a common official language. In column 4, we also add variables proxying for more specific dimension of cultural and institutional distance between countries. They involve a dummy for common legal origin, one for common currency, the number of landlocked countries in the pair, a measure of religious distance, and a measure of genetic distance, taken from Ortega and Peri (2014) and Spolaore and Wacziarg (2009). These specifications identify the role of economic variables, networks, and costs driven by differences in determining potential migration rates. In column 5, we include also the 2000–2010 growth rate of income in the destination country to check whether it affects potential migration. As mentioned above, the comparison of benefits and costs in the decision to migrate should be based on long-run expectations, captured by average differences in income per person more than by recent growth rates. Specification 6 includes two measures of immigration policies: a dummy for those countries with free labor mobility between them in 2000, namely the EU18 countries among themselves and with Switzerland, the Nordic countries (Denmark, Sweden, Norway, Iceland, and Finland) among themselves, and a dummy for those countries having a visa waiver agreement for travel between them (Neumayer, 2006). Finally, in column 7, we include only non-rich countries in Asia, Africa, and Latin America as sending countries, and we analyze whether the determinants of potential migration from poorer countries systematically differ from those estimated using the whole set of countries. The results reported in the tables focus on the role of economic, network, and policy variables. While it is important to control for geographical and cultural variables, those are hard to change or to affect. Therefore, we include them as controls and comment only on some main coefficient estimates, but we do not report their coefficients in the tables.

Migrant Networks and Economic Incentives

Let us first focus on the effects of network and economic variables on potential migration rates. The first two rows of Tables 4 and 5 show the impact of the stock of existing migrants abroad as of 2000 and the effect of the share of people in the country with a household member abroad. While the first variable was constructed based on the data of Artuç *et al.* (forthcoming) and Brücker *et al.* (2013) on the stock of migrants, the second is obtained from the Gallup poll data. It represents the share of natives in country o who said they had a household member who migrated to country d within the previous five years. This allows us to link individuals with their more recent and more direct "connections" then construct an aggregate measure of it. This measure of networks is related more directly to the possibility of natives receiving information about country d and assistance once in the destination. The correlation between these network variables equals 0.16 for the college-educated and 0.43 for the less educated. Both network variables have a positive and significant effect on potential migration for college- and non-college-educated (rows 1 and 2 of Tables 4 and 5). Both explanatory variables are divided by their standard deviation so that the coefficient shows the impact on potential migration rates from increasing the variable by one standard deviation. Table 4 reveals that an increase in the stock of natives in country d by one standard deviation increases the potential migration rate of non-college-educated to that country by 0.73 to 0.95 percentage points, while the effect for college-educated is around 1 percentage point. Increasing the share of people with household members in country d by one standard deviation increases the potential migration rate of college-educated by about 2 percentage points and of non-college-educated by 1 percentage point. Recall that the average migration rate for non-college (college)-educated was 0.49% (0.71%).

Hence, potential migration is very responsive to the stock of existing compatriots and household members abroad. This confirms previous evidence (*e.g.* Hanson and McIntosh, 2010; Hatton and Williamson, 2005) and emphasizes the additional effect of recent household links in encouraging potential migration. For many important corridors, the network effect is a key correlate of potential migration. For example, potential migration rates from Mexico to the U.S. are equal to 16% and 17.5% for college-educated and the less educated. Two-thirds of those values can be explained by network effects. Indeed, the Mexican diaspora in the U.S. amounts to about 5.2 million people, representing 11.2% of the Mexican population aged 25 and over (6.3 standard deviations in the aggregate network variable). The proportion of Mexican households having a household member who migrated in the previous five years is equal to 2% for college-educated and 4.5% for the less educated (i.e., 2.5 and 5.6 standard deviations). Obviously, causal relationships are difficult to establish in a cross-country framework, and our estimates are more correlation than causation. Taken at face value, our estimates suggest that each network effect increases the potential migration rate by 5 to 6 percentage points. As for the Turkey-to-Germany corridor, the potential migration rate of low-skilled Turks equals 3%. Again, two-thirds of this rate (2.2 percentage points) is explained by the network effects. An important caveat is that the stock of migrants abroad may capture not only network effects but also the persistence of bilateral relations that have increased migration in the past and continue to do so. Controlling for that, the measure of people with household members recently migrated abroad has an additional and important effect. It could be more directly connected to the diffusion of information and the presence of potential support at destination, but could also reveal some aggregate collective decision of families due to unobserved factors affecting their willingness to migrate. The fact that we control for country-of-origin effects and that we focus on the aggregate (and not family level) effects reduces the risk of omitted variable bias.

Crucial to our analysis is the role of economic variables in determining potential migration. In the section describing the theoretical framework, we assumed that income per person and the employment rate at destination proxy for the long-term expected gains of migrating as they allow migrants to predict their future income and probability of employment. The large international differences in these variables are likely to be known to potential migrants and hence to affect their preferred destination. It is therefore reassuring to see that both variables strongly affect potential migration rates for both more and less educated. The coefficients are similarly significant for college- and non-college-educated, although somewhat larger for the first group. From Table 4, we see that a difference in income per person of 10,000 PPP US $ in 2000 (which equals one standard deviation in the income per person distribution of the 30 destination countries and corresponds to the difference in income per person between the UK and the U.S.) increases the potential migration rate by 0.20 percentage points for the less educated (for an average of 0.49%) and by 0.30 percentage points for college-educated (for an average of 0.71%). An increase in the employment rate of 10 percentage points (also close to the standard deviation across destination countries) would increase potential migration by 0.05 percentage points for less educated and by 0.10 percentage points for more educated. The estimates are very significant and stable across specifications. Income per capita – for which information is more easily available – has the largest effect, and the response of the less educated to differences in that variable is only 50% smaller than the response of college-educated. This difference can be due to the fact that in richer countries, highly educated get a higher absolute wage premium implying that they would be more willing to migrate (Grogger and Hanson, 2011). This confirms that less educated migrants, when choosing whether to look for migration opportunities, are driven by the same considerations (income and jobs) as college-educated, and their response to those variables is also quantitatively similar to the response of college-educated.

The estimates in Tables 4 and 5 reveal two other important features of potential migration. First, focusing on the last column 7 in which the sample is limited to non-rich countries of origin (outside of Europe, North America. and Oceania), we see that the responses of desired migration rates from these countries to income per person and employment rates in the destination are very similar to the responses obtained with the full sample. College- and non-college-educated migrants from poor countries respond to income and employment at destination in a similar way as migrants from other countries. The only variable that seems to matter somewhat more for potential migrants in poor countries is the stock of nationals having migrated previously to d. Networks measured as the share of natives with a household member abroad, however, have the same impact on poor countries as in the full sample. This possibly implies that the stock of past migrants reveals past preferential relations between the poor country and the destination (driven by cultural, colonial, or other non-observable ties).

The second interesting fact is revealed by columns 5-7. While income per person levels as of 2000 has a strong and positive correlation with potential migration, the growth rate of income per person at destination in 2000–2010 has an insignificant effect. Potential migrants are less affected in their preferences for migrating and where to migrate, by recent/potential economic performance of the destination. The U.S. and Canada remain very attractive destinations for potential migrants from Guatemala, even in decades when their economy was not growing very fast. The marginal effect of growth over a decade on cross-country differences in GDP per person is small and hence does not affect much the pool of potential migrants. This is strongly confirmed by our results. We show evidence below that faster growth increases actual migration rates to a country. Our framework allows us to understand why. Faster growth means more *opportunities* for migrants as new firms and higher productivity generate vacancies and migration opportunities in destination countries. Whereas the flow of actual migrants benefits from that growth, the stock of potential migrants is not much affected.

Geography, Culture, and Policies

If the decisions to be a potential migrant is driven by cost-return calculations only and it is not affected by the probability of securing an opportunity to migrate, we would not expect the policy variables in the destination country, which affect only the opportunities but not the costs/benefits once migrated, to play a crucial role in determining potential migration. Policies are, however, expected to play a role in determining actual migration. Variables measuring geographical, cultural, and institutional distance, on the other hand, should affect the cost of migration through their impact on the transferability of skills and could as such have an effect on potential migration.

    In columns 4 and 5, we include several controls capturing geography, culture, and institutions. We do not show their coefficients in the tables, but we comment on their estimates here. First, the addition of these controls does not change the size and significance of the coefficients of economic and network variables. Second, we should keep in mind that we are already controlling for the past stock of migrants and presence of household members abroad. Those clearly capture a large part of the effect of geography, culture, and institutions, which are slow to change or do not change at all, on past migration. Worth mentioning is that the logarithm of distance is not significant for either more or less educated. Common language is the only variable significant for potential migration rates of both college- and non-college-educated (with a larger coefficient, 0.88, for college-educated than for the less educated, 0.44). No other geographical variable is significant at the 1% level for non-college-educated, while colonial ties (0.48, standard error of 0.17) and genetic distance (t-statistic of -4.93) appear significant for potential migration of college-educated. These checks confirm the relevance of geographical, cultural, and historical ties for bilateral migration as established in the empirical literature (see among others Hatton and Williamson, 2005; Pedersen *et al.*, 2008; Mayda, 2010; Grogger and Hanson, 2011).[10] Here, we are more interested in verifying that after including them as controls for bilateral migration costs, the magnitude and significance of the main economic variables affecting expected gains from migration are preserved. The results of columns 3 and 4 in Tables 3 and 4 confirm that this is the case as the coefficients on the income per person and employment rates remain virtually unchanged.

In column 6 of Tables 4 and 5, we introduce two policy variables. The first is a variable aimed at capturing free labor mobility across countries. The second is a dummy indicating a visa waiver agreement when traveling between the countries. Other papers (*e.g.* Mayda, 2010; Ortega and Peri, 2013) included several measures of immigration policies capturing the restrictiveness of provisions such as visa policies, quotas, or asylum policies to analyze how they affect migration. Here, we take a simpler approach. Since it is very complicated to measure or even rank the restrictiveness of immigration policies, we identify only two policies, which can substantially affect cross-border mobility in general, and for working purposes in particular. Specifically, we consider the elimination of all immigration restrictions to labor mobility between countries and the presence of a visa waiver agreement between countries that allow people to visit without obtaining a visa (shown by Bertoli and Fernández-Huertas Moraga, 2013, to be an important variable in determining bilateral mobility). In the presence of free labor mobility, people from a country can work freely at the same conditions as natives in a foreign country. This type of policy was established across countries of the European Union by the 1992 Maastricht Treaty. Moreover, since the 1990s, Switzerland and the Nordic countries of Europe (Norway, Sweden, Finland, Denmark, and Iceland) have signed bilateral agreements ensuring free labor mobility of their workers with all the EU countries. Hence, we include

---

[10]There is also a large literature analyzing the impact of these bilateral factors on trade. *See e.g.* Ortega and Peri (2014).

bilateral dummies to capture the free mobility arrangements across these countries which were in place as of 2000, the initial year in our analysis.

The estimates in column 6 reveal that neither the presence of free migration policies nor visa waiver agreements affect the pool of potential migrants both for college- and non-college-educated. While the presence of such bilateral agreements may proxy also for other bilateral policies, it makes sense to find that potential migration is not affected by them. Note that while these policies affect the probability of having an "opportunity" to migrate to a specific country, they do not affect costs or benefits from such opportunity. Potential migration reflects preferences, costs, and benefits for bilateral migration choices in the presence of an opportunity. Policies affecting the opportunities to migrate should not affect that calculation.

Robustness Checks

In Table 6, we subject our estimates of the determinants of potential migration rates to a number of robustness checks. The table shows specifications including all the controls from column 5 in Tables 3 and 4, to which we alternatively add different controls or for which we modify the sample in different specifications. Columns 1 to 3 show the results for the less educated, while columns 4 to 6 show those for college-educated. In specifications 1 and 4, we include continent-destination dummies in order to take into account the fact that destination countries in Europe or North America might have particular policies or characteristics in common, and in order to accommodate the possibility that the choice of migration within a continent is correlated (as pointed out by Bertoli and Fernández-Huertas Moraga, 2013). The estimates of the main coefficients are again stable in magnitude and significance. Only the employment rate becomes less significant, which is certainly due to the smaller within-continent variation of this rate across countries. The growth of GDP per person even becomes negative in this specification, confirming that people do not account for recent performance when choosing their "desired" migration countries, but rather compare long-lasting differences in income per person.

Columns 2 and 5 analyze whether considering only "desired" migration rates rather than potential (thus excluding people who actually migrated) changes the effect of economic determinants. This allows us to verify that the subset of actual migrants is not a "special" group among potential migrants in terms of their response to economic incentives. For both college- and non-college-educated, the estimates are similar to those of column 5 in Tables 4

TABLE 6
DETERMINANTS OF POTENTIAL MIGRATION RATES, ROBUSTNESS CHECKS, ONE HUNDRED AND THIRTY EIGHT SENDING COUNTRIES TO OUR 30 DESTINATION COUNTRIES, 2000–2010

Explanatory Variable:	Less educated			College-educated		
	(1) Including destination-continent dummies	(2) Only willing to emigrate as dependent variable	(3) Only most reliable data on willingness to emigrate	(4) Including destination-continent dummies	(5) Only willing to emigrate as dependent variable	(6) Only most reliable data on willingness to emigrate
Stock migrants/population in 2000	0.72*** (0.29)	0.69*** (0.28)	0.71** (0.32)	0.95*** (0.24)	0.62*** (0.14)	0.73*** (0.22)
Stock people with family abroad/population	0.86** (0.41)	0.83** (0.41)	1.20* (0.63)	1.70*** (0.30)	1.50*** (0.26)	2.87*** (0.47)
Real GDP per person (1,000 $ PPP), destination in 2000	0.014*** (0.003)	0.02*** (0.003)	0.02*** (0.003)	0.03*** (0.002)	0.03*** (0.002)	0.03*** (0.003)
Empl/Pop 15+, destination in 2000	0.001 (0.001)	0.005*** (0.001)	0.005*** (0.001)	0.002 (0.003)	0.008** (0.004)	0.009* (0.005)
Growth of GDP per person 2000–2010	−0.002** (0.001)	−0.001 (0.001)	−0.0007 (0.0007)	−0.002* (0.001)	−0.001 (0.001)	−0.001 (0.001)
Standard controls	Origin FE, ln(Pop$_d$)	Origin FE, ln(Pop$_d$)	Origin FE, ln(Pop$_d$)	Origin FE, ln(Pop$_d$)	Origin FE, ln(Pop$_d$)	Origin FE, ln(Pop$_d$)
Geographical and cultural controls	ln(distance), border, common lang.	ln(distance), border, common lang.	ln(distance), border, common lang.	ln(distance), border, common lang.	ln(distance), border, common lang.	ln(distance), border, common lang.

The specification estimated corresponds to column (5) in Tables 3 and 4. Columns (1)–(3) refer to non-college-educated; columns (4)–(6) refer to college-educated. In columns 1 and 4, we include also destination-continent dummies. In columns 2 and 5, we use only the measure of people willing to emigrate relative to the population in 2000 as dependent. In columns 3 and 6, we select those bilateral observations on willingness to migrate that included at least 75 or 37 surveyed people, respectively. The observations are weighted by the country-of-origin population with college education, and we drop migration rates smaller than 0 and larger than the 99th percentile of the distribution. Standard errors are clustered by country of origin. ***, **, and * imply significance at 1%, 5%, and 10% level.

and 5, confirming that those economic variables affect all potential migrants, independent of whether they succeed in migrating or not. Finally, as the data on desire to migrate are based on Gallup polls that include only a few hundred people in some small countries, we include a check on the reliability of those data. In particular, we drop from the regressions all the bilateral desired migration rates based on less than 75 respondents (for the less educated) and less than 37 respondents for college-educated. This reduces the sample (inclusive of all non-missing controls) from 3,744 observations to 3,278. The point estimates of the effects, however, show that the results are robust even to selecting only the most reliable bilateral potential migration rates and that economic and network variables play the same important role.

POTENTIAL MIGRANTS, MIGRATION OPPORTUNITIES, AND ACTUAL MIGRANTS

The analysis so far shows that income per person, employment probability, and the presence of networks from the same country of origin (either measured as the stock of previous immigrants or as the share of natives with a household member abroad) are robust and significant determinants of potential migrants. They contribute importantly to determining the size of the pool of people searching for migration opportunities. But how do these potential migrants turn into actual migrants? What factors affect the actual migration rates on top of the potential migration rates? Which share of potential migrants become actual migrants? These are the questions we will focus on in the present section.

In Tables 7, 8, 10, and 11, we estimate variations of equation (4) in which the dependent variable is the actual migration rate from country o to country d, $m_{o,d}^s$, with the potential migration rate as the first explanatory variable. We include an array of destination country characteristics that may affect migration opportunities and hence the number of actual migrants. We always control for country-of-origin fixed effects. Tables 7 and 8 show the results of the main specifications, for the less educated and college-educated, respectively. Table 10 analyzes whether labor mobility policies, networks, and growth of economic opportunities in the destination countries interacted with potential migrants affect actual rates. Table 11, finally, considers whether actual migration from low-income countries of origin (in Asia, Africa, and South America) responded differently to potential migration and other factors potentially affecting migration opportunities.

TABLE 7

DETERMINANTS OF NET MIGRATION RATES ($m \times 100$) OF THE LESS EDUCATED. ONE HUNDRED AND THIRTY EIGHT SENDING COUNTRIES TO OUR 30 DESTINATION Countries, 2000–2010

Explanatory Variable:	(1) Basic	(2) Control for levels	(3) Include network	(4) Add Free labor mobility 2000 and visa waiver	(5) Free labor, geography, and culture	(6) As (4) using desire to migrate permanently
Potential Emigration rates, Low Skilled	0.046*** (0.009)	0.046*** (0.009)	0.038*** (0.0009)	0.046*** (0.009)	0.047*** (0.0102)	0.058** (0.012)
GDP growth, destination 2000–2010	0.0002* (0.0001)	0.0002* (0.0001)	0.0002* (0.0001)	0.0003** (0.0001)	0.0002** (0.0001)	0.0002** (0.0001)
(Empl/Pop 15+) growth, destination 2000–2010	0.0005 (0.0003)	0.0005 (0.0003)	0.0005 (0.0003)	0.0004 (0.0003)	0.0006* (0.0003)	0.006 (0.005)
Stock people with family abroad/population			0.036** (0.017)			
Free labor movement dummy				0.0106** (0.0051)	−0.0114* (0.0060)	0.012** (0.004)
Visa waiver dummy				0.0108** (0.0047)	0.0076* (0.0042)	0.006 (0.005)
Real GDP per person (1,000 $ PPP), destination in 2000		−0.00004 (0.00007)				
Employment/Population working age destination in 2000		−0.0002 (0.0002)				
Standard controls	Origin FE	Origin FE	Origin FE	Origin FE	Origin FE	Origin FE
Geographical and cultural controls	None	None	None	None	ln(distance), border, common lang,, colony, legal origin, currency, landlocked, religious prox., genetic distance	None

The dependent variable is the emigration rate from country of origin to country of destination, calculated as the sum of total 2000–2010 net migrants, divided by the population of natives in the country of origin as of 2000. Only individuals without college education are included. An observation is a country of origin–destination pair, for 138 origins and 30 (mainly OECD) destinations. All regressions include country-of-origin fixed effects. The observations are weighted by the country-of-origin population without college education, and we drop migration rates larger than the 99th percentile of the distribution. Standard errors are clustered by country of origin.. ***, **, and * imply significance at 1%, 5%, and 10% level.

TABLE 8

DETERMINANTS OF NET MIGRATION RATES ($m \times 100$) OF COLLEGE-EDUCATED. ALL SENDING COUNTRIES TO OUR 30 DESTINATION COUNTRIES, 2000–2010

Explanatory Variable	(1) Basic	(2) Control for levels	(3) Include network	(4) Add Free labor mobility 2000 and visa waiver	(5) Free labor, geography and culture	(6) As (4) using desire to migrate permanently
Potential Emigration rates, High Skilled	0.13*** (0.03)	0.13*** (0.03)	0.12*** (0.03)	0.13*** (0.02)	0.13*** (0.03)	0.17*** (0.03)
GDP growth, destination 2000–2010	0.0008*** (0.0003)	0.0009*** (0.0003)	0.0008*** (0.0003)	0.0006 (0.0004)	0.0006 (0.0003)	0.0002 (0.0003)
(Empl/Pop 15+) growth, destination 2000–2010	−0.002* (0.001)	−0.003** (0.0015)	−0.002 (0.001)	−0.0023* (0.0013)	−0.0024* (0.001)	−0.0027** (0.0012)
Stock people with family abroad/population			0.06 (0.11)			
Free labor movement dummy				0.0056 (0.0145)	0.0235 (0.0216)	0.002 (0.01)
Visa waiver dummy				−0.0338 (0.0208)	−0.0351 (0.0236)	−0.04 (0.024)
Real GDP per person (1,000 $ PPP), destination in 2000		0.0001 (0.0002)				
Employment/Population working age destination in 2000		−0.0006 (0.0006)				
Standard controls	Origin FE	Origin FE	Origin FE	Origin FE	Origin FE	Origin FE
Geographical and cultural controls	None	None	None	None	ln(distance), border, common lang, colony, legal origin, currency, landlocked, religious prox., genetic distance	None

The dependent variable is the emigration rate from country of origin to country of destination, calculated as the sum of total 2000–2010 net migrants, divided by the population of natives in the country of origin as of 2000. Only individuals with college education are included. An observation is a country of origin–destination pair, for 138 origins and 30 (mainly OECD) destinations. All regressions include country-of-origin fixed effects. The observations are weighted by the country-of-origin population with college education, and we drop migration rates larger than the 99th percentile of the distribution. Standard errors are clustered by country of origin. ***, **, and * imply significance at 1%, 5%, and 10% level.

TABLE 9

SAME MATCHING FUNCTION FOR COLLEGE EDUCATED AND THE LESS EDUCATED, CHANGE IN IMMIGRATION FLOWS AND RATES IN THE DESTINATION COUNTRIES

	Net inflow 2000–2010 Less educated			Net immigration rate 2000–2010 Less educated		Net immigration rate 2000–2010 Total	
	Observed	Counterfactual	Change	Observed	Counterfactual	Observed	Counterfactual
Australia	−43,572	156,502	200,074	−0.6	2.2	6.5	8.7
Austria	131,191	245,474	114,283	3.1	5.7	4.0	6.4
Belgium	98,126	190,134	92,008	2.0	4.0	4.4	5.8
Canada	−106,830	203,246	310,076	−0.8	1.6	11.9	13.9
Chile	1,134,916	1,208,874	73,958	16.7	17.8	17.5	18.4
Denmark	84,565	117,438	32,873	2.9	4.0	3.9	4.8
Finland	71,786	97,746	25,960	2.4	3.3	2.8	3.6
France	531,354	1,423,387	892,033	1.8	4.7	2.7	5.2
Germany	343,256	878,725	535,469	0.8	2.0	0.8	1.7
Greece	437,392	532,983	95,591	7.1	8.6	9.5	10.8
Ireland	97,686	178,475	80,789	6.1	11.2	11.7	15.6
Israel	−205,390	−200,132	5,258	−18.7	−18.2	−10.6	−10.3
Italy	474,837	1,164,453	689,616	1.3	3.1	1.9	3.5
Japan	139,541	618,870	479,329	0.2	1.0	0.4	0.9
Luxembourg	18,538	26,751	8,213	10.5	15.2	12.3	16.4
Mexico	49,710	145,167	95,457	0.1	0.4	0.3	0.5
Netherlands	−310,625	−168,669	141,956	−4.3	−2.3	−3.5	−2.0
New Zealand	100,327	213,531	113,204	9.1	19.4	8.9	14.9
Norway	114,426	210,155	95,729	5.2	9.6	7.3	10.6
Poland	−189,459	−187,202	2,257	−0.9	−0.9	−0.7	−0.7
Portugal	424,044	540,023	115,979	6.7	8.6	8.2	9.8
Russian Federation	−1,117,531	−1,049,495	68,036	−2.7	−2.6	−0.7	−0.6
Saudi Arabia	997,625	2,294,148	1,296,523	20.4	46.8	31.1	54.8
South Africa	505,528	740,170	234,642	2.8	4.1	4.2	5.3
Spain	2,328,310	3,588,335	1,260,025	10.6	16.3	12.3	17.0
Sweden	198,125	307,922	109,797	4.7	7.3	7.1	9.1
Switzerland	94,586	292,052	197,466	3.0	9.1	3.1	8.1

TABLE 9 (CONTINUED)

SAME MATCHING FUNCTION FOR COLLEGE EDUCATED AND THE LESS EDUCATED. CHANGE IN IMMIGRATION FLOWS AND RATES IN THE DESTINATION COUNTRIES

	Net inflow 2000–2010 Less educated			Net immigration rate 2000–2010 Less educated		Net immigration rate 2000–2010 Total	
	Observed	Counterfactual	Change	Observed	Counterfactual	Observed	Counterfactual
United Arab Emirates	1,269,853	1,700,601	430,748	248.4	332.6	303.9	374.3
United Kingdom	275,684	1,457,422	1,181,738	0.9	4.6	4.1	7.3
United States	4,629,616	10,387,622	5,758,006	6.3	14.0	5.0	8.6
Total/Average	12,577,615	27,314,708	14,737,093	17.0	36.9	16.1	25.3

TABLE 10
EFFECTS OF INTERACTIONS OPPORTUNITY POTENTIAL ON MIGRATION RATES ($M \times 100$). ALL SENDING COUNTRIES TO OUR 30 DESTINATION COUNTRIES, 2000–2010

Explanatory Variable:	Less educated			College-educated		
	(1) Potential–growth	(2) Potential–policy	(3) Potential–network	(4) Potential–growth	(5) Potential–policy	(6) Potential–network
Potential emigration rates	0.04*** (0.015)	0.0464** (0.0229)	0.039*** (0.011)	0.13*** (0.03)	0.3080*** (0.1115)	0.12*** (0.03)
GDP growth, destination 2000–2010	0.00018 (0.00013)	0.0003** (0.0001)	0.0002 (0.0001)	0.0008*** (0.0002)	0.0008* (0.0004)	0.008*** (0.003)
(Empl/Pop 15+) growth, destination 2000–2010	0.001*** (0.0004)	0.0004 (0.0003)	0.0004 (0.0003)	−0.004*** (0.001)	−0.0022* (0.0012)	−0.002 (0.001)
Stock people with family abroad/population			0.015 (0.051)			0.08 (0.07)
Free labor movement dummy		0.0038 (0.0061)			−0.0348 (0.0372)	
Visa waiver dummy		0.0110** (0.0045)			−0.0019 (0.0233)	
Interaction (potential) x (GDP growth)	0.027** (0.013)			0.017 (0.016)		
Interaction (potential) x (free)		0.0145 (0.0151)			0.0597 (0.0447)	
Interaction (potential) x (visa waiver)		−0.0003 (0.0078)			−0.0716* (0.0404)	
Interaction (potential) x (network)			0.004 (0.013)			−0.01 (0.07)
Controls	Origin FE	Origin FE	Origin FE	Origin FE	Origin FE	Origin FE

The dependent variable is the emigration rate from country of origin to country of destination, calculated as the sum of total 2000–2010 net migrants, divided by the population of natives in the country of origin as of 2000. Only individuals without college education are included in regressions 1–3, while only individuals with college education are included in 4–6. An observation is a country of origin–destination pair, for 138 origins and 30 (mainly OECD) destinations. All regressions include country-of-origin fixed effects. The observations are weighted by the country-of-origin population in the relevant education group, and we drop migration rates larger than the 99th percentile of the distribution. Standard errors are clustered by country of origin. ***, **, and * imply significance at 1%, 5%, and 10% level.

TABLE 11
DO POOR SENDING COUNTRIES HAVE A DIFFERENT EFFECT ON MIGRATION RATES? ($M \times 100$). SENDING COUNTRIES IN ASIA, LATIN AMERICA, AND ASIA TO OUR 30 DESTINATION COUNTRIES, 2000–2010

Explanatory Variable:	Less educated			College-educated		
	(1) Basic with geo controls	(2) Control for income levels	(3) With potential-growth interaction	(4) Basic with geo controls	(5) Control for income levels	(6) With potential-growth interaction
Potential emigration rates	0.06*** (0.01)	0.05*** (0.01)	0.04** (0.02)	0.18*** (0.03)	0.22*** (0.04)	0.17*** (0.03)
GDP growth, destination 2000-2010	0.0006*** (0.0002)	0.0002* (0.0001)	0.0002 (0.0001)	0.0016** (0.0007)	0.0015*** (0.0005)	0.0008** (0.0004)
(Empl/Pop 15+) growth, destination 2000-2010	0.001** (0.0005)	0.0005 (0.0003)	0.001* (0.0005)	−0.006** (0.002)	−0.004** (0.001)	−0.006** (0.002)
Real GDP per person (1,000 $ PPP), destination in 2000		−0.00002 (0.00008)			0.0009 (0.0005)	
Empl/Pop 15+, destination in 2000		0.00007 (0.0001)			−0.001 (0.001)	
Visa waiver dummy		0.014* (0.007)			−0.059** (0.024)	
Interaction (potential) x (GDP growth)			0.03** (0.014)			0.03 (0.03)
Standard controls	Origin FE	Origin FE	Origin FE	Origin FE	Origin FE	Origin FE
Geographical and cultural controls	ln(distance), border, common lang., colony, legal origin, currency, landlocked, religious prox., genetic distance	None	None	ln(distance), border, common lang., colony, legal origin, currency, landlocked, religious prox., genetic distance	None	None

The dependent variable is the emigration rate from country of origin to country of destination, calculated as the sum of total 2000–2010 net migrants, divided by the population of natives in the country of origin as of 2000. Only individuals without college education are included in regressions 1–3, while only individual with college education are included in 4–6. An observation is a country of origin–destination pair, for Asian, African, and Latina American countries of origin and 30 (mainly OECD) destinations. All regressions include country-of-origin fixed effects. The observations are weighted by the country-of-origin population in the relevant education group, and we drop migration rates larger than the 99th percentile of the distribution. Standard errors are clustered by country of origin. ***, **, and * imply significance at 1%, 5%, and 10% level.

Economic Opportunities and Migration Policies

The basic specification (1) in Tables 7 and 8 includes only country-of-origin fixed effects, the potential emigration rate, and growth of GDP per person and of employment probability (employment/population at working age) in the destination countries. Growth in GDP per person between 2000 and 2010 and potential migration rates turn out to be the most relevant and significant determinants of actual migration rates. Growth in the employment rate between 2000 and 2010 appears to have a less relevant impact that is sometimes even negative for college-educated migrants. As a check, we included the GDP level, bilateral geography, and cultural controls and found neither significant effects nor impacts on the other coefficients. Let us focus, therefore, on the two most significant variables: growth of GDP per person and the potential migration rate. What is noteworthy is that while those variables affect migration rates for both non-college- and college-educated, the impact is much stronger and significant for the latter. While an increase in potential migration rates by 1% point produces an increase in actual migration by only 0.04 percentage points for the less educated individuals, it is associated with an increase by 0.13% for college-educated. Similarly, an increase in GDP per person by 20% in the decade (equivalent to 2% per year which is roughly the mean and standard deviation of this variable across destination countries) increases actual migration rates by 0.016 percentage points for college-educated and by only 0.004 percentage points for the less educated. Recall for comparison that the impact of GDP per capita levels at destination on potential migration rates was almost the same for college- and non-college-educated.

Overall, we find that the response of college-educated actual migration rates to growth rates and to potential migration rates is three times larger than for non-college-educated. Hence, on average, a much larger share of college-educated potential migrants turns into actual migrants, and favorable economic conditions at destination increase their actual migration rates much more than those of less educated individuals. This implies, for instance, that in spite of a much higher potential migration rate of non-college-educated from India to the U.S. (around 1%) than from India to Spain (around 0.003%), this will only translate in an actual rate to the US 0.05 percentage points higher than the one to Spain. For college-educated, in contrast, the desired migration rate to the U.S., which equaled 8% relative to Spain (equal to 0.02%), predicts a 1.04 percentage points higher actual migration rate to the U.S. than to Spain. The actual difference in migration rates for college-educated from India to the U.S. and to Spain is 2.7 percentage points, and 40% of it can therefore be explained by the difference in the pool of potential migrants to each country. The difference in potential migration rates of non-college-educated to the two countries, on the other hand, did not explain much of their actual difference.

To illustrate the importance of the difference in realization rates between college-educated and less educated potential migrants, we simulated the net immigration rates under the assumption that the migration opportunity matching rate of the less educated was equal to that of college-educated (i.e., that they had a realization rate of 0.13 instead of 0.04). Our simulation assumes that corridors with zero migrants remain empty. This can be thought as a drastic policy experiment (such a policy is clearly not on the political agenda) that equalizes the migration opportunities of college and non-college-educated. Table 9 presents the simulated realization rates by destination country. Columns 1 to 3 show the change in immigration flows, whereas changes in immigration rates are obtained by comparing columns 4 and 5 (for the less educated) and columns 6 and 7 (for all migrants). The total inflow of less educated migrants to our destinations increases by 14.7 million (+117%) of whom 39% would move to the U.S. The other important destinations are Spain, Saudi Arabia, France, Italy, and Germany. In relative terms, the largest changes in low-skilled immigration rates are observed for New Zealand (+10.3 percentage points), the U.S. (+7.8), Switzerland (+6.2), and in the Persian Gulf countries. The same patterns are obtained for total immigration rates.

It could be argued that measuring migration potential in a bilateral way results in measurement error and hence in an underestimation of the effect of potential migration on actual migration if potential migrants have a clear preference for migrating but a weak preference for specific countries. To assess the severity of this bias, we redefine potential and net migration aggregated over all countries of destination and run a number of specifications keeping only the country-of-origin dimension. In order to avoid too demanding specifications (as we only have 138 observations), we only include the stock of people with a household member abroad and GDP per person in the country of origin as controls. Table A2 in the appendix shows the estimated coefficient of potential rates on actual rates. In the specification with networks and income controls, the estimate of the rate at which potential migrants turn into net migrants is 0.18 for college-educated and 0.03 for non-college-educated. These rates are not too far from those estimated using the bilateral definitions (0.13 and 0.04, respectively), suggesting that the impact on actual migration rates from considering aggregate instead of bilateral potential migration is fairly similar. While bilateral preferences may be imprecise, they still seem to reveal useful information on the potential destination of migrants.

Coming back to our regression results, column 2 of Tables 7 and 8 analyze whether the *level* of GDP per person and the employment rate in the destination country affect actual migration for either skill level, after controlling for potential migrants and GDP growth. The estimates reveal that destination country GDP per person and employment probability do not matter in determining opportunities, *once potential migrants are controlled for*. This confirms the presumption that income levels in the destination country only affect migration through their effect on potential migrants (shown in Tables 4 and 5), as they serve as proxies for present discounted return from migrating. Also, in line with Grogger and Hanson (2011), positive selection in actual migration is positively associated with the GDP level at destination. A 10,000 PPP US $ increase in GDP per capita increases potential migration by 0.30 and 0.20 percentage points for college-educated and the less educated, which, in turn, increases actual migration by 0.026 and 0.008 percentage points (*i.e.*, 0.30×0.136 and 0.20×0.04), respectively. A simple numerical experiment reveals that the total migration flow would be 21% greater if income per capita in the 30 destination countries (an average of 27,606 PPP US $) was equal to the U.S. level (i.e., 39,175 PPP US $). College-educated would be more responsive (+25%) than the less educated (+17%).

Column 3 analyzes whether the presence of family networks affects opportunities to migrate, after controlling for potential migration rates. In Tables 4 and 5, we saw that networks were crucial to increase the pool of potential migrants to a destination country. The impact of networks, measured as the stock of existing migrants or the share of natives with a household member abroad, was estimated to be very large. A one standard deviation increase of the network in country *d* corresponded to a one percentage point higher potential migration rate for college- and non-college-educated (relative to an average of 0.49 and 0.71 percentage points for non-college-educated and college-educated, respectively). Do networks also increase actual migration once we control for potential migration? The estimates in column 3 of Tables 7 and 8 show that their impact on actual migration after controlling for the potential rate is smaller and not always significant. For non-college-educated, the impact corresponds to a 0.03 percentage points for each standard deviation. Considering that the direct effect of networks on potential rates was around 0.9 (for a standard deviation increase) and that potential rates translate into actual rates with a coefficient of 0.04 for non-college-educated, the effect of networks through potential migration ($0.9 \times 0.04 = 0.036$) is as large as the direct effect on creating opportunities for less educated migrants. For college-educated, the effect of their network on migration opportunities was not significant, as they probably become aware of them more easily through other (work or professional) channels. Still, the impact on potential migrants was very large.

Columns 4 and 5 introduce the free labor mobility and visa waiver dummies. In column 4, we include the policy dummies for all those pairs of countries with bilateral agreements as of 2000, the beginning of the period we consider. Free labor mobility could in principle significantly increase actual migration by creating migration opportunities that were previously denied. Similarly, the presence of a visa waiver agreement can make a country more accessible to foreign travelers, especially from less developed countries.

Neither policies automatically imply migration opportunities, jobs, or demand for migrants. The estimates show that both free mobility and visa waiver agreements increased actual migration rates for non-college-educated by around 0.01%, which is a very modest amount. For college-educated, the effects were not significant. This is a first sign that it may take more than simple bilateral mobility agreements to generate migration opportunities. One may also argue that countries agreeing to mutual free labor mobility or visa waiving are those with similar characteristics (Neumayer, 2006), which would result in lower gains for migrants. Hence, a free labor market or a visa waiving agreement does not *per se* need to stimulate mobility across those countries. Finally, one might reason that the 2000s formed a period of slow growth in Europe (with a deep recession and financial crisis toward the end of the decade), which may have discouraged migration altogether. In general, once geographical and cultural proximity are controlled for (distance, border, language, and legal origin dummies), the free labor mobility dummy becomes weakly significant, even for non-college-educated.

Thus, our results suggest that economic growth, more than free labor migration policies, is a proximate determinant of actual migration rates of non-college-educated, once we control for potential rates. Overall, we find that free labor mobility policies and the visa waiver policies did not have a strong impact on migration, on creating actual migration opportunities over the 2000–2010 period, or on increasing the pool of potential migrants.

In column 6 of Tables 7 and 8, we calculate potential migration including only those individuals who revealed a preference for permanent migration. As net migration rates capture long-run permanent changes, they might be expected to be most affected by potentially permanent migrants. In line with this intuition, we find that the impact of permanent potential migrants on actual net migration is somewhat stronger than that of total potential migration (with a coefficient of 0.058 for non-college-educated and 0.17 for college-educated). The effect of the remaining variables remains largely unchanged. The intentions to migrate permanently and their distribution across country couples are in fact very strongly correlated to the overall intentions to migrate.[11]

Interactions with Potential Migration Rates

Economic growth in the destination countries encourages migration flows by creating new opportunities. Was this effect stronger for origin countries that had a larger potential migration rate to that destination? Similarly, did free migration policies and networks interact with the pool of potential migrants from specific origins so that their effect was not linear but larger for countries with more potential migrants? The linear form of equation (4) is a simplification. Including some interaction terms would allow for a different marginal effect of policies and economic opportunities depending on the size of the potential migrant pool.

In Table 10, we interact the "potential migration variable" with the growth of GDP per person at destination (columns 1 and 3), or with the free migration and visa waiver dummies (columns 2 and 4) or with the size of the network of household members abroad (specifications 3 and 6). The interaction variables are divided by their standard deviation, so that the coefficients are easier to interpret. The table shows the impact on non-college-educated (columns 1–3) and college-educated (columns 4–6) migration rates. The only interaction effect that turns out to be

---

[11]Further checks and regressions that we performed and do not report convinced us that potential migration rates (both bilateral and aggregate by origin) are very highly correlated whether calculated using total migration or only permanent migration intensions. Hence, we used total potential migration throughout the paper.

significant is that of GDP per capita growth and potential rates for the non-college-educated (as well as that of the visa waiver dummy with potential rates for college-educated, though only marginally significant and negative). In fact, an acceleration of GDP growth by 1.5% per year in the U.S. relative to an acceleration by 1.5% per year in Spain would generate an interaction with potential migration from India of about 15% in the U.S. and almost zero in Spain, which is about one standard deviation of the interaction. The actual migration rate of less educated from India would thus be 0.027 percentage points larger to the U.S. than to Spain as a consequence of their common higher growth rate but different migration potentials. This also implies, for instance, that growth in the U.S. would attract a much larger number of migrants from Mexico than a similar growth rate in Europe would. Faster growth in Germany would, vice versa, produce a larger effect on emigration for less educated Turkish nationals than would be produced by growth in any other country (as the potential migration rate for less educated from Turkey to Germany was larger than 3% compared to a potential rate of less than 1% toward any other country).

Interestingly, economic growth produced opportunities for actual migration and attracted less educated more strongly from countries with larger potential migration rates. Less educated actual migration appears to be higher for countries with a visa waiver agreement, yet the interaction term with potential migration appears insignificant. Free mobility of labor laws, on the other hand, did not affect the actual migration rates (for college nor for non-college-educated) nor did they affect them differentially depending on migration potentials. The strongest results from the analysis of actual migration are the difference between college- and non-college-educated in the rate at which potential migrants turn into actual migrants. This rate seems to be somewhat affected by economic growth at destination but does not seem to be systematically influenced by free mobility policies or by the presence of networks.

Differences Between Rich and Poor Countries of Origin

In Table 11, we analyze whether the relationship between potential migrants, migration opportunities, and actual migrants is different when considering only poor countries of origin. We select countries of origin in Asia, Latin America, and Africa (omitting therefore the rich continents of the world) and estimate specifications similar to the basic ones in Tables 7,

8, and 9. The basic specification (columns 1 and 4) shows that, as found for the total sample, potential emigration rates affect actual ones, and this effect is much stronger for college-educated (coefficient of 0.22) than for non-college-educated (coefficient of 0.05). The estimated values are close to those estimated for the whole sample and possibly somewhat larger, especially for college-educated. The sensitivity of actual migration rates to growth rates at destination, controlling for potential rates, is also roughly as before, and 3 to 4 times larger for college-educated than for non-college-educated. These results suggest that, for less developed countries, there is no particular intensity of selection of potential migrants into actual ones.

Furthermore, we see that income levels and employment rates at destination (columns 2 and 5) do not additionally affect actual migration rates aside from their impact on potential rates. Moreover, higher growth rates at destination stimulate actual migration, and they have a stronger effect (interaction) on countries with a larger migration potential (columns 3 and 6). Finally, the visa waiver policies have a minor positive effect on migration rates of non-college-educated. The similarity of the coefficients estimated in Table 11 with those for the whole sample in Tables 7 and 8 implies that migrants from poorer countries of origin, especially the less educated ones, are not different from migrants from richer countries in their response to incentives. Similarly, potential college-educated migrants from low-income countries of origin have a much larger probability of becoming actual migrants relative to the less educated. Hence, immigration opportunities in the considered destination countries (affected by the economy, policy and other factors) do not seem to "discriminate" based on the origin of immigrants, but are certainly more accessible for individuals with a college education. Alternatively, more educated people might simply be better in realizing migration potentials by searching for the right opportunities. Understanding better what determines the difference in transforming potential migrants into actual migrants between college and non-college-educated is a very important step to predict the future of migration flows in the world. The data and simple procedures used in this paper are a starting point for this analysis.

CONCLUSIONS

Potential migrants are those people who aspire to migrate and look for migration opportunities. Actual migrants are those among potential migrants, that found and took advantage of a migration opportunity and moved to a foreign country. We first identify the pool of potential migrants and the success of that pool in becoming actual migrants, using original data on the desire (willingness) to migrate and effective net migration from 138 origin countries to 30 major destinations over the 2000–2010 period. We then empirically study the determinants of potential migration and its realization rate, highlighting the role of economic factors, networks, and migration policies.

Interestingly, our results are consistent with rational behavior – the income level and employment probability at destination, as well as the presence of networks of co-nationals, are crucial determinants of the pool of potential migrants. However, in turning potential migrants into actual migrants, the factors that matter most are having a college education and the growth perspectives in the receiving country. According to our estimates, one out of five college-educated potential migrants became an actual migrant (within the considered decade), while only one in twenty potential migrants among non-college-educated finally migrated.

The migration literature has established the value of analytically separating migration aspirations from opportunities to migrate (Carling, 2002). The economic literature, on the other hand, has mainly focused on actual migration rates without differentiating non-migrants by whether or not they are searching for migration opportunities (Grogger and Hanson, 2011). This study connects the two-step approach to migration with economic modeling. We emphasize the most interesting and selective step in the process: from potential to actual migrants. This is a passage that is only understood if we take a two-step approach. We hope that through the use of uniquely large-scale data, additional theoretical sources, and new methodological frameworks, we contribute to further strengthening the two-step approach to international migration.

DATA APPENDIX

We construct bilateral data on actual migration rates ($m_{o,d}^s$) and willingness (or desire) to emigrate ($w_{o,d}^s$) for college-educated and less educated individuals ($s = H, L$), for 138 countries of origin ($o = 1,...,138$) and 30 countries of destination ($d = 1,...,30$) for the period 2000–2010. These rates are expressed as percent of the non-migrant, native population aged 25 and over in country o in the year 2000. Potential migration rates are simply defined as the sum of actual and desired migration: $p_{o,d}^s \equiv m_{o,d}^s + w_{o,d}^s$. This appendix describes our data sources and methodology.

TABLE A1.
SUMMARY STATISTICS FOR EXPLANATORY VARIABLES AND CONTROLS

	Observations	Mean	Standard dev.	Min	Max
Real GDP per person, in 2000 PPP \$, destination	5,363	27,606.65	11,633.00	5,893.64	62,626.35
Real GDP per person, in 2000 PPP \$, origin	5,363	10,392.59	12,829.56	117.22	74,162.94
(Empl/Pop 15 years and older) ×100, destination	5,115	53.72	7.32	38.70	74.40
(Empl/Pop 15 years and older)×100, origin	5,115	57.43	11.03	35.40	85.50
Distance in KM	5,456	7,353.83	4,437.13	114.63	19,539.47
Border Dummy	5,456	0.02	0.14	0.00	1.00
Dummy for common language	5,456	0.12	0.33	0.00	1.00
Dummy for shared colonial past	5,456	0.03	0.18	0.00	1.00
Dummy for common legal origin	5,456	0.25	0.43	0.00	1.00
Dummy for common currency	5,456	0.02	0.15	0.00	1.00
Sum of landlocked dummies	5,394	0.35	0.53	0.00	2.00
Measure of Religious proximity	5,673	0.26	0.25	0.00	0.98
Genetic distance (Spolaore and Wacziarg 2010)	5,672	912.53	647.90	0.00	3,115.87

TABLE A2.
CORRELATION BETWEEN POTENTIAL AND ACTUAL MIGRANTS: AGGREGATE REGRESSIONS ACROSS COUNTRIES OF ORIGIN

	College-Educated		Non-college-Educated	
Explanatory Variable	(1) Basic	(2) Including controls	(3) Basic	(4) Including controls
Potential Emigration rates	0.45*** (0.09)	0.18* (0.11)	0.054** (0.023)	0.031 (0.026)
Stock of people with household members abroad/population		1.31*** (0.29)		0.16 (0.10)
Real GDP per person in origin (1,000 \$ PPP)		−0.0009** (0.0004)		−0.0001 (0.00008)

The dependent variable is the emigration rate from country of origin, calculated as the sum of total 2000–2010 net migrants, divided by the population of natives in the country of origin as of 2000. Each observation is one of 138 countries of origin. The observations are weighted by the country-of-origin population with college education, and we drop migration rates. Standard errors are heteroskedasticity robust.***,**, and * imply significance at 1%, 5%, and 10% level.

Actual migration

Our starting point is the recent IAB database described in Brücker *et al.* (2013). They document the bilateral migration stocks (Stock$M_{o,d}^{s,t}$) of individuals aged 25 and over by education level, from 195 origin countries to 20 destination countries, from 1980 to 2010 in 5-year intervals (t=1980,...,2010). We only use the 2000 and 2010 waves and proxy net

TABLE A3.

ACTUAL AND DESIRED IMMIGRATION RATES OF COLLEGE-EDUCATED AND THE LESS EDUCATED BY ORIGIN COUNTRY

Destination	Net rates 2000–2010 Less educated	Net rates 2000–2010 College-educated	Desired rates Less educated	Desired rates College-educated	Population Ratio of college-educated to Less educated
Afghanistan	0.378	6.177	10.992	19.133	0.080
Albania	9.800	66.976	31.793	37.139	0.077
Algeria	0.869	14.494	14.581	11.298	0.057
Argentina	1.011	5.362	10.009	16.731	0.129
Armenia	1.068	23.480	22.542	27.471	0.250
Australia	0.354	4.507	9.368	13.170	0.264
Austria	−1.683	−1.435	7.172	13.164	0.129
Azerbaijan	−2.652	9.143	9.429	11.751	0.128
Bahrain	0.273	25.890	1.624	1.286	0.039
Bangladesh	0.625	9.568	19.274	39.107	0.043
Belarus	−4.283	3.939	10.854	19.675	0.267
Belgium	0.563	2.863	10.592	14.828	0.313
Belize	2.682	112.886	20.548	23.120	0.082
Bolivia	3.819	12.268	12.754	16.509	0.161
Bosnia and Herzegovina	−8.676	30.384	8.992	12.029	0.074
Botswana	1.911	18.839	13.689	26.923	0.041
Brazil	0.266	2.692	11.186	16.786	0.078
Bulgaria	2.344	9.667	9.399	17.075	0.222
Burundi	0.259	55.932	6.835	100.000	0.006
Cambodia	0.692	93.310	22.932	35.913	0.006
Cameroon	0.535	50.278	23.027	26.316	0.012
Canada	−0.110	4.879	10.531	14.435	0.215
Chad	0.086	6.766	7.625	9.536	0.013
Chile	0.564	2.641	15.608	22.114	0.265
China	0.058	2.132	3.986	16.260	0.044
Colombia	1.259	11.135	25.792	27.996	0.118
Comoros	4.424	62.206	23.615	27.083	0.014
Congo, Dem. Rep.	0.200	17.908	21.740	32.340	0.013

TABLE A3. (CONTINUED)
ACTUAL AND DESIRED IMMIGRATION RATES OF COLLEGE-EDUCATED AND THE LESS EDUCATED BY ORIGIN COUNTRY

Destination	Net rates 2000–2010 Less educated	Net rates 2000–2010 College-educated	Desired rates Less educated	Desired rates College-educated	Population Ratio of college-educated to Less educated
Costa Rica	0.981	4.720	14.774	12.217	0.198
Cote d'Ivoire	1.183	5.692	18.648	31.635	0.114
Croatia	−13.400	15.867	5.505	3.586	0.049
Cyprus	1.019	16.455	8.017	20.576	0.308
Czech Republic	0.223	3.481	6.125	10.748	0.112
Denmark	0.044	5.510	10.245	17.892	0.202
Djibouti	0.163	9.730	15.035	25.041	0.023
Dominican Republic	5.648	28.502	47.102	41.319	0.141
Ecuador	5.656	18.771	17.558	21.474	0.173
Egypt	0.757	17.673	8.988	11.011	0.046
El Salvador	16.468	52.111	30.475	43.006	0.102
Estonia	9.479	34.634	16.532	15.811	0.374
Finland	−0.912	4.077	12.253	17.788	0.158
France	0.391	3.402	10.026	21.906	0.207
Georgia	−4.758	4.129	13.510	17.428	0.128
Germany	0.247	1.977	17.467	19.090	0.244
Ghana	0.391	21.397	38.529	38.106	0.044
Greece	−3.072	2.909	8.294	18.251	0.177
Guatemala	6.856	56.715	21.976	25.288	0.036
Guinea	0.733	16.814	25.030	40.866	0.022
Haiti	3.262	413.808	30.746	46.658	0.009
Honduras	8.275	64.760	27.495	32.201	0.041
Hong Kong	0.048	31.626	12.892	26.892	0.163
Hungary	−0.238	4.948	13.174	12.595	0.143
Iceland	3.630	26.855	17.259	20.385	0.183
India	0.202	6.138	2.151	10.789	0.051
Indonesia	0.034	2.520	2.714	8.042	0.028
Iran	0.001	6.424	15.280	34.391	0.100

TABLE A3. (CONTINUED)
ACTUAL AND DESIRED IMMIGRATION RATES OF COLLEGE-EDUCATED AND THE LESS EDUCATED BY ORIGIN COUNTRY

Destination	Net rates 2000–2010 Less educated	Net rates 2000–2010 College-educated	Desired rates Less educated	Desired rates College-educated	Population Ratio of college-educated to Less educated
Iraq	0.745	11.618	5.714	10.998	0.099
Ireland	2.048	25.211	11.822	18.579	0.298
Israel	0.977	6.125	11.773	19.336	0.622
Italy	-1.128	4.189	11.418	29.441	0.103
Japan	-0.032	0.113	9.924	16.476	0.400
Jordan	5.707	26.634	15.854	21.073	0.168
Kazakhstan	-2.768	18.240	9.080	10.397	0.147
Kenya	0.241	34.199	22.248	34.018	0.023
Korea, Rep.	0.220	4.794	17.631	29.832	0.367
Kuwait	4.772	365.757	3.155	3.810	0.015
Kyrgyz Republic	2.167	18.820	11.721	17.599	0.181
Laos	0.989	39.954	5.569	5.214	0.043
Latvia	-0.148	13.470	15.229	17.260	0.153
Lebanon	2.567	106.875	17.914	20.382	0.051
Liberia	0.566	72.704	36.635	50.322	0.025
Libya	-0.031	20.362	14.197	13.045	0.024
Lithuania	-0.416	10.454	14.590	19.149	0.184
Luxembourg	1.973	10.770	14.294	23.526	0.159
Macedonia	-1.651	2.225	20.411	23.354	0.077
Malawi	0.574	58.055	25.671	22.212	0.005
Malaysia	0.072	7.300	3.694	13.611	0.094
Mali	0.793	30.780	12.955	33.952	0.007
Malta	-0.073	82.980	15.248	32.181	0.066
Mauritania	0.912	24.469	14.241	18.200	0.017
Mexico	8.082	13.677	14.990	21.899	0.134
Moldova	0.284	19.020	23.324	26.176	0.101
Mongolia	-0.253	2.819	11.524	24.488	0.138
Morocco	2.845	30.630	13.345	14.496	0.080

TABLE A3. (CONTINUED)

ACTUAL AND DESIRED IMMIGRATION RATES OF COLLEGE-EDUCATED AND THE LESS EDUCATED BY ORIGIN COUNTRY

Destination	Net rates 2000–2010 Less educated	Net rates 2000–2010 College-educated	Desired rates Less educated	Desired rates College-educated	Population Ratio of college-educated to Less educated
Namibia	4.218	147.195	9.838	0.000	0.023
Nepal	0.130	7.705	9.658	30.391	0.038
Netherlands	0.366	5.904	13.125	17.603	0.292
New Zealand	1.208	10.634	18.953	18.219	0.740
Nicaragua	3.130	20.994	21.204	29.015	0.143
Niger	0.022	4.017	4.457	24.315	0.008
Nigeria	0.086	13.993	38.182	45.891	0.022
Norway	0.102	2.834	10.681	18.430	0.304
Pakistan	1.263	12.676	7.844	19.147	0.076
Palestinian Territory	24.910	462.255	8.352	14.915	0.039
Panama	0.120	−0.456	12.473	18.372	0.261
Paraguay	2.539	14.275	5.643	16.226	0.074
Peru	2.066	6.774	27.216	26.472	0.266
Philippines	1.263	8.927	17.689	36.457	0.338
Poland	0.555	8.927	8.761	10.529	0.143
Portugal	0.459	14.386	8.222	18.336	0.108
Qatar	0.344	7.166	3.943	3.664	0.130
Romania	3.559	21.593	17.650	25.497	0.100
Russian Federation	0.105	0.196	6.168	12.775	1.146
Saudi Arabia	0.102	2.845	1.677	1.138	0.119
Senegal	1.451	42.790	31.836	50.986	0.024
Serbia and Montenegro	6.023	10.734	15.799	14.764	0.150
Sierra Leone	0.604	159.058	36.755	58.638	0.008
Singapore	0.242	17.872	5.143	9.596	0.088
Slovakia	−3.928	5.773	13.226	22.771	0.131
Slovenia	−2.241	0.424	11.271	13.831	0.192
Somalia	2.013	68.930	21.398	24.950	0.015
South Africa	0.141	6.880	8.557	12.060	0.094

TABLE A3. (CONTINUED)
ACTUAL AND DESIRED IMMIGRATION RATES OF COLLEGE-EDUCATED AND THE LESS EDUCATED BY ORIGIN COUNTRY

Destination	Net rates 2000–2010 Less educated	Net rates 2000–2010 College-educated	Desired rates Less educated	Desired rates College-educated	Population Ratio of college-educated to Less educated
Spain	−0.622	1.020	6.926	15.131	0.223
Sri Lanka	0.265	6.927	9.796	17.767	0.159
Sudan	0.476	42.557	15.457	30.189	0.010
Sweden	0.590	3.088	14.710	14.997	0.286
Switzerland	0.501	5.725	8.036	3.627	0.221
Syria	1.235	21.870	16.570	20.079	0.048
Taiwan	0.054	4.110	11.572	21.201	0.255
Tajikistan	0.768	24.293	10.230	15.363	0.074
Tanzania	0.055	23.923	14.821	48.836	0.009
Thailand	0.237	3.912	3.024	4.772	0.057
Trinidad and Tobago	3.520	280.268	14.799	21.332	0.036
Tunisia	0.041	12.257	15.095	21.749	0.058
Turkey	−1.532	4.039	8.785	14.523	0.100
Turkmenistan	−0.213	4.151	5.913	13.173	0.182
Ukraine	−3.318	2.398	11.449	17.524	0.611
United Arab Emirates	5.127	13.111	1.047	3.816	0.196
United Kingdom	0.500	13.984	21.765	27.524	0.147
United States	0.202	0.322	8.223	11.708	1.149
Uruguay	2.447	12.497	9.220	10.507	0.122
Uzbekistan	0.817	11.082	6.428	8.857	0.125
Venezuela	0.536	4.595	6.729	12.209	0.170
Vietnam	0.673	32.555	7.173	15.427	0.024
Yemen	1.514	103.992	16.277	29.681	0.012
Zambia	0.477	37.382	15.698	22.855	0.021
Zimbabwe	2.255	203.604	24.296	33.774	0.010
Average	1.149	33.341	14.221	21.437	0.145

The net migration rate is constructed as described in the text, namely as net emigration 2000–2010 divided by the population of natives in the country of origin as of 2000, and then multiplying this fraction by 100. Countries with negative rates have a net inflow of their nationals (return), countries with net rates larger than 100% (only for college-educated) may have some of their expatriates obtain a degree abroad.

migration flows by taking the difference between the migrant stock in 2010 and 2000: $M_{o,d}^s = \text{Stock} M_{o,d}^{s,2010} - \text{Stock} M_{o,d}^{s,2000}$ (as in Beine *et al.*, 2011; or Docquier *et al.*, 2014).

The IAB database relies on census and register data collected from 20 major OECD destination countries. As for the year 2000, they obtained census or register data from all countries. As far as 2010 is concerned, they obtained census data for eight countries (Denmark, France, Finland, Germany, the Netherlands, Norway, Sweden, and the U.S.); 2010 was extrapolated on the basis of 2005–2006 census data in four other cases (Australia, Canada, Ireland, and New Zealand). In the other eight cases (Austria, Chile, Greece, Luxembourg, Portugal, Spain, Switzerland, and UK), they imputed 2010 stocks on the basis of the 1990–2000 growth rates.

To cover the most important receiving countries of the world (many of which are reported as preferred destinations of would-be migrants), we extend the IAB database and construct estimates of net migration flows to 10 additional destination countries (Belgium, Israel, Italy, Japan, Mexico, Poland, Russia, Saudi Arabia, South Africa, and United Arab Emirates). For these countries, bilateral migration data of individuals aged 25 and over are provided for the year 2000 and by education level in Artuç *et al.* (forthcoming). We combine them with the United Nations database on bilateral migrant stocks from 1990 to 2010 without education breakdown and the 25-year-old threshold. Specifically, we multiply the 2000 bilateral stocks of Artuç et al. by the 2000–2010 bilateral growth factors of the United Nations. This simply means that we assume the growth rate of total bilateral migrant stocks to be identical to that of the bilateral stock of migrants aged 25 and over. We also assume there are 10 percentage points more college-educated in the 2000–2010 net migration flow than in the 2000 migration bilateral stock, an assumption in line with the IAB database.

The database of Artuç et al. also documents the size and structure of the non-migrant population in each origin country in 2000, $N_o^s \equiv \text{Stock} M_{oo}^{s,2000}$. Actual migration rates during the period 2000–2010 are thus defined as $m_{o,d}^s = M_{o,d}^s / N_o^s$.

Willingness to emigrate

The Gallup World Polls identify individuals expressing a desire to emigrate permanently or temporarily to another country. Individual data are available on a yearly basis from 2007 to 2013: We aggregate the seven waves to compute desired emigration rates around the year 2010. This allows us to limit the number of missing cells and increase the accuracy of our estimates. Adding these desired migrants in 2010 to the actual net migration flows will give the potential net migration flows between 2000 and 2010.

A typical Gallup survey interviews about a 1,000 randomly selected individuals within each country. In some large countries such as China, India, and Russia as well as in major cities or areas of special interest, oversamples are collected resulting in larger total numbers of respondents. The data are collected through telephone surveys in countries where the telephone coverage represents at least 80% of the population. In Central and Eastern Europe, as well as in the developing world, including much of Latin America, the former Soviet Union countries, nearly all of Asia, the Middle East, and Africa, on the other hand, an area frame design is used for face-to-face interviewing. As such, the sampling frame represents the entire civilian, non-institutionalized population aged 15 and over covering the entire country including rural areas (with the exception of areas where the safety of the interviewing staff is threatened, scarcely populated islands in some countries, and areas that interviewers can reach only by foot, animal, or small boat). The survey covers 394,459 respondents, that is, an average of 2,761 observations per country. In some cases, the number of respondents is, however, small. As a robustness check, we will only consider countries where the willingness to emigrate has been computed from at least 37 college-educated and 75 less educated respondents.

The Gallup survey documents individual characteristics (such as age and education) and includes two relevant questions on intentions to emigrate; these questions were asked in 138 countries: (Q1) *Ideally, if you had the opportunity, would you like to move permanently or temporarily to another country, or would you prefer to continue living in this country?* And (Q2) *To which country would you like to move?* In line with the actual migration data, we only consider respondents aged 25 and over and distinguish between individuals with college education and the less educated. The skill structure of the Gallup database is, however, different from the one in ADOP and IAB. ADOP and IAB define a high-skilled individual as anyone who has obtained at least one year of college education. In the Gallup survey, education obtained by the respondent is classified using the answer to the question: "What is your highest completed level of education? (possible answers: completed elementary education or less (up to 8 years of basic education), secondary up to 3 year tertiary (9-15 years of education), completed 4 years of education beyond high school and/or received a 4-year college degree, don't know, refused)." Tertiary educated individuals are defined as those who reply: "Completed 4 years of education beyond high school and/or received a 4-year college degree." Since the propensity to emigrate increases with education, we might overestimate the desire to migrate of both high-skilled and low-skilled individuals. By 2013, the 138 countries represented about 98% of the worldwide population aged 25 and over.

The first step consists of computing the aggregate proportion of individuals who express a willingness to leave their country, whatever their preferred country of destination. We denote this proportion by $\widehat{w}^s_{oT}$ (T for all destinations) for individuals of education type s living in country o. To compute desired emigration rates, we aggregate individual responses to Q1 and weigh each observation by the relevant Gallup sample weight. These weights are designed to compensate for the low coverage of certain groups (by gender, race, age, educational attainment, and region) in the whole population. Gallup assigns a weight to each respondent "so that the demographic characteristics of the total weighted sample of respondents match the latest estimates of the demographic characteristics of the adult population available" for the country (Gallup, 2012). The willingness to migrate is given by the weighted proportion of respondents who answered positively to Q1.

In the second step, we use responses to Q2 to disaggregate the number of desired migrants by country of destination. For each origin country o and skill type i, bilateral desired migration rates ($\widehat{w}^s_{o,d}$) are obtained by multiplying the total willingness to emigrate ($\widehat{w}^s_{oT}$) by the proportion of respondents to Q2 who declared that country d is their preferred destination ($\sigma^s_{o,d}$). A few desired migrants did not mention a desired destination (i.e., did not respond to Q2), but this is rarely the case. Given the large response rates to Q2, we ignore those who did not respond to Q2 to compute the bilateral shares. Finally, a few respondents answered to Q2 and mentioned a preferred destination without responding to Q1; we considered that they responded "Yes" to Q1.

Given that we want our actual and desired emigration rates to be expressed as percent of the non-migrant, native population aged 25 and over in the year 2000, we correct for the change in the native population between 2000 and 2010 and compute our index of willingness to emigrate as $w^s_{o,d} = \widehat{w}^s_{o,d} N^s_{o,2010} / N^s_{o,2000}$.

Explanatory variables

The definition and source of the variables used in the regressions are the following:

The stock of people born in country o resident of country d in 2000, in percent of the population of non-migrant natives in o in 2000 ($Netw_{o,d}$). *Source*: See the actual migration section in the data appendix.

The share of people aged 25 and older in and native to country o who report to have a household member abroad times the share of people aged 25 and older in and native to country o who report to have a household member in country d, merged over all available waves between 2007 and 2013 (alternative measure of $Netw_{o,d}$). *Source*: Gallup's World Poll Database (see $w^s_{o,d}$ for more details on data collection). Specifically, the propensity to have a household member abroad is obtained by combining the following questions: "Have any members of your household gone to live in a foreign country permanently or temporarily in the past five years?" and "In which country does/did he/she live?." The intensity of the diaspora connection is thus calculated as the product of the propensity for natives of country o to reply positively to the first question and the propensity that natives of country o report country o as a settlement country for their household members abroad, each time merging all survey waves between 2007 and 2013. Note that these propensities are obtained using sample weights so that the demographic characteristics of the total weighted sample of respondents match those of the adult population in the respective country in terms of gender, race, age, educational attainment, and region (*see* Gallup, 2012). Again, we correct for the change in the native population between 2000 and 2010 in order to express the stock of people with household members abroad as a share of the non-migrant, native population aged 25 and over in country o in the year 2000.

Gross domestic product per capita in the destination country in purchasing power parities in 2005 international \$ (Chain series) in 2000 ($y_{d,2000}$). *Source*: Penn World Tables 7.0.

Employment as percentage of the population aged 15 and over in the destination country ($e_{d,2000}$). *Source*: World Development Indicators and Total Economy Database.

Growth in gross domestic product per capita in the destination country in purchasing power parities in 2005 international \$ (Chain series) between 2000 and 2010 (gy_d^{00-10}). *Source*: Penn World Tables 7.0.

Growth in employment as percentage of the population aged 15 and over in the destination country between 2000 and 2010 (ge_d^{00-10}). *Source*: World Development Indicators and Total Economy Database.

Size of the population aged 25+ in the destination country in 2000 (ln Pop_d). *Source*: Brücker *et al.* (2013).

Set of bilateral variables capturing geographical, cultural, and genetic distance across countries (Dist.$_{o,d}$), including:

Population-weighted distance in kilometers between o and d (taken in logs). *Source*: CEPII Dyadic Distance Database (Mayer and Zignago, 2011).

Dummy for sharing a border. *Source*: CEPII Dyadic Distance Database.

Dummy for sharing a common official primary language. *Source*: CEPII Dyadic Distance Database.

Dummy for sharing a common colonial past. *Source*: CEPII Dyadic Distance Database.

Dummy for sharing a common legal origin. *Source*: Ortega and Peri (2014).

Dummy for sharing a common currency. *Source*: Ortega and Peri (2014).

Number of landlocked countries in the country pair. *Source*: CEPII Dyadic Distance Database.

Religious proximity between o and d, that is, the probability that two individuals randomly selected from o and d share the same religion. *Source*: Own calculations based on CIA World Factbook data on country-specific religious adherence.

Genetic distance between o and d, that is, the probability that two alleles (a particular form taken by a gene) at a given locus selected at random from two populations are different (proxy for time since isolation). *Source*: Spolaore and Warcziag (2009), definitions p. 480–485.

Dummy for free labor mobility between o and d as of 2000 or 2010 (in Policy$_{o,d}$). The corridors which had free mobility in 2000 besides EU15-EU15 involve the EU15 and Switzerland as well as Nordic countries, that is, Denmark, Finland, Iceland, Norway, and Sweden. In 2010, new corridors involve free mobility between (i) new accession countries that joined the EU between 2000 and 2010 (i.e., Bulgaria, Cyprus, Czech Rep, Estonia, Hungary, Latvia, Lithuania, Malta, Poland, Romania, Slovakia, and Slovenia) and the EU15, Switzerland, Poland, and Czech Republic. *Source*: Own calculations.

Dummy for the presence of a visa waiving agreement between o and d in 2004 (in *Policy$_{o,d}$*). This visa waiving dummy is based on country of citizenship rather than on country of birth. *Source*: Neumayer (2006) based on the November 2004 edition of the International Civil Aviation Association's Travel Information Manual.

420 *Immigration Policies and Migrant Mobility*

S96 <small>INTERNATIONAL MIGRATION REVIEW</small>

REFERENCES

Autor, D., L. Katz, and M. Kearney
2008 "Trends in U.S. Wage Inequality: Revising the Revisionists." *Review of Economics and Statistics* 90:30–23.

Artuç, E., F. Docquier, Ç. Özden and C. Parsons
(forthcoming) "A Global Assessment of Human Capital Mobility: The Role of Non-OECD Destinations." *World Development.*

Bahna, M.
2008 "Predictions of Migration from the New Member States After Their Accession into the European Union: Successes and Failures." *International Migration Review* 42 (4):844–860.

Bauer, T., and K. F., Zimmermann
1997 "Network Migration of Ethnic Germans." *International Migration Review* 31 (1):143–149.

Becerra, D.
2012 "The Impact of Anti-Immigration Policies and Perceived Discrimination in the United States on Migration Intentions among Mexican Adolescents." *International Migration* 50(4):20–32.

Becerra, D., M. Gurrola, C. Ayón, D. Androff, J. Krysik, K. Gerdess, L. Moya-Salas and E. Segal
2010 "Poverty and Other Factors Affecting Migration Intentions Among Adolescents in Mexico." *Journal of Poverty* 14(1):1–16.

Beine, M., S. Bertoli, and J. Fernández-Huertas Moraga,
(forthcoming) "A Practitioners' Guide to Gravity Models of International Migration." *World Economy.*

———, F. Docquier, and Ç. Özden
2011 "Diasporas". *Journal of Development Economics* 95(1):30–41.

Bertoli, S., and J. Fernández-Huertas Moraga
2013 "Multilateral Resistance to Migration." *Journal of Development Economics* 102:79–100.

Borjas, G. J.
1987 "Self-selection and the Earnings of Immigrants." *American Economic Review* 77 (4):531–553.

Brücker, H., S. Capuano, and A. Marfouk.
2013 ."Education, Gender and International Migration: Insights from a Panel-dataset 1980–2010." mimeo. URL: http://www.iab.de/en/daten/iab-brain-drain-data.aspx

Carling, J.
2002 "Migration in the Age of Involuntary Immobility: Theoretical Reflections and Cape Verdean Experiences." *Journal of Ethnic and Migration Studies* 28(1):5–42.

Chassamboulli, A., and G. Peri
2014 *The Labor Market Effects of Reducing Undocumented Immigrants.* NBER Working Paper No. 19932. Cambridge, MA: NBER, February 2014.

Clark, X., T. J. Hatton, and J. G. Williamson
2007 "Explaining U.S. Immigration 1971–1998." *Review of Economics and Statistics* 89 (2):359–373.

Creighton, M. J.
2013 "The Role of Aspirations in Domestic and International Migration." *Social Science Journal* 50(1):79–88.

Czaika, M., and M. Vothknecht
2014 "Migration and Aspirations – Are Migrants Trapped on a Hedonic Treadmill?" *IZA Journal of Migration* 3(1). doi: 10.1186/2193-9039-3-1#sthash.Wp8ISHVb.dpuf
Docquier, F., Ç. Özden, and G. Peri
2014 "The Labour Market Effects of Immigration and Emigration in OECD Countries." *The Economic Journal* doi: 10.1111/ecoj.12077.
De Jong, G. F.
2000 ."Expectations, Gender, and Norms in Migration Decision-making." *Population Studies* 54(3): 307–319.
———, K. Richter, and P. Isarabhakdi
1996 "Gender, Values, and Intentions to Move in Rural Thailand." *International Migration Review* 30(3):748–770.
Fawcett, J. T.
1989 "Networks, Linkages, and Migration Systems." *International Migration Review* 23 (3):671–680.
Gallup
2012 *Worldwide Research Methodology and Codebook.* Washington, DC.
Goldin, C., and L. F. Katz
2008 *The Race Between Education and Technology.* Cambridge, MA: Harvard University Press.
Grogger, J., and G. H. Hanson
2011 "Income Maximization and the Selection and Sorting of International Migrants." *Journal of Development Economics* 95:42–57.
Gregg, P., and B. Petrongolo
2005 "Stock-flow Matching and the Performance of the Labor Market." *European Economic Review* 49(8):1987–2011.
Hagen-Zanker, J., M. Siegel, and C. de Neubourg
2009 "Strings Attached: The Impediments to Migration in Albania and Moldova." *Southeast European and Black Sea Studies* 9(4):459–479.
Hanson, G. H., and G. McIntosh
2010 "The Great Mexican Emigration." *The Review of Economics and Statistics* 92(4):798–810.
Hatton, T. J.
2005 "Explaining Trends in UK Immigration." *Journal of Population Economics* 18 (4):719–740.
———, and J. G. Williamson
2005 "What Fundamentals Drive World Migration?" In *Poverty, International Migration and Asylum.* Ed. G. Borjas and J. Crisp. Hampshire, UK: Palgrave-Macmillan. Pp. 15–38.
Helbling, M., and M. P. Vink
2013 "The Use and Misuse of Policy Indices in the Domain of Citizenship and Integration." *Comparative European Politics* 11(5):551–554.
Hooghe, M., A. Trappers, B. Meuleman and T. Reeskens
2008 "Migration to European Countries: A Structural Explanation of Patterns 1980–2004." *International Migration Review* 42:476–504.
Esipova, N., J. Ray, and A. Pugliese
2011 *Gallup World Poll: The many faces of global migration.* IOM Migration Research Series 43, Switzerland, Geneva: International Organization for Migration.

Jónsson, G.
2008 *Migration Aspirations and Immobility in a Malian Soninke Village, IMI.* Working
     Paper No. 10-2008. Oxford, UK: International Migration Institute.
Karemera, D., V. Iwuagwu Oguledo, and B. Davis
2000 "A Gravity Model Analysis of International Migration to North America."*Applied
     Economics* 32:1745–1755.
Manchin, M., R. Manchin, and S. Orazbayev
2014 "Desire to Migrate Internationally and Locally and The Importance of Satisfaction
     with Amenities." paper presented at the FIW-wiiw Seminars in International Eco-
     nomics, 10 April 2014, Austria, Vienna.
Mayda, A. M.
2010 "International Migrations: A Panel Data Analysis of the Determinants of Bilateral
     Flows." *Journal of Population Economics* 23(4):1249–1274.
Mayer T., and S. Zignago
2011 Notes on CEPII's distances measures (GeoDist). CEPII Working Paper 2011-25.
McFadden, D.
1974 "Conditional Logit Analysis of Qualitative Choice Behavior." In *Frontiers in Econo-
     metrics.* Ed. P. Zarembka. New York, USA: Academic Press. Pp. 105–142.
Moretti, E.
2012 *The New Geography of Jobs.* New York: Houghton Mifflin Harcourt Publishing.
Neumayer, E.
2006 "Unequal Access to Foreign Spaces: How States Use Visa Restrictions to Regulate
     Mobility in a Globalised World." *Transactions of the British Institute of Geographers*
     31(1):72–84.
Ortega, J.
2000 "Pareto-improving Immigration in an Economy with Equilibrium Employment."
     Economic Journal 110:92–112.
Ortega, F., and G. Peri
2013 "The Role of Income and Immigration Policies on International Migrations."
     Migration Studies 1(1):47–74.
———, and ———
2014 "Openness and Income: The Roles of Trade and Migration." *Journal of Interna-
     tional Economics* 92(2):231–251.
Papapanagos, H., and P. Sanfey
2001 "Intention to Emigrate in Transition Countries: The Case of Albania." *Journal of
     Population Economics* 14(3):491–504.
Paul, A. M.
2011 "Stepwise International Migration: A Multistage Migration Pattern for the Aspiring
     Migrant." *American Journal of Sociology* 116(6):1842–1886.
Pedersen, P. J., M. Pytlikova, and N. Smith
2008 "Selection and Network Effects: Migration Flows into OECD Countries, 1990–
     2000." *European Economic Review* 52(7):1160–1186.
Petrongolo, B., and C. Pissarides
2006 "Scale Effects in Markets with Search." *Economic Journal* 116(508):21–44.
Pissarides, C. A.
2000 *Equilibrium Unemployment Theory.* Cambridge, MA: MIT Press.
———, and B. Petrongolo
2001 "Looking into the Black Box: A Survey of the Matching Function." *Journal of Eco-
     nomic Literature* 39(2):390–431.

Putterman, L., and D. N. Weil
2010 "Post-1500 Population Flows and the Long-run Determinants of Economic Growth and Inequality." *The Quarterly Journal of Economics* 125(4):1627–1682.
Rogers, A.
1990 "Requiem for the Net Migrant." *Geographical Analysis* 22(4):284–300.
Roy, A. D.
1951 "Some Thoughts on the Distribution of Earnings." *Oxford Economic Papers* 3:135–146.
Ruyssen, I., G. Everaert, and G. Rayp
2014 "Determinants and Dynamics of Migration to OECD Countries in a Three-dimensional Panel Framework." *Empirical Economics* 46(1):175–197.
Sjaastad, L. A.
1962 "The Costs and Returns of Human Migration." *Journal of Political Economy* 70 (5):80–93.
Smith, S. K., and D. A. Swanson
1998 "In Defense of the Net Migrant." *Journal of Economic and Social Measurement* 24 (3):249–264.
Spolaore, E., and R. Wacziarg
2009 "The Diffusion of Development." *Quarterly Journal of Economics* 124(2):469–529.
van Dalen, H. P., G. Groenewold, and T. Fokkema
2005a "The Effect of Remittances on Emigration Intentions in Egypt, Morocco, and Turkey." *Population Studies* 59(3):375–392.
———, ———, and J. J. Schoorl
2005b "Out of Africa: What drives the pressure to emigrate?" *Journal of Population Economics* 18 (4): 741–778.
Wood, C. H., C. L. Gibson, L. Ribeiro and P. Hamsho-Diaz
2010 "Crime Victimization in Latin America and Intentions to Migrate to the United States." *International Migration Review* 44(1):3–24.
Yang, X.
2000 "Determinants of Migration Intentions in Hubei Province, China: Individual Versus Family Migration." *Environment and Planning* 32(5):769–787.

Printed in the United States
By Bookmasters